AF072108

Auction & training venue

Animal health products
Training

Game breeding

Game breeding

Full circle of support for game ranchers

Game breeding, tourism & hunting

Game breeding
Hunting

Hunting

Statutory regulation and registration of game animals

Wildlife Producers Association

In terms of the Goverment Gazette No. 40058 of 10 June 2016, the national Department of Agriculture, Forestry and Fisheries amended the Livestock Improvement Act, Act No. 62 of 1998, changing the legal face of the regulation of game ranching.

This amendment created the possibility that game animals (to date 12 species) be registered in terms of the act, effectively strengthening the concept of game ranching, which takes place on Agricultural land, being considered legally an agricultural activity.

THE NEW
GAME RANCHER

Published by
BRIZA PUBLICATIONS
CK 90/11690/23

www.briza.co.za

P.O. Box 11050
Queenswood 0121
South Africa

First edition, first impression 2016

Copyright text ©: Pamela and Peter Oberem
Copyright photographs ©: Peter and Pamela Oberem with the exception of those detailed in the photo credits
Copyright published edition ©: Briza Publications CC

© All rights reserved. No part of this publication may be reproduced or transmitted in any form or by any means without written permission from the copyright holders.

ISBN 978-1-920217-62-4

Project manager: Johan Steenkamp
Cover design: Ronelle Oosthuizen
Design and typesetting: Ronelle Oosthuizen
Printed and bound by ABC Press, Epping, Cape Town

Disclaimer
Although care has been taken to be as accurate as possible, neither the authors nor the publisher make any express or implied representation as to the accuracy of the information contained in this book and cannot be held legally responsible or accept liability for any errors or omissions.

CONTENTS

FOREWORD vii
ACKNOWLEDGEMENTS viii

CHAPTER 1: Introduction to game ranching 1

History of the game ranching industry in South Africa 1
The four pillars of game ranching 17
    Breeding of game animals 17
    Hunting in South Africa 24
    Game meat production 31
    Wildlife tourism 37

CHAPTER 2: Ecosystems 45

Soil health and veld management in various biomes 45

CHAPTER 3: General game ranch management 65

Planning and management 65
Nutrition in game animals 77
Genomics as a tool for the wildlife industry 91
Predator management 100
Capture methods used in game ranching 106

CHAPTER 4: Species accounts 121

Ungulates 121
    Rhino 121
    African Buffalo 130
    Zebra 147
Hippotragines (horselike antelope) 153
    Gemsbok 153
    Roan 161
    Sable 165
Tragelaphines (spiral-horned antelope) 173
    Eland 173
    Kudu 181
    Nyala 189

Alcelaphine antelope 196
    Blesbok/bontebok 196
    Tsessebe 205
    Wildebeest 211
Aepycertotidae (impalas) 217
    Impala 217
Antelopini (gazelles) 226
    Springbok 226
Small antelope 235
    Cephalophini (duikers) 235
    Neotragini (short, straight-horned) 236
Carnivores 241
    Lion, cheetah and wild dogs 241
Aves 247
    Ostrich 247
Reptilia 253
    Crocodiles 253

CHAPTER 5: Diseases and parasites 269

Basic disease control 269
General conditions 274
Infectious diseases of multiple species 282
Herbivore diseases 292
Insect- (arthropod) transmitted diseases 305
Tick-borne diseases 308
Viral diseases of carnivores 321
Diseases of equines 326
Diseases of suidae (porcines) 328
Important parasites of game animals 330
External parasites of wildlife 339
Poisonings 350

REFERENCES AND FURTHER READING 355

GENERAL INDEX 362

SCIENTIFIC NAME INDEX 366

INDEX OF DISEASES AND PARASITES 369

FOREWORD

Prof. Wouter van Hoven
Emeritus Professor in Wildlife Management, University of Pretoria

Scenario planners are today looking to Africa as being the answer to the rapidly growing demand for food in the world and as the next economic driver of the world's economic future. The reason is twofold: the availability of huge areas of underutilised agricultural land is the first while the demographic imperative of the growing number of economically active individuals is the second. The large African land mass between 30° south and 30° north with the associated positive attributes of high- and regular rainfall, low precipitation and good soils further strengthen this view.

South Africa may not be blessed with the natural resources enjoyed by Africa north of us but it is blessed by its citizens' propensity to embrace modern science and technology as well as by the innovativeness of its lawmakers and people. Forward thinking individuals enshrined the **concept of the sustainable** use of our natural resources in our country's enviable Constitution. As a result, a uniquely Southern African form of agriculture, that challenges many of the conventional forms of agriculture such as dairy or sugar production, developed within the space of two decades.

Today, Game Ranching contributes more than R20 billion to the South African fiscus, contributes to food security in the region by producing more than 150 000 tons of game meat annually and provides more than 140 000 decent jobs.

At the same time, huge contributions to biodiversity and conservation have been made. The contribution of game ranchers to prevent a number of species such as the white rhino, the bontebok, the Cape mountain Zebra, the black wildebeest, to name only a few from becoming extinct in South Africa (and the world), must be applauded.

Similarly, game ranchers are amongst the first to understand and strongly support the need for rural development and land reform in our young country. Their leadership in this important aspects of the democratisation and deracialisation of South Africa's agricultural industry has been noticed and appreciated.

I share the faith of game ranchers in the future of the game ranching industry and in the contribution that this, our unique form of sustainable agriculture, can make to our continent, its economy, its people and to our environment.

Having over the past decade seen the contribution of Drs Oberem and Afrivet to bringing science and experience to the pet owners, farmers and vets in their many informative and useful books I am sure that game ranchers will, as I do, similarly appreciate this new book. Thank you and good luck!

ACKNOWLEDGEMENTS

The compiling authors would like to thank the contributors without whose help the book would not have been written.

They are as follows, in rough order of their contributions:

Breeding and wildebeest: Barry York, livestock and game breeder extraordinaire, of Golden Breeders, and York Safaris.

Tourism: Professor Peet van der Merwe and Jauntelle Els, North-West University, Potchefstroom Campus.

Hunting: Adri Botha, associate of PHASA and current CEO of WRSA.

Ecosystems: Veterinary nutritionist and ecologist Dr Rina Grant-Biggs and her co-author Mike Peel. They tender their thanks to Nemesia Grant and Isak Smit for help with the chapter.

Planning: Gert and Nanette Fourie, wildlife management consultants of Ekofokus in Bela Bela, Limpopo.

Capture: Dr Jacques O' Dell, wildlife veterinarian of the Faculty of Veterinary Science, University of Pretoria.

Predator management: Tim Snow, problem animal consultant and conservationist.

Genetics: Paul Labout, genetics consultant for the company WS^2.

Nutrition: Craig Shepstone, animal nutritionist and game feed consultant for EPOL.

Buffalo: Dr Roy Bengis, veteran wildlife veterinarian, previously at SANPARKS (retired).

Rhino and roan: Rubin Els, outstanding reserve manager of Thaba Tholo Reserve.

Sable, kudu, impala, gemsbok, springbok, blesbok, etc.: Deon Furstenburg, wildlife biologist and owner of the consulting company, Geowild, is a major and valued contributor to the book.

Zebra: Dr Halszka Hrabar, scientist at the Centre for African Conservation Ecology, Nelson Mandela Metropolitan University in Port Elizabeth.

Small antelope: Herman Barnard of the Small Antelope Study Group of WRSA.

Carnivores: Dr Piet Potgieter of the Predator Association of SA.

Ostriches: Dr Johan van Rensburg of Afrivet Business Management.

Crocodiles: Robert Reader of Makwena Crocodile Breeders and Dr Silke Pfitzer of the Veterinary Faculty of the University of Pretoria.

Photo credits

The copyright owners of images are indicated by the use of abbreviations which are explained below. Unmarked images are the property of Peter and Pamela Oberem, or the company Afrivet. Permission was obtained from Dr Koos Coetzer to make use of images in "Infectious Diseases of Livestock", previously published by Oxford University Press. Permission was also given by the Agricultural Research Council to use images from the Tick Monograph series. While all efforts have been made to correctly identify the ownership of images we acknowledge that human errors may occur. Please report any irregularities to the publishers. We would like to give special thanks to Erika Alberts of MPL Media for assistance with image searches.

AdS: A. de Swart
AP: A. Peens
AlR: Arnaud le Roux
B: Bimeda
BI: Bridgeman Images
BK: Bartholomeus Klip
BY: Barry York
BV: Barend Vorster
C: Chemvet
CG: Charles Gilfillan
CV: Clinvet
DC: Deon Cilliers
DF: Deon Furstenburg
DFG: David Gray
DRH: Diana Reynolds Hale
DS: Donkey Sanctuary, UK
EcP: Ecoprint
EP: E. Pretorius
FM: Free Me Organisation
HH: Halszka Hrabar
HvdP: Hans van der Pypekamp

IG: Ignatio Gambin
JB: Joop Boomker
JK: Johan Kriek
JM: Jacques Malan
JvH: Joe van Heerden
JvV: J. van der Vyfer
JvW: J. van Wyk
JW: June Williams
KC: Koos Coetzer
KRC: Keith Collins
LG: Louis Greef
LK: Lucy Kemp
LS: Liesl C. Schoeman
MMF: Malcolm Mc Farlane
MLP: MLP media and associates
MM: Maggy Meyer/ Shutterstock
MP: Mike Peel
MR: Marolien Roux
MS: Martin Schulmann
MvS: Meldt van der Spuy

@MGHP
NZ: National Zoo
OVI: Onderstepoort Veterinary Institute
PW: Piet Warren
QS: Quintus Strauss
RB: Roy Bengis
RGB: Rina Grant-Biggs
RR: Robert Reader
SSK: Shutterstock
SH: Samuel Howett painting courtesy of the Hugh Solomon Pictorial Africana, at Stellenbosch University
SP: Schering Plough
SS: Sarel Snyman
TB: Tertius Bosch
TT: Thaba Tholo/Rubin Els
UN: University of Nebraska
UP: University of Pretoria
WB: Willem Burger
WS: Willem Schack

Illustrations: We are indebted to Ronelle Oosthuizen (RAO) for her excellent drawings and to Pim van Hooft (PvH) of University of Wageningen, Netherlands, for permission to use the illustrations in the genetics section.

CHAPTER 1

INTRODUCTION TO GAME RANCHING

HISTORY OF THE GAME RANCHING INDUSTRY IN SOUTH AFRICA

Peter Oberem

Game ranching is the breeding of wild animal species either extensively on natural ecosystems, or semi-intensively in smaller camps. Although it is practiced in various other countries in the world, in South Africa it has now become an industry or business which makes a significant contribution to the economy, to decent jobs, to food security, to research and knowledge and to conservation. This section outlines the growth, successes and challenges of this industry.

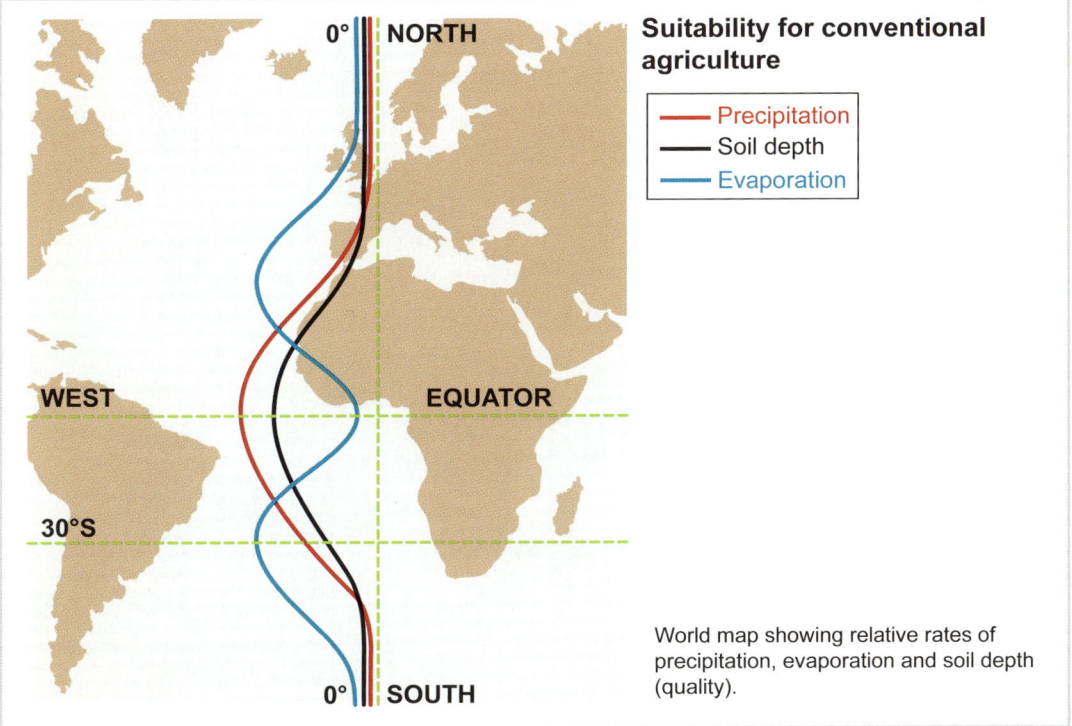

World map showing relative rates of precipitation, evaporation and soil depth (quality).

Introduction

Game ranching has attracted the attention of analysts and commentators because of its huge success and contribution to the economy. In summary its success can be attributed to a number of factors including the fact that game animal species can effectively and profitably utilise the marginal agricultural land on which livestock farmers struggle to make a living.

South Africa is, generally speaking, poorly endowed with the natural resources needed to make it competitive in terms of efficient and competitive agricultural production, due to:
- Low and erratic precipitation.
- High evaporation.
- Shallow and poor soils.

Eighty percent of the 100 million hectares of South African agricultural land is classified as marginal agricultural land and is only utilisable as rangeland for the grazing of ruminants.

South Africa's indigenous animal species have (unlike domesticated livestock) evolved over millions of years in this harsh environment and are better adapted to utilise even poor quality pasture, shrubs and trees, to cope with lack of water, and to resist indigenous diseases, parasites and poisonous plants more effectively.

Natural vegetation or rangelands are therefore adapted to sustainable utilisation by indigenous animals which are also less likely to cause degradation than domestic stock. It is important to note that the 20 million ha currently occupied by game ranches are not established on pristine conservation areas or arable agricultural land but are marginal lands which were degraded by agriculture (overgrazing, ploughing and erosion). Wildlife ranching has therefore expanded the range of game animal species as well as preserving all the species of animals and plants whose survival is promoted by preserving natural vegetation. The activities of wildlife ranching still, however, provide food in the form of game meat, and employment for farm workers while contributing to biodiversity and ecotourism.

Wildlife ranching only came to its own as a form of agricultural business, as opposed to a

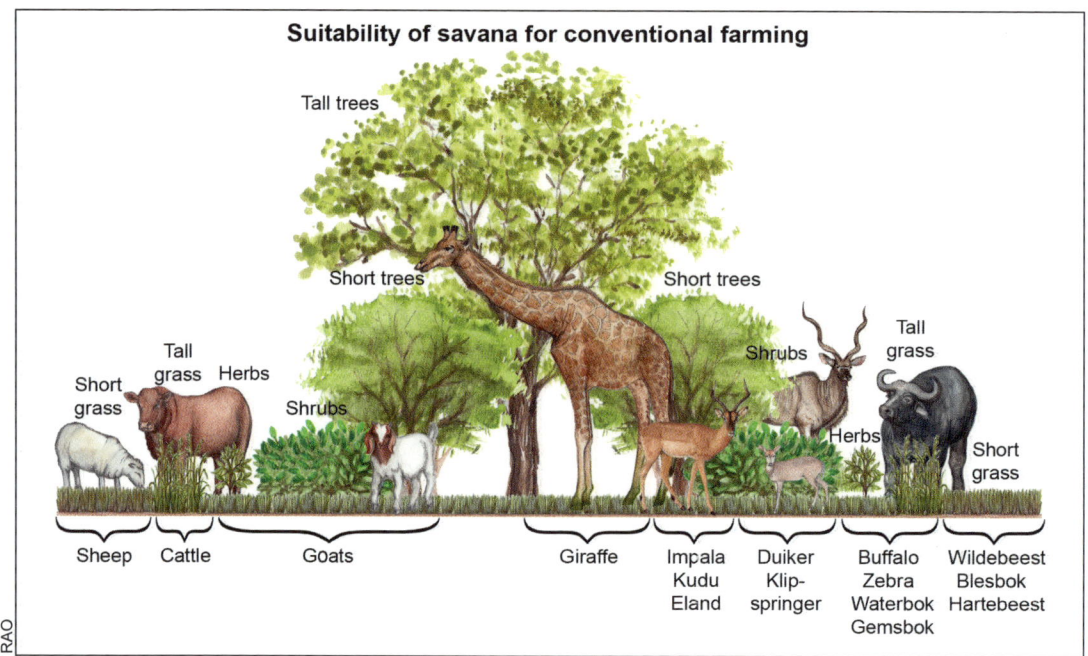

Comparative utilisation of various strata of natural vegetation by game animals compared with livestock.

A painting of the extinct bluebuck antelope.

"Elephant hunt" by Samuel Howitt showing the famous naturalist Le Vaillant hunting an elephant.

small portion of the tourism business, with the proclamation of the Game Theft Act, Act 105 of 1991 in that year. With this confirmation of the ownership of game within specified fences and on permitted (exempted) properties, business principles began to apply to game animals: They became an asset, and in the case of rare species and/or rare colour variants sometimes very valuable assets. This was the spark that ignited the benefits of sustainable utilisation of wildlife and thus wildlife ranching as part of the Green Economy of South Africa.

The subsequent growth was, initially, based on an increase in the number of game ranches and the need to stock them with the common plains game. Income and profits were derived mainly from supplying the increasing number of wildlife ranches with game animals for:
- Consumptive use: Hunting, both local for meat ("biltong"-hunting) and for trophies, the latter by mainly foreign hunters.
- Non-consumptive use for ecotourism.

From the early 2000s, further impetus to the growth and profitability of wildlife ranching was added by the breeding of higher value – rare species and/or colour and morphological variants. The full potential of game meat production, beneficiation and export has yet to be realised and is the focus for the 3rd phase of the growth in the wildlife ranching industry.

Historical background
Settlers, hunters, war and disease

When the first white settlers landed in the Cape of Good Hope in 1652 indigenous southern African game species were plentiful and widespread. For example the Cape or savannah buffalo (*Syncerus caffer caffer*) were found in large numbers in much of Africa south of the Sahara mainly in the savannah and open grassland areas including along the southern coast as far west as Swellendam. There are many historical accounts of the herds of springbuck, black wildebeest and plains zebra extending from "horizon to horizon". The settlers in the Cape were, initially at least, dependent mainly on livestock for their livelihood and survival. Hunting of the extraordinarily rich variety of wildlife was one of the essential skills for settler survival, and it was used to clear land to make space for grazing domestic stock, for trade and to provide meat so that slaughter of domestic animals could be avoided. These practices, together with the view that game animals compete with domestic stock for grazing led to a heavy toll on game numbers. The termination of the practice of "kraaling" and the erection of fences were propagated during the 1870s by Banford, the first Cape colonial veterinarian and his successor, Hutcheon, in order to combat wireworm infestations amongst other diseases in settler livestock. This began to limit the free movement and natural migration of game animals across the country. The conflict of game with livestock led to the demise of the huge population of the quagga, which roamed the Karoo and the southern Free State. The quagga, a subspecies of the plains zebra (*Equus quagga*), was eradicated by farmers who saw them as competitors to their livestock for grazing. Thus, between 1904 and 1930 small stock numbers reached an all-time high of 60 million, in contrast with the less than 25 million small stock which are kept at present in the whole country.

Hunting as a sport as practised by white settlers took a massive toll on the wildlife of South Africa and led to the extinction or near extinction of a number of game species. In the 1800s the last bluebuck (*Hippotragus leucopaeos*), a member of the roan and sable family, was shot in the Swellendam area. It had a restricted habitat between Swellendam and Caledon and was thought to have been a specialist grazer of the grassy renosterveld.

By 1895 the white rhinoceros, the black rhinoceros, blesbok, bontebok, black wildebeest and the Cape mountain zebra had been hunted almost to the point of extinction. The "great" white hunters were celebrated as heroes, in particular those that hunted dangerous animals such as elephant, buffalo and lion, as it was deemed to be a show of manliness. These included celebrities such as the author, Ernest Hemingway and Theodore Roosevelt, the US President who travelled and hunted in Africa following his term in office. These and many other hunters of legend, together with the advancing settlers greatly reduced the numbers of game animals in their paths.

The remaining wildlife population was brought close to extinction by the rinderpest epidemic which swept southwards through the continent in the 1880s (eventually reaching the

The incursion of rinderpest caused massive losses of wildlife and livestock

Cape in 1898) destroying in its path an estimated 95% of the continent's buffalo population and hundreds of thousands of other antelope species. It is estimated that only 10 000 buffalo survived the epidemic in small pockets that did not come into contact with the virus. This viral disease pandemic which decimated the wild game population, ironically led to the disappearance of tsetse fly and with it nagana, at least for a while.

The three year 2nd Anglo-Boer War (1899 to 1902) took a further toll on game numbers mainly due to the "scorched earth policy" which the British used in response to the guerrilla tactics of the greatly outnumbered Boers. This policy of Lord Kitchener resulted in the deaths of Boer and African people, their livestock and the wildlife of the country.

After the Boer War and the rinderpest epidemic had been eradicated the tsetse fly and the disease it transmits (nagana) slowly returned as game and livestock numbers grew, and by 1905 the disease was again reported in Zululand.

The tsetse fly was once again considered a threat to livestock as were game animals which were found to be a reservoir for the trypanosome which the tsetse fly transmits. Some authorities advocated control of the fly, and others advocated the destruction of the reservoir hosts, in effect the slaughter of wildlife. The Natal Parks Board authorised the large-scale slaughter of all game except the white

CHAPTER 1: INTRODUCTION TO GAME RANCHING 5

Paul Kruger monument at the Kruger National Park.

rhinoceros outside the Umfolozi Game Reserve and a "thinning out" of game within the park. During these dreadful years most game animals in the Zululand area were destroyed: between May 1929 and November 1930 (18 months) 26 000 animals were killed around Umfolozi. Between the end of August 1959 and the end of January 1960 (4 months) some 8 000 head of game, mainly warthog, wildebeest, zebra and impala were destroyed.

In Zimbabwe, too, the number of game animals were reduced by hunting between parallel fences 16 km apart. In Swaziland during the 1930s, wildebeest and buffalo were declared vermin because they were so numerous and were carriers of diseases such as foot and mouth disease (FMD), East Coast Fever and Bovine Malignant Catarrh (BMC) or "snotsiekte". Wildebeest were hunted with Vickers machine guns mounted on trucks, and waterholes were poisoned to eliminate them. They were referred to in The Times of Swaziland as "filthy detestable vermin". Large goods buses dubbed the "Impala Express" delivered 1 000 impala carcasses per week to the Johannesburg market for a number of years. Other game meat was ground up and used as feed in a piggery with the aim of exploiting the "free protein". In addition wide swathes of bush were cleared to control the dreaded tsetse fly. Cattle were dipped with arsenic to control ticks with no thought to its lethal effect on the oxpecker population.

Bovine tuberculosis (BTB), a bacterial disease adapted to cattle was introduced onto the continent when cattle were imported from Europe; through contact with livestock it became established in buffalo, also in the Kruger National Park (KNP), Umfolozi, and Hluhluwe and more recently in Marakele in the North-West of the country. The control of bovine tuberculosis (BTB) by the Veterinary Services involves the testing of cattle for the presence of the disease and culling of animals that tested positive. Culling of buffalo, infected or not, was also done based on this policy during and after the 1930s.

All the above factors led to a time where South Africa was left with small numbers of game of certain species: there were just 19 bontebok remaining, less than 2 000 blesbok, 30 white rhinoceros, and 90 Cape mountain zebra. Only three farms in the Free State had small herds of black wildebeest. Other species that were driven close to extinction through a combination of these various effects were, amongst others, black rhinoceros, sable antelope, roan antelope and oribi (see Table 1.1).

The beginnings of conservation

On the 13th June 1894 the President of the Boer republic, S.J. Paul Kruger, proclaimed the first game reserve in Africa, which was called Pongola, in the district of Piet Retief in what is now KwaZulu-Natal Province of South Africa. On 26th March 1898 he proclaimed the Sabi Game Reserve in the eastern Transvaal which today is an extensive park which carries his name, the Kruger National Park (KNP). These parks were the first localised steps in conserving South Africa's natural heritage in government parks and reserves, while outside the parks the decimation of wildlife continued.

Outside these parks, by the middle of the 20th century, the future of wildlife conservation in southern Africa was bleak, to the extent that rural farming properties were advertised with the "advantage" of not having wildlife that

Table 1.1: Population numbers of some game species in private and national parks.

Species	Total in +/- 1950	In parks	On private ranches	Total 2015
White rhino	30	12 000	5 000 (30%)	17 000
Black rhino	30	1 510	450 (23)	1960
Blesbuck	2 000	25 000	>225 000 (90%)	>250 000
Bontebok	19	1 000	>7 000 (87.5%)	>8 000
Sable antelope	450	<500	4 500	>5 000
Roan antelope	150	<200	2 300	>2 500
Cape mountain zebra	<80	1 925	865 (31)	>2790
Black wildebeest	<500	1800	>15 700	>17 500

would compete with livestock for grazing or harbour disease. At this time, all wildlife in South Africa was *res nullius* (of no value) and belonged to the State.

A change of heart occurred when leading conservationists from across the continent met in Arusha to chart a new course for African wildlife. The mood of the "Convention of Nature and Natural Resources in Modern African States" was captured by a South African, Rudolphi Bigalke:

"The indigenous mammals have evolved in the country and are well-adapted to local conditions. Every available food niche is occupied because domestic animals are ruining the country. Why not farm the game?"

Ironically, hunting, which was initially such a destructive force in the history of the country's wildlife, has been one of the drivers of conservation and the development of the game industry (see the section on Hunting). The local or biltong hunting segment is by far the biggest with an estimated 200 000 active hunters, whereas 5 000 to 6 000 trophy hunters (mainly foreigners) visit South Africa annually.

According to Milner-Gulland et al. (2003), a positive correlation exists between population growth of game animals and hunting activities. The authors are of the view that the general growth in the population has also seen a notable increase in the popularity of hunting. Developments such as the ban on hunting in protected areas introduced by the Botswana government, the challenges brought upon Zimbabwe's hunting industry through their largely failed land reform programme and the successive economic slowdown, hunting bans and economic instability in several previously major hunting destinations in Africa are all among the factors that present South Africa the opportunity to grow its hunting industry. The growing middle class in South Africa is another positive for future growth prospects.

Hunting tourism is a major source of income for wildlife business operations (Baldus & Cauldwell, 2004). Hunting involves more than just the actual "hunt" (stalk and shoot, culling, etc.); it also has an extensive value chain which gives rise to supporting industries.

Contribution of the game ranching industry to conservation in South Africa today

The establishment of the game ranching industry has resulted in the conversion of 20 million hectares of marginal agricultural land which was either not arable, was economically unviable, or unproductive, due to erratic rainfall and difficult market forces. Much of this land, from a conservation point of view, had been destroyed by the cow and the plough.

The promulgation of the Game Theft Act, Act 105 of 1991, which conferred private ownership of game, was probably the single biggest driving factor for the growth of the game ranching industry in South Africa. With this Act, wildlife gained value and became an asset to the landowner and consequently game animals became managed as such. Ownership and the subsequent trade resulted in the growth of game numbers which are currently estimated to be at the highest since 1850; the numbers are estimated to be almost 20 million.

Buffalo breeding

In 1997 the National Parks Board of South Africa (SANParks), faced with rapidly spreading BTB in KNP buffalo, initiated a project to breed buffalo free of diseases such as foot-and-mouth disease, corridor disease, tuberculosis and brucellosis.

The aim was to conserve the threatened "Kruger genotype" and to supply other National Parks and private wildlife ranches with "disease-free" buffalo. A long-term breeding project was initiated involving fostering of new-born buffalo calves by dairy cows. The calves were removed soon after birth from their dams and were then extensively tested to ensure freedom from the selected pathogens. These calves constituted a breeding herd from which specific pathogen free (SPF) buffalo could be bred.

Approximately 460 "disease-free" calves were produced during the life time of the project which ended in 2006. The offspring of these original buffalo were translocated to other National Parks and onto private wildlife ranches. The growth in the rare species industry (which includes buffalo, sable antelope, roan antelope and bontebok) has caused a steep and sudden increase in the buffalo numbers and value. Currently there are 35 000 buffalo in the KNP, 370 in Addo Elephant Park, 250 in the Mountain Zebra Park with a total in all parks of less than 36 000. Except for the 370 in Addo, most of these animals are all infected with either FMD, Corridor Disease, BTB and or brucellosis.

In contrast it is estimated that there are at least 60 000 disease-free buffalo on private game ranches or reserves, which is more than double the number which existed 16 years ago (1998) and 4 times the numbers recorded in the whole of the country in the mid-1900s. Similarly other game species have increased in numbers since 1991.

Rhino

The rescue of southern black (*Diceros bicornis minor*) and southern white (*Ceratotherium simum simum*) rhinoceros species, in contrast to the fate of their northern relatives, from the brink of extinction is a familiar story even to the general public. Briefly both southern rhino species had dwindled to worryingly low numbers of less than 100 individuals each when the far-sightedness of a number of conservationists who understood the concept and benefits of sustainable utilisation (most notably Dr Ian Player and private landowners such as Dr Clive Walker), resulted in breeding programs to protect both southern African species. Both the northern species are now practically extinct. Currently South Africa holds 82.3% of all African rhinoceros, 40% of the black rhino and 92.7% of the extant white rhino. Of these private reserves currently own approximately 30% (5 000) white rhino and 23% (450) black rhino. This situation is now under serious threat due to rhino horn poaching by organised crime syndicates which exploded in 2008. This new wave of poaching to supply consumers in Vietnam and other Asian countries for spurious cultural and medicinal purposes, has resulted in mass slaughter of the southern African rhino populations and almost

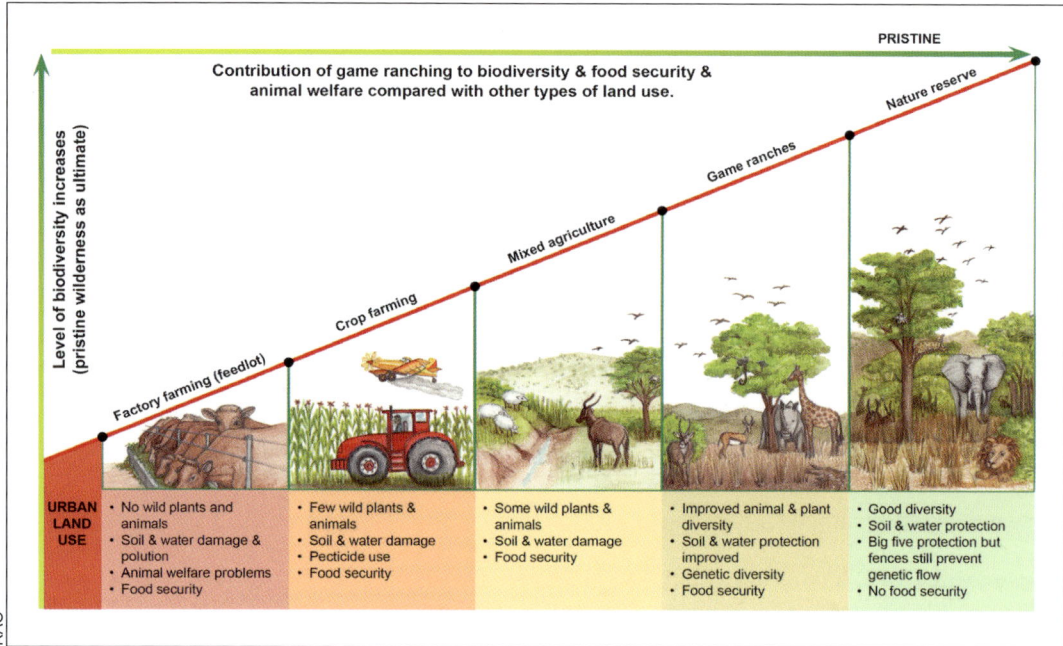

Comparison of biodiversity of various activities.

1 500 animals of the existing populations have been killed for their horns in 2014. It is a huge frustration for wildlife ranchers and conservationists alike that the CITES ban on rhino horn trade has, over the past 30 years, had little impact on this pointless killing, and the wildlife ranching industry is lobbying for controlled sales of horn to supply the product sustainably and legally, and at the same time ensure the survival of the animals.

Predators and other species

With the arrival of the gun in South Africa, farmers, hunters and rural populations have taken their toll on especially large predator species, either for sport, or to protect themselves or their livestock. This is one of the most difficult areas for conservationists and animal lovers to address, because the large carnivores require large areas of land for their survival and need to be adequately contained because of the potential danger to humans and other animals. Unlike other game species which have increased in numbers recently in South Africa due to the South African government's policy of sustainable utilisation, the numbers of predators such as lion, cheetah and wild dogs continue to decline and breeders of these species are faced with the problem of animals with nowhere to go outside of national, provincial and private game reserves. Issues such as lion hunting have become contentious and need open and honest debate, for example what do landowners or breeders do with animals past their reproductive age – should they be hunted to earn revenue for conservation/breeding programs or should they die of old age, or be euthanased? The elephant population faces a similar crisis to that of the predators. From a human point of view the species is large and destructive, and has therefore nowhere to go outside of large wildlife reserves, and even there the numbers have to be controlled to keep ecosystems from being destroyed.

The relaxation of South African legislation again permitting ranchers to keep and move wildebeest (a reservoir of the "snotsiekte" / Bovine Malignant Catarrh virus which is highly fatal in cattle) has led to them again having a value, being an asset and consequently huge increases in the wildebeest populations of both species. This has led to increased conflict with cattle farmers, and to mitigate this research into the development of a vaccine has been spearheaded.

Other contributions to conservation by private landowners have been black wildebeest, sable and roan antelope, bontebok, Cape mountain zebra and many others. But it is not only the larger mammals that have benefited, also oxpeckers, reptiles and insects such as dung beetles and even flies like the oestrid that lives solely in the rhinoceros stomach.

Biodiversity

Many publications have reported on the decimation of game species and game numbers in Africa. A paper published in Ecology, called "Collapse of the world's largest herbivores" reports that between 1970 and 2005, large mammal populations in Africa's protected areas decreased by about 59%, with the current ungulate biomass in Zambian Parks as an example being only 21% of its potential in part due to overhunting. The authors also reported that according to the International Union for the Conservation of Nature (IUCN) 44 of the 74 (60%) largest terrestrial herbivores are listed as threatened with extinction including 12 critically endangered or extinct in the wild, and 43 (58%) have decreasing populations. A very telling point made in this paper is that "Livestock are private goods and so, people invest significant energy to protect it, whereas wild herbivores are typically a public good, often resulting in weak incentives for their conservation and in many cases open access to the resource, both of which commonly result in overuse". Their proposed solutions include reducing uncontrolled consumption of wild herbivores and/or enforced wildlife management such as via wildlife ranching which has proven to be very successful at maintaining sustainably high harvests of wild meat while providing subsistence food resources to local people.

Since the 1970s, West Africa has lost 80% of the wildlife in its national parks, and even more outside. East Africa has lost half the wildlife

The birds are back: With the return of game, oxpecker reintroduction and breeding programs have been a huge success.

in its parks, and some 70% outside them. By contrast, southern African parks (South Africa, Swaziland, Namibia, Zimbabwe and Botswana) have maintained or even slightly increased their wildlife, and after wildlife was nearly annihilated on private land by the 1960s, it has rebounded at least fivefold. In South Africa one third of rhino, approximately 90% of the bontebok, blesbok, black wildebeest, roan, sable antelope, and disease-free buffalo are owned by private ranchers. This is a massive contribution to not only the conservation of rare and endangered species but to all the associated fauna and flora of wild ecosystems, which slowly return when a game ranch is established. Soil, water, plants and animals become an essential part of the web of life: large mammals become invaluable for improving soil fertility, dung beetles and diggers become allies in soil conservation and habitat management, oxpeckers are part of the tick control team and on most ranches, predators are seen as part of the natural culling force. Scavengers are valued for their ability to use and recycle carcasses. Undisturbed uncontaminated wetlands become protected areas for the breeding of rare bird species such as the blue crane, and other waterfowl; vulture restaurants managed by game ranchers provide a safe sanctuary for endangered populations. Bird watchers, nature lovers of all species, photographers, school groups and scientists are able to benefit from these enriched ecosystems which would otherwise be monocultures of crops or livestock in areas with poor soil and erratic rainfall. Game ranches are in effect a sustainable source of income, whether through tourism, hunting, game meat harvesting, training and education or breeding, because they are managing a natural resource rather than depleting it. It is beyond the capacity of a government, burdened with service provision to almost 55 million South Africans to be solely responsible for spearheading the Green Economy. Conservation is an expen-

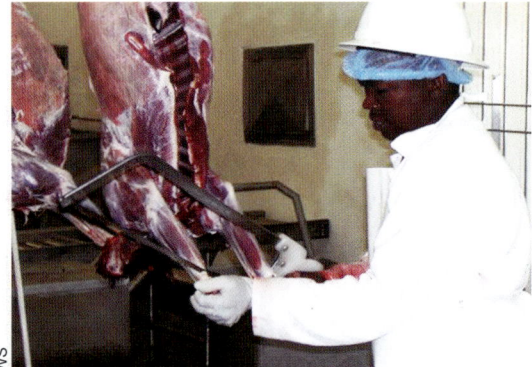
Venison processing in an export abattoir – this industry collapsed due to a foot-and-mouth outbreak in the country.

sive undertaking requiring high levels of capital investment, management and high input costs which now include extensive security. Government departments are mostly understaffed and unable to cope with all the threats and challenges posed by such activities.

Contribution of wildlife ranching to the South African economy

The principle of "if it pays it stays" once quoted by prominent South African conservationist Dr John Ledger, about the future of conservation in Africa has proven to be correct. Once game animal ownership was privatised in South Africa, wild animals took on a value which the landowner could utilise in a sustainable manner either for tourism, trophy or biltong hunting, meat production or breeding rare or desirable species. This resulted in the growth of an industry which contributes to the economy by providing employment.

The current contribution of game ranching to the South African fiscus is more than R20 billion per annum and can be subdivided as shown below.

- Tourism (private Nature, Environmental and Adventure Tourism (NEAT) which makes up a substantial portion of the R100 billion annual tourism revenue earned by South Africa).

- Biltong hunting (R6,3 billion).
- Trophy hunting (R1,2 billion).
- Breeding (R3,1 billion).
- Venison or game meat exports (R400m prior to the ban placed on exports as a result of the failure to control foot-and-mouth disease adequately).

Employment

Private wildlife tourism creates decent job opportunities. Tourism is the largest job provider of all professions worldwide and the third largest industry in South Africa. Currently, 617 287 jobs are provided by the tourism industry in South Africa. Focusing on hunting only, research conducted by Saayman *et al.* reported that hunting in three of South Africa's most prominent hunting provinces (Limpopo, Free State and Northern Cape) is responsible for sustaining up to 31 436 jobs.

Other research has shown that three times as many workers are employed on a wildlife ranch compared to a similar domestic stock farm. In addition, as a result of the higher skill set demand of a wildlife ranch, necessitated to cater for the tourism, for hospitality and hunting components, employees on wildlife ranches generally earn salaries three times higher than those on comparable domestic stock farms.

Food security

As discussed in the introduction South Africa is not ideally suited for agriculture when compared with other countries of the world including in Africa, because of low and erratic rainfall, high evaporation, and poor, shallow soils. Currently it has a government which is unsympathetic to commercial farmers for historical reasons and various economic constraints, such as a volatile currency, relatively high inflation, adversarial and largely unskilled labour force which makes it difficult to compete internationally. Extensive cattle farming, for example, is not currently profitable because farmers are unable to set the price of their own product. Livestock farmers are, therefore, forced to diversify into other areas. Almost half of the 14 million cattle and 25 million sheep and goats in the country are kept on communal grazing and never get to market; they therefore don't contribute to the economy or to the huge demand for meat in the country which requires imports of almost R4 billion annually. Only 16.4% of South Africa's surface area is considered having high agricultural potential. The remainder (65.8%) of the potential agricultural land is regarded as agriculturally marginal (see Table 1.2).

Only half of South Africa's national herd (total livestock population) produces meat commercially, as the other half is owned by small scale pastoralists.

As a result South Africa's annual imports are:
- Beef to the value of R1 billion, mainly from Namibia, Botswana, Argentina and Brazil,
- Mutton to the value of R1 billion, mainly from New Zealand and Australia,
- Chicken to the value of R2 billion, mainly from Brazil.

TOTAL: Meat/protein to the value of R4 billion is imported annually.

Table 1.2: Land allocation in South Africa.

ACTIVITY LAND	SURFACE AREA (in million hectares)	PERCENTAGE OF TOTAL
Potential agricultural land	100.6	82.2
(Viable)	(21.1)	(16.4)
(Marginal)	(80.5)	(65.8)
Other (urban, etc)	21.7	17.8
Total	122,3	100

Table 1.3: Land allocated to agriculture and conservation in South Africa.

ACTIVITY	SURFACE AREA (in million hectares)	% OF AGRICULTURAL LAND	% OF SA
Conservation	28.0	27.8	22.9
(Government)	(7.5)	(7.4)	(6.1)
(Commercial ranches)	(20.5)	(20.4)	(16.8)
Other agricultural land	72.6	72.2	57.3
TOTAL	100,6	100	82,2

It has been determined that South Africa (and the rest of the world) needs to double its food production capacity in the next 35 years while food prices internationally are expected to treble in the next three years and double thereafter every five years. The seriousness of this situation is illustrated by the fact that the responsibility for food security has been taken over by the National Intelligence Agency (NIA).

The game ranching industry in contrast is expanding because it has the Unique Selling Point of having a sustainable resource (wild animals and their habitat), and is currently larger than both the sugar and dairy industries. Also many of the large successful game ranchers are successful business people who generated income to indulge their passion for wildlife by establishing wildlife ranches and using business principles of meeting demand with supply, for meat and animals such as rare species, rare colour variants or "disease-free" animals.

More than 120 000 tons of game meat reach the cities via the informal (not legally accounted for) route of the "biltong" hunter, a further 10 000 tons being contributed by the trophy hunter. In addition, an unknown amount reaches the market directly from wildlife ranches. A significant amount is sold as trimmings and used in many of the processed meat products such as polonies and sausages. This latter market is yet to be expanded to its full potential mainly due to the lack of adequate legislation. Generally, today, game meat is not sold at the premium delicacy price it should be.

South Africa also exports up to R400 million of game meat annually mainly to Europe, an industry that employed more than a thousand people. The recent outbreak of foot-and-mouth disease brought this to a halt and more than 700 jobs were lost. Apart from the job losses caused, this was a huge blow to the economy because for every one kilogram of game meat exported, South Africa earns sufficient foreign exchange to import almost 4 kg of beef.

Contribution to knowledge about wildlife biology

Since the sudden explosion in game prices and the growth in the value of "rare species" and "colour variants" an enormous amount of work has gone into studying various aspects such as genetics, nutrition, habitat and husbandry requirements, diseases, parasites and the characteristics of game meat. Various universities are involved in these studies:
- University of Stellenbosch – game meat and quality.
- University of Pretoria (the faculty of Veterinary Science at Onderstepoort) – diseases, parasites, vaccine development and genetics).
- University of North West – financial aspects of the industry.

CHAPTER 1: INTRODUCTION TO GAME RANCHING

School for the children of workers established on the Wintershoek Game Ranch.

- University of Free State – predator costs and management.
- Tshwane University of Technology – game ranch management.

All these institutions collaborate with Wildlife Ranching South Africa (WRSA) in the fields of research and education.

Social responsibility, community involvement and transformation projects

The game ranching industry currently provides employment for an estimated 140 000 people, many of whom are paid according to the tourist industry rate which is a higher notch than a farm labourer and or domestic worker. In addition many privately owned game ranches and reserves have embarked on programmes to assist social upliftment, for example the provision of schools for local people, clinics, sports fields and training of staff in skills such as taxidermy and the preparation of hides.

Some ranchers have given workers shares in their businesses and even properties, and now they are participating in various projects for the mentoring and development of black game farmers.

A flagship project is WRSA's engagement with the Komani San in the Kgalagadi Gemsbok Park where mentorship and assistance with infrastructure is ongoing.

Workers at Wintershoek receive training as taxidermists.

The challenges to game ranching

There are a number of challenges to the continued growth of game ranching which need to be faced. One of the most serious threats to the industry is the presence of foot-and-mouth disease in the Kruger National Park. Control of FMD resorts under the Veterinary Services Directorate of the Department of Agriculture, Forestry and Fisheries (DAFF). They are, however, hampered by fragmented provincial disease control policies and lack of capacity to attend to their two main objectives, namely disease control and community services. In addition, there is confusion and conflict between National and Provincial Veterinary Services which leads to lack of co-operation between these authorities. As a result full attention and finances are not always directed towards the control of FMD. The latter concerns were addressed and confirmed by the OIE (World Organisation for Animal Health) in their recent visits to and evaluations of South Africa. Since vaccination (as used to protect cattle in the buffer zone) of game species is not a viable option FMD is a major threat to the game ranching industry's future. Should FMD spread into non-infected game reserves and ranches the whole industry would collapse since the control measures will involve eradication of potentially infected species such as buffalo, kudu and impala. Apart from this horrific scenario, eradicating might not be effective in eradicating the disease.

The department's lack of capacity in the area of veterinarians or animal health technicians to attend to test bleeding, to safe transport of blood samples to the laboratories and to attend to the actual transport of negatively tested animals also greatly hampers the movement and thus the business of buffalo ranching in particular. Years of negotiations have to date yielded very limited progress with DAFF. Outdated environmental legislation as administered by the Department of Environmental Affairs (DEA), which was enacted to regulate mainly Municipal, Provincial and National Parks as well as endangered species prior to the establishment of the wildlife ranching industry is not conducive to the business of game ranching. There are numerous laws involved and, as with the Veterinary Services, constraints include the 9-plus-1 constitutional concept where the provinces do not necessarily and rarely follow the National Department's lead. All this additional and unnecessary administration adds to the time, the administrative load and the costs needed to move animals to the obvious

Rhino horn poaching is a serious threat to private rhino owners.

great frustration of game ranchers.

Opposition from some conservationists and a local hunting group to so-called "intensive farming", and to the direction on which the wildlife ranching Industry has embarked, has become a major public debate as the opponents perceive that the growth in the industry and in particular the growth in game prices is making the cost of consumptive hunting beyond their means. They also allege that breeding wildlife species will have negative conservation implications, with particular objections against intensive breeding of valuable rare species and colour variant animals. This ignores the fact that the land used for game ranching was agricultural land that is improving with respect to biodiversity. The main association of wildlife ranchers, WRSA, has a Code of Conduct and Notes of Best Practice to mitigate against any negative aspects that might occur. Critics claim that the game ranching industry is a "pyramid scheme" which will ultimately collapse. This is refuted by agricultural financiers who point out that a pyramid scheme is one in which the market becomes saturated, leaving the investor with a product which has no value (see Economic contribution).

The hunting fraternity itself is coming under increasing criticism due to a mounting dislike among the public of in particular hunting of so called "iconic" species such as lion as well as what is perceived as unnecessary hunting (trophies). Unprofessional and unethical conduct by hunters and hunting outfitters does not help the poor image of hunting in any way and could destroy this industry.

The scourge of rhino poaching is placing South Africa's rhino population at the real risk of eventual extinction. Since 2008 when there were 83 rhino poached there has been a precipitous rise to the 1 215 in 2014. There are 320 private rhino reserves that occupy 2 million ha of ranch land. Apart from the impact on rhino numbers and the loss of genetic material, the impact of poaching is estimated by the Private Rhino Owners Association (PROA), a Chamber of Wildlife Ranching South Africa, to be R350 million in direct asset loss – dead rhino – to private ranchers alone. In addition to this, security costs the ranchers R300 million per year and this ignores other expenses like veterinary bills and other management interventions like feeding animals to keep them close to secure spots on the ranches. Roughly 40 reserves have stopped rhino ranching due to the high costs of security (estimated to be R272 million per year), safety concerns and the trauma of poaching incidents. The CITES ban on the sale of rhino horn which was imposed in 1977, has had no impact whatsoever, and private owners argue that alternative strategies must be sought.

In addition rhino poaching is causing a huge economic drain on the country with respect to loss of income of farmers, insurance, expenditure on security services and funding raised by public. Land reform policies continue to be an uncertain and troubled political area. Although Government has engaged in conservative land reform policies thus far, the threat of land grabs and radicalisation of jobless youth is placing pressure on politicians to have more radical policies. This uncertainty is a negative factor for the industry and vacillating attitudes by politicians make it difficult to plan for the future. The perceived threats and uncertainty are greatly hampering investment in land, agriculture as a whole and especially in wildlife ranching where the true contribution of the industry to the country is not well understood by many politicians.

The future of game farming

There are no signs that the game industry is a bubble which will collapse in the next decade. The prices of sought-after animals continue to increase. For example, the sales on auction of buffalo over the past 10 years have increased 7 fold to 358 individuals for a total value of R360m in 2013. To put a "consumptive" perspective on this, the income from hunting in 2011 was 47.5% of the total income for buffalo for the year (52.5% of the total thus at auctions for live breeding animals). The record price paid for a buffalo bull so far is R40m, which shows that there is still a market for good buffalo genetics. Agricultural economist Ernst Janovsky, head of Agribusiness at ABSA, predicts that even if the market for sought-after animals such as disease-free buffalo become "saturated" (and it is far away from that situation), the animals still have intrinsic value as would livestock, so there would be no resultant "crash" as is seen with pyramid schemes.

See the transcript of his 15th July radio interview on the youngest trends and future prospects for South African Agriculture (in Afrikaans) on Moneyweb (http://www.moneyweb.co.za).

Breeders of valuable and sought-after species are selecting progeny based on certain characteristics such as body size and conformation, typical masculinity, reproductive efficiency and where applicable, horn length since these animals command the highest prices both for hunting and thus as breeding animals. In collaboration with geneticists WRSA has revised its Code of Conduct and disciplinary procedures, and developed "Notes of Best Practice" for many ranching activities, including breeding for its game rancher members to ensure that the industry limits any negative aspects such as inbreeding, a reduction of genetic diversity and any deleterious genes such as albinism or depigmentation of the skin.

It is foreseen further that other modern technologies such as diagnostic techniques, "stud" breeding software and vaccines against various previously non–preventable diseases will revolutionise game farming to the benefit of the industry and conservation. Selection for deleterious characteristics will not favour the game-ranching industry.

A move away from regionally-based (based on a region being classified as FMD infected or free) to commodity-based trade policies (based on the ability of a product to transmit the virus) used by the member states of OIE will also add further impetus to the industry's remarkable growth and its contribution to the South African economy and conservation of various species.

As techniques to study the genetics of species develop and as the understanding of the information gained improves, conservation and game farming can be managed more scientifically and contribute to the successful breeding of rare and endangered species.

Role of Wildlife Ranching Association of South Africa (WRSA)

Two game ranching associations in South Africa are currently looking after the interests of their members. The largest and only national body is Wildlife Ranching South Africa (WRSA) which lobbies government on legislation, creates study groups on the ranching of certain species, initiates research into genetics of game breeding, diagnostics and vaccination against diseases, and provides information to educate the public, an essential part of the conservation process.

WRSA functions are all funded by WRSA members. They also publish a magazine which informs and educates members and the public about their industry but also about conservation issues. WRSA has taken on one of the roles of conservation which is education.

Transformation and land reform within South African society, agriculture and in particular the wildlife industry is essential to ensure the future. Based on business models in Angola and Zimbabwe where local people took custodianship of areas repopulated with wildlife after decades of conflict and war for the purposes of sustainable utilisation this is a feasible model.

WRSA has committed itself to assisting in transformation projects and has set the following goals for 2021:
- Contributing R75 billion to the South African fiscus.
- Employing 300 000 people in decent jobs.
- Producing 250 000 tons of game meat, contributing to food security.
- Exporting R1.5 billion worth of game meat.
- Contributing to biodiversity and the Green Economy through expanding the wildlife ranching footprint to more than 30 million hectares.
- Stocking farms with 30 million head of game.

WRSA provides its members with information, study groups, and support in certain areas such as rhino poaching and assistance with legal matters.

For more details about WRSA:
www.wrsa.co.za.

THE FOUR PILLARS OF GAME RANCHING
BREEDING OF GAME ANIMALS
Barry York

This sector of the wildlife industry involves the breeding and trading of game animals. It has grown exponentially since the legalisation of game ownership by private ranchers, and is rapidly becoming, financially, the largest sector of the wildlife game industry for various reasons. Some of these reasons are the availability of disease free buffalo together with the increasing popularity of colour variants of various antelope and a few other species. Some of the advantages of this sector have been identified by economists of ABSA's Agricultural department:

- This animal husbandry activity is unique, not just in Africa but in the rest of the world where wildlife are decreasing in numbers.
- It is attracting foreign investors.
- It is labour intensive.
- It is cash based.
- It has stimulated the development of other industries and activities, such as feed production, disease and vaccine research and even game meat production (good value chain).

Breeding valuable wild animal species provides a sustainable income.

Breeding is especially suited for ranches with no ecotourism potential because of the lack of aesthetic appeal. Wild animal breeding by private owners makes a significant contribution to conservation which is increasingly difficult for government to support and provides diverse genetic material for repopulating isolated wild animal populations such as in KNP. KNP's animals are not only isolated but are infected with introduced diseases such as TB (lion, buffalo and kudu) and brucellosis (buffalo) which impact on their breeding potential, while most of the privately owned wild animal populations serve as a reserve of non-diseased animals.

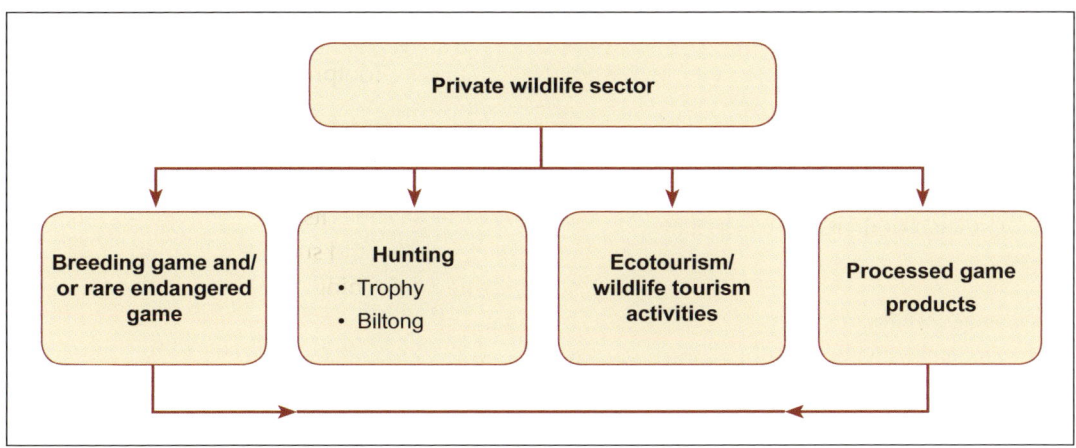
Figure 1: Four pillars of game ranching

The reasons for choosing to breed wild animals whether extensively or semi-intensively in camps are varied:
- Lifestyle and occasional income: Owners wishing to create a private nature reserve and do occasional hunting or capture to control numbers. This generally earns a small income and involves high overhead costs, which can be supplemented by eco-tourism and/or occasional hunting or sales.
- Sustainable income from breeding: Ranchers in marginal areas where livestock ranching is uneconomical, who have opted for ranching valuable species in semi-intensive systems. Animals may be bred and sold:
  - as stud animals to other breeders,
  - to restock hunting ranches.
- Breeding for conservation purposes, for example Cape Mountain zebra, the large cats and wild dogs, etc.
- Sustainable income from venison harvesting: Ranchers who make a sustainable living from providing venison for local and overseas markets.
- Breeding for specific products such as ostrich or crocodile leather, meat and others.

Table 1.4

TYPE OF ANIMALS BRED	PERCENTAGE GAME RANCHES
Plains game species (common species) e.g. impala, springbok, zebra, hartebeest, gemsbok, etc)	25%
Less common species (nyala, lechwe, bontebok)	25%
High value species (sable, roan, disease-free buffalo)	30%
Colour variant antelope	5%

Most of the discussion in this section refers to herbivore breeding, so the reader is referred to species chapters for details on non-herbivores. The type of breeding system practiced on a game ranch will determine the management style. There are basically two different management systems which are used for breeding game animals, namely extensive and semi-extensive systems. In general, extensive systems are minimal input, used for hunting, tourism, lifestyle and conservation, while semi-extensive systems are used for endangered, rare or highly sought-after game species. The activities of the breeder sector of game ranch breeders is summarised in Table 1.4.

Advantages and constraints of extensive game ranching

The average size of a game ranch in South Africa is roughly 2 600 ha, depending on the biome, as in more arid areas the carrying capacity is lower and the size of a commercially viable property would need to be larger. The extensive nature of a game ranch is not only defined by the size but by the management style, which would include a single undivided large fenced area stocked with a variety of suitable game species.

These systems lend themselves to being combined with tourism, occasional hunting and venison harvesting but are not very efficient in terms of animal production for a number of reasons:
- Wild animal populations that are not well managed have a higher proportion of males than is necessary for efficient reproduction. Fewer producing females in these populations result in low numbers of offspring in relation to the total number of animals carried on the property.
- Game ranches no matter how large, do not allow for the free migration of animals which would be necessary for them to

migrate and obtain the nutritional needs for optimum production. Nutritional stress when either the quality or quantity is low, results in poor levels of reproduction, slow growth rates with increased mortality and predation levels. Malnourished animals are less resistant to both internal and external parasites, and are subject to their accompanying diseases.

- Continuous grazing by both domestic or wild animals even at low stocking rates leads to combinations of overutilisation of certain areas, and underutilisation of others. Both overgrazed denuded areas and undergrazed areas with tall unpalatable moribund grasses lead to veld degradation, a lower carrying capacity, increased risk of soil erosion, reduced effective rainwater absorption, inefficient mineral cycles and decreased biodiversity.
- Losses through disease, predation or other causes are often relatively high and may go unnoticed in extensive areas. Rare species such as roan, sable and tsessebe cannot survive high predation levels.
- Genetic deterioration such as inbreeding and subsequent loss of diversity cannot easily be managed in an extensive system.

These limitations can to some extent be addressed by removing excess males through hunting or capture, providing feed supplements such as licks, using fire where too much moribund vegetation and bush encroachment occur, closing of water points and controlling predators. But, in general, financial returns from an extensive game ranching system that has been stocked with more common species, which allows recreational hunting or live sales of animals to game capture operations, are low and they seldom cover the day to day running costs of the property. This is true for both small and large game ranches where the actual production side of the business is not financially viable and must be subsidised by some other income stream.

Comparison of the productive capacity of extensive and semi-extensive breeding systems

Extensive systems

The production levels of a 1 000 ha ranch where animals are managed according to conservation principles and are left to fend for themselves with minimum interference can be assessed with the examples discussed.

Definitions

Extensive ranching/systems: Refers to a natural environment that is of sufficient size for the management of free roaming wildlife populations, irrespective of whether it is fenced or not; that meets the ecological requirements of the wildlife populations occurring on such land; where no or minimal intervention is required in the form of the provision of water, supplement food (except in times of drought), control of parasites or predation, or provision of health care.

Semi-extensive wildlife system: Refers to an environment that is of sufficient size for the management of self-sustaining wildlife populations, irrespective of whether it is fenced or not or whether it meets the ecological requirements of such population or not, but where human intervention is required in the form of the provision of water, supplement food, control of parasites or predation and/or provision of healthcare.

Wildebeest are used here as an example because they are suited to extensive ranching being hardy, low maintenance animals which can utilise unpalatable grasses on leached sandy infertile soils of old lands.

- A carrying capacity of one livestock unit (1 LSU or a beef cow equivalent = 10 ha) will carry 2 wildebeest or one wildebeest per 5 hectares.
- Wildebeest calves are born to a ratio of 50% male and female.
- Animals achieve 75% of their mature body weight at 2 years (puberty) and mature mass at 3 years old.
- Heifers calve at 3 years of age and reproductive females have a 50% conception rate.
- Female to male ratio on the ranch will be 60:40 since more males are hunted.
- Mortality rate for young animals up to weaning age is 5% and 2% for older animals
- Average wildebeest life span is 10 years

Given these parameters on a 1 000 ha ranch one could run a herd of 200 wildebeest, comprised of 80 males and 120 females, of which 70% or 84 females would be sexually active with a calving rate of 50%. One could expect 42 calves minus 5% mortalities which leaves 40 calves a year. A 2% mortality overall for older animals leaves 36 animals or an 18% increase of the herd. An annual increase in animal numbers on extensive game ranches in SA is estimated to be 15–25%, which is a low level of production.

Given the above, selling the 36 excess animals at R3 000 each would result in an income of R108 000.

Semi-extensive systems

To achieve economic viability and optimise sustainable economic production the current tendency is to produce rare or expensive species in semi-extensive systems. This means keeping animals in large camps which allow free movement but in which they can be identified, supplemented, better protected against predators and breeding can therefore be better controlled. Semi-extensive systems improve the production in a number of ways:

- Optimising grass production through rotational grazing and fertilisation by dunging.
- Improving production of animals by supplementation.
- Improving genetic management to ensure genetic diversity and improved vigour.
- Protect vulnerable species from predation.

Using the example given above of wildebeest under the extensive system, under semi-extensive management where the grazing is managed by camp rotation, dunging and

Table1.5: Estimated economic contribution for live game trade and a few related activities (after ABSA, 2015)

Description	Live sales and related activities (value of animals sold)	
Estimated economic contribution in 2014	Formal auctions	R1.8 billion
	Informal sales	*R8 billion
	*Commissions (only from formal sales)	*R55 million
	*Capture and translocation (excluding pharmaceutical equipment, etc.)	*R200 million
Total		**Excess of R10 billion**

*estimates

Extensive breeding of common red-coloured impala.

Semi-intensive breeding of black and saddle back impala.

supplementation, the carrying capacity is increased (1 LSU is now 4 ha) so the number of animals can be increased from 200 to 500.
- The breeding ratio can now be adjusted to the optimal bull:cow ratio (1:30) which is 16 bulls for 484 females.
- Heifers on improved nutrition now calve at 2 years so 80% females are reproductive = 388 cows.
- An improved calving rate of 90% minus 5% allowed for mortalities means an increase of 321 animals compared with the 36 animals per year on extensive systems giving an income of R 963 000, an increase of almost 10 fold. If these happen to be differently coloured wildebeest, e.g. golden wildebeest then the income will increase even more dramatically.

Animals bred are traded either informally from rancher to rancher via direct sales or via agents or formally via auctions. The breeding contribution to the industry and the country's GDP is in excess of R10 billion which can be subdivided as in Table 1.5.

Economic risks and benefits

These animals were either raised on extensive or semi-extensive ranches and sold to similar properties. Semi-extensive systems will initially incur increased initial outlay for the purchase of

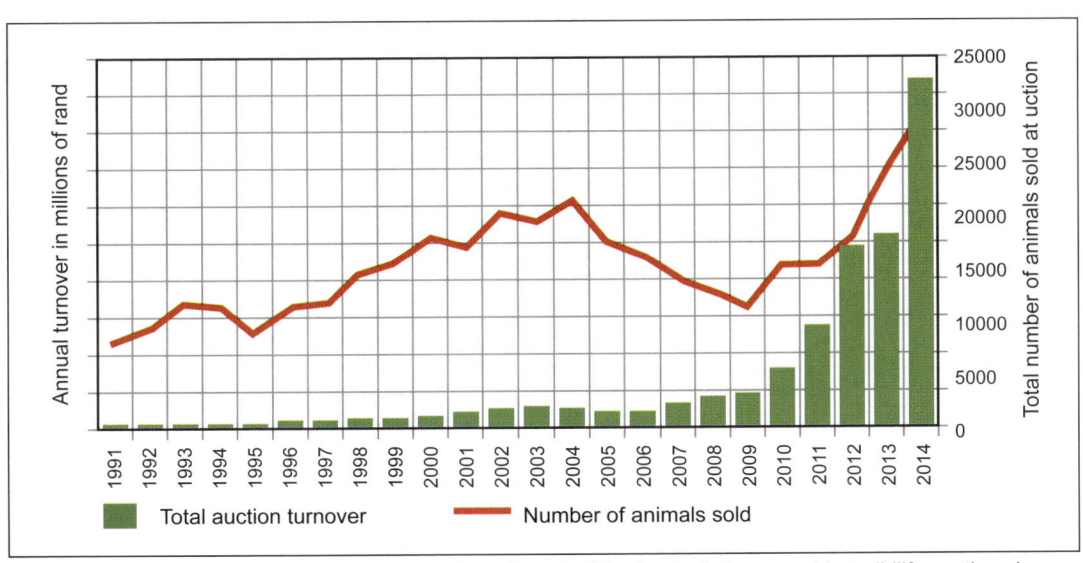
Annual turnover in millions of rand and the total number of wild animals that were sold at wildlife auctions in South Africa from 1991 to 2014 (after ABSA, 2015).

Sable antelope in unsuitable habitat and unacceptable conditions. Note the close contact with cattle which are a potential source of brucellosis and tuberculosis.

Sable in suitable habitat with good camp management.

animals, fencing, and feed troughs; additional overhead costs such as supplement feed, transport and other management aspects must also be budgeted for, but if the animal involved is in demand, for example a golden wildebeest or a split golden wildebeest (carrying the recessive golden gene) compared to a blue wildebeest, the additional overheads are offset by the increased selling value of the individual animal (blue wildebeest bull R3 000 compared to a golden wildebeest bull from R800 000 to R3 400 000, or a split heifer pregnant to a golden bull at R225 000).

Management considerations in semi-extensive camps

Breeding animals under semi-extensive conditions requires good initial planning, good supervision and a respect for the welfare and basic needs of the animals under one's care. A "profiteering" approach to breeding to exploit current high prices commanded by some species will backfire on the rancher involved because animals not adapted to the environment or whose needs are not met will not thrive or breed and mortalities usually eventually result. The habitat (biome) must be suitable for raising the specific species, for example impala are not suited to arid areas, while springbok are not suited to sourveld conditions. Other specific requirements of the species which has been chosen for breeding must be borne in mind. For example, kudu do not do well at all in small camp systems while sable thrive if they are given the recommended minimum space, and the composition of the social structure of breeding herds is borne in mind to prevent injuries due to bull and cow aggression. Mixing of herbivore species must be done with caution. All these aspects are discussed for each species in Chapter 4.

Breeding camps must always be correctly constructed for the specific species, and with the animal's welfare in mind, providing the correct space, feed, water spacing, shelter from adverse weather conditions, protective fencing. Raising animals in backyards or vegetable gardens, un-rehabilitated old lands, and feeding on the ground or from old bathtubs and the like are not suitable practices for professional breeders of valuable game animals. Camps must always be the correct size per species, and must be rotated to provide sufficient natural grazing and prevent build-up of diseases such as coccidiosis, worms such as wireworm and ticks carrying *Theileria* spp. Zero-grazing feed supplementation (no forage) should never be a long term plan for game animal breeding because it defeats the object of game ranching which is sustainable use of the natural resource (grazing) and promotion of biodiversity. Supplementing whole rations

Minimum camp sizes recommended for different main veld types, for one breeding herd / breeding couple, of one species only.			
Animal species	Kalahari Karoo	Bushveld Savannah	Grassland Highveld
Gemsbok, eland, red hartebeest, buffalo, white rhino, mountain zebra	200 ha	75 ha	50 ha
Blue-/golden wildebeest, sable, roan, tsessebe, plains zebra, Black wildebeest, waterbuck	75 ha	40 ha	30 ha
Springbok, impala, blesbok, mountain reedbuck	75 ha	20 ha	15 ha
Nyala, oribi	50 ha	12 ha	12 ha
Common reedbuck, bushbuck, Klipspringer	30 ha	10 ha	7 ha
Duiker, steenbok, suni	20 ha	2 ha	2 ha

is very expensive and in addition it does not promote optimal use of natural grazing. The supplements used must be suitable for the species and must be fed in the correct amounts according to the recommended method (see guidelines under Nutrition).

Genetic management in semi-extensive systems

Striving for genetic diversity in wild animal populations is a serious challenge for game breeders; in many cases species have been on the brink of extinction, and the small remaining population has reached a "genetic bottleneck" or low genetic diversity. Having a low genetic diversity may make the animals susceptible to disease conditions and may result in poor viability of young. It is now particularly important given the challenges of global warming which will test the ability of animals to adapt to changing environmental circumstances.

The difficulties of dealing with founder groups with low genetic diversity include insufficient knowledge about genetics of game animals, controversies about the status (existence or not) of sub-species, politics about keeping nature "pristine" and complying with statutory regulations. The game industry instigated research into wild animal genetics which has made a whole new body of knowledge accessible to game ranchers and breeders in conservation projects. A genetics section is therefore included in this book.

The growth in popularity of breeding animals with rare and uncommon coat colours has drawn criticism from purist conservationists who feel that these "unnatural" animals should not be bred. Genetics experts agree that these colour variants are merely the result of the rich variation of nature, which is now more commonly seen due to the increased numbers of game animals (>20 million head, more than ever since 1850) closer inspection by game ranchers and selection by breeders for their scarcity, beauty and value. However, breeding animals for specific characteristics such as coat colour and horn size should be done with a good knowledge of the dangers, learned from experience in the livestock industry, of line-breeding which can result in the disadvantages of in-breeding, such as infertility and predisposition to disease. Fortunately, the body of knowledge on genetics in wildlife is growing and the breeder has the opportunity to learn and to consult experts on these issues making it possible to limit in-breeding and mitigate any possible negative consequences.

HUNTING IN SOUTH AFRICA
Professional Hunters Association of South Africa (PHASA)

Hunting, sustainable use and bio-diversity conservation

With an estimated 19 000 white rhinos in South Africa in 2015, representing around 90% of the world's total rhino population, few people are aware that trophy hunting played a pivotal role in the expansion of rhino across South Africa and many people consider trophy hunting one of the biggest contributors in preventing the *white rhino from becoming extinct.*

During the early Sixties leading conservationists recognised that for rhino numbers to increase, their habitat had to grow beyond that of the few provincial parks where they occurred and that an economic incentive was needed for landowners to keep rhino on their property. In order to achieve this rhino were put back on the hunting list which, thanks to the large amount of money hunters were prepared to pay for the privilege, resulted in rhino populations ballooning. This was the beginning of South Africa's remarkable conservation success story.

Thanks to legislation allowing for the private ownership of game and limited, sustainable trophy hunting, the total head of game in South Africa soared from around 500 000 in the early Sixties to some 20 million today, of which 16 million are privately owned. At the same time private game reserves in the country increased from only four in the Sixties to an estimated 10 000, covering an estimated 20.5 million hectares of land. In comparison, all South Africa's national and state parks comprise only 7.5 million hectares. Private game farms therefore own three times more land dedicated to wildlife and four-fifths of all the game, managed under very successful and effective conservation programmes, than all the state-owned parks and reserves combined. Game has overtaken cattle, which now number only some 14 million, and vast tracts of land have been reclaimed from livestock-rearing and agricultural use for wildlife conservation. This is unheard of anywhere else in the world and it is almost entirely due to trophy hunting. Additionally, due to the demand by trophy hunters, species such as the bontebok, black wildebeest, roan antelope and sable, which were once very scarce, have been successfully reintroduced to areas where they had become locally extinct.

Policy of leading conservation bodies on sustainable use

Most leading conservation bodies (as opposed to animal rights and welfare groups) consider controlled, sustainable and legal trophy hunting as a valuable conservation tool. These include the Convention for the International Trade in Endangered Species (CITES) and the International Union for Conservation of Nature (IUCN), the latter being the world's first global environmental organisation and the largest professional international conservation network. The IUCN has made the following policy statement:

Conservation of biological diversity is central to the mission of IUCN, and accordingly IUCN recommends that decisions of whether to use, or not to use, wild living resources should be consistent with this aim.

Both consumptive and non-consumptive use of biological diversity are fundamental to the economies, cultures, and well-being of all nations and peoples. Use, if sustainable, can serve human needs on an ongoing basis while contributing to the conservation of biological diversity.

Position of the South African government

Trophy hunting is legal in South Africa and the activity is endorsed and fully supported by the Department of Environmental Affairs, among others, as a vital component of the country's overall wildlife conservation strategy.

Tourism, of which trophy hunting forms an important part, is a priority economic sector in the government's Medium-Term Strategic Framework, which identifies, among others, the following overall priorities:
- Creating decent work and sustainable livelihoods.
- Rural development, food security and land reform.
- Building cohesive and sustainable communities.

Furthermore, South Africa's New Growth Plan identifies tourism as one of the six core pillars of growth. The Industrial Policy Action Plan (IPAP2) indicates that tourism is one of the areas expected to contribute to the development of, among others, rural areas by growing the economy and creating jobs.

Hunting: the economy and communities

Preliminary figures for 2013 indicate that hunting alone contributed R8 billion to the South African GDP. Live game sales generated a further R1 billion. These figures do not take into account capital expenditure and other value chain contributions (e.g. taxidermy, hotels, shopping, side trips, etc.). The value chain sustains 140 000 jobs. Approximately 8 000 overseas hunters visit South Africa every year, each spending on average R140 000 per visit.

Rural communities in Africa benefit directly from controlled, legal trophy hunting. These benefits include direct revenue (license and concession fees), infrastructure developments (schools, roads, clinics, etc.) paid for by hunting companies, job creation and skills transfer and improved food security (through the provision of meat and crop protection against problem animals). Most hunting in South Africa takes place on private land and as such does not affect local communities to the same extent as in other parts of Africa.

Rhino conservation by private owners was initially driven by permitting trophy hunting.

Trophy hunting in particular is an excellent vehicle to drive BBBEE in the professional hunting and wildlife industries through training, skills development and education. Transformation, particularly in poor, rural communities, is of critical importance, which the hunting and wildlife industry is giving serious attention to.

In contrast non-consumptive photographic ecotourism has been highly promoted as an alternative to hunting but the reality is that this sector is already saturated. Non-consumptive ecotourism is also not commercially viable in large parts of Africa given that photographic ecotourism is dependent on a specific combination of factors which is difficult for most game farms to achieve: high densities of game, the presence of the Big Five and scenic beauty as well.

Hunting – ethics and morality

The concepts of ethics and morals are often confused. While both relate to "right" and "wrong" conduct, morals are subjective and differ from culture to culture as well as from person to person. Ethics, however, refer to a

Trophy and skin processing are byproducts of the hunting industry which earn income and create employment.

Overseas hunters bring foreign currency into the country and spend a substantial amount.

set of rules applied by external sources such as laws, traditions, customs and professional codes of conduct.

There are, from a philosophical and academic perspective, arguments on both sides of the spectrum insofar as the morality of hunting is concerned. PHASA respects every individual's choice not to partake in any activity, including hunting, with which he or she may not feel comfortable.

The animal rights/animal welfare movements (as opposed to true conservation bodies) approach the morality of hunting largely from the perspective of their own emotions and the individual animal while ignoring the indisputable evidence that most conservation success stories are by and large the result of sustainable utilisation programmes.

Hunters could counter argue that it is immoral to put the interest of individual animals above that of the species, ecosystems, overall wildlife populations and rural communities. This counterargument is particularly potent considering that wildlife would be confined to our national parks and a few private reserves if hunting practices were prohibited.

> "… hunting is moral if it contributes to man's welfare, the welfare of the ecosystem. To refer once again to Whitehead's remark, hunting is moral if it is in the end life-sustaining."

Professor Theodore Vitali, quoting Alfred North Whitehead, one of the most respected 20th Century philosophers.

International hunting tourism: South Africa as a hunting destination

South Africa is the premier hunting destination in Africa. It has an unrivalled diversity of species — more than 45 major plains game species and all of the Big Five may be hunted here. Endemic species include the vaal rhebok, black wildebeest, bontebok, blesbok, Cape mountain zebra, Cape bushbuck, Eastern Cape greater kudu and Cape grysbok. A large variety of game birds, some presenting very challenging shooting, are on licence with generous bag limits.

SA extends from the cold South Atlantic Ocean to the warm Indian Ocean, and together with a varied topography, offers an astonishing variety of natural environments. The arid Karoo and Kalahari, the unique Cape fynbos region, the coastal forests along our eastern seaboard, the snow-capped Drakensberg and Eastern Cape mountains, the central grasslands, and the magnificent bushveld and savannah areas in the eastern and northern parts of the country all offer unique and captivating experiences. There is a misperception that all hunting in South Africa takes place on small, "high-fenced" properties. Hunting concession sizes are, in fact, on the increase because landowners are purchasing more property to add to their existing properties, especially in marginal agricultural areas, forming conservancies and are dropping fences between their properties. Communities are buying into the concept of conservation through sustainable utilisation and are opening their large tracts of land to trophy hunting.

A number of provincial nature reserves offer hunting in large, unfenced areas with free-ranging game populations. The "dangerous" game-hunting in some of these reserves is of the finest on offer in Africa today. In certain parts of the country, a significant portion of hunting takes place on unfenced private land that is home to free-ranging game populations.

South Africa has so much to offer and every foreign hunter, regardless of their specific requirements or preferences, will find a suitable hunting destination to meet their needs.

The role of professional hunters and hunting outfitters

A professional hunter guides and is responsible for the safety, well-being and conduct of a "client" during the course of a safari. A "client" is a person who is not normally resident in South Africa and who pays to hunt here. The safari is arranged ("outfitted") by a hunting outfitter or hunting contractor. The outfitter employs the professional hunter for the duration of the safari.

In order to legally operate as a professional hunter and/or hunting outfitter, one must be in possession of a valid permit, issued by the provincial authorities for the province where one will operate. Professional hunter permits may only be issued to South African citizens, permanent residents or persons in possession of a work permit, in terms of the Aliens Act. To qualify for a permit, one must have attended a professional hunting school, and successfully completed and passed the professional hunting course, which includes theoretical and practical exams. An outfitter permit may only be issued to a person who is a licensed professional hunter. In addition, such a person must have operated as a professional hunter for at least three years, or be a landowner. Permits are renewed periodically. In order to qualify for renewal, the professional hunter and hunting outfitter are required to submit a minimum number of returns, in respect of hunts conducted. The renewal periods and minimum returns vary from province to province.

Professional hunters and hunting outfitters have important responsibilities. They must ensure that the necessary permits, licences and other documents are obtained, so that the clients have them in their possession and may hunt legally.

Professional hunters must see to the welfare of their clients and be responsible for their safety while in the camp and hunting area. They must guide clients during the hunt and ensure that they do not contravene the law.

Hunting outfitters must ensure that all written agreements are in place, that a licensed professional hunter guides the client, and provide facilities and services that meet stipulated requirements. Professional hunters must ensure that all trophies are skinned and prepared according to the correct methods. Outfitters must obtain the necessary permits to transport and export their clients' trophies.

Of particular importance are the responsibilities of the outfitter when advertising hunting opportunities. Any misleading or ambiguous information must be avoided. For example, the terms "Greater Kruger", "KNP" or any wording implying that the animals on offer are in any way part of the Kruger National Park's population, should not to be used in any advertising or marketing of hunts in the APN reserves or other areas adjoining the Kruger National Park. Outfitters may not advertise or market hunts for which they do not have lawful hunting rights.

The import of firearms, hunting permits and the export of trophies

It is important to note that rules and regulations in respect of firearms import permits, hunting permits and trophy export/import permits, as well as airline policies on firearms carriage, change from time to time. Hunters booking flights to their hunting destination, are advised to verify airline firearm carriage policies, prior to making a booking.

Firearms importation: A temporary import permit is currently required to bring firearms into South Africa. It is recommended that a pre-approved permit be obtained. Various institutions, including PHASA, offer a service to process the application on the international hunting tourist's behalf before arriving in South Africa. Services include meeting the person at the South African Police Service (SAPS) office at OR Tambo International Airport with the pre-approved permits and assistance with clearing firearms.

Hunting permits: Most species can, as a general rule, be hunted in terms of a so-called "Exemption Permit" or equivalent permit. A hunting permit and/or hunting licence is required for all species not included in an exemption permit, which will depend on whether an open or closed hunting season applies to a particular species.

The international hunter, professional hunter and outfitter must complete a Professional Hunter Register for each hunt. The register must list all hunting permits, including exemption permits, and it is of the utmost importance that registers be completed accurately (with a correct physical address for the client — PO Box addresses will not be accepted; and with first and last names spelled correctly — Bill, instead of William, is unacceptable) and signed by the professional hunter, the outfitter and the client.

Trophy export: South Africa has sound conservation management strategies in place. As a result, there are virtually no restrictions on the export of trophies from animals that were legally harvested. The following documentation forms part of the supporting documentation in the export permit application process:

- A copy of the Professional Hunter Register, signed by the client, the professional hunter and the hunting outfitter.
- All hunting permits (depending on the species/province where the hunt took place): original signed by the client.
- A CITES/TOPS hunting permit, if applicable: original signed by the client.
- CITES import permit into foreign countries for CITES Appendix I species (if applicable).
- Nature Conservation Exemption Permit or CAE (Certificate of Adequate Enclosure).
- Transfer of hunting rights from landowner to hunting outfitter (if not hunting on own property).
- Permission to hunt from landowner/outfitter to client.

For CITES Appendix I species, the client must first apply for a CITES IMPORT permit from their local issuing authority. This permit may be obtained after the safari. On receipt of the import permit, a copy should be forwarded to the client's taxidermist/clearing agents in South Africa, in order to apply for the CITES EXPORT permit. The export permit will not be issued without a copy of the import permit.

For CITES Appendix II species, the permit application procedure is the other way round: the South African taxidermist/forwarding/dip and pack agents apply directly for the CITES EXPORT permit, after which the CITES IMPORT permit will then be issued by the client's home country.

The European Commission has implemented new regulations for the importation into the European Union of lion, elephant, white rhino and hippo trophies, which came into effect on 5 February 2015, and in terms of which the

> **The following species, listed on CITES Appendices I or II, require Special Hunting Permits (only the more commonly hunted species are listed here):**
> - **Appendix I:** Leopard, black rhino, black-footed cat and Cape mountain zebra.
> - **Appendix II:** Hippo, elephant, lion, crocodile, bontebok, caracal, Hartmann zebra, white rhino, all monkeys, all baboons, blue duiker, African wild cat and red lechwe.
>
> The following species, listed under the TOPS Regulations, require a TOPS (Threatened or Protected Species) hunting permit, in addition to the provincial permit (only the more commonly hunted species are listed here):
> - Leopard, lion, Nile crocodile, oribi, common reedbuck, bontebok, black wildebeest, elephant, black rhino, white rhino, blue duiker, roan antelope, serval, suni, tsessebe, Cape mountain zebra, Sharpe's grysbok, brown and spotted hyena.
>
> The hunting outfitter must take out these hunting permits and the client MUST SIGN THEM PRIOR to the hunt commencing. Both must ensure that all particulars contained in the permit are correct and accurate, including the correct full names and physical address of the client. CITES/TOPS-listed animals may not be hunted without the specific CITES/TOPS hunting permit which has all correct details on hand. Some of the species are listed in both the CITES Appendices and TOPS, in which case one integrated export permit may be issued. The TOPS regulations were revised during 2015, with input of the hunting and wildlife industry.

client (or the clearing agent) must apply for an import permit before the consignment may be released for shipping.

Local hunters

At the turn of the 1900s stock and crop farmers viewed game as obstacles or even pests and huge numbers of game animals were hunted for meat and so-called "pest control".

Around the 1900s farmers realised the value of wildlife and hunters were prepared to start paying for their hunts. In the late 1900s a group of hunters realised the importance of "self-regulation" of the sport of hunting and formed a hunting association. Today, South Africa has more than 25 hunting organisations which are all membership driven, each with a constitution, code of conduct, disciplinary bylaws, and other codes of best practices as pertaining to the specific association. Membership of these organisations is sadly not compulsory by law.

However, one can never underestimate the role the associations play in keeping their members informed of the latest rules and regulations of which the following are only a few:

Firearm licensing for hunting purposes

Any potential firearm owner needs to attend a firearm training course through an accredited training institution in order to obtain the necessary certificates to apply for a competency certificate from the South African Police Services.

Only once a person is in possession of a competency certificate, will he/she be able to apply for a firearm licence. An occasional hunter can apply for a maximum of 4 firearm licences (excluding semi-automatic firearms).

Hunters (not registered for doing business in hunting) must have dedicated hunter status in order to license more than four firearms (including one self-defence firearm) and any semi-automatic firearms.

Dedicated hunter status is being awarded by accredited hunting associations once the person has passed the proficiency grading theoretical and practical shooting tests of the association.

Professional Hunter (PH) status may be awarded to professional hunters in possession of a valid professional hunters permit issued by the relevant Nature Conservation Authority. The PH status may only be issued to the person by an association accredited with the SAPS for professional hunting purposes.

The recipient of the Dedicated and/or Professional Hunter status need to comply with specific requirements as set out by the association awarding the status, which includes amongst others membership in good standing. The association must submit an annual report to the SAPS and members who do not adhere to the criteria, will lose their specific status, which could result in them losing firearm licences issued in terms of that specific status. Firearm owners must ensure they apply for the renewal of competency certificates and firearm licences from the SAPS within 90 days before the expiry date.

Hunting licences/permits/permissions

Each province in South Africa has its own set of legislation, including annual hunting proclamations. The proclamations clearly specify the hunting seasons which might even vary by species, and bag limits for bird shooting. Legislation is amended from time to time and proclamations change from year to year. In some provinces, a hunter only needs a hunting licence when hunting on a farm which is not exempted; in other provinces a hunter always needs a hunting licence and in certain instances the species to be hunted must even be identified on the permit. This is not only applicable to antelope hunting, but also bird shooting. It is therefore extremely important to ascertain beforehand whether a hunting licence is necessary and where to purchase it from.

To hunt certain species, one needs to be in possession of a TOPS permit. Some landowners have TOPS permit books, from which they can issue the permit to the hunter. Should the landowner not be in possession of the TOPS permit book, the hunter must apply from the provincial nature conservation offices in advance.

The hunter should always ensure that the landowner issue him with a "Permission to hunt and transport game" document, before leaving the farm with the carcasses. Permits are also necessary for the transport of warthog. This must be confirmed with the landowner in advance. It is extremely important that the hunter has his firearm licences and all the necessary permits as listed above in his possession. It would be a sad day to be stopped on the road by Police, and have not only the meat but also your vehicle and firearms confiscated because of permits not being in place. During 2013, the hunting and wildlife industry and the Department of Environmental Affairs have agreed on the following definition for responsible hunting:

- Conducted within the parameters of applicable legislation.
- Conducted in a manner which protects and promotes the sustainable utilisation of wildlife.

In summary all of the 250 000–300 000 hunters in South Africa and all the professional hunters and international hunting tourists hunting in South Africa, have a responsibility to comply with legislation and hunt in a manner to ensure sound wildlife populations, and safe an ethical hunting.

For more details on handling and export of trophies contact:
ceo@phasaco.co.za

Game meat can be utilised as high value products such as filet and carpaccio, but the processing and marketing is still hampered by various factors.

GAME MEAT

GAME MEAT* PRODUCTION IN SOUTH AFRICA

Peter Oberem

Introduction

The game ranching industry stands on the 4 economic pillars of breeding, hunting (local meat and foreign trophy), ecotourism and the production and sales of products such as game meat, curios, skins and beneficiated goods. Game meat production, beneficiation, marketing and exports have underexploited potential for supplying high quality red meat and meat products to the local market and to earn substantial foreign exchange from exports. South Africa imports meat to the value of R4 billion annually. The increasing population and the higher demand for meat as the population's standard of living improves will consequently require that its production capacity will have to double in the next 15 years (while food prices are expected to treble in the next 3 years and double thereafter every 5 years). Therefore, utilisation of game as a source of highly nutritious and healthy meat makes excellent sense.

Until fairly recently, game meat used to be regarded as a by-product of the hunting industry – it was given to farm workers or sold illegally at low prices because consumers did not know how to prepare it and were unaware of its nutritious value. This product, prized by the overseas market because of its organic nature and healthy characteristics has therefore been largely ignored by local consumers. The development of the game meat industry has been hamstrung by legislative problems and failure to control foot-and-mouth disease outbreaks.

History of the game meat industry in South Africa

Export industry

Before being interrupted by the February 2011 foot-and-mouth disease (FMD) outbreak, SA exported a relatively small amount, more than 400 tons (at R90/kg = R360 million), of boneless, packed game meat to EU-approved export abattoirs. Prime cuts were exported at an average of about R90/kg (current exchange rate). Prices ranged from loins at €15, 4-piece cut (denuded) at €8.50, goulash at €4 and shoulder at €3.50 p/kg delivered to EU port

---

* The term "game meat" is used to differentiate the South African product from the New Zealand "venison" which is derived from farmed deer. New Zealand exports almost R4 billion of deer meat to Europe annually.

frozen. With the trimmings and bones sold locally, exporters realised about a combined income of R60/kg for the whole carcass. Most of the meat was derived from springbok (70%) with kudu (10%), blesbok (10%) and zebra (5%) with eland and blue wildebeest making up the rest. The FMD outbreak and the consequent 5 years' loss of the export market, cost the country more than R1.5 billion in foreign exchange and more than 700 jobs were lost. The ban is still in place despite the fact that the OIE have declared South Africa a FMD-free zone in June 2015 and after the OIE audit in December 2015.

Local market

Currently the sale of game meat is illegal unless done in approved private or export abattoirs. To address the growing demand for game meat in South Africa as well as an overall need for red meat by a growing population the wildlife industry engaged with the Department of Agriculture, Forestry and Fisheries (DAFF) almost 10 years ago, on the development of a legal framework for the harvesting of game meat for sale on local markets. In South Africa meat hygiene, quality and safety is controlled in accordance with the Meat Safety Act of 2000. The basis of this Act is that a dead animal may not be taken into an abattoir and as a result government legal advisers stated that game meat could not be accommodated in a separate regulation as part of this Act, since a regulation must be subservient to the Act itself. They therefore recommended that a separate game meat scheme to be facilitated/administered by the WRSA be drawn up. The proposed Game Meat scheme was drawn up and published for public comment in 2013. WRSA was informed that the Game Meat scheme would be published and enacted by the end of 2013, however, government has backtracked on this decision. In the interim high quality meat is going to waste. WRSA has therefore begun the process of registering its own internationally approved quality control system. This was registered during July 2015 and details are available from WRSA.

Table 1.6: Game meat exported in 2008 (before FMD outbreak).

SPECIES	TOTAL AMOUNT (tons)	PERCENTAGE CONTRIBUTION
Springbok	710	41
Blesbok	401	23
Gemsbok	40	2
Kudu	131	8
Red hartebeest	18	1
Zebra	58	3
Impala	43	3
Eland	15	1
Black wildebeest	144	8
Blue wildebeest	143	8

Table 1.7: Comparison of various nutrients in game meat and domestic stock.

PROPERTY	GAME MEAT	DOMESTIC STOCK (BEEF AND/OR MUTTON)
Energy per mg	545	969
Fat content %	4.3	25 to 39
Protein %	34	22
Zinc per g	2 820	2 629
Magnesium	25	19
Selenium per mg	2.2	1.8
Potassium	352	314
Copper	190	88
Cholesterol per g	82	86

The nutritional and other qualities

Much research has been done on the nutritional qualities of game meat. It has been shown to be highly nutritious, low in fat and cholesterol, high in protein, iron and other essential minerals. Dr Maretha van der Merwe of Tshwane Municipality (doctoral thesis) has shown that the hygiene of the slaughter process in the veld is comparable with that achieved in livestock carcasses in abattoirs, and because game meat has a lower pH than either beef or mutton, it does not support bacterial growth as well as domestic species meat and so has less spoilage and a better shelf life.

Dr Maretha van der Merwe has studied and highlighted the healthy properties of game meat when compared with red meat of livestock.

Table 1.8: Nutrient composition of game meat compared with various domestic stock.

SPECIES	Fat (kcals)	Calories/mg	Cholesterol
Game	2.42	143	82
Beef	9.28	211	86
Pork	9.66	212	86
Chicken	7.41	190	89

Table 1.9: Nutritional composition of some game species compared with some domestic species.

Species	Moisture (g/100g)	Protein (g/100g)	Fat (g/100g)
Springbok	74.7	23.7	1.7
Eland	75.8	–	2.4
Impala	75.7	22.5	1.4
Blesbok	75.5	23.5	1.7
Black wildebeest	77.0	–	2.3
Mutton	60.7	13.9	21.6
Pork	55.0	13.9	17.6
Beef	64.4	19.2	14.2

– no value available

Feeding a nation: how game meat can address South Africa's meat shortage

South Africa faces the huge challenge of feeding a growing population while at the same time being a nett importer of both red meat and chicken. Since half the national herd are kept on communal land and never reach the market, achieving food security in the future is a huge challenge to South Africa. Commercial beef farming is currently not economical and farmers are abandoning cattle farming for game farming. Mutton farming is being increasingly abandoned due to stock theft problems.

The alternative for providing more red meat is keeping animals in feedlots which has many problems of its own. Intensive or factory farming involves keeping animals in crowded conditions which is conducive to the development of diseases. It also necessitates stressful transport of animals over long distances. "Factory farming" is becoming a huge problem in the USA as it causes environmental pollution of water, soil and air (see "Farmageddon" by Philip Lymbery), as well as an animal welfare concern.

Game meat on the other hand is a sustainable resource. It is organic and arguably the "kindest meat" of all since the animals are free ranging, and killed quickly and cleanly with minimal stress and suffering. The animals are not medicated with dips, hormones or antibiotics and are therefore truly organic natural meat sources. Full utilisation of the carcass prevents wastage and provides materials for by-product industries (tinned meat, compost, curios, pet treats and leather).

Current and potential contribution of game meat to food security in South Africa

It is estimated, based on figures from hunting and culling exercises, that the game industry delivers 170 000 tons of game meat to the country annually.

An EU-funded study carried out by Afrivet/LED showed that the Waterberg district alone has a potential of delivering 60 000 head of game which at 60kg/head totals 3 600 tons of game meat per annum, which if sold at R75/kg will contribute R180 million of turnover. Profit is generated from the added value (beneficiation: increases the turnover from R35/kg to up to R400/kg for specific products such as smoked, sliced eland leg). The success of game meat provision, however, is reliant on a consistent supply, a quality product, critical mass and in a user-friendly form.

An investigative study has shown that the Western Europe game meat/venison market potential is >100 000 tons per annum. New Zealand sells 35 000 tons to Western Europe as a delicacy at premium prices. The industry in NZ comprise of 4 000 deer farmers with 1.7 million deer (50% of the world's farmed deer). In 1983 a cooperative, the Cervena Appellation, was founded which has 1 500 supplying farms with a total production of >40 000 tons of venison per annum of which >25 000 tons to the value of >R4 billion depending on the exchange rates at the time, is exported to Europe. At R100/kg it is clearly mainly prime cuts.

Once the ban on export of game meat from South Africa to Europe has been lifted WRSA

Intensive meat production is efficient but has many negative impacts on animal welfare, health and environmental problems .

through its efforts and facilitation hope that SA will be able to rival New Zealand given that our product has better marketing attributes. The WRSA goal is to reach 10 000 tons by 2021 generating foreign exchange of R1 billion annually.

Constraints to game meat production and sale/exports

There are various constraints to the game meat sales and export market which need to be addressed by the following:
- Consolidation of the fragmented supply chain: suppliers need to work together to provide a constant supply.
- Veterinary Services must meet the OIE requirements for FMD control.
- Mobile abattoirs to complement the lack of approved game meat facilities.
- Training and certification of professional commercial harvesters is needed.
- Quality control measures should be put in place; WRSA has developed a proposed Quality Assurance Programme.
- Strong and co-ordinated marketing campaign both locally and for export market is needed; this should include consumer education on how to use/cook game meat.

are not all necessarily enforced for local use they are valuable guidelines to ensuring healthy and quality game meat.

Some of these basic guidelines are:
- Animals intended for game meat harvesting are shot in the head to ensure quick and clean death, and ensures that lead shot does not contaminate the meat.
- After an animal is shot it must be bled out by cutting the jugular veins within 5 minutes. This is important because carcasses not bled out properly will have a dark colour, and poor taste and shelf life.
- The carcasses must be hung to assist the bleeding out process.
- Evisceration must take place at the field depot within 2 hours to prevent bloating (should be done sooner with springbuck as they will discolour) and possible contamination from the viscera. Head and feet are then removed.
- At this stage a partial meat examination of the viscera is done; both the viscera and the carcass must be marked/numbered to ensure that in the abattoir, when the skin is removed, the viscera and carcass can be matched (traceability).
- The skin must be removed in a controlled environment (at abattoir for export) or in the mobile abattoir. In small farm abattoirs it can be done immediately after evisceration.
- When moving the skinned carcass from the slaughter area to the cold room it is critical to prevent contamination, therefore as little handling as possible. In the cold room, the carcass temperature must be under 7 °C within 24 hours in order to control growth of bacteria especially *Salmonella* spp. but must not be cooled too quickly; it should not fall below 10° C within 10 hours because this will cause "cold shortening" which results in toughness.

- Full utilisation of the product (from top to tail) must be promoted so that all parts of the carcass are used, including heads, offal and tongues for consumption, horns and hooves for curios or "bone meal", rumen content to make compost, skin for leather (curios, furniture, shoes, car seats, clothing).
- Value adding should be prioritised so that products like carpaccio, salami, smoked sliced cold meats, sausages, patties, biltong and precooked meals are manufactured on top of the high end prime cuts.
- The product is sold at a premium as it is healthy, organic and a speciality dish.

Harvesting game meat

Game animals, unlike domestic livestock, are generally shot in the veld where they are then partially processed. Only the final processing, namely skinning and carcass inspection, is done in an abattoir. The destination of the meat (export or local consumption) will determine specific requirements (mobile, local or export abattoir). A Veterinary Procedural Notice (VPN) or regulation published by Veterinary Services lays out the procedures that must be followed when game meat is harvested for export. These are good standard procedures and while they

Harvesting of game for game meat.

Mobile abattoir for game meat processing and inspection.

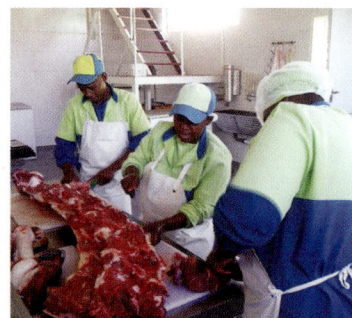
Trained staff working in an approved private game meat abattoir.

Basic considerations when setting up and running an abattoir

Most of the processing of game meat takes place in the veld and the only step in the processing chain that takes place in the abattoir is the removal of the skin and the final meat inspection. However, if building an abattoir is necessary for whatever reason, it should be done in consultation with an expert (see contact details below) because this requires conforming with various rules and regulations enforced by many institutions that include the Veterinary Services in the province, environment impact assessment from DEA, rezoning the land by local authorities, approval and Registration at Veterinary Services.

As soon as a carcass, whole, halved, or quartered leaves the abattoir gate, the meat, its transport and any further processing falls under the jurisdiction of the Department of Health in accordance with the Foodstuffs, Cosmetics and Disinfectants Act, Act 54 of 1972 and its new regulation 962.

The premises must be approved with respect to layout, ease of cleaning, temperature control, workflow, staff control, the suitability of the receiving area, easily cleaned and disinfected surfaces, regular monitoring of bacterial load (the standard used is referred to as Pick 'n Pay standard for bacterial contamination). Workers health, health monitoring, training and overall suitability is important. It is important to consult experts in putting these plans together. There are also specific packaging regulations, Regulation 146 focusing on the sell by date.

Important public health issues

In general free-living game are less likely to be a public health risk assuming that there is good hygiene on the farm and freedom from livestock diseases such as bovine tuberculosis and brucellosis. However, the viscera must be inspected and must be traceable back to the carcass of origin if any problems are found.

The most important conditions for which game meat is examined are cysts in muscle (human and carnivore tapeworms), cysts on viscera (hydatids), *Trichinella*, tuberculosis in lungs, lymph nodes and other viscera, and liverfluke in the liver and bile ducts, lung- and heart worm for aesthetic reasons.

As with other meat which is processed, carcasses can be contaminated during handling and processing with streptococcus, staphylococcus and salmonella by humans if good practice is not implemented.

For more information on WRSA's Game meat initiatives and quality assurance system with regard to processing and marketing contact www.wrsa.co.za. For planning of meat processing and abattoirs please contact Dr Tertius Berg: trts.bergh@gmail.com or 082 902 8914.

Wildlife tourism must provide close encounters with wild animals, comfortable and interesting accommodation and photographic opportunities.

WILDLIFE TOURISM

Jauntelle Els and Peet van der Merwe

Game farm tourism forms part of sustainable wildlife tourism and plays a major role in nature conservation. Wildlife tourism plays an important part in the world tourism industry, is growing rapidly and holds high potential for economic growth. The combination of benefits that are offered by South Africa in general and the unique experiences on offer at game farms makes the country one of the top tourism attractions for local and international tourists. While the opportunities are unlimited it is essential that game farm owners carefully consider what type of enterprise will best suit their game farm and to manage resources responsibly to be sustainable. It is also important that the rate of consumptive use of renewable resources are well managed and clearly understood among game farm owners to ensure that the biological resources are sustainable.

Introduction

Tourism is generally described as the largest industry in the world because of its contribution to global GDP, and the huge number of people it employs (OECD, 2009). This is one of the fastest growing industries, and is increasing in developing countries. In Africa, for example, cultural and environmental tourism grew from

2% to over 11% of the total African exports between 1980 and 2003 (OECD, 2009). Within the global tourism industry, nature-based tourism is rapidly growing and holds high potential for wildlife-based economic growth. As a result, this is one of the few trade/service sectors in which poor countries have a clear comparative advantage as a result of their often rich natural resources' base such as South Africa (OECD, 2009).

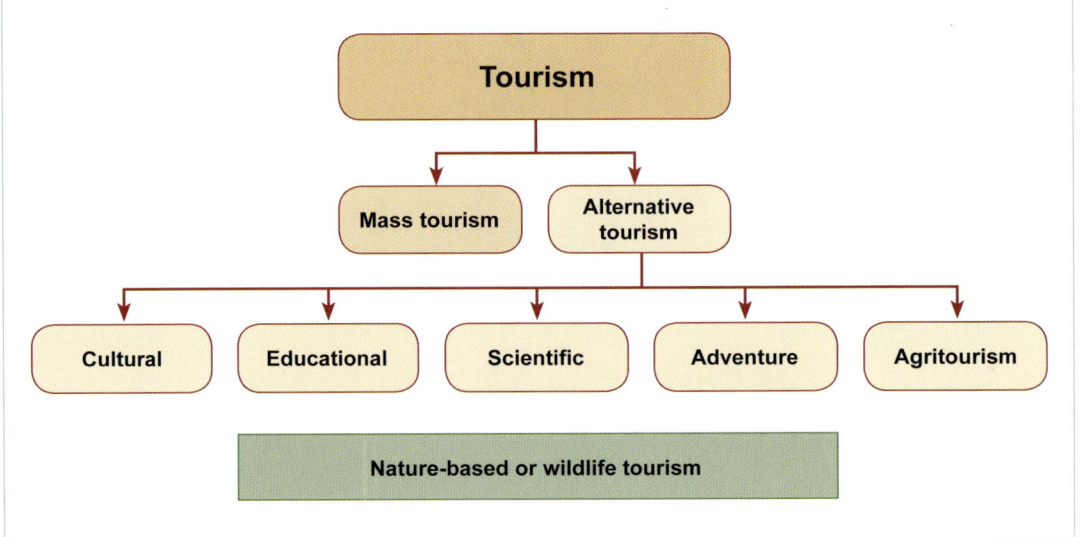

Figure 2: Alternative tourism (Source: Wearing & Neil, 1999:3).

The tourism industry can broadly be divided into two categories, namely mass tourism and alternative tourism (Figure 2). Mass tourism involves large numbers of tourists visiting an area and refers to visits to cities, beachfronts, amusement parks and other places where the sustainability of tourism is dependent on tourist numbers. Mass tourists seek to replicate their own culture in institutionalised settings with little cultural or environmental interaction in authentic settings. The success of mass tourism lies in the interaction between the tourists, requiring the destination to adapt to the tourists (Page & Dowling, 2002; Wearing & Neil, 1999).

Alternative tourism, on the other hand, aims at experiencing natural, social and community

DEFINING WILDLIFE TOURISM

According to The Cooperative Research Centre (CRC) for Sustainable Tourism (2001) and Higginbottom (2004) wildlife based tourism can be described as "tourism that involves encounters with non-domesticated animals either in their natural environment or in captivity. It includes a wide range of activities, such as bird-watching, whale-watching, general wildlife viewing, visiting zoos and aquaria, snorkelling to view underwater life, hunting and recreational fishing". Activities can be consumptive and non-consumptive. The interaction with the animals include activities that is historically classified as non-consumptive such as photography and feeding, as well as those involved with the capture and killing of the animals. Consumptive activities include hunting (in the terrestrial environment) and recreational fishing (in the aquatic environment). In this manner wildlife based tourism can also be described as "an area of overlay between nature-based tourism, ecotourism, and consumptive use of wildlife, rural tourism, and human relations with wildlife" which is illustrated in Figure 2 (Page & Dowling, 2002).

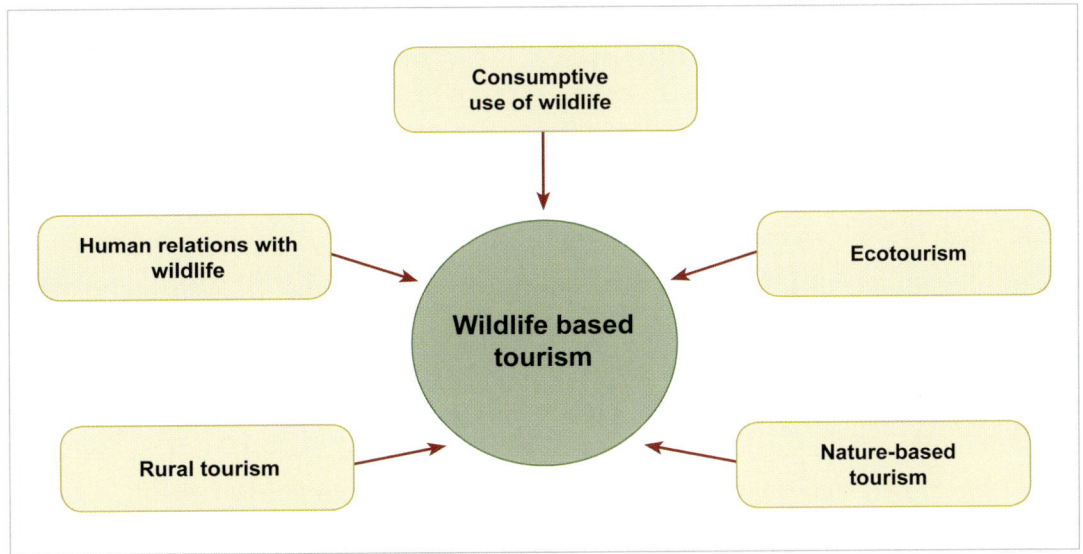

Figure 3: Wildlife tourism (Source: Page & Dowling, 2002)

values, and which allows both hosts and guests to enjoy positive and worthwhile interaction and shared experiences (Wearing & Neil, 1999:3). Alternative tourism focuses on aspects such as culture, education, science, adventure and agri-tourism, and includes nature/wildlife-based tourism. These types of tourism experiences are quite diverse – from scuba diving on coral reefs to wildlife safaris in Africa. Wildlife tourism concentrates on fewer numbers of tourists, but a better quality experience where tourists can learn more about nature, for example a guided walking safari, horse trails, hiking and hunting. For many countries, wildlife tourism plays an important role in sustaining economic benefits whilst supporting wildlife conservation and local communities. For this reason, governments, the tourism industry, private sector as well as researchers have more interest in tourism based on visitors interacting with wild animals.

Observing wild species in their natural habitat in Africa has been an attractive focus for the tourism industry for a long time (Allen & Branna, 2004). Novelli states that over the past hundred years, the African continent has circumscribed extraordinary growth in wildlife tourism activities, in both consumptive and non-consumptive categories (Novelli 2005).

The accelerated growth in wildlife-based tourism in South Africa can be attributed to the presence of attractive landscapes, good weather and combination of people, history, wildlife products, cultures and demand for hunting (The International Hotel School, 2014). The main goal of wildlife tourism is to create a sustainable tourism product that provides the maximum number of benefits to all contributing parties, which may include the conservation of wildlife and the natural surroundings, improvement of the surrounding community's way of life via economic injections and education, as well as economic benefits to other contributing parties.

"Wildlife tourism consists of a variety of activities within its boundaries and caters for a wide range of needs in different ways. Some forms of wildlife tourism are a bigger attraction to tourists than others, and sustainable environmental practices are very important (Page & Dowling, 2002). The positive effects of wildlife-based tourism on the environment and wildlife are the use of marginal agricultural areas for nature

conservation. However, inappropriate development caused by mass tourism can degenerate protected areas and destroy local communities. In order to practice successful wildlife-based tourism it is crucial to find the equilibrium between visitors' enjoyment and conservation needs. Often the tourism industry focuses on activities that generate income at the expense of the environment and the conservation." (Freese, 1998).

Consumptive wildlife-based tourism includes the sport of hunting and fishing. Consumptive wildlife tourism such as hunting generates income from permits, and hunting fees, hunting equipment and hiring of vehicles (Milner-Gulland, & Mace, 1998). Income is also generated from non-consumptive wildlife-based tourism from activities such as park fees, services, admission fees, sales of materials, leases, and other tourism-related entrepreneurship (Freese, 1998). Non-consumptive wildlife tourism can however impact wildlife and their habitats. Photographers, for example, can often be more invasive than the general tourist (Klein, 1993).

Impacts of wildlife-based tourism

The impact of wildlife-based tourism can either be positive or negative and it can be both tangible and intangible. There are four main mechanisms through which the positive effects work, namely: financial contributions, non-financial contributions, socio-economic incentives and education. These contributions can take place in conservation and animal welfare or both. Some forms of wildlife-based tourism contribute positively to conservation (Shea, Abbott, Armstrong & McNamara, 1997).

The impacts of wildlife-based tourism can be divided into three main categories, namely economic, ecological and socio-cultural (Figure 4).
- **Economic:** Wildlife-based tourism impacts on the economy of a country in terms of job creation, foreign currency, and the development of infra- and superstructures and for these reasons wildlife-based tourism has economic value.
- **Ecological:** When development takes place in terms of infra- and superstructures, these developments have various impacts on the fauna and flora as well as on the environment in general. These developments can also have various advantages and disadvantages and impact studies are therefore important.
- **Socio-cultural:** Tourists bring their culture along with them which can influence locals either positively or negatively.

Advantages of wildlife tourism

The following are advantages of wildlife tourism:
- **Benefits to conservation:** Since the early 1980s when private wildlife tourism (game farm tourism) started to escalate, it had a significant impact on the growth in the number of game in South Africa. As a result, it added value to conservation areas in South Africa. Currently, more land is under private conservation ownership (game farms/private nature reserves) than the land surface of all the national and provincial parks put together.
- **Positive impact on nature:** Farms on which game farming and wildlife tourism take place are cleared of old and unused infrastructures in order to protect the attractiveness of the location (the game farm) for tourists visiting the farms. The land is therefore rehabilitated to its original state.
- Creates job opportunities: Tourism is the largest job provider of all professions worldwide, but only the third largest industry in South Africa.
- **Creates entrepreneurial opportunities:** The wildlife tourism sector creates a variety of entrepreneurial opportunities for the potential entrepreneur. Different entry

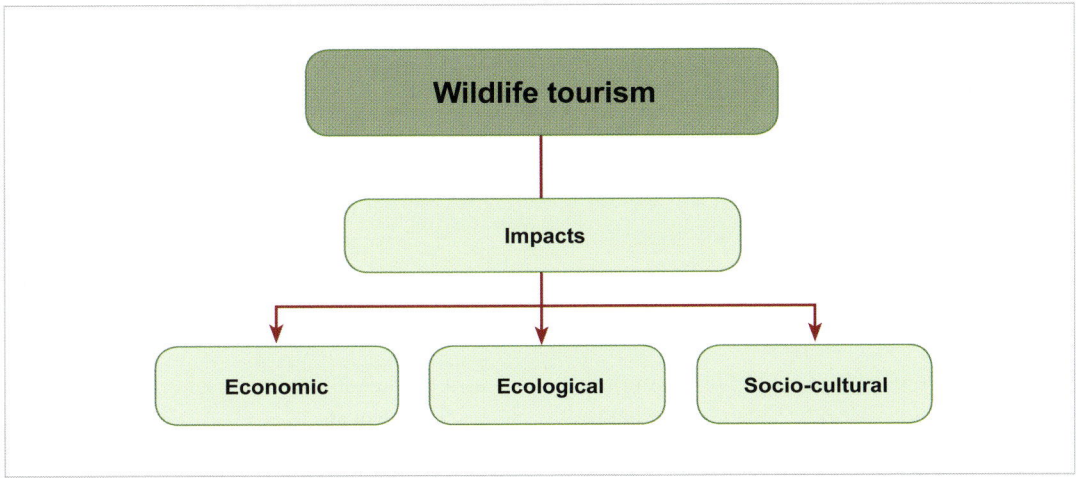

Figure 4: Impacts of wildlife-based tourism (Source: Van der Merwe, 2014).

levels to the tourism industry facilitate the development of small, micro- and medium-sized enterprises (SMME). Due to wildlife-based tourism activities such as hunting, game breeding, game capturing, game transporting, breeding of endangered species and taxidermy evolved.

- **Develops infrastructure:** As the demand for more products and structures grows, it offers the opportunity for more and better infrastructures to be created, especially in rural areas, for example roads, water and electricity supply. As a result of wildlife-based tourism hundreds of ordinary cattle farms in South Africa have been transformed into game farms. Game ranches and nature reserves with lodges created more infrastructure and development than normal cattle farming.
- **Generates foreign currency:** Trophy hunting, foreign wildlife tourists and breeding of scarce species generates foreign income for product owners and provinces where game farms are situated.
- **Creates a value chain:** It leads to conservation, taxidermy, meat processing, game breeding, and production of leather products.
- **Broadens education:** Tourists learn about new cultures, people, places, nature, conservation, species and other aspects they might not have known before.
- **Reinforces preservation of heritage and traditions**: Cultural and heritage tourism acknowledge the fact that heritage and traditions should be preserved.
- **Leads to visual and structural changes:** New uses are found for marginal, unproductive land, the re-use of neglected buildings (for example, old and vacant farm houses), as well as the regeneration and/or modernisation of the building environment on farms (Mason, 2008:75).

Disadvantages of wildlife-based tourism

There are, however, also negative impacts of wildlife-based tourism. According to Knight and Cole (1995:35), there are four extensive causes of impacts, namely habitat modification, harvest, disturbance and pollution. They also point out a pecking order of immediate reactions, effects that have a long term impact on animals and animal populations.

When the tourism industry grows rapidly it could be seen as a threat to wildlife and ecosystems (Croall, 1995); it is therefore important that wildlife-based tourism is well managed, is sustainable and have minimal impacts on wildlife and their supporting ecosystems (Green & Griese, 2004:81). Even though wildlife-based tourism is environmentally friendly, unwitting damage can be caused by wildlife tourists despite their concern for wildlife issues and conservation. Negative impacts can vary from short term effect to long term impacts. Developments like roads and eco-lodges can cause more disturbances which will affect wildlife behaviour (Green & Griese, 2004:82).The following are disadvantages of wildlife-based tourism:

- **Leakages:** There are concerns that funds raised from wildlife-based tourism such as hunting and breeding sometimes do not end up in the pockets of local businesses and communities. For example, owners who do not live in the immediate area do not use local service providers (for example, taxidermists or butchers), or employ workers from neighbouring countries, such as Zimbabwe and Mozambique.
- **Unethical practices:** Irresponsible game farm and lodge owners, who allow illegal and unethical practices, such as the hunting of caged animals or shooting game unethically, pose a threat to the industry (Ivns, 2007)
- **Biodiversity:** Habitat destruction and loss can cause changes in the composition of species if not managed sufficiently and adequately by owners (Mason, 208)
- **Increase in land value:** The cost to develop game farms, game ranches and nature reserves is tremendous. This automatically increases the value of the land, making it too expensive for people from the region to acquire. Coupled to this is the fact that numerous businessmen, who actually do have the capital, buy game farms as an investment, thus further increasing the value of land.

The private sector and wildlife-based tourism

Over the past few years, there has been a growing interest from the private sector in using wild animals within multi-purpose systems, including the production of meat coupled with added activities such as hunting, wildlife/ecotourism and breeding. This has contributed to the emergence of game farming/ranching as a sustainable land use alternative to more conventional livestock farming systems. The private wildlife industry is based on four pillars, namely animal husbandry, hunting, wildlife/ecotourism and game products (Figure 4). The other three pillars are discussed in other sections.

Wildlife tourism can be defined as follows: "Tourism based on encounters with non-domesticated animals. These encounters can occur in either the animals' natural environment or in captivity. It includes consumptive and non-consumptive activities." (Higginbottom, 2004).

Wildlife tourism has become one of the leading and fastest growing sectors of the tourism industry. It is estimated that wildlife-based ecotourism is growing between 10 and 15% per annum. The wildlife-ecotourism segment accounts for billions in value added. Its indirect multiplier effect (in industries such as airlines, taxidermy, 4x4-trails, outdoor equipment and hotels) is of a roughly similar size.

There is huge potential for future growth in wildlife-based ecotourism on game ranches, mainly because its market share of the total tourism industry is relatively small in South Africa. Game ranches with a high level of diversity which have a large number of species, any of the Big Five present, and open areas with good viewing opportunities, for example on viewing decks at permanent water holes, will be the most attractive for wildlife tourists.

Close encounters with the big five provide excitement and photo opportunities for tourists.

Game ranch tourism can also offer other additional activities:
- Hiking trails combined with game and bird watching.
- Photographic safaris.
- Farm holidays.
- Hospitality (conference facilities; traditional cooking opportunities or experiences, etc.).
- 4x4-trails, canoeing and abseiling for the more adventurous tourist.
- Promotion of unusual attractions, such as caves, waterfalls, ruins of previous civilisations.
- Provision of different types of accommodation, rest camps, tented chalets, chalets, luxury lodges, campsites, old farmhouses with an interesting character.
- Horseback safaris, walking safaris, mountain bike trails, donkey cart trips.
- Educational tours where the tourist can learn more about nature.
- Curio shops where local people can sell their products.

Prospects for the future of wildlife tourism

Conservation is a key element for sustainable wildlife tourism and therefore all stakeholders involved, including governments and other partners, are crucial and have special roles in guaranteeing proper legislative protection and resources for conservation.

For the day-to-day outcomes habitat managers, which include conservation NGOs, private landowners, protected area managers, and traditional owners, have a high responsibility to manage wildlife-based tourism and to assure sustainable utilisation. The involvement of community groups is also very important because they offer political, financial and intellectual support for wildlife-based tourism ventures. Government needs to support this type of tourism by providing adequate legislation with effective resources: capacity building, enabling best practice codes and guidelines are needed from the authorities.

Research is however needed into the potential negative effects of wildlife tourism on various species and there should be collaboration between researchers, industry and management on this issue.

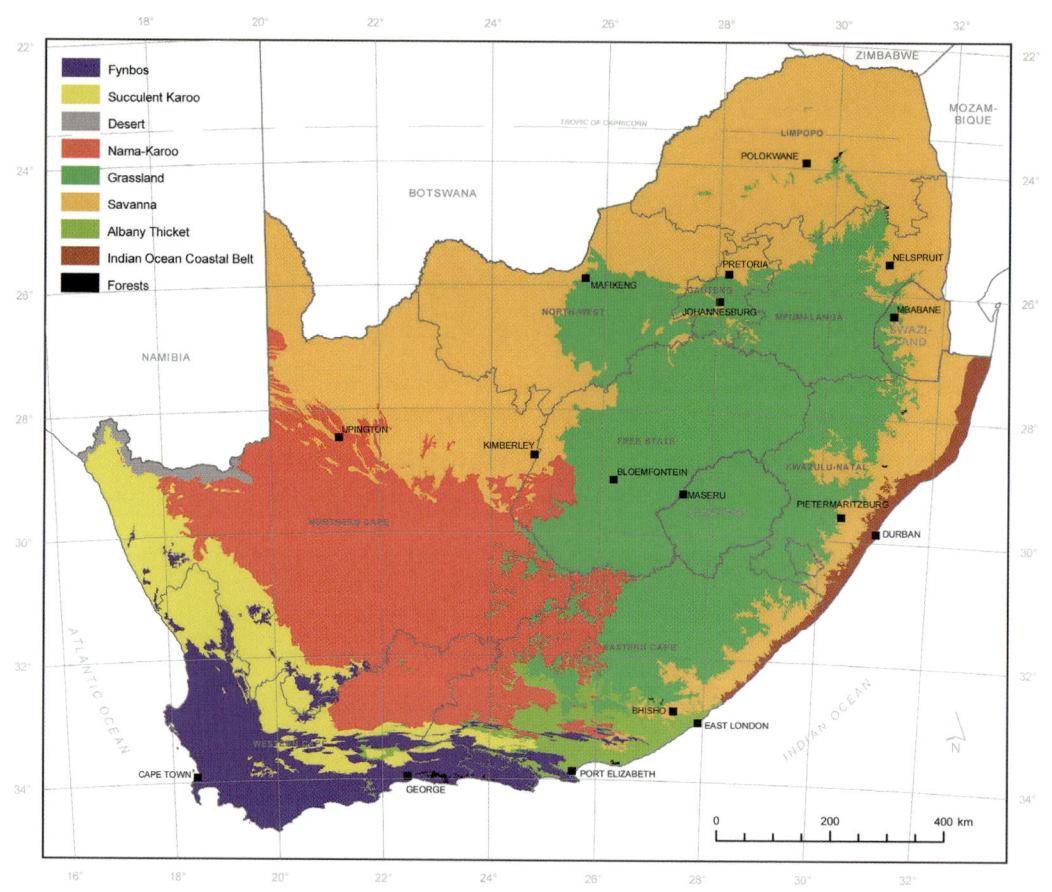

Figure. 2.1: The vegetation types (grouped as biomes) of South Africa (from Low & Rebelo, 1996) (http://pza.sanbi.org/vegetation).

MUCINA, L., RUTHERFORD, M.C., POWRIE, L.W., VAN NIEKERK, A. & VAN DER MERWE, J.H. (eds), with contributions by REBELO, A.G., CAMP, K.G.T., LOTTER, M.C., HOARE, D.B., BOUCHER, C., BREDENKAMP, G.J., VLOK, J.H.J., EUSTON-BROWN, D.I.W., JURGENS, N., DU PREEZ, P.J., LE ROUX, A., SCHMIEDEL, U., SCOTT-SHAW, C.R, VAN ROOYEN, N., DOBSON, L., PALMER, A.R., GELDENHUYS, C.J., LLOYD, J.W. VAN DER MERWE, B., BEZUIDENHOUT, H., SIEBERT, F., SIEBERT, S.J., GOODMAN, P.S., WINTER, P.J.D., HELME, N., SMIT, J.H.L., DESMET, P.G., PFAB, M., MCKENZIE, B., SCHOLES, R.J., MANNING, J.C., VAN WYK, E., ZAM BATIS, N., LECHMERE-OERTEL, R.G., ECKHARDT, H.C., LUBBINGE, J.-W., MATTHEWS, W.S., MCDONALD, D.J., SMIT, W.J., BENNETT, R.G., JONAS, Z., LOMBARD, A.T., DE FREY, W., ROBESSON, R., OELLERMANN, C., GROBLER, A. & BOONZAAIER, I. 2014. Vegetation Field Atlas of Continental South Africa, Lesotho and Swaziland. Strelitzia 33. South African National Biodiversity Institute, Pretoria.

CHAPTER 2
ECOSYSTEMS
Rina Grant-Briggs and Mike Peel

SOIL HEALTH AND VELD MANAGEMENT IN VARIOUS BIOMES

Farming with game is more complex than farming with domestic stock because of the wide variety of species and their specific habitat and dietary requirements. Management should aim to facilitate an increase in wildlife through an improved water cycle, increases in plant available moisture, nutrients and ultimately a resilient functional grass sward and associated tree layer. The purpose of this chapter is to provide:

- New perspectives on understanding habitats at the finer scales at which management actions are exercised.
- Aid in identification of the different habitats and their possible values.
- Advice on how to evaluate soil health and deterioration.
- Advice on appropriate approaches to determining stocking densities

Understanding habitats and requirements of different species

Vegetation types can be grouped into biomes with similar characteristics. Once you have established the biome that your game farm is located in, it will help you determine the type of animals that would thrive there. A relatively broad but useful recent classification is used here. (See Figure. 2.1.) Note that even though a farm is located in a specific broad biome, various elements of different biomes and habitats may be present on any one farm (e.g. patches of grasslands in otherwise Nama Karoo vegetation).

Biome descriptions (from Low and Rebelo, 1996)

Forest biome

Forests are restricted to frost-free areas with a rainfall of more than 525 mm in the winter rainfall area and more than 725 mm in the summer rainfall area. Forests rarely burn and tend to occur in patches. The vegetation is dominated by large trees with a variety of lower vegetation types in the sub-canopy, but very little vegetation is found on the ground due to the dense shade. Forests play and important role in providing wood, but are also attractive tourist sites. There are several game reserves in the Sand Forest such as Mkuze Game Reserve and these forests provide suitable habitats for several game species such as kudu, bushbuck and nyala.

Thicket biome

This vegetation type forms a closed shrubland with low trees that are mostly evergreen. Many species have spines forming impenetrable thickets. Various thicket types provide suitable habitat for game farming. Valley thicket occurs mainly along the river valleys of the Eastern Cape and have rainfall of 400–800 mm. Soils are sandy clays to deep clay soils. These dense habitats are suitable for browsers such as kudu and bushbuck, but where areas have been opened up plains game such as zebra are also found. The spekboom succulent thicket have an average rainfall of 250–300 mm. Soils here are derived from sandstone, quartzites and shales and are generally shallow. A wide variety of game is farmed and conserved here.

Savanna biome

This is the largest biome in South Africa and supports the widest variety of game species. The vegetation consists of a grassy ground layer which is interspersed with a distinct layer of woody plants at various height classes. Where this woody upper layer is near the ground the vegetation may be referred to as Shrubveld, where it is dense as Woodland, and the intermediate stages are locally known as Bushveld. Rainfall varies from 235–1 000 mm per year and the amount of frost varies depending on the locality. Many of the major geological and soil types are found in various localities in this biome, and may differ from farm to farm. The grass and tree combination is maintained by fire and herbivores and can vary from grass dominated to woody dominated depending on the amount of fire or herbivory. This biome provides grazing for domestic stock and game and many game farms and conservation areas are found in this biome.

Grassland biome

This vegetation type is found mainly in the high central plateau of South Africa. The vegetation consists mainly of grass with isolated patches of trees and shrubs in localities where they are protected from frost and fire. In areas with a rainfall above 625 mm and where soils are more acidic the grasses tend to be "sour". These grasses are generally more productive, grow tall but tend to be more fibrous or woody (high lignin content) and become unpalatable in winter. These grasses are, however, palatable early in the summer season when the grass is young, short and nutritious. Regular fires and/or intense grazing keep the grass in this short palatable state.

Sweet grasses occur in lower rainfall areas and more alkaline soils and although their biomass is lower these grasses are palatable throughout the year. This biome is very suitable for plains game and large herds can be seen on game farms and in conservation areas. This biome has a very high biodiversity and has been earmarked as a priority conservation area, also since large tracts of this biome have already been transformed by agriculture and urbanisation.

Nama Karoo

This biome occurs on the central plateau of the western half of South Africa. Most of it is between 1 000 and 1 400 m above sea level. Geology is varied and the rainfall varies between 100 and 520 mm. Soils are lime rich and shallow and are very prone to erosion. The vegetation consist of grasses and dwarf shrubs. The large herds of springbok and other game that used to occur in the area are no longer seen due to changes in land use. However, there are still many game farms and conservation areas in this biome and the area is very suitable for springbok, gemsbok and other arid adapted game.

Succulent Karoo

This unique vegetation type occurs mainly along the west coast at an altitude below 800 m. Soils are shallow and lime-rich. This area receives winter rainfall between 20 and 290 mm per year (interestingly, reasonably consistent in any particular locality), and summer temperatures may be above 40 °C. Fog plays an important role in providing moisture to plants and frost seldom occurs. The vegetation is dominated by succulents but annuals form impressive displays when they flower in spring. Because of the poor grass cover, this is not a very good game farming area, but springbok and gemsbok do well here at low densities.

Fynbos

This area is well known for its importance in biodiversity due to the endemic vegetation with 7 000 plant species. Many of these plants are endangered due to land use changes and invasion by alien plants. The soils are generally very poor and low in nutrients except for the small area of renosterveld where large game used to occur. In general, even this vegetation type is not recommended for game farming.

Requirements of game species

Wildlife in Africa has evolved to make use of the variety of habitats available. They are adapted to utilise specific vegetation types, dependency on water differs and they also have different ways of digesting their food.

Interaction of game species with their environment

See Table 2.1 for information on examples of the species representing the different types of adaptations.

Differences in digestion

Wild herbivores can be classified as either ruminants or hind gut fermenters. Ruminants have a rumen which is a large digestion tank with bacteria. Grass is collected by biting and is only chewed at a later stage (chewing the cud). Ruminants can therefore spend relatively little time collecting their food in areas where they may be threatened by predators, and can then chew and digest their food in areas where visibility is higher and where they are safer from predators. In the rumen, bacteria help to digest the cellulose in the grass that cannot be digested by forestomach mammals. Ruminants can therefore make use of very low quality material, but need time to digest the plant material properly. When the quality deteriorates too much, ruminants cannot ingest sufficient food for their needs and lose condition and eventually die.

Hind gut fermenters on the other hand, have to chew their food where they collect it and are therefore more exposed to predators. However, the low quality cellulose is digested in their hind gut where food is passed relatively quickly. These species are not as limited by low quality food as ruminants as they can go on feeding until no forage is left. These species should therefore be considered as more of a risk to veld deterioration when resources are very limited.

Forage preference

Herbivores can also be classified according to their food preferences:

Grazers

These species generally have fairly broad mouths and relatively large rumens, adapted to a diet mostly consisting of grass. They are most limited by nutrients in winter when the protein levels of grass is very low.

Browsers

Browsers focus on eating leaves from woody plants, and as such have relatively small muzzles to be able to select their forage and avoid spines (thorns). They mostly have large salivary glands that assist in neutralising the digesting-inhibiting tannins that are high in browse species. They become compromised in spring and early summer in particular, when few leaves of high quality are available resulting in relatively low energy intake (biomass low) but with high protein intake (high quality). When they are seen apparently "grazing" on open veld, they are invariably eating forbs or small woody plants.

Mixed feeders

These game species adapt their diet from graze to browse as the quality of the grazing deteriorates (i.e. mostly graze in summer and browse in winter). They are therefore very adaptable species and often the most numerous species on game farms. Their size and muzzles are intermediate between grazers and browsers as are their rumens.

The interaction of herbivores with forage and other herbivores (according to Collinson and Goodman)

Herbivores interact with their environment and can change it to their own benefit. Their interaction with their environment can change depending on the environment and therefore herbivore type is not included in Table 2.1. The examples given here are to help you interpret the plant-animal interactions that you may observe.

Type 1 herbivores

Select palatable grass species from the tall grass sward, and in large numbers they can change the type of vegetation from tall to a more palatable short grassland. However, large numbers may cause a decline in the more palatable tuft grasses. Examples of this type of herbivore are elephant, white rhino, buffalo and zebra.

Type 2 herbivores

Prefer taller grasses as forage, and decrease in number due to the changes brought about by the Type 1 herbivores. Examples of these are roan, sable, tsessebe, waterbuck, common and mountain reedbuck and grey rhebuck. Many of these species also require dense, tall grass stands to hide their young calves, thus the disappearance of such areas will make the young animals more vulnerable to predators.

Type 3 herbivores

Thrive on the changes that may be brought about by the Type 1 herbivores as they prefer the shorter high quality grasses. Wildebeest, warthog, hartebeest and springbuck are examples of this type of herbivore.

Type 4 herbivores

May respond to changes brought about by Type 1 and 3 herbivores, but do not change the grassy part of the system themselves. These are mostly browsers and include species such as giraffe, kudu, black rhino, eland, bushbuck, duiker and steenbuck.

This classification may not be true for all species depending on the type of habitat but can be useful as a guideline to determine species mixes. To maintain a healthy productive system, the effects of the Type 1 and 3 herbivores, as well as their population sizes should be monitored carefully.

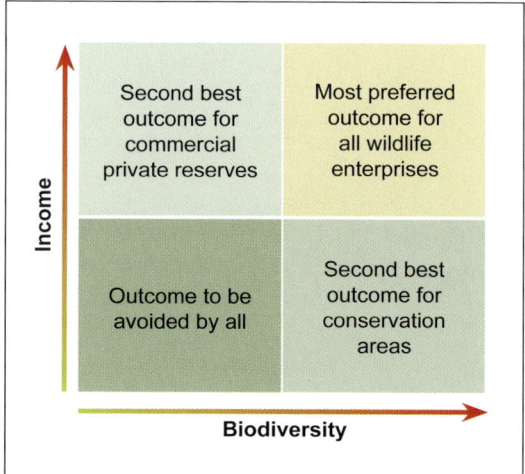

Figure 2.2: Balancing between the desired outcomes of biodiversity and income is challenging and choices have to be made between optimising income and biodiversity.

In any enterprise it is important to decide what the goals are and then to manage as effectively as possible towards these goals. Evaluating whether these goals are being achieved is an ongoing process and adjustments where necessary are part of learning and achieving.

Conservation of biodiversity has become an important goal environmentally. Biodiversity is defined as the variety of plant and animal life in the world or in a particular habitat. Farming with wildlife can make a positive contribution to biodiversity where the landscape is not altered to promote a specific species and is not degraded, allowing different species to co-exist. However, it is almost impossible to optimise for income and biodiversity as illustrated in Figure 2.2. The resources and consequence of management decisions for biodiversity, or for income, must be taken into account. Choices for income often involve improving visibility of game for tourism by providing water or opening vegetation. This change in the landscape can have detrimental effects on biodiversity that is often associated with changes in vegetation species and cover which affects the distribution of smaller mammals, reptiles and birds.

Understanding habitats available for game ranching

Healthy soils and habitats are the foundation of wildlife and other rangeland enterprises.

Some general principles

Although soils and habitats differ with geology and rainfall, there are some basic principles that are true everywhere. Bare soils cannot capture rain, as rain drops tend to splash and compact the bare soil, and tend to run off, taking some of the top soil and the organic matter on the surface with them. Soil covered by vegetation and organic matter softens and distributes the impact of the raindrops, and allows the water to infiltrate into the soil. Furthermore, plants themselves provide organic matter when their leaves and seeds drop and when plants die back. Soil organisms such as soil bacteria, as well as earth worms and even termites, process the fallen material to make the nutrients available for absorption by plant roots, while dung beetles process animal droppings in the same way, ensuring that the nutrients are recycled to keep the system healthy and productive.

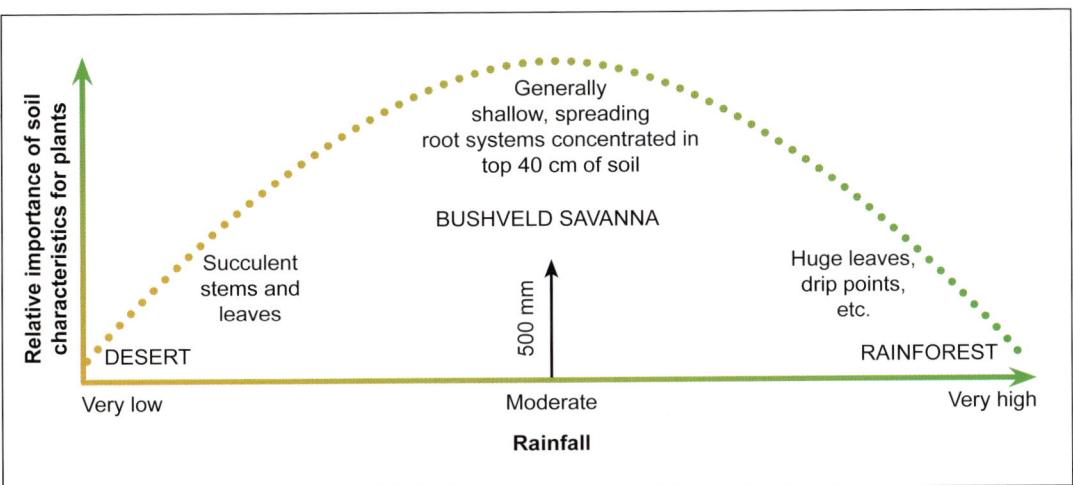

Figure 2.3: There is a strong link between vegetation pattern and soil type and rainfall, and hence the game species that can utilise these areas. (Venter 2003)

Table 2.1: Vegetation types where game species occur with a short description of their preferred habitats, dietary preference and water dependence. (From Skinner and Smithers 1990.)

Species	Preferred habitat							Habitat requirement	Dietary preferences	Water dependency	Digestive system
	Forest	Thicket	Savanna*	Grassland	Nama Karoo	Succulent	Fynbos/Renosterveld				
Eland	√		√	√	√				B	L	R
Kudu	√	√	√		√			Thickets	B	L	R
Nyala		√	√						M		R
Bushbuck	√	√						Thickets	B		R
Blue wildebeest				√				Short grass	G	H	R
Black wildebeest				√	√			Open grass plains in the Highveld savanna	G	H	R
Tsesssebe				√				Ecotone	G	H	R
Blesbok				√	√			High grasslands	G		R
Bontebok							√	Grasslands	G	H	R
Gemsbok			√		√			Arid grasslands	G	L	R
Sable				√				Tall grass in open woodland with vleis.	G	H	R
Roan				√				Require open grassland with tall grass	G	H	R
Waterbuck				√				Associated with water	G	H	R
Reedbuck				√				Reedbeds	G	H	R
Impala				√				Woodland with open patches	M	H	R
Springbok				√	√	√		Open arid grasslands	M	L	R
Red duiker	√							Riverine forest	B	L	R

Species								Habitat	Diet	Water	Digestive
Common duiker	✓	✓	✓		✓	✓	✓	Dense bush	B	L	R
Suni			✓					Dry woodland with thickets	B	L	R
Sharp's grysbok			✓					Scrub and low grass	B	L	R
Steenbok			✓					Open grassland with cover	M/B	L	R
Oribi				✓				Open habitat	G	L	R
Klipspringer				✓	✓		✓	Rocky outcrops	B	L	R
Grey rhebuck				✓				Rocky hills and mountain slopes	G	H	R
Mountain reedbuck				✓				Dry, grassy slopes with scattered bushes	G	H	R
Buffalo		✓	✓		✓			High forage biomass and shade	G	H	R
Plains zebra			✓					Open areas of woodland	G	H	HG
Cape mountain zebra					✓			Mountainous areas	G	H	HG
Black rhino	✓	✓	✓					Well-developed woodland and thickets even in arid savannas	B	H	HG
White rhino				✓	✓			Short grass, flat terrain, wallows	G	H	HG
Elephant	✓	✓	✓					High biomass forage	M	H	HG

Dietary preference: G = grazer
B = browser
M = mixed feeder

Water dependence L = low
H = have to drink regularly – this will decrease when animals feed on succulent vegetation

Digestive system R = ruminant
HG = Hind gut fermenter

Soil types are closely linked to geology. Sandstones for instance erode to form sandy soils, while volcanic rocks such as basalts, dolerites and gabbros tend to erode to clays. Figure 2.3 illustrates the links between soil type, rainfall and vegetation, with the closest links at a moderate rainfall such as the Kruger National Park. In these areas the change in vegetation very closely reflects the change in geology and soil type (Sappi Tree Spotting, Venter in the Kruger Experience). This link becomes less evident in low rainfall areas such as the Kalahari and Karoo and in high rainfall areas such as the forests of the Natal coast.

How does this knowledge apply to your farm?

Within broader vegetation types such as illustrated in Figure 2.3, and especially in the large part of the savannas of South Africa that fall in the central part of the graph in Figure 2.3, each farming unit also consists of patches with more or less clay and soil moisture. These different patches have different functions and production potential depending on the specific season and type of wildlife.

By improving your understanding of the distribution and role of these specialised habitats you can improve the chances of achieving the production and biodiversity goals of your wildlife enterprise.

Soils can be broadly divided into sandy soils, which tend to be lower in nutrients, with nutrient concentrations increasing as the particle size decreases and other attributes change towards the other broad type, clay soils. On the other hand, the water captured in sandy soils is more readily available to plants than in clay soils. This is the reason that broad-leaved trees and shrubs such as bushwillows dominate sandy soils while finer leaved thorn trees occur most commonly on soils with a higher clay content. Sandy soils tend to occur on crests in undulating landscapes such as granites and quartzites, and the broad leaves are mostly defended by chemicals such as tannins that cause leaves to be less palatable. Clay soils are more common in valleys where the small soil particles are washed down slopes and accumulate. They are also found in the plains of basalt landscapes and where there are dolerite and gabbro intrusions. Fine-leaved thorn trees grow preferentially on these clay soils and as

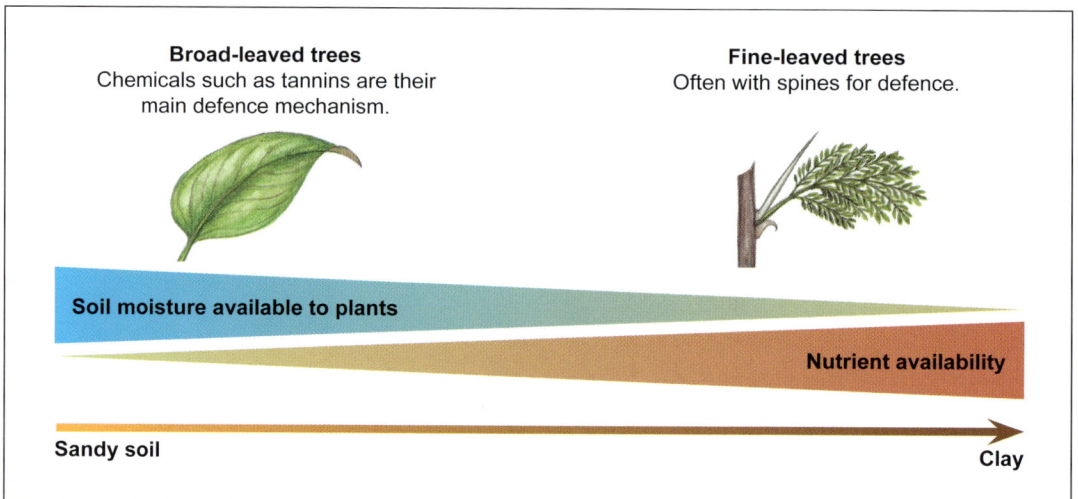

Figure 2.4: The relationship between soil type and nutrient availability, soil water availability and vegetation. Fine-leaved in the figure.

they are very palatable, they are defended by spines. This pattern is illustrated in Figure 2.4.

Protein is an important ingredient of wildlife diets. Physiologically, short growing grass is higher in nitrogen than tall more mature grass. During the growth season, patches of young growing grass plays an important role in the nutrition of most grazers, especially those that prefer shorter grasses such as wildebeest, zebra, impala and warthog. As long as there is sufficient soil moisture, these species can create and maintain patches of short-growing grass that often resemble lawns. This is promoted by grazing and fertilising (through dung and urine) these patches regularly. Because the grass on these patches always seem to be very short, they have been suspected of indicating areas of degradation or overutilisation. However, the growth points of the grass species that grow in these areas are very close to the ground and these grasses can be grazed regularly without detrimental effects. These type of patches could therefore increase the animal production during the plant growth season, allowing the animals to build-up body condition and thus ensure reproduction.

Even though these short grass patches are favoured by grazers in the growth season, they become dormant with very low biomass in the dry season. Animals therefore have to survive on areas with the higher biomass of taller grass tufts in the dry season. In low and moderate rainfall areas, the quality of the dry forage on the veld provides sufficient energy to maintain grazers, while supplemented hay or grazing of higher quality may have to be provided in the high rainfall areas where grasses are more sour and less nutritious, e.g. in the Natal highlands. Mixed feeders such as impala and nyala change their diet from grass to browse and are therefore able to generally maintain their condition better than grazers such as buffalo that are dependent on a high biomass of grass for maintenance. Many tufted grass species do not thrive if continuously grazed, as their growth points are higher and can be damaged by repeated grazing. The area covered by tall grass tufts should therefore be much larger than the short grass areas in order to provide the necessary forage for grazers throughout the year.

Habitats providing high quality resources to grazers in the growth season

Habitats that are more often selected by grazers in the plant growth season, and therefore kept in this short, growing, more nutrient-rich state during the growth season, are:

Sodic sites

These are open patches in granitic landscapes that tend to be higher in salts and clays than the surrounding vegetation. These areas often look barren and do not seem to be very productive, however many grazers and even browsers prefer these areas as they tend to provide forage with higher nutrient concentrations. In areas with predators, these areas are also safer to spend time ruminating as visibility here is good.

Termite mounds

Termites increase the soil moisture and nutrients in their mounds. Grasses growing on these mounds are also higher in nutrients, and are often utilised selectively by grazers, especially later in the growth season.

Short grass patches on clay rich soils

Any factor that concentrates grazing pressure on clay soils in a relatively small area can lead to the formation of short grass patches or lawns. Waterpoints and drainage lines tend to concentrate grazing, and grazing lawns can thus often be seen along rivers and around watering points. *Cynodon* is often the dominant species in these short grass patches and is well adapted

A sodic patch in the Kruger National Park.

In private reserves adjacent to KNP, sparse grass cover is well utilised as long as green tufts are available.

A termite mound in northern Kruger National Park, showing distinct areas of shorter grazed grass on the mound and a small radius around it. Grazers are often seen on these mounds.

A typical area of cleared land in Addo National Park. Although these areas do not represent the natural vegetation they are preferred foraging sites of many of the game species there, and areas of short lawn type grass is created within these old lands.

In Golden Gate National Park animals such as the Red Hartebeest create and maintain patches of short grass where they prefer to forage.

Short grass patches are also developed and maintained by grazers such as wildebeest and zebra on gabbros and basalts in the Lowveld.

Tall trees are important nutrient pumps in the savannas, and areas of short grass are often seen below these trees, where they provide high nutrient forage.

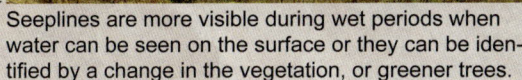
A typical Highveld wetland. Grasses are tall and tough and form an important dry season resource.

Seeplines are more visible during wet periods when water can be seen on the surface or they can be identified by a change in the vegetation, or greener trees.

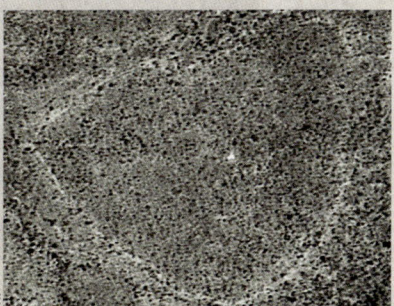
The aerial photo illustrates the location of seeplines relative to the broad-leaved woodland on the crest and fine-leaved *Acacia* in the valley bottom.

to being grazed on a regular basis. The same pattern can be seen in patches on the basalt plains when grazers tend to select certain patches on which to forage. These patches are also often covered in lawn-type grasses that are very palatable.

Old lands and cleared areas

In many areas the vegetation was cleared for agricultural purposes. These open lands have often been fertilised and these open more productive areas can provide favoured foraging sites for grazers even if the areas are subsequently acquired for game farming. The attractiveness of the patches is very well illustrated in Addo National Park.

Tall trees

In areas with an annual rainfall above about 200 mm and below about 800 mm trees that are taller than 5 m tend to draw water and nutrients from deeper down the profile to the soil surface. Grasses growing under these trees are therefore more palatable and nutritious, and a small patch of short grass can often be seen surrounding larger trees in these areas.

Habitats providing important dry season resources

Some areas that stay wet can provide soil moisture even during the dry periods. Grass is therefore greener in these areas and provide an important source of high quality grazing later in the season. Examples of these type of habitats are:

Wetlands

A wetland is an area that is saturated with water, either permanently or seasonally. Soils in such areas have specific characteristics and are often dark due to organic matter captured in the soil.

Drainage lines are very distinct in arid areas such as the Karoo and are often essential for survival of animals.

Seeplines

Seeplines are a characteristic occurrence along catenas (rocky hill crest surrounded by a valley or drainage line), and found where broad-leaved tree species that grow on the hills are replaced by fine-leaved trees of the valleys and drainage lines. These seeps form because the sandy soils from the crest, formed by erosion of rocks such as granites, meet the clay soils.

Water, captured between the sand particles is forced onto the surface by the less permeable clay soils and superficial rocks. These areas are often more open than the surrounding vegetation and in some areas Silver Clusterleaf (*Terminalia sericea*) tend to dominate (this pattern is illustrated in Sappi Tree spotting Lowveld) and in the aerial photo.

Drainage lines

The size of drainage lines differ from small streams to large rivers. These are all in lower lying areas where the water that does not percolate into the soil accumulates. The areas surrounding drainage lines are invariably higher in soil moisture and provide green grass into the dry season.

Other important resource habitats

Ecotones

An ecotone is the region of transition between two biological communities, often on very similar soils such as clays. Ecotones between such two habitats are often richer in species than either (Oxford Dictionary).

Rocky outcrops

Rocky outcrops are specialised habitats where the soils are shallow. In the Highveld these areas provide protection from frost and therefore are the only areas where clumps of trees can occur.

Winter resources

Although large parts of the grassy plains are not much utilised during the growth season, they are an essential source of bulk forage during the dry season. It is very important to ensure that this resource is sufficient to provide the forage required.

CHAPTER 2: ECOSYSTEMS

Ecotones are typically more open areas between drainage lines and the upland woody vegetation on clay soils. These areas are important habitats especially for rare game such as roan antelope.

Rocky outcrops are specialised habitats where soils are shallow. In the Highveld these areas provide protection from frost and therefore are the only areas where clumps of trees can occur.

These tall grass areas are very important dry season resources during the absence of high quality green leaves.

Management of these habitats

A healthy soil is one of the most important indicators of a healthy habitat, while an associated good plant cover provides roots to bind the soil, preventing the loss of the top soil and organic material due to wind or water erosion. To determine whether an area is in a healthy state one therefore needs to look at plant composition, cover and indicators of the loss of soil and organic matter from the area. These methods (see Trollope and Peel for more detail) can be augmented with an assessment of soil indicators using a simplified landscape assessment based on the methods developed by Tongway and Hindley (landscape function analysis or LFA).

The purpose of such an assessment is to evaluate the state of the vegetation and the soil along a representative transect (line) down the slope in the area to be evaluated. The transect length (which should be at least 50 m) will depend on the density of the plants and size of bare soil stretches between vegetation patches when these are present.

This survey can also be expanded according to the more detailed landscape function assessment of Tongway and Hindley.

An example of soil rich in organic matter. Water will penetrate this soil well.

Website for landscape function assessment of Tongway and Hindley:
http://www.researchgate.net/publication/238748160_LANDSCAPE_FUNCTION_ANALYSIS_PROCEDURES_FOR_MONITORING_AND_ASSESSING_LANDSCAPES_With_special_reference_to_Minesites_and_Rangelands

Method for landscape assessment

Include patches of vegetation and bare soil along a line transect that follows the slope of the landscape.

At 1 m intervals measure the distance from a point on the line to the nearest perennial grass. In arid areas with mainly annual grasses or forbs, the distance to annuals (including forbs) should be added to the measurements.

Record any signs of soil loss or water runoff along the transect, as well as any obstructions that will stop water and soil from being lost from the area.

Determine the average distance to tuft for each habitat of concern and keep this record to compare data in future.

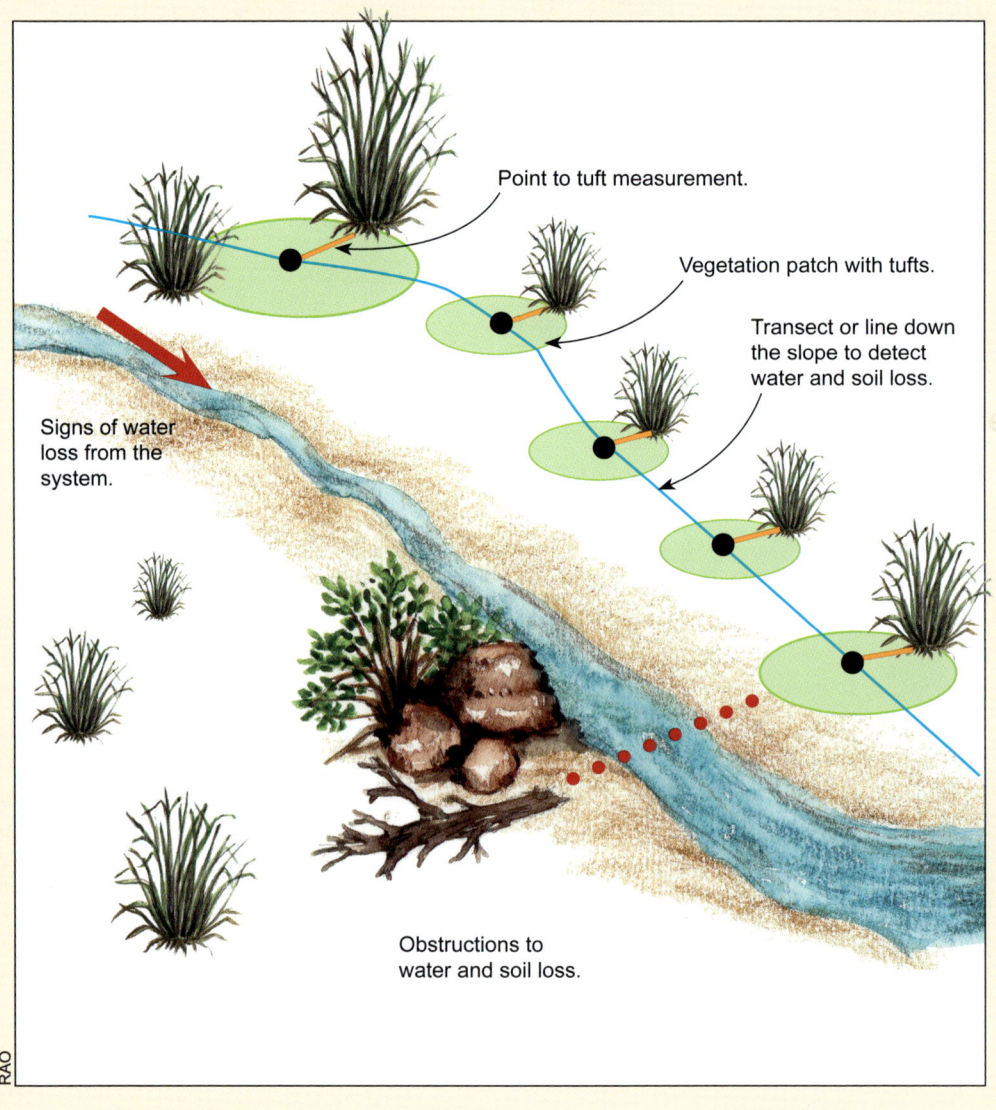

Interpretation

Even though the density of grass tufts will vary hugely in different rainfall zones and soil types, one would as far as possible strive to manage in a way which keeps the distance between tufts (point to tuft measurement) as small as possible for the relevant rainfall regime. If there is a clear indication that soil is being lost, or that there is an increase in the average distance between tufts, then it would be appropriate to consider rehabilitation measures such as brush packing. If none is observed, the area is most likely in a healthy state.

From practical experience in savannas, Winston Trollope, a practical fire and savannah ecologist, suggests that the potential for erosion is as reflected in the table.

Erosion potential	LOW	MOD	HIGH
Distance from point to tuft in cm	<3cm	3-5 cm	>5 cm

Rehabilitation

Rehabilitation or intervention should be considered whenever an increase in distance between plants or a loss of top soil can be detected. This is often caused by inappropriate utilisation as discussed above. Compaction due to the creation of game paths or roads and tracks can also lead to erosion when not maintained or carefully planned. Certain areas such as sodic sites are more sensitive to disturbance and should be avoided totally when driving off road or when tracks are being developed for use on a farm. One should also consider evaluating these sites more regularly for signs of degradation.

Once an area is degraded or eroded more concerted effort needs to be made to rehabilitate the area. The different approaches are well described in "Caring for natural rangelands" by Ken Coetzee. Each manager needs to look at the options that will work best for his farm. The main purpose of rehabilitation is to increase plant cover and soil organic matter. The first action needed is often to stop water and top soil being lost from the system. Brush packing works well to recover areas where soil is being lost over a large area, but where deep erosion channels are still absent. The brushes decrease the rate of water flow and capture soil and organic matter enabling grass seeds to establish. The brush also protects the grass and forb seedlings that establish from grazing by large herbivores. Deep erosion channels need to be addressed with more sophisticated methods such as gabions and specialised advice is required to understand where to place these structures to address the problem (i.e. poorly planned or executed erosion control methods can worsen rather than alleviate the problem).

The simplified landscape function assessment can also be used to evaluate the effectiveness of the rehabilitation effort. A decrease in the distance between plant tufts and less evidence of soil and organic matter loss would be an indicator of improvement.

Clearing of alien plants

Alien plants are a threat because they do not have natural enemies that control their growth and propagation, while the indigenous plants have various insect and other enemies that play a role in their control. There is an increased awareness of the threat of alien plants and the Working for Water Programme is making a concerted effort to clear areas of these plants. Helpful manuals and advice is available from working for water website and offices. (https://www.environment.gov.za/sites/default/files/legislations/guideto_clearing_invasive_alienplants.pdf.)

Alien species such as black wattle (*Acacia mearnsii*) often form very dense stands outcompeting the natural vegetation. The shade in these stands also precludes the growth of grass, and areas that are invaded are thus not available for grazing.

Many of these alien trees and plants are also very unpalatable and cannot be seen as forage for browsers. Some of the other most widespread species are the Port Jackson willow (*Acasia saligna*), rooikrantz (*Acasia cyclops*), blackwood (*Acacia melanoxylon*), lantana (*Lantana camara*) and triffid weed (*Chromolaena odorata*). Because of the bare and exposed soil under these stands of alien trees there is an increased risk of erosion, which should be taken into account when the alien plants are removed. In general clearing alien plants is a huge and ongoing task that can be very costly, so one should as far as possible try to avoid purchasing areas that are heavily invaded. However, many of the alien plants are distributed along water courses, and in this way new plants establish in areas where they were not a problem before.

Be very cautious when using herbicides as these chemicals may have detrimental long term effects on human health and the native vegetation. When available, biological control approaches are often very effective although these act slowly and are unlikely to eradicate the alien plants totally.

Bush control

As many of the areas that are under wildlife management are encroached or very densely wooded, many managers find it necessary to clear areas to increase the availability of grazing, and to improve game viewing. This must be done with care to avoid unintended consequences, such as a loss of grazers due to predation, increase in bush density due to coppicing, and erosion when clearing was done in the wrong areas.

A general principle is that grasses inhibit the growth of young woody plants. Any factor that decreases grass cover such as very heavy utilisation by grazers, or droughts, can create an opportunity for woody species such as sickle bush and black thorn to establish, and once they have established and grown to above grass height, their shade inhibits grass growth and they become very difficult to control. The questions that one should ask when contemplating bush control are as follows:
- Was the area historically open?
- Will there be a favourable grass response to treatment (related to soils) in the medium to long-term?
- Will the objectives for control be achieved?
- Will the management action be economically viable?

Fire is a tool that can be used to control the growth of woody species. However, sufficient grass biomass is needed to support a hot enough fire to cause top kill of the woody species. Also the heat generated by a fire varies not only with biomass but also with the growth stage and biomass of the grass; the drier the grass, the hotter the fire it can sustain. Weather conditions are also important. Hot, dry days support much hotter fires than cool, misty days. Fires are also cooler and often die as temperatures drop and humidity increases towards the late evening (dew point). Hot, windy days are best avoided as fires are very difficult to control under such conditions.

Remember, most of the African tree and shrub species re-coppice after fire, therefore fire frequency has to be considered. This is especially important in higher rainfall areas where a strict fire regime is required to maintain open areas.

No golden recipe is thus available; drier areas need less frequent fires than high rainfall areas, but soil type and woody composition will also influence the frequency of fire required to maintain the vegetation as an open savannah. Fires do not occur in forest and thicket areas and cannot be used as a tool in these vegetation types.

Management of wildlife density

Wildlife management can be very challenging, especially on fenced small and medium-sized units, such as game farms and even consolidated conservancies, because their natural movement to better resources is restricted. To avoid degrading the natural resources on which the animals rely, managers have to estimate the number and type of animals that can be supported on a property. Knowledge of soil types and habitats, as well as animal and plant-animal interactions is critical for sound decisions. As savannahs in Africa are very dynamic, using simplistic or rigid figures to indicate stocking capacity are misleading and may easily be an over- or underestimate depending on the rainfall and veld condition of the farm.

The number and type of animals should be considered on a regular basis taking at least the forage quality and biomass into account, but animal behaviour and physical condition may also indicate when animals are stressed. An important reason why the determination of stocking densities is not straightforward is the particularly fine scale patchiness of many game farms. The seasonal variation and differences in rainfall cycles and patterns, as well as the less than complete knowledge we have of nutritional and social requirements of wildlife, further complicate this issue. One needs to remember that there are limited management options when farming with game, as game animals cannot easily be herded or moved, and one needs to rely on attractants like licks, waterpoints and green grazing created by fire, to try attract animals away from heavily utilised areas when this is desirable. In the face of this complexity it is nevertheless helpful as a first step to know how much food is available and how much your particular selection of game species will require. As explained there is no single answer and we can only attempt to help you to initially make a judgement from which you can start to learn, and adapt management as you understand the animals and their interaction with the farm better.

Determining the forage biomass available to animals

Available biomass is but one aspect that determines the number and species of animals that can be supported, but it is one of the more simple measures and an easy place to start. Ideally one may like to measure the forage available for each species according to their preferences, but this is an impossible task at this stage, yet the more representative the measurements of the available forage, the better the idea you may have of the numbers that can

Table 2.2: Determining the forage requirements of the game species on the farm. Herbivore requirements (from Meissner 1981).

Energy requirements listed are for females suckling young	
Species	Energy demand
	MJd-1
Black wildebeest	28.9
Blesbok	18.1
Blue wildebeest	41.4
Buffalo	106
Eland	96.9
Elephant	374
Hippo	206
Impala	16
Springbok	9.24
Tsessebe	28.9
Warthog	24.8
Waterbok	36.4
White rhinoceros	265
Zebra	67.8

Determination of grass biomass (standing crop)

Grass is generally the limiting resource in game areas. The first step is therefore: To estimate the amount of the grass biomass available at the end of the growth season around May in summer rainfall areas.

The more representative this measurement is of what is available to grazers the better your calculations for the grazing and mixed feeder complement. Therefore one should try and assess a representative sample of different habitats across the farm to arrive at an overall estimate of the amount of forage (kgha^{-1}) available for herbivores and for the use of fire (if that is considered as a management tool).

- Grass biomass can be measured by estimating biomass based on experience of amount of hay produced per hectare or by cutting a square meter of standing hay and determining the dry weight.
- Biomass can also be determined using a Disk Pasture Meter.
- The disc pasture meter (or DPM) is an aluminium instrument used to measure the compressed height of the grass. Based on research, the available grass biomass per hectare (kg grass/ha) is then calculated using the formula developed for this purpose (or the table in the appendix). This is an easier alternative to cutting, drying and weighing grass samples for measuring biomass.
- The compressed height should be measured at at least 50 points representing the forage expected to provide nutrition to animals until the next growth season (see the Trollope references for details).

Calculate the amount of biomass (standing crop). (Note: This figure does not reflect the forage available as animals select palatable species and leave the unpalatable species and material.)

When using the disk pasture meter:
- For each transect determine the average compressed height for the 50 points on the transect.
- From research we know that grass biomass (kg/ha) = -3019 + 2260x (square root) (average disc height of 50 readings) (cm).
- Calculate the average biomass for all the measured transects.

Determine the total amount of grass biomass available in suitable forage patches by multiplying the average grass biomass by the number of hectares of forage available.

Estimate the forage available by taking the frequency that preferred grass species is encountered along the transect into account. More information on species preferences is available in Van Oudtshoorn (2014).

Take the type of grazing or veld into account: Sweet veld is more palatable than sour veld and animals can utilise up to 80% of this veld type, while sour veld is much less palatable and only about 50% is utilised.

be supported. The text box (p 70) supplies some guidelines to help you to use information from your farm to determine the numbers and types of grazers that you might reasonably be able to support on your unit. See the attached list of further reading for more information on the different methods available.

Determining the number of browsers that can be supported is more difficult as the measurements of browse and available biomass is more complex and it may be more useful to look at the body condition of the browsers in order to determine whether the animals are receiving sufficient nutrients. Detail on the method is available in Smit 1996 and Dreber 2014.

To calculate the energy required to feed herbivores for a year:

1. Energy required per year = (energy requirement of each species from Table 2.2) x population size of each species present x 365d (MJy^{-1}).
2. Divide the total energy required by 10.5 (estimated energy available from dry forage as calculated by Lombaard 1966) to determine the kilogramme biomass required.
3. Correct the forage biomass available by taking the frequency that preferred species occur into account. Also correct for the veld type – all the biomass calculated is not available as forage.
4. Also take into account that mixed feeders such as impala and springbuck will not need grass for the entire period and their requirements should be adjusted according to the observations of the period these species concentrate on grass as their main source of forage.
5. Subtract the amount of vegetation required (kg) from the amount available to give an idea of the degree to which the grass will be able to meet the requirements of the grazers and to what extent the grazer composition should be changed.

To finally determine the best mix of game species for the farm, knowledge of the habitats available for the different species, climate and landscape need to be taken into account. By monitoring animal performance for your goals (perhaps production if that is key) and responses of the vegetation to the game species, you will be able to evaluate the outcome of your estimates. If the intended goals (high income or high income and high biodiversity as illustrated in Figure 2.2) are not achieved, the species mix and numbers might need to be adjusted as necessary.

Water provision

Water distribution is an important factor in how animals move and utilise the landscape. In large conservation areas such as the Kruger National Park an increase in available water was associated with an increase in wildlife numbers. However, even in this large area many animals died of hunger during the big droughts. Managers therefore need to carefully consider how they can balance food and water resources on their farm as they are both essential for survival. One approach is to adjust animal numbers according to the limitations of the most limiting resource in order to avoid losses. It is advisable to have some areas further from water than others to allow for species that are less water dependent. Also make use of natural drainage lines and water points as far as possible as the soils in these areas are often more resilient to heavy utilisation than areas where water does not occur, such as on the crests.

Disc pasture meters (DPM) can be ordered from Brian Clarke (Eastern Cape, South Africa) info@alus.co.za or Tel 076 813 0122.

CHAPTER 3

GENERAL GAME RANCH MANAGEMENT

PLANNING AND MANAGEMENT

Gert and Nanette Fourie

Before purchasing a game farm the potential rancher should be clear about which one (or combination) of the four pillars of the industry will be practiced. This will determine where the farm should be located, which animals can be kept, and what management system will be adopted. This section provides a guide to all the aspects which must be reviewed when planning to buy a game farm, as well as the ongoing management of the game ranch after its establishment. There are also a number of game management experts available to assist new game farmers to plan and monitor the progress and sustain ongoing management of the business or ecosystem.

SELECTING A FARM

Location: If the owner does not intend to live on the farm it should preferably be easily accessible for good management purposes, but bear in mind that not all areas are suitable for game ranching. The positive and negative factors influencing game farming in the region should be borne in mind. The buyer requires a fair knowledge about the climate and habitat offered by the specific region as well as the requirements by the specific species that will be introduced on the farm. Understanding the historic occurrence of the species will be an excellent starting point and will indicate the intrinsic suitability of the habitat offered to those species. The best approach is to introduce animals according to natural available habitat rather than manipulating the habitat or conditions according to the species that the landowner wants to keep. Today, however, through intensive breeding, many species that did not occur in an area naturally are kept and bred successfully in areas outside their historic and natural areas of distribution. By food provision, providing cover in some cases and artificially controlling predation and acquiring permits for the keeping of these animals from nature conservation authorities, animals can be kept successfully on the farm.

Biomes

Each biome has a different suitability for game farming and must, therefore, be realistically evaluated.

Savannah biome: The savannah biome is one of the most suitable to game farming because of the wide diversity of animals which can be kept. Small-sized farms are from 100–1 000 ha,

medium 1 000–5 000 ha and large farms from 5 000–15 000 ha. Suitable veld types in the savannah biome are:
- Mixed bushveld in the Limpopo Province, Mpumalanga and North-West Province.
- Sweet bushveld in Limpopo Province.
- Waterberg Mountain bushveld in the Limpopo Province.
- Mopane bushveld in the Limpopo Province.
- Lowveld bushveld in the eastern parts of Limpopo Province, KwaZulu-Natal and Mpumalanga.
- Sub-arid thorn bushveld mainly found in the Eastern Cape.
- Kalahari bushveld in the drier western parts of North-West province.
- Northern Cape coastal bushveld in KwaZulu-Natal.

Karoo biome: This area has limited potential for game farming due to lack of suitable habitat for a larger variety of animals, as well as a low capacity in terms of available food. Large areas of a few thousand hectares are normally required to run a sustainable game farm. Smaller microhabitats such as drainage lines or riverine forest with higher tree cover become more suitable for a higher variety of game.

Forest biome: These areas are not suitable for game due to a limited amount of food within browsing height of animals, as well as lack of enough suitable habitat. Grazing is normally also very sparse. Very few game farms are found in these areas.

Thicket biome: This biome is very suitable for shrub-feeding animals, but less suitable for grazers. However, thicket may form a mosaic with the grassland and savannah biomes in the Eastern Cape. This type of habitat provides sustainable provision of food during all seasons, especially for browsers. Land sizes vary from a few hundred hectares to 10 000 ha.

Grassland biome: This area is very suitable for grazers, but not for shrub-feeding animals (except in smaller micro-habitat areas). Some of these areas have rocky outcrops with woody plants or valleys where more trees and shrubs are found, thus offering better cover and protection as well as food for animals. More and more game farms are being developed in these areas.

Appropriate size: Studies undertaken on mostly open natural areas for most game species indicate the roaming and territorial areas used by these species in the wild. Conservation authorities use this information as a minimum requirement: For most larger game species, the requirement is a minimum of 200 ha and in some cases 400 ha. Therefore, introducing animals on smaller land sizes is not allowed without special permits. Buyers of land should ensure that the land on which they intend to farm their species of choice fulfils the requirements set by the specific provincial authority. If the land is smaller, a special permit application for the keeping or breeding of the specific animals will be required.

Despite the legislative requirements it is of course also of importance to ensure that the intended animals to be introduced can be sustained by the land. The habitat requirements, condition of the habitat and the size of the land should be investigated before the farm is purchased. If the intention is to have an economical unit based on hunting or live sales of animals where selling relatively large numbers of animals on a regular basis is required, the carrying capacity together with the size of the land will be determining factors.

The use of semi-intensive systems for breeding projects has made it possible to farm economically on smaller scale farms. On these smaller scale farms a large portion of the land may be utilised for breeding and although these activities have financial benefits it may come at a price – exclusion of certain animals and possible reduced biodiversity on the farm to ensure optimal production of one species. The ideal is a property that is large enough where a higher

The moist sour bushveld of the Waterberg is a suitable biome for game ranching.

biodiversity conservation approach can be offset against the intensive conditions on the farm.

Size of a property is also directly linked to maintenance costs and if a property is merely purchased for lifestyle and personal relaxation, maintenance costs of a large farm may become a burden for the owner. On the other hand, the scale of operation should also be considered. The same equipment and the same cost will have to be obtained for a 100 ha compared to 500 ha, however, the scale of cost (cost per hectare) on the smaller farm is much higher.

Condition of the land: This is probably the least well understood aspect when buying a property for game farming is considered. The conditions may appear good to the inexperienced eye but statistics have proven that the majority of farms in South Africa have poor veld conditions. The grass sward may for instance appear to be good but it could offer poor quality grazing. In high rainfall areas in particular regions, merely appraising the grass cover visually may be misleading.

Poor management results in overgrazing, or selective overgrazing, damage to important browse due to fire, disturbance or loss of the soil. The impact of poor management will have varying effects in different regions and the ability of the area to recover is sometimes referred to as the "elasticity of recovery" – in some areas the recovery is quick and the land is

Erosion and alien plants such as bankrotbos (*Stoebe vulgaris*) will be costly for the landowner to repair and eradicate respectively.

reverted to its original status, whereas in other areas it may never recover fully or the recovery may be slow, taking decades to revert to the natural state.

In general, soil damage is the most serious because eroded soil cannot be naturally replaced within a foreseeable timespan. Repairing serious soil erosion is extremely costly and it may even not succeed for various reasons. It may take hundreds of years to replace tall fire-damaged trees. Recovery of the grass sward is normally of shorter duration and may be achieved fully within five to ten years if no damage to the soil occurred.

Dense invasion by alien plants can reduce the carrying capacity and this can also be a very costly problem to resolve, so it is also essential to consult specialists in this regard.

Availability of water: The majority of farms in South Africa obtain water from underground resources by means of one to various boreholes on the property while some properties have the advantage of a permanent river. A primary borehole that delivers enough water for the daily requirements plus a back-up borehole is normally essential for the operation of a game farm.

A house or lodge for 4 to 6 people will use 2 000 litres of water per day and if gardens are maintained the usage may easily escalates to 10 000 litres depending on the size. Animals on the farm will consume approximately 3% of their body weight of water per day. By knowing the stocking rate on the farm, the weight of the animals on the farm can be calculated and the daily water requirement can be determined. This figure will have to be doubled to accommodate evaporation.

When inspecting a property with game ranching in mind, the water resources should be evaluated properly in regard of waterholding capacity, and the extend and state of the equipment – pumps, pipes, etc. The borehole should also be tested/certified if there is doubt about the capacity. Also take into account that the water source is not indefinite. Water levels in certain areas may be receding due to the demand in the area and a borehole that used to provide sufficient water years ago, may not still have the same capacity. Water from a borehole should be considered a shared source and consideration should be given to neighbours and other people relying on the source.

An often neglected aspect is the quality of the water and therefore a prospective owner should ask for water quality tests. Tests should ideally be undertaken once per year and will indicate the suitability of use by humans and animals.

Seasonal and permanent water sources are a valuable resource on a game farm.

Animals: If the new owner is simply seeking a lifestyle farm, a good variety of animals present on the farm and in most cases a preference for non-dangerous animals will be a given. A good variation in habitat types will consequently be important. Ranching could also be focused on regular tourists and a more commercial approach. Again the variety in habitat types and variation in game species will be important. Depending on the size of the property and the activities offered, dangerous animals can be introduced, especially if the main activity on the ranch is game drives and some or all of the big five animals can be seen.

A ranch offering hunting opportunities will require a higher number of popular hunting animals and depending on the type of hunters a variety of species, especially trophy males. The requirement for an animal to grow to trophy size will be habitat in optimal condition. Meat hunters will not seek a variety of species but rather a high number of a few species should be on offer. For this reason a farm with good carrying capacity but not necessarily high variation in habitat is required.

Some animals adapt well to most types of habitat, while others are more selective and sensitive to the habitat. If the prospective landowner intends to breed specific species, he must ensure that the habitat is suitable for those animals and that the veld has the capacity to sustain them. This will ensure optimal

The grass cover and carrying capacity of a farm must be determined for each herbivore species.

performance of the intended breeding animals. The prospective buyer should have a clear knowledge of the capacity to sustain animals before buying the property.

The carrying capacity is determined by the combination of grazing capacity (grass is normally the main source of food) and browsing capacity. The browse capacity is determined by woody plants (trees and shrubs), the type of species present as well as availability (within reach of animals) and acceptability of the forage. A higher variety of plants on the farm will also offer better forage availability throughout the year since not all species shed their leaves/pods/fruit at the same time of the year. Likewise the grazing capacity is also dependant on the type of grasses and the dry mass available to animals. It is of importance to note that in some cases by means of selective overgrazing, some preferred grasses are depleted and other non-preferred grasses then become dominant. The grazing may appear abundant but in reality the quality may be low and limiting. Fluctuation in carrying capacity can occur from one year to the next due to management, rainfall, and other factors such as frost, fire, termites, etc.

Carrying capacity can be expressed in different terms: one common reference is hectares required to carry a grazing animal unit (blue wildebeest) or a browsing animal unit (kudu) without deterioration of the veld. Depending on the area where the farm is situated and the condition, these values may vary between 3 ha/GU and 15 ha/GU for grazers and between 6 ha/BU and 25 ha/BU for browsers.

In intensive breeding projects, the carrying capacity is slightly less important because of the role of supplementary feeding as a management tool. Buying a farm with the preferred animals already on the property is always a bonus, since animals are already adapted to the habitat while those that are introduced from other regions normally experience a period of stress and needs to habituate to the new environment. This period of adaptation is often associated with some mortalities and it may take months before the newly introduced animals have organised into social groups and are functioning optimally. Already established game species that are doing well is especially important with regard to animals that are difficult to establish, for example gemsbok in higher rainfall bushveld areas or nyala in relatively cold areas. Having these animals established on a farm is a plus point. Also bear in mind the role played by tick-borne diseases such as heartwater and babesiosis when bringing in new animals (see the chapter on diseases).

Live animals are sold to a limited extent at auctions: most valuable species are sold on catalogue or at private auctions which allows one to become acquainted with the breeding history and disease status of the animals. Wildlife agents are another source of mainly plains game (more common species); these agents are required to be registered with APAC (Agricultural Produce Agents Council) that regulates their activities and allows for redress in the case of animal mortalities or diseases.

If a farm is already stocked the animals may be inbred, especially if the owner followed a low interference approach. As a rule of thumb it is always safe to replace a number of males of each species with males from a new genetic pool and thereby ensure a game population with a healthy genetic diversity. Where animals need to be introduced or where new genetic material is introduced it is of importance to source these animals from similar areas (similar habitat and climate) to ensure that they adapt easily. However, avoid buying animals from adjacent farms because they often tend to return to the original property.

There are legislative issues regarding the acquisition and translocation of rare game species to a new or existing farm. A regulation implemented by the government to protect these species from irresponsible management/handling is TOPS (Threatened or Protected Species Regulation) – this regulation restricts the movement, introduction, capture, handling, hunting, import or export of certain species without special permission and permits. In some cases a proper detailed study and motivation by a professional is required before animals can be introduced on the farm.

General infrastructure: Without taking the cost in consideration, the best option is to buy a farm with no infrastructure and to plan and establish the infrastructure correctly from day one. This will include taking the ecological factors, the objectives of the owner and future management into consideration.

Unfortunately few farms are planned well and when buying a farm, the new owner inherits some of the mistakes of the past. On the other hand, the cost of developing a farm with the correct road network, a good water distribution network and correct water presentation, proper layout and positioning of fences and bomas, loading facilities and camps as well as suitably well-planned and positioned houses/lodges and stores is a very expensive exercise and not always accounted for in the price of the farm.

Buying a relatively well-developed farm at a reasonable price is therefore a bonus and it will be considerably cheaper to rectify some of the mistakes rather than doing everything from scratch.

The flipside of the new owner developing the land is off course overcapitalisation – beware of overcapitalising of the property since the value of the infrastructure may never be recovered when the farm is sold. Electricity is vital for various functions on the game farm, so uninterrupted availability should be investigated. In most rural areas irregular supply due to load shedding or weather conditions will necessitate back-up sources such as generators and solar installations.

Other aspects of infrastructure that must be considered are:

Fencing: Fencing is a very expensive item for game farms, so the buyer must thoroughly check to ensure first of all the suitability of the fencing. The main purpose of the fence is to keep animals inside the farm and in some cases to keep other animals out of the farm. Different game species require different types of fencing. Not all animals jump over a fence but some will simply break/jump through or crawl underneath the fence. Kudu, eland, impala and sometimes waterbuck and nyala will jump – sometimes successfully jumping over but in many cases jumping high into the fence, either going through or breaking some of the strands on higher levels. Ideally for these jumpers a strong fence of 2.4 m in height should be erected, and enough strands and droppers close enough to ensure that the fence is strong enough on point of impact is important – spacing between droppers and strands not further than 10 cm apart at height levels 1.4 m to 2 m. The strength of the fence is also determined by the distance of the line poles (y-standards or poles planted in between straining posts). Other species breaking the fence on lower levels like wildebeest, rhino, buffalo and waterbuck will also require 10 cm spacing on lower levels and spacing of droppers not more than 1 m apart. Additionally, an electric fence with strands at height levels 800 mm to 1.2 m may be helpful in keeping these animals away from the fence.

Rusty wire and droppers will result in breakages and repair expenditure.

"Crawlers" that go underneath fences are difficult to control and in most cases only the larger creepers like gemsbok, hartebeest, sable and springbuck should be kept in by ensuring strands are 50 mm to 100 mm apart, droppers are 1 m apart and holes under the fence are fashioned in such a way to allow only warthog and other small antelope to go through (various methods are used).

Any electrification of fences, especially at very low heights, should be considered only with proper motivation and responsibility since smaller animals can be electrocuted and natural migration of these smaller animals will be directly affected by the electric fence. Electric fences will thus have a direct affect on a farm's biodiversity and the surrounding environment. Electrification of certain areas (e.g. breeding areas) on the farm is acceptable but it is highly recommended to have an area available for free movement of all smaller animals for obvious conservation reasons.

Finally fencing must be neat, with all poles in line, upright and well anchored. Any rust or breakages of wire will indicate that the fencing may have to be replaced.

Bomas for quarantine, capture, holding or management: Having a boma on the farm is not essential but it is very handy to have and it makes game management so much easier. A boma is essential for a farm containing buffalo because if they are to be translocated, veterinary requirements stipulate a 30 day quarantine period during which the buffalo need to be tested regularly. Temporary bomas are also sometimes used and it can be moved to a better position should it be required and can also be removed for aesthetic reasons. A permanent boma has other advantages and can be constructed much stronger and build in such a way that the handling and holding facilities are much better than a temporary one. However, should it be determined that the boma was constructed in a wrong location, moving it will be difficult and costly. A good test by the prospective buyer is to find out how regularly the boma has been successfully used.

Employee accommodation: On game farms these buildings are often neglected and of low quality. It is part of the social responsibility of the owner to provide suitable accommodation for workers. Game farm employees are cooperatively responsible for a multi-million rand operation and their quality of life may directly affect their performance. Dilapidated structures on a farm are also aesthetically unpleasing and definitely impact negatively on the value of the property. Also consider the position of the housing – a manager needs to be close enough to the workshop and main operational area and should preferably have cell phone reception and radio communication in cases where security is paramount. The general workers should be situated closer to the road to avoid unnecessary traversing through the farm. Housing situated within sight or earshot of the main access road/gate on the farm may contribute to the security on the farm.

Roads: A network of roads on the farm giving access to most areas makes management so much easier and improves overall experience of the farm. Roads that are wrongly planned, poorly constructed and ill-maintained may however become a headache and quite an expensive part of the maintenance cost. The buyer should be wary of farms with seriously eroded roads and roads with poor drainage that will require re-filling and serious ground moving to correct. A scenic circular main road that avoids fences and offers a variety of views and elements of surprise is ideal.

Workshops, stores, cold rooms and abattoirs: No farm can function without a workshop. There will always be something that needs to be fixed or worked on such as patching tyres, servicing a tractor, fixing pipe fittings or boreholes, repairing broken equipment, etc. Therefore, a workshop of reasonable size (depending on the size of the farm) is essential. Another essential requirement is an area where feed can be stored. Supplement feeding will be part of the management on most farms and a proper protected area with reasonable volume is required for this purpose. These two structures can be ideally positioned close to an office for a manager (if required) and not too far from the manager's house. Cell phone reception and availability of electricity will be essential.

A cold room and abattoir are not essential but a huge advantage to have on a farm – even if hunting is not an option on the specific farm. Animals may have to be culled or a post mortem on an animal that died without obvious cause may have to be undertaken. These structures should not be constructed close to accommodation since it may be associated with unpleasant smells and flies. It should preferably be constructed closer to the main operation/workshop area. Avoid close proximity to feed stores since flies associated with the abattoir may spread diseases and contaminate feed. If commercial hunting is undertaken, guests will spend some time near or around the abattoir area and therefore the appearance and position should be well considered.

Neighbours: All farms have neighbours of some sort who can add or detract value to or from the business or lifestyle game farm. Animals breaking through fences, runaway fires and security problems are but a few of

Roads must be well planned and kept in good condition.

the common issues that will have to be dealt with. A study of all the surrounding areas is important since it may influence the security situation on the farm – water may be affected or polluted due to activities in the area such as mining or housing developments, or land reform and communal land claims may cause local disturbances. Ideally the prospective landowner should stay overnight on a property to get an idea of any disturbances which will affect the business or atmosphere of the farm. Having other game farmers as neighbours is ideal because knowledge can be exchanged, combined purchases, such as feed, can be beneficial, services and cost of game marketing can be shared.

Land claims: Due to inequalities in the past, a land reform programme is followed by the government of South Africa that aims at restitution, land tenure reform and land redistribution that will compensate those that were previously disadvantaged. All these terms may sound very intimidating to the prospective landowner. Although the constitution currently protects land rights, rumours of land claims tend to lower property prices in an area. Furthermore, if a land claim is successful, the implications for the landowner may be relocating and the sense of loss at having to leave behind a meticulously well-managed project. An agent or specialised attorney should be requested to do a proper

Combining livestock and game species must be properly planned and considered.

investigation into the history of property in the area. Transformation partnership (BEE) ventures for social upliftment could be considered to involve local communities.

Equipment: When purchasing a farm it is essential to have the required equipment to maintain and improve the farm. It could be beneficial if all the loose items and equipment are included in the purchase price of the farm. On the other hand, taking over old equipment from the previous owner can mean endless misery – inoperable or ineffective equipment can not only be costly to replace but can take up valuable production time on the farm and quality time from the owner.

The required equipment vary considerable in type, quantity and size depending on the size and activities on the farm. A few essential pieces of equipment will be a tractor and trailer, mower/slasher, firefighting equipment, brush-cutters and chainsaw, mobile generator, welder, compressor and all the smaller tools required to do fencing and steelwork.

Security: Most game ranches are located in rural or remote areas where there is little or no preventative policing. It is essential to have a good backup communication network such as satellite phones or radios to be able to communicate with neighbours and local police. Private security firms are expanding their services into rural areas and they provide on-farm services, road block patrols and surveillance, as a tool to prevent poaching of targeted species such as rhino. Private security services is very expensive. Ranchers can organise co-operative neighbourhood watch patrols. Other practices are locking of gates, installing of an alarm system at critical sites such as rhino camps and cell phone monitoring towers to detect the presence of intruders

Combining game with livestock: A combination of game and livestock may be a huge advantage, or a huge liability for the game/stock farmer. Cattle play an especially important role as bulk grazers on a game farm. If no wild bulk grazers like buffalo or rhino or hippopotamus are present, the role that livestock play in providing a shorter grass layer are beneficial to other species. They do, however, need more intensive management than game animals in the form of tick control and vaccinations. Therefore, proper cattle handling facilities are required on the farm. This infrastructure may interfere with the game farm operations and may negatively impact the aesthetic value of the farm. Furthermore, the smaller inner fences used for cattle may also cause some serious injuries to certain animals such as giraffe. Where regular feeding of game is required, cattle may consume this feed long before the game get to it.

Disease: This is always a concern when mixing game and cattle: Wildebeest will infect cattle with bovine malignant catarrh virus (BMC) or snotsiekte, if not separated by a minimum distance of 1 km. Even more serious is the threat of cattle diseases for valuable game species such as buffalo, sable and roan. If cattle are used for veld management they should be free from bovine tuberculosis and brucellosis, be separated from neighbouring farms by maintaining proper exclusion fences between neighbours, and maintained as a closed herd by testing any new introductions for possible diseases.

However, cattle have been successfully combined with game through correct management. Where different camp systems for game breeding are present, cattle may be very easily combined with game by following a daily rotational program to allow all the game to feed successfully without cattle interfering. On open farms, a large number of cattle may be introduced in an area for a short while to graze heavily and then moved out again. Some farmers have implemented a corridor for cattle around the farm, thus ensuring a fire break and be able to manage the cattle more effectively.

Financial aspects and planning: The cost of developing infrastructure, introducing game and management in relation to the expected production potential will determine if a return on the investment is possible. Income can be generated by annual population control. Game can either be sold as live animals or offered as hunting opportunities. Hunting is a form of tourism and this aspect together with other forms of ecotourism will require a good farm location, excellent infrastructure and a well-oiled management team to attract visitors. Among other forms of income generation that have become very lucrative, is specialised breeding of rare game species. This endeavour will, however, require high initial capital investment, excellent knowledge of the animals and specialised managerial expertise. Over the last ten years many game farms have developed from very unprofitable lifestyle properties into lucrative businesses, creating unmatched returns on investments in the investor world. The very lucrative business of rare animal breeding has drawn investors from all industries because it offers investors the option to combine a lifestyle investment with an excellent business opportunity. The potential form of income that will be generated on the farm will be determined by:

- Whether the location of the farm influence the activity and form of income.
- What the unique characteristics are that the specific farm offers and what should be focused on to optimise the potential.
- What infrastructure is required to implement activities and what the cost will be to upgrade the existing infrastructure if inadequate.
- The ecological capacity of the farm and the estimated production potential of animals.
- The running costs and basic overheads of a standard game farm.
- The market sector in which the farm will be active.

Specialists can be consulted to undertake a feasibility study of the planned activity on the farm. Many game farms turn into big black holes of expenses. In order to prevent this a proper budget should be prepared and adjusted over a period of time. If a manager is appointed, keep in mind that a basic knowledge of accounting skills is essential to manage the farm within the budget provisions and restraints.

Ongoing management

Ecological monitoring: Similar to any successful venture, game farm management should be focused on improving and optimising the conditions on the farm. Conditions on the farm change due to external factors such as fluctuations in climate, occurrence of fire, game population dynamics, and other ecological events. Only management is a stable factor and should be able to deal with fluctuating conditions on the farm.

It is impossible to remember exactly the condition of the vegetation a few years ago without quantitative information. Therefore, a proper ecological monitoring program that measures and compares subsequent years should be implemented. The grass sward is checked by a scientifically based method that can be repeated in the future and changes in species composition, grass cover and the

Fire-fighting equipment is essential for all farms.

Game counting is an important part of game ranch management.

biomass over a period of a few years are recorded. The woody component (trees and shrubs) takes longer to change unless a drastic event like a hot fire transforms the structure. Monitoring regularly will show whether the available volume of food within reach of browsing animals is changing. Densification of the woody layer is common on many game farms. The extent should be monitored regularly to be aware of the situation and to take appropriate action.

Specific monitoring points are selected on a farm to ensure that monitored records can be compared using the same fixed points repeatedly. Although a specialist should ideally be commissioned to do the monitoring at regular intervals, the landowner or manager should also undertake monitoring regularly (annualy or bi-annually) using the fixed-point photography method. Comparing photographs of different years of exactly the same position on the farm will at least indicate drastic changes and management can be adapted accordingly.

Fire is a useful ecological management tool (see *Habitat management*) but must be used responsibly (consult the Fire Act administered by the Department of Agriculture, Forestry and Fisheries – DAFF). Irresponsible and unplanned burning can cause habitat damage, devastation of property and endangerment of animals and people. All game ranchers should be members of the local Fire Protection Agency (FPA). Permission must be obtained from a FPA to burn veld as this can only be done at certain times of the year and under fire-safe conditions. Some associations invest in fire-fighting equipment which can assist in controlling accidental fires. Every game farm should have basic fire-fighting equipment in the form of a water tank mounted on a trailer with a hose and pump. Backpack sprayers and bought or home-made "beaters" are also useful especially on rough terrain. Fire fighters shoud wear appropriate protective gear. Note that fire extinguishers are ineffective for use on veld fires because they help spread the fire. All equipment must be kept ready and in good working order at critical times of the year and staff must be properly trained in using the equipment. Making fire breaks at the start of the dry season is essential to prevent spreading of fire from neighbouring farms onto the farm, and these must also be made around all buildings, valuable equipment and camps where animals are housed.

Game monitoring: Because game cannot be counted and monitored in the same way as livestock, other methods have to be used to monitor their condition and the population dynamics. The landowner needs to monitor the population growth since not all deaths and births can be recorded. Furthermore, it is important to know what sex ratio is present in the game population and what percentage of the animals can be harvested annually. The terrain and type of vegetation will determine the method to be used – for instance, if the farm is small with relatively open grassy plains, the animals can be monitored relatively accurately from vehicles.

A farm with dense vegetation and more variable terrain will require a different method. In this case a helicopter survey may be the only way to monitor the animal numbers. Note, however, that it is almost impossible to see all animals from a helicopter and these surveys will only provide an indication of numbers and trends. Absolutely correct numbers cannot be determined this way. These counts may indicate certain trends, especially when counting is repeated with the same helicopter, persons counting, flight patterns and time of the year.

Also make use of "known group" methods – people working on the farm will get to know certain herds and by regularly counting and recording this data, this may become one of the most useful pieces of information to determine numbers and trends.

During lambing and calving seasons, the number of young seen from vehicles or on foot can also be recorded and by determining the percentage of newborn lambs and calves in relation to the adults and extrapolating this information, an indication of the reproduction percentage and success can be determined.

Technology also makes it easier to use alternative measures. Using trap cameras at various points on the farm, certain groups of animals, compositions and animal condition can be determined and monitored.

Economic monitoring: Keeping within budget guidelines, comparing actual expenditure, keeping stock records, recording births and mortalities, comparing target reproduction percentages, annual sales and all other financial aspects will help assess if the objectives were achieved or not. If the farm has a manager this person should be able to do the recording and reporting.

Management and staff training and monitoring: Game farm staff will only perform as well as they are trained. Lately more and more courses are offered to train unschooled employees and investing in the staff's skills improvement may save a lot in the long run. The staff should have basic knowledge of tracking, hunting and slaughtering, firefighting, basic vehicle maintenance, machine and equipment operation, fence and road maintenance, and also a basic knowledge of the animal and plant species on the farm.

Even well-trained staff and well-educated managers may not be able to realise the full potential of a farm without a proper management program. If the manager or owner is unable to do the planning themselves, it may be worthwhile to obtain an expert's assistance. An annual planned program depicting all the season-related activities on the farm will ease management's task. Plan ahead, on a monthly and even on a weekly basis. By having a weekly or daily schedule on which certain activities are pre-established, will ensure these activities are undertaken and executed timeously.

Contact Gert and Nanette Fourie at info@ekofokus.co.za

NUTRITION IN GAME ANIMALS
Craig Shepstone

Animals require specific nutrients to keep their bodies functioning effectively, which is referred to as homeostasis.

The nutrients involved include protein, fats, carbohydrates, minerals, trace minerals/elements, vitamins and water.

Depending on the physiological status of the animal, the amount of each specific nutrient will differ:
- Mature non-breeding animals will require a maintenance diet while
- young growing animals, and pregnant and lactating females, will require a higher level of nutrition.

In this section the nutrition of the main groups of herbivores encountered on game farms is discussed, namely ruminants and hind gut fermenters.

Herbivore nutrition

All herbivores have the ability to convert vegetation to energy to sustain vital functions but they do this in different ways. Herbivores can be divided into foregut fermenters (ruminants and pseudo-ruminants) and hind gut fermenters. Pseudo-ruminants which include the hippopotamus, the camel and the llama are not discussed in this section.

Ruminant herbivores in South African game ranching include the bovines such as buffalo, the giraffe and all the antelope species. Ruminants ingest plant material with minimal initial chewing, so the plant material has to be reduced to fine particles by repeatedly regurgitating and physically chewing the ingested forage, before rumen bacteria can break it down.

Examples of ruminants: Bulk grazer (buffalo), browser (nyala) and short/medium grass grazer.

Examples of hind gut fermenters: white rhino, black rhino and zebra.

Rumen microbes ferment the cellulose and hemicellulose components of the plant material into volatile fatty acids namely acetic, butyric, propionic and lactic acids. Volatile fatty acids are the main energy source for ruminants and they are absorbed into the animals' blood stream through the papillae in the rumen wall. Most of the dietary protein gets converted into microbial protein, which is the main source of protein for the ruminant. Lipids are digested in the small intestine and amino acids are absorbed here. Most ruminants, unless their feed contains a high moisture content, need to drink regularly to provide the large amount of water needed for the suspension of the food and microbial culture in the forestomachs.

Ruminants can be subdivided into:
- browsers,
- grazers and
- intermediate feeders (animals that graze and browse).

Small antelope which feed on succulent food like fruit and flowers are referred to as concentrate selectors – their nutrition will be dealt with in the small antelope section. The bulk and roughage eaters (grazers) are generally found in grassland habitats, where they utilise grass of a relatively low quality. Grazing animals generally have a slow rate of digestion and a large rumen and abomasum. Roughly 80% of the intestinal mass is made up by the small intestine (duodenum, jejenum and ileum) which is mainly involved in the absorption process.

Browsing ruminants select juicy concentrated food and are found in areas with more shrubs and trees, eating feed composed of mostly leaves, flowers and fruits from forbs, shrubs and trees. In contrast to grazers they have faster feed fermentation rates, a smaller rumen and abomasum, and dense even ruminal papillae; 70% of the intestines are made up of the large intestine (caecum and colon), allowing for more hind gut digestion.

Ruminants take roughly 12 hours to digest green forage, but as forage dries out in the winter and protein content falls, the rate of digestion slows and the supply of nutrients from the rumen decreases. The animal then has to mobilise fat and protein from body stores in order to produce energy for survival. This results in loss of condition and muscle mass.

Hindgut fermenters (HGF) are monogastric animals which after initial digestion in the stomach use the large intestine as a microbial fermentation chamber for the fibrous plant material content. Examples of HGF game animals are zebra, elephant, black rhinoceros (browser) and white rhinoceros (grazer). In contrast to the ruminants, HGF animals chew their food with well-developed molars, which allows acid digestion of the protein component in the stomach to polypeptides and amino acids. Lipids and carbohydrates are digested in the small intestine and amino acids are absorbed here. The undigested fibrous component of the feed passes into the caecum where cellulose digestion takes place by microbial action, producing volatile fatty acids like acetic, propionic, butyric and lactic acids. In white rhino the natural diet contains high levels of fibre and a low to moderate protein content, while in black rhino the protein content of the diet is higher and the fibre content is lower.

The role of natural forage in herbivore nutrition

Natural forage or veld provides optimal nutrition for the combination of grazers and browsers adapted to that particular biome or habitat. However, many game farms are rehabilitated cattle farms which have been overgrazed by livestock and used for crop farming. The challenge for the new game farmer is to determine how many animals can be kept on the land (the stocking rate) to ensure optimal habitat utilisation, avoiding overgrazing or overbrowsing

Grazers use different resources of vegetation when compared to browsers.

which can result in shortages of feed for game animals especially in different seasons.

The traditional method for determining stocking rate is the carrying capacity (CC) method which was originally developed for livestock farming. It expresses the capacity in animal units (AUs) or in herbivore large stock units (LSUs). In practical terms an LSU needs the intake of 9kg dry matter which represents 8.3 MJ of metabolisable energy per day. CC is the unit of vegetation required to maintain a single animal unit over an extended number of years, without any negative effect on the vegetation or soil. A LSU is the equivalent of a steer (ox above two years) with a mass of 450 kg, with a live body mass gain of 500 g/day on grass forage (veld) with an average digestible energy efficiency (DE) of 55% (to maintain this 75 MJ per day is required). When optimising veld management, it is crucial that the CC of the farm be calculated prior to introducing the animals.

Using the LSU-method is, however, not a very accurate method of determining the carrying capacity of a piece of land, because the system does not allow for ecological separation of animals and overlooks the potential of maximum veld utilisation by the complementary resource-use habits of different wild ungulates, for example, the fact that grazers use different resources of vegetation when compared to browsers. Dekker *et al.* (1996) designed a system for multiple species situations. The grazing unit and browsing unit were therefore defined: "A grazing unit (GU) with the metabolic equivalent of a blue wildebeest and a browsing unit (BU) with the metabolic equivalent of a kudu. (For more accurate methods of calculating forage biomass and optimising habitat utilisation refer to Section 2).

In totally natural systems animals can migrate from one area to another after forage of better quality. This allows the animals to obtain all the essential nutrients for maintaining body condition and reproducing. Forage quality in any particular grass, forb, shrub or tree species generally decreases as the season dries out. During the dry season plants mobilise nutrients for seed production and storage (in the roots) for the next season, resulting in the leaves drying out and becoming more lignified (woody). These seasonal changes affect the nutritional quality of the forage. Because most game farms are fenced they are unavailable to areas where there is more palatable grass (for example from sour veld to sweet veld).

If animals like sable antelope are confined to sour veld regions for example, with little or no supplementation, the animals will not be able to maintain their body condition or reproduce with regularity. Browsers in fenced-off areas are also affected by seasonal changes, as deciduous trees have little or no available browse on them, and some evergreen trees produce tannic acid which binds the ingested protein making it unavailable to the kudu and other browsers. This may result in death from starvation.

Boma feeding, seasonal licks and supplementing in semi-intensive camps.

General principles of supplementation of game animals

The ideal of every game farmer is to utilise the natural forage on the property to the optimum, not only because this is necessary for healthy habitat utilisation and maximum biomass production, but because additional feeding is extremely expensive, labour intensive and carries some risks. Supplementation must therefore be done after due consideration of the cost:benefit ratio. The main reasons for supplemental feeding are:
- Seasonal supplementation to maintain condition.
- Emergency feeding during droughts or after fires.
- Short term boma feeding for translocated animals.
- Feeding in semi-intensive breeding systems.
- Boma feeding during quarantine.
- Supplementation of mineral/vitamin deficiencies.

The need for supplementation is determined by the factors discussed above as well as the type of ranching which is done. Some general principles and guidelines are discussed in this section. Commercially available supplements in the form of pellets, cubes, blocks or licks are available to complement the natural forage or roughage supplied to the animals daily, and are not intended to replace the grazing or available browse. Generally speaking supplementation should not exceed 1/3 of the animals' dry matter intake. Full feed recipes are available for animals confined in camps and bomas which have no access to natural forage (see textbox for definitions of various feeds). Supplements and semi-ad lib feeds must always be fed with roughage; examples of suitable roughage are veld or pasture grass, cereal (unpitted) and legume hay (lucerne), silage and browse.

Commercially available pellets or cubes are formulated to contain the correct amount of digestible protein, energy, macro- and trace minerals for that particular animal species, age, sex and physiological phase. The recommended intake per class of animal is given by the manufacturers. Some game farmers formulate their own rations using various raw materials. This requires a good working knowledge of nutrition to prevent imbalances and rumen-related problems such as acidosis due to high intakes of easily fermentable carbohydrates (starch).

Mineral and vitamin deficiencies

Herbivores on natural forage seldom develop vitamin deficiencies because their microbial flora are able to synthesise these micro-nutrients. The exception is vitamin A, the level

Sable bull with a copper deficiency before (left) and after (right) treatment.

of which drops once forage dries out. Animals fed on dry hay may therefore need vitamin A supplementation if this is not added to other feed supplements.

The mineral phosphorus drops in winter forage in summer rainfall areas, which can lead to pica or eating of the bones of old carcasses or tortoise shells. Since phosphorus is an essential mineral for animal growth and production, its deficiency will reduce performance and pica behaviour will expose the animals to botulism (see Diseases). Licks containing a balanced calcium:phosphate mixture should therefore be given in areas where animals are dependent on dry winter forage.

Soils in South Africa have shown to be deficient of some trace elements including iodine, copper, cobalt, manganese and molybdenum (Maree and Casey, 1998). Copper deficiency has been diagnosed in sable in Limpopo Province. Affected animals showed a yellow-grey discolouration of the hair coat but after treatment with a copper supplement the colour returns to the normal black or brown. There are also reports of selenium deficiencies causing deaths in sable, but the primary cause is usually a lack or roughage. When specific deficiencies are diagnosed in such cases supplementation can be done using injectable trace elements or added to rations in consultation with expert consultants/veterinarians.

Extensive or semi-intensive supplementation: Dry season supplementation on veld is done for all game, in particularly sourveld and mixed veld areas, and sweetveld areas where protein and energy components of the natural forage declines the drier it gets. Protein blocks, and lucerne hay can be supplied as protein sources. Supplement valuable animals on a larger game farm/reserve with protein pellets which can be placed where animals tend to congregate (see discussion on suitable feed containers later). In the green season mineral licks containing phosphorous, calcium and trace minerals should be used. Apart from their attractiveness to herbivores salt blocks are not very useful as mineral supplements because they are deficient in all the other minerals except for sodium and chloride and may contain heavy metals and sand. Prevent tannic acid poisoning by feeding products containing polyethylene glycol (PEG) which can be added to drinking water (Browse Plus or GameMin for Browse).

Intensive supplementation: Animals kept in camps with little or no grazing for management purposes will need full rations suitable for the particular species. In these cases cubes, pellets or self-mix feed fed together with high quality hay are given on a daily basis. Alternately a total mixed ration (which includes chopped hay with lengths greater than 2.5 to 3.5 cm) can be given on an *ad lib* basis.

Species specific recommendations

Ruminants: Protein supplementation is given in dry seasons to increase the voluntary intake of forage. Suitable dry season protein supplements are commercial protein pellets or cubes, protein licks, blocks and lucerne hay (in small amounts). Do not feed lucerne hay as the sole roughage source. When supplementing forage with hay the fibre length must be >2.5 to 3.5 cm, to ensure optimal fermentation, rumination and digestion. Green lucerne must not be fed due to the risks of developing "red gut" (see under Diseases).

Feed grade urea can be fed as a cheap non-protein nitrogen source in the dry season. Game licks, pellets, self-mixed recipes with small amounts of urea, have been used successfully on game farms, but should only be used where there is sufficient natural grazing. Urea licks need to be managed carefully. Poor mixing and overdosing can cause poisoning in ruminants. When urea is dissolved in water it can be drunk which will lead to poisoning.

Supplementing ruminants with self-mixed feeds and/or pellets which contain grain and proteins must be done carefully. Animals need to be adapted to these diets because they can develop conditions like acidosis, red gut, etc. These feeds must be fed gradually over a 5-week period, to allow the rumen to adapt.

Hindgut fermenters: Rhino and zebra can be supplemented with commercial diets formulated for horses, in which no more than a third of the total energy should be obtained from the concentrate portion. Large pellets (>1.0 cm diameter) are used for grazing species such as white rhino, while smaller pellets are readily manipulated by browsing species. Obesity can be a concern if the energy component is too high, so it is ideal to use a body condition scoring system, using prominent bony structures like the spine, hip bones or shoulder blades to assess nutritional status of the animals.

Rhino must never be fed poor quality hay, for example straw which contains high levels of fibre, because this can cause health problems. Exclusive use of lucerne hay and small grain hay for black and white rhinoceros may lead

---

Definitions of feed types

Full feeds: Total mixed ration made commercially or on the farm to supply the coarse fibre needed for rumination and or fermentation, to supply the necessary nutrients like energy, protein, fat, macro and trace minerals and vitamins needed on a daily basis.

Semi-*ad lib* feeds: Self-mixed diet made commercially or on the farm, supplying approximately two-thirds of the requirements in the diet, the balance being natural forage, hay or other roughage supplied separately.

Supplements: Including self-mixed diets made on the farm and purchased products, consisting of nutrients packaged together for a specific purpose.
- **Protein supplementation:** Dry/winter months: Pellets or cubes, blocks, fine meals, self-mixed diets including energy, macro, trace minerals and vitamins.
- **Mineral supplementation:** Salt, macro and trace minerals (green month supplementation), also known as summer licks, in the form of fine-powdered salt mineral licks or blocks.
- **Trace mineral supplementation**: Trace mineral and vitamin supplementation including Stress Packs, trace mineral blocks, mineral and vitamin supplementation via water.

Pregnant and lactating animals may need supplementation.

to mineral imbalances, colic and diarrhoea. When possible, freshly cut grass can be added to the ration, but this must not be cut too short as this can possibly result in constipation. Feed should always be fed in troughs or bins and never placed on the ground because this will result in soil ingestion, which leads to colic.

Urea cannot be converted into protein by HGFs so there is no rationale for feeding them NPNs.

Feeding reproductive animals

Successful reproduction of animals is dependent on a high plane of nutrition and good body condition at the time of breeding, calving and lactation. Body weight and condition are measured by weighing/scoring the animals on a regular basis. Reproductive success is optimal when little or no nutritional fluctuations occur around ovulation, fertilisation and embryo implantation (short duration events), calving and during milk production. A negative energy balance indicated by a loss in body weight and body condition, will lead to a lower fertility level which will cause extended post-calving anoestrus periods (failure to come on heat) and resulting in extended calving intervals.

Processes like growth, foetal development, calving, lactation and uterine involution all demand energy. To increase the probability of re-conception shortly after calving, mothers must receive an increase in nutrients 3–8 weeks before giving birth and 3 months thereafter.

It has been shown that buffalo and sable heifers on a higher plane of nutrition come on heat 3 to 4 months earlier when compared to published historical data.

Overfeeding, for example increasing nutrients in the first two trimesters of pregnancy, can lead to obesity of the dam and overgrowth of the foetus, both of which cause birth difficulties. Obesity in bulls/rams will cause laziness to breed and poorer semen quality.

The contamination of feed supplements with toxins such as gossypol (from cotton plants) or mycotoxins can have a detrimental effect on fertility. Mycotoxins will grow on feed that becomes damp during storage. There are commercially available in-feed toxin binders and toxin deactivators which can be added to feed to prevent this.

Practical pointers in feeding pregnant animals:

- Do not overfeed supplements in the form of pellets or self-mix feeds to breeding animals during the first two trimesters as this can cause dystocia.
- Injectable mineral supplementation must be done strictly according to recommendations

Pellets made from green lucerne are not suitable for grazers.

because overdosing can cause the death of the mother and the embryo.
- For optimal milk production ensure each animal gets their share of the feed every day, this can be done by putting out more bowls than animals and following a strict routine at feeding.
- Buffalo heifers which have received optimally balanced feed (supplement plus roughage) may reach physiological maturity early but may be too small to calve effectively. They may have to breed at a later stage.
- In order to keep all the female animals at optimal production and reproduction, reduce feed-related stress and oversupplying feed to animals that don't need it. Bulling seasons (keep bulls with cows for 2 to 3 months) can be used to synchronise the cow herd so all the cows can calve within a 2 to 3 month period. This allows the group to be fed the most suitable ration.

Feeding during translocation/boma containment

Commercial game farming often involves moving wildlife from one farm or location to another following auctions or direct sales. Before and after being moved, the animals are usually kept in a confined area, known as a boma. Animals are stressed and feeding routines are disrupted which can be especially problematic in ruminants because the rumen microbes will start dying off, the animals' condition will progressively worsen and fatalities may result. In general the combination of a Stress Pack (see later) together with high quality lucerne hay will encourage animals to eat soon after being placed in a boma or released on the farm.

Animals transported over long distances are usually dehydrated so fresh water must be freely available and water points must be placed so that all animals have access. In order to mitigate the effects of stress the use of Stress Packs (combinations of vitamins, electrolytes and other liver metabolites) can be added to the water to assist animals to return to normal eating patterns as soon as possible. This will prevent loss of body condition. GameMin Capture and Boma from Afrivet is an example of a "stress pack" product designed for game.

If animals are kept in bomas for protracted periods, reduce the amount of lucerne offered by mixing grass hay and lucerne hay as follows: browsers 50:50 and grazers 70:30. Molasses meal (8–16%) can be added to improve palatability and reduce dustiness. Boma feeding is discussed in detail later in the chapter.

Practical aspects of supplementation

Feed is one of the most costly overheads on a game farm, so correct management of this resource is absolutely vital. Supplementation can only be cost effective if the correct product for the animals is purchased, the quality is ensured and maintained, and the product is fed correctly.

The practical tips on the following page will help to ensure that feed is utilised correctly.

Buying feed and feed supplements: Supplements or feeds purchased should be registered under Act 36/47 from reputable firms that can guarantee quality and consistency, and offer technical on-the-farm assistance. When purchasing any bagged feed or raw material, record the manufacturing/bagging date and keep some of the tags for reference. Avoid using old feed or raw materials. Keep some of the bag tags in case you need to make a future query. Use all old feed and/or raw material prior to using new feed – follow the "first in, first out" approach. When purchasing roughage and raw materials used in mixes, such as lucerne, grass, oat hay, maize, chop, sunflower-oil cakes, soya-oil cakes, wheaten bran and dry brewer's grains, buy from a reputable source and obtain a certificate of analysis where possible. Ensure that all supplements, licks and self-mix rations are suitable for the particular species.

Changing feeds: Animals need a period of adaptation to new feed and this has to be done slowly, over a period of about five weeks, to prevent conditions like acidosis and red gut (see Diseases). The new feed must be added to the old feed in weekly increments of one fifth in the first week until the animals are eating the new feed on its own in week five.

Feeding sites: When a particular spot in a camp is used continuously as a feeding site, a build-up of pathogens such as coccidia, worms, and fungi can result. There will also be a concentration of faeces and urine which will attract flies. If these feeding sites are in a boma or a dedicated feeding/drinking area in a camp, develop this area so it can be easily cleaned and disinfected. The water trough must not be too close to the bowls. Allow the animals a short walk so that the amount of feed that falls from an animal's mouth into the water is limited.

Regularly clean all water troughs and remove the faecal build-up at the feeding site. If the feeding site is on dry ground in the camp, move it regularly or have more than one point in the camp where the animals are fed. By moving the feed bowls from one area to another, and by closing off one of the water points when there is more than one water point in a camp, you can prevent areas from being overgrazed – the animals will use more of the camp.

Ensuring correct intake: When feeding supplements or full rations, ensure each individual animal eats the predetermined recommended amount of feed (see Feed bowl management below). The aim of supplying supplements in cube/pellet or meal form, is

Terminology used in feeding wild herbivores

- **Hay:** dried grass, grass hay like *Eragrostis teff*, *E. curvula* ("oulandsgras"), *Cenchrus ciliaris* (blue buffalo).
- **Cereal hay** (oat hay).
- **Legume hays:** lucerne, cow pea ("akkerboon"), medics, etc.
- **Grain:** maize, oats, wheat, sorghum, triticale, barley.
- **Silage:** derived from maize, sugar graze, wheat and other grass silages.
- **Pelleted speciality products:** species specific pellets/cubes/meals designed to supplement the animals with the necessary protein, energy, minerals and vitamins which natural grazing or roughage cannot provide.
- **Browse:** supplemented small shrubs and tree branches with leaves for browsers in small enclosures.

to give the animal a small amount of feed that will help them digest the roughage available to them in the camp. It is critical that no individual animal overeats the concentrated product. Ad lib feeding of pellets/cubes is strongly discouraged and will prevent proper rumination due to short fibre lengths, possibly leading to rumen disorders and possible deaths. Ad lib diets must be mixed with long fibre hay for ruminants.

Feed bowl management (not hay): When feeding pellets, cubes, self-mix supplements and semi-ad lib feeds, use the recommendations of the feed manufacturer or nutritionist. Using this information accurate feed intake can be calculated camp for camp. Ensure enough feeding space and or feed bowls for animals. For larger animals with horns place bowls 2.5 animal lengths from each other in either a block, rectangular or chessboard type pattern, which ensures limited contact between animals while feeding. One bowl per animal and for every 4 animals another bowl – this is critical for animals where dominance is observed and species where both male and female animals have horns. For large numbers of smaller animals supply enough feeding space by using long troughs, place these troughs in a rectangular-like chessboard type pattern.

Only feed the animals when they are near the feed bowls to allow monitoring, and this will prevent food being overconsumed by "early birds." Remove all supplementary feed that is not utilised after feeding. If there is left over feed, feed less the next day (subtract the amount left over from the calculated amount), this usually happens when green regrowth is available in the camp. Move feed bowls regularly to prevent overuse of an area, and accumulation of faeces and parasites.

When permanent feeding points are used, clean the areas regularly. Don't place feed bowls to close to water points. Clean feed bowls regularly.

If tyres are used for feeding they must be cleaned regularly.

Prevent feed selection and feeding pellets and hay together: It is not advisable to supply animals with two or three different types of concentrate and/or lick in the feeding area (cubes/pellets from different manufacturers, blocks, mixed feed placed together). The supplementation should be kept as simple as possible for proper management. A well-balanced mineral lick and supplement/semi-ad lib feed should be supplied to the animals for the green and the dry season respectively. Don't feed lucerne and cubes/pellets in the same bowl at the same time, as animals will not receive their individual requirements. Keep hay in hay racks or separate hay bowls

Feeding roughage and long fibre feeds: Hay can be fed ad lib, and is best placed in separate bowls or on a hay rack which keeps it off the ground. Remove hay that falls onto the ground for hygienic purposes.

Ensure that all baling string or wire is collected and removed from the feeding area, because these can be ingested and cause trauma. Placing hay on the ground encourages its use as bedding which is wasteful and in addition it may become mouldy causing mycotoxicosis. Do not use any roughage that has visible signs of fungal growth or mouldiness. Fungal growth and mycotoxins (fungal toxins) associated with it are often found in lucerne and hay that is stored directly on the ground/concrete floors;

similarly, bean and peanut pods often house fungi (store hay on pallets). Roughage like soya bean, peanut and other legume hays can be used if the products are free of mycotoxins. If in doubt, use a mycotoxin binder when using such roughages in any form of feeding. Never feed cubes/pellets and fine meals to wild herbivores on a semi-ad lib or full-belly basis, as the fibre length in these products are normally too short.

Mycotoxin binders should be added to all self-mix recipes. If self-mix recipes need to stand for periods longer than two or three days, the addition of a mould inhibitor is advisable. The addition of an active yeast product will aid in the control of rumen pH (reducing the risk of acidosis) and will enhance fibre digestion.

Good quality grass hay should be the largest proportion of any grazing herbivore's diet. In situations where hay needs to be supplied in a camp or boma, storage and management of hay is vital. Mouldy or dusty hay can cause pneumonia and colic.

If the grass hay available is low in crude protein, 10–20% legume hay (lucerne) can be added to the diet to ensure the correct amount of protein is supplied. Ideally, all hay needs to be analysed by a laboratory for macronutrients to assess what the animals are eating. This will help in deciding how much legume hay to mix into the ration. Browsers can be fed a mixed ration of grass hay:legume hay percentage of between 60:40 to 50:50; broadly speaking this mimics the ratio that would be consumed in the wild. To attract the animals to eat the roughage mix and to limit dust use the above mentioned ratio's but add molasses meal (max 16%), and or a fine spray of water (max 8%).

The exclusive use of lucerne hay and small-grain hay for any herbivore is discouraged as it may lead to nutrient and mineral imbalances, colic and diarrhoea.

The use of tyres as feed bowls: These feed bowls are normally turned-over tyres with the top rim cut off and a piece of conveyor belt, cement or corrugated iron used to prevent the feed from falling out. With most turned-over tyres, the tread is on the inside of the bowl. However, the grooves and indentations create an area where fungus and bacteria can grow once feed has caked there. In addition, the base of the bowl, which is often a block of conveyor belt or piece of corrugated iron, is frequently bolted or positioned on the inside of the bowl so feed doesn't fall out. Unfortunately, this creates a flap where food can accumulate and get old, creating a suitable environment for fungal growth. If using tyres keep the smooth side of the tyres as the inside of the bowl by simply cutting the side wall off and trimming off any protruding wires. Attach a piece of conveyor belt on the underside of the remaining side wall so that there is no lip hanging over the edge on the inside of the bowl. The smooth interior reduces the risk that feed can cake onto it, limiting mould growth. Concrete can also be used as a base. Corrugated iron is not ideal as it can rust and the sharp edges can cause wounding. Sharp, rusty points on feeding or drinking troughs, or protruding wire, can cause small wounds that can lead to *Corynebacterium* abscessation. Clean out all bowls regularly removing any caking of feed. Do not add new feed on top of old feed.

Quality control of feed

Diets for game feeding must have the correct composition to meet the needs of the animal, must be digestible and palatable. The quality of the feed can be assessed in various ways. Physical examination is an easy and effortless way of picking up any abnormalities and excess dustiness. In addition the farmer can do regular sampling and submission for chemical analysis (proximate analysis or NIR). Assessing the quality of the feed does not assess the digestibility but determines if raw materials used are of consistent quality.

Sampling procedures

Hay samples – collect samples from at least 5% of the bales in the hay stack, or 12–15 samples from the lot should be sampled. The most representative sampling method is to use a bale corer, this allows you to collect the sample in a cross section. If grab samples are taken, the bale needs to be cut to allow a cross-section sample. Ensure thorough mixing of samples prior to taking subsamples for analysis.

Bulk grain samples – collect 12–15 samples from a lot as widely spread as possible. Ensure thorough mixing of samples prior to taking subsamples for analysis.

Sacked feeds – collect at least two samples from 5 to 7 different bags. The use of a sack probe is best or take samples as the bag is emptied out. Ensure thorough mixing of samples prior to taking subsamples for analysis.

Storage and delivery of feed

All dry or semi-dry feed (cubes, pellets and other bagged or baled feed products) must be stored in a well-ventilated storeroom or container, away from direct sunlight. If containers are used place them under a roof and make ventilation holes for decent air flow. In very humid environments use a dehumidifier when storing dry or semi-dry feedstuffs, since moisture can lead to fungal infections of feed. All storerooms and containers must be rodent, insect and bird free. Storage of all feedstuffs in storerooms, containers or under roof (open air) storage areas must be on pallets (or a similar method) – away from direct contact with the floor (whether soil or concrete) and walls.

All raw materials delivered, including hay, cubes and pellets and other bagged feed products, delivered by truck on the farm should be covered with a watertight tarpaulin. Bagged products in direct contact with the tarpaulin, and some of the bags at the bottom of the stack may be moist, either from condensation or water that has moved in during transit (above the wheels). So when offloading inspect these bags, place bags with signs of moisture aside and use them first.

Silage needs to be stored in a oxygen free environment, ensure silage bunker management is optimal, to prevent loss due to spoilage and mould growth.

Feed tag checking

The feed tag provides valuable information to the farmer. If produced by a reputable company which has registered their product under Act 36/1947 (the product must have a V number) it should include the net weight of the product, the product and brand name, date of manufacture and batch number, species, guaranteed analyses for crude protein %, moisture %, presence and amount of NPN i.e. urea, fat %, crude fibre %, calcium % and phosphorous %. The tag also details a list of ingredients, the directions for use, any medication content, precautions and withdrawal period.

Water: quality and supply

When considering water supply and quality, it is important to ensure that an adequate amount and quality of drinking water is available at all times. Water can be obtained from a number of sources – above ground from rivers, dams and wetlands, underground water obtained via boreholes.

When considering the quality of drinking water supplied to the animals, it is important to understand that its suitability as drinking water is often overlooked and is therefore not always satisfactory. In general, the mineral content of water used for livestock is the same as that required for human consumption, but since the water sources used for animals on a farm are often different from those used by humans, it can be useful to have borehole or river water analysed for its suitability as a water source. The table contains rough guidelines for good quality water.

Parameter	Maximum permissible level
Solids	5 000 ppm
pH	5,6–9
Sodium	2 000 ppm
Calcium	1 000 ppm
Magnesium	500 ppm
Chloride	3 000 ppm
Sulphate	1 000 ppm
Fluoride	6 ppm
Nitrate	400 ppm

(From Maree and Casey, 1998)

Poor quality water can affect the health of animals and occasionally causes poisoning. Various problems associated with water supplies in South Africa are discussed below:

Brackish water: Brackishness is a problem in certain areas of the country. This is caused by the presence of high levels of various salts as a result of local geological conditions in underground water. The salts involved can be sodium chloride, magnesium chloride, sodium sulphate or magnesium sulphate. Animals forced to drink brackish water show decreased water and also food intake; they can also suffer from diarrhoea due to a high concentration of magnesium salts. The brackishness of water is aggravated when the water pumped into troughs evaporates during the day, increasing the concentration of salts. Regular cleaning of troughs will result in the water being less unpalatable. Since not all boreholes in these areas are brackish, one should look for the most palatable water for animal drinking water, or make use of rainwater when possible.

Nitrates: Certain areas in the country have high levels of nitrates in underground water, particularly areas like the Springbok Flats near Pretoria, certain areas in Limpopo and the northwestern Cape. Nitrate contamination of water sources such as streams, dams and underground water can also be caused by run-off from fertilised lands or sewerage contamination. Chronic nitrate poisoning can result from high levels of contamination.

Fluoride and other metals: Fluoride may be present in high levels either naturally, for example in the Northern Cape, or due to contamination by mining activities. Fluorosis is an uncommon cause of poor performance in livestock, but has been known to cause skeletal problems in cattle, namely fractures and lameness, and lowered fertility and milk production may also be seen. Mining activities in farming areas can also cause contamination of water sources with other heavy metals such as lead and arsenic, which may affect production or cause toxicity.

Eutrophication: Dams which are heavily utilised by game animals become contaminated with faecal material which raises the nitrate content. This is referred to as eutrophication and this condition can become dangerous for game animals especially during drought periods. The growth of a green alga-like bacterium (cyanobacterium, *Microcystis aeruginosa*) can cause poisoning which leads to fatal liver damage (see under Poisoning). Mud wallows for buffalo and rhino can be created in the dry season but should not contain enough water for them to drink from these. More than one wallow should be created so that they can be alternately dried out to prevent parasite build-up, eutrophication and other possible health issues.

Water supply in camps

It is essential to supply animals living in camp systems, small camps/bomas with sufficient fresh clean water on a daily basis, preferably supplied in large water troughs and not in man-made earthen dams (species preferences

A suitable water trough, but it is placed too close to the fence and seems to be leaking which is a disease and parasite risk.

are discussed in Chapter 4). For small animals a dripper bottle, a small dish or bowl can be used but these must be kept clean and free from bedding and faecal matter. For larger animals water bowls or troughs are used, where the water level is regulated with a ball valve. Ensure these troughs are cleaned regularly to prevent a build-up of algae. Ensure that water troughs do not leak and cause muddy areas which encourage the build-up of coccidia and internal parasites.

Sufficient water troughs must be provided to prevent aggression and the positioning is also important, for example, water points near fences can result in injuries because animals cannot escape confrontations.

Water and feed testing services are available in various parts of South Africa. Some service providers are given below:
- Central analytical laboratories (CAL), Krugersdorp: Testing of feed products, grains, and hays.
- Institute of Soil Climate and Water: Water, soil, bone, tissue samples.
- Envirotech, Brits: Heavy metals in feed.
- Water Research Commission: Testing of water samples.

GENOMICS AS A TOOL FOR THE WILDLIFE INDUSTRY

Paul Lubout and Pamela Oberem

Modern genetic techniques (genomics) continue to make a major contribution to breeding strategies in wildlife populations, both for conservation and the wildlife industry. Before genomics were available, authorities and breeders faced with small populations of endangered animals, had to make difficult decisions about breeding from these small gene pools or selecting certain characteristics.

The new genomic techniques have allowed geneticists to gather information about the genetic characteristics not only of various species but the various populations (meta-population) of a species within South Africa. Genomics has also clarified the genetic basis of some of the coat colour variants that are seen in certain species and which have become very popular, and can identify the markers for other desirable characteristics such as horn length and body size. This section discusses some of the ways in which genomics can assist the game farmer/conservationist.

Who's your mommy? Various genomic techniques can be used to determine parentage, species, genetic diversity and various phenotypic characteristics.

The birth of genomics

Most readers are familiar with the account of the Austrian monk Gregor Mendel (1800), who in the process of carrying out cross-breeding experiments with pea plants, discovered some of the mechanics of inheritance. Mendel observed that there was some "particulate body" which carried inherited characteristics and that these bodies re-assorted during the replication which takes place in the gametes or sex cells. His observations were a remarkable achievement because the DNA molecule and its organisation into separate genes hadn't yet been discovered. It was only in the 1960s when Watson and Crick first described the huge molecule DNA which lay in the nucleus of the cell that the science of genetics was officially born. Scientists were able to examine the nucleotide subcomponents of the DNA helix, and found that certain DNA segments or genes carried heritable characteristics. Researchers went on to compare the DNA sequences of individuals, locate specific genes as loci for physical, metabolic or disease characteristics and look at relationships between different species. The latter provided the evidence which finally proved that Darwin's Theory of evolution was indeed correct. The DNA technology now available is so powerful that it can be used for forensics to detect very small amounts of DNA at crime scenes (polymerase chain reaction "PCR"), to identify bodies from tissue remnants and to accurately determine the parentage of individuals. Some of the molecular techniques which are available to wildlife breeding systems for making various management decisions are discussed below.

Mitochondrial DNA techniques for identification/verification

This is one of the most controversial areas of genetics, not just for taxonomists, but for wildlife conservationists and breeders: What constitutes a species and a subspecies is still a difficult area of science, and every decade sees a reclassification of species and subspecies. This is confusing both for the breeder and authorities who have to make a decision on the permissible importation and translocation of a particular species.

Mitochondrial DNA analysis is one of the techniques used for species identification or verification. The mitochondria are located in the cytoplasm and their main role is energy production. They also have a small amount of their own DNA which is referred to as mitochondrial DNA (mtDNA). The small genome of the cell's mitochondrion divides independently of the cellular DNA, and is also an important tool in the study of genetics and evolution. In most animal species the mtDNA is transmitted though the maternal line, via the ovum during sexual reproduction (the male mtDNA is contained in the sperm tail which breaks off before its entry into the ovum). Therefore, all maternal descendants will carry the same loci or sites on the DNA (excluding mutations which occur with time).

Mitochondrial DNA studies have been used for example to re-evaluate the designation of species based on morphology: An example of this was the revaluation of the classification of the four designated African buffalo species. Analyses of mitochondrial DNA of all 4 morphologically designated species showed that in effect there were only two species, the Cape buffalo and the Forest buffalo (van Hooft).

Microsatellite markers for genetic diversity and parentage

Microsatellites are stretches of DNA on the chromosomes that consist of nucleotide repeats in tandem, of a simple sequence of nucleotides (e.g. "CTTGCCT" repeated a number of times in succession). The number of tandem repeats

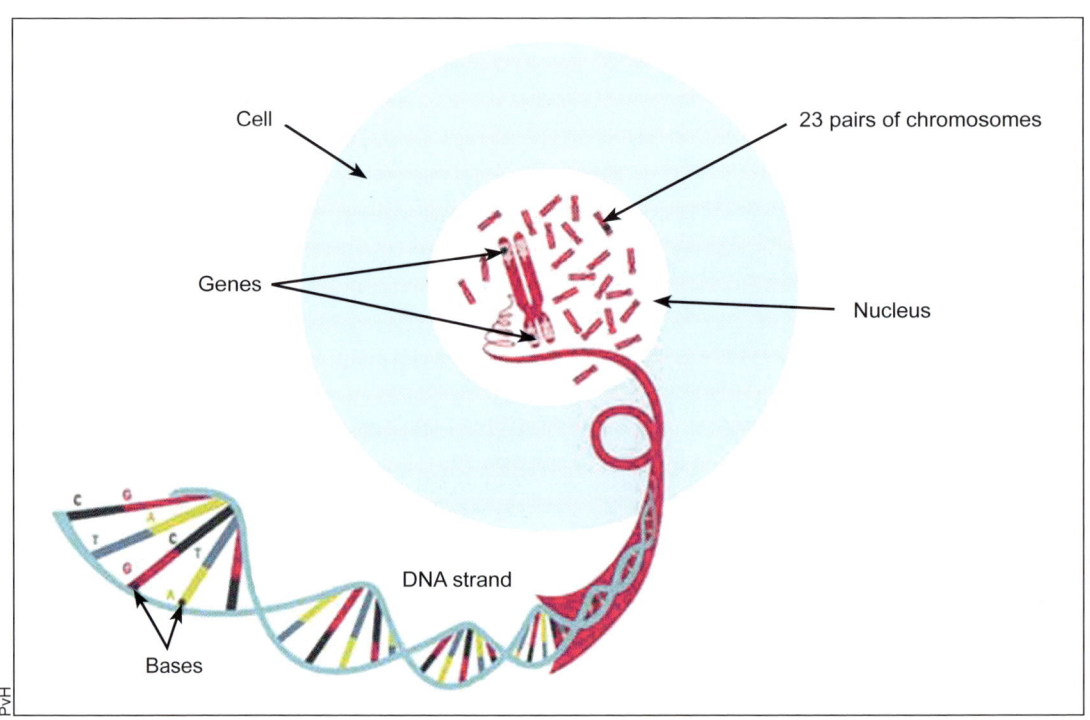

Genomic jargon: The diagram illustrates the various terms applicable to genomics.

found in any given microsatellite marker varies between individuals just as their physical appearance does. Microsatellite markers are the basis for individual identification, generally in forensic applications, for paternity analysis in humans and for the majority of animal parentage testing performed today. The various forms of a given microsatellite that are identified by differences in repeat number are referred to as alleles and are inherited in a Mendelian fashion. Each animal has only two alleles for a specific microsatellite, one inherited from its dam and the other from its sire (Table 3.1). The alleles found in an offspring must correspond to those of the presumed parents on a 50:50 basis.

Accurate parentage testing requires breeders to identify possible parents since, if considering a randomly selected large group of individuals, there could be more than one that qualifies as a parent. As an example, human paternity testing was originally developed as a means to verify that a named individual could or could not be the father of a given child. At most it was meant to determine if one of several men could be the father of a child. The same rules hold true for animal parentage testing. A good application for animal parentage testing is verification that the dam is correct and which of a number of sires on a particular farm could actually be the correct sire.

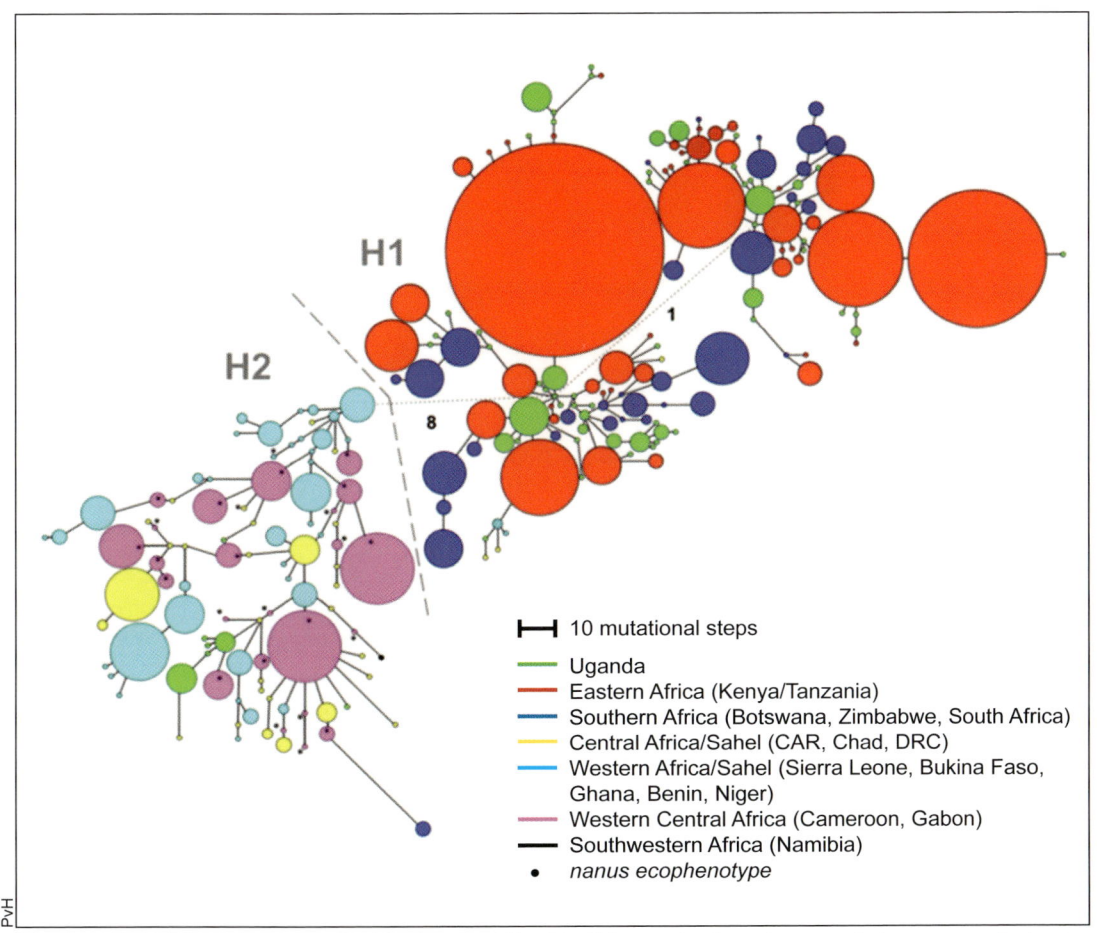

Mitochondrial DNA analysis was used to show that the 4 buffalo species based on morphology were in fact only 2 species genetically.

The accuracy of most animal parentage tests is greater than 99% when both parents are included in the analysis and drops to around 95% when only one parent is included in the analysis. However, this accuracy will decrease when the potential parents are part of a large group of closely related animals. Again, an animal closely related to an actual parent could possess marker alleles that make it appear to be the correct parent. To prevent erroneous parentage qualifications, breeders need to submit samples from all possible parents when first requesting parentage verification. If more than one sire and one dam qualify as parents of an offspring, the laboratory can then test with additional DNA markers to determine the actual parents.

Microsatellite markers have also been used to determine the genetic diversity of Cape Buffalo (*Syncerus caffer*) in South African reserves and ranches since the numbers of Cape Buffalo had been so decimated by the introduction of rinderpest in the 1800s that this was believed to have caused a "genetic bottle neck" or reduction in the number of alleles in the various isolated populations.

Analysis of samples from a number of ranches as well as national parks showed that the genetic diversity on most ranches and in the Kruger National Park was high, while in Addo and St Lucia it is low. This information allows conservationists to manage isolated populations more effectively.

Table 3.1: Determining parentage using microsatellite markers: Microsatellite markers from the putative mother and father are compared with those of the offspring: The offspring must have one allele each from the proposed dam and sire.

Marker	Calf Alleles		Dam's alleles		Sire's alleles	
BM 1824	178	178	178	184	178	210
BM 203	202	202	202	206	202	202
BM757	182	182	182	190	182	194
BM 804	132	132	130	132	132	132
CT 10	104	110	108	110	104	108
CT 12	128	132	132	138	128	136
CT 13	153	169	153	153	159	169
CT 17	148	150	150	158	148	158
CT23	212	212	212	212	212	214
CT 25	158	166	142	158	136	166
CT 27	102	120	114	120	102	114
ETH 10	206	206	200	206	206	206
MCM 58	153	153	147	153	153	155
OARFCB 48	158	162	158	166	160	162
SPS 115	253	259	257	259	253	257
TGLA 122	130	136	140	136	136	140
TGLA227	61	61	61	61	61	61
TGLA 53	155	159	157	153	153	159

DNA markers (SNPs) and genome libraries

To identify genes which influence characteristics such as coat colour, horn length, health and viability, geneticists use segments of DNA referred to as markers. These are called "single nucleotide polymorphisms" or SNP (commonly known as "snip"). SNP genetic tests focus on detecting precise single nucleotide base pair differences among the billions of nucleotide base pairs that constitute the genome.

Performance or appearance characteristics markers can be identified when they can be correlated with specific snips. This is why recording and measurement for a number of important traits (like horn growth) from birth through to maturity is essential. SNPs that are related to a trait can then be identified and characterised. These SNPs can be included in a DNA testing panel for game species and used to improve selection for these traits. The ability

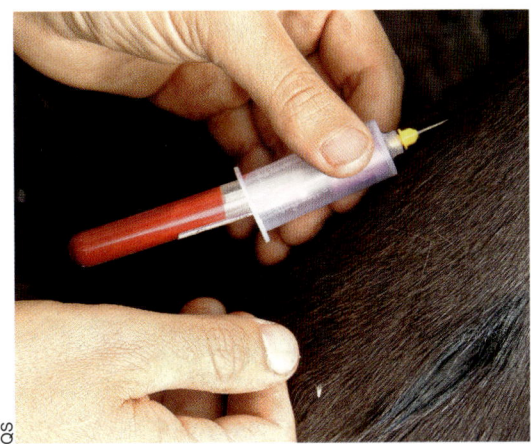

Blood is one of the body tissues which can be used for genomic analysis.

to identify the presence or absence of genes that are known to influence production traits will enable game farmers to increase income and profit by maximising production through genotyping "founder" animals.

SNP alleles differ from each other by only a single nucleotide base pair. Development

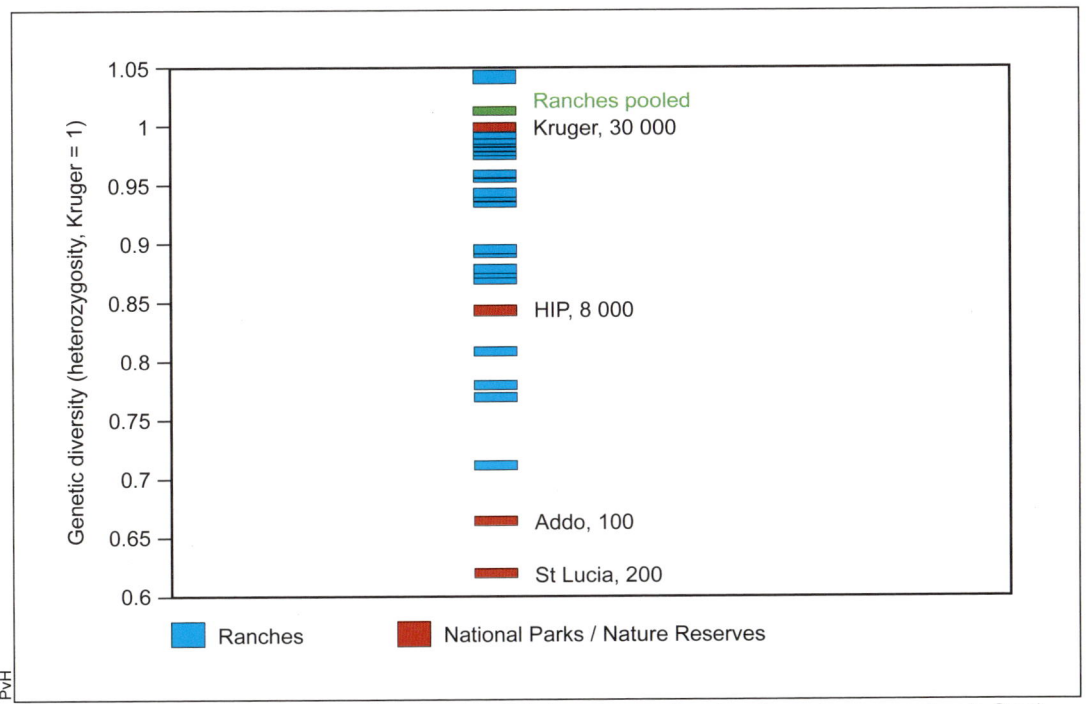

The diagram compares the genetic diversity of buffalo in various national parks and game ranches in South Africa.

of genetic databases or libraries, not only for genomic data but also pedigree, physical traits (colours, heritable defects), and performance characteristics, is essential for the development and genetic management of wildlife species. The genomic data is worthless without databases of physical traits and genetic values of multiple gene traits as association studies between genomic information (SNPs) and genotype/phenotype to determine which SNP affect which traits positively or negatively. These specific SNPs are then used in marker-assisted selection to enhance existing selection methodologies. SNP information can also be used to estimate genetically determined performance characteristics that increase the accuracy of selection especially in young animals where information is limited or in sex limited traits such as milk production (Holstein) and lack of horns in females of certain wildlife species (nyala, kudu, etc.).

Managing genetic diversity on game ranches

Because wild mammal populations can no longer move freely, managing the genetic diversity of wildlife poses a special challenge to the wildlife industry. Preserving genetic diversity of a species is important because this allows them to adapt to changing conditions. The maintenance of genetic diversity implies sufficient variation on a genetic level to avoid the loss of fertility and general fitness. In small populations that are being kept in isolation for a long time with limited introgression of new unrelated males on a regular basis, there is always the danger of inbreeding. Among other things, inbreeding leads to the loss of genetic fitness, increased mortality in young animals, reduced fertility and depressed growth. This phenomenon is known as inbreeding depression.

Genetic diversity can be measured in a number of ways: By recording the relatedness of animals (pedigree) or looking at the level of heterozygosity (diversity) on the molecular level. Mere exchange of animals between populations is only of value if animals are unrelated, breeding successfully and their progeny survive to reproduce. Cheetah, lion, roan and rhino suffer from low allelic diversity, because of habitat loss and/or overhunting and/or incorrect diversity management.

Effective population size, which can be defined as the number of individuals that actively contribute to breeding or to the genetic make-up of the next generation, is very important. The number of breeding animals present in the herd influences the rate of inbreeding in each generation. The level of inbreeding per generation should be maintained below 1% (livestock populations below 3.125%).

From a management point of view, it is best practice for a wildlife rancher to only keep those wild animals that are ecologically adapted to their region and are known to have occurred there historically. Wildlife ranchers can keep animals that did not occur historically by adapting their environment to suit their needs. This will ensure that competition between ecologically equivalent animals is eliminated, for example between the sable antelope and the gemsbok. The aim should also be to keep healthy breeding herds to satisfy all the nutritional and social requirements of the animals. It is recommended that when wild animals are utilised commercially, and there are fewer than 50 breeding animals on a wildlife ranch, males should be replaced biannually by unrelated males (as determined by DNA relatedness tests) or from unrelated herds (without genetic tests this method is questionable).

Wildlife ranchers should also preferably re-establish complete breeding herds instead of fragmented ones or small groups of unrelated individuals because it can take some time for new social groupings to form.

The problem of hybridisation

Hybridisation is the term used to refer to the crossing of two animals of different species. An example would be crosses between black and blue wildebeest, which gives rise to the so-called red wildebeest. However, the Biodiversity Act (Act 10 of 2004) prohibits the hybridisation of closely related, but ecologically distinct, types of wildlife (ecotypes): Examples of this are the separate ecotypes of springbok which are said to occur in Angola, Kalahari and the rest of South Africa.

Wildlife ranchers are therefore tasked with ensuring that "hybridisation" does not take place on their properties. This can be done by effective separation of animals that can potentially hybridise, by maintaining genetically viable populations and separating closely related groups into different camps. Within herbivores in general, hybridisation between currently designated species and even subspecies is possible, and such hybrids are often fertile. For example, members of the zebra group can interbreed and produce fertile hybrids.

Similarly, hybrids between species of the genera *Kobus* (lechwe, waterbok, kob and puku) or *Tragelaphus* (bongo, greater kudu, bushbuck, lesser kudu, mountain nyala, nyala and sitatunga) are known to be fertile or infertile depending on the species involved. The recessive golden colour variant of the blue wildebeest is typically found in some areas of southern Africa. Red wildebeest are said to be a hybrid between the blue and black wildebeest.

Some other examples of known or possible hybrids between wild species include:

- **Fertile hybrids:** African wild cat and domesticated cat, blue wildebeest and black wildebeest, bontebok and blesbok, roan and sable antelope.
- **Infertile hybrids:** Tsessebe and blesbok, red hartebeest and blesbok, eland and greater kudu, black rhinoceros and white rhinoceros, Hartmann's mountain zebra and donkey.
- **Possible hybrids:** Plains zebra and Cape mountain zebra, Cape buffalo and Indian water buffalo, nyala and greater kudu (see Species Accounts).

A zorse or hybrid of a zebra and horse.

Coat colour and pattern variations

Coat colour variation occurs in wild species as in domestic species. It is the result of a small variation in the genetic sequence of the DNA molecule which is referred to by geneticists as a mutation. The term "mutation" does not imply unfitness but merely a variation from the "norm". Most coat colour mutations are harmless and may be adaptive should the survival of the animals new colour become an advantage.

Many coat colour or pattern variations have been described in wild animal species worldwide; in some cases the mutation on the melatonin gene has been determined. For some of the coat colour variants seen in African wildlife, the actual mechanism of inheritance has been elucidated: Examples are the recessive genes for black coats in impala, golden colour in blue wildebeest, and the king cheetah coat pattern. These are recessively transmitted coat colours which follow the Mendelian law of dominance/recessive inheritance.

The wide variety of pattern variation seen in the antelope population in reserves and game farms is probably due to the overall increase in animal numbers which increases the probability of "variants". The genetic nature of patterning such as "saddlebacks", spotting, striping, etc., have not yet been clarified, but they are probably caused by genes such as those found in domestic animals, including cryptic genes which mask, dilute or modify coat colours (see proposed theory for appearance of saddleback patterning in section on impala). These genes therefore do not function in a simple Mendelian fashion.

Some game farmers have selected coat colour or pattern variants for breeding because the animals are rare, attractive and sought after by other breeders. Line breeding is used to establish herds of colour variants; this means that animals with a particular chosen characteristic, for example black coat in impala, will be mated with another black-coated impala. Line breeding was the breeding system used to develop all domestic breeds, for example in beef cattle, body weight was the characteristic for which farmers selected. This was very effective in producing breeds for specific purposes, but had some disadvantages. Because the animals are very closely related, the breed is genetically homogenous (little genetic diversity) and can be subject to other problems such as physical deformities or tendencies to disease. When this occurs, the animals are said to be "inbred". Inbreeding is one of the dangers of line breeding and it must therefore be practiced using genetic information about animals used for breeding.

The "King" or striped pattern (right) found in cheetah is caused by a gene which is recessive to the dominant "spotty" gene (left).

Some helpful genetic terminology

Allele: An allele is the alternative form of the same gene, one inherited from each parent. For example, alleles for colour could be BB, Bb or bb (see geneotype).

Artificial selection: Humans select breeding stock as parents of next generation, this is done both in game ranching and conservation where males are introduced into populations to promote genetic diversity.

Colour variants: These are naturally occurring variations of colour in wild and domestic animals. Many are recessive and so "normal" colouration predominates in most populations.

Hybridisation: This is the crossbreeding of two closely related species which results in viable offspring. The offspring may however not be fertile, e.g. zebra x donkey (zonkies, debras).

Crossbreeding of subspecies: According to the biological species concept, mating between different subspecies of the same species will be able to produce functional and fertile offspring. Current academic thinking, sometimes called the "discontinuous mind", does not take into account the dynamic, never-ending process of evolution, nor does it take into account the continuum that exists genetically between subspecies. The crossbreeding of subspecies is therefore generally frowned upon by authorities and a school of academics supporting the philosophy of sub-speciation.

Genetically engineered or transgenic animals: This term is used to describe animals in which DNA of other unrelated species have been inserted. So far this has proved impossible in mammals and the only transgenic animals are fish, such as zebra fish into which genes for fluorescence have been successfully transferred from jellyfish to produce a patented "Glo"-fish which glows in the presence of water pollution.

Genotype: This refers to the alleles of a specific gene pair, for example the genotype for the colouration of a blue wildebeest (*Connochaetes gnou*) could be BB, Bb or bb.

Inbreeding: A mating system between animals that is more closely related than the mean of the population from which they originate. In small populations that are being kept in isolation for an extended period with limited introduction of new males on a regular basis there is always the danger of inbreeding. Among other things, inbreeding will lead to the loss of genetic diversity and could lead to the loss of genetic fitness, increased mortality in young animals, reduced fertility and depressed growth.

Line breeding: Line breeding is a form of breeding that attempts to maintain a high frequency of individuals with specific genetic qualities in a population. The animals involved tend to have high genetic relatedness with one or more ancestor.

Natural selection: Progeny are selected by natural processes based on their adapatation to environment.

Outbreeding: A breeding strategy used to address inbreeding problems in a herd, in which distantly related animals of the same breed or type are bred, to provide genetic diversity.

Phenotype: The phenotype or appearance of the blue wildebeest in the example above would be blue (BB or Bb), or gold variant (bb).

PREDATOR MANAGEMENT

Tim Snow

Effective predator management is the process of correctly identifying the problem animal, rather than eradicating every single predator and at the same time, ensuring that the measures applied are humane, legal, ethical, wildlife friendly and target specific. Research has shown that non-lethal preventative measures are more effective than lethal controls in the medium to long term (Snow, 2008). An intensive study carried out on Madikwe, using radio collars to track the activity of black-backed jackal showed that predation of ungulate young was minimal under these circumstances (Harrison-White, in press). The study further showed that when problems did arise under certain conditions the problems of predation could be solved with minimal intervention. It should however be understood that every situation is unique, so a combination of management methods or controls may be needed, always bearing target specific action in mind.

The bat-eared fox is a valuable ally to the farmer but is often one of non-target species killed in gin traps.

Predation or scavenging?

Game ranchers may experience some losses due to predators, which is particularly problematic when raising valuable or vulnerable species such as small antelope and rare game species such as able, roan or tsessebe. Problem animal management specialists caution that one must distinguish predation from scavenging, so that the right "culprit" (if there is one), can be managed appropriately. If a kill is not witnessed there are various key indicators that one can use to determine whether the animal has been killed by a predator or scavenged post mortally and these clues often provide a guide to the identity of the predator. This can be done by thoroughly examining the external signs on the carcass and doing a post-mortem examination, to distinguish scavenging from predation. These signs are summarised in the table below which has been modified with permission from the publication *Farmers and Predators* published by the Endangered Wildlife Trust. In confined spaces such as breeding camps, the use of cameras is probably the most efficient way of identifying predators and distinguishing them from innocent scavengers.

In addition to the above there are several additional distinguishing parameters:
- Bleeding around wounds only occurs while the victim animal is alive, so absence thereof indicates that the animal was dead by the time it was eaten.
- Frothing may be visible in the trachea when prey has been suffocated.
- An absence of milk in the "milk stomach" of a lamb indicates a still-birth rather than death by predation.
- The absence of wear on the hooves of newborns indicates that they died shortly after birth, before they were able to walk.

The most common damage-causing animals

The predators most commonly involved in stock/game predation are caracal, domestic dogs, black-backed jackal, and leopard to a lesser extent. While many game ranchers view the presence of leopard with trepidation many conservationists believe that leopard may in fact have a positive ecological effect by controlling the numbers of these smaller predators. The inter-specific competition is fierce, and predators fight and kill one another for scraps at kills. Predator population dynamics are poorly understood, especially inter- and intraspecific relationships, home range/territorial sizes and overlap with other species. Wildlife biologists maintain that an absence of larger predators leads to an upsurge of jackals and caracals.

Predator potential and predation habits of carnivore species

Species	*Predator potential	Prey size	Guts	Bite wounds	Bones	Other evidence
Domestic dog	High	Up to 400 kg	Ripped and partly eaten	All over body (random)	Long bones chewed	Scattered remains, no throat marks, face and ears chewed
Caracal	High	10-25 kg	Intact/ripped	Bites on throat or back of neck	Rib ends chewed	Wool plucked, skin not eaten, red hair on prey
Black-backed jackal	High	Up to 50 kg	Partly eaten	Bites side of neck, hindquarters of large prey	Chews rib ends	Face and ears chewed, skin flaps left, forelegs detached
Cheetah	Low	From 10 kg	Intact/ripped open	Bites on throat	Rib ends chewed	Skin and gut untouched
Leopard	Low	From 10 kg	Intact/ripped	Back of neck, throat bitten	Rib ends chewed	Plucked, skin and gut untouched
Brown hyena	Low	Up to 50 kg	Party eaten, strewn about	Huge bites on back of skull, and hindquarter	Skull crushed	Eats all except guts and hooves, bones crushed
Spotted hyena	Lower	Up to 400 kg	Guts partly eaten	Flanks, udder, back	All bones crushed	Messy carcass, few remains because of pack activity
Lion	Low	Any size	Eats guts	Throat bites	Large bones intact	Massive tissue damage
Wild dog	Low	Up to 400 kg	Eats guts	All over body	No bones remain	No carcass remains

Specific protection and prevention

Caracal take small antelope and their young. They can be controlled effectively by protecting target species by using predator proof-fencing. Predator-proof fencing is a long-term cost effective solution and has been available for a while, but improvements have been made recently which make fencing more affordable.

The fence should have a base mesh to prevent burrowing under the fence and should be packed with stones to give added stability. Overhangs which can be electrified may be necessary to prevent animals climbing over the fence. Electric off-sets may minimise burrowing, but low off-sets have a very negative effect on snakes and tortoises. Obviously fences must be well designed and maintained to be effective

Species	*Predator potential	Prey size	Guts	Bite wounds	Bones	Other evidence
Raptors (Martial eagles)	Very low	Poultry, prey less than 5 kg, may scavenge	Never eat stomach	Single puncture marks on head, neck, shoulders or back	Pluck meat around bones	Pluck wool, feathers, eat from behind foreleg towards head, internal organs
Vultures	None	Scavenge carcasses	Clean carcass	-	Need hyena to crush bones	Carcass picked clean
Bat-eared fox, aardwolf	None	Eat insects/ termites	Teeth are weak and unable to scavenge large prey	-	-	-
Wild cat and serval	None	Eats rodents sometimes poultry	-	-	-	-
Black-footed cat	None	Eats rodents	-	-	-	-
Otters	None	Mainly fish eating	-	-	-	-
Honey badger	None	May raid poultry and hives – occasionally captive small antelope	-	-	-	-

*Note that this refers to livestock but can be used as a rough guideline.

A sheep killed by domestic dogs.

Jackal are most problematic during antelope calving/lambing periods.

and much information with regard to design is available. Fences should be tailored to specific needs. Proper planning can save huge costs on this expensive overhead cost.

Caracal can also be trapped by means of cage traps baited with their favourite prey. White chickens are a good bait attraction, but it may take 100 trap-nights per caracal captured, since they are extremely wily. The animals will refuse to enter a trap if the smallest of errors are made by the trapper. The floor of the cage should be carefully covered with fine soil and leaf matter from the immediate area, and the sides of the trap covered to provide a "tunnel view" of the lure. Caracal have an exceptional sense of smell so smoking, urinating near the trap site, or wearing boots contaminated with diesel will alert them to human presence. Leopards are known to prey on caracals and will usually keep their numbers in check and hence this predator balance becomes an important aspect for game farmers to consider. The leopard which causes some damage through predation may also generate income through game drive sightings by tourists.

Domestic dogs can be very destructive especially in packs, because they tend to maul a number of animals for sport rather than killing a single animal for prey. Farm dogs should therefore be confined at night to prevent them marauding since even pet dogs may take to hunting for sport. Problem dogs can be effectively removed by baiting cage traps, but shooting can be much more difficult in the field. Feral and stray dogs are possibly the greatest threat to domestic livestock and small game in rural areas, yet because they are a companion animal, many farmers overlook the extent of damage they can cause.

Jackals take small antelope and are a problem specifically during lambing periods, predominantly in spring when young jackals are brought out from their dens by parent animals and the family hunts as a pack. The threat diminishes into autumn as the pack structures disintegrate, but young and inexperienced jackals can also cause damage. Where valuable species are involved they should be protected by jackal-proof fences which are correctly erected. Attention must be given to gates as poorly designed structures may provide creep-through opportunities. Jackals are too wily to be cage-trapped. Shooting jackals is usually not a solution to the problem since the niche created by their killing is rapidly filled by others and selects for the "superjackal," an animal

Angel, the Anatolian shepherd dog, looking after his herd.

Electrified breeding camp designed to exclude predators.

which becomes very adept at avoiding hunters and by-passing other eradication strategies. According to conservationists populations of jackals are usually kept in check when leopards are present on a property. Some problem animal researchers recommend using carcasses as a decoy for jackals during the lambing/calving season.

A variety of collars have been developed which make use of the predator's aversion to scent, light and noises. Some of the collars available give physical protection, or emit scent. Newer technologies are also available such as cellphone-connected collars (Cellwatch) which trigger an alarm when animals are chased, but collars may be impractical for game farmers.

The use of lights and noise may be used in breeding camps. Scent emitting units such as "Skaapwagter" have been reported to be useful but should be used tactically, for example at times of increased danger such as during the lambing season, to prevent habituation by predators. This tactical use is critically important because most of these devices depend on neophobia or the fear of something new. If predators become accustomed to them, the surprise and fear value is lost.

Guard animals, for instance donkeys and ostrich are effective at deterring predators. The Anatolian shepherd dog has shown to be an effective predator guard; when these dogs are raised with a herd or flock they become protective towards their charges and will drive off predators. They are used by livestock owners in Namibia to drive off cheetah and have been used in Limpopo to guard valuable antelope species. For more information on Anatolian shepherd dogs contact Cheetah Outreach (Deon Cilliers 082 853 1068; deoncilliers@vodamail.com) for suitable dogs. The Maluti dog (*Africanis*) is also said to a valuable guard dog if suitably trained. These dogs are obtainable from Boavida Kennels (Matthew Berry 082 869 9366; boavida@saol.com).

Eradication

Eradication or removal of predators by capture and translocation must be carefully considered bearing in mind the type of predator and the likelihood of the success of the enterprise. Systems Thinking must be applied, i.e. analyse the cause and effect of the predation, and the cause and effect of management actions and controls undertaken.

Ground hornbill are often the victims when poison is used for predator control.

most certainly, such translocations disturb the carnivore ecology at source and destination, and may lead to exacerbated predation.

It is now illegal to hunt predators with packs of dogs, setting of gin traps, and "coyote getters". According to researchers leg-hold traps with an adjustable tread plate can be effective if used correctly without causing pain and mutilation. These "soft-traps" have off-set jaws and rubber stoppers to prevent leg fractures and loss of circulation in the affected limb (see under Capture Methods). The use of poison baits is illegal and is one of the most common and destructive causes of poisoning non-target animals, including endangered birds such as blue cranes and ground hornbills. "Coyote getters", or M44 devices contain a trigger mechanism which, when pulled, shoot a toxin into the mouth of the predator or scavenger. They are not target specific and the trigger mechanism makes them illegal in terms of recent firearm legislation.

Merely killing predators causes an ecological "sink effect" which means the predation niche is soon re-filled by a surplus from elsewhere. Viewing several farms and a district more holistically can hold long-term benefits for farmers, and predator populations tend to stabilise when they are not constantly persecuted. The efficiency of moving predators from one area to another is debatable. In many cases cats return to their original area but

Conclusion

Eradication should always be the last option for the game farmer who is committed to keeping a balanced ecosystem, since predators play a valuable role. Often their removal merely creates new opportunities for other predators to exploit.

Removing "innocent bystanders" in the environment on a game farm will not solve the problem and merely cause environmental imbalance. There are a number of predator management consultants who can give advice and targeted solutions for preventing predation.

Wildlife Poisoning Prevention & Conflict Resolution NGO
Tim Snow • 082 802 6223,
snowman@bundunet.com
www.wildlifepoisoningprevention.co.za

CAPTURE METHODS USED IN GAME RANCHING

Jacques Henry O'Dell

Introduction

Modern day game ranching or farming cannot take place without some form of game capture at some time, whether this is for management or veterinary purposes. The method used will be determined by various factors (see below). In essence the method selected needs to be effective, safe and economically viable and must be selected by the operator according to the specific circumstances. However, some general guidelines can be given and the factors to be considered are discussed below.

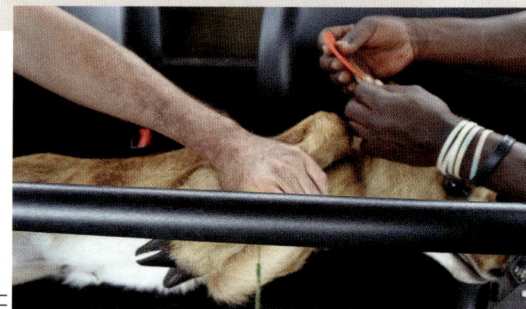

Hand capture of newborn sable for ear tagging. Hand capture is also used for small to medium antelope habituated to vehicles.

Some factors to consider in selection of a specific capture method

The choice of a particular capture method is a function of a combination of factors which after being weighed up and considered will lead to the selection of a particular method or combination of methods:

- Species: A suitable method must be selected for the species to be captured (see specific recommendations in the text).
- Tameness: Habituated animals will be easier to capture by net guns, passive capture or darting from vehicles if they are habituated to the presence of humans. Bear in mind that tamed males of certain species may be highly dangerous.
- Condition of animals: Heavily pregnant females or animals in poor condition may not be able to handle chemical capture or chasing over long distances without suffering ill effects.
- Safety and skill of personnel: Game capture is a highly skilled operation which requires well trained and experienced staff to make a success of the operation, and minimise injuries to both animals and humans.
- Value of animals: In this case there will be less concern about costs and the least risky method will be adopted. On the other hand, capture and treatment of individual animals for conditions of poor prognosis may not be economically worthwhile.
- Environmental conditions: Rough terrain is unsuitable for certain types of game capture. Ambient temperature must also be considered because driving animals as well as transporting them in hot weather can lead to heat exhaustion and subsequent losses.
- Behaviour and herd structure: In general herbivores have a good herd instinct which makes mass capture suitable since the animals tend to follow a leader.

Some reasons for game capture on game farms

There are several reasons why a game farmer might decide to capture game. These include:

Removal of excess animals: Animals need to be sold or relocated to another camp or farm. This can be done with various mass capture methods including net capture and plastic boma capture. Plastic boma capture is the best method for capturing large numbers of animals, of various species, in the shortest space in time. This is, however, not entirely selective or cost effective when one wants to capture and remove specific individuals.

Removal of specific animals: If specific animals need to be selected from a group then net gun capture or darting might be more cost effective. If time is not an issue then the various methods of passive capture will be most cost effective.

Management procedures on groups of animals: When the management procedure involves physical handling of many animals then net capture is an option. When only a select few animals need to receive attention then net gun capture or darting is a better alternative.

Management procedure on healthy individual animals: Horn measurements, notching or tagging, performed on healthy individuals is best done after darting the animal.

Treatment of sick or injured individual animals

When attending to a sick or injured animal darting is a common capture method. However, severely ill animals are at risk when capture drugs are administered to them, and some animals may die as a result. Injured animals losing their footing may injure themselves further as is the case with minor sprain or fractures. A good alternative is a combination of passive capture and darting, in which the animal is not chased and has limited space to run and exert or injure itself. This can only be done where permanent passive capture structures are in place.

Treatment or preventative treatment on a number of animals

Management procedures on groups of healthy animals are best done by mass capture methods. Permanent passive capture bomas could be used to aid in the rotation of herds between camps. When medicines need to be given to the entire herd they could be lured into the passive capture bomas, where the medicated feed or water can be given.

Game capture methods

Game capture methods could be divided in two broad categories, namely physical and chemical capture.

Physical capture or restraint

Physical capture or restraint involves procedures and methods where animals are captured in or by specific equipment and may include some degree of physical restraint by a person. Some of the methods may be applied to the capture of only a single animal whereas some methods are designed for the capture of many animals, known as mass capture.

Individual animal capture methods

Hand capture: This method is effective to capture small to medium antelope like impala and nyala. The animals must be habituated to the close proximity of vehicles. It should be done on dark, moonless nights. A combination of two or more spotlights is used to blind the animal or herd and while being blinded the capturers quickly run towards the blinded antelope without breaking the beam of the light. They grab the antelope above the hock and hold on until support staff arrives which help to blindfold and restrain the animal further. It is difficult to select specific animals from a group. If lambs, lactating or heavily pregnant ewes and other unwanted antelope are caught by accident, they should be released without delay. Excessive force and power should be avoided when restraining small antelope. Normally after catching one, or a few animals from a herd, the herd becomes extremely skittish and one has to move on to find another herd should more animals need to be captured. Depending on the reason why the animal is captured, it is advisable to administer a tranquiliser as soon as possible after capture.

Hand capture after chasing animals on foot, horseback, motorbikes or vehicles, driving them to the point of exhaustion is not advisable or ethical as many of these animals succumb to capture-related complications like capture myopathy (see Complications below).

Net gun capture: The net gun is a customised bolt action rifle, normally .308 calibre. There are 4 barrels, each pointing at a different angle. Weights attached to the corners of the square net, are then loaded in to the barrels. The net rests in a basket that sits between the four barrels, each pointing at an angle away from each other. Propulsion of the weights after firing the blank pulls the net open and forward. The idea is to shoot over and in front of the animal; the animal then runs into the net, becoming entangled. The capturer quickly restrains the animal further with the aid of a blindfold and ropes or hobbles. Hobbles are easy and quick to use. Once properly restrained the animal is then untangled from the net. Depending on the reason why the animal is captured, it is advisable to administer a tranquiliser as soon as possible.

This capture method allows for the selective capture of specific individuals. A net gun in the hands of a skilled person is one of the most effective and least stressful methods of capture with the lowest mortality. It is most effective for small to medium-sized antelope in relatively open terrain. It can be used for larger antelope when two or more capturers are able to attend to the animal in the net. Net gun capture is more cost effective than chemical darting (see below). In situations where animals need to be darted, but running and exertion should be kept minimal, the net gun can be used in combination with darting. This not only has some benefit for the animal, but also saves on helicopter time. It is also a good adjunct to net capture (see below) because animals that escape the nets can be netted from a helicopter while a ground crew then restrains the animals. Just as effective as the net gun can be, so it is also one of the most dangerous tools in the hands of an inexperienced operator. Deploying the net in the helicopter or the net catching the skid or rotors or deflecting from the ground to hit the helicopter can lead to serious accidents. Poor aim can lead to mortality if the heavy weights hit the animal. The odd traumatic injuries like bruises, scrapes and cuts do occur when the animal becomes entangled in the net. Although uncommon, leg and neck fracture can occur as a result of the animals becoming entangled and tumbling.

Leg-hold traps: Humane leg-hold traps clasp the foot or leg of the animal when the animal steps on the pressure plate. This method is mostly used for capturing predators for research projects and the odd problem animal. This may be necessary in the case of game ranching where a problem predator leads to the death of animals in a camp. Killing predators should be left as a last resort and all attempts should be made to capture and relocate the animal. In order to catch animals with foot traps one may need a permit from the provincial nature conservation office. The operator of leg-hold traps must be well acquainted with these laws before attempting this method (see legal issues below). The predator in question could be lured to the area with bait, sound or pheromones. One can set the trap with an alarm system that sends a signal to the capturer as soon as an animal is captured in the trap. The animal, depending on the species could then be restrained physically or chemically. In the case of leopard, never leave the vehicle when darting the animal, as if it comes loose from the trap it will most certainly attack. Leg-hold traps are non-specific and one cannot select a specific individual animal. Sometimes a completely unwanted species may become trapped. There

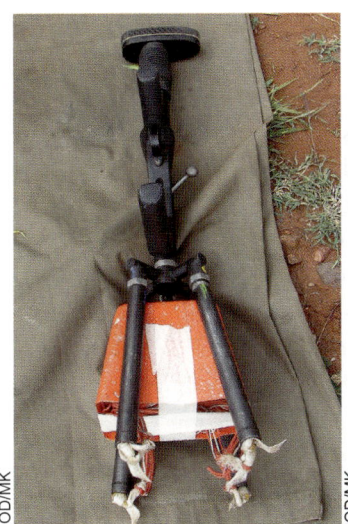

Left: A net gun with the net folded in basket and weights already loaded in barrels (note the angle of the barrels). Right: Cage trap for small-sized predators.

is also lots of controversy over the degree of pain and suffering animals endure with this method. If this method is selected, the time an animal is trapped should be kept to an absolute minimum. Traps should be monitored at least a few times a day, but be aware that monitoring too often will lead to an unsuccessful capture as the animal may become spooked.

Cage traps: Cages of various designs and sizes are mostly used to capture predators, primates and crocodiles. These cages have a place on game ranches and could be used when problem animals need to be removed from breeding camps. As with leg-hold traps, cages are non-specific in selecting the animal or species that is captured. The cages are set in an area which the quarry frequents. They often need to be baited for an extended period of time by placing the bait on the pressure plate. Cage traps are considered to be more humane than leg-hold traps, and if designed correctly pose fewer risks to both the animal and the capturer. On predator-breeding farms, cage traps could aid in the physical restraint of smaller predators like cheetah. Cage traps are built as part of the camp, and used much the same as a "cattle crush". These cages allow for small procedures like injections or blood collection to be performed without chemically restraining the animal. Additional poles could be used to further restrain the animal within the cage. Cage traps can also be used to capture mini antelope in thick forest, by placing them along the paths used by these species. This method is time consuming as it may take a long time for the antelope to use this path and the success rate is variable. As with leg-hold traps, it is recommended to set an alarm system that notifies the capturer as soon as an animal is trapped. Traps need to be inspected regularly, at least a few times a day, even if the alarm has not gone off. Inspect the cage from a distance so as not to disturb the area.

Mass capture

Plastic boma capture

This method designed by Jan Oelofse has revolutionised game capture. Since its advent in the late 1960s, hundreds of thousands of animals have been captured by this method. Its main advantage above all other methods, is that a large number of animals can be captured in a very short time. The basic design of the plastic boma is in essence a large funnel built of durable plastic material. The plastic material is supported by cables and nets. A main curtain is used to close the mouth of the funnel as soon as the animals are in the boma. As the animals are driven up the funnel a series of curtains across the boma is closed behind them. The animals regard the plastic material as a solid wall and seldom attempt to escape through it. The end of the funnel consists of a solid wall crush, made with either metal, strong wood or conveyor belt. Once in the crush animals could either be worked with, or driven directly up the loading ramp and on to a transport vehicle.

This method can be used to capture almost all game species including small antelope such as impala and some large species like buffalo and giraffe. Ostriches, warthog and even predators such as wild dog have been captured in plastic bomas. It is the most cost effective method for capturing herd animals. When capturing "digging" species the funnel must be well secured to the ground. For jumping species such as impala and kudu, the side walls need to be high enough for them not to try and jump over the boma. Giraffe bomas need to be high enough for them not to see over. Buffalo bomas need to be strong enough to keep the milling herd from breaking through the sides.

The basic design of the boma is the same for most species. Site selection is very important, and may differ slightly between the different species captured. The boma should ideally be erected the day of the capture. Alternatively it can be erected in the late afternoon with the capture taking place early the next day. Putting up a boma a few days before a capture, especially on smaller game farms, will make animals wary of its presence and they will avoid moving in that direction. The boma should be erected away from water holes or other areas that the animals frequent. The boma needs to be placed in an area with adequate vegetation. The vegetation should not be too thick otherwise erection of the boma is difficult. It also interferes with the ability to herd and work with animals inside the boma. The area around the entrance of the funnel needs to be fairly open and clear of tall trees. This is to allow the helicopter to apply maximum pressure on the animals so they enter the boma with some speed. There should be enough vegetation to allow the side walls and curtains to be camouflaged. Big trees to support the cables of side walls and curtains are a bonus.

Most animals prefer to run along known paths, thus constructing the boma with a well-used game path running down the middle should be done where possible. Avoid areas with a steep topography, rocky terrain, dongas, or lots of aardvark holes. The capture site should be accessible to heavy transport vehicles. Design the boma so that the crush and loading area is in an open area and if possible close to or even on a road. One of the single biggest success factors for capturing animals with the plastic boma is the wind direction. Although this can change at any moment, all attempts should be made to design the boma so that the wind blows directly in to the funnel.

Plastic boma capture is most successful when a helicopter is used to herd the animals into the funnel. Horseback and motorbikes can be used, but are not nearly as effective. Animals should not be chased over long distances as this will lead to exertion and death. Once animals have escaped from a plastic boma the chance of recapturing them is slim, so success on the first attempt is essential.

The mixing of various species in a single capture should be avoided at all costs. Also avoid building the boma close to perimeter fences, power lines, telephone poles or tall trees that could interfere with the helicopter operation.

The inside curtains are usually operated by people on the ground. Once the animals have passed the line or the helicopter has given the

Capture using a plastic boma

Top: The animals are driven down the funnel towards the crush. Bottom left: The animals are processed in the crush in which solid shields are used to protect the operators from injuries. Bottom right: The curtains are closed behind the animals driving them into the crush.

signal, they are closed by sprinting with them to the opposite end. Animals are then herded up the funnel by several people holding on to a single large section of loose plastic. With dangerous species like buffalo the curtains are closed by pulling ropes while safely sitting on the outside of the boma. The buffalo can be herded in to the crush area using vehicles.

Depending on the reason of the capture, the animals could be driven on to the transport vehicles directly where they could then be tranquilised, or they could be left in the crush area to receive their specific treatment or tranquiliser. Sometimes individual animals are knocked down in the crush area either by pole syringe or by darting. The animals can then be worked with after which they are loaded on to the transport vehicles, or released back in the same farm or camp.

Modifications of the plastic boma method are used to capture and handle large groups of animal in small breeding camps. Animals are herded to one side of the breeding camp, after which the camp is divided into smaller sections by closing a plastic curtain. The process is repeated until the animals are in a small area where they could be handled. As with the conventional plastic boma, they could be

Variations on net capture

Drop nets: Black wildebeest being walked to a truck after capture and tranquilisation.

chased in to the crush area and loaded on to a vehicle or they are immobilised either by pole syringe or darting and could then be handled for whatever reason they were captured. This variation normally requires no helicopter. Motorbikes could be handy to quickly chase animals to the required area. Depending on the size of the camp, lots of plastic sheeting may be required.

Net capture

Several variations of net capture exist including linear nets, net bomas and drop nets. With all methods of net capture some form of chasing is required. Animals normally hit the nets hard, and injuries do occur. As soon as animals enter the nets, the capturers need to restrain them, preferably a minimum of two people per animal, depending on the species involved. Blind folds and hobbles need to be put in place immediately. The main operator has to administer the tranquilisers as soon as possible. Net capture can be used for almost all species, apart from the very big and strong species like kudu and eland. These species tend to injure themselves and the capturers. Nets differ in their height and mesh size and each species requires a different net type. In general the bigger the species captured, the higher the net and the larger the mesh. The smaller the species the lower the net and the smaller the mesh. Mini antelope like suni are actually captured in fish gill nets, supported by larger nets.

Drop nets: the simplest form of net capture. Sections of net varying from only a few meters up to 200 m can be used. As soon as the animal hits the net it drops down from its anchoring position and the animal becomes entangled. Short sections of net could be used in thickets for species like impala, nyala and bushbuck. Longer lines could be used in open area for species like blesbuck, springbuck and black wildebeest. Several lines could be placed behind each other, allowing the opportunity for the escapees to become entangled in the next net. Animals are usually chased in to the nets by motorbikes, vehicles or helicopters. Drop nets are the most traumatic method of capture, and should be used as a last resort.

Linear nets: similar to drop nets, except that the nets do not drop from their anchoring position. They are most effective in thick vegetation to capture species like bushbuck, nyala and duiker amongst others. The net is set in the shape of a shallow arc and animals are driven in to the net by rows of people making a noise, shouting and beating sticks and drums. As soon as animals hit the net, the capturers,

Linear nets used to capture red hartebeest: Note the use of drop nets in between to prevent piling.

A net boma used to capture impala: As soon as the animals hit the nets they can be tranquilised.

lying in ambush close to the net physically restrain the animals until it is blindfolded, hobbled and tranquilised. Linear capture could also be done in more open terrain, but the success may vary. Long nets on open plains and animals being chased into the nets with motorbikes, vehicles or a helicopter could be attempted. A better option to capture species on open areas is the net boma.

Net boma: has a fairly square shape, with three of the sides of the boma consisting of linear nets. The fourth side will consist of plastic curtains. Animals are chased into the boma, usually with a helicopter or alternatively by vehicles, and then as soon as they enter the boma, the plastic curtain is closed. Animals then move away from this curtain and into the nets. Short drop nets could be used at various positions inside the boma. This will prevent all the animals from piling in to one section of the net boma. Piling of animals into and on top of each other leads to severe injuries like leg and neck fractures. As with the plastic boma, net bomas are most effective when animals are chased with the wind, and along a game path.

Passive capture

There are several methods of passive capture, and many variations of these can be used. One could differentiate between temporary passive capture structures and permanent passive capture structures.

Temporary passive capture structures

These structures are erected for a "once-off" capture, and include boma traps, net bomas, pop-up and drop-down bomas.

Boma traps: vary in layout, size and strength, depending on the species targeted. Temporary passive bomas are handy for capturing large groups of animals ranging from warthog to hippo. Bomas for small to medium antelope may be built with plastic sheeting, whereas hippo bomas need to be constructed from steel. The boma is built close to an area the animals frequent. They are lured to the area with food, initially placed in the vicinity of the boma and as animals become habituated the food source is moved closer, and eventually enter it. Once the desired species and number of animals enter the boma the gate can be closed behind them. Gates could either be pop-up gates, drop-down gates or swing gates. This could either be done manually, by hand or by ropes and pulley system. Some gates could also be set to close automatically. The aid of small cameras allows one to do this from a distance, thus not disturbing the animals. Once the animals have entered the boma they could either be loaded on to the transport vehicles, or darted, depending on why they were captured.

Passive net bomas: similar to standard net boma capture, the difference being with passive net boma capture there is no driving of the animals in to the boma. The net boma is constructed around an area which the animals frequent, for example a small irrigated pasture. The net is put in place over a period of time, so animals become habituated. Several gates where plastic curtain is used are left in place. Animals enter through these gates. Once the required number of animals have entered, the gates are closed and the animals panic and run in to the nets. Handle as described above.

Drop-down and pop-up bomas: have a similar construction but most of it consists of plastic sheeting. These bomas are usually constructed around an already active feeding or drinking site. It is best to design the boma so the feeding or drinking site is right in the centre of the boma. With drop-down bomas the plastic sheeting is neatly rolled up, and suspended in the air by aid of metal poles and cable. Once animals enter the boma, and are feeding or drinking at their leisure, the trigger releases the plastic sheeting causing it to drop down to the ground within a second or two. The advantage of this method over boma traps is that animals normally become habituated to this method much sooner as the presence of the boma is less obvious. With the pop-up boma the plastic is down on the ground, sometimes buried in a small trench. As soon as animals are feeding or drinking, the release causes the plastic to shoot up. Sometimes animals are reluctant to walk on and step over the sheeting on the ground, and it may have to be concealed with a small layer of dirt. Pop-up bomas are best for species that tend to dig or crawl their way out of structure like sable and wildebeest. Drop-down bomas are best for species that tend to jump over obstacles. With these methods, some of the more alert individuals may have time to escape from the boma before it has adequately closed. With drop-down bomas the plastic sheeting needs to be secured to the ground as soon as the boma is closed.

Permanent passive capture structures

Permanent passive capture structures could include all of the temporary structures, but only left out in place indefinitely. Depending on the type of construction, like hippo boma traps, this works really well. The trap door mechanism is deactivated until it needs to be used, allowing the animals to get used to it. Other bomas that work with sensitive release mechanisms, such as pop-up or drop-down bomas should ideally not be left in place for a long time, as failure of the mechanism will result in failure of the capture. Weathering of the plastic will also occur.

Permanent structures are similar to boma traps, but with a stronger construction, and these work especially well in small camps where antelope need to be captured for a variety of management procedures. The design of these is similar to permanent holding bomas, and could even be used as is, or incorporate holding bomas. Construction with wooden poles, steel and conveyor belting rubber seems to be the most durable. The height of these structures would depend on the species targeted, but a height of 3 m is ideal. The size of these bomas need not exceed 30 m x 30 m. The feeding and or drinking point of the camp should be near the boma with additional water trough inside the boma. When animals need to be captured the water trough outside the boma is closed and the feed moved inside the boma, forcing the animals to enter. Different gate options could be used. As soon as the targeted individual or group is in the boma then the gate is closed. Passive capture bomas of one camp could connect with bomas of the neighbouring camp. This makes camp management such as rotation easy and cost effective. Feeding of

Sturdy temporary passive boma under construction for capture of hippo.

animals should ideally not take place inside the capture boma on a permanent scale as this will lead to the build-up of parasites and other diseases. Ideally they should be fed in the vicinity of the boma and only lured in once in a while and when capture is planned.

Chemical capture or restraint

Chemical capture or restraint basically entails the administration of certain drugs, known as the capture drugs, to the animals, either in their feed, or via some form of injection. Capture drugs are made up of various drug classes or groups and include all the potent narcotics, tranquilisers and sedatives. These are drugs used to inject animals with, either by hand, or remotely via a dart, in order to produce a state of immobilisation. Animals may or may not be anaesthetised, depending on the class of drugs used. The ideal immobilising drug, used in a dart, should have the following characteristics: Be potent, have a rapid knock-down, stable under adverse environmental conditions, be safe, have minimum side effects and have a reversal agent. Capture drugs also include the sedatives and tranquilisers used to calm animals down when they are transported or placed in temporary holding facilities like bomas. These can be administered without knocking the animal down.

Capture drugs

"Knock-down" drugs

Opioids: The most important class of drugs used in game capture is the opioids. There are two common opioids used in South Africa, namely etorphine hydrochloride (M99®, Captivon ®) and thiafentanil oxalate (Thianil ®).

These drugs are mostly used as potent knock-down drugs in the dart, or sometimes pole syringe. Hand injecting these drugs should be done with caution. They are extremely potent and potentially dangerous to humans and should only be handled by experienced and adequately trained persons. Intoxication of these drugs would lead to the inability to breath, asphyxiation and eventual death. Respiratory depression also occurs in animals especially impala, giraffe and rhino, and caution must be applied with the use of potent opiods in these species. The advantage of the opioids is that they are reversible, either totally, or partially. Partial reversal with drugs like butorphanol tartrate (Torbugedsic®) or diprenorphine (M5050®) in some species like impala and rhino is standard practice. Giraffe could either be partially reversed, when they require some medical attention, or fully reversed when they need to be loaded and transported. To fully reverse the effects of the potent opioids in animals naltrexone (Trexonil®) is used.

This is also the drug of choice for accidental intoxication of humans. As a precaution, eating, drinking and touching ones mouth or eyes should be avoided during the capture. Wash hands thoroughly after a capture.

Cyclohexylamines: These drugs induce a state of narcosis in the animals and if given in high doses could result in general anaesthesia. Common examples include ketamine (Anaket-V®) and tiletamine (Zoletil®, tiletamine in combination with zolazepam – see Sedatives). They are mostly used in the dart for predators, in combination with a sedative, for example Zoletil®. The volume of drug required to knock-down antelope is too large to fit in a dart and they are thus seldom used as the primary knock-down drug. They are sometimes used in combination with the opioids. They can, however, be used as the primary knock-down drug before the animal can be injected with larger volumes, for example by pole-syringe. These drugs are less potent than the opioids and as a result have a longer knock-down time. There is no antidote for the cyclohexylamines.

Sedatives and tranquilisers

These two drug classes have differing mechanisms but the end result is a calming effect on the animal. One difference is that at high doses, sedatives produce a deeper state of sedation whereas tranquilisers will produce the same level of tranquilisation at higher doses, but often with significant side effects.

Sedatives: These are represented by two groups, the benzodiazepines like diazepam, zolazepam and midazolam, and the alpha-2 adrenergic agonists like xylazine and medetomidine. Zolazepam is used in combination with tiletamine in the drug Zoletil® and is mostly used for immobilising predators. Other alpha-2 adrenergic agonists like medetomidine is also used in combination with Zoletil® or ketamine for predators. Diazepam should not be used in the dart when combined with other drugs. It has value in sedating impala, springbuck and other species after mass capture methods. Midazolam is often used in the dart or when baiting for predators. Alpha-2 agonists have profound effects on the blood pressure of animals and should be used with caution in game. There is also an increased risk for regurgitation, and possible aspiration, when using them at high doses in large species like eland and buffalo. Both groups have reversal agents.

Tranquilisers: Tranquilisers can be classified as short or long acting. Short acting tranquilisers such as azaperone (Stresnil®) are often used in combination with opioids when darting cloven-hoofed animals, rhino, elephant and hippo. The other short acting tranquiliser, haloperidol and the long acting tranquilisers, zuclopenthixol acetate (Clopixol-acuphase®) and perphenazine enanthate (Trilafon LA®) should never be used mixed with other drugs in the dart for example. Azaperone is only effective for about 2–4 hours, an ideal when a group of animals need to be darted, so as to keep the other animals tranquilised. It works well when used to tranquilise animals that need to travel short distances. Haloperidol has an effect lasting around 8–12 hours. It can be used in combination with azaperone when animals need to travel further, or when they are confined in temporary holding bomas. Zuclopenthixol and perphenazine is usually given to animals if they are housed in bomas for a longer period of time. Zuclopenthixol lasts for about 3 days, and is normally sufficient in most cases of boma housing. Perphenazine lasts for up to 7 days and could be used when housing extremely wild animals in a boma for an extended period of time. The long acting tranquilisers should only be administered in the muscle, thus darting animals with these drugs are risky. Care should be taken when administering tranquilisers to animals as there is no reversal for these drugs. Overdosing could lead to severe side effects.

The capture drugs are scheduled medicine only permitted to be used and administered by authorised persons (see Regulations below).

Methods of administering capture drugs

Drugs in food: This method is mostly used for carnivores and primates. The degree of restraint would depend on the type of drug used, the amount consumed, and the species involved. This method is seldom used to gain full restraint over an animal, but is useful when nervous animals need to be sedated or tranquilised before they are captured by another method such as darting. Certain drugs like diazepam could be given to antelope in their food before being darted. This would allow the darter to approach the normally skittish animals to within darting distance. The same method could be used to drug lions and other predators when they need to be darted.

Injection: Injection by hand as an adjunct to hand capture, net gun capture, cage traps and net capture to administer capture drugs is common practice. This should only be attempted by skilled personnel and only once the animal is adequately restrained (as per the capture methods above). Hand injection of predators in cage traps should only be done by experienced persons and should be avoided with lightning quick species like leopard. Rather consider pole syringe, or better yet, darting (see Darting below). Common routes of hand injection include in the veins (intravenous), in the muscle (intramuscular, IM) and under the skin (subcutaneous, SC). Other routes like in the tongue (intralingual), in the nasal passage (intranasal) and in the abdominal cavity (intraperitoneal) are less commonly used. The quickest effect takes place after administering a drug intravenously followed by the intramuscular and subcutaneous routes. Some drugs need to be administered by a single

Pole syringe injection after mass capture. Note the operator marking the animal to prevent it being injected again.

method only as this will influence their effect. The long acting tranquilisers like perphenazine, for example, need to be administered IM only. This allows for a slow release of the drug. Giving the drug IV, by accident, would not have the desired effect, and it places the animal at risk of an allergic shock reaction and death. It is thus good practise when administering drugs by hand injection to aspirate blood into the syringe before injecting.

Pole syringe: The pole syringe is basically an extended version of hand injection. It is useful where animals are not restrained by hand, and the animals need to receive some form of capture drug, such as capture by leg-hold traps, cage traps and plastic boma capture. With this method the exact route of administration is not ensured. Pole syringing animals are normally jabbed from above, thus the most common injection sites include the back and rump area. These are well-muscled areas and drugs would mostly end up in the muscle. There is a possibility of drug being administered in the vein or under the skin, leading to delayed drug action, no drug action or adverse drug reactions. Adverse drug reactions are always a risk when administering long acting tranquilisers by pole syringe, but for example in plastic boma capture there is no other alternative.

Darting

Darting is a very common method of administering capture drugs to animals. Different dart systems exist, each with its positives and negatives. There is no single system of choice.

Darting can take place on foot or from a vehicle or helicopter. This would be determined by the species pursued, the state of habituation of the species, the size of the camp/farm amongst others. Darting takes place in camps, bomas and sometime even after plastic boma capture, and carries the same risk as pole syringing as it cannot guarantee an IM injection. Every effort should however be made to hit a large muscle group. It does sometimes happen that the drug is administered in to a vein or artery, and less frequently in to bone, and when using potent knock-down drugs this would cause the animal to go down quickly, often with some degree of adverse effects. Close attention should be paid when this does occur. Poor dart placement leading to SC injections could lead to prolonged down times with other complications like hyperthermia or capture myopathy.

Drugs that should go strictly IM must rather be avoided in darting.

Darting can be used in any species. The smaller the species the higher the risk of injury from the dart. Small, lightweight darts should be used where possible, or alternative capture methods should be considered. Hitting bone in small and even larger animals could result in fractures. This together with other injuries are risks associated with darting.

Darting blue wildebeest after mass capture.

Laws and regulations surrounding game capture

There are several laws, regulations, rules and standards dictating the way game capture methods are applied. These are in place to protect both the animal and the personnel involved in the capture. Game capture could be a dangerous venture but abiding by the laws, sticking to the rules and regulations and maintaining a high standard will ensure a safe and effective capture.

- In South Africa the management of wildlife is governed by provincial and national (Department of Environmental Affairs) nature conservation departments. One of the important acts is the National Environmental Management Biodiversity Act (NEMBA), Act no. 10 of 2004 of which the Threatened or Protected Species (TOPS) regulations fall under. This Act and regulations determine which species may be captured and translocated and under what conditions. Depending on the province, there is a strict capture season for mass capture. Capture may only take place out of season in the event of an emergency.

Darting rhino from a helicopter.

A permit might be necessary for the farmer to keep a specific species. Another permit may be required to capture that species and perhaps a different permit to transport that species. Veterinarians attending to injured or sick TOPS species also need a TOPS permit.

- The control of scheduled drugs and medicines is governed by the Medical Control Council (MCC) of South Africa. The Medicines and Related Substances Act, Act no. 101 of 1965 prescribes the way in which controlled drugs should be handled, and who may handle these drugs. This is based on the schedule of the drug in question which in turn is determined by a range of factors. Act 101 of 1965 together with the Veterinary and Para-veterinary Act, Act 19 of 1982, regulated by the South African Veterinary Council (SAVC) states that capture drugs may only be used by specific individuals.
- All capture drugs, apart from the reversals/antidotes which are Schedule 4, fall under Schedule 5 or 6. Schedule 5 and 6 capture drugs may only be handled by a veterinarian registered with the SAVC. Only a registered veterinarian may administer these drugs to a patient.
- No layperson may handle, own or be in possession of these drugs. There are a select few Schedule 5 sedatives and tranquilisers that veterinarians may prescribe to patients of bona fide clients. These include azaperone, haloperidol, zuclopenthixol acetate, perphenazine enanthate and diazepam.
- Animal welfare issues surrounding capture are governed by the National Society for the Prevention of Cruelty to Animals (NSPCA) under the Animal Protection Act, Act no. 71 of 1962. There are no laws or rules governing the capture and transportation of wildlife (apart from Act 101 of 1965). This is unfortunate as it allows opportunities for unlawful conduct. There are however some standards (South African National Standards, SANS) for the relocation and housing of wildlife. These are available from the South African Bureau of Standards (SABS) as SANS 1884-1 and SANS 10331.
- Helicopter pilots are governed by the Civil Aviation Authority (CAA) and in order to perform any method of game capture, need to be "game rated".

CHAPTER 4
SPECIES ACCOUNTS

UNGULATES
- Rhino
- African Buffalo
- Zebra

RHINOCEROS
Rubin Els

Rhino are odd-toed ungulates belonging to the Order Perissodactyla which includes zebra. Two distinct genera are recognised each with a number of subspecies:

***Ceratotherium simum* White rhino**
- North western white rhino of north Africa (now extinct)
- South western white rhino of southern Africa

***Diceros bicornis* Black rhino**
- North western rhino of North Africa (now extinct)
- Eastern black *D. b. micheali* (Kenya and Tanzania)
- South central black *D. b. minor*
- South western black *D. b. bicornis* South Africa and Namibia

Habitat and distribution

White rhino: The natural habitat of white rhino is bushveld with patches of short grass which is their preferred diet, thickets and a source of water. Their main distribution areas are the north and eastern parts of the country but some game ranchers have introduced them into areas such as the Free State. This species has a broad mouth which allows them to take in large quantities of grass at a time. They are bulk feeders with a preference for short grass but

Conservation status in Africa
White rhino: 20 404 remaining (18 910 in SA) Endangered
Black rhino: 5 044 remaining (2 044 in SA) Highly endangered

White rhinoceros are bulk grazers that favour short grass.

Black rhinoceros have a pointed upper lip which assist them with browsing on leaves.

will also seek out the taller buffalo grass which grows in the shade. In the dry season they will take medium length grasses but avoid thatch grass species and *Aristida* spp. (steekgras).

Black rhino: The natural distribution of black rhino is historically widespread almost throughout the whole country where sufficient browse is available, including arid areas such as the karoo and desert habitats. They have a pointed upper lip which is suited for browsing trees, shrubs and even the bark of various trees.

Game ranching with rhino

Rhinos are megaherbivores which play an enormously important role in ecosystems and are therefore valuable on any game farm in suitable areas as they are bulk feeders and contribute significantly to biodiversity. In addition as one of the Big Five they used to be a source of Wildlife Tourism for game farms. However, the practice of keeping and breeding rhino is under threat because of poaching which is discouraging farmers from keeping these animals. Those rhino owners who have continued breeding the animals have mostly opted to dehorn their animals to protect them from poaching which nullifies their value for ecotourism.

Apart from their contribution to biodiversity rhino can also be of significant economic importance if rhino horn could be farmed on a sustainable basis to meet the demand by Asian countries, which is currently fuelling large scale extermination of rhino throughout Africa. As far as horn production is concerned white rhino produce more horn material per year than black rhino which have smaller horns. White rhino are also more docile and less nervous than blacks, and therefore easier to maintain from a husbandry point of view. Rhino trophies are also potentially an important source of income for owners.

Behaviour and handling

White rhino are normally docile and easy-going animals. The males are strictly territorial and will demarcate and scent-mark their boundaries diligently. The territories are defended vigorously, which may lead to serious injury or even death for the loser of a territorial battle.

Rhino cows vigorously defend their young against intrusion, especially when surprised. A safe distance and respect must be shown at all times, whether it be from a vehicle, by horse, bicycle or on foot. This safe distance will vary, depending on the expertise of the persons involved, the individual animals and the specific situation. Using this management approach will save lives and equipment.

Cows have home ranges so are not bound by territorial limits as are the bulls, and they move freely through several territories in search of ideal food. They can cover vast

Rhino are megaherbivores that have an important role in ecosystems.

distances overnight if disturbed, or in search of food or water. Ovulating cows can be covered by several bulls, as they move through their territories.

Black rhino are normally secretive and nervous animals. They are highly intelligent and will pick a fight with anybody, anything or any animal, at the drop of a hat. They are normally found in singles, pairs (mother and calf, or same age subadult pairs) or threes (mother, calf and previous calf or mating bull). They are, however, more social than first believed. Young rhino can be injured during courtship rituals, if they get in the way of the courting bull. This usually stems from inexperience.

Initially the bull is vigorously refused by the cow, until she is ready and completely receptive. This may take a few days. During this period, there is some risk to the calf. It may take a knock or two from the bull, if it really gets in the way. The mother will normally fend for her young, but one knock on a shoulder may break a leg, or the youngster may experience horn puncture wounds. It is recommended that male offspring of 18 months and older, be removed to another, safe enclosure or camp. Young bulls can annually be added to a bachelor camp, where they can be kept safe from the territorially dominant bulls. In the absence of females, young bulls can be added and successfully merged, with older even adult, non-breeding bulls. Horn growth and growth statistics can be monitored in this group. Sales, hunting and future breeders can easily be earmarked and selected from this bachelor group.

Breeding systems for rhino

Black rhino are not territorial animals as such, but rather move within home ranges. The home range will not be defended as vigorously as a territory, but fighting may still occur between individuals, either during courting or chance meetings. Their home ranges are quite expansive and due to their nervous dispositions, intelligence and fiery temperaments, one would reason that they would not be ideal for intensive breeding systems. They do surprisingly well in zoos and small breeding camps, ranging from 20 to 400 hectares, if these are well planned and embrace effective husbandry practices. They need sufficient browse, drinking water and wallows to cool down, and sufficient thickets for shelter. Irrespective of the thickness of the bush, small breeding camps will be denuded of shrubs and trees, within a few years, if the animals are not rotated to other camps. Surprisingly, they will turn the thickest bush into parkland savannah, within a few years of constant browsing.

The smaller the breeding camp, the more intensive and pinpoint management is required, to the point where even the breeding bull may need to be removed and introduced again, with each breeding cycle. One bull to

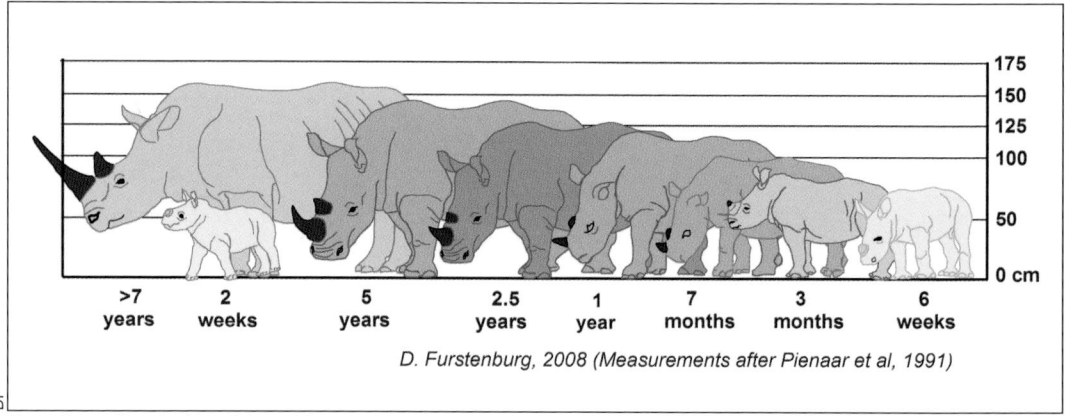

Growth profile of white rhino with age.

two or more cows, is the ideal ratio for intensive breeding systems, depending on the size of the enclosure.

One bull to two cows in 30–50 ha, can easily be managed (subject to permits from the provincial Conservation departments, who prescribe a minimum of 1 000 ha for black rhino and 400 ha for white rhino), with rotational camps, and on condition of the bull being removed after breeding.

Extensive breeding systems need less micro-management, but remain more difficult in monitoring the animals. This results in less data being captured for individuals, such as exact birth dates of calves, calving intervals, and injuries or diseases which need to be identified soonest.

White rhino: Their docile dispositions allow these animals to be bred intensively as well as extensively, but they are surprisingly susceptible in captivity to stomach ulcers which may lead to internal bleeding, poor appetites and even death, if not diagnosed and treated early. Contrary to expectations, under the correct management and husbandry systems, black rhino tend to settle down quicker in captivity than white rhino. White rhino have been known to breed successfully in small breeding camps and zoos, under good management, with good husbandry systems in place. It is normally more challenging, due to more than one bull generally being required. Single bulls may become lethargic in their reproductive cycles, which is countered by the presence of another bull. This does not need to be another dominant breeding bull – purely the presence of another adult or sub-adult bull, tends to keep the breeding bull invigorated. In zoo-like situations, it was found that even the presence of another bull in an adjacent enclosure, would stimulate and vitalise the breeding bull.

It is therefore advisable to have more than one bull in a breeding group. This is best achieved by including at least two bulls in the founder group, when acquiring the animals at onset. Remove excess young bulls annually for their safety. Sexual maturity is reached at about 4–5 years, depending on body size. Females kept under optimal conditions, can be pregnant for the first time at 4.5 years of age. They live to 35-45 years and should be able to breed until they pass away. Under optimal breeding conditions, a rhino cow (white or black) should produce 15 to 20 calves in her lifetime. The normal inter-calving period is 3 years, but under game ranching conditions, females with inter-calving periods of 20-24 months (one calf every 20-24 months), should be selected as primary breeding animals (obviously in conjunction with other desirable traits like body size, temperament, horn size, motherhood viability, reproductive soundness, etc.).

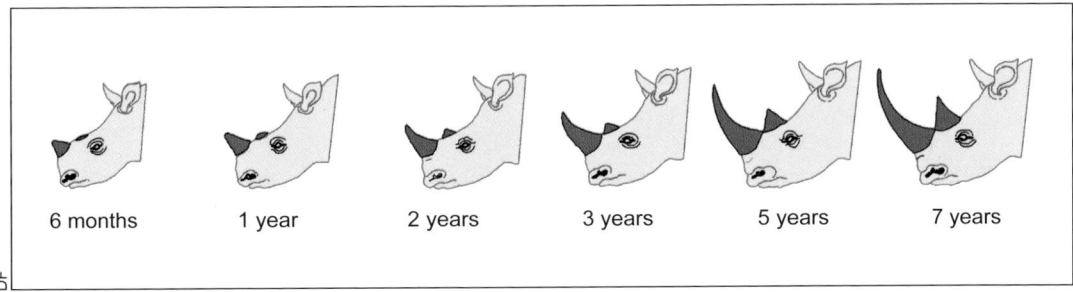
Horn growth of rhino.

Calves separate from the mothers (sometimes enforced by the mother), upon the mother calving again. The bond between mother and calf is exceptionally strong. Separated calves will be scent-tracked by sniffing and vocalising by the mother. Mothers may search for a lost calf for days, before giving up. Often a calve is found next to the decomposing body of a white rhino mother. The bond between mother and calf in the case of black rhino is, however, less strong. Black rhino calves, separated from their dams are often lost due to hunger, thirst and predation because the mother flees without heeding the calf. She may then look for the calf when danger has passed but soon gives up the search.

Scent introductions

There is generally much less risk to introducing white rhino to an existing herd, than with black rhino. Staggered introductions (adding animals to an existing herd), is seldom ideal, but the risk can be managed in several ways:

New breeding bulls: Remove the old (and territorial bulls, in the case of white rhino) first. Place the old and new bulls in a neutral camp/enclosure, for a while. Settle any new females, before introducing old and new males, simultaneously. Scent introductions also assist greatly in reducing risk of fighting or skirmishes with staggered introductions. This is done by scattering fresh manure from the new animals, into the territories/home ranges, of the old/established animals. If the new arrivals are kept in a boma, fresh manure should be collected from the outside animals to scatter into the enclosure of the boma animals. This should be done for several days or weeks, depending on the duration in camps, of the captive animals. When the animals are released and they encounter the older/established animals, they would have been "introduced" already.

Translocating to a new property: Scatter large volumes of their manure along boundary fences and waterholes, before releasing the animals onto the property. This promotes the animals settling in and prevents them from breaking through unfamiliar fences or boundaries. It also encourages drinking at water holes where their or other familiar dung is spread around pans or boundary fences. Enough manure from home ranges or territories should be transported along with the translocated animals, for use on the other side.

Supplementary feeding

It remains good practice from a husbandry, economic and animal welfare perspective, to give supplementary feeding to rhino during the dry times of the year, as well as during drought periods. It is of primary importance that wildlife ranchers be successful grassland/pasture farmers, firstly, before commencing to be successful game ranchers. The one precedes the other, and virtually guarantees success, whilst if veld management is ignored, game ranching may not be as successful or sustainable over a prolonged period of time. White rhino

are bulk grazers requiring 60–100 kg of food per day. They spend nearly half of their day feeding. They must have sufficient good quality natural veld grass at all times. Lucerne hay is readily accepted after some initial persistence. Mouldy lucerne or grass must never be fed as rhino are prone to aflatoxicosis, which causes organ failure and can eventually be fatal.

Supplementary feed must be given during the dry months, when the protein levels of plants, naturally decreases from around 10% to around 2%. A protein lick without urea assists the animal in digesting the dry feed and converting it into protein. In the event of enough quality grass being available, very little lick is needed to maintain body condition throughout the season. Hard compressed licks placed in tight-fitting lick holders prevent rhino from overeating and subsequent painful, often fatal colic.

Supplementary feed prevents the animals from losing weight over the dry season, and therefore expending more energy in gaining body weight again in the wet season. An animal which maintains a constant body weight and condition throughout the year, will have a more constant calving rate. It equates to more calves being born, over a shorter period.

Supplements also prepare the animal's gut flora so that when it is captured for sale or for recuperation after injury or sickness, it will not have adaptation stress in the boma. This counters stress and body condition loss, which is normally prevalent in captured rhino. Less stress means a smaller chance of developing stomach ulcers.

As a rule, rhino should not be dewormed upon capture, as the anthelmintics kills the bots (the larvae stage of the *Gyrostigma* fly) in their stomachs, which assists them in a uniquely symbiotic relationship digesting their food. However, the same bots, may become detrimental to the rhino in the case of animals in poor physical condition. Deworming after

DEHORNING RHINO AS A DETERRENT TO POACHING?

Removing the horns of rhino to prevent poaching is in theory an excellent deterrent because it reduces the incentive and increases the risk of capture or harm to the poacher. A study conducted in Zimbabwe to dehorn rhino as a deterrent indicated that it could be effective as a management tool provided it was done aggressively without leaving any remaining stumps, and it was used in conjunction with ongoing law enforcement and regular monitoring of the animals. They recommend further that to maximise effectiveness, as many rhino be dehorned as possible and that private owners as well as state-owned organisations should have coordinated dehorning programs. Veterinarians at the Onderstepoort Faculty of Veterinary Science have perfected a method which leaves very little horn behind: Under anaesthetic both horns are cut off with a chainsaw and an angle grinder is used to lower the profile closer to the germination layer from which the horn originates. This method leaves a more pleasing profile than if the horn is merely sawed off. The process must be repeated every 2 years because the horns will regrow. Rhino owners must ensure that horns are kept in safe places such as bank vaults for their own security.

Dehorning can be a deterrent to poaching when combined with other methods.

the animals have taken to food supplements would then be essential. The eggs of the *Gyrostigma* fly can be seen as small, oblong shapes, found on the head and neck regions, but also often around the base of the horn.

Dry lucerne is a valuable and convenient supplement for rhino. Large consignments can be fed in a long line along the shoulder of a road, to feed groups of rhino at a given point. The portions should be quite bulky, but must not be placed on sandy soil. Sand intake can cause impaction of the stomach, which could lead to colic. Similarly, game pellets must be fed in robust containers like tyre feeders and not on the ground.

Balanced phosphate licks will prevent animals from eating bones, sand and termite mound clay to satisfy phosphate or mineral shortages. Licks are mostly utilised by rhino and other game, during the wet season. Persistence in providing licks will be rewarded by the animals taking them readily, and this will ensure correct mineral levels. Salt blocks do not provide the correct balance of minerals.

Common health problems

As mentioned above feed-associated problems such as sand impaction, aflatoxin poisoning from mouldy feed, botulism due to pica or bone eating are common. Rhino are also susceptible to cyanobacterial poisoning (Microcystis) (see Chapter 5). Other diseases seen in rhino are clostridial myositis (sponssiekte), and occasional infection with insect borne viruses. Rhino are also susceptible to heat exhaustion, when capturing and transporting animals during very hot conditions.

WALKING OFF INTO THE SUNSET?

Pelham Jones, Private Rhino Owners Association (PROA)

After being saved from the brink of extinction South Africa's two rhino species face this possibility once more. Whether they can survive this latest onslaught, brazen slaughter of animals for the sale of rhino horn on the black market, seems to rest mainly in the hands of private rhino owners.

The role of PROA in conserving rhino

South Africa has 82% of the world's rhino population – 18 910 white rhino and 2 044 black rhino. Private farms own 27% (5 000) and 23% (450) respectively and play a significant role in the conservation of rhinos. However, private owners are under siege, because despite the annual expenditure of roughly R200 m on security, the exorbitant prices obtained for rhino horn on the black market makes poaching a high risk/high return business. Huge expenditure on veterinary dehorning procedures can still fail as a deterrent (see Dehorning), as poachers are willing to kill animals for small horn stubs and often maim or kill rhino calves to silence their distress cries when mothers are shot. Almost all private owners have had to witness horrific scenes like this but also experience enormous financial losses and huge frustration at the failure of all the efforts poured into countering poaching. The numbers continue to rise annually even at the time of writing (see statistics below).

Poaching statistics

The graph below illustrates the precipitous rise of poaching of rhino in South Africa since 2008 which now totals 4 000.

Failed strategies

In 1977 CITES banned the trade on rhino horn, but by 1992 COP 18, reviewing the status of rhino conservation in Africa which showed that 100 000 had been poached in Africa, declared:

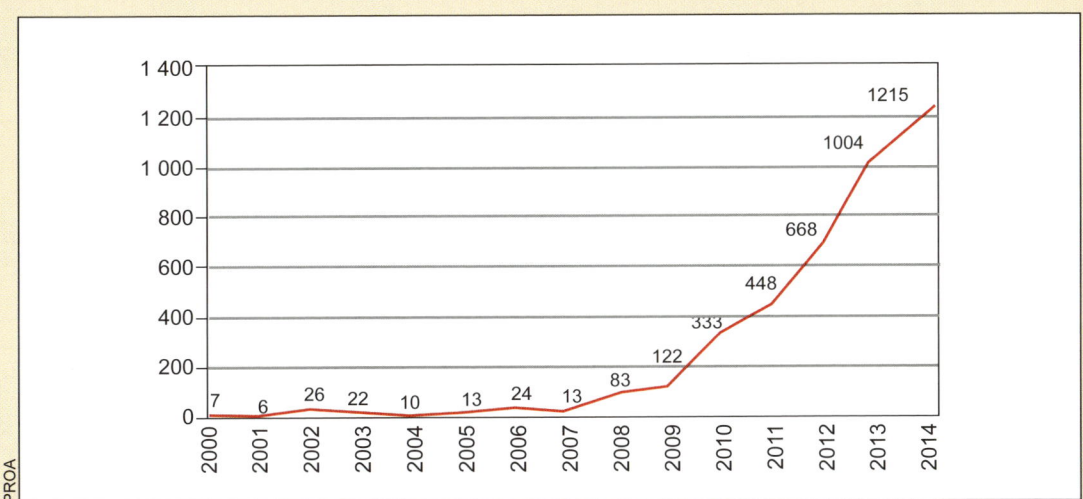
Rhino poached in South Africa.

"Banning the international trade of rhino products has failed to provide protection to rhino in the wild and should be abandoned as a viable conservation process."

In 2008 poaching suddenly exploded in South Africa, forcing the Department of Environmental Affairs to devise a security strategy in 2010, which despite their best efforts did not have any impact on annual losses. In 2011 the DEA asked for public participation to devise strategies for collapsing the illegal trade.

Proposed solutions and obstacles to stop poaching

At the current rate of rhino poaching both species will be extinct by the next decade. PROA has proposed the sustainable sale of rhino horn in particular of the massive and worthless stockpiles owned by SANPARKS which could be used to fund conservation, to immediately bring down the black market price. The controlled sale of horn is proposed in which DNA tagging is used to allow legal trade. The long term strategy is therefore to reduce demand, removing the exclusivity of an illegal product and further lowering the price of horn which will make rhino poaching a high-risk activity with relatively low profit.

The initiative to legalise controlled rhino horn trade is hampered by over 3 000 NGOs, NPOs and commentators on social media who subsist on public donations ostensibly to "Save the Rhino". These entities fearing loss of subsidies oppose legal trade. They have no viable alternative solution, insisting that the status quo be maintained even though poaching shows no sign of abating. Of these commentators 99% are not rhino owners, so it serves their purpose if poaching continues because they can retain their funding. For PROA losing the war against rhino poaching is unthinkable and every conceivable effort must be made to end the slaughter.

Dead rhino cow with calf.

AFRICAN BUFFALO (*Syncerus caffer*)
Roy Bengis

Physical characteristics

African buffalo are robust ruminants that have a massive body, short neck, stout strong limbs and a broad bare muzzle. The adults are coloured black or seal brown, and calves are generally born dark brown, often changing to yellow-brown after several months and then gradually darkening to reddish or chocolate-brown. Hair coat is generally dense but smooth in calves, becoming sparser in older animals. Both sexes have horns, and in adults the size and shape of the horns is highly variable. In bulls, the bosses and about a third of the inner part of the horns is heavily rugose and the remainder is smooth. The horns of females are always lighter in build and the boss is less well developed. The ears are large and round and fringed with long hair, and the tail is long and tufted. Shoulder height is 138–160 cm, and bulls weigh in at 650–850 kg, while cows tip the scale at 500–700 kg. The inguinally located udder of the cow has four teats. Male genitalia are easily visible. The front hooves are larger than the hind, which can also be seen in the spoor. Buffalo seldom live longer than 15 years under free-ranging conditions, but may live longer in captive or intensive conditions where feed is supplemented.

From birth to about the 9th month of age, buffalo calves have a total of only 20 deciduous teeth (there are no deciduous molars), which are progressively replaced by a set of 32 permanent teeth during the next six years. There are no upper incisor teeth, these being replaced by a dental pad as in most ruminants. Aging of buffalo is usually done by taking into account shoulder height, horn development

African or Cape buffalo.

and examining of the teeth. In the live animal it is often difficult to visualise the premolar and molar teeth to assess eruption or wear, so most people assess age by the sequence of eruption of the permanent lower incisor teeth and their subsequent wear. The deciduous central incisor teeth are replaced by the permanent incisor teeth at 2.5 years of age. The second incisor is replaced at 3.5 years, the third at 4.5 years and the corner incisor is replaced at 5.5 years. All permanent incisors will be in wear by 6 years of age.

As the buffalo ages, the incisors wear down progressively from their original sharp, spatulate form, to a more rounded wearing surface where the infundibula are visible, and finally, to mere nubs at the gum-line in aged animals. However, for accurate aging after 8 years, one needs to be able to visualise and assess the wear of the permanent premolar and molar teeth. While eruption of teeth follows a biologically programmed temporal sequence, the actual wearing down of teeth is very much a function of soil type, veld type

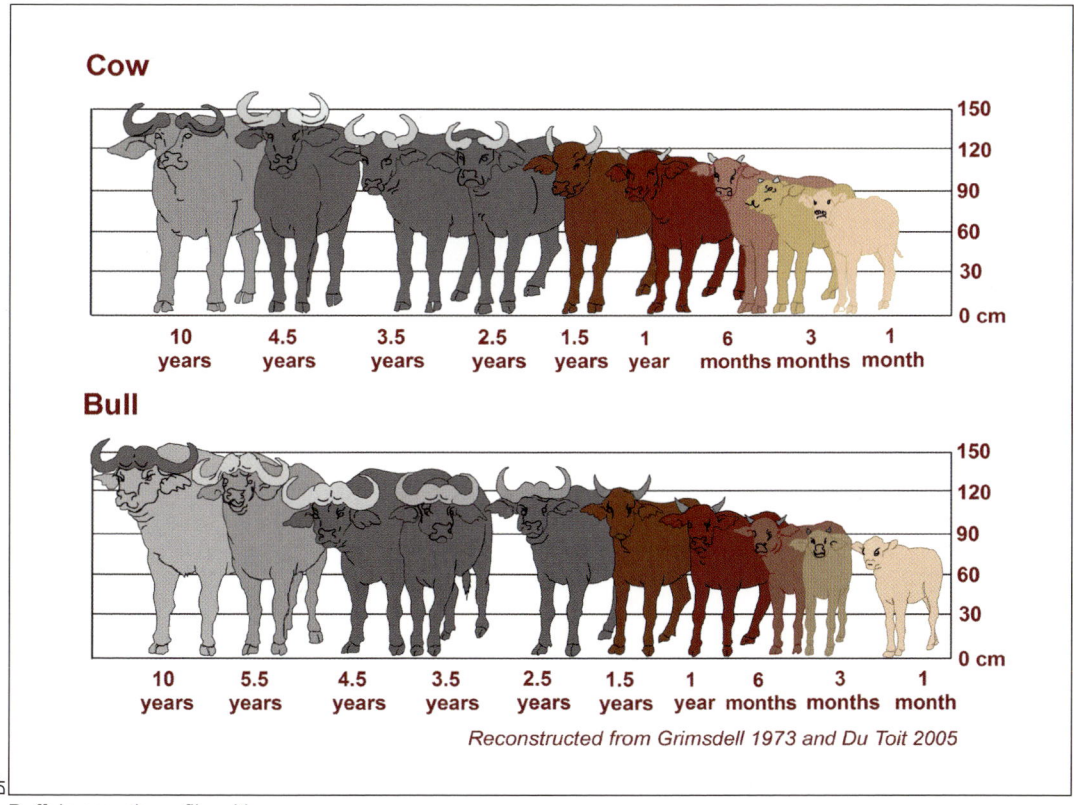

Buffalo growth profile with age.

and vegetation. Buffalo teeth wear down much more rapidly on abrasive sandy soils typically found in granitic, calciferous or sandstone areas. In addition, an excess of certain trace elements such as fluorine and cadmium may have negative effects on the structure and rate of wear of buffalo teeth.

Biology

African buffalo are found in a wide variety of vegetation types and therefore are adaptable to a range of habitats. They do not naturally occur in arid areas with an annual precipitation of less than 250 mm. Their three basic necessities include adequate grazing, permanent surface water and protection from the elements, including shade during the heat of the day and thickets to escape inclement weather. Buffalo need to drink water every day. They reach maximum densities in well-watered savannahs, swamps and floodplains, but also occur in numbers in certain montane grasslands and forests. Good buffalo habitat is generally a composite mosaic of dense cover with shade, woodlands and open savannahs. Buffalo are bulk grazers, able to subsist on grasses too tall and coarse for most ruminants and are less partial to tender shoots than most ruminants. They also browse to some extent, more so in the dry season when grass is scarce or of poor quality. Buffalo, with their wide incisor row and mobile tongue can consume large amounts of grass in a short period of time, and in tall pasture, they play a pioneering role in savannah grazing succession, reducing grasslands to the height preferred by more selective feeders. In addition, a mobile herd of buffalo plays an important role in trampling and breaking the outer soil crust which facilitates penetration of grass seeds and water.

Comparative images of incisors

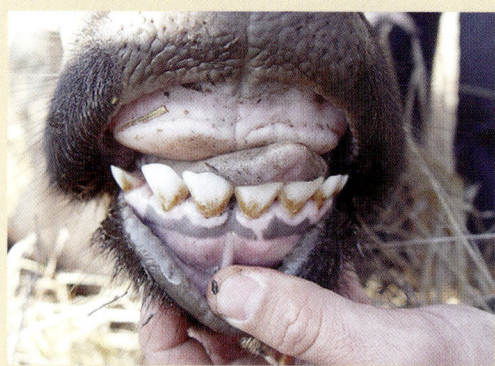

< 2 YEARS: All incisors present are deciduous (milk) teeth. No permanent incisors have erupted yet. In these cases age should rather be assessed by horn development and body size.

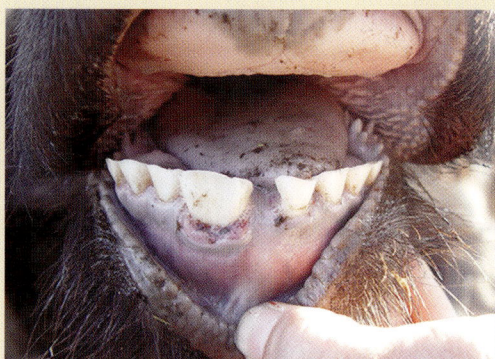

2 ½ YEARS: First central permanent incisor has erupted. The paired incisors may erupt singly or at the same time.

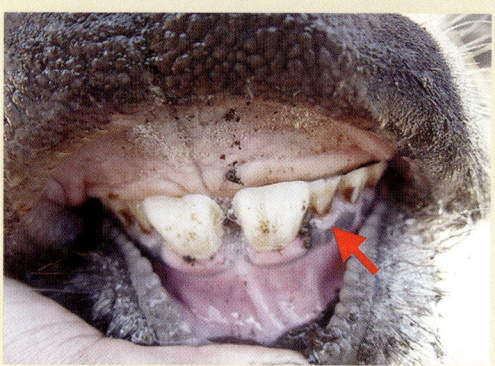

3 YEARS: The permanent central incisors have both erupted and are in wear. Notice the obvious difference in size and shape between the deciduous and the permanent incisors.

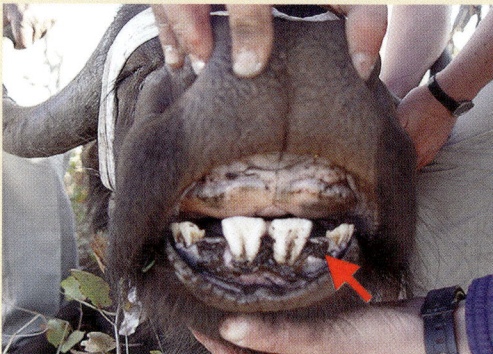

3 ½ YEARS: The first set (central) incisors are in wear, and the second set are erupting on either side of this first set.

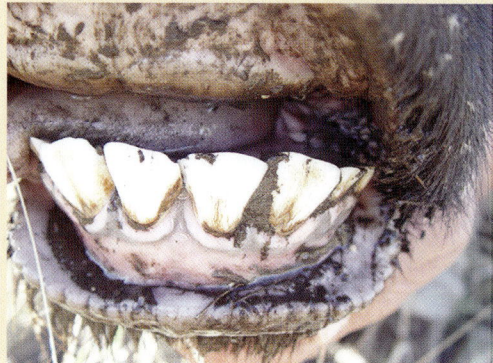

4 YEARS: Two sets (4 teeth) of permanent incisors are visible and in wear. Once again, notice the obvious difference in size between the permanent and milk teeth.

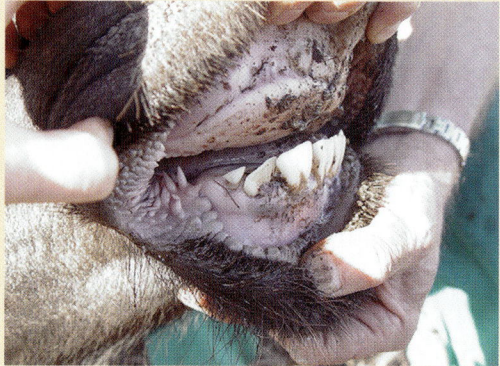

4 ½ YEARS: The first two sets of permanent incisors are obvious and in wear, while the third set is just erupting and visible – often one side first.

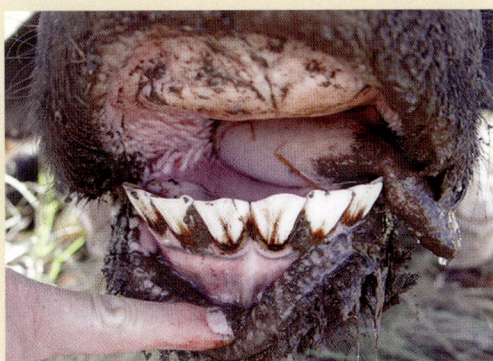

5 YEARS: Three sets (6 teeth) of permanent incisors are now in wear. Notice that the last (corner) milk tooth incisor is still present.

5 ½-6 YEARS (full mouth): At 5 ½ years of age, the corner (4th set of incisors) erupt, and all four sets of permanent incisors are in wear by 6 years of age. Notice that the teeth are all still spatulate and sharp-edged and infundibula not yet visible.

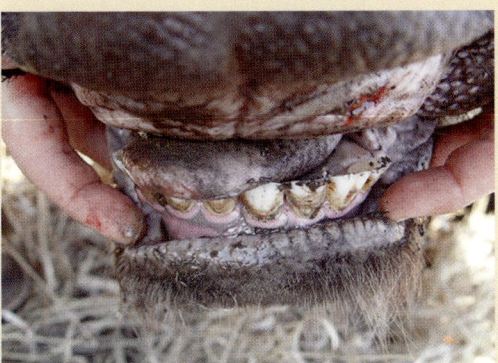
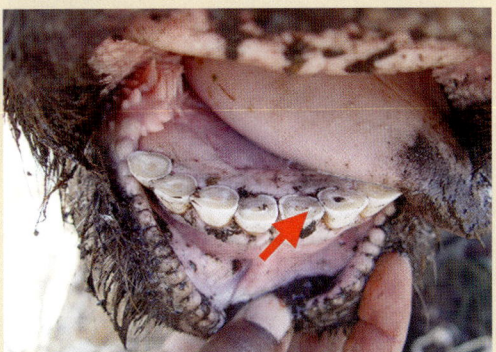

6-10 YEARS: Notice that the wearing surface is flattening on all four sets of incisor teeth. Infundibula slowly become visible. With adult bulls, it is important to note body size, thickness of neck, boss development and fusion – to fine tune age assessment in this age class.

> 11 YEARS (old buffalo): All incisor teeth are rounded and well worn. Infundibula are visible on the worn surface of all the incisors. Buffalo in this age class generally start losing condition.

Behaviour

Buffalo are gregarious, non-territorial and occur in large mixed herds with a male dominance hierarchy. In large protected areas, herds of several hundred are commonplace and aggregations of over 1 000 animals are not uncommon. In natural systems, buffalo are distributed in discrete population units which remain in separate traditional home ranges. The size of these population units is determined by the nature of the habitat and primary productivity of the ecosystem. The population unit is composed of the major breeding herd, one or more bachelor herds which separate from the main herd during the dry season and rejoin just before the mating season, and sedentary old bulls which no longer join the main herd.

The basic units of the buffalo breeding herd are stable kinship groups or cohorts of presumably related cows, each being accompanied by successive offspring up to about 3 years of age, although the sub-adult males tend to associate in subgroups. Each cohort is usually accompanied by several adult bulls that are also ranked according to age and dominance status. A kinship group generally consists of 15–35 individuals and is thus made up of the female family unit and the male subgroups.

At certain times of the year when resources are scarce, a buffalo herd may exhibit fission/fusion behaviour, whereby the large herd breaks up into smaller foraging units as a survival mechanism. Later, when resources improve during the early rainy season, these smaller groups may coalesce, sometimes with buffalo groups other than from their natal herd. This is an important mechanism for "gene flow". In the Kruger National Park, small groupings of pubertal sub-adults (heifers and bulls) were occasionally observed to leave their natal herd and then later join up with different herds, many kilometres away.

Reproductive biology

Heifers reach puberty at about 2.5–3 years, and generally have a first calf at foot from 4–4.5 years of age. The gestation period in buffalo is 330–345 days. The inter-calving period may be as short as 15 months after exceptional rainfall years, but may be as long as 20 months as a result of lactation suppression of oestrus or poor grazing during the dry season. In Southern Africa, most calves are born between December and May with a peak in February/March.

Bulls reach puberty at 3–4 years, but generally only enter the dominance ranked reproductive competition when they are mature (5.5 years and older).

In Southern Africa, the mating season lasts about 4 months, starting in mid-December. Pro-oestrus lasts about 2 days during which the cow may be closely attended by several bulls in dominance succession, but she will not stand to allow physical mating. By the time the oestrus female is ready to mate, she would usually be attended by the most dominant male.

Management

There are three main management systems employed for buffalo:

- **The true free-range extensive management system.** This is seen in National Parks and in the larger private reserves and conservancies, which are usually multi-species conservation areas. In these systems, buffalo rarely ever receive nutritional supplementation, although watering points may be established to distribute the availability of surface water. Hay, feed blocks or licks may be provided during droughts. In general, stocking rates of 10–20 hectares per Livestock Unit is aimed for, depending on availability, and distribution of grazing, surface water, shelter, veld type and veld condition scoring. These systems generally require minimal management which may include fence and road maintenance, water provision, veld assessment and a periodic census of the population. Occasionally, population management to reduce numbers may become necessary.
- **The semi-intensive management system.** This system is what we most commonly see in private buffalo ranching enterprises – where relatively small buffalo herds (< 50 animals) are kept in large camps (50–500 hectares) where they are partially reliant on natural grazing and water is provided. Supplementary feed is also provided, but the scale of supplementation will depend on body condition score, seasonal rainfall and veld conditions. These semi-intensive buffalo ranches require an intermediate level of management, including fence and road maintenance, water provision, veld assessment, feed supplementation,

Perimeter fencing used for buffalo containment.

tick management and camp rotation. Rotational grazing of large camps can be achieved by manipulating water points or feeding sites to encourage the buffalo to move between camps. Bull rotation may be practiced to avoid prolonged line breeding or inbreeding. In some areas of the country, tick management may become necessary. Biosecurity aspects of fencing between camps become even more important if there are more than one herd of buffalo on the registered property. Where possible, it is important to create double-fenced biosecure exclusion zones between the herds. These exclusion zones, though expensive are important to prevent diseases spreading between herds and generally also function as access and patrol roads and firebreaks. In addition, perimeter fencing of the ranch, at the interface with neighbouring wildlife ranches or cattle farms are extremely important to prevent spread of diseases.

- **The intensive buffalo management system.** These breeding establishments generally have small groups of buffalo that are kept in small camps (1–5 hectares) and these animals are totally dependent on the farmer for daily feeding, water and shelter. In this form of buffalo farming/breeding, management is similar to cattle stud breeding farms, except that the physical structures such as fencing, gates and chutes need to be much more robust and designed to contain and facilitate manipulation of these large aggressive ruminants. These animals require daily management for feeding, watering and cleaning of camps, as well as routine veterinary interventions such as endo- and ectoparasite control, vaccination and treatment of clinical cases when necessary. Separation of animals may also become necessary from time to time and the buffalo should be made accustomed to regularly moving through a linking crush (chute) into a small adjacent camp. This will facilitate procedures such as applying "pour on" medications, vaccinations, separations, treatments and cleaning up accumulated dung. Shade trees should be protected from debarking.

Buffalo holding pens and boma management

No matter from which of the above three management systems the buffalo originate, if they are to be moved to another property, auctioned, sold or transported, they will need to be placed in a boma system to facilitate marking and identification, pregnancy testing, treatment for internal and external parasites,

Example of buffalo holding pens.

and for compulsory disease testing prior to movement (see later in text). Bomas are also useful for managing sick or injured buffalo. Buffalo are herd animals and should never be housed alone – they should always have one or more companion animals in the boma.

The holding pens must be solid permanent structures, and the perimeter fence must be at least 2 m high, is usually constructed of tanalith treated poles with gaps in between (place one–miss one). The poles can be bolted to a basic frame consisting of vertically concreted metal straining posts 5 m apart with two horizontally running poles about 40 cm and 180 cm from the ground. This structure avoids planting all the poles and thus reduces risk of poles rotting and termite attack. Steel cables, supported by solid members, is another option. Each boma unit should always consist of two compartments, approximately 25 x 20 m linked by an externally controllable sliding gate to facilitate daily cleaning and feeding. This size boma should be adequate to accommodate 8–10 (maximum) adult buffalo. The sliding gate separating the two compartments also provides for manipulating and safe handling of individuals or groups of immobilised animals, allowing the rest of the group to move away into the second compartment.

The sliding gate must be solidly constructed, easy to operate and equiped with a quick securing device. Each compartment should also have an external access gate and all gates must be wide enough to allow passage of a "bakkie" or tractor. At least one third of each compartment should be covered in shade. Shade cloth (80%) can be used as well as natural shade provided by trees. If shade trees are present, the trunks must be protected from debarking caused by constant rubbing by the animals.

A continuous water supply controlled by a ball valve should be available in each compartment. The water troughs should be constructed against the fence with a small section protruding to the outside. With the slope of the bottom of the trough towards the outside, this allows for easy cleaning. A central hay-rack allows for "all round" feeding, but has the disadvantage that it needs to be filled one or more times per day, and it may also make darting of individuals more difficult. Two articulating hay racks on the sides of each compartment is the alternative and makes hay replenishment much easier, but there must be enough feeding space to avoid competition by dominant animals. Hay racks should also be covered by impervious roofing material in order to prevent rain from soaking the fodder and to reduce mud formation and water pooling around the hay rack.

A catwalk along one side of each compartment is very useful for observing and darting animals. When wild buffalo (off the veld) are first introduced into these holding pens, the sides should be closed with capture plastic sheeting to reduce visual stimuli, and noise must be kept to a minimum. For the first three days, the connecting gate between the two compartments is left open and hay is supplemented when necessary, but no attempt should be made to clean the compartments. As the buffalo acclimatise to their confinement and new surroundings, the plastic can be progressively rolled down and later removed completely.

As one introduces the daily feeding and cleaning of the compartments, it is extremely important to develop and follow a routine. The buffalo learn the routine very quickly and stress is reduced to a minimum.

Nutrition

Adult buffalo generally need 10–15 kg of good quality hay and 25–45 l of water per day depending on season and environmental temperatures. In their natural environment, buffalo are mainly long grass feeders and show a preference for grasses of the genera *Themeda, Panicum, Digitaria, Setaria, Cenchrus* and *Schmidtia*. With this in mind, regular "veld condition" assessment should be practiced in extensive systems to avoid overgrazing and veld deterioration. "Standing crop" and grass species composition are the determinants of veld condition and should be regularly monitored. In these extensive management systems, buffalo nutrition is occasionally supplemented during droughts. Buffalo will learn to utilise licks and game blocks in extensive and semi-intensive management systems. Certain specific macro and trace elements may be added to these licks and blocks in areas that have known deficiencies.

In semi-intensive management systems, supplementation of natural grazing with cultivated tef (*Eragrostis tef*), oulandsgras (*Eragrostis curvula*) and oat or lucerne hay, generally takes place on a daily basis but the scale of supplementation may vary, depending on veld condition, season and rainfall. Game pellets may also be given.In intensive management systems buffalo must be fed on a daily basis. Tef, oulandsgras, lucerne and oat hay are the major constituents of the feed.

The amount of lucerne or oat hay fed should not exceed 20% of the total hay on offer. If there is hay left over after a 24 hour feeding period, then the animals are being fed too much, and there will be wastage.

Buffalo are mainly long grass feeders.

If the buffalo start losing condition, then they are being fed too little. In intensive management systems, concentrates in the form of specially formulated game pellets are frequently fed. They are used to flush body condition, to supplement calf nutrition, to assist in recovery of injured or sick animals, and importantly, to lure animals between pens, through chutes or into crates. These game pellets or cubes can also be used as a vehicle by which anti-parasitic medications and mineral or vitamin supplements may be given. Adult buffalo can be given up to 2 kg of game cubes/pellets per day when necessary, but this is dependent on the formulation and manufacturer's recommendation.

Capture, handling and transport

Basic considerations and precautions

- The adult African buffalo has a 20 mm thick hide that demands the use of long (minimum 40 mm), thick (minimum 2 mm diameter) needles to deliver the immobilising agents intramuscularly. A retaining barb on the needle is recommended for field work.
- Buffalo have large muscle masses on the shoulders, neck and hindquarters, that provide ideal darting sites.
- Bleeding sites include the jugular vein and tail vein, and the ear veins are useful for administering top-ups, stimulants or antidotes.

Supplementation of natural grazing.

- Buffalo do not tolerate heat well because of their relatively small surface area to body mass ratio and dark colouration. Avoid working during the heat of the day. Early mornings are the best time for capture operations, and late afternoons can work, but be aware that buffalo usually drink in the afternoon and there is a greater risk of regurgitation, and also beware of failing light at sunset.
- Avoid capturing buffalo shortly after heavy or prolonged rain showers when the ground is wet and soggy. When chased under these conditions, buffalo often develop musculo-skeletal problems due to excessive muscular exertion in the saturated slippery conditions.
- Exercise care when immobilising heavily pregnant buffalo cows. They appear to require higher doses, and are more prone to bloat or regurgitate.
- Avoid capturing buffalo shortly after they have drunk water, as significant problems due to regurgitation and aspiration may result. If animals do regurgitate, the attendant must immediately lower the head and an antibiotic cover should be given prior to reversal.
- If ambient temperatures are above 25 °C ensure that adequate water is on hand to wet and cool the immobilised animals. If temperatures rise even further, cut short the capture operation.
- Avoid prolonged recumbency in all adult buffalo. If it is unavoidable, change the position of the hindquarters, rotating from one hip to the other at regular intervals, to relieve pressure on blood supply to the lower legs. These animals should be treated with an anti-inflammatory drug prior to reversal.
- Buffalo are enormously strong and must always be treated as potentially dangerous. The potential danger associated with darting out of bull groups or cows with small calves should not be underestimated as they can be particularly unpredictable.
- Ensure that a stomach tube and/or adequate 15 ga needles are available to relieve bloat if it occurs.
- Ensure that sufficient trained helpers are available so that each immobilised buffalo has an attendant to maintain correct sternal positioning, to lift the head, monitor breathing and to call for assistance if necessary.

Chemical capture

Buffalo are generally captured using a "cocktail" of drugs which include a narcotic component and a tranquilliser/sedative component. The narcotic components most commonly used include etorphine (M99), thiafentanil (A3080) and fentanyl citrate, which may also be combined in various ratios. These are Schedule 6 medications (Act 101 of 1965) and it is a legal requirement that an experienced wildlife veterinarian must be in charge of making up the darts required, and be present for the entire operation. These drugs are highly dangerous and accidental human exposure can be fatal. It is also extremely important that the meat of animals that may have died during a darting operation should not be eaten or provided to staff, because of the presence of narcotic residues. The tranquilliser components most commonly used are azaperone or midazolam. Xylazine, detomidine or medetomidine can also be used, but may result in regurgitation, problems with thermoregulation and incomplete reversal when animals are antidoted.

When working with groups of buffalo, hyaluronidase is frequently incorporated into the cocktail to speed up absorption of the drugs. It is important to ensure that adequate doses of all the components are used, to effect a rapid "knock-down". In the veld, buffalo can be darted from a vehicle, a hide or from a helicopter.

Once the animals are down, the ground team must move in swiftly and roll all the buffalo into a natural sternal position and blindfold them. Each buffalo should have an attendant, and an experienced wildlife veterinarian should circulate among the buffalo to check on breathing, circulation and positioning of body and limbs, and to treat animals when necessary.

Animals that are excessively rigid and swaying their heads tend to fall over into lateral recumbency. These animals need top-up sedation with ketamine or midazolam, and their body position can then be corrected. Animals that are breathing very slowly and appear to be excessively drugged can be given Dopram (short acting) or butorphanol to stimulate respiration.

Practical capture drugs should be reversible, and specific antidotes to reverse one or more components of the capture cocktail are essential. These antidotes are Schedule 4 medications and are usually given intravenously, but may be given intramuscularly. The most commonly used antidotes include diprenorphine (M50/50) and naltrexone. The reversal occurs very quickly (within minutes) and all helpers must be safely back on the vehicles or out of the boma when the antidote is given. All blindfolds must be removed after antidoting. Antidotes are also available for some tranquillisers/sedatives such as xylazine, detomidine, medetomidine, diazepam and midazolam.

Mass capture

Buffalo are easily herded using a helicopter and can be successfully captured using the same plastic sheeting plus netting funnel, chute and corral technique used to capture other social herbivores, except that more robust structures are needed for the corral and chutes. Natal Parks Board/Ezemvelo Wildlife have successfully used this technique in the Hluhluwe/Imfolosi Complex for a number of years, to capture entire herds of buffalo (40–90 animals) in order to test them for bovine tuberculosis. This technique was also successfully employed in the Sabi Sand Game Reserve in 1999, to vaccinate large numbers of buffalo during an anthrax outbreak.

Transportation of buffalo

There are strict movement controls for buffalo in many African countries. In South Africa, the owner/manager of the buffalo is responsible for

Vehicle used for transporting buffalo.

obtaining the necessary Provincial export/import permits as well as the final State Veterinary movement permit, and the capture operator or veterinarian in charge must ensure that all requirements including disease testing are complied with – prior to the start of the operation.

Single immobilised and blindfolded buffalo may be transported short distances on a stretcher on the back of a bakkie or trailer. For longer distances, individual animals may be transported awake but tranquilised inside a suitable closed trailer. Transporting family groups and young bulls is usually done in a purpose-built transport truck with multiple compartments separated by very strong vertically or horizontally sliding doors. Family groups and similarly-sized animals can travel together in a compartment. Adult bulls are usually accommodated in separate compartments.

The floors should have an anti-slip grid covered by bedding, or ideally be covered by woven rubber mats. Soft bedding such as sand, straw and mixtures of the two, can create problems in trucks with horizontally sliding doors, by impacting or impeding the doors' runways or channels. Trapdoors in the roof of each compartment are essential for dissipating heat after loading the animals and for controlling the temperatures during transport. They are also useful for viewing, monitoring or treating the animals when necessary.

The truck drivers must be trained to have a specific driving style, with slow pull-aways, easy cornering and gentle stopping. The buffalo should be inspected through the trapdoor every few hours. If there is need to stop in transit during the heat of the day, the truck should be parked in the shade. Ideally, buffalo should be accustomed to confinement in a boma at the farm of origin prior to transport, and then be further confined for a few days in a larger, possibly less permanent structure at destination, in order to settle down prior to a passive release.

Buffalo should always be transported tranquilised, the tranquilliser being given by dart or by pole syringe in the loading chute or in the truck compartment, via the trapdoor. The tranquillisers generally used include azaperone (short-acting 2–4 hours), haloperidol (intermediate acting 8–12 hours) or Acuphase (long-acting 2–3 days), or a combination.

Disease problems

Disease problems in buffalo fall into three categories, namely State controlled diseases, other common buffalo diseases, and finally diseases associated with intensification of buffalo farming or ranching.

Buffalo associated and State controlled diseases

Unfortunately, buffalo are the natural carriers of African strains of foot-and-mouth disease (FMD) and corridor disease (CD) in South Africa and most large free-ranging buffalo populations are persistently infected and permanent carriers of one or both diseases. Infected buffalo generally show no symptoms or signs of infection. It must be stressed that these two diseases are buffalo-associated diseases, and buffalo are the ultimate source of all outbreaks of these diseases in cattle.

Foot-and-mouth disease is a highly contagious viral disease transmitted by persistently infected buffalo, and may infect all cloven-hoofed livestock, with severe economic consequences for the farmer, the district, the zone and the country. Corridor disease, which is generally fatal in cattle, is transmitted by brown ear ticks that have fed on an infected buffalo.

More recently, several important buffalo populations in southern and eastern Africa have become infected with bovine tuberculosis (BTB) and/or bovine brucellosis. These two diseases are originally cattle diseases, and were probably introduced onto the African continent with imported cattle.

BTB is a chronic bacterial disease that affects mainly the lungs and lymph nodes of buffalo. It has a long incubation period (months) and the disease then develops slowly and progressively, and may take years to kill its victim. An infected buffalo is continuously infectious to other buffalo in the group (see Chapter 5).

Bovine brucellosis is a chronic bacterial infection that may have a long latent period before it becomes apparent. It affects mainly the reproductive organs, and in heifers and cows this leads to late term abortions. The aborted foetus, foetal membranes and placenta are an immediate source of infection for other buffalo in the herd.

The fluids discharged from the uterus after birth are also a source of infection for several weeks after the abortion. The infected cow once again becomes highly infectious during her next calving, even if a live calf is born. Some buffalo with brucellosis develop hygromas or knee swellings.

FMD, corridor disease, bovine TB and brucellosis are listed as "controlled animal diseases" as defined in the Animal Diseases Act (Act 35 of 1984), for which control measures have been prescribed in the Act and its Regulations. For the buffalo rancher/breeder the following pertinent extracts from the Regulations are important:

Regulation 20 – Restrictions on the movement and keeping of buffalo

- 20 (1)(a) – No person shall, except under the authority of a permit issued by the responsible State Veterinarian, and in accordance with the conditions specified in this permit, move or remove live buffalo from the land on which they are kept to any other land.
- 20 (3) – This permit for the removal or movement of buffalo shall be issued only if the land to which the buffalo are to be moved is registered as contemplated in Regulation 20 A (see below).
- 20 (6) – No permit shall be issued for the movement or removal of live buffalo out of the control areas for corridor/buffalo disease (in the Limpopo and Mpumalanga Province Lowveld and areas of Northern Kwazulu-Natal) OR the infected zones or protection zones of the control areas for foot-and-mouth disease (in the Limpopo and Mpumalanga Province Lowveld).
- 20 (8) – No buffalo may be moved onto the same land where cattle are being kept, and no cattle may be moved onto the same land where buffalo are being kept. Contact between cattle and buffalo shall be prevented.

Regulation 20 A – Registration of land for keeping of buffalo

The following control measures are prescribed for keeping of buffalo:
1. No person shall keep buffalo on any land which is not registered by the National Director of Veterinary Services for this purpose.
2. Application for the registration of land for keeping of buffalo shall be made by the responsible person in charge of the land concerned, on the applicable form which is obtainable from the office of the responsible State Veterinarian.
3. Land for the keeping of buffalo shall only be registered if that land is fenced in in a game proof manner for buffalo according to the requirements of the Nature Conservation Authority concerned. Land for keeping buffalo situated within an animal disease control area shall also be electrified to the satisfaction of the responsible State Veterinarian.
4. The Director shall consider each application on merit and issue a certificate of registration to the responsible person concerned, if he is satisfied. A non-transferable WR-number for that property or portion of a property appears on the certificate.
5. Regarding this certificate of registration:
    - It shall be valid only in respect of the land specified therein.
    - It shall lapse when buffalo are no longer kept on the land concerned.
    - It may be withdrawn by the Director if the holder thereof is convicted of an offence concerning registration, keeping or movement of buffalo.
    - It is not transferable to other land.
    - It may be transferred to a new owner, provided he applies therefore in the prescribed manner.
    - It may on application, be amended to provide for an extension of the land.

If buffalo are found on unregistered land, they shall be removed or destroyed by the responsible person concerned, within the period and in such a manner as determined by the State Veterinarian in an order served on such a person. If the responsible person refuses or fails to comply, the State Veterinarian may seize the buffalo concerned and dispose of them in a manner determined by the Director.

Another "notifiable" disease that has recently been seen to affect buffalo and other wild ruminants is Rift Valley fever (RVF). RVF is a mosquito-borne viral infection of ruminant animals that causes abortions, neo-natal mortalities and some adult mortalities in livestock and wildlife. Rift Valley fever outbreaks in livestock generally track high rainfall periods and occur in a cycle of 7–11 years. An effective vaccine is available for high value animals.

Other diseases

Buffalo, together with giraffe and white rhino are the preferred hosts for the adult stages of the brown ear tick (*Rhipicephalus appendiculatus*) and the bont tick (*Amblyomma hebraeum*), and high tick burdens may be seasonally found on buffalo. Older buffalo or buffalo weakened by disease may show large scaly patches of hair loss (mange) caused by either *Psoroptes pienaarii* or *Sarcoptes scabeii* mites. In younger age classes of buffalo, nodular demodectic mange lesions (resembling lumpy skin disease) is common, the skin nodules usually present on the neck and shoulder areas. Large ulcerative lesions, up to 30 cm in diameter, are also commonly seen in summer on the shoulders and back of adult buffalos. These are caused by a worm parasite called *Parafilaria bassoni* (see Chapter 5). These lesions heal over time, frequently resulting in scarred hairless patches.

Buffalo carry a variety of internal parasites, which are rarely a problem in free-ranging animals. These include a large variety of "round-worms", flukes, and tapeworms.

Buffalo with hygroma caused by bovine brucellosis.

Warts caused by the bovine papilloma virus are occasionally seen on the head and neck, and sometimes affecting the hairless regions around the udder and sheath of adolescent buffalo.

Diseases/parasites of buffalo that are of public health importance

These include some intermediate stages (cysticerci and hydatid cysts) of tapeworm parasites generally found in wild carnivores and domestic dogs. These cystic lesions may occur in the muscles, heart muscles, liver and lungs of a buffalo carcass, and may be infectious to humans and domestic dogs. In addition, protozoan sarcocysts are commonly present in the musculature of the tongue and upper oesophagus of buffalo.

Larvae of the nasal "tongue worm" parasite of carnivores are frequently found in mesenteric lymph nodes, larger blood vessels and liver of buffalo. For these reasons, domestic dogs on wildlife ranches should be regularly dewormed, and should not be given free access to game camps.

Bovine TB, brucellosis and Rift Valley fever can all affect humans, and carcasses/organs with lesions should not be used for human consumption. People should also wear rubber gloves if handling organs or foetuses from suspect animals.

Diseases associated with intensification of buffalo ranching/farming

In extensive and semi-intensive multi-species systems, buffalo generally have low to moderate parasitic burdens and are continually moving away from areas they have seeded with these parasites. In addition, many of the parasitic ova and larvae are removed when ingested by "non-patent" species such as zebra or rhinos that share the environment. In intensified buffalo farming systems which are generally mono-species systems, the daily movements of buffalo are limited and this may result in a build-up of ectoparasites (ticks, lice and mites) and endoparasites (worm eggs and larvae, and oocysts) in the environment. In these situations very heavy burdens of these parasites may develop, resulting in clinical disease. Treatment of buffalo with acaricides and dewormers before entering the intensive systems may reduce future risk, but regular inspection of buffalo for tick burdens and pooled faecal sampling to monitor endoparasitic loads is essential. In the long run, deworming and tick control must become part of normal management in these systems.

Under intensive conditions with regular management activities such as darting, moving through crushes or into crates and vehicles, buffalo are exposed to knocks and bumps and bruising. These may result in one of several *Clostridial*-diseases such as malignant oedema, quarter evil or gas gangrene – which are acutely fatal toxaemic conditions. These are preventable by vaccination with polyvalent Clostridial toxoid vaccines in accordance with manufacturer's instructions for cattle. Buffalo being moved to anthrax endemic areas should be vaccinated against anthrax, and those being moved to phosphate deficient areas should be vaccinated against botulism.

Buffalo raised under intensive tick-free conditions may lose their natural resistance to certain tick borne diseases such as Corridor disease and heartwater, and if released onto veld with moderate to heavy tick loads, they may actually develop clinical disease and die. To prevent this such buffalo should be afforded "trickle exposure" to ticks by releasing them in the "low tick" season (usually winter) or low level prior exposure before direct release onto the veld. Release of these "tick naïve" buffalo onto veld with moderate tick loads should especially be avoided in the summer months (December to May).

In addition, buffalo that have been raised under intensive mono-species systems have also been known to die of snotsiekte (malignant catarrhal fever) after released onto properties with wildebeest or sheep. To prevent this, buffalo and sheep should not be farmed on the same property, and when such buffalo are moved onto a multi-species ranch with wildebeest, this move should not take place during the wildebeest calving season and for three months after this calving season.

Economics

Buffalo are ecologically important because they are bulk grazers which occur in large herds. Through short-term, mass-grazing pressure, these herds are capable of opening up tall rank grass cover, to the benefit of other species which are more selective or short grass feeders.

Buffalo are also important from the eco-tourism point of view, being a member of Africa's charismatic "big five", which are much sought-after for viewing, photography and hunting. For these reasons, buffalo have been much in demand by the wildlife industry. In the early 1980s, when the private ownership of wildlife became a reality, the only buffalo available to the private wildlife ranching industry were a few surplus "disease-free" buffalo from Addo National Park or from Provincial Reserves that had previously received Addo buffalo. In 1989, an entrepreneurial wildlife rancher negotiated a "pilot project" with the National Director of Veterinary Services, with the object of breeding "disease-free" offspring from corridor disease infected buffalo parent stock from KwaZulu-Natal. The rationale was that brown ear ticks did not occur in the Northern Cape because the elevation, semi-arid conditions and winter frosts made it climatically unsuitable for these vectors of corridor disease. The project was approved subject to certain restrictions and was an immediate success. Following this, a few more similar projects were started in the other parts of the Northern Cape and western Free State which were considered "vector free" areas. In 1990, bovine tuberculosis was detected in the south western Kruger National Park (KNP) and its rapid spread northwards, prompted South African National Parks to apply for a "pilot project" to assess the possibility of breeding "disease-free" buffalo calves from FMD- and CD-infected parent stock.

The objectives of this project were to preserve the Kruger buffalo genotype in the face of the huge BTB threat, and to supply other National Parks with suitable habitat and needs, with "disease-free" buffalo of the Kruger genotype.

A pilot project designed by and under the supervision of the State Veterinary Office at Skukuza was approved. The project design made use of several disease mitigation strategies. These included:

1. Only bulls and cows free of BTB and brucellosis would be used. These buffalo were kept under extensive free-range conditions in a large, fenced breeding enclosure (4 000 ha) just south of Satara rest camp in the KNP.
2. Several months before calving, the pregnant cows were brought to an intensive boma system that had been erected at Skukuza.
3. A few days after calving, all calves were ear-tagged and micro-chipped, and blood samples were collected for baseline disease/antibody status screening. These calves were all raised by their biological mothers.

"Disease-free" buffalo breeding project.

4. The bomas and the buffalo cows and calves were kept tick free for the duration of the project in order to avoid transmission of CD from the cows to the calves. The bomas were surrounded by a 10 m de-bushed and regularly mown exclusion zone (box in a box system)
5. The buffalo calves were then prematurely weaned and removed from their biological mothers when the FMD antibody levels, obtained from their mothers, started to wane. These calves were then placed in a separate bio-secure facility, in calfhood cohorts according to size and approximate age.

This project was successful and the first eleven disease-free calves were produced in 1998. SANParks then applied for permission to erect a satellite facility on private land near Phalaborwa. This was successfully accomplished, and in the year 2000, a total of 61 calves were produced by these two facilities. In addition, a second private facility was registered near Phalaborwa, where newborn calves were removed from their biological mothers at birth and then raised by Jersey cow surrogate mothers. This was also a success, producing 19 "disease-free" calves in its first year. These successes prompted several wildlife ranchers in the FMD and CD Control Areas to follow suit, and by 2001, three breeding projects were registered in Mpumalanga, and a proliferation of breeding projects occurred in Limpopo Province. It was a challenge for State Veterinary Services to control, service and monitor this rapid proliferation of projects, some of which were not even registered.

To manage this new emerging industry, the National Directorate of Veterinary Services created a formal Buffalo Advisory Committee, made up of experienced National and Provincial State Vets. They in turn drafted an official Protocol for the keeping, breeding and movement of buffalo in South Africa, and this included an important section containing explicit guidelines for "disease free" buffalo breeding projects.

Unfortunately, the performance of certain disease-screening tests were not optimum and some breeders did not conform to the protocol or took short cuts. This resulted in numerous "break-through" infections involving all four diseases at origin (fortunately inside the FMD and CD control area), and break through infections mainly of corridor disease, but also some BTB cases outside of the control areas. This prompted State Veterinary Services to call a meeting with all the buffalo project owners and managers in December 2001, and at the meeting it was agreed that breeding projects that make use of infected breeding stock would be phased out by 31 December 2011, thus giving the buffalo breeders 10 years to consolidate their investments.

During those 10 years, further break through infections occurred in the facilities at origin, and also at destination on wildlife ranches outside the disease control areas (mainly of corridor disease). The official buffalo protocol was amended several times, and diagnostic methods and tests were improved. However, the success story is that by the time the closing date for the "disease free" breeding projects arrived in December 2011 {Regulation 20(6)},

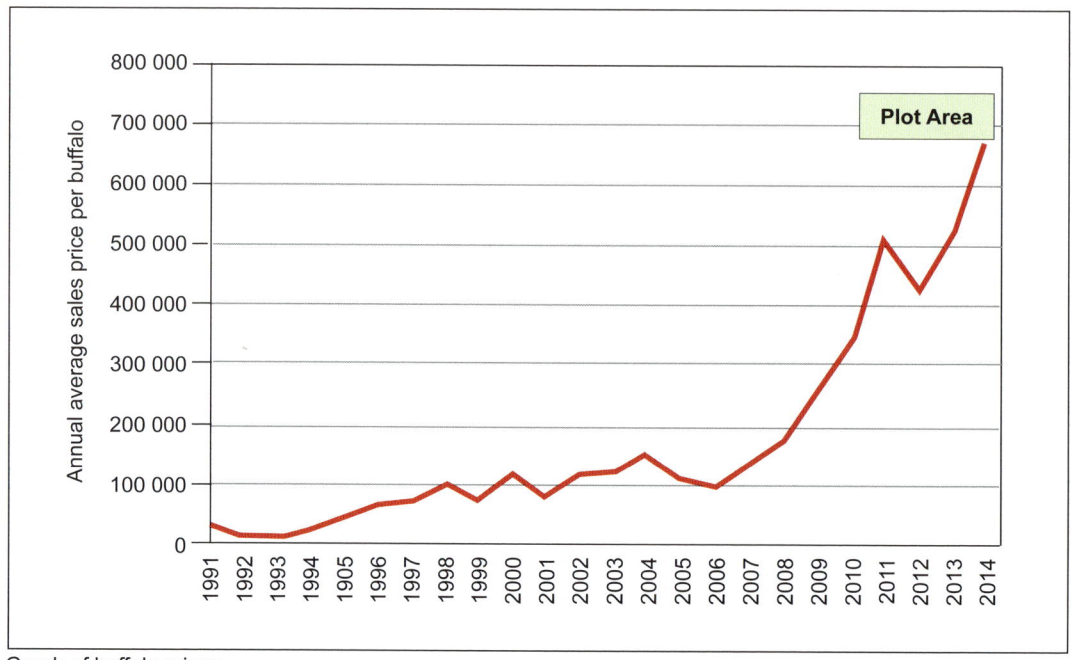

Graph of buffalo prices.

there were in excess of 27 000 privately owned, "disease-free" buffalo on private land in South Africa.

Initially, most breeders and purchasers of buffalo were aiming at the ecotourism (Big 5) and hunting industry markets, and this is reflected in the buffalo prices of the period: Between 1989 and 1996 average buffalo prices increased from R6 000 to R62 000 *(Report: Centre of Wildlife Economics – Univ. of Potchefstroom)*. Thereafter average buffalo prices increased slowly but progressively from R74 000 in 1997 to R134 000 in 2007, a doubling in 10 years.

From 2008 onwards there has been an exponential rise in buffalo prices, partially due to the entry of many more Lowveld "disease-free" buffalo and some East African buffalo onto the market, and by 2014 the average price paid per buffalo on game sales/auctions reached R670 000 *(Data sourced from Vleissentraal and unpublished data from Univ. of Potchefstroom)*. In addition, since approximately 2008, the emergence of buffalo breeders who have focused on genetic line breeding of selected animals for certain phenotypic traits such as body, horns and boss size, has resulted in a second tier of prices on a much higher trajectory.

In conclusion, the private buffalo industry is in a very healthy state, with currently more than 30 000 privately owned "disease-free" buffalo on private land. The future of this industry lies in the hands of the buffalo ranchers and breeders, and any short cuts with regards to movement requirements, bio-security, and disease testing may be short cuts to disaster. Wildlife ranchers must be aware that the introduction of one infected animal may ruin their enterprise. They should also be aware that prolonged genetic line-breeding or inbreeding of animals for specific phenotypic traits may unmask certain undesirable "linked" genes, which may negatively affect characteristics such as heat resistance, tick resistance and disease resistance or other metabolic or immunological processes.

ZEBRA
Halszka Hrabar

Quagga pattern of a plains zebra.

Speciation

Three species of zebra exist:
- Grevy's zebra (*Equus grevyi*),
- Mountain zebra (*Equus zebra*) and
- Plains zebra (*Equus quagga*).

Mountain zebra consist of two subspecies:
- Hartmann's mountain zebra
- Cape mountain zebra

Current plains zebra taxonomies divide the species into six subspecies, three of which occur south of the Limpopo River.

Plains zebra subspecies

- The quagga, the southernmost subspecies was, however, driven to extinction by the end of the 19th century (ca. 1883) by overhunting and competition with livestock.
- Burchell's zebra.
- Chapman's subspecies.

Grevy's zebra, the largest of the three species, historically ranged from Southern Eritrea and Djibouti, through Ethiopia, south into northern Kenya and southern Somalia. This species has, however, undergone a substantial reduction in range in recent history, due to limited access to water, habitat degradation and loss, competition for resources and hunting. It currently only remains in northern Kenya and southern Ethiopia. Grevy's zebra occupies arid and semi-arid grass/shrubland and prefer stony plains or hills, short grassy flats or broken country where there is permanent water accessible every 1–3 days. Compared with plains zebra, Grevy's zebra can inhabit areas where vegetation is much less abundant and more variable and they are less water dependant than plains zebra, enabling them to occupy an interzone between the arid-adapted wild ass and the water-loving plains zebra. Unlike plains and mountain zebra, Grevy's have no permanent adult bonds or herd system. Adults may live alone on territories (breeding males defend large resource territories), bachelor groups or mixed herds.

The quagga project

While the extinct quagga was previously considered as a separate species based on morphological evidence, research has now firmly established that the quagga is a subspecies of the plains zebra. After the very close relationship between the quagga and surviving zebras was discovered, the Quagga Project was started in 1987, in an attempt to "bring back an animal from extinction and reintroduce it into reserves in its former habitat". Nineteen animals were selected from reserves in Namibia and South Africa, choosing animals with demonstrable reduction in striping over the rear of the body or legs, or with a tendency to a darker background colour. Offspring either showed heavier striping, lesser striping, or similar striping patterns to their parents, and those with heavier striping were removed as part of the selection process. After running for 24 years the programme was on its fourth generation of progeny and was producing individuals with a degree of striping reduction which approximate the striping pattern typical of some museum specimens of quagga. Despite the success of the project in producing animals which are phenotypically similar to the extinct quagga, adaptive attributes which the quagga might have had, have not been accounted for and individuals can therefore not be referred to as "quaggas". The heart of the quagga's range was the semi-arid and temperate Karoo, which would have required a degree of adaptation to this specific environment, for example.

Plains zebra

Habitat and diet

The plains zebra is the most abundant and widespread equid in the world today, found from as far north as Ethiopia, down through East Africa and into southern Africa. Subspecies are morphologically distinct and in general the extent of stripe pattern decreases from north to south while body size increases.

Almost exclusively grazers, plains zebra are strongly associated with grasslands and savannah woodlands. Many populations are seasonally migratory, tracking flushes of vegetation caused by rainfall. Plains zebra are usually a dominant member of the ungulate community within its range and plays an important role in the overall dynamics of its grassland habitat. Due to their hindgut digestive system, zebra are able to utilise coarse vegetation of low nutritional value, as long as it is abundant. Typically, plains zebra move into a grassland ahead of other grazers and by removing the older growth layer they open it up to more selective ruminants such as wildebeest. Their ability to exploit a greater range in grass quality also enables them to occupy a larger variety of habitats (although they are selective for certain grass species). Their range is, however, dependent upon standing water as all adults need to drink at least once a day.

Behaviour

Plains zebra have a two-tiered social organisation. The core social group is the "harem" (breeding group), consisting of a single stallion and one to six adult females and their dependent offspring. Females within a harem are unrelated as offspring of both sexes disperse at sexual maturity. Harems are stable units, with females tending to remain together in the same harem for much of their reproductive lives. Males without harems live in bachelor groups. Multiple harems and bachelor groups join together to form herds (consisting up to thousands of animals in large conservation areas) which are unstable, with associations among harems changing over hours to days.

Males are not socially mature (able to attract and acquire females) until about 4–4.5 years old and prime breeding stallions are under 12 years old. Females are fully reproductive by three years old. The gestation period of plains zebra is 12 months, resulting in less seasonal reproduction than for most other African species. Foals are born year round, peaking during the rainy season. On average, the inter-foal-interval is around 14–16 months. Overall, foal sex ratios are 1:1, but temporal biases have been found in populations, such as a male foal bias late in the rainy season (when females are in peak condition) and a female bias in subpopulations experiencing below average rainfall over prolonged periods. Plains zebra therefore follow the predictions of the Trivers-Willard hypothesis, which states that for polygamous species such as zebra, mothers in good condition should produce more sons. All factors affecting female condition, such as social rank, rainfall, population density, etc. can therefore influence the production of male or female offspring. Foal sex ratio could hence potentially be used as an indicator of nutritional stress in a population, as a repeated female bias could mean that adult females are in suboptimal condition.

The social system of plains and mountain zebra also has implications for the population dynamics and genetics of the species. Long tenures of harem stallions result in some males never getting a chance to breed, thereby reducing the effective or genetic population size, for example. However, evidence from studies on plains zebra show that a change in the breeding herd stallion has a significant negative effect on the subsequent inter-foaling-interval of females. Furthermore, translocation of females and a change in harem stallion had

How the zebra species got their stripes

The explosive growth of the study of evolutionary developmental biology (also known as Evo Devo) has enabled scientists to explain how genes drive the highly complex formation of the embryo.

One of the most interesting insights gained from this science is into the development of the striped coat colour in the embryo; this arises from the migration of melanocytes or pigment cells in specific bands during the development of skin of the embryo.

Zoologist Johnathan Bard developed a model for predicting why the different zebra species have different numbers of stripes. He suggested that if the stripes are generated at the same interval, for example every twenty cells at slightly different times in each species, this will produce different numbers of stripes and sizes. If the stripes arise early in the embryo (28 days) they would give rise to fewer and broader bands as in the plains zebra which has 26 stripes, while if they arose in larger embryos (28 and 35 days) they would give rise to more stripes (43) in the mountain zebra and 80 in Grevy's zebra.

Plains zebra

Hartmann's zebra.

Grevy's zebra.

an even more dramatic effect, raising the inter-foaling-interval to a mean of 38.9 months. This is therefore an important factor to consider in harvesting strategies, as the killing of herd stallions can result in reduced fecundity arising from social stress. It should also be noted that because females within each harem are genetically not related, genetic diversity within the effective population is relatively high.

Mountain zebra

A number of characteristics distinguish mountain zebra from the plains zebra, including the grid-iron pattern of stripes above the tail, a lack of shadow stripes (which occur on plains zebra in southern Africa) and a distinct dewlap. There is sexual dimorphism between the sexes – the mare being larger than the stallion. The underbelly is white in contrast to that of the plains species in which the stripes are continuous onto the midline. The following differences distinguish the two subspecies:

Hartmann's: Larger and heavier than the Cape mountain zebra (stallions weigh 298–343 kg versus 250–260 kg respectively) and the mane comes further forward between the ears than in the Cape mountain zebra.

Cape Mountain Zebra: The black stripes are generally wider than those of Hartmann's and the dewlap is more pronounced.

Historically, Hartmann's mountain zebra ranged from south east Angola, through Namibia and into the Northern Cape Province of South Africa, occurring in the mountainous transition zone between the Namib Desert and the central plateau in Namibia. Endemic to South Africa, Cape mountain zebra were widespread in the mountains of the Western and Eastern Cape provinces of South Africa. It is postulated that the ranges of the two subspecies were separated by an area devoid of mountainous habitat between the northernmost point of the Cedarberg and Bokkeveldberg ranges, and the southernmost point of the Kamiesberg range. Hybridisation between the two species was identified as one of the major threats to the Cape mountain zebra in 2002, due to a number of extralimital Hartmann's populations within South Africa. It is therefore not permitted to keep the two subspecies together. Similarly, hybridisation between plains zebra and mountain zebra has recently been confirmed. These two species should therefore also not be kept together.

Habitat

Mountain zebra inhabit rugged, broken mountainous and escarpment areas up to around 2 000 m, for which they have evolved exceptionally hard and pointed hooves compared to other equines. They are reliant on sufficient surface water, which they drink daily and are predominantly grazers, only browsing if forced to do so. Although they are bulk feeders and feed on course fodder, they are highly selective and prefer the large-tufted, leafy perennial species such as red grass (*Themeda triandra*), narrow-leaved turpentine grass (*Cymbopogon pospischilii*), dropseed grass (*Sporobolus fimbriatus*) and buffalo grass (*Panicum stapfianum*). They do not graze as closely to the ground as many antelope species that may be found in the same habitat (bite height at 40–80 mm), hence they tend to avoid the closely grazed "grazing lawns" favoured by blesbok, black wildebeest and springbok (Grobler, 1983). Although fynbos is abundant throughout the historic range of the Cape mountain zebra, fossil evidence suggests that such vegetation is unlikely to support dense populations and access to open grassland is therefore crucial in maintaining large Cape mountain zebra subpopulations. In optimum habitat, with an annual rainfall of 350–450 mm, the stocking density should not exceed one animal per 27 ha and this should be reduced in lower rainfall areas. Access to wooded ravines and shallow caves is important for shelter against rain and cold in winter, as they are particularly vulnerable during this crucial period. Penzhorn (1984) found 91% of deaths in a Cape mountain zebra study occurred in winter, primarily following snowstorms.

Excessive hunting and habitat loss to agriculture left the Cape mountain zebra numbers in a critical status in the 1950s with fewer than 80 individuals remaining, in only three relict populations.

Since the 1950s numbers have gradually built up through active conservation programmes, and the total extant population in 2015 now consists of no less than 4 790 animals in 76 subpopulations. Fifty six of these subpopulations are on privately owned land, but the majority of the population (69%) remains in formally protected areas.

In Namibia, the establishment of artificial water points has allowed Hartmann's mountain zebra to occupy previously unsuitable habitat, such that their present range differs from that in historical times.

Hartmann's populations also underwent a decline in numbers, decreasing by 50% from 1998 to 2008, but have increased successfully in recent years, from an estimated 25 000 in 2008 to 70 000–90 000 individuals in 2014. Low genetic variation within the subspecies is a key threat to Cape mountain zebra, caused by the population having undergone an extreme genetic bottleneck and all subpopulations being isolated due to fencing, resulting in no natural gene flow between subpopulations. In addition the social structure of Cape mountain zebra, in particular the long tenure of herd stallions, reduces the effective population size still further (number of breeding adults).

A meta-population approach to management, involving translocations between subpopulations to ensure continued population growth and genetic diversity is therefore necessary for the Cape mountain zebra. Furthermore, on establishing a new subpopulation, a founder population of at least 14 animals is recommended so as to ensure the genetic viability of the subpopulation. Introducing an

Cape mountain zebra in natural habitat.

excessively small number of founder individuals can also be a wasted effort, as this tends to result in either failed reintroduction or poor population performance in the long term.

Breeding behaviour

Like the plains zebra, the social system of mountain zebra consist of breeding herds (harem) of one stallion and one to five mares (most commonly 2–3 mares, normally unrelated) and their offspring. "Bachelor" groups are constituted by both sexes, however, a characteristic unique to mountain zebra. Harems remain stable for long periods, and once a female has become firmly established in a harem, she tends to remain there until death (periods of up to 17 years are reported). Herd stallions tend to have a long tenure, averaging seven years, but usually for life. They are generally only replaced when in poor condition and females often then disperse independently after the death or supplementation of the breeding stallion.

Breeding herds may also split up if the herd becomes too large. Social hierarchies exist in breeding herds, with the stallion being dominant and a linear hierarchy among females. Hierarchical order in mares is generally according to the order in which mares join the breeding herd. Dominance is important, as reproductive success of dominant mares is higher than subordinate mares, largely due to a higher mortality rate of foals from subordinate mares – often caused by aggressive behaviour by the dominant mare.

Foals of both sexes disperse from their natal group to join bachelor groups, thereby preventing inbreeding in a social system where male herd tenure tends to be long (compared to most other harem-forming species).

Fillies disperse at an earlier age than colts (average age of 18 months versus 24 months respectively) and colts also remain in bachelor groups for longer than fillies (on average, 54 months versus 29 months respectively). Fillies will leave a bachelor group to either join an existing breeding herd or establish the nucleus of a new herd with one of the stallions from the bachelor group. Excess males in a population therefore play an important role by enabling the formation of new breeding herds and a larger number of smaller harems result in a larger effective population (as more males are contributing towards breeding).

As with plains zebra, mountain zebra mares foal year round but peak around the raining season, with up to 85% of Hartmann's foals born between November and April. The age at first reproduction has been reported as early as two years to as old as five years and the reproductive potential of Cape mountain zebra is, on average, one foal every 25 months.

Given the reproductive lifespan of around 15 years, a mountain zebra mare may produce up to eight or nine foals in her lifetime. The annual rate of increase for populations is 8–12% in the absence of predation. Foal sex ratios are 1:1 overall but female body condition (influenced by social rank, rainfall, etc.) does appear to influence the production of male or female foals. Unlike plains zebra, however, nutritionally stressed females tend to produce more male offspring. Populations with a continued male foal bias may therefore be resource limited.

Diseases and parasites

Equine sarcoids are virus induced tumours which are a common condition in equids; they have been found especially in inbred populations of mountain zebra.

The growths are confined to the skin and directly underlying tissues, but can occur as single or multiple lesions in different forms, ranging from small wart-like lesions to large ulcerated fibrous growths. Lesions can occur at any site on the body but most commonly occur in the areas around the genitals, the thorax, abdomen and head. Although only the odd case has been reported from some populations, the virus reached epidemic proportions in two populations, namely in the Gariep Nature Reserve and Bontebok National Park where 22% and 53% of the population was infected respectively.

Treatment of sarcoids is difficult at the best of times and almost impossible to manage in a free ranging population of wild equids. Monitoring of the incidence of sarcoids in the various sub-populations is ongoing and until such time that the understanding of the epidemiological factors that result in sarcoids is better understood, it is recommended that animals with visible lesions be euthanased as they are thought to act as a source of infection.

Conservation achievements

- Mountain zebra were down-listed from Endangered to Vulnerable by the World Conservation Union (IUCN) in 2008.
- Cape mountain zebra are currently in the process of being further down-listed to Near-Threatened.

HIPPOTRAGINES (HORSELIKE ANTELOPE)

- Gemsbok
- Roan
- Sable

GEMSBOK (*Oryx gazella*)

Deon Furstenburg

Speciation

Gemsbok are endemic to the south-western arid region of Africa and are also known as oryx. They are classified in the family Bovidae, subfamily Antilopinae, tribe Hippotragini, genus *Oryx*.

The genus is divided into four species and four subspecies of which only the gemsbok or southern oryx occurs naturally in South Africa. The species are:
- *Oryx gazella gazella*, the gemsbok or southern oryx of southern Africa.
- *O.g. blainei*, the Angolan gemsbok of Angola.
- *O. beisa beisa*, the Beisa oryx of northeastern Africa.
- *O.b. callotis*, the fringe-eared oryx of the central parts of East Africa.
- *O. dammah*, the scimitar-horned oryx of northern Africa.
- *O. leucoryx*, the Arabian oryx of Arabia and Iraq, also known as the white oryx.

There is still doubt about the validity of the subspeciation of the Angolan gemsbok although it is recognised by the Rowland Ward trophy register. The Angolan gemsbok seems to be merely a phenotype of the gemsbok and not a subspecies. There is also a dispute over the recognition of the species *beisa*. Some authors are of the opinion that it should be a different subspecies of *gazella* but this remains to be confirmed by genetic characterisation.

Two coloured variants of the typical gemsbok are recognised in the commercial game industry, the Burchell's golden gemsbok and the royal (red) gemsbok. The golden variant originated naturally and Fred Burchell, related to the late Dr William John Burchell after whom the Burchell zebra was named, established the first golden gemsbok (free roaming) breeding herd at Dewad Sud near Keetmanshoop in Namibia. The original golden animals were obtained from free-roaming populations scattered across the southern regions of Namibia.

IUCN Conservation Status

- Gemsbok, Beisa oryx, Fringe-eared oryx = Lower Risk, conservation dependent (LR/cd)
- Scimitar-horned oryx = Endangered (EN)
- Arabian oryx = Critically endangered (CR)

154 THE NEW GAME RANCHER

Typical gemsbok.

Scimitar-horned oryx.

Arabian oryx.

Beisa oryx.

Colour variants of oryx

Golden gemsbok colour variant.

Royal or red gemsbok colour variant cow with calf.

The origin of the royal gemsbok is thought to be a result of selection and camp-breeding. A specific breeding project to maintain royal gemsbok colouration is managed by Dr Johan Kriek from Kriek Wildlife Group. Severe cases of genetic inbreeding with golden gemsbok are apparent on several commercial game farms, mostly resulting in weak and deformed horn growth. Golden gemsbok are being crossbred with normal gemsbok on a large scale, and cases have been found of crossbreeding with scimitar oryx and being offered for sale as golden gemsbok, which would probably be infertile.

Current distribution and numbers

The endangered scimitar-horned oryx of the Sahara, believe to be the ancestor of all extant gemsbok and oryx species, was tamed by the ancient Egyptians for commercial farming. It was recently introduced into game farms in the U.S.A. and into the State of New Mexico where it is roaming freely. The Arabian oryx is confined to the coastal zones of Arabia and Iraq where it has become critically endangered, mostly due to civil warfare.

The Beisa oryx is restricted to Somalia and the lowlands of eastern Ethiopia. The fringe-eared oryx, a subspecies of the Beisa oryx, only occurs in southern Kenya and the northern parts of Tanzania, while the southern gemsbok is widely distributed throughout Botswana, Namibia, southern Zambia and the western and southern regions of South Africa. It has also been introduced into Zimbabwe and the eastern bushveld and savannah areas of South Africa. Introductions into the Eastern Cape Province to the east of longtitude 24°45' E

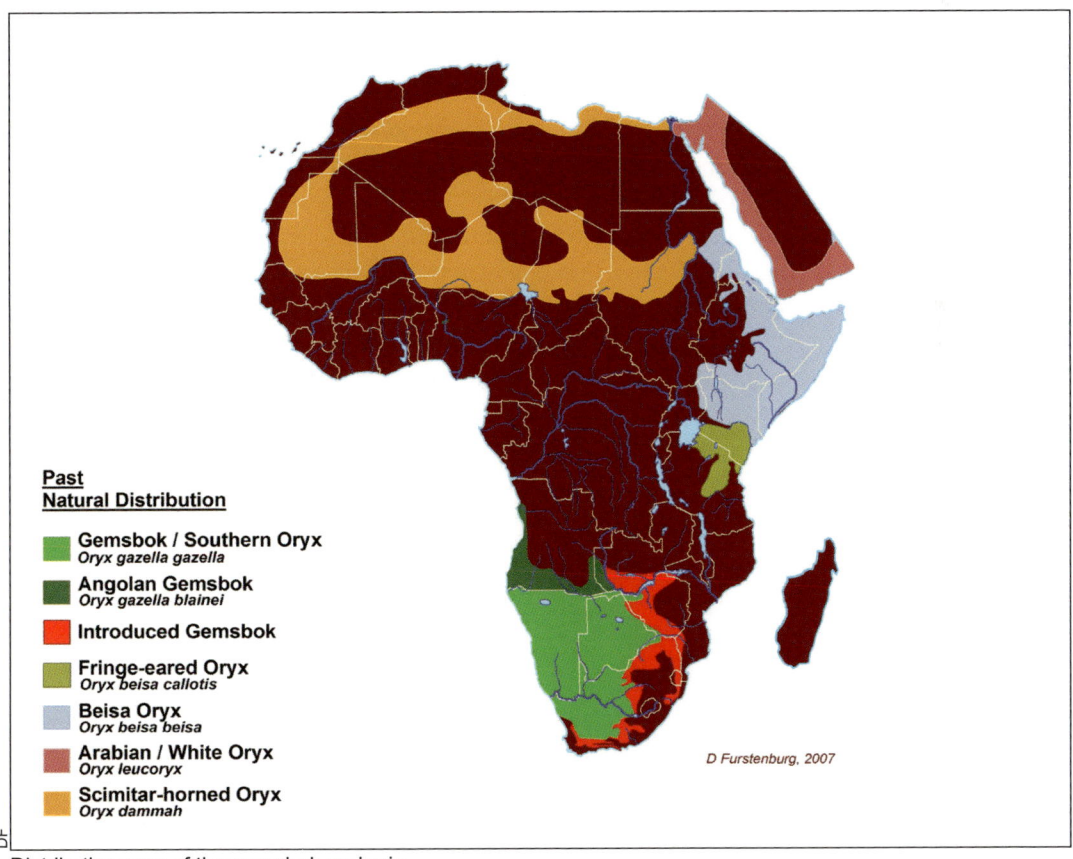

Distribution map of the gemsbok and orix.

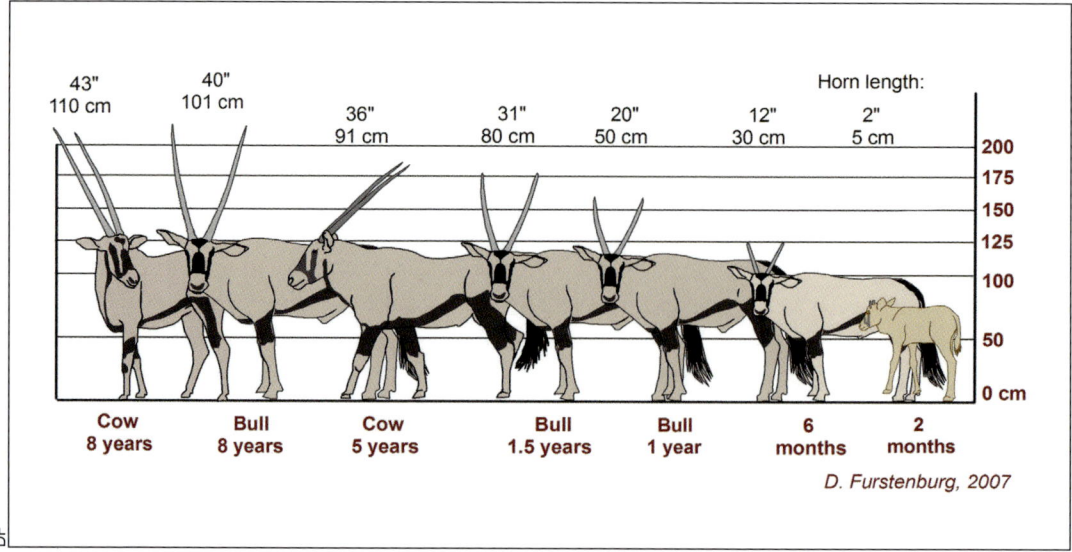
Growth profile of gemsbok with age.

do not do well due to high levels of parasite infections and the cold, wet winter spells. During the drier times of the Pleistocene two million years ago, the distribution ranges of the northern and the southern gemsbok species were probably continuous in Africa but became divided (3 600 km apart) by global climate change. Estimates of the present global gemsbok numbers are 373 000. The overall trend is an increase in gemsbok numbers on private farms, conservancies and protected areas. In Namibia the estimated population increased from 55 000 in 1972 to >164 000 in 1992 and is still increasing.

Rowland Ward records and horn characteristics

Horns are present in both sexes and are long, almost straight and heavily grooved with smooth ends. The cow's horns are longer, thinner and usually narrower with a lesser tip-to-tip width than that of the bull. The best trophies are found in cows rather than bulls and the greatest quality is found in the southern gemsbok. Horn buds appear shortly after birth and reach a length of 2–3 cm at six weeks. The average adult horn length is 38–42" and the Rowland Ward trophy status is reached after 6.5 years in cows and after 8 years in bulls. Gemsbok does not do well in captivity nor in camp systems. Inbreeding in herds and environmental stress in marginal habitats are major problems and as a result deformed horns has become a common phenomenon – this correlates with the slow trend of Rowland Ward top 10 trophies recorded. The gemsbok population is genetically diverse and probably reached its ceiling as far as trophy size is concerned. The Rowland Ward no. 1 (49$\frac{1}{2}$" from Askam in the Northern Cape by S. Marais in 1985) has not been beaten after 30 years

Behaviour

Gemsbok are most active on cool mornings, late afternoons and moonlight nights. They tend to stand in the shade of trees during hot midday hours or, in the absence of shade, limit heat absorption by turning their bodies lengthwise with the rays of the sun. Gemsbok cope with intense heat by raising their body temperature by 4 degrees to 42 °C for up to four-hour periods and thus prevents loss of body fluids in the normal process of evaporation cooling in mammals. The nasal tract and the black

Gemsbok in optimal natural Kalahari habitat.

skin areas are equipped with a network of fine arteries which serve a thermo-regulatory function. Body contact between individuals is rare and gemsbok do not associate readily with other game species. Gemsbok are master crawlers under fences breaking open holes as small as 30 cm by forcing the forequarters through. In Namibia it is general practise not having the bottom strain of cattle fences lower than 30 cm and having fence droppers not driven into the ground but loose, as to allow gemsbok free crawling and movement across larger land area.

Gemsbok are semi-gregarious forming mixed groups of 5–40 individuals that include several territorial bulls as temporarily associates, adult non-lactating cows and subadult cows. Family groups on the other hand consist of 4–12 animals including lactating cows and calves and sometimes a territorial bull. Bachelor herds are 2–7 bulls of all ages and then the solitary territorial bulls. Gemsbok groups are nomadic, wandering long distances across large areas so their home ranges cannot be defined or measured. As they utilise the entire area within the boundaries of fenced land, a minimum land area size of 1 200 ha is recommended. Adult bulls have permanent territories of 420–890 ha that are poorly demarcated, because the boundaries tend to follow morphological terrain structures such as drainage lines, hills, koppies and dunes. Solitary bulls rarely enter another's territory, so fighting between free-roaming bulls is unknown. A bull will occasionally join a mixed group that wanders across several territories and returns to its territory at a later stage. Sometimes bulls intentionally break branches and shrubs with the horns to demonstrate their dominance. Gemsbok have good vision detecting danger from a distance of 2 km. When alerted or threatened, they stand on high slopes or dunes for observation of their surroundings. In bushveld they hide in thickets for months without being spotted. During dry periods the groups tend to split into smaller units that reassemble when conditions become more favourable.

Family bonding is poor and groups are thus unstable with individuals constantly interchanging. In desert habitat gemsbok often sense rain falling far away and migrate towards the new plant growth in aggregations of several hundred animals.

Gemsbok in suitable (slashed) short temperate grassland (Free State) which offers some cover.

Sourveld grass habitat is unsuitable for gemsbok.

Cows only mate with a territorial bull after 2.5 years. Mating takes place any time of the year and a single calf is born after 9 months gestation. The mother hides the young in thicket vegetation or under a bush for 3–6 weeks and returns daily for suckling. The calf is frequently moved between hiding places that can be up to 3 km apart. The calf weans at 3.5 months. In optimal conditions a cow may reproduce every 10 months, five calves in 4 years. Bulls become sexually mature at 1.5–2 years and start mating at 4.5–5 years when they establish territorial status. They remain territorial until 7.5–8 years age when replaced by younger mature males. In the absence of male competition male maturity is extended up to 12 years. Post mature bulls join either bachelor herds or mixed groups.

The natural annual population growth ranges from 5–12% in the marginal habitats of the eastern Cape and the mixed bushveld to 33% in the optimal habitats of Botswana. An optimal habitat of 1 000 ha at 280–300 mm rainfall can sustain 50 gemsbok. In the absence of bull competition the natural mating ratio is one bull to 12 cows. An adult gemsbok animal-unit of 210 kg equals 0.47 Large Stock Units (LSU) multiplied by 65% for its portion of grazing, giving 0.31 LSUs per animal and 0.80 Browser Units (BU) multiplied by 35% for browsing, giving 0.28 BUs per animal.

Habitat and dietary requirements

The natural preferred habitat is dry, karroid scrubland, semi-desert shrub vegetation, arid grassland and semi-arid open savannah such as Kalahari sandveld. Broadleaved short grasses surrounding pans are highly favoured. In the Kalahari sandveld, gemsbok prefer the arid sweet grass on the sand dunes while springbok prefer the dry river beds between the dunes. Their basic needs are a sandy soil, short annual sweet grasses, perennial broadleaved forbs, dwarf shrubs, low density large shrubs and an annual rainfall of 50–300 mm.

Gemsbok only use thicket and closed woodland for refuge against potential danger, bad weather and for hiding young calves. Moist drainage lines especially on alluvial and clay soils, tall grasses and forests are totally avoided.

Gemsbok often roam on steep, dry mountain slopes. They are not dependent on surface drinking water but will drink 4–7 l per day

Breeding camp of good size (800 ha) and suitable habitat in mixed bushveld with a variety of other species.

when available. They do not drink from livestock troughs with raised edges but only at ground level. Gemsbok are mixed feeders of both grass and browse and they consume large quantities of roughage with high fibre content.

During droughts they become highly selective and can destroy the veld by digging up bulbs and roots. The diet generally consists of 70–85% grass and broadleaved forbs and 25–30% browse of low growing shrubs.

Although intermediate grass (8–30 cm high) is frequently grazed, short grasses (2–6 cm) of sweet species are preferred. Mixed veld with a high proportion of sour grasses is marginal, while moist sour veld is entirely unsuitable.

Breeding systems

With large-camp systems (500 ha and greater per camp) more than one breeding family can be stocked provided that the number of adult bulls may at no time be less than three, and if only one breeding family is stocked then only one adult bull, but never two bulls in one camp as it will create fierce fighting.

A similar strategy of rotational stocking in 500 ha camps as illustrated and described for the springbok is recommended (see section

Breeding camp in suitable mixed bush habitat but at 25 ha it is too small.

on Springbok). Gemsbok are not very well suited to small camp systems. They should not be confined to areas less than 50 ha per camp. They should be rotated every 8 months between two 50 ha camps, per breeding herd (one adult bull of 4–10 years age and 20 cows of 3–10 years). The rotation ensures good natural veld condition and minimises the build-up of unwanted parasites.

With small-camp systems the male calves need to be removed from the breeding herds to a separate male camp before reaching 1.5 years to prevent injury from conflict with the adult bull, but not before seven months to allow proper bodily development.

A similar management strategy as illustrated and described for the impala, but with larger 50 ha camp sizes (see section on Impala). In general, gemsbok have a low impact on veld condition but with mismanagement, a lack of surface drinking water and at a high animal density they become destructive, high-impact users that can degrade veld condition dramatically. In Namibia in particular, high densities of gemsbok can be more destructive than cattle.

With camp systems animal movement are restricted, therefore supplement feeding and water need to be provided – a minimum of two water holes per camp and one feeding station per gemsbok group per camp.

The feeding stations should be rotated bi-weekly between 2–3 different locality sites to prevent dung and parasite build-up at the feeding sites. Feeding buckets should be placed in a full circle (not in a line) and 5–7 m apart – one bucket for each animal in the group. The feeding buckets must be moved by 0.5 m with every feeding. Feed must not be placed on the ground.

Feeding stations and water holes must never be closer than 50 m from any fence or infrastructure. In the case of planted pastures in camps, altered sections of the pasture need to be slashed down to a maximum height of 12 cm to provide suitable grazing grounds for gemsbok. Small-camp systems with gemsbok should never be shared with any other game species; in camps larger than 500 ha gemsbok can be combined with other species but separate feeding stations need to be provided.

Diseases and parasites

Gemsbok are adapted to arid environments and are therefore susceptible to tropical diseases such as heartwater. They also lack the grooming behaviour that helps them eliminate external parasites and cannot tolerate high levels of parasite and tick infestations.

Mortalities are seen in the Waterberg area of Limpopo due to *Theileria hippotragi*. Gemsbok do poorly in the Eastern Cape, and subtropical bushveld due to heavy tick loads.

In sourveld areas gemsbok are subject to feeding stress.

Additional information

Comprehensive information on gemsbok biology by the same author is available on E-Book, the
Game Species Window.
www.amazon.com. pp 5001–5324.
Genetic advice on gemsbok breeding: Wildlife Stud Services www.ws2.co.za
Geo Wild Consultants www.geowild.co.za

ROAN ANTELOPE (*Hippotragus equinus*)

Rubin Els

Currently there are five roan subspecies recognised, including *H. equinus equinus*, the species which occurs in South Africa. Their numbers have increased in South Africa from the estimated 150 animals in the 1950s to more than 2 500 animals thanks to breeding programs by private landowners.

Description and biology

Roan are large, shy antelope with a sandy-coloured coat, long ears and black and white markings on the face. Both sexes have backward curving heavily ringed horns which are more robust in the bulls. As they are specialist grazers their natural habitat is savannah woodland with medium to tall, sweet grasses and permanent water sources. Historically their main distribution was in the KNP and Waterberg area of Limpopo, but have been successfully introduced into other areas.

These antelope are extremely habitat sensitive and can be driven from their home range by pressure exerted by other species. According to Frost the precipitous decline seen in numbers of roan in KNP (450 to 60) was due to short grasses replacing long grass. Veld management is therefore extremely important for breeding roan effectively. Roan are one of the most underrated species in Africa. Although they are the second largest antelope after eland, they are not as attention grabbing as sable. However, these beautiful antelope will thrive when given the right food, water, space and attention.

Under natural conditions they occupy large home ranges in order to select suitable grazing areas. They may be driven out of areas if there is too much activity by warthog, impala, zebra or wildebeest. They will return to the area again, when less populated. The males will defend their harems of females against other males and will do so with much vigour. Fights for dominance, can lead to serious injury and sometimes occasionally death.

Roan bull showing the horns and typical black and white mask.

Roan cow in suitable savannah habitat in Thabazimbi-district.

Roan do well in small-camp systems given the correct conditions and nutrition.

Predator fencing may be necessary to protect vulnerable young calves.

Breeding systems

Roan form herds of 8–25 animals, but exceptional groups of up to 80 animals have been recorded. They have a strong social herd structure whereby a matriarch, or dominant cow, rather than the bull, is the leader of the herd. Roan do well in intensive breeding systems, but require meticulous and constant management. The Department of Environmental Affairs stipulates a minimum of 400 ha for free-living herds; camps of 35–50 ha are ideal for precise management.

These small camps should be well rotated at 8–12 months. A sex ratio of one bull to 10–15 cows, is usually ideal, which amounts to a herd size of around 20–30 animals, in the enclosure. If herds are bigger (20–40 cows per bull) and camps are accordingly larger, management of newborn calves becomes increasingly difficult. Reproductive females tend to calve around the same time, so it is a challenge to find and mark (ear tag or microchip) new calves spread over a large surface area.

Calves are normally found and marked within the first three days after birth when they are in hiding and easy to catch. Within five days, they become strong enough to outrun humans and would then need to be immobilised in order to be marked. This is not a recommended practice.

Roan mothers will defend their young vigorously and aggressively against humans especially during capture and marking, and other animals like jackal, caracal, hyena, and even unwary porcupines. Recommended practice with aggressive mothers is to take the calf into the cab of a vehicle closing the doors and windows if necessary! The marking procedure can then be performed, and the calf restored to the mother, from the safe confines of the vehicle. Roan have a gestation period of 280–290 days, or around nine months. Good breeding stock have inter-calving periods of around 10 months. Roan are seasonal breeders, but have been known to reproduce throughout the year, under optimal conditions.

Young bulls must be removed by 12 months to prevent injuries from the breeding bull. Breeding bulls should be rotated every two to three years, to prevent inbreeding with daughters. Alternatively, young heifers should be removed from the herd within 18 months after birth. Roan do not tolerate newcomers. Once a herd is bonded, it is extremely risky to add any animals to the herd.

A new group can be bonded into a family unit by darting (chemical immobilisation) the individuals and then waking them up all together, into a new camp which is therefore neutral territory. A small holding facility, within

Feed bowls are filled from outside the fence minimising human contact.

Hay is placed in feed racks from a vehicle.

a breeding camp, works exceptionally well. The newly formed group is then left together for about four weeks. Due to the stresses imposed on them by the immobilisation process, and the relocation to a new area, amongst strange animals, they will be forced to find security in each other's company. Once the group is securely bonded as a unit, they can be released into the breeding camp, or extensive area.

Feeding

Provide individual feeding bowls for pellets or game cubes, rather than communal bowls and these should preferably be elevated from the ground. These bowls can be cleaned and sterilised regularly to maintain hygiene. A rule of thumb is 1–2 kg of this feed per animal per day, depending on the size and reproductive stage of the animal. Larger animals and adult cows with suckling young, need more than young animals, especially during the cold and dry months.

Providing supplementary feed, before sunset, in cold winter months, assists greatly in providing energy to generate heat in combatting night and early morning cold. Grass and lucerne supplement feed can be provided in communal hay racks, or similar feeding troughs, preferably raised from the ground. Always ensure the availability of sufficient, high quality grass, in natural grazing, or dry hay form. Lucerne hay is a valuable supplement but should rather not exceed a ratio of 50% to grass. Grass should not be limited, but provided in sufficient quantities at all times. Long fibre in natural grass (not refined through a mill), provides a natural barrier against internal parasites.

Supplementary feed (especially a tasty antelope cube or lucerne) is an exceptionally powerful management tool. Roan accustomed to feed can be manipulated for various management reasons, such as luring them into rotational grazing areas or capture systems. They are easily monitored at feeding points, and this facilitates data recording. External parasite loads, injuries, body indexes, udder health and condition analysis of suckling mothers, as well as a multitude of other observations can be made at feeding stations.

Roan will take phosphate and protein licks after some perseverance because they are averse to strange scents. They enjoy salt licks, but salt should preferably be added in proportional balance in licks, which supply trace elements and minerals as well. Sudden changes (especially dry and brown to green) or a sudden increase in protein levels will cause the condition "red gut" which can wipe out a whole herd. Ensure that drinking troughs are cleaned weekly, or even daily, if possible.

A management system which uses stainless steel or cement bowls along the fence allows for constant monitoring of the animals.

Common health problems

Roan antelope are susceptible to a multitude of diseases, the most common being pneumonia especially after transport or handling, redwater, laminitis as a result of excess concentrate feeds, red gut and damage due to tick bites. Infection by *Theileria hippotragi* is the cause of mortalities of calves under six months. It is transmitted by red-legged ticks (*Rhipicephalus evertsi*).

Any stress conditions such as infection, malnutrition, physical injury, pain, weaning or social stress may trigger cases in all roan of all ages. The cases are usually fatal as there is no specific treatment (see Sable antelope and Chapter 5 for more discussion on prevention of *T. hippotragi*). Roan are very susceptible to anthrax, especially when drought causes exposure of the anthrax spores. Roan can be vaccinated for anthrax and clostridial diseases.

Predation by caracal, jackal and hyena can be a problem, so predator proofing of small camps may be necessary.

In some areas roan calves may develop *Theileria hippotragi* infections but develop immunity after a few months of age.

SABLE ANTELOPE
(*Hippotragus niger*)

Deon Furstenburg

Young Zambian sable bulls.

Speciation

The genus *Hippotragus* contains three species:
- *Hippotragus leucophaeus*, the extinct Cape blue buck.
- *H. equinus*, the roan antelope.
- *H. niger* the sable antelope.

Four sable subspecies are recognised:
- *H. n. niger*, the southern sable antelope found in southern Africa, Zambia, Zimbabwe and southern Tanzania.
- *H. n. variani*, the giant or royal sable of central Angola.
- *H. n. kirkii*, found in Tanzania and central Africa to the west of the Rift Valley.
- *H. n. roosevelti*, the eastern sable antelope of Tanzania and Kenya to the east of the Rift Valley.

As with many other African game species, the speciation of the sable antelope is in dispute which affects both its commercial market value as well as its conservation status as implemented by governmental legislation.

The present-day sable population shows a tripartite pattern of genetic subdivision representing West Tanzanian, Kenya/East Tanzanian and Southern African locations (Pitra *et al*, 2002). Past allopatric fragmentation, caused probably by habitat discontinuities associated with the East African Rift Valley system and global climate changes, together with intermediary episodic long-distance colonisation and restricted, recurrent gene flow have resulted in the present sable-genome which encompasses a 10.4% genetic variation between the different present sable populations.

An extensive, but geographically circumscribed and unidirectional hybridisation event in the past resulted in an extreme intraspecific admixture difference of 18.2% among morphologically monotypic sable antelopes from West Tanzania (Pitra *et al*, 2002; Vaz Pinto *et al*, 2015). The genetic studies by Robinson & Harley (1995) do not provide conclusive evidence of the subspeciation of sable to the south of Tanzania. Pitra *et al.* (2006) question the legitimacy of subspecies status of the giant sable, with the most closely related sable individuals found in central Tanzania, some 2 000 km apart.

Despite the taxonomic dispute the present sable phenotypes namely the giant sable, the West Zambian sable, the East Zambian sable, the Matetsi/Southern sable and the East African sable have definite differences in socio-economic market value (the name Matetsi is derived from a rural village in the northwest of Zimbabwe). The giant sable is undoubtedly a flagship species for conservation initiatives, also being the national symbol of the Angolan natural heritage.

IUCN Conservation Status
- Southern sable: Lower Risk, conservation dependent (LR/cd)
- Zambian sable: Vulnerable (VU)
- Giant sable: Critically endangered (CR/en)
- Eastern sable: Endangered (EN)

Southern sable bulls.

Charlie – the sable with horns of over 1 m in length.

Current distribution and numbers

Until the 1950s when their numbers fell to less than 800, the southern sable's distribution was restricted to subtropical woodland savannah. Extinction of the species was prevented by a major relocation carried out by the S.A. National Parks Board and the S.A. Department of Nature Conservation during the 1970s. By 1976, sable numbers were restored to 1 200 in the Kruger National Park, and by 1983 to 2 060, with an additional 1 300 outside of the Park. More recent numbers are the 1999 estimate of 75 000 global population, between 200 and 400 giant sable in 2007 and the current IUCN Red Data List estimate of 54 000.

As a result of dwindling numbers sable antelope suffered a severe lack of genetic diversity which reduced their quality and trophy size. This has been addressed by breeding programs such as the Gravelotte Sable Study Group

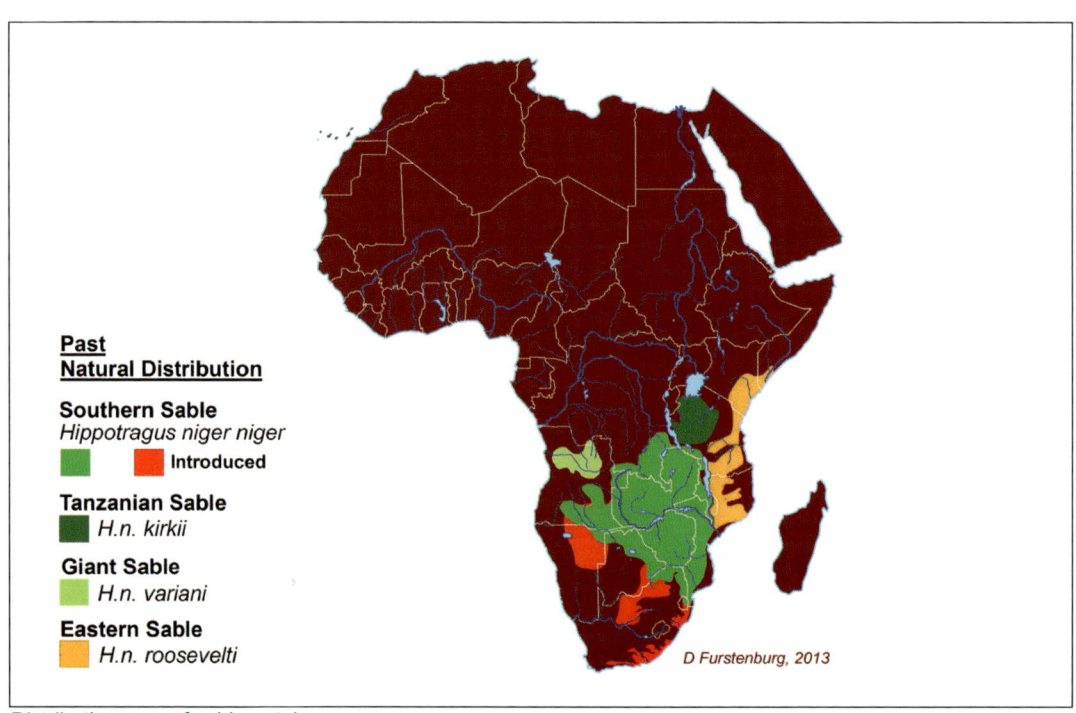
Distribution map of sable antelope.

and its members to restore the former genetic quality of the sable antelope by enforced cross-breeding. This has been successful as in August 2012 a sable named Charlie, bred by Mr Piet Warren, measuring horn length 50.25" (1.26 m) was auctioned at a record price of R12.2 million. The exponential increase in prices of sable reflects the demand for good quality animals, both as hunting trophies but also for stocking of game farms for breeding and game reserves for ecotourism.

Rowland Ward records and horn characteristics

Because of the popularity of sable as trophies there is great interest and focus on horn length, quality, growth and genetics. The Rowland Ward record trophy (55$^{3/8}$") was a southern sable hunted in 1989 at Tshokwane in the Lowveld (SA) and not from a giant sable.

Pre-1900 average hunted trophy size = 44.22", 1900–1924 = 47.12", 1925–1949 = 45.77", 1950–1974 = 44.44", 1975–1999 = 44.40" and 2000–2015 = 42.75" – in other words there was roughly a 10% deterioration in average horn length over the last 100 years

Table 1: Geographic distribution of Rowland Ward (RW) trophies (adapted from Rabie, 2011)

Rated	Country	Number of RW trophies	Avg. trophy length
1	Zambia	338	45.76"
2	Namibia	8	45.30"
3	Malawi	6	45.08"
4	Zaïre	13	44.90"
5	South-Africa	41	44.82"
6	Zimbabwe	348	44.27"
7	Botswana	189	44.22"
8	Tanzania	92	43.94"
9	Angola	88	43.80"
10	Mozambique	13	43.80"
11	Unknown	23	

(Rabie, 2011). The quality of the southern sable population in South Africa declined from the Rowland Ward number one to fifth ranked in 2011 (Table 1).

The horns of sable grow vertically from the skull for the first third of the length and then turn backwards to form a long curve of

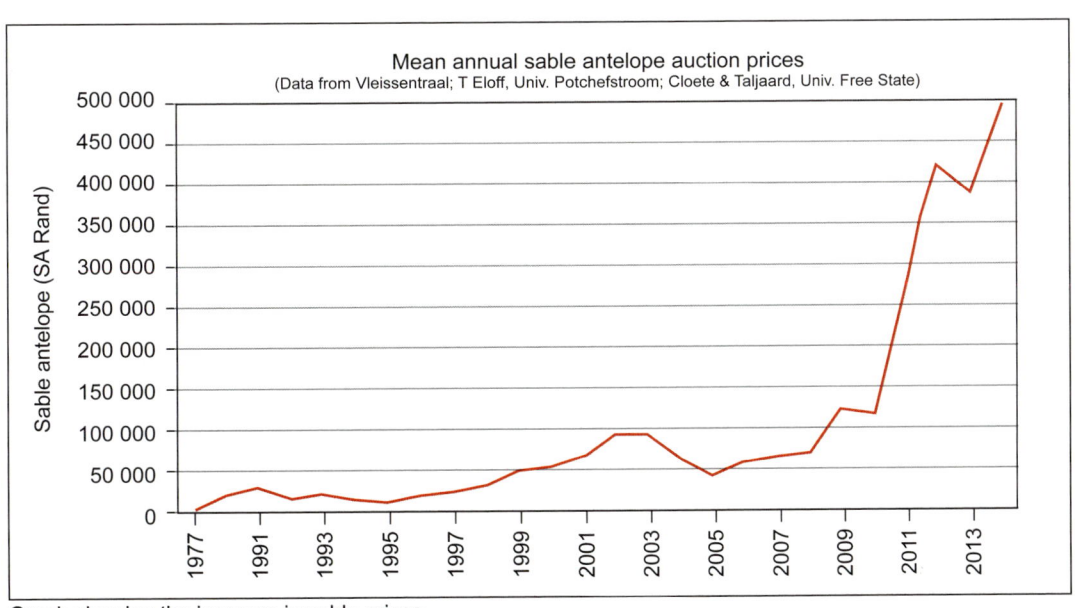

Graph showing the increase in sable prices.

Table 2: Performance of young sable bulls in terms of horn growth rate (Rabie, 2011)

Age	Below–average			Average			Above-average		
Months	mm/day	min length	max length	mm/day	min length	max length	mm/day	min length	max length
0-12	0.8	-	11.3"	0.9	-	13"	0.95	-	13.5"
13-18	0.9	12.8"	19.1"	1.0	14.2"	21"	1.05	14.9"	22.3"
19-30	0.8	17"	28.3"	0.9	19.2"	32"	0.95	20.2"	33.7"
31-42	0.7	24.8"	34.7"	0.8	28.4"	39.7"	0.85	30.2"	42.2"
43-48	0.65	32.3"	36.9"	0.75	37.2"	42.5"	0.8	39.7"	45.4"
0-48	0.72	-	40.8"	0.82	-	46"	0.85	-	48.2"
Adult			42"			47"			50"

85-110°. They are heavily grooved for 85% of the length and have smooth tips. Generally, the first grooves begin to show at an age of two years. Poor forage quality and social stress may limit horn development in some environments.

The Gravelotte Sable Study Group has developed a benchmark standard for the quality of breeding sable (Rabie, 2011):

- Coat colour – A glossy light-brown or red-brown are preferred for adult females, and glossy dark auburn to jet black for adult males. Females tend to become progressively darker during pregnancy (less fertile females tend to be lighter in colour).
- Testicles of bulls should be evenly sized and with a scrotum circumference of 22–26 cm.
- Genetic value % index for female horn length: 24" = 0%, 25" = 5%, 26" = 10%, 27" = 25%, 28" = 40%, 29" = 50%, 30" = 60%, 31" =70%, 32" = 85%, **33" = 100%**, 34" = 120%, 35" = 150%, 36" = 200%, 37" = 220%.
- Horn apex length (smooth area between the first ring and the horn tip); the longer the apex the greater the quality. For bulls the apex should be a minimum of 20 cm, preferably longer than 25 cm.
- Horn curve: The less the curve of females the greater the quality; for bulls the higher upward, the straight before curving backwards the greater the quality.
- Horn cross section should be round in heifers younger than 5 years. Female horns longer than 32" tend to become oval in cross-section; for bulls the cross-section should be oval and for an adult bull the cross-section should measure 80 x 45 mm at the 20th ring.
- Space between the rings; the further apart the greater the quality.
- Rings should preferably be shallow and smooth, rather than deep and well defined.
- Circumference at the horn base should be 15–17 cm for adult females and a minimum of 9.5" (23.7 cm)–11" (27.94 cm).
- Tip-to-tip horn-measurement of outstanding bulls is greater than 14.9" and up to 30".
- Horn length of breeding bulls should be a minimum of 43".
- The longer the horn the better the quality, given the performance ability of the animal is also good.
- When selecting young bulls, the horn growth rate up to the age of 28 months is crucial (Table 2).

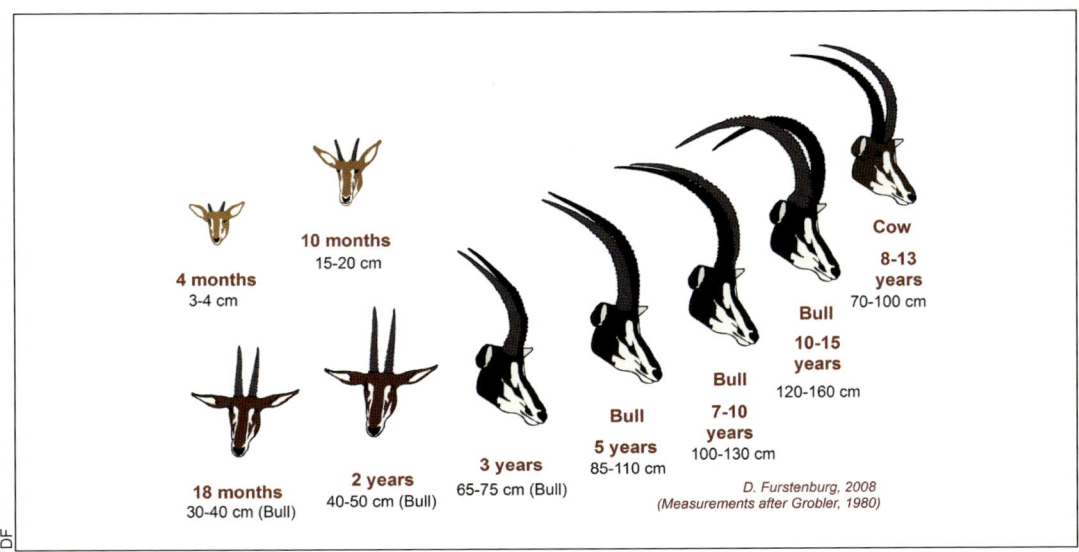
Sable antelope trophy development

Behaviour

The natural home ranges of sable family herds and bachelor bulls vary from 200–400 ha; the ranges of adjacent herds rarely overlap each another and dominant adult bulls are strictly territorial during the rutting season, aggressively defending a temporary territory of 25–40 ha. They form stable family groups of 6–40 individuals with a mean of 14. Matriarchal systems are maintained with a strict hierarchical order of aggressive female dominance; cohesion between family members is tight and females may bond for life.

Heifers become sexually mature at two years and mate at 2.5 years; young bulls reach sexual maturity at three years and are then aggressively expelled from the herd by the dominant bull. Under free-range conditions during the mating season from May to July, a dominant bull of >6 years will mate with 2–5 adult cows of >2.5 years. Calves are weaned after 8 months and generally reach a mature mass of 200 kg at 6 years. The natural population density in an optimal habitat with an annual rainfall of 400–500 mm, is five sable per 100 ha; densities of 9 per 100 ha increases the risk of increased aggression between adult bulls and towards other animal species. Sable are inactive at night when they shelter under the canopy of trees.

Habitat and dietary requirements

Sable antelope have highly specific natural habitat requirements. They prefer abundant stands of dense, intermediate to tall grasses 45–150 cm high of both sweet and sour species, as found in mixed veld, open savannah woodland with scattered large trees and a lower stratum of moderately dense shrubland (400 to 600 trees per hectare; 40% tree and shrub canopy cover at 0–2 m height, 20% at >2–3 m, 5–8% at >3–4 m and 10% at >4 m, flat to slightly undulating topography. The soils in preferred areas are drained, dry, and sandy and are usually derived from granite and quartzite.

The animals need clean surface drinking water for daily consumption (within 1 km roaming radius). Sable will avoid open grassy plains and short grass, having a preference for the tall grass ecotones found surrounding termite mounds and along seepage lines at the foot of hills and koppies. Sable are very susceptible to the deterioration of veld during

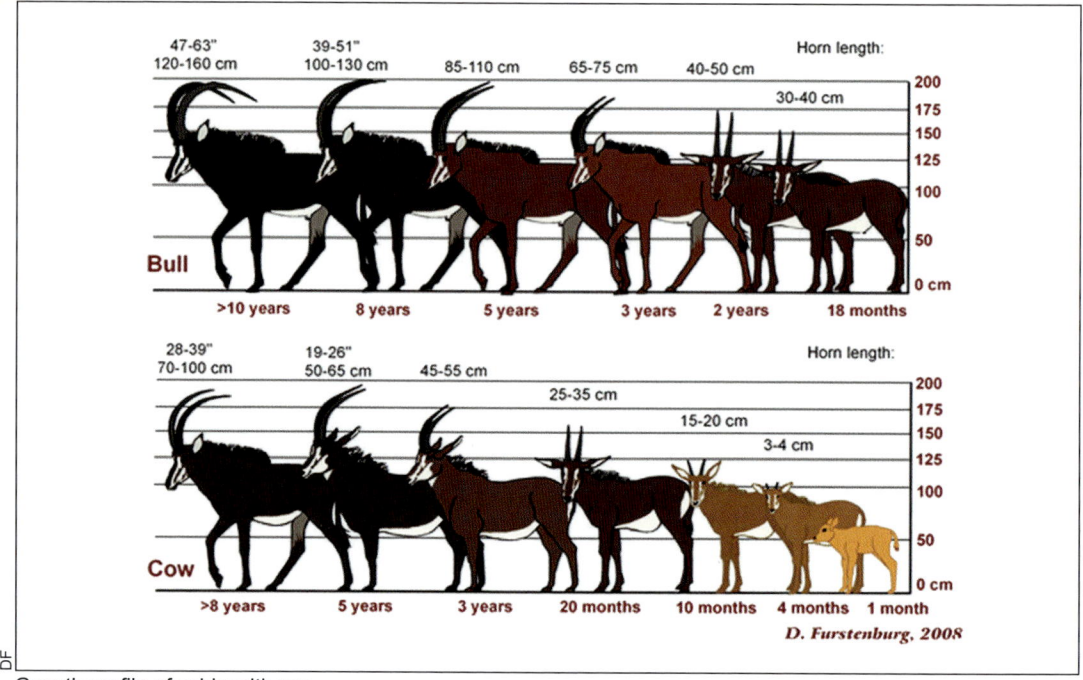
Growth profile of sable with age.

droughts. They are also intolerant of severe cold so they need patches of thicket vegetation in which they can shelter against cold and the wind chill factor. An adult sable is equivalent to 0.6 large stock grazing units (LSU), multiplied by a grazing ratio of 85% of its diet, which computes to 0.51 LSUs per animal, and 1.45 browse units (BU), multiplied by a browsing ratio of 15% of its diet which computes to 0.22 BUs per animal.

Sable teeth wear rapidly after 10 years and many sable die after 13 years from starvation as their molars are worn down to the gums and therefore non-functional. Supplemental feeding is essential in a marginal habitat during the dry winter months.

Breeding systems

Small-camp production systems for sable should be designed to eliminate male competition, optimise female reproduction, increase fecundity and eliminate mortality. In an optimal habitat which does not require daily supplementary feeding, the size of breeding camps should be no less than 80 ha (or preferably two camps of 50 ha each, rotational stocking), while in marginal habitats such as the Kalahari, a minimum size of 200 ha is advised.

The minimum camp sizes should always be in terms with the territorial needs of the animal, being 25–40 ha. A minimum single camp size of 40 ha, or a rotational system of two 30 ha camps per breeding herd is recommended in which animals are rotated between the camps at eight month intervals (the camps are rested for eight months). Camp sizes of 15 ha units or less are unsuitable.

The soil in small-camp systems must always be well drained and dry because sable are highly susceptible to endo-parasites and coccidia which thrive in damp conditions. The camps should not adjoin marshland, floodplains, drainage lines and foothills which are subject to inundation. Endoparasites are also a problem when camps are situated on southern mountain slopes and in areas with greater than 600 mm annual rainfall.

Individual breeding camps should not share fences but should be at least 10 m (preferably 20-30 m) apart or double fenced in order to prevent social stress between the dominant bulls. Alternatively, breeding camps may be alternated with other game species such as roan, tsessebe and red hartebeest.

Natural mating ratios are a maximum of five cows per bull and family sizes are on average 14 (all ages included); breeding camp stocking ratios should therefore not exceed 20 cows per bull, the optimum being 15 cows per bull. Animals in good condition and of superior genetic quality and reproductive potential should be constantly selected for breeding, and inferior animals removed. Non-breeding animals must be kept in separate camps for harvesting. All new-borns should be hand-caught several hours after birth, when they are hidden by the females in grass thickets. They can then be marked and treated preventatively for disease conditions (see Theileriosis in Chapter 5).

Calves wean naturally at eight months and inter-calving period is 12 months. All male calves must be removed soon after weaning to an alternative holding camp to prevent injury from the breeding bull. Some owners tend to remove calves from the mothers as early as six months old to reduce the inter-calving period and induce sooner mating, but this can reduce the cow's body condition, and is not recommended.

Some breeders tend to rotate breeding bulls between families/camps for genetic management but this must be done with caution as some bulls may kill females when moved between families. Due to the strict family bonding and hierarchy of females, introducing new members into family groups is difficult. The matriarch may attack newly introduced strangers. When introducing a breeding bull to an existing family it is best to move the whole family to a new camp where the new bull is then introduced, as this focuses the attention on the new environment. The same tactic can be used for introducing new females or otherwise they can be kept in an adjacent camp, and fed next to the separating fence. When darting sable cows in a small-camp system it is best to first dart the breeding bull as he often attacks drugged females during an operation.

Suitable camp habitat for sable.

Genetic quality management involves a complicated and strict protocol of crossbreeding of offspring between two breeding herds and periodic exchange of breeding bull material. For advice on genetic improvement of sable see the note at the end of the chapter.

Supplementary feeding becomes essential on veld with an annual rainfall of below 400 mm, as well as in small camp systems. The animals must be gradually introduced to the new food source over a few weeks and the daily requirement must not be exceeded to prevent the development of problems. Sable must consume a portion of crude fibre in the diet to maintain proper rumen digestion functioning. Therefore it is crucial for any supplement pellet feeding to also include sufficient crude fibre so a wildlife nutritionist should be consulted.

Dried lucerne can be fed in small quantities as roughage. Feeding stations need to be moved fortnightly in order to prevent a build-up of endo-parasites in the vicinity. Each camp must be equipped with at least two drinking points, small concrete hollows with their edges at ground level. These drinking holes must be cleaned weekly as clean water is essential. Supplement feed must be provided in single

Unsuitable grazing and camps.

Catching and tagging newborn sable.

buckets (one bucket per animal) placed in a large circle (never in a straight line) at least five meters apart to avoid social interaction and ensure even consumption. Buckets must be moved daily at least one meter to prevent parasite build-up. Feed must never be placed on the ground as soil can be ingested causing colic and impaction.

Diseases and parasites

In contrast to the roan antelope (*Hippotragus equinus*) of the same genus, the sable antelope is rarely infected by anthrax. However, they are susceptible to a number of other infections and conditions. Intensively raised sable calves are susceptible to *Theileria hippotragi*, a tick borne condition. Since there is no registered drug for the treatment of this condition control is aimed at the tick vector: Experts recommend moving cows to camps which have been rested for 18 months, or treating newborns with pour-ons until they are over two months of age (see Theileriosis in Chapter 5).

Young sable kept in bomas are prone to developing intestinal coccidiosis which can be prevented with good hygiene or treated on the advice of a veterinarian. Another potentially serious problem which arises in small breeding camps is the wireworm (*Haemonchus*, see Chapter 5 for discussion and control).

Outbreaks of brucellosis have been seen in sable herds due to contact with infected livestock (see Brucellosis in Chapter 5 for discussion and control). Clostridial myositis (sponssiekte) has caused several sable die-offs.

Sable are prone to pneumonia which develops when they are subjected to nutritional stress and chilling as a result of drenching. They are also susceptible to frostbite in the marginal habitats of the cold, frosty areas of South Africa and ear tips, nostrils and the outer tissue of the lips can be destroyed. This does not kill the animal but causes permanent scars that reduce the animal's trophy status and commercial value. In habitats such as the central regions of the Eastern Cape Midlands where the diet lacks sufficient trace metals such as copper, the hide colour fades from dark brown or black to a dirty yellow-white, which reduces the animal's commercial market value. Copper deficiency can be treated by administering a mineral supplement.

Sicklebush (*Dichrostachys cinerea*) has formidable thorns which can cause severe hoof injuries in sable as well as other species such as roan and nyala, so when bush clearing is done the branches must be collected into piles rather than leaving them scattered on the ground.

Additional information

Comprehensive information on sable biology by the same author is available on E-Book, the *Game Species Window*. www.amazon.com. pp 12541-12887. Genetic advice on sable breeding: Geo Wild Consultants www.geowild.co.za or Wildlife Stud Services www.ws2.co.za).

TRAGELAPHINES (SPIRAL-HORNED ANTELOPE)
- Eland
- Kudu
- Nyala

ELAND (*Tragelaphus oryx*)
Deon Furstenburg

Speciation

The eland is the largest African antelope and its name has its origins in the Dutch word "eland" meaning elk. Numerous investigators have explored the possibilities of domesticating the eland as it is large, has a high reproductive rate, is easily tamed and not dependent on water sources. However, under natural farming conditions eland have proved inferior to cattle due to their spatial requirements and their social hierarchy. Eland were originally classified in a separate genus *Taurotragus*, but taxonomists recently placed them in the genus *Tragelaphus* based upon evidence of hybridisation with the greater kudu (*Tragelaphus strepsiceros*) and the sitatunga (*T. speckii*), as well as mitochondrial DNA studies and allozyme analysis. There are two species in the genus *Tragelaphus*:
- ***Tragelaphus derbianus*** – the giant or Lord Derby's eland that is confined to the northern savannah regions with two subspecies:
  - *T. d. gigas* to the east of the distribution range.
  - *T. d. derbianus* to the west.
- ***Tragelaphus oryx*** – throughout the southern savannah regions with three recognised subspecies (phenotype colour variants):
  - *T. o. oryx*, the Cape or southern eland.
  - *T. o. livingstonii*, Livingstone's eland.
  - *T. o. pattersonianus*, the East African or Patterson eland.

Recent genetic studies indicate these subspecies are phenotypic differences, being only colour variants of the Cape eland. As for the sable antelope and the buffalo the genetic variation within localised populations is great and the genomic difference between the three different eland phenotypes (colour variants) is too small to be considered subspecies.

The typical form is the Cape eland of South Africa which has no stripes. In northern Botswana, Zimbabwe and southern Mozambique, hybrids and crossbreeds between the southern Cape and Livingstone's eland have 1–5 vertical body stripes.

IUCN Conservation Status
- Cape eland: Lower Risk, Least concern (LR/lc).
- Western Lord Derby eland: Critically Endangered (CE).
- Eastern Lord Derby eland: Endangered (EN).

Cape eland bull.

Lord Derby eland bull.

Livingstone's eland have 6–12 vertical white stripes, 9–12 mm wide on the flanks but lack the prominent, dark brown marking on the forelegs. East African eland are rufous-fawn with 8–14 narrow stripes, 4–8 mm wide down the flank and a white chevron above the eyes on the forehead. The Lord Derby has 8–16 stripes, 4–8 mm wide.

Hybrids of the southern Cape eland and the East African eland which have the same rufous colouring but are without stripes are common where distributions overlap. Lord Derby's eland have a rich terracotta, reddish-brown to chestnut colour with 8–12 narrow stripes, a distinct dark brown to black blaze around the bottom half of the neck and a short black mane stretching down the neck to the middle of the back. The east African eland is more reddish in colour and has a distinctive black mane down the spine and below the belly.

Translocations throughout southern Africa have probably caused phenotype mixing. The lack of stripes on some eland in central east Africa may be due to the hybridisation accompanying overlapping distributions. Adult Cape eland cows have a mass of 400–560 kg and a mean shoulder height of 150 cm, compared to adult bulls at 650–940 kg and a shoulder height of 160–180 cm. The forequarters of the body are notably larger and heavier than the hind and as a result, the front feet are larger. A large dewlap descends from the throat of adult bulls. Eland are much smaller in the Drakensberg Mountains of KwaZulu-Natal where the males only reach a maximum mass of 500 kg. The difference in size is the result of poorer nutrition and greater energy expenditure required in this habitat.

Male eland and female greater kudu can produce a viable male hybrid, though it is not known if it is sterile. A crossing of an east African eland (*T. o. pattersonianus*) with an east African kudu (*T. s. bea*) in the San Diego Zoo Safari Park proved to be sterile.

Current distribution and numbers

Eland have a wide distribution in Africa with the giant or Lord Derby eland inhabiting the Sahel from the far west through to Cameroon and southwestern Sudan. The distribution of the common eland stretches from eastern Sudan, Ethiopia and Somalia to the savannahs of central east Africa and down to the Cape Peninsula. Total numbers are estimated at 136 000, about 50% of which occur in protected areas and 30% on private land. Population trends are varied in protected areas, increasing on private land and decreasing elsewhere (20%). Population density estimates obtained by aerial counts in areas where the species is moderately common and generally range from about 0.05–0.4/km². Higher density estimates (0.6–1.0/km²) have been obtained in some areas.

Lord Derby eland cow.

Rowland Ward (Charl Kemp, 2011).

Rowland Ward records and horn characteristics

The growth tips of horns can be seen 10 mm above the coat at birth. Both sexes carry slightly diverging, straight horns that are smooth and lie in a flat triangle when viewed in cross section. They have a keel-like ridge on the anterior and posterior edges that turn like the thread of a screw towards the tip, forming two tight twists of a spiral. At 15 months the first signs of the spiral become evident at the horn base, with a length of 70 cm being reached at 18 months for cows. The horns of cows are longer and thinner than those of the males. They thicken and become progressively heavier with age.

The Rowland Ward minimum trophy quality of 35" may be reached after 3.5 years for cows and for bulls only after 10 years. Genetic diversity of eland is good and there has been an increase in trophy quality: No. 1 in 2014 (47$\frac{1}{2}$", SW Pienaar), no. 2 in 2011 (46$\frac{3}{4}$", Charl Kemp, Grootfontein, Namibia) and no 3. in 2005 (46$\frac{1}{4}$", F.J. Weyers, Thabazimbi, Limpopo).

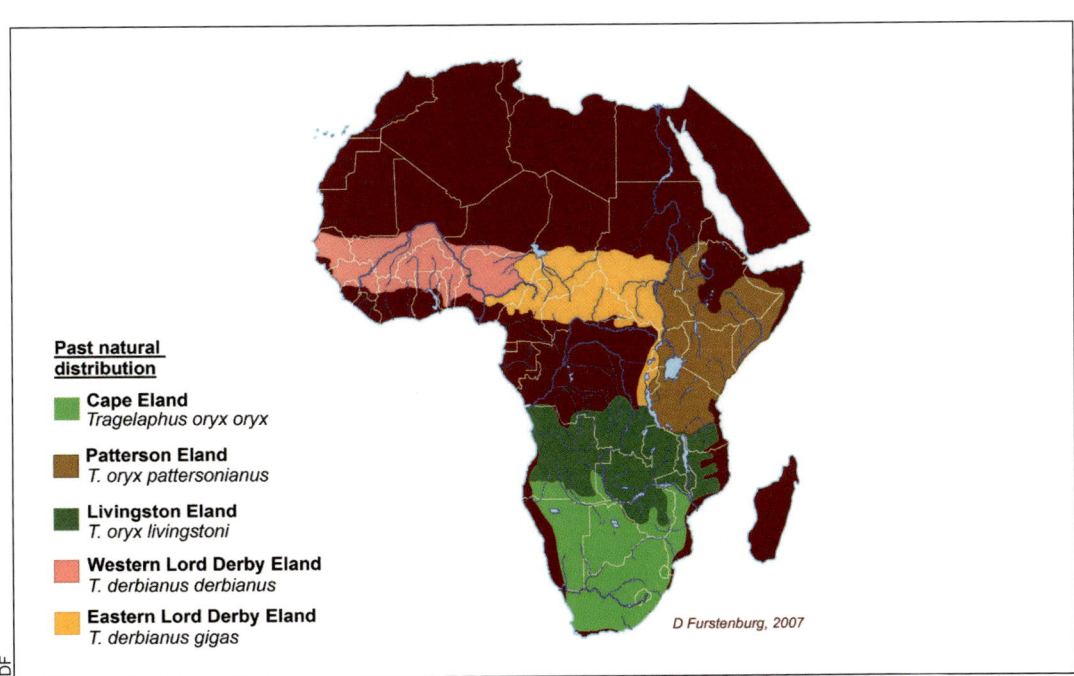
Distribution map of the eland.

Table 3.

Mean age related growth rate for the Cape eland					
Age)	Shoulder height (cm)		Live body mass (kg)		Horn length (cm)
	Cow	Bull	Cow	Bull	
Birth	45	55	25	32	1
1 month	65	75	52	56	3–4
3 months	90	110	85	93	10–15
6 months	108	137	155	165	25–38
9 months	120	140	165	182	30–50
1 year	135	157	207	224	37–65
2 years	140	160	300	326	40–70
3 years	145	164	350	474	45–80
4 years	148	167	410	650	50–90
5 years	150	170	450	740	55–100
6 years	150	170	460	780	60–110

Behaviour

The Cape eland are diurnal and are most active in the morning and late afternoon, while Lord Derby eland are predominantly nocturnal, lying under cover during the day. Adult bulls will give a lively display of aggression, but fighting and bodily contact rarely occur in nature. Eland are generally shy animals but can be tamed. A fence height of 1.5 m are easily cleared but 1.8–2 m height can be jumped breaking the top strands with the drag of the hind feet. They are nomadic, migratory animals without fixed home ranges, usually occurring in small groups and move several hundred kilometers per year seeking quality food. On game ranches eland generally roam the entire area irrespective of its size and cross all the habitat types.

Eland adapt well to smaller environments but require supplementary feeding. In the absence of supplements, eland should not be kept on land units smaller than 3 000 ha. Under favourable conditions, such as on grass plains, very large herds of 300–1 000 animals occur consisting of satellite family groups of 15–50 animals. During the calving season the females form nursing groups that include yearling subadults. At the end of the season adult bulls rejoin the family herds and remain until the start of the next calving season, when they break away. The bulls maintain a strict hierarchy of dominance while they are in the family herd. Young, non-breeding bulls of 2.5–5 years form bachelor groups of 5–10 individuals and adult bulls form small herds of 3–6 individuals outside of the mating season.

Natural sex ratio is one adult bull per 8–12 mature cows. Mating occurs throughout the year but shows a slight peak in summer from November to March. The gestation period is nine months, calves being born throughout the year with a peak in summer. Cows give birth to their first calf at 30–42 months. A cow can produce 10–13 calves in her expected lifespan of 14–18 years. The calf follows the mother and the herd within four hours, forming a crèche with others within the herd. Lost calves have little chance of survival, as cows do not

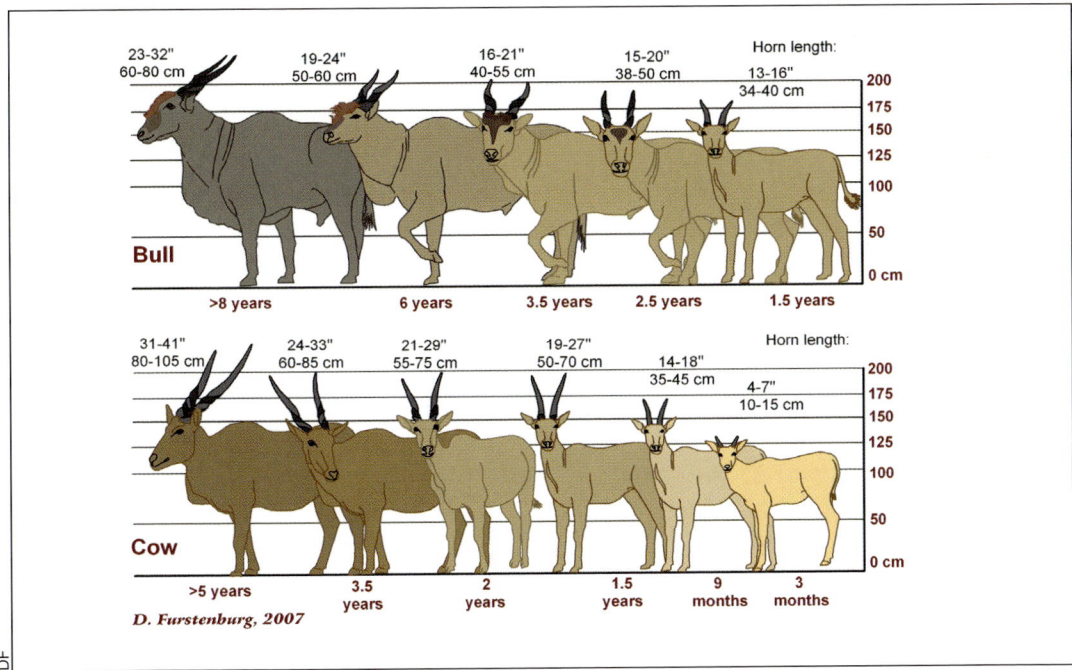

Growth profile of eland with age.

act as surrogate mothers. Calves start to feed on vegetative matter at one month and are weaned after four months. The adult body size is reached at five years.

Survival of calves in nature is low: 33% in Kenya, 34% in the Drakensberg and 68–79% in captivity. In the absence of large predators on the eastern Highveld of Mpumalanga, the survival rate of year-old calves is 84%. Average natural, annual population growth varies from 11 to 38% depending upon rainfall, veld condition, and predation pressure and population density.

Recommended stocking density is 27.5 ha/animal at 400 mm, 22 ha per eland in optimal habitats at an annual rainfall of 450–550 mm, and 21.3 ha/animal at 650 mm. The large stock equivalent of an adult eland cow is 0.8 with 2.1 browser units (BUs) and up to 2.0 LSUs and 4.6 BUs for a bull, depending on the size of the animal. A minimum of 3 000 ha of natural feeding is required to meet the dietary and spatial needs of an eland.

Habitat and dietary requirements

Cape eland utilise a wide variety of habitats including Kalahari sandveld, most of the semi-arid regions of Namibia, Namaqualand, Karoo succulent scrubveld, southern subtropical savannah bushveld, Eastern Cape valley bushveld thickets, highveld sour grassland and Cape fynbos. They are equally at home in semi-desert scrubveld as in woodland, bushveld and montane grassland and do well on plains grassland and the outskirts of marshlands and estuaries in coastal areas.

Eland are found at areas with annual rainfall of 250–1 200 mm and at altitudes from sea level in the Eastern Cape, to 1 800 m in the montane grasslands of Zimbabwe, and 4 000 m in eastern Africa. They are not water dependent but will drink regularly if available. Kloofs and bush thickets are an important form of shelter against rain and the winter cold, especially in mountainous areas. Eland can tolerate light snowfall and temperatures to -6 °C but only for

Cape eland in optimum sweet, open bushveld habitat.

Cape eland in marginal Karoo veld in the Oudstshoorn district.

short periods of 2–3 days, after which time they move downhill to sheltered kloofs. In contrast to the Cape eland, Lord Derby eland are predominantly associated with denser, wooded habitats with more shade. Eland require food with high protein content as they have high metabolic rates, a narrow thermal neutral zone and lose large quantities of urea in their urine. As a result, they need alternative resources in different seasons. They are mixed feeders that can switch from browse to graze when the grass becomes green and rich in protein and *vice versa*. Eland are able to adapt to various grassland habitats including montane grassland of the Drakensberg. Congregations of 40–300 animals occur on grass plains but they scatter into smaller groups of 3–20 animals in bushveld areas. Grass always forms more than 33% of the dietary intake at any time of the year, but can be as high as 92%. Eland will graze on short to medium height grass (6–35 cm) of both sweet and sour species. They favour burnt areas and are often the first animals to move to new grass growth on recently burnt veld.

Highest nutritional stress occurs during late winter (cold dry season) and coincides with advanced pregnancy. This emphasises the importance of allowing eland to roam in areas of a sufficient size to meet their requirements of a protein rich diet. This diet consists of a wide variety of plant species including trees and shrubs such as *Combretum* spp., *Burkea africana*, *Bauhinia* sp., *Diplorhynchus condylocarpon*, *Lonchocarpus capassa*, *Acacia* spp., *Dichrostachys cinerea*, *Sclerocarya birrea*, *Ximenia caffra*, *Strychnos* sp., *Securingia virosa*, *Grewia* spp., *Ehretia rigida*, *Boscia albitrunca*, *Colophospermum mopane*, *Euclea* spp., *Terminalia* spp., *Portulacaria afra*, and more. Dry, fallen leaves of browse are regularly eaten. In mountainous areas they tend to move downhill in dry periods, and uphill during wet periods.

Breeding systems

Being a migratory species eland need large areas and tend to perform poorly in camps smaller than 150 ha. The absolute minimum camp size recommended for a breeding herd of 30 eland is 75 ha. It is ideal to rotate one breeding herd between two 75 ha camps at 8 month intervals. Such a system is suitable for sharing with another game species such as a breeding herd of 30 blue-(golden) wildebeest, or a breeding herd of 30 impala, or with 40 nyala. If shared with another game species it is important that all animals are moved simultaneously when rotating between the camps as to allow the non-stocked camp a full 8 months rest of no grazing. This rotational stocking strategy sustains good natural veld conditions. A minimum of two drinking holes must be provided, spaced evenly over the camp size and must never be closer than 50 m from any fence or infrastructure. Feeding buckets must be loose standing, to allow them to be moved 0.5 m daily to prevent moisture and parasite build-up under the buckets. Never feed directly on the ground as to avoid soil and

Boma confinement and handling of eland are problematic and most often result in mortalities. Note the pipes on the horns to prevent injuries.

gravel intake which cause rumen compaction. Feeding buckets are to be placed in a circle rather than a straight line and 5–10 m apart to prevent fighting and to prevent the dominant animals eating the majority of the quality feed that need to be shared for all of the herd. Feeding sites must be rotated bi-weekly between at least three different stations/localities in the camp, and never closer than 50 m from any fence. If the camp is shared with another game species it is crucial that supplement feeding be provided simultaneously at least at two (preferably three) different feeding stations to prevent inter-species conflict and fighting.

Adult breeding bulls become highly aggressive towards other bulls and will enter fierce fights often resulting in lethal injury. Young male offspring need to be removed from the breeding camps between 10 and 14 month age, preferably not before 8 months. A mating ratio of 1 adult bull (>5–12 years) to 30 cows (>2–10 years) is recommended. Older bulls and cows should be regarded as post-mature and removed from breeding camps.

Eland can access fodder at a greater feeding height by using their horns to break branches from trees and shrubs. This activity results in the destruction of vegetation and can be detrimental, especially during dry seasons. Sub-adult bachelor bulls (2.5–5 years) that become socially frustrated are prone to break branches, so their numbers need to be limited. Free-roaming eland must never be placed directly into a camp system smaller than 150 ha. If they need to be placed in camps a three step plan must be adopted gradually reducing the area to the target size. Eland translocated directly from a sub-tropical or bushveld region to a high rainfall, montane grassland habitat can adapt but will experience a high number of mortalities. It is preferable to purchase eland from catalogue sales where the animals are not pre-captured and held in auction bomas. They cope poorly in bomas unless they are sedated which is undesirable. Aging adults tend to lose their hair, resulting in the overall colour becoming bluish-grey due to the skin reflecting through the coat.

Diseases and parasites

Eland are susceptible to *Brucella abortus* so must be separated from cattle unless livestock have been certified free from brucellosis. Other important conditions in the species are tick-borne diseases: They are susceptible to redwater and heartwater, and so should not be translocated from areas free of these diseases, such as the Karoo, into endemic areas. *Theileria taurotragi* which is also tick-transmitted causes sporadic losses when there is heavy tick infestation. It has caused many eland deaths.

They are intolerant of heavy tick infestations and in areas such as the mixed and sour bushveld of the Waterberg, chemical control may be needed.

Additional information

Comprehensive information on eland biology by the same author is available on E-Book, the *Game Species Window*. www.amazon.com. pp 3975–4350.
Genetic advice on eland breeding:
Wildlife Stud Services www.ws2.co.za
Geo Wild Consultants: www.geowild.co.za
Derbianus Game Breeders:
www.derbianusgame.co.za.

KUDU (*Tragelaphus strepsiceros*)
Deon Furstenburg

Speciation

Kudu originated in the northern hemisphere, and their fossils have been found in Pliocene and Pleistocene deposits across Europe and Asia. Only in recent historic time did they spread to the African savannah or miombo-biosphere. Kudu are thus still actively developing as a species as they continuously adapt to new environments and habitats. There are two different species:
- *Tragelaphus imberbis* – lesser kudu.
- *Tragelaphus strepsiceros* – greater kudu.
    - *T. s. strepsiceros* – southern greater kudu.
    - *T. s. bea* – East African greater kudu.
    - *T. s. cottoni* – western greater kudu.
    - *T. s. chora* – northern/Abyssinian greater kudu.

Top: Trophy bull 72$^{5/8}$" – Rowland Ward no. 2, Namibia, 2001 (4 half-turns). Right: Trophy bull 72" – Welverdiend, Hoedspruit, 2011 (4.5 half-turns).

There is dispute about recognising of the Eastern Cape variation of the southern kudu as a different sub-species. DNA analysis of a few kudu individuals in the Grahamstown region has revealed some genetic difference to other kudu from the Limpopo Province. However, this difference has not yet been accepted as significant enough to justify a separate subspecies.

IUCN Conservation Status
- Lower Risk, conservation dependent (LR/cd).

Distribution

Kudu used to be distributed all across South Africa, from the Limpopo River down to Cape Town, excluding the highveld and mountainous sour grassveld regions. They were eliminated from many of these areas by the rinderpest, exploitive hunting, wars, bovine tuberculosis, fencing, and drought. The subsidence of disasters and epidemics heralded the recovery of their population and the range of the species is still enlarging at present. The Eastern Cape kudu became isolated from the rest of the population as a result of human settlement and therefore retreated to the thickets of the valley bushveld areas of the Sundays and Great Fish River valleys. It is at present being artificially managed as a subspecies based on size and trophy quality. Global warming is favouring

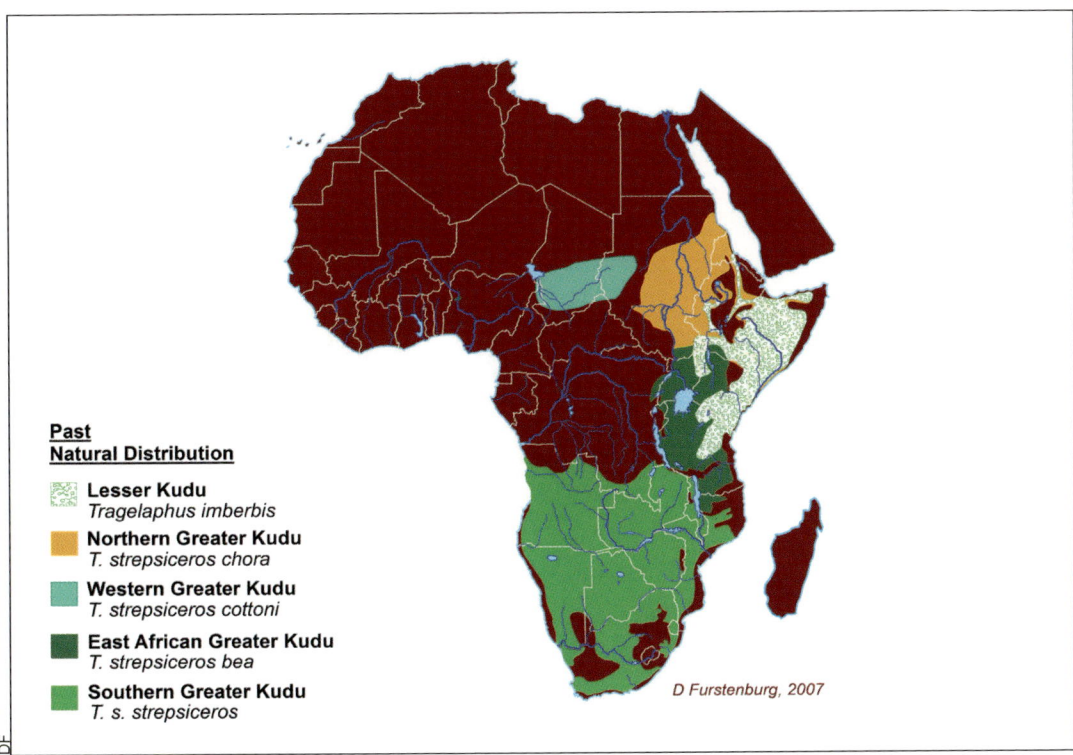

Distribution map of kudu in Africa.

the encroachment and development of *Acacia karoo* shrub and trees along the drainage lines and floodplains of the Karoo and the Eastern Cape Midlands providing new habitat for kudu. Kudu distribution is rapidly reaching its former distribution due to the expansion of the game industry over the past two decades and if left to natural environmental dynamics, subpopulations created by humans will unite. It is of crucial importance that this spread should not be inhibited by statutory translocation legislation, as it is a natural process of co-evolution with both habitat and animal changing in relation to global warming.

Economic aspects

Kudu are one of the main game species which are sought after for their trophies, hence the focus on horn growth rates and size, and the Roland Ward records. As with the impala (*Aepyceros melampus*) they are also sought after for biltong hunting. In the mid 1990s, the increased trade value of rare species such as sable, tsessebe, nyala and buffalo begun to replace the economic value of the kudu, but in recent years (since 2010) kudu started gaining commercial value again. The breeding of kudu has been mainly under free-range conditions in protected areas, rather than in breeding camp systems. The ravages to their population and distribution apparently did not cause a decline in genetic diversity, because six of the top 10 Rowland Ward trophies are listed within the last 17 years.

It should be noted that the decrease in trophy value and genetic diversity of the Eastern Cape kudu is not a result of isolation and a population bottleneck, but rather of long-term selective hunting pressure. Sustained hunting of kudu which has been an annual cull of between 15 and 30% of the population size each year, has reduced the trophy quality by more than 40% over a period of 12 years, thus depleting its prime genetic material.

Time line of top-listed Rowland Ward trophies

Year	Ranking	Measurement	Location	Person
2014	No. 3	72 1/2"	Namibia	Dewald Joubert
2011	not listed	72"	Welverdiend, Hoedspruit, RSA	unknown
2005	No. 6	68 3/8"	Soutpansberg, Limpopo, RSA	G.M.Y. Al-Hamad
2002	No. 7	68 1/4"	Alldays, Limpopo, RSA	D. Tallman
2001	No. 2	72 5/8"	Hochfeld, Namibia	J. Rohrer
1998	No. 5	68 7/8"	Marble Hall, Mpumalanga, RSA	N. Coetzee
1963	No. 1	73 7/8"	Mozambique	C. Caldres (picked up)
1916	No. 4	69 1/4"	Lydenburg, Mpumalanga, RSA.	P.G. Rous
Unknown	not listed	82"	Unknown	unknown

Measurements from 400 kudu carcasses during 1989–1996 as part of the Kirkwood study revealed the number of half-turn spirals of horn growth to be correlated with animal age. There is no scientific proof for claims that narrow horns relate to bush dwelling or montane kudu and wide horns to plains kudu, as the two forms are found in both habitats. However, narrow-horned kudu are more mobile in thickets and are seen moving more frequently in thicker vegetation, whereas a wide-horned kudu tends to conceal itself rather than to move. The horns of a kudu are constructed in such a way as to give the animal constant eye contact with the tips. Horns are borne by males alone and although cows occasionally have horns they are under-sized or deformed. In general, the Rowland Ward minimum qualifying trophy quality is only reached after seven years, the quality increasing with the depth of the spiral. The horn quality can be easily estimated by looking from tip to base along the inside core; the greater the diameter of the spiral, the better the quality.

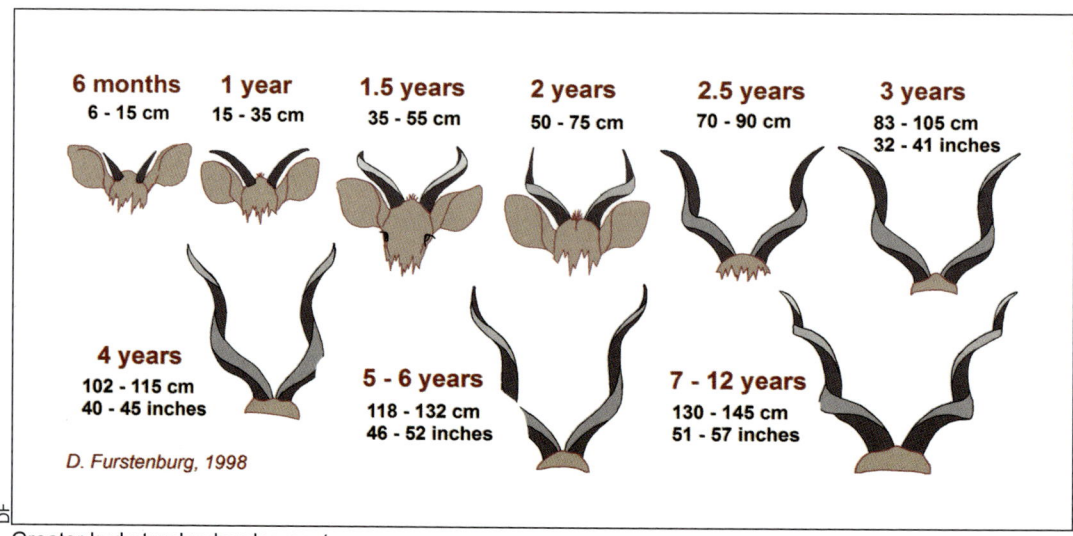

Greater kudu trophy development.

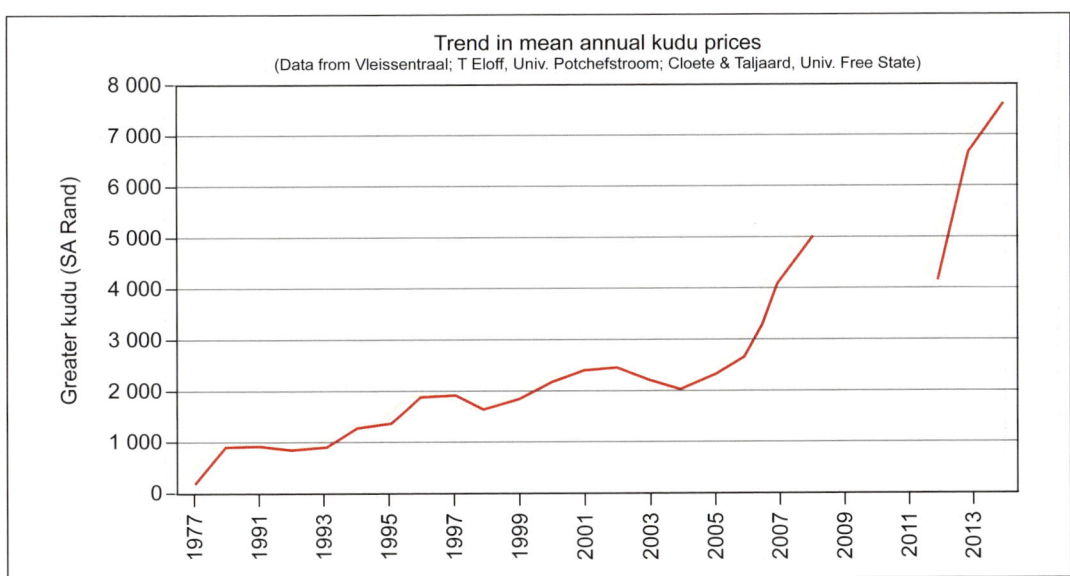

Trend of kudu prices.

Main features of kudu

The shoulder height of adult cows ranges from 119–141 cm (average 134 cm) and of bulls from 128–152 cm (size depends upon the post-mature age). Due to differences in the climate and forage of the local habitat, kudu from the Eastern Cape are markedly smaller than elsewhere in southern Africa. In the Eastern Cape population the mass for 220 adult cows >3 years varies between 110 and 210 kg with a mean of 136.8 kg compared to 155 kg for those in the eastern Lowveld of the Kruger National Park. The maximum mass for kudu cows is reached at 4–5 years, whereafter they become highly vulnerable to nutritional quality, and seldom live longer than 9 years. From five years age onwards the body condition deteriorates with age.

Kudu bulls reach maximum body size/mass of 260–315 kg only at the end of their natural lifespan of 12–16 years. After social maturity is reached at four years, bulls continue to grow. The natural life span of kudu bulls has been reduced to an average of 9–11 years.

The greater kudu has 9–10 vertical white stripes on each side of the body flank, the eastern African greater kudu 6–8 and the northern greater kudu 4-7. The colour of the coat differs, being a pale greyish colour in the southern greater kudu, a comparatively richer colour in the eastern African greater kudu and much paler in the northern greater kudu. The lesser kudu does not have a mane. After eight years the coat colour of bulls becomes greyish-blue and their hair becomes dull and less dense. The hair of the adult cow becomes dull and begins to wear away after five years, hairless patches appearing after 6–7 years.

Habitat and dietary requirements

Kudu are free-roaming antelope. They perform optimally at an annual rainfall of 500–700 mm that provides for a high diversity of fodder plant species, with tree and shrub density being the most critical parameter governing their choice of habitat. Kudu prefer broken bushveld or a woodland of deciduous plants with scattered thicket bush clumps for refuge. In general they do not do well in small camps and in habitats of homogenous vegetation with little plant species variety. Important parameters for kudu are savannah bush environment with 50–80%

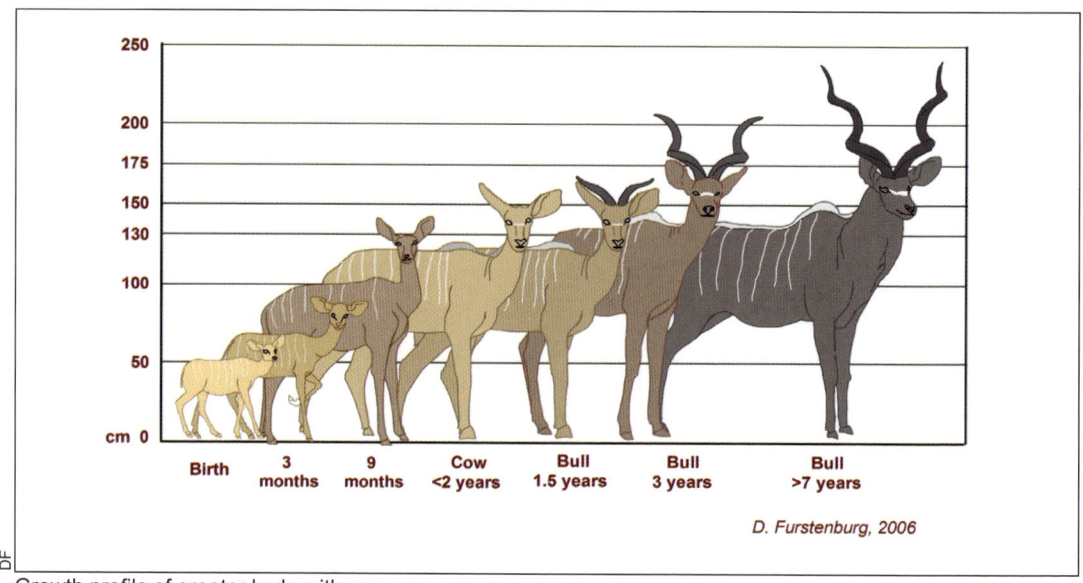
Growth profile of greater kudu with age.

Table 1.

Age	Mean age related growth rate for the Greater Kudu (460 eastern Cape kudu carcasses from 1989 to 1998, Furstenburg, 2000)			
	Live body mass (kg)		Horn length (bull)	
	Cow	Bull	(mm)	(Inch)
Birth	13	13	0	0
6 months	50	60	5–80	0.2–3
1 year	90	95	51–432	2–17
1.5 years	105	120	178–635	7–25
2 years	120	140	483–787	19–31
2.5 years	125	160	635–889	25–35
3 years	130	165	838–991	33–39
4 years	140	180	1 041–1 143	41–45
5 years	145	205	1 143–1 245	45–49
6 years	138	220	1 245–1 295	49–51
7 years	130	240	12 70–1 346	50–53
8 years	130	250	1 295–1 372	51–54
9 years	128	260	1 346–1 397	53–55
10 years	125	265	1 346–1 422	53–56
11 years	120	270	1 372–1 448	54–57
12 years	----	275	1 372–1 473	54–58
13 years	----	280	1 397–1 473	55–58

Kudu bull.

Kudu ewe and calf.

tree canopy, that is 600–1 100 trees per hectare. Closed thickets of more than 1 300 trees per hectare reduce kudu performance drastically. Kudu bulls do take refuge in forest, but they provide minimal to no food for kudu. *Acacia* spp., especially *Vachellia karroo*, *V. tortillis*, *V. sieberana*, *Senegalia nigrescens*, *S. galpinii* and a few others form the bulk of kudu fodder.

Other important trees include *Combretum apiculatum*, *Dichrostachys cinerea*, *Grewia occidentalis* and many more. The encroacher species *Senegalia erubescens* and *S. mellifera* are not eaten by kudu and need to be controlled by bush-clearing means. Kudu are seldom found in completely open country (grass forms <12% of kudu diet), although they may be temporarily attracted to it by dicot broadleaf forbs and dwarf succulents. They need a selection of vegetation that includes:

- Palatable, deciduous, woody plants as a dietary staple during the wet season.
- Soft-stemmed, dicot broadleaf forbs and the new growth of woody foliage year round, particularly during the lactation phase of cows.
- Relatively palatable evergreen or late deciduous, woody plant foliage during the dry season.
- Protein rich fruits and pods in the dry season.
- Woody plants that produce new foliage in advance of the first rains.
- Relatively unpalatable, evergreen woody plants that can be used as a last resort when all other food reserves are depleted during extreme droughts, e.g. noors (a succulent cactus) in the Eastern Cape xerophytic valley bushveld.

Both plains and mountainous terrain are suitable provided the necessary fodder plants are avilable. Kudu are highly susceptible to the defensive production of tannins in *Acacia* and *Combretum* trees, which is one of the reasons why they don't do well if confined in small properties. It has been shown that kudu are able to make a fermentation switch from foregut digestion in wet summer to hindgut digestion (fibre digestion) in the dry conditions of winter in order to overcome the natural decline in nutritional quality.

Behavioural and breeding characteristics

Kudu are extremely shy, sensitive and nervous by nature. Disturbances, handling and movement

Typical optimal *Acacia* sweet bushveld kudu habitat (800–900 trees per ha).

of humans, vehicles and other species must be restricted to promote their well-being. As a result they are highly susceptible to capture myopathy during capture and translocation. For the least impact on production hunting or cropping must be done in August to September for cows and September to December for bulls. May to July is the rutting and lactating season and no hunting should be allowed. After September most adult cows are more than 3.5 months pregnant and hunting is not recommended.

Moist cold spells or sudden temperature changes will cause kudu to move away from lower lying areas, to warmer hill slopes where they can avoid prevailing winds. During hot sunny days kudu will keep close to the shade of trees and on cold winter days stay in thicket vegetation. Kudu display a variety of browsing behavioural patterns (Furstenburg 2005 & 2015); adult bulls tend to browse higher up on slopes than adult cows. Several studies have shown that kudu is not migratory nor territorial but inhabits a static home range of 90–350 ha extending to 600 ha during drought, shared by individuals of both sexes.

Family bonding is weak and group structures are unstable as members constantly drift between adjacent family breeding groups, the mean family group size being 4.5. The social structure comprises of family breeding groups (1–2 socially mature bulls, 2–4 adult cows, 1–3 youngsters), bachelor groups (2–6 subadult bulls of 2–5 years), socially mature male groups (2-4 bulls of 5-8 years) and post-mature groups (2–6 non-breeding bulls over eight years).

Most mating takes place during the rut from May to early July when 1–2 socially mature bulls accompany each family group. In good rainfall years the rutting period can extend throughout the year. Bulls reach sexual maturity at 22 months, social maturity at 4.5 years, post-maturity at 9–10 years and have an expected lifespan of 12–16 years. Outside of the rutting season the mating bulls join mature bull groups, but will frequently leave to join family groups for a short period. Females reach sexual maturity at 18 months and normally start mating at 3 years.

The gestation period is 8.5 months and generally 94% of calves are born between late December and early March. Eastern Cape kudu cows show a natural fecundity of 93–96%, with a mean birth rate of 84% and only 62% of the calves survive to be weaned. The maternal instinct of kudu cows is poor when compared with that of other antelope, as mothers leave the calves to find their own cover. The cow returns for suckling 2–4 times daily but if disturbed may abandon the calf for a day or two resulting in high calf mortalities during cold spells. Because calves younger

Left: Kudu at Addo browsing on bushveld thicket. Right: Supplementation of post-mature kudu bulls sharing a 150 ha camp with nyala and blue wildebeest. This is one of three feeding sites in the camp and there are multiple feeding buckets to limit social competition.

than seven months cannot jump higher than 1.2 m, they are often abandoned when the mothers are disturbed.

Breeding management

Kudu do not do well in small-camp systems. The minimum camp size recommended is 150 ha, preferably 250 ha. The natural optimal sex-ratio is one breeding bull (5–8 years) to 4 cows (3–6 years). The natural home range of kudu is 90–350 ha which is mainly for browsing reasons. A practical solution on farms with small-camp systems is to erect internal camp fences at 1.8 meter height (will contain most other breeding animals except impala and eland) which can be jumped by kudu allowing it free movement across various camps.

For optimal breeding and production on farms it is vital to remove young non-breeding bulls and all post-mature trophy bulls (older than 9 years) from the population.

Stocking rates and supplementation

Sustainable stocking rates on natural veld are 40 ha/kudu in mixed bushveld (Nylsvley and Kruger National Park), 33 ha/kudu in dry mopane sweet bushveld, and in the Eastern Cape valley bushveld 15 ha/kudu at 300–340 mm rainfall, 10 ha/kudu at 340–360 mm rainfall, 8 ha/kudu at 360–400 mm rainfall and 4 ha/kudu at 470–700 mm rainfall. For each adult kudu an annual natural tree-fodder supply of 1 500 edible trees (minimum size 1.5 m high, 1.5 m canopy diameter), maintaining >30% of their foliage throughout the dry winter season are needed (Furstenburg, 2000 & 2005).

A dietary protein intake of 9–11% and 19–23% fibre should be maintained throughout the year as kudu require 9 700 kilojoule energy intake per day. It increases by 30% for lactating cows emphasising the high quality of nutrition needed for kudu, consumed at 8–9 kg wet/fresh natural plant matter per day per kudu.

Overstocking can be suspected when 38% of all edible foliage has been removed below 1.7 m height and/or a browse line appears on the vegetation at or above 1.7 m, and signs of poor body condition and mortalities are likely to follow. Supplementation of the diet during drought should not rely on concentrate mixture alone but should be based on good quality lucerne in order to supply the necessary fibre as well.

The amount of supplementation should not exceed 20% of the natural daily diet consumption rate, the difference to be obtained from good condition veld. While kudu can adapt to a gentle, slow change of climate and veld condition but are intolerant of rapid changes in food quality.

Table 2.

Stocking density benchmark for greater kudu, in relation to annual rainfall, and to tree/shrub density; expressed as number of hectare (ha) needed per animal (Furstenburg, 2000)

Rainfall (mm)	% Foliage per tree/shrub	Number of ha needed per kudu (related to tree/shrub density per ha):				
		2 500 plants/ha	2 000 plants/ha	1 500 plants/ha	1 300 plants/ha	800 plants/ha
120	10–20	12.0	13.7	13.7	15.4	29.4
170	15–30	11.8	13.3	13.3	14.3	28.6
220	20–40	11.1	12.5	12.8	13.3	27.0
270	30–50	10.0	11.1	11.8	12.5	20.7
310	40–60	9.1	10.0	10.0	11.1	16.7
340	45–70	7.7	9.1	9.1	10.5	14.3
360	55–80	6.7	8.3	8.3	10.0	12.5
380	60–85	5.3	7.4	7.4	8.7	11.1
410	70–90	4.0	5.3	6.3	7.7	10.0
450	75–95	2.5	5.0	5.0	5.9	8.3
500	80–100	2.0	3.3	3.3	4.0	7.4
550	90–100	1.7	2.2	2.5	2.5	6.7
600	100	1.3	1.7	2.0	2.0	5.0

Diseases

Nutritional stress and starvation, with subsequent pneumonia, is the one factor contributing to the majority of all kudu mortalities. This is a particular problem during cold wet spells following on drought periods. Kudu are susceptible to anthrax, foot-and-mouth disease, bovine tuberculosis, and rabies which causes sporadic outbreaks with high mortalities. Kudu can tolerate a tick load of up to 5 000 mature ticks per animal, but these may increase tenfold when animals come under nutritional stress. They become heavily infected especially with the brown ear tick (*Rhipicephalus appendiculatus*) which can cause ear damage.

Kudu biology information

Comprehensive information on kudu biology from the author is available on E-Book, the *Game Species Window*.
www.amazon.com. pp 12541-12887

NYALA
(*Tragelaphus angasii*)
Deon Furstenburg

Nyala bull in mixed bushveld.

Speciation

There are eight different species of nyala including the southern African nyala (*T. angasii*) and the mountain nyala (*T. buxtoni*). No subspecies of either are recognised.

The closely related mountain nyala of Ethiopia is similar to the kudu in appearance and build. It is found 2 740 m above sea level in the Chercher, Arusi, Bale and Amorro mountains, weighs 204–227 kg and has an average shoulder height of 134 cm. Although uncommon and very rare, nyala can hybridise with both bushbuck and kudu as is the case for all of the tragelaphines.

Description

The nyala antelope shows a marked sexual dimorphism in size with a large male and a much smaller female. As a result the male is known as a bull in common with the larger antelope species and the female an ewe in common with the smaller antelopes. Young males have colour patterns similar to the females' which protects them from the aggressive behaviour of the dominant male. The nyala bull is one of the most colourful antelopes of the African continent. It is a medium-sized antelope with a build similar to that of a bushbuck and the face of a kudu. The adult nyala bull weighs 92–126 kg, has a shoulder height of 104–121 cm and an apron of exceptionally long hair. Their pelage colour varies from a light chestnut to a chocolate-brown that darkens with age to a dark greyish-black. There are 10–14 vertical, parallel, white stripes on the flanks. Nyala ewes are much smaller, weighing only 54–68 kg and have a shoulder height of 82–106 cm. Ewes are often mistaken for bushbuck ewes. They are a bright chestnut-brown and lack the furry coat of the bull.

Occasionally nyala males are born without the genetic marker of the typical black colouring of adult bulls. Such colour variants recently found themselves a valued place in the commercial game markets and are referred to as nyala red-bulls.

Current distribution and numbers

The nyala occurs naturally in the southeastern countries of Africa, including Malawi, Mozambique, Zimbabwe, and in South Africa in northern KwaZulu-Natal and along the banks and floodplains of the Limpopo River.

IUCN Conservation Status
- Nyala: Lower Risk, least concern (LR/lc).
- Mountain nyala: Endangered (EN).

Nyala ewe in thicket.

Nyala red-bull variant Lower Sabie Kruger National Park, 2004.

The game industry has introduced nyala to most parts of South Africa as well as large areas of northern Namibia. At present, the largest introduced populations are to be found in the Great Fish River Valley of the Eastern Cape and in the George and Oudtshoorn districts of the Western Cape Province. Except for a small population thriving in the Tswalu Reserve in the Kalahari in the Northern Cape, nyala are naturally restricted to environments that are both humid and well wooded.

While nyala populations were severely depleted in the past, total population numbers are now being estimated at 32 000 almost entirely restricted to protected areas and private land. Population trends are generally stable or increasing and long-term survival will be enhanced by the current efforts to rehabilitate wildlife areas such as Gorongosa, Banhine and Zinave National Parks, Gaza Province and the Maputo reserve in Mozambique.

Nyala has spread recently into the Tuli Block farms of Botswana due to the introductions onto private farms on the South African border. In Swaziland nyala became extinct by the 1950s but since have been successfully reintroduced. The numbers of the mountain nyala population has dropped critically to below 2 500 and is still declining.

Rowland Ward records and horn characteristics

Only adult bulls have well-developed horns. These are lyre-shaped with two full spirals, are smooth and have distinctive white tips 6–8 cm long. Horn buds appear after six months and reach a length of 20 cm at 15 months. The first spiral is complete at two years and Rowland Ward minimum trophy quality is reached after five years. Occasionally ewes are found with rudimentary, malformed horns. An ewe with a mass of 114 kg and a trophy of 32.5" was once recorded in the Imfolozi Game Reserve in KwaZulu-Natal.

With the expansion of the game industry over the last 20 years the overall quality of nyala has improved. The Rowland Ward maximum trophy size has increased from only 12 trophy entries exceeding 30" and the old record being $32^{7}/_{8}$" (1902, P.I. Phelan, KwaZulu-Natal), by adding 44 entries greater than 30".

In 2014 a so-called nyala bull from Marken, measuring $34^{5}/_{8}$" was auctioned for R1,65 million at Oljaco Game Dealers Pens in Vaalwater. The animal showed obvious visual characteristics of being hybridised with a kudu. The animal was evaluated prior to auction by veterinarians only, hence lacking any inspection by zoological scientists.

Nyala kudu cross.

The outcome of the DNA analysis of the much doubted animal's bloodline was never shared in public media. To the authors knowledge the sale was later declared void being in doubt to the genetic purity of the species.

Behaviour

Nyala are predominantly active during the day in optimal habitats, but become nocturnal in open, marginal habitats or with increased human interference. During daylight hours they tend to keep to thickets and move out at night to feed on adjacent, more open ecotones. Nyala crawl under obstacles rather than attempt to jump over them. However, when captured in bomas a bull can clear a canvas curtain of 1.8 m. Different nyala groups often gather together in sharing a good fodder source, temporarily tolerating each other's presence with little aggression. No territorial behaviour but the home ranges of both bulls and ewes are permanent and overlap to a great extent. The size of home ranges depend on the suitability of the habitat and the abundance of fodder ranging from 15 ha in succulent valley bushveld, to 60 ha in the closed, sandy woodland of the Imfolozi Game Reserve and 400 ha in Mozambique. Nyala are not migratory and only make small moves when veld conditions deteriorate. Even under severe

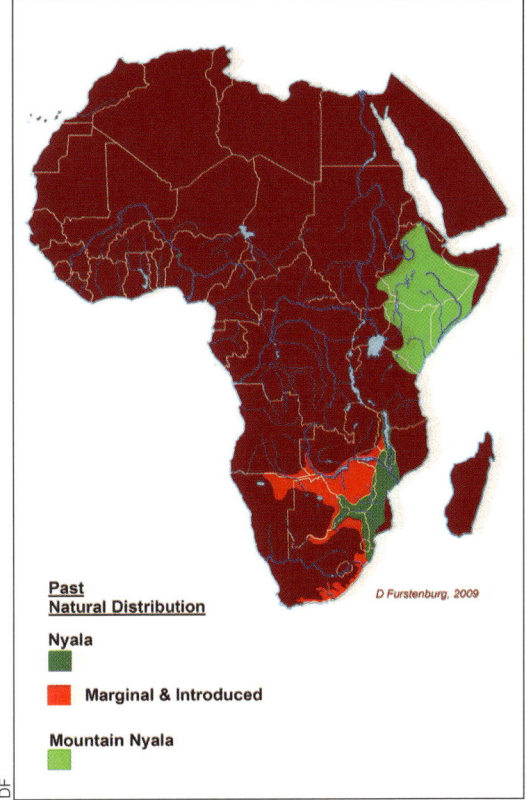
Distribution map of nyala.

This Nyala trophy 32$^{7}/_{8}$" shot in 1902 in KwaZulu-Natal was Number 1 for 28 years.

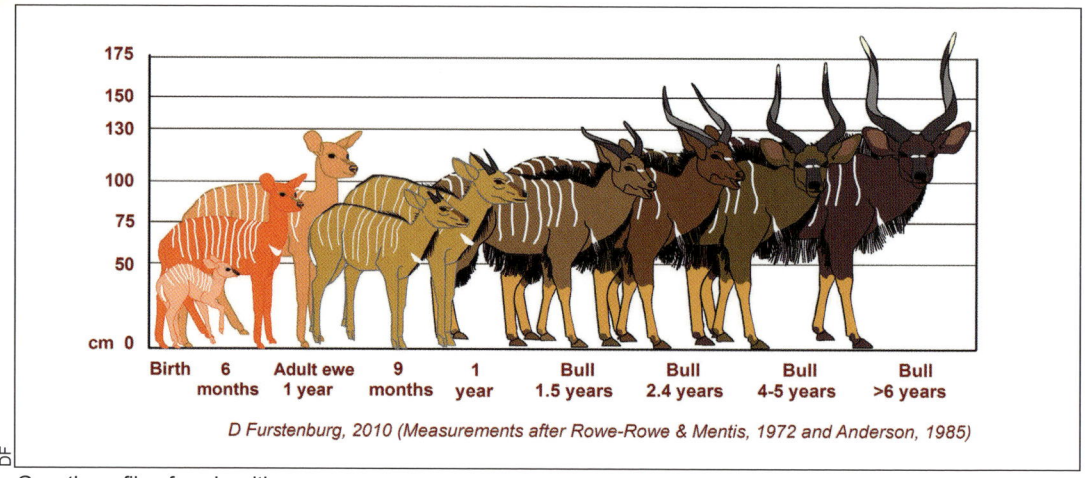

Growth profile of nyala with age.

conditions they will not leave the area but die in the vicinity. Young animals disperse to new areas when the stocking density becomes overcrowded.

Nyala are semi-gregarious, forming small groups of 3–15. Bulls form groups of 2–8 with a hierarchy of dominance. Breeding families consist of 3–15 individuals, including adult ewes, subadults and with or without 1–2 adult bulls. Single adult ewes often leave the group temporarily to guard their hidden lambs. Post mature bulls become solitary and often associate with other game species such as kudu, waterbuck and small impala groups. Group structures are unstable as members constantly move between groups. Mating is not seasonal and lambs are born throughout the year. Adult bulls (>3 years) frequently leave their groups and accompany a breeding family for several days for mating with ewes >1.5 years. More than one bull may join the same family and after mating, remains for another 2–3 days before leaving to rejoin a bull group. A single lamb of 4.2–5 kg is born after a gestation period of 220 days and hidden for 2.5 weeks by the mother. The lamb weans at three months. Under optimal conditions, a nyala ewe can give birth every 9–10 months. Young subadult males leave the breeding groups between 1 and 2 years and join bull groups.

In common with bushbuck, nyala production and density depends on the suitability of the habitat and the fodder supply. Natural nyala densities vary from 1.5 to 30 ha/animal. Recommended stocking is 2.5 ha/nyala at an annual rainfall of 550–650 mm. The natural mating ratio is one bull to 2–4 ewes to be raised to seven ewes for maximum production. The maximum expected lifespan is eight years for ewes and 11 years for bulls.

Habitat and dietary requirements

Abundant shade, bush cover and nutritious browse are the essential elements that are found mainly in thicket, closed woodland and riverine bush. Riverine woodland and floodplains with bushy clumps are preferred. Tropical conditions with a moist climate provide the most suitable environment. Nyala spend 70–90% of their life in thicket. However, they also thrive in marginal habitats such as dry savannah providing that a mosaic of thicket bush clumps exists and that permanent water is available within a radius of 800 m.

A constant supply of fresh drinking water and a large diversity of browse and broadleaf forbs and a minimum of 15% thicket are essential. The less the thicket component of the

Optimal habitat is sweetveld riverine bush and thicket clumps surrounding dams. (D. Furstenburg)

habitat, the more nocturnal the nyala become. The grass layer must consist of short to medium height (4–23 cm) sweet grass species. Nyala cannot survive at below 300 mm rainfall, at temperatures below -2 °C or in sourveld areas. They have adapted well to the semi-arid sweet succulent valley bushveld of the eastern and southern Cape at 380–450 mm rainfall. Nyala occupy the same feeding niche as the bushbuck, and if allowed to overpopulate, tend to displace them. Nyala do not pose a threat to bushbuck if managed at lean stocking densities, and in common with them, are highly sensitive to captive handling and to droughts.

Nyala are highly selective, mixed feeders, eating a large variety (up to 108 species recorded in Mozambique) of sweet grasses, forbs and browse. In common with the impala, the nyala can change from 90% browsing to 70% grazing, particularly short to medium (<23 cm) sweet grass species. In general, grass contributes 12–30% of the dietary intake. Important browse species include several *Acacia* spp., *Ziziphus mucronata*, *Grewia* spp., *Dichrostachys cinerea*, *Colophospermum mopanae*, *Capparis sepiaria*, *Spirostachys africana* and *Adansonia digitata*. Fruit, pods and flowers, the soft new growth of grass and broadleaf forbs are very important – dry grass are totally avoided.

Nyala drink 3.5 l of water per day. In very dry, marginal habitats a population may gradually adapt and become increasingly selective towards dietary moisture and drink less fresh water, but this reduces breeding and production potential. In dry periods nyala consume both wet and dry lucerne supplements. Fallen, dry pods are an important protein source during a dry winter. Take special note that nyala is extremely sensitive to change of and limited quality of nutrition. Mortalities are common when translocated to a marginal and/or less nutritional environment, e.g. from sweetveld to mixed or sourveld habitat.

Breeding systems

Intensive nyala production in camps of 50-100 ha has proved to be highly successful in both optimal and marginal habitats. They are extremely productive on planted pastures consisting of a mixture of 2–3 varieties. A nyala breeding herd can be kept in a camp of as little as 3 ha providing that it is the only animal species in the camp and that adequate high nutrition supplement food are provided daily. Three to four breeding families with one breeding bull per family can be kept together in larger camps greater than 50 ha provided that fodder and nutrition are adequate and that all non-breeding bulls older than 2 years be removed

Nyala thriving in sweet succulent valley bushveld of the Eastern Cape where they were introduced. (D. Furstenburg)

In marginal habitats of dry grass and mixed veld, nyala may need daily supplementation. (D. Furstenburg)

from the camp. Nyala bulls are much more tolerant of each other than any other antelope species and often sharing the ewes of the same breeding family. Conflict and confrontations are generally only a visual display of power and with little aggression. Aggression is more common towards other animal species than to members of its own species, and mostly restricted to time of drinking and feeding from buckets at feeding stations.

Rotational eight month stocking between two camps in systems where the camps are smaller than 20 ha is recommended. Unlike sable, eland, roan, buffalo, and impala rotational stocking with nyala has little effect on ecological veld condition, but is desirable to minimise and control parasites and diseases by prolonged periods of rest from game, as their moist shady habitats favour these organisms.

Nyala can share camps with other species if a few basic guidelines are followed:
- Camps should be larger than 50 ha (preferably 75–150 ha).
- Feeding stations need to be spaced in different habitat forms within the camp.
- Multiple feeding stations, one per species must be provided simultaneously (3 species – 3 stations, etc.).
- Feeding must be delivered at all feeding stations at the same time of day to allow animals to feed with least inter-species conflict.
- When rotating between camps all species must be moved simultaneously.
- Never mix any species in a confined space such as when using passive capture bomas.

Mobile boma erected for several weeks in nyala camp.

Sharing camps with other species can be done successfully if sufficient water sources and feed stations are provided.

Avoid human contact during feeding time as this causes habituation and leads to aggression.

- When sharing multi species in camps a minimum of two drinking water holes must be available at all time as some animals will dominate and others will die of dehydration.
- Provide one bucket per animal at feeding stations, and preferably place the buckets in a full circle and minimum 5 m apart.
- Feeding stations and drinking holes must never be closer than 20 m from any fence or infrastructure if only nyala is kept in the camp and at least 50 m away when the camp is shared with other game species to allow space for escape from inter-animal conflict.

Capture and handling

Nyala are easily handled and captured in permanent passive capture bomas. Feeding pellets inside a passive boma over time lures nyala to enter and exit at will through gates as narrow as 1 m. Forced capture by chasing nyala into confined bomas leads to injuries and high mortalities. Nyala generally react badly upon forced handling and they are highly sensitive to transportation. When translocated it is recommended to nurture them at optimal conditions for extended periods in a small camp (1.5 ha) before releasing them in larger camps or free-roaming.

Diseases and parasites

Nyala are highly sensitive to stress produced by rapid cold fronts accompanied by rain and wind. In a dry winter season, these conditions combined with poor nutrition result in severe hypothermia and mortality.

Nyala are also severely affected by capture myopathy when handled and transported, and sudden changes of diet during capture and relocation may cause clostridial enteritis and death. Although not susceptible to heartwater, heavy tick infestations can affect body condition.

Additional information

Comprehensive information on nyala biology by the same author is available on E-Book, the *Game Species Window*. www.amazon.com. pp 9892-10166.
Genetic advice on nyala breeding:
Wildlife Stud Services www.ws2.co.za
Geo Wild Consultants www.geowild.co.za

ALCELAPHINE ANTELOPE

- Blesbok/bontebok
- Tsessebe
- Wildebeest

BLESBOK (*Damaliscus pygargus phillipsi*)
BONTEBOK (*Damaliscus pygargus pygargus*)

Deon Furstenburg

Speciation

The blesbok evolved on the plains of South Africa and are endemic to the country, where they roamed in such numbers that their herds stretched to the horizon.

The popular name "blesbok" refers to the distinct white blaze on the forehead and the nose. The genus *Damaliscus* has two species:

- *D. pygargus,* formerly known as *D. dorcas*, with two subspecies:
  - *D. p. phillipsi*, the original blesbok.
  - *D .p. pygargus*, the more recently evolved bontebok.
- *D. lunatus* with five subspecies:
  - *D. l. lunatus*, tsessebe of southern Africa.
  - *D. l. tiang*, the tiang of the eastern regions of the Sahel.
  - *D. l. topi*, the topi of East Africa.
  - *D. l. jimela*, the nyamera of the lakes area of the Rift Valley in eastern Africa.
  - *D. l. korrigum*, the korrigum of West Africa

Due to a sudden, unfavourable climate and habitat change, blesbok split into a major northern group (roaming across various habitats) and a small southern group some 300 km apart with the Cape folded mountains in between the southern group isolated to a single habitat. The latter developed a different colouration and became the more habitat-specialised bontebok. Because they were stretched to the coastal plains of the Western Cape they were exploited by hunting from European Cape-settlers long before the blesbok population further inland.

Because blesbok and bontebok are subspecies they interbreed readily and they can crossbreed with any of the *D. lunatus*-subspecies, but these offspring are infertile. However, blesbok cannot crossbreed with the red hartebeest which is of the different genus *Alcelaphus*, contrary to anecdotal accounts by hunters of encountering blesbok-red hartebeest crossings. These were most likely hybrids between topi or tsessebe, both of which are infertile crosses.

All blesbok-bontebok crosses are probably fertile and reproduce a second and third generation, causing a significant threat to the genetic purity of both species. Several populations of privately owned blesbok and bontebok have already been deregistered by

Typical blesbok colouration.

Blesbok bontebok cross.

authorities as they are not suitable for trading due to this "hybridisation".

Dr Desiré Dalton and her team at the Molecular Wildlife Genetics Unit at the National Zoological Garden (NZG), recently developed a DNA typing test consisting of eight species specific and five cross species microsatellite markers confirming the purity of bontebok and blesbok populations. The so-called bontebok tested to date indicate a frequency of hybridisation of 40% with blesbok. DNA testing has now become the test required by government for the accurate identification and genetic integrity of bontebok and certification is required by law for the trading and translocation of bontebok.

Colour vaiants

White blesbok have been recorded from various locations as from the late 1960s. A herd of more white blesbok (counting >200 in 2001) was established in the Mpofu Game Reserve in the Eastern Cape back in 1974. As with impala, the black and white forms in blesbok are due to recessive genes which tend to be rare in natural populations due to the dominance of the "normal" colour, dark brown with black tint and white. The natural coat colour varies from light to dark brown but lacks the dark plum shading that distinguishes the bontebok. The saddle and the rear of the buttocks are a dull yellow-brown. With commercial breeding in camp systems the appearance of recessive colour genes are selectively favoured and enforced by specific management.

Various colour variants of blesbok occur and are traded at high value in the game industry (under various changing commercial names), varying from common white and copper to yellow, black, bont, apache, silver, white saddleback and yellow saddleback. Unlike for impala and springbok the genetic mechanisms for the different colour variants of blesbok have not yet being defined nor described. The colour and pattern of blesbok colour variants varies considerably between farms.

Current distribution and numbers

Historical documents relate that hundreds of thousands of blesbok were once seen in the northeastern Karoo and, in lesser numbers, in

IUCN Conservation Status
- Blesbok: Lower Risk, Least concern (LR/Lc).
- Bontebok: Vulnerable (VU).

Black blesbok.
Bont variation.
Copper variation.
Silver variant.
Yellow saddleback.
White saddleback.
Yellow variant.
White blesbok herd.

the central highlands of the Free State, Gauteng, Mpumalanga and Zululand. The largest concentration was found in the northeastern Free State where they were hunted for their hides by European pioneers and the region became known as the "Riemland" after the leather thongs cut from the skins. Historically, blesbok had a wide distribution between the southern latitudes of 33°40' and 25°40' from the Winterhoek Mountains of the Eastern Cape to the Magaliesberg Mountains in Gauteng; and to the east, from the highveld of Mpumalanga to the Tugela River Valley of Kwazulu-Natal. The furthest documented, western sighting was near Hanover in the Western Cape. Ecologically, there was no reason why small groups of blesbok could not migrate temporarily further west to the periphery of the Karoo, especially during periods of good rainfall.

The natural distribution ranges of the blesbok and the bontebok subspecies are divided by a corridor 250–320 km wide with extremely arid

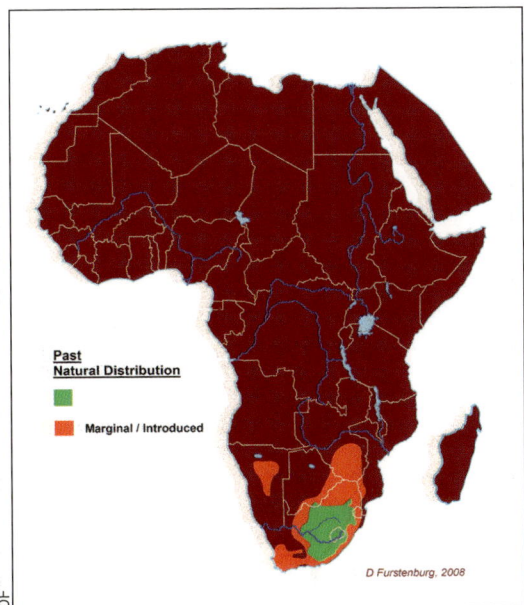
Distribution map of blesbok.

Differences between horns of ram (left) and ewe (right).

Karroid veld, the bontebok being less tolerant of environmental change which limited its distribution. Excessive hunting had reduced blesbok numbers to about 2 000 by the late 1800s. Since then it has made a spectacular recovery, mainly on private farmland, and it has been successfully introduced into marginal habitats across the major part of South Africa, the central regions of Zimbabwe and Botswana, and the northcentral areas of Namibia. These areas include fynbos, coastal plains, open bushveld and semi-Kalahari habitats.

Estimated blesbok population numbers for 1999 was between 235 000 and 240 000 (of which 97% occurred on private land) and increasing. Current estimates put the numbers of bontebok at around 3 500 of which only 1 500 animals occur within the historical range of the subspecies.

Rowland Ward records and horn characteristics

Although blesbok numbers decreased drastically as a result of heavy hunting, they were preserved as different populations on various farms, and remain genetically diverse. Both genders bear well-developed lyre-shaped horns that bend backwards from the skull and then turn outwards away from the body until the tips point upwards or slightly forward. The horns are heavily grooved for 85–90% of their length and have smooth tips.

The horns of adult rams are thicker at the base and are lighter in colour than those of the ewes. In rams the horn base thickens with age until they almost meet, while in ewes the bases remain separated by a gap of 2–3 cm. The adult horn length varies from 38–50 cm and Rowland Ward trophy status can be reached after 6 years. The current trophy record being 20 $5/8''$ by Thomas A. Hunt in 1988. Rowland Ward No. 2 is 20 $3/8''$ from Reivilo, North-West in 2005, No. 3 of 20 $1/4''$ from Lichtenburg in 1999 and a new No. 6 of 20 $1/8$ recently by N. Plumpton.

Behaviour

Blesbok are diurnal antelope, less active during the cold winter months when large groups spend hours either lying in the sun or in the shade of trees. In the cooler highveld regions blesbok are independent of shade and survive in open grassland, but in warmer regions they need shade against the heat of the sun.

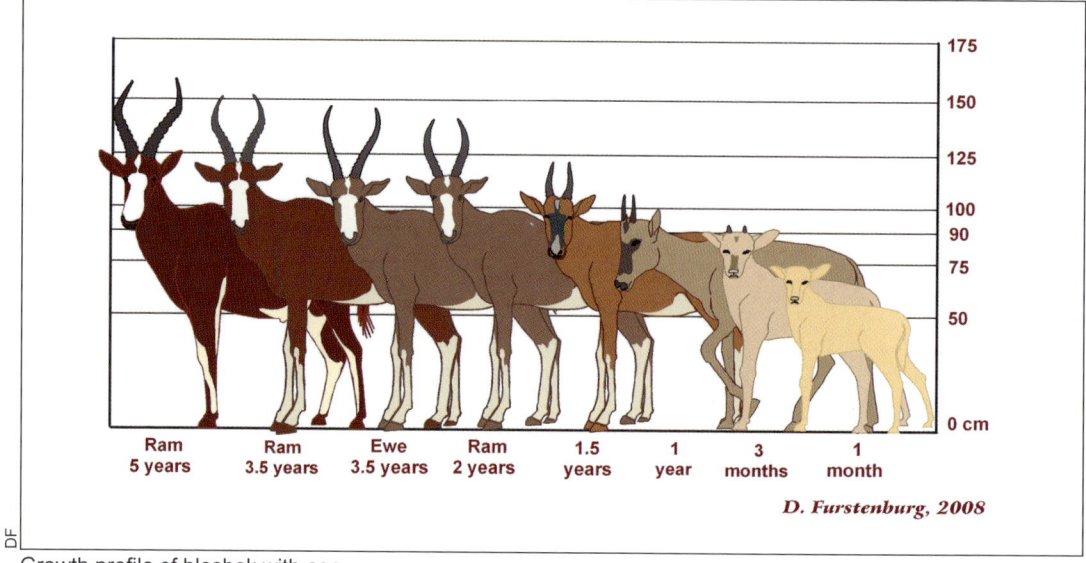

Growth profile of blesbok with age.

Grazing is usually restricted to the cooler daylight hours when large herds break up into smaller groups which remain separate throughout the night, and rejoin in large herds again during the warmer sunny hours of the day. With the onset of the spring rains the adult rams start competing with each other determining their social rankings and such contests can sometimes be fatal. In the mating season (March to May) adult rams (4–8 years) establish individual territories (0.9–4.1 ha) in open, heavily over-grazed veld or brackish areas. Some rams remain around their territories long after the mating season only because the habitat is trampled and open and optimal for their feeding needs. During these times, territories are not defended. As one territory seldom produces enough food outside of the rutting season, adult rams rotate and move between territories of other rams.

Family groups and harems (20–120 animals) have home ranges of 150–400 ha, but they sporadically migrate in search of alternative resources when the food source is depleted. Family groups consist of subadult females of all ages, young males (1–2 years) and post-mature ewes (>7 years). Harems include 4–25 adult ewes (2.5–7 years) and their lambs (10–18 months), and often a territorial ram. Bachelor groups consist of subadult rams (2–4 years) and one or two adult rams (>4 years). Adult ram groups consist of non-territorial rams (4–8 years) and post-mature rams (>8 years). In some populations, especially on smaller game farms, there are less distinctive differences between bachelor and adult ram groups and both categories can be united into a single group; the same applies to family and harem groups.

A ram (4–8 years) mates with 8–12 ewes (2.5–7 years) from different harems as they pass through his territory. The bulk of the lambs are born between November and January with additional births extending into May, after a gestation of 7.5 months. The ewe remains with the group during lambing and within 20 minutes the lamb runs with its mother. Lambs are not hidden and are weaned after 4 months but remain dependent on the mother until 6 months. After 12–18 months the subadult females leave to join a family group and after 10–12 months the young males leave to join a bachelor group. Adult body size is reached from 28–36 months.

Blesbok grooming.

The annual population growth ranges from 18–55% depending upon rainfall, veld condition and level of predation. In an optimal habitat of 1 000 ha with an annual rainfall of 450–550 mm, 67 blesbok can be sustained. At a higher rainfall of 650–700 mm, 110 blesbok may be sustained. Breeding ratio for maximum free-roaming production is one ram for 12 adult ewes. A greater ewe ratio results in fewer ewes being covered resulting in a reduced production rate, and an increase in the ratio of young males and a decrease in the number of mature males. This causes the age structure of the males in the population to become younger each year and results in a decline in the development of potential trophy animals. A stocking rate of three blesbok per hectare may be allowed for temporary aggregations on burnt veld without the risk of a permanent impact on the veld condition. One adult blesbok animal unit (AU) is 70 kg which equals 0.23 large stock units (LSUs) and 0.56 browser units (BUs). When introducing blesbok three adult rams should be included in the breeding group to reduce the dominance by one male as he will chase a challenging ram to exhaustion, and killing all male offspring in the population before they reach sexual maturity. Blesbok have very poor defences against predators and it is well known that their young suffer severe mortalities from various predators, while adults are often attacked by leopard and cheetah.

Blesbok repeatedly use the same routes to and from feeding grounds and water, which creates a network of footpaths that can cause veld degradation. During moist, summer months, blesbok aggregations of up to 650 animals frequently form. Such mass aggregations include all group structures but individual groups remain intact within the larger gathering, creating the effect of several islands. Danger is detected by vision rather than by smell. Bodily contact between blesbok individuals is rare and individuals groom themselves by rubbing the body with the muzzle or horns or by nibbling the skin with the incisors. Blesbok are more popular for meat and "biltong" than for their trophy value. The preferred season for harvesting, hunting and culling of blesbok is early winter, immediately after the mating period which ends in May and before the animals start to lose body condition.

Habitat and dietary requirements

The preferred habitat is the higher altitude grassland plains found in the central and eastern regions of South Africa with an annual rainfall of 400–800 mm. Unsuitable habitats are karroid veld without a grass stratum, thickets, forests, dense bushveld, closed woodland and tall grass stands. Open woodland and savannah are marginal. The most important habitat features are sufficient short-grass veld (<15 cm high) with a mixture of both sweet and sour grass species, a wide range of scattered non-woody forbs, sandy soils and a daily supply of drinking water.

Blesbok are well adapted to mountain plateaus with a mixed short grass stratum and a high rainfall. In the warmer subtropical

Typical cool temperate historic blesbok habitat in the central Free State.

conditions of most savannahs, trees for shade are essential for blesbok survival and reproductive performance. Although blesbok can survive on sourveld, these habitats are marginal and result in a reduced performance. Steep slopes and rocky surfaces are totally avoided. Blesbok are highly selective grazers of short grasses of <6 cm. Sweet grass species are preferred although blesbok adapt well to mixed veld where sour grass species constitute up to 65% and sweet grass as little as 35%. The diet consists of 95% grass and 5% dicot forbs and browse. Blesbok prefer the young summer growth of grasses in burnt veld and cultivated lands and will travel long distances to reach these. After the first winter frost blesbok lose up to 15% of their body mass due to the reduction in nutritional value and digestibility of grass.

Blesbok tend to avoid moribund grass that has not been grazed for longer than a year and will not feed on grass tufts from a previous season's growth. The species composition of the diet changes markedly between seasons. Only the very young, new growth of sour grass species is eaten. In winter, blesbok roam and feed across the entire home range but in spring and early summer vast numbers concentrate on burnt veld. In the Gauteng area the main grazing is red grass (*Themeda triandra*), love grass (*Eragrostis curvula*), black seed grass (*Setaria nigrirostris*), couch grass (*Cynodon dactylon*) and the *Chloromelas* sp.

Breeding systems

Blesbok are migrators by nature and prefer to roam rather than being confined to specific areas. They dislike sharing habitat with other game species and should be kept alone in camps that are smaller than 75 ha. With free-roaming blesbok stocking load should be limited to a maximum of 1 blesbok per 4 ha and a population ratio of one male to three females (all ages). In large camps greater than 150 ha a small population of three breeding families (20 animals plus a ram each) and a small bachelors' herd (4–10 rams) may be kept together, providing that the number of breeding rams may under no circumstance be less than three, otherwise it will result in fights resulting in the deaths of young males. Ideally mixed or sourveld should be burnt annually in spring to stimulate new grass growth which provides high quality fodder. Camps should therefore be divided into two burning blocks by means of a fire break so that burns can be alternated. Sweetveld can be slashed/mowed instead of burnt, but large patches of grass must be kept short, below 15 cm height all year round. Mowing of veld is best practised in mid or late summer.

Always provide at least two drinking holes per camp and feed at one feeding station for every group of blesbok in the camp simultaneously; for example, for two breeding herds and one

Blesbok in marginal suitable, sub-tropical mixed bushveld.

Blesbok fenced to prevent digging and predation.

bachelor herd three feeding stations must be provided. Provide one feeding bucket per animal placed in a full circle and 5 m apart. Move the feeding buckets daily by 0.5 m to allow the moisture under the buckets to dry out to prevent parasite build-up. Feeding stations and drinking holes must never be closer than 30 m from any fence or infrastructure.

Any camp smaller than 100 ha should be regarded a small camp and with only one breeding herd of blesbok (maximum 35 animals) and 3–5 adult rams of same age. Camps smaller than 50 ha (absolute minimum camp size is 30 ha) should be restricted to no more than 25 blesbok and only one breeding ram, in which instance all young males born must be removed from the camp at the age of 10 months, to prevent aggressive fighting injury from the ram. They should not be removed before weaning at six months. With small-camp systems two camps are needed per blesbok breeding herd, or at least three camps for two herds in order to facilitate rotational stocking at 6–8 month intervals. Small camps should never be shared with any other game species. Veld rotation using bulk grazers such as cattle is helpful. This ensures even utilisation of less palatable grasses in the camps and thus limit the risk of selective overgrazing of the desired palatable grasses by the blesbok.

If blesbok are stocked at rates higher than one per 4 ha large areas become grazed down to grass root level, bare patches of soil and eventually erosion result, animals lose condition in winter, calf survival declines and calving rates fall, social problems become exaggerated and parasite infestations increase. To prevent overstocking it is essential that surplus blesbok be taken off annually. At low to moderate densities, blesbok can be maintained on sourveld which cannot support domestic stock in winter.

Blesbok are crawlers and fences need to be well secured at ground level, also to prevent jackal from entering. Jackal predation on blesbok young may prevent growth of populations.

Diseases and parasites

Blesbok evolved in cool temperate climates where less parasites occur but allogrooming helps to rid them of excessive tick loads. They are often kept on farms in close contact with livestock and sporadic cases of diseases such as vibrionic abortion (*Campylobacter jejuni*), and bovine rhinotracheitis virus may occur.

Blesbok are host to a number of roundworm species and may acquire those of livestock. It should be noted that blesbok can be a reservoir of the larvae of *Goedoelstia*-flies, which are the cause of "uitpeuloog" in cattle. Copper deficiency has been diagnosed in free-roaming blesbok in Karoo National Park, Graaff Reinet.

BONTEBOK – back from the brink of extinction but what are they?

Blesbok and bontebok are considered to be subspecies or races of *D. pygargus* which have been geographically and historically separated and have adapted to different habitats.

They are similar in appearance and crossbreeding occurs when animals are held on the same properties (note that the term hybrid for the offspring is therefore not correct *sensu stricto* – see Definitions):

Bontebok are said to be characterised by the following colouration (Frost, 2014):
- Unbroken white blaze (subdivided by a complete brown bar in blesbok).
- Prominent white socks (blesbok have white inside legs only).
- Prominent white belly compared with blesbok.
- Purplish gloss on the flanks which is absent in blesbok.
- Horns in both sexes are black while those in male blesbok are lighter in colour.

Since 1988 bontebok herds were registered as "pure" using a photographic method developed by Fabricius *et al*. In 2011 DNA analysis was developed to determine the subspecies of an individual bontebok and this individual testing is used to obtain a registration certificate of "purity".

Presently, bontebok are also listed as a Threatened or Protected Species (TOPS) in terms of the Threatened or Protected Species Regulations (GNR 152 of 23 February 2007). According to the "Threatened or Protected Species" regulations bontebok is classified as a vulnerable species and a permit is required for any restricted activity such as breeding, hunting, transporting, importing or exporting of these animals.
Bontebok study group WRSA.

Typical bontebok colouration.

Additional information

Comprehensive information on blesbok biology by the same author is availableon E-Book, the *Game Species Window*.
www.amazon.com pp 297-591.
Genetic advice on blesbok breeding: Wildlife Stud Services www.ws2.co.za
Geo Wild Consultants: www.geowild.co.za

TSESSEBE (*Damaliscus lunatus lunatus*)
Deon Furstenburg

Speciation

Contrary to popular perception tsessebe are most closely related to the blesbok/bontebok (*Damaliscus pygargus*) and not hartebeest which fall in the genus *Alcelaphus*. The genus *Damaliscus* has two species, namely:
- *Damaliscus pygargus*, formerly known as *D. dorcas*, with two subspecies:
  - *D. p. phillipsi*, the blesbok and *D. p. pygargus*, the bontebok.
- *Damaliscus lunatus* with six subspecies:
  - *D. l. lunatus*, the tsessebe of southern Africa.
  - *D. l. tiang*, the tiang of the eastern regions of the Sahel.
  - *D. l. topi*, the topi of Tanzania.
  - *D. l. jimela*, the East coast topi of Somalia and Kenya.
  - *D. l. korrigum*, the korrigum of West Africa.
  - *D. l. superstes*, the Bangwela tsessebe of Zambia (recognised recently as a new species by Grubb, 2005 and Cotterill, 2003).

Current distribution and numbers

In South Africa tsessebe (*D. lunatus lunatus*) formerly roamed the savannah plains and grasslands to the north of Suikerbosrand and the Vaal and Orange Rivers, as far west as Kuruman. At present the largest population is found in the Kruger National Park and several small groups have been successfully introduced to many reserves and private ranches throughout the bushveld region, including the savannahs of Kwazulu-Natal. Currently their numbers are increasing especially on private land, while most other subspecies are decreasing.

Rowland Ward records and horn characteristics

Both sexes bear fully developed horns that bend horizontally forming a sideways bow, and from this the naming *lunatus*. The bow slope slightly backwards and the horn tips are parallel to each other. Deep grooves are apparent from the base until two thirds of the length. Bull trophies measure on average 11.8–15.7". The world record Rowland Ward No 1 tsessebe trophy has been holding for 81 years – it was hunted by A. Curado in Angola in 1934. Trophy No. 2 of the same size $18\frac{1}{2}$"

IUCN Conservation Status
- Tsessebe, Bangwela tsessebe, East coast topi, tiang = Lower risk, conservation dependent (LR/cd).
- Korrigum = Vulnerable, conservation dependent (VU/cd).
- Topi = Near-threatened, conservation dependent (NT/cd).

Tsessebe bull.

Tsessebe cows with calves on old lands under sucession.

was hunted in Botswana in 1967 (48 years). Trophies No. 3 and 4 are both from Zambia (both measuring $18\frac{1}{4}$") hunted in 1998 and 1981 (17 and 34 years), and are Bangwela tsessebe. No. 5 is also from Angola (measuring $18\frac{1}{8}$") in 1972 (43 years).

There has been little increase in trophy size in the past 34 years. This lack of trophy development can most probably be ascribed to a decrease in population size that resulted in a mosaic of fragmented isolated distributed small herds and hence a genetic bottleneck in the past 100 years, as well as a very long period of little interest in the breeding and redevelopment of tsessebe as a species.

Interest in tsessebe breeding only started in recent years and are well behind the major of other game species in the industry. Tsessebe holds a great potential of increased genetic development and improvement by manipulated proper managed breeding systems. The best trophies are found on solitary bulls at the outskirts of the population.

Behaviour

Tsessebe are semi-gregarious animals which occur in small family herds associated with one territorial bull. Other groups consist of solitary post-mature nomadic bulls and small bachelor herds of 3–6 young bulls. Families consist of 2–3 mature cows and 1–3 year old calves.

The bull is often found separate, 50–300 m away from the family, standing on an elevation displaying dominance, whilst constantly keeping an eye on the family. Aggressive bull fights are rare, but when it does happen both opponents will stand on bended knees engaging each other with the horns. When danger approaches they ran out in the open, stop briefly to evaluate the situation and then flee for distance.

Tsessebe cannot jump fences but they are master crawlers, finding holes under fences and enlarging them. When reaching 3 years bulls leave the bachelor herds and become solitary nomads until 4.5 years after which they establish permanent own territories of between 150–400 ha, which is also the home range of the bull. Each family herd associates with one territorial bull and both the bull and the cows participate in the marking of the territory. The same bull may dominate for an entire year and the home range of the family will extend the territories of a maximum of three bulls. Old bulls become solitary nomads and often associate with other animal species such as zebra, waterbuck and blue wildebeest. Tsessebe typically create resting sites in their territory which they create by digging with horns and front feet.

Migrations do occur but only during times of severe drought and food shortages. Temporarily

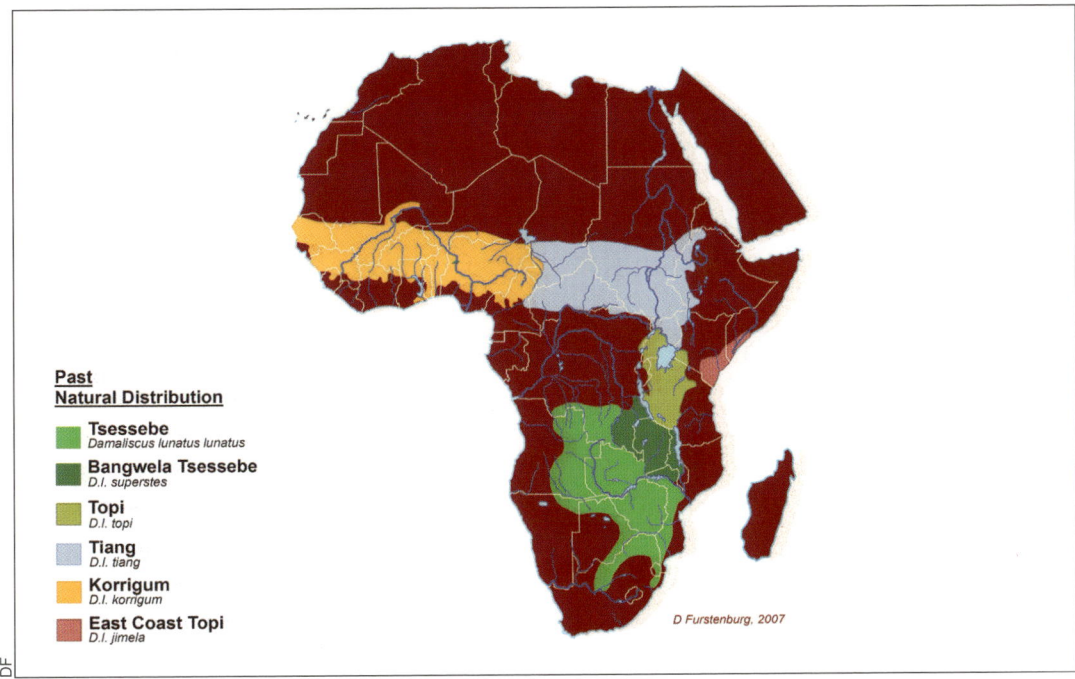

Distribution map of tsessebe.

mass herds numbering up to 200 are often formed during severe droughts.

Tight family bonding exists between members within families and year old bull calves get driven away aggressively by the bull when nearing the next mating season. They then join bachelor herds. Bachelor herds are nomadic on the outskirts of the family herds and on the boundaries between the ranges of the territorial bulls.

The cows of each family mate with only one territorial bull, older than 4 years. Mating season is from January to March and the majority of calves are born as single calves from mid-September to early December, after a gestation of 8 months. The calf is not hidden but follows the cow and the herd after a few hours. Heifers remain with the family for several years and as the family grows larger, it eventually splits into two forming a new family.

Little is known about calf mortality rates and the growth of natural populations. The small herd sizes and fixed territories create a limit on the stocking capacity and not the vegetative carrying capacity of the habitat. The maximum density is calculated to be 15 ha per adult animal at 400 mm annual rainfall. An adult tsessebe represents 0.38 Large Stock Units. Annual natural population growth is mostly affected by rainfall and is estimated to vary from 12 to 25%. If tsessebe are to be stocked in relation to the vegetative carrying capacity only, then the spatial limit would most certainly be exceeded putting the animals under social stress that will limit reproduction.

Tsessebe is the second fastest antelope after the red hartebeest and can reach a running speed of 100 km/h. It has tremendous stamina, the run starts normally as a jog gaining momentum until full speed that can be maintained for a few kilometres.

Habitat and dietary requirements

Tsessebe have evolved in subtropical climates and cannot adapt to temperate climates, or the open grasslands of the Free State. Tsessebe cannot survive on highveld sour grassland and they avoid sour bushveld. Most important

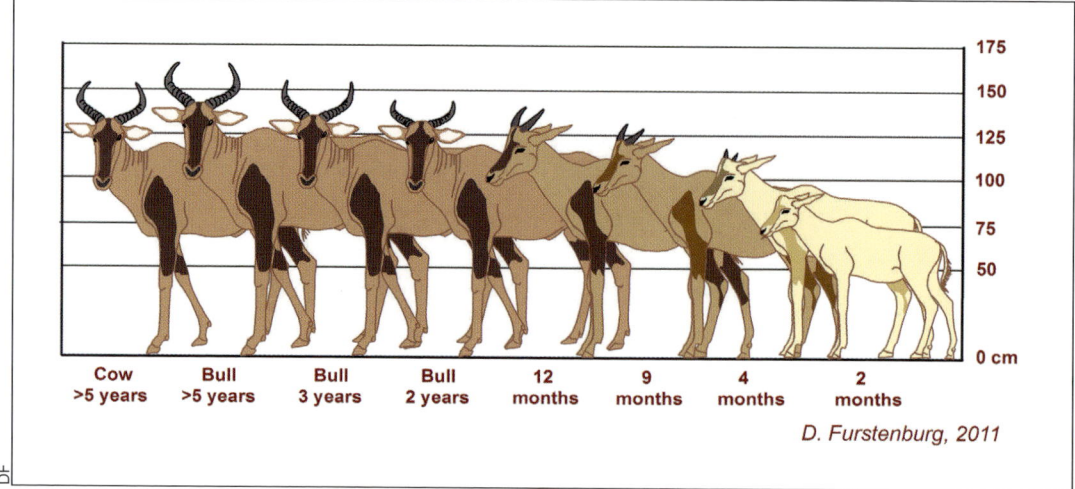

Growth profile of tsessebe with age.

requirements are fresh drinking water daily, palatable medium height to tall (23–60 cm) sweet grasses (sweetveld), scattered shade for midday resting, and marshy drainage lines. The ideal habitat is a marshland surrounded by a stretch of sweetveld grass extending into an open woodland ecotone. Hills and slopes are avoided and they cannot tolerate cold environments. During droughts they migrate to floodplains and marshes, returning to the home grounds after the first summer rains.

Bush encroachment is a major source depleting population numbers and declining the natural distribution range because they rely on vision for escaping danger – they will therefore move away when the bush closes up. Overgrazed veld is also marginal unsuitable to them.

Tsesssbe do not adapt easily to integrated mixed animal and livestock management systems, but prefer non-crowded larger free-roaming space, with little competition from other animal species. They will graze wetland grasses of up to 3 m tall, especially of the species *Sorghum verticilaster*. The diet comprises 70–95% grass and the rest of broad-leaved forbs. They select new growth above 8 cm from the ground and towards softer leaves on the stems of taller grass, but they do not consume any bulk roughage material. Tsessebe will migrate to reach burnt veld but only enter once the new growth has reached above 8 cm. Overall tsessebe behaviour has little impact on veld conditions. Preferred grasses include *Themeda triandra, Panicum coloratum, Panicum maximum, Cenchrus ciliaris, Digitaria eriantha, Heteropogon contortis, Schmidtia bulbosa, Urochloa mosambicensis, Sporobolus centrifugus, Eragrostis* sp., *Aristida* sp., *Ischaemum brachyatherum, Setaria woodii* and *Sorghum versicolor*.

Breeding systems

The tsessebe is highly specialised and does not adapt easily to habitat change. Likewise it does not adapt easily when translocated and/or introduced to a new or different habitat. They do not adjust well to the temperate habitats of the Free State and/or the dry habitats of the Western and Northern Cape. They are very prone to malnutrition and lose body condition rapidly with a sudden change of diet composition and/or diet quality. Sudden climate change, especially wet cold fronts can cause serious mortalities.

Tsessebe do not perform when kept together with any other animal species in an intensive breeding camp of less than 100 ha which is one of the reasons tsessebe has not yet established

Typical natural optimal habitat of tsessebe in mixed open woodland, with a marsh/vlei in the background and a semi-sweet grass stand of 45 cm height, on clayish soil in Mookgophong district.

Marginal Kalahari habitat, sweetveld and karroid scrub, on poor soil; overgrazed and competition with other grazers (rhino) has led to poor condition condition in Kimberley district.

greatly in the game industry. Farming with tsessebe is best done in free-roaming systems greater than 400 ha at an annual rainfall of 350–600 mm, with a minimum of three water holes and a minimum of three feeding stations. On 600 ha natural veld a maximum of 35 tsessebe should be kept, consisting of four family herds of 6–8 animals each and a bachelor herd of 5–6 non-breeding bulls and 2–3 nomadic post-mature bulls. Stocking and carrying capacity is not only determined by veld condition and feed plants but rather the 15 ha social spatial area required per animal, with a 20% overlap. A free-roaming system may be shared with several other game species.

Large-camp systems (75–200 ha per camp) are recommended for tsessebe breeding, stocked with two breeding herds of 6–10 animals, two breeding bulls and 2–5 selected subadult non-breeding bulls. Surplus young males should be removed annually. A minimum of two waterholes and three feeding stations are required. Feeding stations must be rotated between two different sites every two weeks to limit dung and parasite build-up at the sites. Feeding sites and waterholes/drinking holes must never be closer than 30 m from any fence or infrastructure. One feeding bucket per animal in the herd, placed in a full circle 5–7 m apart. Feeding buckets must be moved 0.5 m every day to avoid parasite build-up in the micro-moisture underneath the buckets. No other game species should be kept with the tsessebe herd.

Small-camp breeding systems must be a minimum 30 ha large, preferably 40–70 ha because tsessebe need social space and are subject to stress in smaller camps. With small camps it is best to allocate two camps per breeding herd, applying rotational stocking at 8 month intervals between the two camps. This herd should comprise 10–15 animals plus one breeding bull per two-camp system. All young males must be removed from the herd and the camp between the ages of 10–18 months.

Tsessebe calves are fragile and need maternal care up to 10 months of age, but from 18 months the males run the risk of confrontation with the breeding bull. The two-camp system must never be shared with any other game

Starter herd of two cows, one bull and a calf in a 30 ha camp with sweetveld, clay soil (grass 35 cm) and adjacent marshland (Swartruggens).

species. One feeding station being rotated bi-weekly between two sites and two water holes per camp (meaning 2 feeding stations and 4 water holes per two-camp system per breeding herd), and a minimum 30 m from any fence. One feeding bucket per animal placed in a circle.

Handling

Tsessebe are difficult animals to capture in bomas, so should be darted from a vehicle in a small handling camp. Darting from a helicopter will predispose them to capture myopathy and they may die up to 3 weeks after the capture operation.

Tsessebe are not easily tamed and when wounded become very fierce in camps, or in extensive areas can cover vast areas very quickly. Bulls often break their horns from digging up soil in displays of aggression.

Diseases and parasites

Tsessebe are immune to tick-borne diseases, and are rarely troubled by ticks because they groom constantly, especially at rest when standing or lying under the shade of trees. They are highly sensitive to wet cold spells and thus highly susceptible to pneumonia, which is why they do poorly in most regions of temperate climate and in all highveld regions. If kept in sourveld tsessebe tend to easily starve from feeding stress as well as suffer from botulism. These antelope are prone to capture stress and myopathy.

Additional information

Comprehensive information on tsessebe biology by the same author
is available on E-Book, the *Game Species Window*.
www.amazon.com pp 14302-14564.
Genetic advice on tsessebe breeding:
Wildlife Stud Services www.ws2.co.za
Geo Wild Consultants www.geowild.co.za

Wildebeest are exceptional at utilising short grass pastures in various biomes.

WILDEBEEST
Barry York

Introduction

Wildebeest belong to the tribe Alcelaphini which they share with hartebeest, tsessebe, blesbok and bontebok. Historically wildebeest lived in high densities on open plains and blue wildebeest migrate extensively across the African grasslands in search of water and grazing unless confined by fences.

The two species which occur in South Africa are the:
- black wildebeest and
- blue or brindled wildebeest.

Biological and economic value of wildebeest

Large herds of wildebeest are highly beneficial for the grassland and savannahs of Africa: The most nutritious grasses have evolved from the impact of these large herds of animals grazing, trampling, urinating and depositing dung on an area for a relatively short period of time, before moving on and allowing rest and regrowth of the grass sward. This cycle of relatively short duration high animal impact, followed by a longer recovery period, has a positive effect on the reseeding of grasses with improved ground litter cover and soil humus which leads to more efficient mineral and water cycles. This utilisation of the grass covering ensures a healthy, productive savannah ecosystem with little soil erosion or bush encroachment.

As well as making exceptional use of grasslands, wildebeest with their long limbs, and large surface area per unit mass are adapted to facilitate body cooling. Their smooth shiny coats reflect infrared radiation and the pigmented skins are resilient to UV rays. In addition, they are fertile, disease resistant and require little by way of parasite or disease management.

Wildebeest are utilised by game ranchers for breeding especially of beautiful colour variants such as the golden form which currently fetch very high prices on auctions. For this reason "goldens" are the ideal entry level game ranch animal for upgrading a breeding program with relatively low initial capital outlay.

In terms of meat production, whether for biltong or venison, wildebeest outperform most other species per unit of land. Wildebeest trophies are in demand from discerning hunters. Horn growth or trophy size slows down and stops with sexual maturity so top quality animals may be hunted from 2.5–3 years old. Two separate species occur in South Africa.

Black wildebeest in natural habitat.

Blue wildebeest with gold colour variants.

Black wildebeest (*Connochaetes gnou*)

Description

Black wildebeest are a buffy brown colour with a white tail. They are smaller than the blue wildebeest with distinct forward curved horns, white tail, a stiff mane and bristly chest and muzzle. Gold variants of this species were seen in the Eastern Cape where they were shot when black wildebeest were placed under the TOPs regulations of the DEA.

Habitat and distribution

Black wildebeest were numerous and widespread over central grassveld areas but were driven almost to extinction by hunting, disease and agriculture which reduced their numbers to 500. The conservation efforts of some farmers increased their numbers so that private farms and reserves could be restocked. There are currently 20 000 animals with 80% occurring on privately owned land.

They are best suited to the highveld plain grasslands of South Africa being selective grazers of short grasses with a preference for open plains without trees or shrubs. Biomes in which long grasses predominate or very arid areas are not suitable for black wildebeest (Frost, 2014).

Blue or brindled wildebeest (*Connochaetes taurinus*)

Various subspecies are recognised on the basis of differences of coat colour or markings.

Blue wildebeest: *C. taurinus taurinus* the blue or brindled wildebeest is the subspecies which occurs in South Africa. The coat colour varies from dark grey to brown, with a silvery sheen. A series of darker bands are found on the forequarters, which has given rise to the alternative name of "brindled".

Cookson's: *C. taurinus cooksoni* found in the Luangwa Valley in Zambia, is almost identical to the blue wildebeest but has a white dot on either side of the nose.

White-bearded gnu: *C. taurinus albojubatus* found in Tanzania and Kenya is almost identical to blue wildebeest but has a white throat mane.

Nyasaland gnu: *C. taurinus johnstoni* occurs currently in Mozambique, Zambia and Malawi. Most have a white band across the nose, but intermediates between these and white-bearded and blue wildebeest are seen.

Description

Blue wildebeest have a black mane and tail and a grey-blue hair coat with the hair on the limbs tending to show a brown or golden sheen. The horns curve out horizontally and then turn

The King's wildebeest is a localised colour variant of the blue wildebeest, with a grey body and white face.

upwards and inwards. Colour variation in the blue wildebeest is an interesting phenomenon, and curiously enough these are not regarded as a subspecies. The variation seen occurs naturally and some have been selected by game ranchers for breeding. The following variants have been described:

Golden or voss wildebeest: This is a recessive colour variation of the blue wildebeest, which has been recorded for decades in South Africa, along the Limpopo basin and the Tuli block. The name "vos" refers to the Afrikaans word for chestnut. It is thought that this colour variation is an adaptation to the hot dry climate in the areas where they were first described. Based on research work done in yellow-coloured cattle (Bonsmara) it is thought that the gold/yellow colour is an adaptation to the intense heat and resistance to high levels of UV radiation from sunlight. Light, shiny, coloured hair is very efficient in reflecting infrared rays. Many genetic variations including colour are therefore adaptive characteristics which enhance the functional efficiency of an animal to survive a constantly changing environment. Genetic variations are therefore strongly supported by the International Convention for Biodiversity.

King's Wildebeest (Bont wildebeest): These colour variants occur among blue wildebeest herds found in the western part of the Limpopo River basin. Their bodies are grey in colour with distinct white faces, ears, mane, beard and tail with many patches having a lighter patch on the side of the body. The lack of pigmentation found on the white areas can be a risk in the subtropics and may result in cancer problems especially among older animals.

Golden King Wildebeest (bronze wildebeest): These animals have a pattern similar to that of the King's wildebeest and differ in that the body is a copper-bronze colour, with pigmented skin and a golden mane, face, beard and tail. Mating between these and golden wildebeest produce all blue calves.

Prince wildebeest: These have a distinct white patch on the centre of their foreheads and/or a white stripe running down the face, sometimes with a pink nose. These variants occur on game farms in the Cradock region of the Eastern Cape where they continue to appear despite attempts to eliminate them.

Ghost or white wildebeest: White wildebeest are found among all wildebeest populations in Africa. They may not be typical albinos since some have pigmented skins and seem to vary in hair colour from white to grey with some red hairs at the top of their hooves. Those that lack skin pigment are not well adapted to local conditions of high UV radiation. Crosses between white and golden wildebeest produce blue offspring.

A hybrid cross between a black and blue wildebeest.

Bulls must be selected for fertility.

Red wildebeest: This "hybrid" or colour variant has been seen where black and blue wildebeest are found on the same property. The animals are fertile and produce viable offspring, which raises the question of whether *gnou* and *taurinus* are actually two separate species. The crosses are considered undesirable by conservation authorities, and so the two "species" may not be kept on the same property.

Habitat and distribution

Blue wildebeest are adapted to the savannahs of southern and East Africa. They are almost entirely grazers adapted to utilising short grass.

General breeding management

Wildebeest exhibit high levels of fertility in both sexes. There is a distinct breeding season with most calves being born in December and January after a 8.5 month gestation period. Aggressive, masculine bulls with a high libido give up to 35 calves in a single breeding season. Testicle size and volume is a good indication of fertility. The most fertile bull recorded has a testicular circumference of 34 cm and regularly sires 30 calves. Typically mature males have a testicular circumference of 25 cm. It should be noted that horn size may not be correlated with fertility, as has been shown in Afrikaner-cattle, so the selection parameters for fertility should receive preference. Bulls are sexually mature at 2.5 years old and are characterised by the eponymous "gnu" vocalisation.

Females on a good level of nutrition calve for the first time at two years old and will calve every year. A calving percentage of 90% is often achieved in a well-managed herd. Wildebeest cows are renowned for their ease of calving and high survival rate of their calves. However, overfed fat cows may develop calving problems, so the body condition must be carefully monitored. Cows are extremely protective of their offspring which are able to run within ten minutes after birth. They remain with the mothers until they are weaned. Smaller predators such as caracal and jackal have little impact on the survival of young. Mothers produce sufficient milk resulting in excellent calf growth rates. The calves reach 55% of the mother's mass at weaning.

Well-nourished animals have a good growth rate on a high roughage diet and can achieve up to 80% of their mature mass at one year of age, reaching their mature mass by 2.5 years old. Wildebeest are highly valuable as meat production animals for the biltong hunting market.

Golden cow with calf.

Breeding bull in camp with grass and natural vegetation.

Behaviour and handling

Wildebeest have a very strong herd instinct so it is easy to move them when rotating grazing areas on semi-intensive systems, which is beneficial for veld and pasture management, and disease and parasite control. Those raised in semi-intensive systems in large camps easily adapt to extensive conditions. Bulls are highly aggressive particularly if hand-raised and must always be treated with caution.

Semi-intensive breeding camps

Factors influencing the size or area of grazing camps to be erected include the carrying capacity of the land, herd sizes (single or multi species), number of camps per herd and social structure of the animals concerned. On a farm with a carrying capacity of 10 ha per livestock unit equivalent (LSU) breeding high value wildebeest in single sire herds of one bull and 31 female animals, the area required would be 160 ha (2 wildebeest per LSU). Based on this calculation one could erect 4 camps of 40 ha or 8 camps of 20 ha each.

The system of 8 camps per herd may be optimal in terms of grass production but the larger camps of about 40 ha are preferable as they allow adequate space for movement of animals within the grazing area, when fighting for social dominance takes place or when darting animals from a helicopter is required. Camps smaller than 20 ha are not recommend for wildebeest.

When designing the layout of grazing camps one should where possible separate different veld types or ecological areas that may require different management strategies. It is important to note that breeding bulls should not be separated by only a single fence as they often fight through and destroy the fence, sometimes with fatal consequences. This fighting along fences can be avoided by having double fencing or passages between camps, alternating camps with different game species or separating herds of the same species with camps that are being rested. Camps and gates should be designed so as to facilitate the movement of animals from one area to the next with the minimum amount of stress for the animals. This can be achieved by closing off water points or moving feeding troughs from one camp to the next and leaving the relevant gates open.

Where wildebeest cows and calves have become separated in adjacent camps, they have been known to kill themselves on the fence in an attempt to rejoin each other. In order to avoid this situation wildebeest should where possible be moved in a diagonal direction, through the camp corners.

The erection of 6 to 8 camps with a central passive capture boma or adjoining, swing gates in a four-camp system can be used to facilitate this process.

Nutrition

Wildebeest are almost exclusively grazers and seldom or possibly never browse. They can generally be stocked at the rate of two wildebeest per LSU.

Historically, wildebeest migrated to obtain optimal nutrition, but on game ranches do well in sweetveld areas where grasses have a high nutritional value provided there is sufficient grazing available. In mixed and sourveld areas phosphate licks can be provided in summer and protein supplements given in winter.

Wildebeest prefer young, short, nutritious grasses and do well on fertilised old lands where grasses such as kweek (*Cynodon dactylon*), Smutsfinger and Rhodes grass are sown/grown.

Adequate nutrition is most important for optimal production and where good grazing is limited wildebeest do best on a high roughage diet with a total digestible nutrient content (TDN) of 60%, and a crude protein content of 10–12%.

Good quality hay must be freely available at all times if grazing is in short supply. Wildebeest are not adapted to the high energy diets fed in cattle feedlots and can develop various digestive problems which result from carbohydrate supplementation such as acidosis and vitamin B deficiency. Soft buffalo type dung instead of the normal pellet type faeces is the first sign of nutritional problems in wildebeest.

Diseases and parasites

In their natural habitat wildebeest are extremely hardy animals. Even in semi-intensive camp systems, if they are rotated on a regular basis they seldom develop internal parasite infections and do not need tick control. If placed on irrigated pastures, however, they may well develop heavy burdens of worms which can be fatal.

Wildebeest occasionally develop clostridial myositis, botulism and are susceptible to anthrax. They can be vaccinated against these diseases in semi-intensive systems where management systems make this possible.

Cases of theileriosis (*T. hippotragi*) have been seen in young wildebeest under certain conditions. Allowing mothers to calve in tick clean camps (free of animals for 18 months) will reduce the chances of these infections (see chapter on Chapter 5).

The most important negative aspect of farming with wildebeest is that they are healthy carriers of the alcelaphine herpes virus (Al 1) which causes bovine malignant catarrh (BMC) or "snotsiekte" in cattle. The virus is shed by young wildebeest at weaning and can infect cattle up to 1 km away. The virus causes an almost invariably fatal disease in cattle, which brings game owners and livestock owners into conflict and makes it impossible to run cattle and wildebeest together. An attenuated vaccine is currently being tested which could alleviate the problem. Currently the only control measure is to keep a distance of 2 km between wildebeest and cattle herds.

Wildebeest are seldom victims of plant poisoning since they appear to avoid indigenous toxic plants such as gifblaar.

AEPYCERTOTIDAE (IMPALAS)
- Impala

IMPALA (*Aepyceros melampus*)
Deon Furstenburg

Speciation

Impala have become the most abundant of all game species on private land in South Africa, because they have always been an important source of venison.

In the dry southwestern regions of southern Africa, the role of the impala is replaced by the springbuck (*Antidorcas marsupialis*). Impala are the most important prey animal for large predators and is often managed to provide a buffer preventing the killing of more valuable game species.

The basic body form of the impala has remained almost unchanged since the Miocene (6.5 million years ago) and there has never been more than one species at any given time. Such evolutionary stability is astonishing considering that the closely related *Alcelaphine*-antelopes (blesbok, hartebeest and wildebeest) that share a common ancestor with the impala have split into new species at least 18 times. The body form bears a resemblance to many other bovids and taxonomists consider it to be the archetypical antelope.

The genus *Aepyceros* has only one species – *melampus* – and seven formerly recognised subspecies, only three of which are accepted by the Rowland Ward trophy register as having distinguishable morphologic differences:

- *Aepyceros melampus melampus*, the well-known southern impala including the former subspecies *A. m. johnstoni*, *A. m. katangae* and *A. m. holubi*.
- *A. m. suara*, the East African impala from central, eastern Africa including the former subspecies *A. m. rendilis*.
- *A. m. petersi*, the black-faced impala from northern Namibia, southern Angola and northwestern Botswana.

Typical southern impala ram.

Southern impala ewes.

Black impala.

Saddleback impala.

Based on molecular biology only two extant impala subspecies are recognised: The common impala (*A. m. melampus*) and the black-faced impala (*A. m. petersi*) (Nersting and Arctander 2001; Lorenzen et al. 2006). The two subspecies is of equal body size and no difference other than coat colour. The East African impala is only a phenotype of the common impala and not a subspecies.

Colour variants

Various colour forms of impala are known in the commercial game industry and trading at enormous value (under various changing commercial names), varying from black to saddleback, black-faced, white-speckled, white-flanked, pale white and white. Black-coloured impala have been photographed by tourists in the Kruger National Park as far back as 1976. It has subsequently been shown that the black colouration is a natural recessive gene that appears sporadically among impala, but in large free-roaming populations it is diluted because of the dominant red colour.

IUCN Conservation Status
- Impala: Lower Risk, conservation dependent (LR/cd).
- Black-faced impala: Vulnerable (VU).

With commercial breeding in camp systems the recessive black gene emerges and is selected by some breeders.

Table 1 illustrates the genetics of black and red colours of impala coat colour. Crossing two animals with heterologous (recessive) black genes Rb will produce a phenotypic ratio of three red-coated impala (two splits) and one homologous black-coated animal.

Table 1: The genotypes and phenotypes of crossing black impala and a "split"

Alleles of dam and sire	R	b
b	Rb	bb
b	Rb	bb

Note: Capital letter indicates dominance and lower case the recessive characteristic.
Rb: Red coat (referred to as "black splits").
bb: Black.

The crossing shown above will result in 50% black lambs and 50% red-colour lambs, wheras crossing two split blacks will produce only 25% black lambs (RbxRb: RR, Rb, Rb and bb). Note: The black-faced subspecies resembles similar colouration found for heterologous animals (referred to in the trade as "splits") and for saddleback impala, and may be just another colour variant being isolated for an extended period of time.

CHAPTER 4: SPECIES ACCOUNTS

Black-faced impala subspecies (*A. m. petersi*).

This is illustrated in the Punnet square cross:

Alleles of dam and sire	Sb	SR
SR	SSRb	SSRR
Sb	SSbb	SSRb

SSRb or SSRR are saddlebacks (75% in this cross). SSbb are blacks (25% in this cross).

Current distribution and numbers

Impala are endemic to the African continent. The current distribution range from East Africa through to South Africa remains largely unchanged from the historical range. In the past, the southern and east African impala were naturally distributed throughout the eastern regions of central and southern Africa including Kenya, Uganda, Tanzania, Zaire, Zambia, Angola, Botswana, Zimbabwe, Mozambique and the lowveld, bushveld, savannah and the Kalahari regions of South Africa.

Black-faced impala are restricted to the southwestern regions of Angola and the northwestern regions of Namibia, with

Saddleback genetics

The genetics for the "saddleback" patterning of impala is thought to be caused by a gene which is associated with the recessive black gene, but masked by the presence of two black recessive genes. The saddle pattern therefore appears when the genotype has two saddleback alleles (SS) associated with one recessive black allele (the other allele being a red gene).

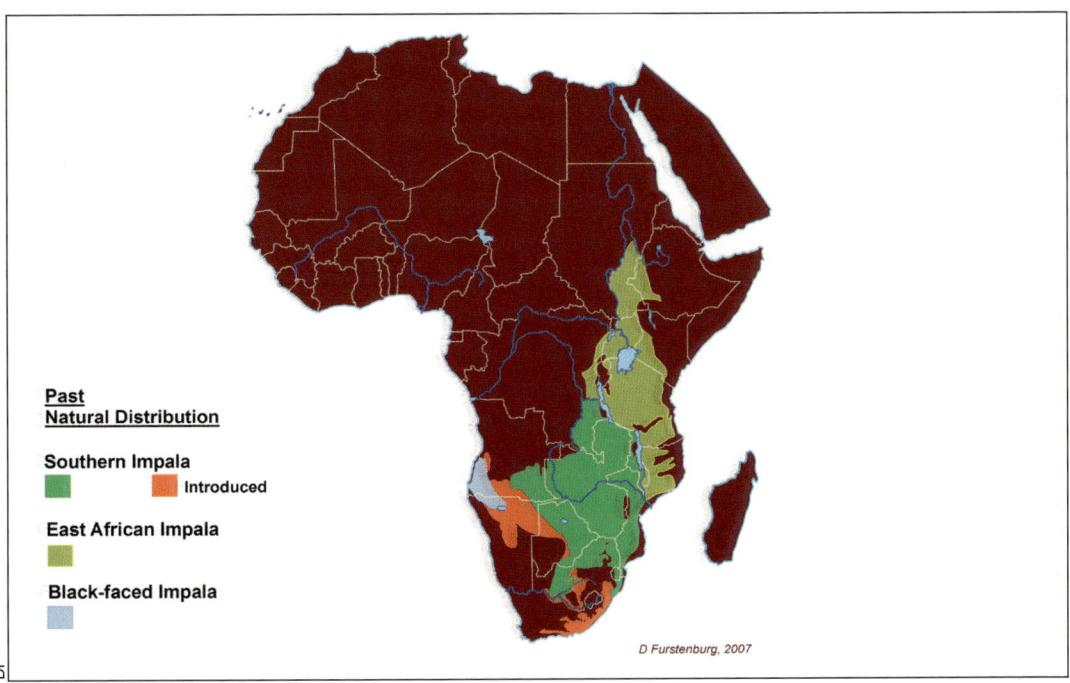

Distribution map of impala.

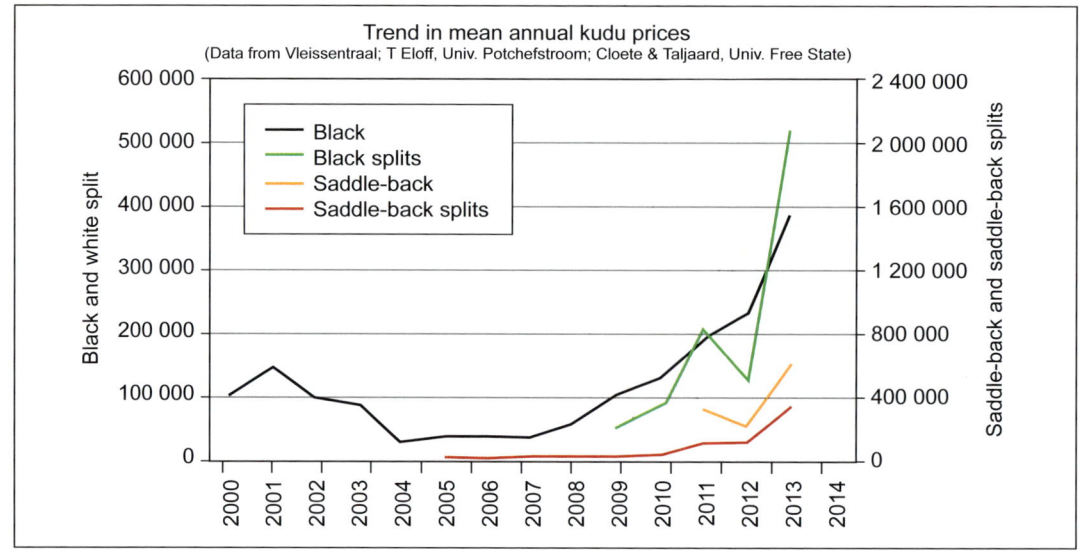

Impala prices.

scattered pockets occurring along the western Zambezi River. In the late 1800s and early 1900s, southern impala were more numerous in South Africa along the riverine and drainage lines to the northeast of Kuruman.

In 1970 impala were successfully introduced into an area stretching as far south as Uitenhage and George. They were also introduced into the Free State and the eastern Karoo and are now found in all nine provinces of South Africa.

Impala managed to survive and increase in numbers throughout the settlement period of historic and modern human development and succeeded in this co-existence due to its ability to alternate between grass and browse feeding, which allowed it to disperse into the ecotone habitats between grasslands and woodlands. These ecotones have increased owing to the spread of man and his farming practices that include overgrazing by livestock and the fertilisation of pastures on riverine banks together with the natural impact of global warming. The present status of the global impala population is estimated at 2 million of which about 50% are on private land. There are roughly 2 200 black-faced impala (IUCN 2015).

Rowland Ward records and horn characteristics

Horns are lyre-shaped, over 50 cm long and are coarsely grooved on the front surface for up to 75% of the total length. The last quarter

Mean age related growth rate for Southern Impala			
Age	Live body mass (kg)	Horns	
		Length (cm)	Number of grooves
Birth	4.5	0	0
2 months	7	0	0
4 months	12	0.5–4	0
6 months	16	10–15	0
1 year	25–30	20–30	1
1.5 years	30–35	32–40	4–6
2 years	33–40	38–48	9–13
2.5 years	36–45	42–54	15–18
3 years	38–50	46–58	16–22
4 years	40–55	50–64	18–24
5 years	40–58	>52	20–24
6 years	40–64	>52	20–24

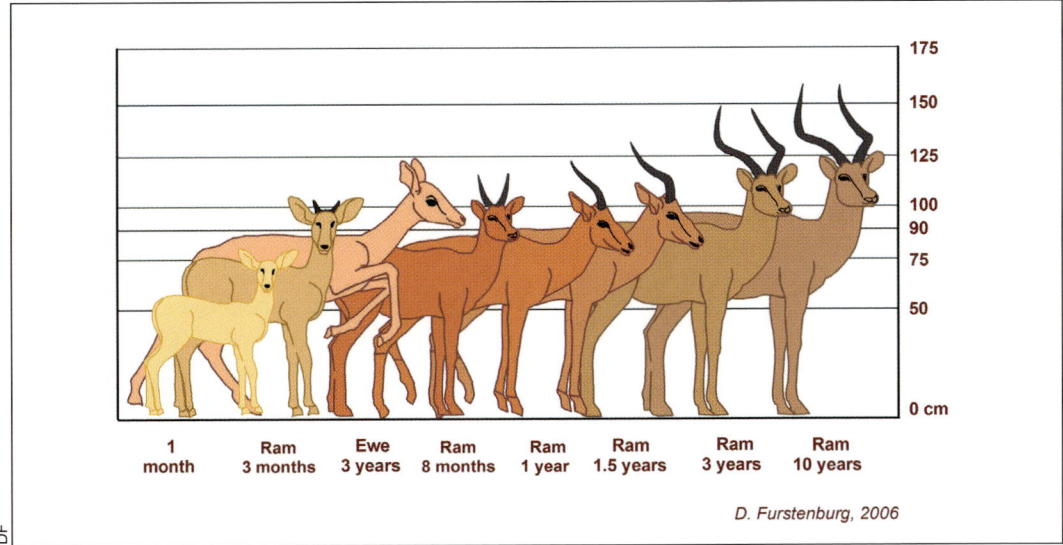
Growth profile of impala with age.

of the horns is smooth. The number of grooves on the horns relates to the animal's age and can be used as a method for age determination. Well-developed horns are only found in rams but ewes with inferior, rudimentary, deformed horns occasionally occur.

The Rowland Ward trophy status of 23 5/8" is only reached after five years, the record being 30 7/8" from Steenbokpan, Limpopo in 2003 hunted by R.N. Diplock. Black-faced impala have similar, but smaller horns whereas those of the East African impala are of a better quality, being longer with a distinctive wide diameter and a much greater tip-to-tip spread than the southern impala.

Behaviour

Impala are known to associate with other gregarious animal species such as blue wildebeest (Connochaetes taurinus), zebra (Equus spp.), chacma baboon (Papio ursinus), waterbuck (Kobus ellipsiprymnus) and giraffe (Giraffa camelopardalis), which is thought to be a symbiotic relationship. When bred in camp systems sharing with larger game such as sable, roan or wildebeest, impala often get injured or killed from aggressive interaction of the other species at drinking holes and feeding stations. Black impala are generally more timid than common impala and tend to keep to thicker bush and shelter.

Impala are area-bound and the same group (6–30 animals) is frequently found in the same vicinity. The mean distance for 24 hours movement being 2.5–3 km. Home ranges are stable year round and vary from 200–700 ha depending on the veld condition and the stocking density. Impala are not migratory and roam approximately 8.4 ha/24 hour-cycle keeping within 1.6 km from drinking water – they often starve at a dried-up water hole instead of migrating to seek an alternative water source. Feeding is restricted to daylight hours and during hot daylight hours they keep to the shade of trees. Socially mature rams establish temporary territories of 4–10 ha only during the rut. Bachelor herds form during the rut between January and April, consisting of sexually mature, but socially immature rams. Temporary nursing groups of youngsters form on the outskirts of the family herds and are accompanied by 1–2 adult ewes. Herds form of post-mature rams of 2–4 years that are mostly of trophy quality.

Breeding

Rams reach sexual maturity at 16 months and ewes at 13 months, but social maturity (age of first mating) at 3 years for rams and 1.5 years for ewes. The gestation period is 185–205 days. The lambing season differs with the geographic area, being from October to January in South Africa when 90% of the lambs are born within a short period of 3–5 weeks. Lambs only associate with their mothers for suckling and spend the rest of their time in nursing groups. Dominant rams become aggressive as the rut approaches at the end of January. Declining daylight hours stimulate an increased hormonal production that enables fat (known as blubber) to accumulate in the neck, enlarging the neck of the male that, in turn, triggers oestrus in the adult ewes. Territorial rams try to retain their family herds generally for a period of 8–12 days and thereafter become weak and displaced by another challenging opponent. After 4–6 weeks the ram becomes exhausted, and abandons its territorial behaviour. After 8 years rams become post-mature and join small post-mature groups.

Natural mating ratio is one mature ram to three mature ewes, giving an annual population growth of 23% at 300 mm annual rainfall, to 48% at >600 mm. The lambing efficiency of two year old ewes is only 60%, in 3–7 year old ewes it is 97% and for ewes >8 years of age it declines to 70–80%. The mean lifespan is 8–12 years.

Habitat and dietary requirements

Impala are associated with a bushveld, savannah or open woodland habitat, mainly on alluvial and volcanic clay soils at an annual rainfall of 400–700 mm. Habitats with a diverse tree and shrub composition are favoured, especially if it includes *Acacia, Combretum, Terminalia, Dichrostachys, Grewia* and *Mopane* trees and shrubs species. Impala tend to avoid rocky outcrops, mountain slopes, open grasslands, marshlands, arid environments, riverine thickets and forests. They do not tolerate arid climates. Ecotones on the perimeter of riverine thickets and closed woodland are more suitable. Overgrazed veld provides prime habitat as it increases the number of annual broad-leaved forbs which are preferred fodder for impala.

Impala are mixed feeders being both a browser and grazer of high quality fodder and are highly selective in choice of both plant species and plant parts. Most important is the nutritive quality and palatability of the plant material. The ratio of browse to grass varies with the season and depends on rainfall and habitat. A low crude-fibre diet of <40% is required, together with high protein content of 8% in winter and 16% in summer when females are lactating.

A property of 1 000 ha with good quality forage can sustain 300 impala at an annual rainfall of 400 mm, and 600 impala at 600 mm rainfall. An impala animal unit (AU) of 50 kg equals 0.17 large stock units (LSUs) and 0.38 browser units (BUs). Each impala animal unit requires a minimum of 2–4 ha spatial area in an optimal habitat, with 650 edible shrubs or trees of >80 cm canopy diameter and a sustained canopy height of 50–150 cm. This index can be used to calculate the carrying capacity and animal load for any given land unit after determining the browse composition and density of the unit.

During moist conditions feed consists of predominantly short (<8 cm), sweet grasses forming 79–92% of the diet, together with herbs, dicot forbs and little woody browse. In dry winter conditions the lignin content of grass increases and the diet changes to 32–67% woody browse. During winter there is an increase in the rumen wall thickness and an enlargement of the ruminal papillae from 6 to 11 mm resulting in an enlargement of the

Optimal habitat for impala.

absorption surface. A change in the acidity of the rumen fluid from pH 6.7 to 5.8 and a simultaneous enrichment in the protozoan composition of forestomachs increases the fermentation of the crude-fibre content. These physiological changes revert with the onset of a moist summer; this allows the impala to be a concentrate feeder in a variety of different habitats year round. The daily protein requirement for adult ewes increases from a non-lactating level of 0.5 to 22.0 g at the time of birth.

The daily food consumption of adult impala ranges from 0.9 kg dried matter in a dry winter to 1.9 kg in a moist summer. Impala are strongly attracted to the new growth on recently burnt veld in a close vicinity to the home range. Impala do not migrate and cannot be lured over long distances.

Like kudu and giraffe, impala need to feed across a large diversity of fodder plants as they are severely affected by secondary metabolites such as condensed tannin and glycosides. Studies in the mixed bushveld of the Limpopo found up to 87 dietary plant species for one impala population. Fallen pods are an important source of stored protein during the dry winter months.

Territorial mating rams do not feed during the rut but rely entirely upon their stored reserves. They start to feed again once the short mating period of 4–6 weeks is over or when an opponent displaces them from their territory. In order to build up body reserves of stored energy for the rut, the socially mature rams increase their food intake during the late summer months of January to March. Energy reserves are stored as a protein deposit in a layer of "brown" fat called blubber that surrounds the neck muscles and causes a visible thickening of the neck.

The preferred browsing height is 40–100 cm but overstocking results in the developing of a distinct browse line at 130 cm, eradication of the herbaceous layer and the replacement of palatable decreaser grass species by unpalatable increaser species. This results in a decrease in ground cover. Impala have a high impact on veld condition as a result of their selective feeding behaviour and their gregarious nature.

Supplemental feeding

Impala accept supplemental and artificial feeding and will take both dried lucerne and concentrated antelope cubes. When there are mineral deficiencies they eagerly take concentrated mineral salt licks. Approximately 4 litres of water are drunk every second day limiting them to an area within 1.6 km of the nearest water. Impala do not readily drink from artificial livestock troughs, so drinking holes need to be designed close to ground surface and more than 30 m away from any fence or infrastructure.

Breeding systems

Until recently the focus of impala breeding has been selection of colour variants which are in demand. It is predicted that the next era of impala breeding will see a shift to impala trophy and genetic improvement as is being done

Good impala breeding camp systems.

with the sable, buffalo, kudu and the golden wildebeest. Impala do not do well in camps smaller than 20 ha, recommended minimum camp size is 25 ha and preferably two camps per breeding herd of no more than 30 females and one breeding ram each. Impala should not be forced to share camps with other larger game species because they will be injured at communal drinking holes and feeding stations.

Inbreeding due to line breeding of colour variants results in numerous negative effects relating to fitness and quality (Lubout 2015). See the suggested management strategy (on the following page) for impala in semi-intensive impala breeding in camp systems.

Some of the worst cases of mismanagement of game animals in breeding camp systems are generally found with impala and are illustrated in the examples below:
- Pellets made from green lucerne risking dietary problems.
- Feeding from unsuitable containers such as bath tubs resulting in crowding, poor access and fighting.
- Impala kept on open old lands with no cover from winter cold.
- Feeding green lucerne thrown on ground.
- Water holes placed only 3 m from fence, with little space for escape during social confrontations, resulting in injury.
- Separating herds with see-through shade cloth so rams continuously fight through fence.
- Housing impala with other species resulting in injuries to the smaller animals.
- Housing in unsuitable enclosures such as vegetable gardens, backyards with no grazing and no protection against cold.

Diseases and parasites

Impala are prone to develop some diseases when transported and kept in camps if these are not managed correctly. They develop pneumonia (especially when infected with lung worms) after translocation, and coccidiosis frequently appear with impala kept in bomas. However, roundworm infestations of up to 60 000 can be tolerated without negative effect. Free-living impala are susceptible to diseases such as foot-and-mouth disease and anthrax. Ticks are seldom a problem because their teeth allow them to groom effectively. Occasional cases of sarcoptic mange are seen.

Management strategy for two breeding herds of impala as to sustain better veld condition and to improve genetic animal quality

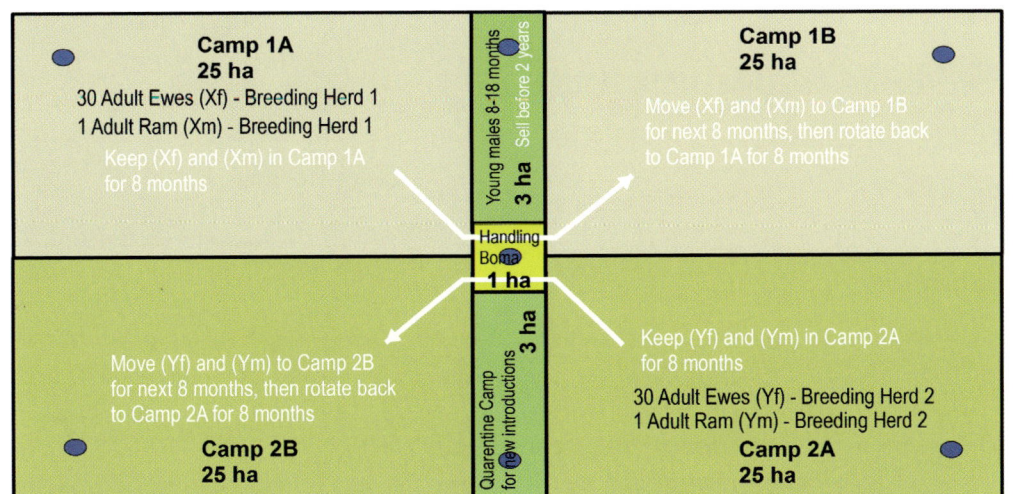

* Rotate each herd at 8 month intervals between the A & B sections of the camp as to sustain veld condition
* Stock the camps diagonally across as to prevent the two herds sharing the same fence
* Ram Xm and Ym from different genetic origin / farms
* Ewes Xf and Yf from different genetic origin / farms and from different origin than the rams
* After 2 breeding seasons alter the rams between Camp 1 & 2
* After next 2 breeeding seasons alter the rams again
* After 2-3 breeding seasons the ewes in Camp 1 can be replaced by the female F1 offspring from Camp 2 and vice versa
* Remove all male offspring from breeding herds at 8-10 months age to prevent fighting
* Sell young male offspring before 2 years age
* All new animal introductions must be kept in quarentine at least 2 months before mixing with local animals (biosecurity)
* This system can be extended to 3 or more breeding herds to the better of genetic quality management
* Placement of water / drinking holes, furthest corner from boma and very important minimum 30 m from fence
* Feeding buckets (1 per animal, placed in a circle), alternate feeding between two locations - at drinking hole and close to boma (20 m away from any fence)

Suggested management strategy for impala in semi intensive breeding systems

Additional information

Comprehensive information on sable biology by the same author
is available on E-Book, the
Game Species Window.
www.amazon.com pp 7782-8147.
Genetic advice on tsessebe breeding: Wildlife Stud Services www.ws2.co.za
Geo Wild Consultants: www.geowild.co.za

ANTELOPINI (GAZELLES)
- Springbok

SPRINGBOK (*Antidorcas marsupialis*)
Deon Furstenburg

Typical springbok colouration.

Speciation

The springbok is endemic to southern Africa where it fills an ecological niche and socio-economic role in the arid and desert southwestern parts. The impala (*Aepyceros melampus*) fills a similar role in the subtropical woodland and savannah of the northeastern parts of the region. Springbok remained the most important game meat during centuries of European colonisation. Millions of springbok were harvested/hunted for biltong and food between 1750 and 1896 coinciding with the mass migration-treks (Le Roux, 2015). Countless tales have been told of the millions of springbok that formed colonies several kilometres in diameter moving at speeds/distances of up to 140 km per day through the Karoo and Namaqualand.

- The springbok belongs to the genus *Antidorcas* with only one species *marsupialis*. Originally three subspecies were distinguished:
- *Antidorcas marsupialis marsupialis*, the southern or Cape springbok of the southwestern Cape region.
- *A. m. hofmeyri*, the Kalahari springbok of southern Namibia, Botswana and the northwestern parts of South Africa.
- *A. m. angolensis*, the Angolan springbok of northern Namibia and southern Angola.

In 1975 Robinson concluded that there was little support for the continued recognition of springbok subspecies. More recently, measurements of skulls from springbok to the north of the Orange/Vaal River system showed a significant phenotypic difference in size to those from the south and were thought to be due to major differences in diet and climate. The debate resurfaced in 1996 and two phenotypes have been proposed:

- *A. m. marsupialis*, the southern springbok found to the south of the lower Orange River and the Vaal River including the Free State and most of the Eastern and Western Cape Provinces.
- *A. m. hofmeyri*, the northern or Kalahari springbok found to the north of the Orange and Vaal Rivers including the northern parts of the Western Cape, Gauteng, Limpopo and North West Provinces and the Kalahari regions of Botswana, Namibia and Angola.

In the commercial market springbok from Namibia are traded currently as Damara springbok. Attempts to increase body size by crossing northern springbok with the southern gave varying results in different regions. Ranchers in the arid Karoo claimed that these attempts were successful, but in the more temperate savannah environments further to the southeast it had little effect on the body size. The introduction of the larger, black

---

IUCN Conservation Status
- Springbok: Lower Risk, conservation dependent (LR/cd).

Various colour variants of the springbok

White variants. Black variant. A coffee colour springbok lamb.
Copper variant. Maroela/ivory. Cream.
King. Bont.

springbok to the south was more successful with a sustained production of offspring with a larger build.

Colour variants

Various colour variations of springbok are known and traded commercially at high value in the game industry under various changing names including common, black, white, copper, cream, blue, maroela/ivory, coffee, king and bont. Animals trading as "Kalahari" and "Damara" refer only to geographic origin and not to any colouration. White and black mutants have arisen naturally and has been recorded in the Cape as early as the settlement of Jan van Riebeeck. As with impala the black and white colours in springbok are recessive. In large free-roaming populations these colours disappear due to the dominance of the normal colour. White springbok have pigmented skin and horns unlike albinos which have a health risk for the development of skin cancer.

There is some confusion regarding copper and coffee springbok: The first "copper" springbok was seen in the mid-1990s in the eastern Cape in the Grahamstown/Port Alfred region; the animal was a beautiful distinctive rich dark copper-brown on the back with a bright white belly and much sought after, but are now called coffee springbok. Those now referred to as copper have a copper-coloured back and a light brown belly.

Current distribution and numbers

Springbok are associated with dry environments and are limited to the dry regions of Namibia, Botswana, Angola and the western and southwestern areas of South Africa. They were exterminated over much of their natural range during the course of the late 1800s as a result of hunting and the effects of rinderpest. It is estimated that they numbered close to a billion before this and were therefore the most numerous antelope that have populated the planet. Since the mid-1990s springbok were reintroduced widely to private land and protected areas throughout its former range. The largest numbers occur on private game farms, mainly in the highveld of the Free State and Gauteng Provinces and the Karoo and Kalahari thornveld of the Western and Northern Cape Provinces. The most southern natural distributions recorded was at Van Rhynsdorp in the Western Cape, and at Port Alfred in the Eastern Cape.

Currently the numbers of springbok are estimated at 730 000 in Namibia, 10 000 in Angola, 100 000 in Botswana, 75 000 in the Free State, 75 000 altogether for Gauteng, Limpopo and North West, 1 000 000 in the Karoo and about 100 000 in the Cape provinces outside of the Karoo. The total population size in southern Africa is estimated at between 2 and 2.5 million.

Rowland Ward records and horn characteristics

Both the ram and ewe bear well-developed lyre-shaped horns. They are parallel at the base, then curve backwards and then sideways and close sharply towards each other at the tips forming two hooks. The horns are heavily

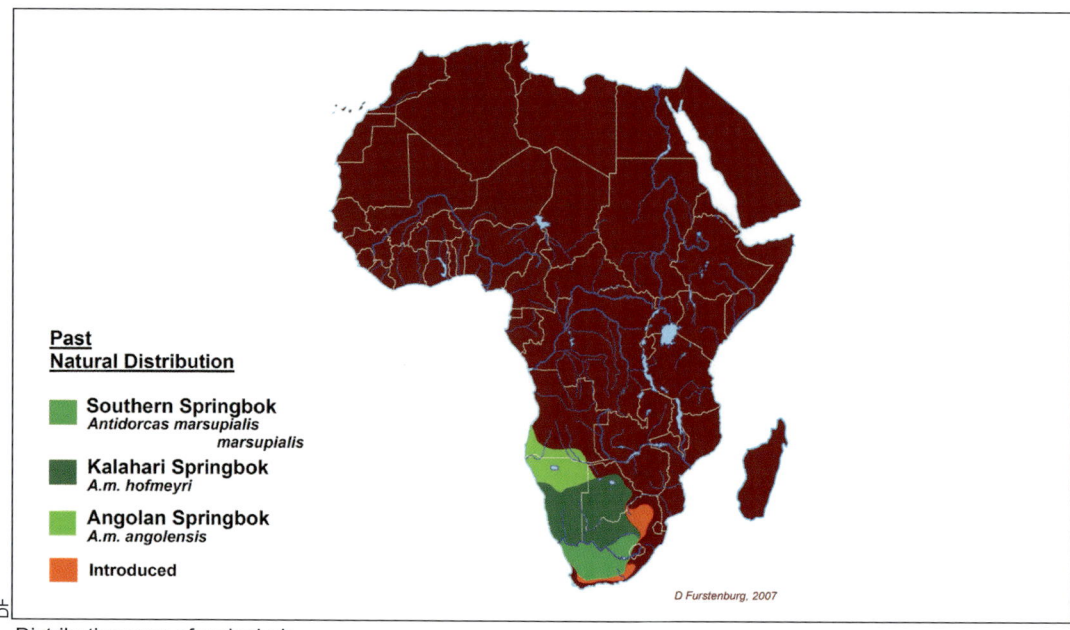

Distribution map of springbok.

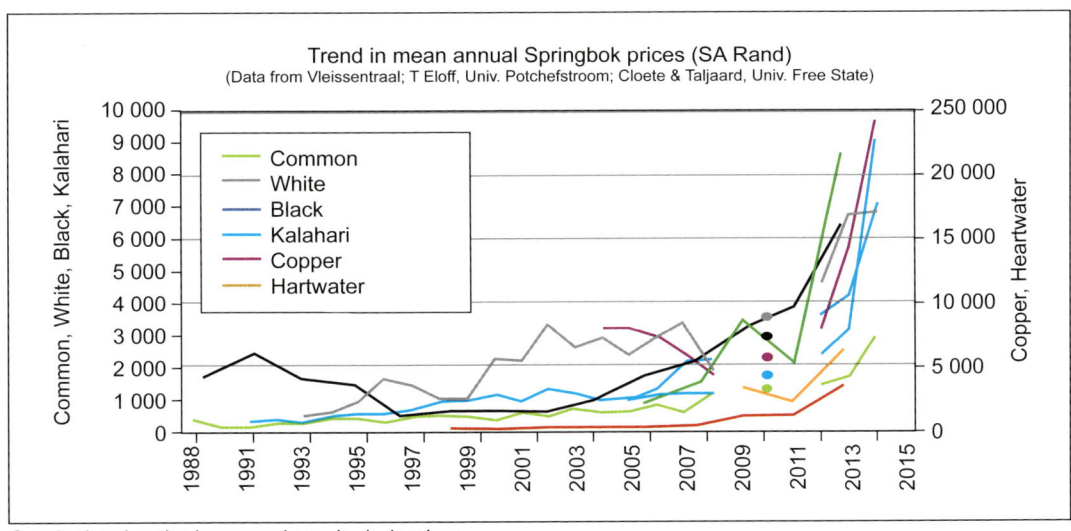

Graph showing the increase in springbok prices.

grooved for 60–75% of the length and have smooth ends. The horns of ewes are distinctly thinner, straighter and further apart at the base than those of the rams. Trophies reach full development at an age of 20 months and Rowland-Ward trophy status after 5 years. The 19³⁄₈″ trophy shot by B.L Steenkamp in Namibia in 1973 was the Rowland Ward No. 1 for 40 years (now No. 2) before it was replaced by the current No. 1 record of 20¹⁄₂″ of Zottan Pecsi. The 19¹⁄₈″ of W.H. Allhusen shot in 1961 near Beaufort West, Western Cape still remains No. 3. The huge population size of the springbok metapopulation has ensured

Springbok trophy development

Mean age related growth rate for Springbok		
Age	Live body mass (kg)	Horns Length (cm)
Birth	3.5	0
2 months	6	0
3.5 months	10–12	3–5
9 months	18–25	5–9
1.2 years	28–35	13–18
1.5 years	29–37	17–24
1.8 years	30–40	19–26
2.5 years	32–42	21–30
3 years	33–44	28–35
4 years	34–46	30–40
6 years	35–48	32–45

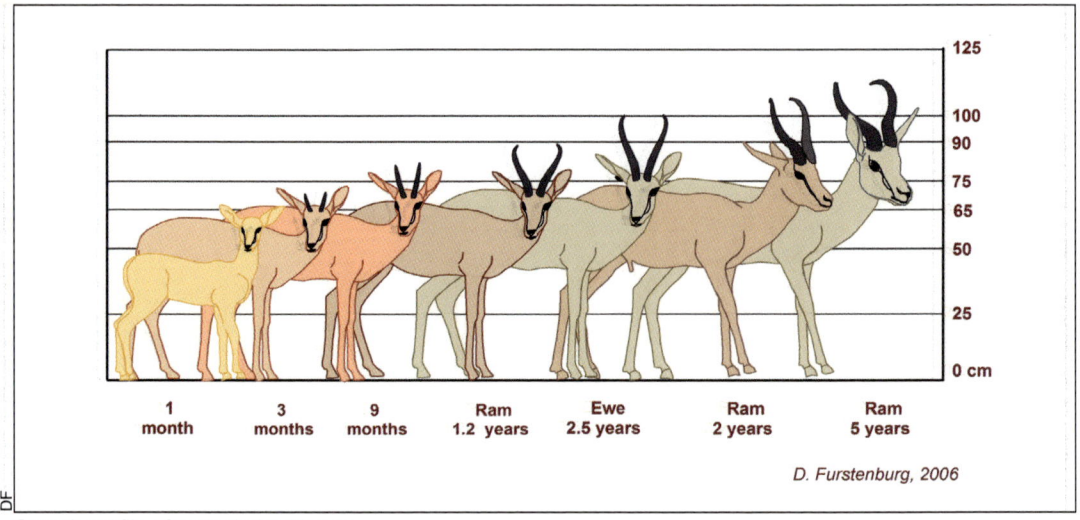

Growth profile of springbok with age.

their genetic diversity and they fare better in this than almost all other game species. It is therefore unlikely that trophy quality can be improved in this species unlike the scenario of the sable antelope.

Behaviour

Springbok are social and gregarious, forming family groups of 5–100 individuals during dry winter periods and aggregating into temporary mass herds in summer. A family herd consists of adult ewes, subadult females and juveniles of both sexes. Adult rams (>2.5 years) only become territorial during the rut in late summer and autumn; during the rest of the year they join family herds or become solitary nomads. Territories (2–6 ha) are aggressively defended and the ram will attempt to confine any passing family herd to its territory for as long as possible. During the lambing season the year-old subadult rams leave the family herd to form temporarily bachelor herds.

During dry winters springbok tend to break up into smaller herds. In desert habitats, herds travel long distances to feed on the vegetation that appears after localised rainfall.

Springbok are diurnal and are most active in the early morning, the late afternoon and the early, dark evening hours. Hot, midday hours are mostly spent lying down or standing ruminating. If threatened a flight speed of 88 km/h is reached, accompanied by long leaps of up to 5 m and 2 m high. Unlike impala (*Aepyceros melampus*), springbok do not readily associate with other game species.

Apart from the sporadic "treks", springbok do not follow a seasonal migration route as for the white-bearded blue wildebeest in the Serengeti. Family herds tend to stay in a fixed home range of between 300 and 800 ha. Some minor, nomadic populations still exist but are rare. In the Western Cape to the west of Colesberg a herd of 400 to 1 200 springbok constantly move in an enormous area including several farms. These "trek-springbok" are not confined by livestock fences and jump, crawl under or break any fence in their path. Commercial herds are content to remain enclosed and have a totally different behavioural pattern that may indicate the beginning of domestication. Farmers regard "trek-springbok" as problem animals that interfere with general livestock and game farming management.

Mature rams have a mean weight of 41 kg and ewes 37 kg. In general, trek-bokke are 6 kg lighter than the non-migratory animals.

Optimal Kalahari habitat, note the dry *Rhigozum* browse scrub between medium height sweet grass.

In marginal habitat with tall sweet grassveld (humid north-western bushveld) the animals seek out over-grazed open spots.

Breeding

Springbok mating seasons differ between years as a result of changing climatic conditions and the resultant difference in the nutritional quality of forage. Most births occur during the peak rainfall period of the year after a gestation of 5.5 months. Ewes gain sexual maturity at six months but start to mate after ten months with adult territorial rams older than 2.5 years. Lambs join crèches for the first three weeks and wean at three months. With optimal climatic conditions an ewe can produce one lamb every 8 months, and when nutritionally stressed as during droughts ewes abort foetuses of up to 4 months development. Adult body size is reached at 18–20 months age. Annual natural population growth rate ranges from 28–42% depending on rainfall and veld condition. An optimal natural habitat of 1 000 ha with an annual rainfall of 250–350 mm can support approximately 450 springbok.

For free-roaming animals the maximum mating ratio is one mature ram to 7 mature ewes. There may be a decline of trophy quality if the ram/ewe ratio is greater as the male population becomes younger overall. An adult springbok animal unit (AU) is 40 kg and is the equivalent of 0.15 large stock units (LSU's) and 0.37 browser units (BU's). In order for a herd to survive, each springbok AU needs a minimum of 1.5–3 ha of suitable grazing and 454 edible shrubs with a canopy diameter >80 cm.

Habitat and dietary requirements

The preferred habitat is found mainly in the western region of southern Africa which is arid with dry grassy flats, Karoo scrub, salty pans, dune pathways and semi-desert shrubland. The broadleaf, sweet, short grasses surrounding water pans are favoured. In the Kalahari, the dry river beds are preferred over the areas between dunes. The most important habitat parameters are the availability of perennial short, sweet grasses and forbs, woody scrub with a high mineral content, sandy soil, a low shrub density (no thickets) and an annual rainfall of 50–450 mm. Dense thicket and closed woodland, rocky surfaces, mountainous areas, forests, tall grass stands and moist, alluvial clay soils are avoided and not suitable for springbok. Surface drinking water is not essential as springbok gain sufficient water from the diet.

Springbok are concentrate/mixed-feeders that consume sweet short grass (to 8 cm in height), forbs, succulents and browse. Grasses

The author hand-grooming a springbok ram in typical springbok habitat – short sweet grass on dry sandy soil with scattered browse shrubs.

and forbs form the bulk of the diet during moist summer periods but in dry winter they consume mainly browse and succulents. Springbok cannot tolerate the high crude fibre content found in most grasses during winter and of sourveld grasses. Most important food selection criteria are nutrient quality, palatability and digestibility of plant matter. Springbok cannot survive in sour veld. Important dietary species include:

Grasses: *Panicum* spp., *Eragrostis* spp., *Brachiaria* spp., *Pennisetum* spp., *Sporobolus* spp., *Digitaria* spp., *Enneapogon scoparius*, *Themeda triandra*, *Cynodon dactylon* and *Stipagrostis uniplumis*.

Forbs and shrubs: *Monechma* sp., *Rhigosum* sp., *Psoralea* sp., *Zygophyllum* sp., *Grewia* spp., *Solanum* spp., *Acacia* spp., *Pentzia incana*, *Chrysoeoma tenuifolia*, *Rhus ciliate*, *Boscia albitrunca*, *Ziziphus mucronata* and *Colophospermum mopane*.

Succulent forbs, for example "vygies" of the Mesembryanthomaceae plant family, cacti, and bulbs such as tsammas and gemsbok cucumbers serve as important water sources. Adult springbok needs 1–1.5 liters of moisture per day. Springbok are independent of drinking water when the moisture content of the diet is greater than 10%. Fog and dew are licked from stones and the surface of vegetative material in early morning. Springbok are adapted to low water availability by reabsorbing water, resulting in concentration of the urine.

Breeding systems

Springbok with migratory instincts (trekbokke) cannot be farmed on private land while non-migratory animals or "houbokke" can be kept in large-camp systems. As a species they do not adapt well to small camps, but like eland, red hartebeest and gemsbok they prefer to roam large areas, an evolutionary adaptation to surviving in harsh dry conditions.

Springbok can with some effort be habituated using a constant supply of quality supplement food. When purchasing springbok for semi intensive breeding the buyer should choose animals which have been habituated rather than free-roaming animals which may become stressed and injure themselves in small camps.

In their natural environment (Karoo, Kalahari and/or sweet climate climax grassveld) springbok need 500 ha camps with a herd size of 80 springbok per camp. With a six-camp design, it is better to stock only four camps with 80 springbok each (5–6 breeding rams per herd) and rotating all herds simultaneously

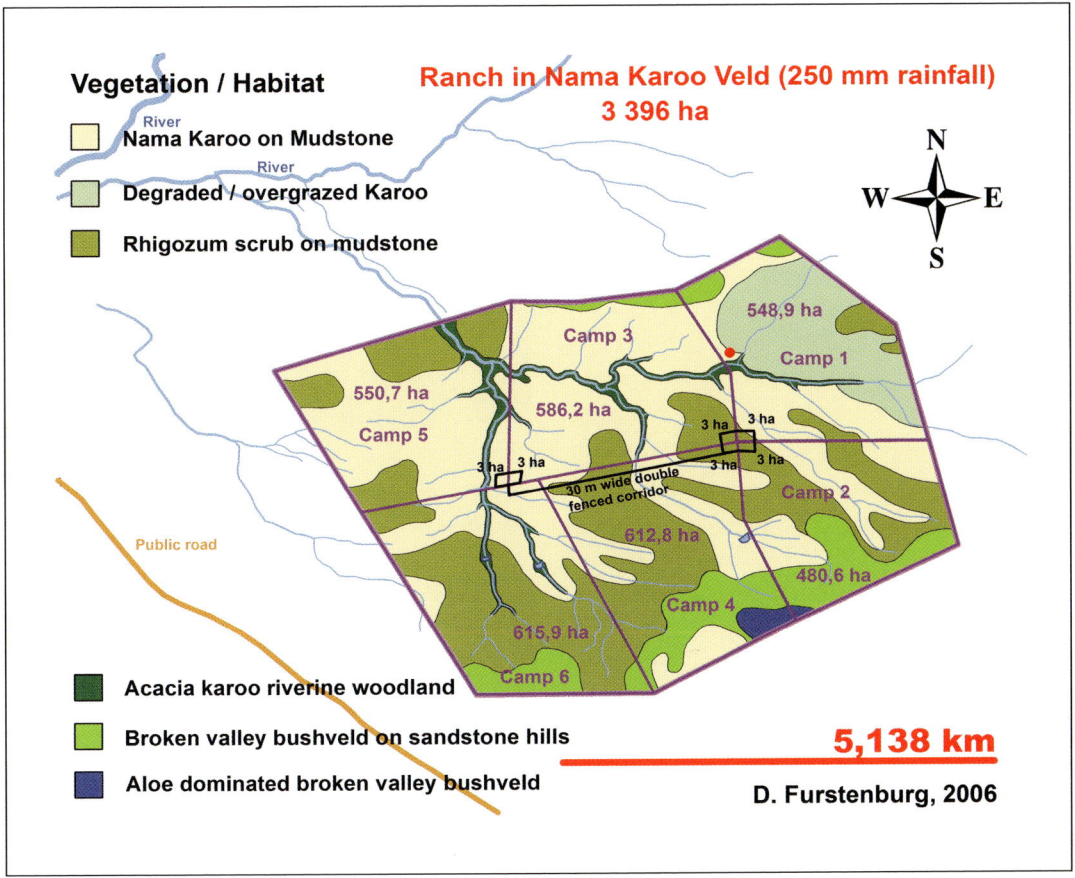

Example of an extensive camp system for springbok production in the Nama Karoo.

between the camps every four months. Example, see illustration of a real farm system on the following page:
- Stock camps 1 and 2, and 3 and 4 simultaneously each (camps 5 and 6 resting);
- after four months move animals from 3 to 5, from 4 to 6, from 1 to 3 and from 2 to 4 (camps 1 and 2 resting);
- after another four months move animals from 5 to 2 (cross switch), from 6 to 1 (cross switch), from 3 to 5 and from 4 to 6 (camps 3 and 4 now resting);
- continuously repeat the process.

Note the 3 ha handling camps and corridor for the feeding and passive moving of the herds. Once every two years rotate the breeding rams between the herds to improve genetic fitness in the population. With small-camp systems the minimum recommended camp size is 30 ha for 1 breeding ram of value and 20–25 females. Take note these animals must be semi-tamed prior to introduction and should not be introduced from a large-camp or free-roaming system (high risk of stress related adaptation). Breeding rams may fight when being adjacent to other breeding camps.

Small camps for breeding springbok must never be restricted to moist areas, along drainage lines or in marshy areas without access to dry sandy environment on higher ground. Also take note that springbok camps must consist predominantly of short grasses (< 12 cm) which will discourage tick burdens and internal parasites. Supplementation outside the natural habitat must be done carefully with professional advice.

Feeding buckets should be spaced in a circle and 5 m part, one bucket per animal. Buckets must be cleaned daily and moved 0.5 m to prevent parasite built-up underneath. Feeding stations must be altered every two weeks between 3 different localities in the camp. Each camp must have at least two well-spaced drinking holes. Feeding buckets and drinking holes must never be closer than 30 m from any fence or infrastructure as to allow space for escape when gathered animals get agitated with each other. Male lambs must be removed from the herds in small-camp systems before the age of 10 months to prevent fighting from the breeding ram, but not before 6 months (weans only at 5.5 months). Surplus valued rams are to be removed and kept together for conditioning in a ram camp of no less than 15 ha. Springbok should not be mixed with other species.

Diseases and parasites

Springbok are known for their susceptibility to heartwater. Animals raised in heartwater endemic areas are not necessarily resistant – this has led to major disputes in the past between buyers and sellers.

Roughly 4–8% of a susceptible population become resistant to heartwater when translocated, and the rest will die within 6 months depending on the rainfall and tick load. When purchasing animals into an endemic area, request a veterinary certificate which indicates that they are naturally immune or have been successfully vaccinated. Auctioneers generally neglect providing these when offering so-called heartwater resistant animals.

Springbok groom themselves regularly by rubbing the body with the muzzle or horns and nibbling the skin with the incisors to remove ticks. They are not, however, well adapted to tick burdens and deaths have been recorded due to tick paralysis caused by *Ixodes rubicundus*.

Endoparasites may occasionally build up in springbok populations introduced into marginal habitats which can cause severe losses.

Springbok are fragile, susceptible to horn and bone fractures during capture and prone to capture myopathy. Passive capture is therefore the best method to use for springbok.

Additional information

Comprehensive information on springbok biology by the same author is available on E-Book, the *Game Species Window*.
www.amazon.com pp 13403-13761.
Genetic advice on tsessebe breeding:
Wildlife Stud Services www.ws2.co.za
Geo Wild Consultants www.geowild.co.za

SMALL ANTELOPE

- Cephalophini (duikers)
- Neotragini (short, straight-horned)

CEPHALOPINI: THE DUIKERS
Herman Barnard

The duikers belong to the tribe Cephalopini and are allocated into three different genera, as indicated below. They are browsers and also eat leaves, fruit, seeds, mushrooms, occasional insects and small vertebrates. Duiker are an important source of prey for raptors and predators. Despite their low reproductive rate, none of the South African species are considered endangered. However, their numbers are believed to be declining due to deforestation, loss of habitat, human settlement and agriculture.

Grey or common duiker.

There are three endemic species in SA:

Bush/Common (grey) duiker (*Sylvicapra grimmia*): Grey duiker are widespread throughout SA even in arid areas, as long as browse in the form of forbs and bushes is available. It is very adaptable and can be found in most types of habitat. It is also often found close to human habitation and kraals where it scavenges on leftovers. Rams are usually smaller than females with a shoulder height of about five cm and a mean bodyweight of about 17 kg. Females reach a shoulder height of about 57 cm and average body weight of 21 kg.

Blue duiker (*Philantomba monticola*): Blue duiker are confined to the eastern coastal forests and are adapted to a diet of forest fruits, fallen leaves, seeds and mushrooms. They are a favourite species for zoos because they are easily tamed and quite adaptable to captivity. It prefers forests with a dense canopy in the high rainfall regions of KwaZulu-Natal and along the coastal lowlands along the east coast of South Africa right into the Western Cape. It can also be found in the forests of Swaziland and further north in eastern Zimbabwe, Mozambique and Malawi. The blue duiker is the smallest antelope of southern Africa. Males have an average shoulder height of 34 cm and an average body mass of 4.5 kg, while ewes can stand 1 cm taller and have a mass of 5.5 kg. The blue duiker has been classified as "Rare" and is protected by CITES regulations in terms of international trade. Blue duikers adapt well to captivity and there are several successful breeding projects throughout the country.

Red duiker/Natal red duiker (*Cephalophus natalensis*): Red duiker are shy antelope adapted to the coastal forests of Natal. It

Klipspringer in natural habitat.

Colour variant klipspringer with white spotting.

prefers riverine habitat but can also be found in savannah bushveld. The geographic distribution in South Africa is limited to the northern and southeastern parts of KwaZulu-Natal, Swaziland and the Lowveld of Mpumalanga. There is also a population in the Soutpansberg in Limpopo Province. Red duiker males reach a shoulder height of 43 cm and a body weight of 12 kg, while ewes can be slightly bigger at 45 cm shoulder height and 12 to 14 kg body weight.

Neotragini: Small antelope with short straight horns

The following species are endemic in SA:

Oribi (*Oribi oribi ourebi*): They are found in the eastern parts of South Africa in savannah, open woodlands and grasslands. They are selective feeders of forbs and grass. Their population is declining, since they are under threat from poaching, particularly by "traditional" hunters using packs of dogs.

Klipspringer (*Oreotragus oreotragus*): Because they are adapted to living on rocky outcrops they are found throughout most of the country except the central Free State and North West Province. They are browsers living on a wide variety of bushes and shrubs, as well as seeds, fruit and fallen leaves. Because of their habitat they are less subject to threat by human activities, but rams are sought after by trophy hunters.

Steenbok (*Raphicerus campestris*): They are found throughout South Africa, even in arid areas where they utilise short palatable grass and browse such as leaves, fruit and pods, and seek bush for the cover they need. Steenbok are often shot by crop farmers as they damage newly emerging crops such as maize, pumpkins, water melons and the like.

Cape grysbok (*Raphicerus melanotis*): The Cape grysbok is confined to the southern and eastern Cape area where they are selective browsers on fynbos and graze to a lesser degree.

Livingstone's suni (*Neotragus moschatus livingstonianus*): Suni are found in the northeastern part of South Africa's coastal forest and thicket where they browse on forest leaves and fruit.

General

The small antelope belong to two main tribes as discussed above. With a few exceptions most are adapted to specific habitats, in particular to forests and woodland because of their browsing habits. The small antelope are mainly browsers with some species taking soft sweet or selected grasses. Some are totally independent of water sources because of the moisture content of

An example of a camp complex suitable for small antelope.

their feed. Although none of the small antelope in South Africa are considered endangered. Their populations are mostly in decline due to habitat destruction (forests), poaching, conflict with crop farmers, indiscriminate poisoning and hunting. Orphan lambs are often encountered and can be successfully raised if they have received colostrum.

There has been a resurgence of interest in breeding small antelope by game farmers who want to stock farms depleted by hunting or persecution. Some horned species are hunted for trophies. Permits for keeping small antelope are required from relevant authorities for outside their normal habitat.

Colour variants

Colour variants are rare among the small antelope but include:
* Black and white forms of steenbok.
* White saddle klipspringer.

Breeding systems and management

Camp complex and camps: The camp complex fencing should be erected to a height of 2.4 m with a small bonnox fence on which electrified strands should be added to keep out predators. Inside this complex the smaller individual camps should also be of small bonnox wire type and similarly electrified on the outside. These inner fences need only be normal cattle fence height of 1.3 to 1.5 m. This will not, however, suffice for the klipspringer which unlike the other species are "jumpers" as opposed to "crawlers". Because of the mostly small breeding territories occupied by small antelope rams they do well in small breeding camps. The size of the small inner camps will depend on the species involved.

Generally, a good size camp for small antelope is 1 ha provided the habitat is suitable. Blue duiker can be kept in camps as small as 20 m x 20 m or 400 m^2. These camps must have sufficient trees, shrubs, and long grass inside for these shy species to hide in or under and to provide food and shade especially during the summer. A more open portion should be made for where their feed and water bowls are placed. Shelter for the animals in the form of small tents, huts or caves made of bales of straw can be placed in camps to allow the animals to escape from human disturbance and deal with stress until they have become adapted to the breeding/containment camp. Most males are strongly territorial so camps of the same species should not adjoin each other to prevent aggression and stress. Even hand-tamed animals need bush or long grass cover

Suitable feeding station for small antelope.

Release of klipspringer from a suitable crate.

in their camps in which they can hide away from disturbances or stressful situations. In some species such as red and grey duiker and steenbuck, rams can be kept with more than one ewe, sometimes as many as 10, while blue duiker breed in monogamous pairs naturally. However, they may behave differently in captivity.

The small antelope and especially their young are vulnerable to predation especially by caracal but even by small opportunist predators such as honey badgers, so appropriate fencing and other protective measures must be employed to prevent attacks from over or under the fence.

Large trees close to the outside of the camp complex and high fence will provide a means for caracal to leap into the camp complex. The inner short fences are no obstacle to this predator. Fencing must be "digger proof" as the small antelope will otherwise easily escape through holes dug under fences by animals such as warthog. Most species such as steenbok are fence "crawlers" and will dig their way out of poorly constructed camps. Klipspringer are, as the name suggests, good jumpers so their camps must be designed accordingly.

Capture: Duiker and some other small species will, if frightened, tend to rush at fences, injuring themselves or even break their necks. Placing bales of hay against fences will help prevent injuries until the captives are habituated. Capturing these small and delicate animals is a serious operation if one is to prevent injuries and even death. Most commonly nets are used, stretched across the camps and a group of helpers chase the antelope as calmly as possible into the nets where they become quickly entangled. Projectile nets can also be used. Blue duiker, because of their small size can even be caught with a scoop net similar to one for catching butter flies. Working swiftly and calmly they are disentangled from the net, held and placed into a sack with just the head sticking out of the bag. They should then be given a long acting tranquiliser by a veterinarian, and then released into the newly prepared and clean crate.

Transport: These are generally very shy animals and as they are so small the normal equipment used to transport game is not suitable. Specific transport crates are manufactured and used. They have the following dimensions: 80 cm long x 60 cm high x 35 cm wide. The front, back and top can open and there is an inspection window on the sides. When transporting the small antelope a good bedding of fresh lucerne should be used. Eight crates can usually be loaded onto the back of a 1 ton bakkie. During warm or hot weather

Blue duiker enjoy supplements of certain fresh fruit and vegetables.

Small antelope orphans like this steenbok can be successfully hand-raised using basic guidelines.

it must have windows that are kept open and if available the window between the cab and the back can be opened and the air conditioner used to supplement the flow of cool air.

Release: On arrival, preferably in the evening at the new accommodation which must be provisioned with fresh water and suitable feed, the crate is placed inside the camp with the exit facing into the camp. The door is quietly opened and the animal is left to emerge on its own, which may take as much as 5 minutes.

Animals from the Karoo or Kalahari do not initially do well in the small camps described above. They should be transported at night and released early the next morning very quietly into camps of at least 5 ha. They must be quietly monitored and fed/watered daily until they adapt. Losses can still be expected so capture from these areas is not recommended.

Nutrition

Their preferred natural browse is the best source of nutrition for small antelope, but if this cannot be provided, fresh fruit, vegetables (chopped carrots and apples) and lucerne should be provided initially. Soft commercial antelope pellets (Epol) well-suited to small antelope can be offered in small quantities until the animals have learned to accept it. When animals are adjusted to pelleted rations the quantities can be increased to ensure adequate intake of protein. They eat a small amount in a day (200 g) but it should be given ad lib making sure that there is very little left at the end of the day. A little roughly chopped lucerne (25 mm sticks) should also be given. Similarly, a small mineral lick block can be used in each camp. If the camps are well vegetated and suitable, the antelope will take very little of the offered feed, preferring the forbs, leaves and fruit growing naturally. Forest species like blue and red duiker are more dependent on fruit in their diets so they can be given a limited variety of suitable fruit and vegetables such as carrots, apples or pumpkins.

Tropical fruit, which contain high levels of starch and sugar, should be avoided as it will cause acidosis. Wild fruit species are suitable because they have high levels of roughage and low starch levels. Although some small antelope species are independent of water sources in the wild, clean fresh water should be provided daily since the feed provided (especially pellets) may not contain sufficient moisture. Both feed and water should be provided in small, heavy bowls (never on the ground) and must be properly cleaned daily. The water bowl should be deep enough and placed in a shady spot to ensure the water does not get too warm during the day.

Releasing a duiker from a capture crate.

Raising orphans

Fresh cow or goat milk has been used successfully to raise orphaned small antelope, but the ideal is to add cream and eggs for extra fat and protein (add 20 ml of fresh cream plus 1 egg yolk to 1 l of milk), but this must be done consistently as changing the diet composition will lead to digestive problems. Feed 10 to 15% of bodyweight per day divided in many little feeds. Start with about 6-8 feeds per day. Do not overfeed as this will cause milk to run into the rumen, where it cannot be digested properly. The addition of a probiotic seems to help reduce problems such as diarrhea. Bottle teats for human infants seem to stimulate a better sucking reflex, so the small ones can be used for pet animals. Bottle-fed animals may need to be taught to suck and will need ano-genital stimulation to induce defecation and urination. Baby antelope start sampling browse and green grass quite early so they should be put in outside enclosures as soon as possible. Be aware that male lambs when habituated to humans may become very aggressive and horned species can inflict severe injuries, so limit contact with them to the minimum.

Daily routine

Check fencing to ensure there are no holes made by diggers such as warthog. Ensure all feed and water bowls are cleaned and replaced. Observe animals quietly for abnormal behaviour.

Diseases

The small antelope appear to be resistant to tick infestation and tick-borne diseases in most areas. Worm infestation is not usually a problem in free-living small antelope. However, when kept in camps in close proximity to other species, especially domestic animals, duiker may develop worm infestations which can be problematic. Any signs of diarrhoea should be investigated by doing faecal analysis. Faecal samples can be collected quarterly and examined for worm eggs. If either signs of disease or a spike in worm egg numbers are detected, the animals in that camp must be treated with a registered, safe anthelmintic which can easily be added to the feed. Poor hygiene in small breeding/holding camps will result in a build-up of pathogens such as coccidia and fungal contamination of feed.

Some small antelope species are very delicate, especially when transported and handled, and may develop capture myopathy and pneumonia as sequels. Animals should be purchased or acquired from experienced professionals who will minimise stress. Constant supervision is necessary to identify any signs of disease timeously.

Additional information
WRSA
Small Antelope Advisory Committee
info@wrsa.co.za
012 335 6994
Herman Barnard 082 335 6441

CARNIVORES

- Cheetah
- Lion
- Wild dogs

CARNIVORES

Prof Piet Potgieter of SA Predator association

Ann van Dyk, famous cheetah breeder, with one of her "ambassador" cats used for education.

There are three large carnivores which are bred in South Africa by various organisations: Lion (*Panthera leo*), cheetah (*Acinonyx jubatus*) and the African wild dog (*Lycaon pictus*).

These animals are under severe threat because of fragmentation and shrinkage of their natural range lands and conflict with humans, both in farming situations and due to human safety concerns. Farmers generally don't want them on their land and the general public don't want them roaming free so there is literally nowhere for these animals to go, except for the limited government owned conservation areas and private landowners who keep them for tourism and other purposes.

Even in reserves as large as the 37 000 ha Welgevonden in the Waterberg district, the introduction of a small lion pride has necessitated special management to ensure their survival. Their introduction and increase in numbers (to as few as 12) threatened the long term existence of their main prey species in the reserve, viz. blue wildebeest, eland, warthog, red hartebeest and kudu, necessitating the purchase of huge numbers of these animals just to ensure their own survival and sufficient food for the small pride.

Cheetah and African wild dog have been the subject of a number of conservation projects to prevent their extinction. While in Africa the geographic range of lion has shrunk by as much as 82% and their numbers in the wild have declined by 68% over the past 50 years, lion numbers in South Africa have increased by 30% in the last decade.

Of huge concern, however, is that the wild lion population is infected with bovine tuberculosis and captive bred lions may therefore be a valuable source of "disease-free" animals.

IUCN Conservation Status

- Lion: **Listed as vulnerable**. IUCN does not count any "non-wild" animals in its population estimates and hence does not take the privately owned animals in South Africa into account when determining the status. The west African sub-population of 645 animals is listed as **critically endangered**.
- African wild dog: **Listed as endangered**, with less than 5 000 left in the wild.
- Cheetah: **Listed as endangered** with as few as 12 000 in the wild.

Breeding large carnivore species

Breeders have opted to keep and breed these species for a number of reasons, including conservation of the species, as a tourist attraction, to supplying to zoos and other private owners or for consumptive reasons such as for hunting. There are legal requirements, both national- and provincial for keeping and breeding these species, specifically the size of properties, fencing requirements, etc. Aspiring breeders must comply with these regulations in order to obtain permits to keep and/or breed these animals. Acquiring a good knowledge of the behaviour of the species (all of which are potentially dangerous), spatial requirements, breeding management, nutrition and diseases is a prerequisite to keeping these species. They are all prone to diseases of domestic dogs and cats (see Chapter 5) and need intensive vaccination programs, deworming and constant (expensive) veterinary monitoring to ensure that their young grow properly and remain healthy. All staff must be suitably trained to prevent mishandling and fatal accidents.

The source and presentation of suitable feed (fresh meat in most cases) is challenging and more complicated than in most other species, such as herbivores. "Backyard" breeders who take short cuts in raising these species will be faced with huge financial losses and legal action by welfare societies.

Hunting of captive bred carnivores

The decision of some owners to allow hunting of the animals they breed (in particular lion) has drawn criticism from various quarters. "Canned hunting" which is defined as the hunting of recently released tame, sometimes even drugged animals, has been forbidden in South Africa since 2007 and lion hunting like all other forms of hunting is strictly regulated. Only 2–5% male lions of the lion population in South Africa are hunted. Conservationists are concerned that the banning of lion hunting and in particular trophy hunting as a whole will lead to an overall decline in wild animal numbers, especially lion, which are because of their specific requirements difficult and expensive

TROPHY HUNTING

What the IUCN says:
According to Ivo Vegter, Daily Maverick journalist, Rosie Cooney who serves on one of the conservation committees of the IUCN, says that bans on trophy hunting in Tanzania, Kenya, and Zambia accelerated loss of wildlife due to removal of incentives for conservation.

She warns that the same is occurring in Botswana and if imposed on South Africa will lead to the loss of private game farms which cover 3 times the surface area of government run conservation areas. This will lead to a reversion to livestock and crops and hence degraded habitats. If well-regulated trophy hunting is permitted this will ensure the survival of wild species.

Lion trophies are purchased by overseas hunters and collectors.

Captive lions make a valuable contribution to the gene pool of the species.

to keep. Hunters of so called "wild" lion tend to target the biggest and best maned (mature) lion, thereby damaging the social structure of a pride that may lead to an "outside" male taking over the pride and kill all the young of the previous (hunted) male.

Keeping and breeding lion

The South African Predator Association estimates that there are currently between 5 000 and 6 000 lion in private ownership in South Africa – more than double the number of lion "in the wild" in the country. Significantly, these privately owned lion represent almost 20% of all lion in Africa (approx. 30 000). Lion may be kept for a number of reasons:

Tourism: These are generally large properties and extensive systems with sufficient space and prey species to sustain a pride of lion. Depending on the environment the area required will vary from five lion per 1 000 ha to six lion per 10 000 ha. Judging from the example of Welgevonden, above, these may be over optimistic estimates for South African conditions. Clearly, unless there are specifically fenced areas, this form of ranching cannot be combined with the breeding of valuable rare species or valuable antelope of different colours. In deciding whether to introduce lion to such properties for tourism purposes, the cost in animals predated (which could have been hunted or sold) must be compared with the increase in number and value of tourism bed nights sold.

Exhibition and/or breeding: A natural pride of lion is generally kept in dedicated, adequately fenced areas within larger game ranches. The pride will require careful management, in particular "housing" and provisioning of food and water. The food generally consists of fresh meat which is supplemented with a vitamin and mineral powder, in the form of whole carcasses with all the internal organs intact from domestic stock or wild antelope, or whole chicken, with or without feathers. Chickens fed must be free of *Salmonella*, *E. coli* and antibiotic residues.

Whole carcasses with the internal organs intact provide all the vitamins and minerals required by lion but it must be fresh and free of drug and or pesticide residues. This is fed, depending on the sex, age and size of the lion once or twice a week, at a rate of 4kg/adult lion/day (28kg per week). Animals can also be shot on the ranch for this purpose. Meat can be frozen and thawed when required. After

Hand-raised cheetah eating kitty kibble (note king cheetah on the right).

defrosting, supplements (usually vitamin and mineral powders) which are commercially available are added to the meat. The food is best placed on a concrete slab that can be regularly cleaned and disinfected to prevent a build-up of disease-causing organisms. Bones not consumed should be regularly removed and destroyed (burned), also for hygienic and health reasons. Obesity is common in captive lion due to overfeeding. Monitor the condition of the lion and adjust the amount fed accordingly. Horse and donkey meat is very lean and may not contain sufficient arachidonic acid to meet the nutritional requirements of lion. Lion are more resistant to hepatic lipidosis than cheetah for instance so one need not trim the fat off the meat.

If the license is specifically for exhibition (not breeding purposes) the authority will require that one or both the sexes be sterilised to prevent breeding. It is important to consult an experienced veterinarian in this field as some techniques may lead to incomplete sterilisation and/or aberrant behaviour.

The intricate social and reproductive behaviour of breeding lion should be understood. Genetically unrelated young adult lion should be well introduced in different camps prior to allowing them to mix. Lion are in fact prolific breeders, and the off-spring must be removed from the pride at the age of 24 months as would be the case in nature. Animals bred in such a manor can be kept for further breeding but eventually some will have to be sold to other breeders, conservancies for tourism purposes, zoos throughout the world, or to ranches that offer lion hunting.

A male lion is a much sought after trophy. More than 1 000 are hunted in Africa annually, about two-thirds of these in South Africa. Almost 1 000 skeletons are exported, about 75% thereof to Asia. The dwindling numbers of wild lion in Africa, of which only just more than 10% are mature adult males older than five years, cannot sustain the demand for animals suitable for trophy hunting. Surveys have shown that almost 50% of hunting clients show no preference regarding the type of hunts they plan and hence due to the overlap there is little doubt that the breeding of lion in South Africa has reduced demand on the hunting of "wild" lion.

Keeping and breeding cheetah

There are an estimated 10 000 to 12 000 cheetah left, 25% of these in Namibia. In South Africa, cheetah are kept both extensively in the larger reserves, for exhibition and for breeding.

Cheetah are a popular species for ecotourism.

African wild dog.

There is a small market internationally in both national and private zoos for cheetah, especially the rarer king cheetah.

The fencing principles are the same as for lion and wild dog with small amendments such as that the fences are electrified with four strands on both sides at heights of 20 cm, 40 cm, 80 cm and at the top. These fences must also be 2.4 m high with jackal proofing up to 1.2 m. Although cheetah are not diggers the fences also must have a concrete foundation of about 50 cm deep to which the fence is fixed/hooked to prevent animals like warthog creating openings that can be exploited by the cheetah. Although in Namibia an inward overhang at the top is not legally required, it is recommended. While camps of as little as 2 000 m² are adequate for one animal as cheetah are "runners", camps of 1 ha each are preferable. When kept for exhibition only, the males generally are implanted to prevent breeding. In this case groups/siblings that grew up together can be kept together.

When kept for breeding the females are kept in separate camps, each preferably in two rows with a 4 m passage in between. The males are kept in separate camps and are "released" one at a time into the passage to detect females in oestrus. If the pair show interest the male is let into the female's camp. If no interest is shown a second male can be used to make sure that no female is ready for breeding.

Cubs in the wild normally stay with the mother for 18 months, but in the breeding programmes they can be removed from the mother from 6 months' of age ensuring that she will come into oestrus earlier. The feeding principles are the same as for lion (above) and wild dog (below) with each cheetah being fed about 7 kg of meat (carcass/chicken) per week every second or third day. Excess fat should be removed if meat from domestic stock is used as cheetah are susceptible to hepatic lipidosis. Their condition should be monitored and the amount of food provided adjusted accordingly. They can also receive part of their diet in the form of commercial cat food (Iams or Ekanuba). As with the wild dogs, cheetah on commercial food may develop diarrhoea.

Keeping and breeding African wild dog

African wild dog, also known as the Cape hunting dog or as the apt "painted dog" is the second most endangered carnivore in Africa with only approximately 400 animals in South Africa. It is now extinct in 23 of its sub-Saharan former range states. As with the lion, a decline and fragmentation of their habitat, their conflict with man and his livestock and diseases contracted from domestic carnivores has led to their persecution and near extinction. Susceptibility to diseases like rabies and distemper have taken an added toll. Added to that, like lion being pack animals and voracious feeders they are very difficult to keep extensively on any game ranch except for the very large ones. Unlike lion though, they are not sought after for hunting meaning that there is little or no demand and hence very limited sales of live animals.

Consequently, they are kept mainly on very large tourism orientated game ranches or for exhibition purposes in which case they too should be sterilised with the consequential aberrant behaviour as seen with lion. In principle, the management of African wild dogs is the same as given above for lion with a few obvious differences, like size and the consequent amount of food required.

When kept for breeding, socially they need to be kept as a small pack (up to 30 individuals in nature) in which only the alpha-pair breed, producing litters of 12 or more pups. The diet of the puppies is supplemented very early on, after about only 3 weeks with regurgitated meat brought by the other pack members. They too require specific fencing, because they tend to bite and pull at it or burrow under it. Specifications for permits and for the fencing requirements should be obtained from the local provincial department responsible for Environmental Affairs.

The camp should not be less than 1 ha in area. The fences, constructed of 60 mm diamond mesh, must also have a concrete foundation to which the fencing is hooked, as well as three strands of electrified fencing at ground level, at 30 cm and at 130 cm above ground. A feeding hatch, or pulley system to provide food, and a small capture camp with a remote-controlled gate should also be included. The camp should have trees and shrubs for shade (or some form of shading constructed) as well as a small sunken concrete dam in which they can cool off during warm weather.

A separate facility to provision clean and cool drinking water is essential. A den/cave should also be considered in which the dogs will rest and pup.

African wild dogs are mainly carnivorous, scavenging only occasionally. They should thus be fed fresh carcasses (or portions thereof) once a day providing 2 to 3 kg of meat per adult in the enclosure. Most of the food can be replaced by good quality commercial dog food. In both cases, clearly, the condition of the dogs over time needs close monitoring in order to adjust the amounts provided from time to time.

Fencing

Because they are potentially dangerous predators, the Department of Environmental Affairs has very strict fencing laws for keeping lion and other big wild cats or dogs. This is one of the most important and expensive aspects of keeping large predators. The fencing requirements are species specific and this limits the ranchers' ability to change from keeping one species to another.

Lion tend to be crawlers, not jumpers. The 2.4 m, 17 strand heavy duty fence needs to have either a rock- or concrete embedded foundation and apron on either side of 50 cm in depth. The fence must be supplemented with four electrified strands (30 cm, 60 cm, 150 cm, and 230 cm above ground) as well as a 30 cm inwardly-angled overhang. At least half a hectare per lion is required.

Permit requirements and fencing guidelines must first be obtained from the nearest provincial office dealing with Environmental Affairs. Failure to ascertain and to adhere to these requirements will lead to long delays and possibly a major waste of money.

AVES
- Ostrich

OSTRICH (*Struthio camelius*)
Johan van Rensburg

The ostrich is a flightless bird indigenous to Africa, Syria and Arabia. It is an herbivorous bird with specific adaptations to dry hot conditions although it flourishes on open savannah woodlands.

Early settlers to the Cape hunted and killed the birds for their feathers to the extent that in 1822 the Cape colony declared the birds protected to prevent them from becoming extinct. The first ostrich was tamed in 1863 and ostrich farming in the Klein Karoo became a profitable agricultural activity because the birds, unlike most livestock, could survive the periodic droughts in the area. The period between 1875 and 1880 is described as the "First Ostrich Boom" This was driven by the demand for feathers as a fashion item and this product was for many years one of South Africa's most important exports. War and changing tastes in fashion conspired to cause the collapse of the feather boom and by the 1930s the number of birds kept for farming had declined from one million to 23 000.

In the 1940s the value of ostrich leather was discovered which led to increasing interest in ostrich farming. The Klein Karoo Agricultural Co-operative (KKLK) was established in 1945 to regulate and protect the industry, which was then deregulated in 1993 to create a free market system on the request of KK International (KKI) and the first export ostrich abattoir was opened

Ostriches were initially farmed to produce feathers (1) but now the main product is ostrich leather (2) and meat.

to supply ostrich meat to Europe. Since then outbreaks of avian influenza have impaired the ostrich meat export industry but research by Elsenburg scientists and KKI veterinarians have resulted in improved strategies for biosecurity and disease control of the industry.

A breeding group of ostriches.

The main products of the modern ostrich industry are leather, meat and to a lesser extent feathers, as well as eggs for use as curios. This section gives a brief outline of the production process of ostrich farming in South Africa.

Reproduction

In South Africa ostrich farming follows different operational systems. Various internal and external factors dictate the development of a specific system on a farm. Market conditions are probably the biggest influential aspects pertaining to which production system to follow. Other important influences are climatic conditions, farm location and size, and management skills. On some farms various hybrids of different systems are used.

Approximately 70–80% of farmed ostriches are maintained in breeding flocks with sizes ranging from 50–100 birds. In these flocks the male to female ratio is approximately 6:10.

The length and frequency of mating sessions may differ but in general mating will occur in spring months (September–November). Peak egg production occurs in late winter to early spring (August–September). Reproduction is influenced by photoperiod and nutritional status of the birds. Under natural conditions a female would lay 8–15 eggs per clutch in a nest.

Eggs are collected on farms in different ways. The egg collection strategy is mainly driven by the type of mating system. On farms where an intensive system is followed, eggs are collected daily and incubated artificially.

Farm workers are specifically designated to work specific camps during the collection period as to prevent disease transfer and consistency on the farm. This method also minimises the external and environmental influences on the quality of the eggs. In more extensive farming conditions, eggs are collected approximately every second day, in

Ostrich eggs can either be incubated artificially or naturally.

which case the longer exposure to the elements do affect the quality (sterility and hatchability) of the eggs. Males reach sexual maturity at 3.5 years and females at 2.5 years. The fertility of breeding birds in their first breeding season is often poor. Full breeding potential is reached around the third breeding season. Even though females can start producing eggs at 18 months, in general this is not the case in South Africa. Improved feeding and bird selection makes it possible to select for early sexual maturity in both sexes.

Breeding birds are joined the end of May/June and it usually lasts until the end of January the following year. In May the number of daylight hours is too short to effectively initiate sperm production and female follicular development. This results in an asynchrony in reproductive activities. Some males and females are more sensitive to the change in daylight length and thus are synchronised sooner.

Mating can occur more than once a day. The male shows a peculiar behavior pattern in that soon after mating he will start preparing the nest. Females lay their eggs mainly in the afternoon but under high intensive conditions they may also lay in the late afternoon. Up to 10 ostriches could be kept in a 0.25 ha paddock, still with satisfactory egg production.

Egg production starts off slowly but as the season progresses more breeding birds will come into production. By the end of July just about the entire flock should be in production. The total breeding and production season is about eight months on intensive breeding farms.

On the more extensive breeding farms this period may last up to ten months. Egg production peaks in August/September. There is a natural short decline in production of about 3–4 weeks but thereafter production increases gradually with a second peak in December. After December production declines sharply towards the end of January. Fertility and production decrease naturally during autumn. Male and females are then separated at this time for a rest period until the next breeding season starts in May/June. A female could lay a maximum of 15 to 16 eggs per month under intensive and good genetic selected conditions. In general the average production is 8 to 10 eggs per month.

On intensive breeding farms where genetic selection and closer attention is given to reproductive performance, the farmer will make use of breeding trios. In this case a single male is placed in a breeding paddock of minimum 0.25 ha with two females. The females will lay their eggs together in one nest but each female has a specific egg form and weight. In these cases the nominated farm workers give even more attention to detail

Ostrich chicks can be raised intensively or given to a breeding pair.

Tractor tyres must be disinfected to enforce biosecurity on a farm.

regarding egg collection to help in the selection for production and fertility. It is important that breeding birds are not disturbed during the breeding season and handling is limited to the resting period which is from February to April/May. A fully balanced ration is fed to breeding birds for 8 months (245 days) and maintenance rations during the rest of the period (120 days).

Hatching

Presently the artificial incubation of ostrich eggs is the most commonly used system. Eggs are collected in the late afternoon and stored. Eggs can be stored up to seven days before placement in the incubator. The optimal temperature for storage of ostrich eggs is 15 to 20 °C, with a relative humidity of 75 to 80%. Eggs are collected soon after laying, because the absence of a cuticle on the outer surface of an ostrich egg makes it vulnerable to microbial contamination and spoilage.

The hatchability of ostrich eggs is influenced by various factors at different stages of incubation. Eggs are disinfected soon after collection and moved to a store room. Eggs are either washed, fumigated, or disinfected by ultra-violet light.

Vircon S™ is the product of choice of many hatcheries and eggs are either sprayed or fumigated using this product.

Eggs are heated prior to storage and after disinfection for approximately 4 hours at 36 °C. This is an optional process but it ensures higher hatchability. This heating process acts as a simulation of the natural process before the female starts to incubate them. The heating also helps to initiate the development of the embryo.

Eggs are placed in the incubator with the air cell either horizontal or vertically. The air cell is visualised with the aid of a light in a dark room. Temperature is the most critical incubation parameter. The incubating temperature is 36 °C with fluctuations not exceeding 0.5 °C. The incubation period is 42 days and the humidity in the incubator should not exceed 28%.

After five weeks of incubation the eggs are transferred to the hatchers for the last week before hatching takes place. During this period the eggs are not turned. In general the average egg production is 50 eggs per female with a hatching percentage of around 60%.

Rearing of chicks

Chicks can be reared either artificially or naturally by breeder birds. Good quality chicks weigh about 750 g at hatching and this weight has a very distinctive effect on future survival and production. Under artificial conditions, ostrich chicks are kept at a temperature of

Birds are slaughtered for meat and leather at the age of 10–14 months

26 °C for the first two weeks. Thereafter they are slowly exposed to the natural environment taking temperature fluctuations into consideration. After hatching, they are kept in different types of housing systems in groups of up to 100 birds. Chicks are given free access to feed and water and is fed twice a day (mornings and afternoons). The type of ration fed to chicks is determined by their body mass. A set routine is followed to keep stress to a minimum. Biosecurity at the rearing units is very high and access is not easily granted.

Chicks may also be reared naturally by a breeding pair. Soon after hatching chicks are placed with a breeding pair and moved into a lucerne paddock. Up to 50 or more can be placed with a single breeding pair. If more than 25 chicks are placed with a breeding pair, extra shelter must be provided. Chicks are reared by the breeding pair up to the age of 3 months. From 4 months of age the outside space should be approximately 40 m^2 per bird. The stocking rate of young birds on pasture could be 100 birds per hectare. Older birds can be kept at a stocking rate of 20 birds per hectare. In both intensive and extensive production systems, birds are raised to the slaughter age of 10 to 14 months.

Production

Meat and skins are the most important sources of income representing approximately 90% of the total income. Feathers make up a small percentage. Good quality feathers are harvested from adult breeding birds. The quality of skins is driven by the absence of skin damage and the size and form of the nodules on the skin.

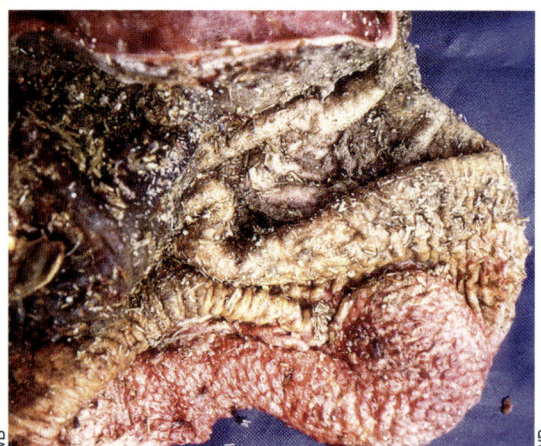
Proventriculitis caused by the ostrich wireworm (*Libostrongylus douglassi*).

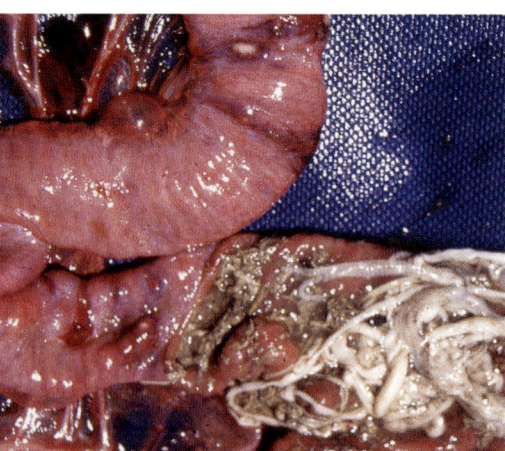
The ostrich tapeworm (*Houttynia struthionis*) can cause runting in young ostriches.

The potential income from a single breeding unit (one male and two females) is around R15 000. It can be taken that a breeding unit will produce around 57 chicks at a cost of R180 per chick excluding incubation costs. Feed cost represents the biggest cost item (83%) in the production system.

A breeding bird consumes approximately 960 kg feed per year. Income generated per bird is around R3 100 of which R2 000 constitutes the skin value; R1 100 the meat value, and additional income is generated by feathers. Birds slaughtered at 10 months represent the highest income generating group, producing on average 41 kg meat, 140 dm^2 skin and 1.5 kg feathers. A skin weighs between 1.0 and 1.5 kg.

Diseases

Ostriches are subject to many of the virus and bacterial diseases occurring in poultry and vaccination programs must be instituted with the help of specialist veterinarians.

The birds are susceptible to avian influenza which, because of the potential for spread of the virus to human populations, poses the most serious threat to the industry, because outbreaks necessitate large scale slaughter of infected birds.

Biosecurity is therefore strictly implemented on intensive farms. The bloodsucking wireworm (*Libostrongylus douglassi*) can cause severe and fatal infections.

A regular deworming program must therefore be applied. The tapeworm (*Houttynia struthionis*) can cause runting of young ostriches.

Additional information

Breeding, management, nutrition, health, economics and biodiversity are available in the
Ostrich Manual of the SA Ostrich Business chamber
(Volstruis Handleiding).

REPTILIA
- Crocodiles

INTENSIVE CROCODILE FARMING
Robert Reader and Silke Pfitzer

Introduction

Intensive crocodile farming can be divided into four main activities: keeping of large breeding adults, collection and incubation of the eggs of female breeders, raising of hatchlings and then raising grower crocodiles which are then harvested for their skins at around 2–4 years of age. Each of these functions requires special facilities and considerations. Some farms only carry out certain parts of these functions and other farms fulfil all functions themselves.

The main product of intensive crocodile farming is the belly skin. Crocodile skin is usually sold to buyers who export the product in order to make high value fashion goods such as shoes, handbags and belts. Intensive farms can also supply meat, live crocodiles, curios made of various crocodile parts and host tourists on the farm.

The biology of the Nile crocodile (*Crocodylus niloticus*)

In order to farm effectively with crocodiles it is important to understand the biology and unique characteristics of the animal. In nature Nile crocodiles inhabit river systems or wetlands in the warmer areas of the continent, where they function as predators in an aquatic environment. Their bodies are covered in scales, some of which contain bony osteoderms that aid in protection and thermoregulation, but the absence of these on the stomach makes the skin soft and smooth and sought after as leather. The shape of the head allows crocodiles to lie on the water surface with minimal exposure, with only eyes and nostrils above the surface. When crocodiles swim, their eyes are protected by a transparent third eyelid which is moved over the eyeball.

IUCN Conservation Status

There are only a few large natural populations of Nile crocodiles (*Crocodylus niloticus*) left in South Africa in Mpumalanga, Limpopo Province and in KwaZulu-Natal. Nile crocodiles are under threat mainly due to human persecution but also due to habitat destruction and water pollution. Many of the natural populations are still under pressure today despite conservation efforts. Due to commercial farming crocodile numbers have not only increased but the animals have become very valuable assets on breeding farms.

The eyes are reflective by spotlight, a characteristic which can be exploited during capture. In addition to having keen eyesight and smell, crocodiles also possess sensory pits all along their skin, which pick up minute vibrations of the water and allow crocodiles to locate their prey.

Crocodile teeth are replaced about every 20 months or so; the jaw muscles can generate enormous crushing power so that even with leverage it is virtually impossible to open the mouth of a 2 m long crocodile. However, in contrast the muscles that open the jaw are comparatively weak, so the jaws even of large crocodiles can be secured using insulation tape or bicycle tubes. Gastroliths or stones and the strong stomach acids enable digestion of flesh and bones. However, this effective digestion is slowed at ambient temperatures below 25 °C.

The Nile crocodile can grow to a body length of 5.499 m and reach a weight of 905.7 kg, and being one of the most aggressive of all crocodilians, breeders need to take extreme care when handling these animals. They do, however, become accustomed to a set routine in captivity which helps to eliminate stress and enables their management.

Planning a crocodile farm

There are a number of important issues to consider before embarking on intensive crocodile farming. Aspiring farmers should visit as many different crocodile farms as possible before building enclosures or settling on a design. Dependent on the type of farming chosen (breeder, hatchlings, yearlings and/or growers) consideration needs to be given to the type of structures or facilities that need to be provided. Current modern day farming practices also apply to the crocodile industry. Economic considerations, evaluation of structures and the type of nutrition are crucial when deciding on the type of facility to be provided. There are a number of basic factors to take into account when considering crocodile farming and these must be carefully weighed before embarking on intensive production:

Climate: In the wild, crocodiles prefer a warm climate and need wetlands, or a river system with deep pools and sandy banks. Because they are cold-blooded, they avoid areas with prolonged winter frost which impairs their digestion and growth. Where the climate is not ideal, artificial heating may need to be supplied which adds to the overhead costs. Energy efficiency, good isolation and energy supply is therefore essential. In a controlled or intensive system, the environmental temperature required is between 30 and 32 °C for hatchlings, yearlings and growers. Breeders are usually kept in outside enclosures in earth dams or cement dams where one cannot readily control the temperature. Therefore, in colder climates, these dams need to be at least 2 m deep so the water can form a thermal protective barrier. Selected farm sites should therefore preferably be in a warm subtropical to tropical climate in order to save heating and building costs and to ensure that breeders have ideal conditions for breeding.

Planning and site selection: The selected site for a fully-fledged commercial crocodile farm that produces crocodiles in all stages should at least be 10 ha and must be suitable for building of the various necessary enclosures. The required infrastructure consists of water storage tanks or dams, heating facilities such as boilers, food storage and preparation rooms, staff ablution areas, skin storage sheds, chemical storage rooms and slaughter facilities. A water treatment plant, offices and security facilities are also considerations. Authorities may require an Environment Impact Assessment (EIA) to be conducted before building or may request building plans only. In consultation with the Department of Water Affairs, the plans for water usage for the projected future must be indicated and especially the intended methods

A crocodile farm must have a reliable source of good quality water.

of waste water disposal. The farming site should preferably be close to a feed source such as an abattoir, feedlot or chicken farm. Alternatives to fresh meat as feed source are mentioned in the section on nutrition. The work force is also an important component of any crocodile farm and has to be accommodated within reasonable distance of the farm. Effluent plants may be needed to deal with waste

Water source and quality: A sustainable source of sufficient good quality water is essential for the establishment of a crocodile farm. In South Africa the authorities generally insist that breeder farms are some distance from rivers to avoid crocodiles escaping into natural waterways during flooding. The water supply from rivers is therefore usually channelled along canal systems or obtained from springs and boreholes to supply the ponds of the various age groups. The water must be aerated or recycled to keep it oxygenated, because polluted water may be a source of disease. Water quality should be analysed during the planning stage to identify any potential problems beforehand. Crocodiles need water for drinking and at least 1.5 m deep pools for mating.

Reliable electricity supply: Depending on the location of the farm, hatchling and grower houses might have to be heated and therefore hot springs would be an ideal heat source. In absence of hot springs, a boiler system heated by wood or coal can be utilised for heating. Three phase electricity is necessary for the running of incubators, cold rooms and freezers for feed storage. Good insulation of buildings will make heating more cost effective. Computerised systems adapted from vegetable or flower farming operations are used nowadays on many farms, to control the temperature and ventilation in crocodile houses.

Safety and security: Crocodiles are very powerful and aggressive animals, and can pose a danger to human safety unless properly contained. All outdoor crocodile enclosures need to either have a wall or fence around them. If a fence is used, galvanised welded mesh is recommended and it should be sunk into the ground as crocodiles can dig their way out of an enclosure. Crocodiles also climb and therefore external fences and walls have to be 1.5 m high or have to be equipped with an overhang. Good security is also needed because crocodiles are valuable assets and theft is a major problem. Biosecurity is an essential feature of crocodile farming enterprises, therefore access to crocodile farms should be strictly controlled. Crocodile handlers and farm workers should be suitably trained to handle accidents and breakouts. Small crocodiles have to be protected from predation by birds, monitors and other wild animals.

Legal requirements: There are a number of laws and regulations that pertain to the crocodile farming business and should be taken into account when planning and operating a commercial crocodile farm. The provincial Department of Environmental Affairs must be contacted for a "Threatened or protected species" (TOPS) standing permit according to the National Environmental Management: Biodiversity Act (NEMBA), Act 10 of 2014. The transport of crocodiles within South Africa falls under movement permits: Movement within SA is under the jurisdiction of provincial authorities while exports are controlled by the Convention on International Trade in Endangered Species (CITES).

Nile crocodiles of South Africa are listed on appendix 2 of CITES, which allows for the skins produced on commercial crocodile farms to be sold and traded on the international market. A CITES permit needs to be applied for if crocodiles are slaughtered for the export market and a CITES tag with unique number is allocated to each skin and remains on the tail until a final product is manufactured. The item manufactured is also then issued with a CITES tag to ensure traceability throughout the process. Further, a health certificate from state veterinary services might be required in order to export raw skins or trade in live animals on the international market. If crocodiles are to be hunted, a hunting permit is required from the relevant provincial authorities.

Market and economics: The skins of Nile crocodiles are used for the production of luxury products and therefore command high prices. The meat is a by-product but is sought after overseas and a good export market exists for meat of high standard. There is also a local market for crocodile meat, crocodile fat for cosmetics and body parts for traditional medicine. Many crocodile farms also cater for tourism and crocodiles are simply displayed or even trained to do tricks. These farms also often produce and sell curios that are produced locally of crocodile products such as leather and teeth to the tourist market.

South Africa currently has several tanneries specialising in tanning crocodile skins in order to produce high end market leather products. Most skins, however, get exported in their raw form and are tanned overseas to produce luxury products for the big fashion houses such as Hermes, Gucci, Prada and Louis Vuitton. The Far East has a growing market for crocodile skins. Farmers also sell live crocodiles to other skin farmers, as well as to the conservation and hunting industry.

Between 180 000 and 200 000 Nile crocodile skins are exported annualy from South Africa. Currently the bench mark price of crocodile skins in the industry is quoted in US dollars and the current value is $167.50 per skin.

Business model: In South Africa the eggs of the Nile crocodile may not be harvested from the wild. Crocodile farms therefore keep breeders to produce their own eggs or otherwise buy hatchlings produced in surplus by other breeders. In the current economic climate a crocodile farm can operate profitably if it produces 1 500 A-grade (flawless) skins per year, or a total of 3 000 skins of which 50–75% are A-grade. Skin prices decrease with the number of flaws detected by a grader. To produce 3 000 skins, 3 500 eggs have to be produced per year. Therefore 150 breeders are needed or alternatively hatchlings have to be

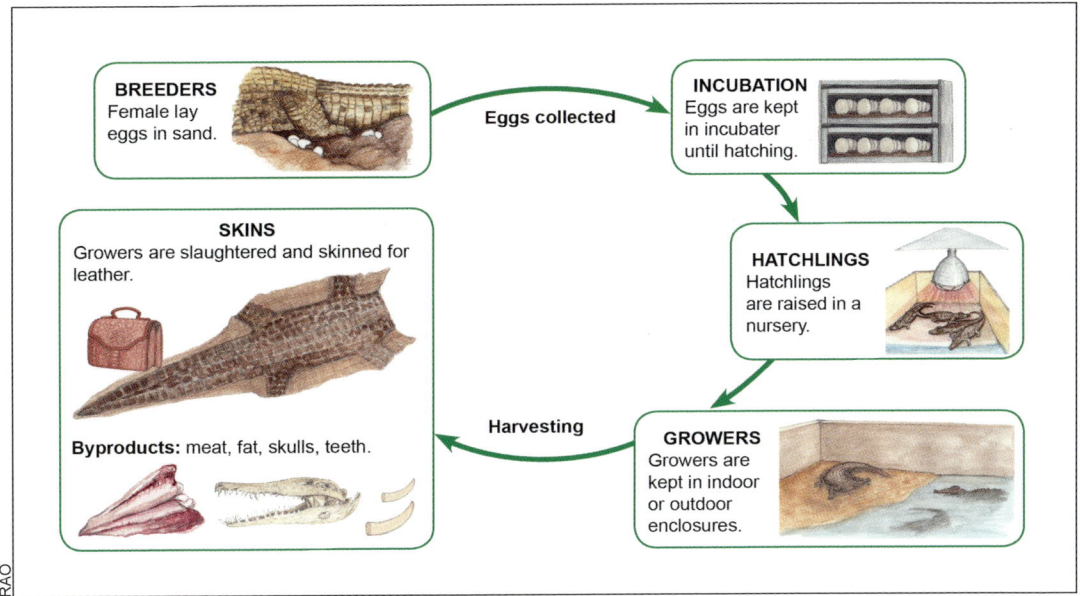
Flow diagram of activities on a crocodile farm.

bought in at a going rate of USD10–20 per hatchling. Usually crocodiles reach slaughter age/size at about 3–4 years, but this is subject to fluctuation as large skins are in demand some years while in other years smaller skins are in demand. In total, a crocodile farm that produces 1 500 A-grade skins would generally have 12 000 crocodiles when ready to supply skins for the market.

Organisation of the crocodile farm

Enclosures on a crocodile farm have to be suitable for the class and size of crocodiles that have to be accommodated.

Adult breeding crocodiles are kept usually in large enclosures with deep dams and sandy ground where they are able to mate and lay eggs. Once females start laying eggs, the eggs are collected and incubated artificially.

Hatchlings are transferred to indoor, usually heated, ponds where they are fed on a suitable diet. At about 10–12 months the hatchlings are referred to as growers and should now be 0.8 to 1 m long. They are then transferred to grower enclosures, where they are fed until they attain a suitable size for the market (usually at about 3-4 years of age). The skins are then evaluated by the export agent for their quality and a price is determined. Growers are then slaughtered and tanned either by the farmer or by a second party tannery. Growers that are nearly ready for slaughter are referred to as finishers, and may be housed individually during the last 3–6 months in order to ensure good skin quality.

Breeders

Facilities: Good results are achieved when the enclosures used for breeders are kept as close to natural conditions as possible by using earth dams. Natural earth dams are also aesthetically pleasing, environmentally friendly, and can be used as a tourist attraction. However, they cannot be cleaned easily and it is difficult to monitor such large groups of crocodiles for recording purposes (nesting successes, fertility, etc). Whether one adopts the natural approach or uses cement dams with designated feeding sites, the area must be properly fenced as discussed under Safety and Security. The area

Keeping breeders in a natural dam will give the best performance and is attractive as a tourist feature.

of the breeding dam must be sufficient to allow smaller animals to escape aggression especially during the breeding season. Sufficient feeding areas such as platforms must be provided to prevent competition and ensure that all animals have access to food. In natural earth dams, a natural food source in the form of *Tilapia* and catfish in the dams can be provided for the summer months. Adult crocodiles are not fed during cold periods or before transport. Obesity of breeding crocodiles can lead to low fertility, so care must be taken not to overfeed dominant animals as a tourist attraction. Large waterbodies, such as breeder ponds, should be cleaned at least once per year. Breeding ponds have to be at least 1.5 m deep to allow crocodiles to mate effectively and to ensure proper thermoregulation during cold winter temperatures. Sand banks are also necessary because the female digs a nest in which she deposits her eggs. The sand of these banks should be at least 1 m deep.

Breeding management: Breeding crocodiles can be held in large groups or in smaller groups. A sex ratio of one male to 5–8 females is recommended. If several males are held in a large enclosure, it must have lagoons, islands, etc. to be used as territories, otherwise males will fight during the breeding season and cause injuries or even death to each other.

Adult crocodiles should not be disturbed during the mating season from May to August and during the egg-laying season from September to December. Any management or translocation procedures should therefore be carried out during the first quarter of each year.

Mating: The mating season varies slightly from area to area, but generally takes place from May to August. Nesting takes place between September and December and crocodiles hatch between November and March. Female Nile crocodiles are considered sexually mature at a length of about 2.3 m or roughly 8–10 years. Males mature later at about 3 m body length and 12–15 years of age. Mature males are territorial and aggressive towards each other, especially during the mating season. In many instances younger or smaller crocodiles which are competing with territorial males are driven out.

Fights can cause severe injuries and even death. Crocodiles mate in the water after a courtship display. Mating takes place repeatedly which ensures that the majority of the eggs are fertilised. Eggs can be fertilised by more than one male.

Incubation of eggs.

Hatchlings need ponds of clean water for drinking and thermoregulation.

Egg-laying: Following the mating season, clusters of hard-shelled oval eggs are deposited in nesting sites which are usually holes dug in the sand by the female. The first clutches of young females are often small and not all eggs are fertile. Mature females can lay around 60 eggs per clutch and usually only one clutch of eggs is produced per season. Healthy, well-adapted crocodiles will lay large fertile eggs every year. Once the female starts laying, the eggs must be collected every day. The nest sites can be identified by observing soil disturbance, guarding by the female, or signs of urination near the hole. Surveillance equipment such as cameras are useful for identifying new nests. Staff must be vigilant during egg-collecting as females can defend their nests aggressively. Hitting a plastic pipe on the ground can be used to distract a nesting female, but breeding crocodiles should not be unnecessarily stressed during this procedure. The eggs must be removed without being turned and must be placed in a container in exactly the same position as it was removed from the nest.

Incubation of eggs: There are various options and techniques to incubate eggs. Some farms incubate on open trays or with the natural nesting material or moss. Currently the most common method in South Africa is to incubate eggs carefully packed into Styrofoam boxes filled with sterile vermiculite. This is the material of choice and it provides insulation, retains moisture, allows for gas exchange and prevents crushing. The incubator must maintain a constant temperature of between 28 °C and 34 °C to ensure optimum growth of an embryo. Temperatures below 28 °C can result in arrested development, or runting, and temperatures above 34 °C can cause deformities and coagulation of the egg. At the upper end of the range mainly male hatchlings are produced, while those incubated at lower temperatures will generally produce female hatchlings.

The growth rate of a male is higher than that of a female and generally farmers strive for higher temperatures to ensure higher production of males for the skin market. Relative air humidity should be monitored and kept at least above 80%. The incubation period is generally 90 days from the time that eggs have been laid.

Close to the 90 day period baby crocodiles will start to call and start hatching. At this stage the particular entire nesting box should be removed to another facility/room to avoid other nests hatching prematurely as they are stimulated to hatch by the calls of hatchlings.

Hatchlings

Facilities: Hatchlings are kept in groups in hatchling facilities which are usually inside a building but some farms in warmer climates also operate hatchling enclosures outdoors with underfloor and water heating. Enclosure must ensure protection from predation and provide maintained correct temperature. Strict hygiene and biosecurity must be applied to prevent diseases because hatchlings are very vulnerable at this stage.

Usually animals of one clutch are kept together as a group during the hatchling stage. The temperature should be maintained at 30–32 °C. A wall of 1 m in height is sufficient to keep hatchlings from escaping. Small ponds are provided to allow hatchlings to thermoregulate, drink and bath.

Generally between 40 and 250 crocodiles are kept together in groups depending on the enclosure size.

Management: Usually hatchlings are removed from the hatchling house at about 10-12 months of age when they are close to 1 m in length. An all-in-all-out system is the preferable system for any crocodile house, especially for hatchling houses where diseases can be a problem and lead to major losses. Hatchlings may have to be stimulated to accept their food by moving it around or other methods to simulate the predation instinct (see under Feeding crocodiles).

After the 10–12 month old hatchlings are removed from the hatchling house and put into the grower enclosures, the house is cleaned, disinfected and left empty for 1–2 weeks, before new hatchlings are brought in. Hatchling enclosures should be cleaned with suitable detergents and the water changed at least once daily.

Disinfection with a suitable non-toxic product must be done at least weekly. Some

Stocking densities of hatchlings and growers

Stocking densities depend on the enclosure design and the age group of crocodiles held in the enclosure. Bear in mind that all animals must have access to water, sun, shade, hiding places and a feeding area. If a specific group of animals is very aggressive, stocking density should be reduced to prevent injuries. Huchermeyer (2003) proposed the following formula for the stocking density of Nile crocodiles:

- $p = (n \sqrt{m})/5$ where p is the required pen size in m^2, n is the number of crocodiles per pen and m the average mass in kg per crocodile.

A low stocking density is recommended that usually promotes a better skin quality of the animals while overstocking will lead to damage of the skins as well as stress, disease susceptibility and decreased growth rate, so there is no economic justification for this. The enclosure size stipulated for crocodiles kept as pets and in zoos in Europe (length of the crocodile x 2 equals the length and width of the enclosure) is not suitable for use in intensive farming.

Crowding or piling will damage the skins of growers.

Growers

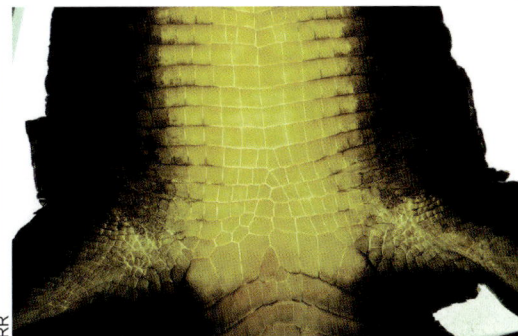
Skin

types of feed may cause a build-up of fat on the skin. In this case cleaning detergents can be used to wash the crocs and they must then be hosed down to wash the product off. A quaternary ammonium such as F10 is suitable as a detergent and disinfectant.

Growers

Facilities: At the age of 10–12 months hatchlings are transferred to the grower pens. Some management systems regroup growers on an ongoing basis but it should be borne in mind that this leads to social stress of these animals as they have complex social hierarchies within a group. On some farms growers are kept in large outside enclosures where up to 1 000 animals are held and a large waterbody such as a dam is provided, while others keep growers indoors in small groups of about 40 animals. The choice of system will depend on the climate, water availability and personal preferences.

Management: The grower enclosure must be cleaned regularly and excess feed should be picked up daily. Many farmers actually build two dams within one enclosure. This ensures that the animals can always retire into water to escape management procedures, to thermoregulate and to drink. All management procedures must be done calmly and quietly because stressful situations lead to "piling" (climbing on one another) which damages the belly skin.

Finishing: In the last 3–6 months before slaughter growers are called finishers. On some farms finishers are moved to low density pens or single pens to allow the skin quality to improve and grow a bit more. The single pen system is used in Asia, America and Australia and is also becoming popular in southern Africa. It has the advantage that crocodiles are hardly handled during this stage and thus are not stressed by handling or social stress. The cleaning of these ponds is automated to reduce stress and handling.

Slaughter and skinning

Crocodiles are harvested when they reach the required size. Crocodiles can be inspected randomly to verify whether there are defects in skin quality and whether such defects can be rectified through treatment. Some farmers supply live crocodiles to agents who skin and market crocodiles on their behalf, while others who have direct contracts with the buyers do slaughter and skinning themselves.

Slaughter process: The slaughter of crocodiles should be carried out by trained personnel and in accordance with animal welfare requirements.

Slaughter and culling protocols can be found in the relevant SANS 631:2009 documents relating to Crocodiles in Captivity. Crocodiles shall be slaughtered in a designated hygienic facility and screened from the public. The crocodile is rendered unconscious by means

Crocodile skins in storage awaiting grading.

of a headshot with a suitable calibre rifle such as a .22, or the animal can be stunned into unconsciousness with an electric stunner or captive bolt.

The spinal cord is then severed immediately with a knife between the skull and the first cervical vertebra. The brain is destroyed by means of pithing. Pithing is the insertion of a metal rod or a sharp-pointed instrument into the brain of the animal. The crocodile can then be left to bleed out.

Skinning: Crocodiles are skinned according to prescribed methods, removing any fat or meat. The skinning process is extremely important as the belly skin produces the income. The slightest cut into the belly skin will render it worthless. Therefore skinners have to be very well trained. The prescribed cuts to harvest the belly skin can be slightly different and sometimes depend also on the buyer. The harvested, salted belly skins must be kept in cold storage to prevent damage by rodents and fungal infection, while awaiting the grading process.

Farmers that wish to slaughter and skin themselves should visit experienced operators before attempting the procedure. Grading of skins is generally done by the buyer's agent: The determination of the grading of the skin and the price is where new farmers experience the most difficulties.

Skin grading and obtaining the correct market prices is a difficult process requiring skills and a good knowledge of the skins industry. New farmers generally enter into agreements with farmers who have established markets and knowledge.

Crocodile meat: As with all meat for human consumption processing must be carried out within the confines of the Meat Safety Act, which stipulates high standards for slaughtering and processing.

The cost of setting up a commercial abattoir is huge and currently there are only three main abattoirs that produce crocodile meat, mainly for the export market.

Properly harvested crocodile meat is healthy, high in protein and low in cholesterol. The domestic market is fairly underdeveloped at this stage but has huge potential.

Efforts are being made to allow crocodiles to be slaughtered in less prescriptive rural abattoirs and to transport the carcasses to registered abattoirs for processing and packaging for the local market. Many farmers do not take meat into account as a feasible revenue source, so many merely feed the carcasses back to their crocodiles as a food source which is undesirable from a health point of view.

Other aspects

Feeding crocodiles – general principles

Crocodiles are fed according to their age and the ambient temperature as follows: In winter, the weather forecasts must be consulted and feeding held back if a cold front is imminent. Crocodiles should not be fed when the ambient temperature is under 25 °C because the food will stay in the stomach where it rots and leads to a fatal septicaemia.

Grower crocodiles can go without food for several weeks and adults can go without food for one year. Hatchlings on the other hand are kept at constantly high temperatures to ensure good health and cost effective growth and thus hatchlings should be fed daily with a break during the weekend so that their stomachs can empty completely. The feed should be consumed within 30 minutes and leftovers cleaned up.

Feeding meat

Red meat carcasses or chicken as well as fish are suitable feed for crocodiles. These carcasses must not contain medications such as ivermectin and non-steroidal anti-inflammatories, antibiotics, barbiturates or capture drugs which can be poisonous and leave residues in meat. Many farmers feed crocodile carcasses which can lead to transmission of various diseases, such as coccidiosis especially in hatchlings. It is also a potential source of trichinella which is a public health threat in crocodile meat.

Food intake depends on the temperature but as a rough guide the following can be used:
- Hatchlings of less than 0.5 m body length consume about 0.15 kg of meat per week per animal.
- Growers of about 1 m body length consume about 0.5 kg meat per week per animal.
- Adult crocodiles in summer can be fed about 5 kg of carcass every 7–10 days. Entire carcasses should be fed that contain skin and bones as well as stomach contents, which mimics the natural diet and usually contains enough vitamins and minerals to keep adult crocodiles healthy. If it is not possible to feed entire carcasses, it is best to analyse the feed that is available and develop a supplement in consultation with a nutritionist (see below).

It is very important that the carcasses used for feed are fresh and hygienically slaughtered. If meat is retrieved from abattoirs, this should always be done in consultation and agreement with the responsible meat inspectors as meat is declared unfit for human consumption for different reasons and the movement of condemned meat can lead to spreading of diseases. Any kind of animal flesh fed to crocodiles has to be kept cool or frozen and should not be rotten or rancid. Rancid fish, for example, should never be fed to crocodiles as it could lead to steatitis or yellow fat disease which can be fatal.

Supplies of fresh meat can be obtained from chicken farms or abattoirs, or red meat feedlots and abattoirs. Fish can be used as a primary meat source if one is situated close to a large lake.

Feeding fresh meat to crocodiles has some difficulties especially in hatchlings and growers. Fresh meat is not easily eaten by hatchlings because it sticks to the ground. Small crocodiles will not eat an entire carcass unless it is minced, so they may lack vital vitamins and minerals. Fresh meat also contains a lot of water and therefore the nutrient intake could be improved by adding nutrients in the form of dry carcass meal to the diet of hatchlings and growers. The meal can therefore be mixed together with the minced meat and pressed into moist pellets, the size of which will depend on the size of the animals. In the beginning the fresh meat content is often higher (90%) and can then be reduced.

The farmer should submit samples of the main food being fed to their crocodiles for laboratory analysis. This will in consultation with a nutritionist allow cost effective supplementation of the diet if necessary. For example, growers that are close to the finishing state might need extra zinc or vitamin A and biotin in their diet to ensure a good skin quality.

In America, many farms now feed commercially available dry alligator pellets that have been scientifically formulated. This has the advantage that farmers do not have the problem of organising, transporting and storing fresh meat. The pellets are always of the same quality and do not contain any harmful residues and thus the meat would be suitable for human consumption.

The pellets are dry and thus the stomach of the animals fills up with more nutrients and less moisture (lean beef muscle meat contains only about 23g protein and 73g moisture per 100g meat); the higher dry matter content of pellets leads to higher nutrient intake and better growth. The rolling action of pellets also stimulates the small hatchlings to start feeding.

Feeding behaviour

Crocodiles, especially growers and breeders, become very excited and aggressive during feeding time. Ensure that feeding space is large enough so that all crocodiles can get to the feed. Hatchlings may need some movement of the food or "prey" to encourage them to eat. This can be done using a laser light or moving the food along the ground.

Crocodiles larger than 1 m can be caught by hand.

Handling and transport

Nile crocodiles are naturally aggressive animals, which can make their handling difficult. Although they seldom vocalise and cannot communicate with facial features, they do feel pain, fear and stress. They do, however, get used to their caretakers and will adapt to a routine from a young age. This helps to keep stress at a minimum level, especially for subadults.

Crocodiles should be handled as little as possible and in a calm manner. Any handling can lead to stress and skin injuries and thus it is not only a welfare issue but also implies economic losses to the farmer.

Crocodiles up to 1 m can be caught by hand. Crocodiles larger than 1 m can be caught by hand or by using a steel noose which is placed

Using the stunner to catch a grower croc.

over the jaw or neck and tightened. Today most commercial farms make use of the electric stunner or e-stunner to catch crocodiles for management procedures. This apparatus has been approved as a tool for this purpose on the SABS standard SANS 631 and a recent study confirmed that it reduces stress because it speeds up management interventions 10-fold. The e-stunner delivers an electric charge of low voltage and high amperage to the brain and renders the animal immobile and unconscious for about five minutes. This time can be used to tape the jaws closed and management procedures such as slaughtering, grading, regrouping, loading, etc. can be done. However, the e-stunner should be used by well-trained personnel only and if applied wrongly, it can cause serious injuries and welfare issues.

For veterinary interventions immobilising drugs can be delivered using the pole syringe method. This is generally done on land to avoid drowning. Large crocodiles can also be caught in traps or from a boat by means of large hooks on a heavy duty fishing line. These hooks can be hooked on the body surface of the crocodile and it can then be roped in with a fishing rod until it is close enough to attach a noose. Crocodiles should be caught as fast as possible as prolonged struggling, especially in large crocodiles can lead to exhaustion, anaerobic metabolism and to high lactate levels and muscle damage which can be fatal.

Hatchlings can be transported in temperature controlled Styrofoam boxes. Subadults should be transported in individual crates, canvas bags or in crates made out of large diameter pipes as can be bought in any hardware or irrigation store.

Blindfolding the animals during transport helps to reduce stress. Containers used should allow sufficient airflow for respiration, and temperature regulation. The temperature should not rise to more than 32 degrees over a long period of time and not lower than 20 degrees. Note that anything above 35 degrees and below 12 degrees could be lethal. The legs can be tied to prevent scratching or lying on top of each other. The leg restraints must not restrict blood flow, which can be a challenge. The jaws are usually secured in all age groups except for hatchlings, using insulation tape or rubber straps but again this must not restrict the blood flow of the jaw. Crocodiles that have not been starved before capture and transport might on rare occasions vomit, so tying a piece of rope or a small stick between the jaws will prevent vomitus from being inhaled. Large crocodiles can be transported in individual wooden boxes which for air transport, must be International Air Transport Association (IATA) compliant.

Copies of the IATA regulations can be downloaded from www.iata.com. Large crocodiles in dark, secure, individual crates do not need to be tied up or blind-folded.

Important diseases

Many diseases of crocodiles are stress-related and triggered either by unsuitable temperatures, handling stress or social stress combined with management issues such as lack of hygiene and water quality problems, etc. However, crocodile specific pathogens introduced onto disease-free farms may lead to outbreaks of disease. Therefore, strict biosecurity measures have to be taken on crocodile farms. Preferably farms should work on all-in-all-out farming systems with cleaning and disinfection of the different enclosures inbetween.

Hatchlings should be isolated from the rest of the farm and have their own dedicated facilities, staff, and equipment. Overalls, gumboots and disinfecting footbaths at each entrance for any section of a crocodile farm are important aspects of biosecurity as in any intensive farming business. If new crocodiles are brought in, they should be placed in quarantine to prevent the spread of diseases such as mycoplasma and coccidiosis by unidentified carriers.

It is important to consult a veterinarian or pathologist if disease outbreaks do occur to get a definitive diagnosis and thus to be able to start adequate treatment and to estimate and prevent future losses.

At present there are a number of important conditions which are discussed briefly.

Crocodile pox: Infection with crocodile pox virus mostly affects hatchlings and grower crocodiles up to 2 years of age. The virus causes brown crusty lesions in the mouth, on the head and on the body. Often these lesions heal spontaneously but there might be a low mortality. Healed lesions can, however, cause scarring, resulting in the downgrading of skins which will lead to loss of income. Other similar conditions are bacterial or fungal skin disease so a veterinarian must be consulted to confirm the diagnosis. Prevention of crocodile pox is done by implementing strict biosecurity, hygiene and disinfection of young crocodiles in particular.

Adenovirus infection: This disease affects mostly crocodile hatchlings under 5 months of age, causing mainly hepatitis. Common symptoms are lethargy and loss of appetite. Deaths may occur especially during colder winter months. A post mortem with histopathology can confirm the disease. The virus is thought to spread between hatchlings and therefore strict hygiene and biosecurity are of importance to prevent the disease. Water from rivers inhabited by wild crocodiles can also be a source of infection, so only clean water should be used, especially for hatchling crocodiles. Stress caused by cold must be avoided.

Mycoplasmosis: *Mycoplasma crocodyli* and *M. alligatoria* have been identified as a cause of arthritis in crocodiles of 1–3 years of age. Affected animals are often reluctant to move and sometimes cannot leave ponds when they are drained. Pneumonia, poor condition and loss of appetite can also be seen. Diagnosis is based on the history and post mortem findings. Quarantine of new animals is essential as the disease is carried without symptoms by healthy crocodiles. Collecting eggs from the wild can also introduce the disease. Treatment with suitable antibiotics is effective and can alleviate clinical signs, but relapsing does occur.

Chlamydiosis: Chlamydiosis affects mainly hatchlings and can develop in two forms: Acute hepatitis and chronic conjunctivitis. This disease has also been identified in combination with mycoplasmosis and adenoviral hepatitis in farmed crocodiles. This disease can be acute and hatchlings might die without showing any clinical signs. Chronic cases can show a swelling and opacity of the third eyelid with accumulation of fibrinous exudate and conjunctivitis. The eyes of these crocodiles can appear white and crocodiles can become blind. Treatment of the chronic form of this disease can be attempted with suitable antibiotics, given orally in feed or as an injection. The disease is probably maintained by asymptomatic carriers, so quarantine is essential and stress must be prevented.

Coccidiosis: Crocodiles have their own specific species of coccidian parasites. They become infected by contact with infected crocodiles or feeding of crocodile meat. Coccidiosis causes intestinal inflammation which can lead to swelling and blockage of the intestines. Animals appear bloated and lethargic, they take on a runted appearance and might survive for several months. Some animals might die acutely without showing signs of the disease. A post mortem can confirm the presence of the disease. Coccidiosis can be confused with other forms of enteritis such as salmonellosis or *E. coli* infections which can commonly occur in hatchlings and are often associated with stress, lack of hygiene or both. Affected animals can be treated with coccidiostats.

Runting: This is a non-specific, but common phenomenon in hatchling and juvenile crocodiles and it can be defined as the failure to grow. It is common to encounter a small amount of runts within a group of hatchlings. However, if a large number are encountered or if this contributes to mortalities on a farm, management issues must be investigated. A combination of management and other factors may contribute to the problem:

- Anorexia (not eating) because feed is not suitable and of the wrong consistency.
- Genetic causes: Certain individuals may be runts because of genetic traits.
- Poor incubation conditions: Poor yolk sac absorption due to poor incubation conditions and inadequate temperatures will also cause failure to grow.
- Age of mother: Hatchlings of very young breeding females usually are smaller and less vigorous compared to those of large, mature females.
- Environmental factors: Cold temperatures, stress and a high stocking density may contribute to runting.
- Chronic infections: Infections, including some of those discussed in this chapter, could also cause runting.

Clinical signs of runting are the failure of individuals to grow compared with others of their age group. The neck of a runt is usually drawn in and the abdomen might appear distended. Pathological findings are usually non-specific with visible depletion of the body fat. Runts should be separated from the larger animals to prevent bullying.

Additional information

WRSA crocodile interest group
Industry statistics:
http://www.bloomberg.com/bw/articles/2013-10-24/a-crocodiles-bumpy-road-from-farm-to-handbag

CHAPTER 5
DISEASES AND PARASITES
Pamela and Peter Oberem

BASIC DISEASE CONTROL

This section on diseases of game animals is not intended to be an instruction manual for game ranchers because diagnosis and treatment are always best left to the veterinarian. The focus on game ranches should be on early detection and prevention of disease as far as possible.

Biosecurity is of the utmost importance and is discussed under the risk management section but some basic principles are highlighted here because failure to ensure this may cause huge economic or genetic losses of rare animals:

- Introduction of animals susceptible to tick-borne diseases: Game ranchers in areas where tick-borne diseases are endemic must enquire into the origin of the animals to be brought in, because susceptible species will die acutely unless they have been immunised.
- Introduction of infected animals or infected animal material: Bear in mind that bringing in animals of unknown origin, or infected carcasses for feeding to predators or scavengers may introduce diseases such as TB or brucellosis.
- Exposure to infected livestock either on the farm or adjoining farms: When livestock and buffalo in particular are grazed alongside, buffalo in particular are at risk from diseases such as TB and brucellosis. When allowing livestock of neighbours to utilise grazing the disease status of the animals must be provided or investigated.

Use reputable and experienced game capture outfits who will deliver animals without undue stress, injuries and mortalities. Always enquire about the nutrition of animals to be purchased so they can be given periods of nutritional adjustment if necessary (see Nutrition, Ch. 3).

Disease investigation

It is important to investigate the cause of game animal deaths on a game farm, in particular if a number of animals die over a short period of time, or affect animals of different species as this often presages anthrax outbreaks. Postmortem investigation is usually best left to experts since diseases can be spread by opening infected carcasses and there are various zoonoses which may be a threat to the operator (anthrax, rabies, echinoccocosis, and tuberculosis). Specialised techniques and protective clothing are required for performing these investigations. When possible, submit the carcass to the local vet or request a veterinary investigation. If this is not possible the game owner can look for various external signs on the carcass which may reveal clues to the cause of death.

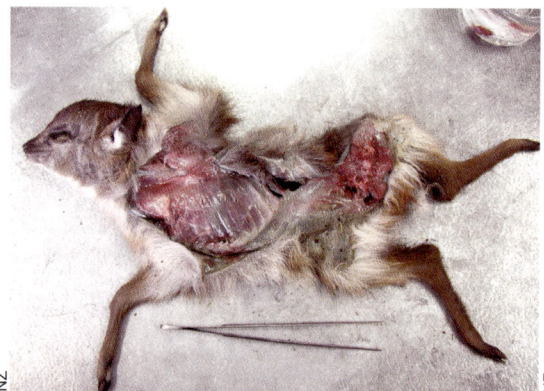
A postmortem examination of a carcass provides useful information to the game rancher.

Gross pathology and histology on the organs can reveal a specific diagnosis as in this case of liver damage caused by *Microcystis*-poisoning of a zebra.

For example, severely worn teeth in ruminants will indicate old age which can result in starvation. High tick burdens, although not always a cause of death in animals, can also be an indication that the animal was too ill or too weak to groom.

External wounds are often a clue to the cause of death. Predators such as leopards bite animals on the neck, causing suffocation. Other wounds that can be found are those caused by fighting among male antelope, which can cause severe, fatal stab wounds. Taking photographs of the carcass can be useful.

Vaccination

Vaccination of wild species is mostly "extra-label", in other words the vaccines have not been tested for safety and efficacy in wild animal species. Wildlife veterinarians are permitted to carry out extra-label vaccination and have considerable knowledge of which current vaccines can be used with safety. Vaccination programs or campaigns against specific diseases should therefore always be done under veterinary supervision. This is particularly important in wild carnivores, since the live modified viruses used for domestic animals may actually cause disease in wild canid species.

As a result of some recent developments vaccination against diseases that threaten wildlife and livestock may become a very important tool in the control of diseases and even parasites in game. For discussion of specific vaccines, see under the appropriate diseases.

Raising orphan animals

Hand-raising orphaned wild animals is a very time-consuming, meticulous and often heart breaking process. It also requires specific knowledge about the nutritional requirements of the species to be raised, and the physiology of young animals.

Additional information

For game farmers in remote areas or those who wish to gain some expertise, postmortem kits with the required protective clothing and training are available from the
University of Pretoria (Onderstepoort)
Prof. Nick Kriek
082 908 6035 nick.kriek@up.ac.za

It should preferably be undertaken by experienced professionals, under the supervision of veterinarians or nurses, or by foster mothers if available. The latter option is preferable in species which become dangerous when hand-reared.

Bear in mind that raising a young animal causes imprinting on humans which can be problematic later in its life, causing aggression or non-socialisation with their own species. This is a particular problem in primates, carnivores and some antelope that become very aggressive.

There are a number of general basic principles involved in raising orphaned wild animals.

Chilling: Young carnivores are born blind, helpless and unable to maintain their own temperature for the first week of life. They must be dried off, and kept warm in an insulated bed. The young orphans of other species also need to be kept in warm, draught-free conditions with dry comfortable bedding which insulates and protects them from injury.

Dehydration: The newborn animal may be dehydrated if it hasn't fed for a while. Evaluate by using the "skin fold test" and correct if the animal is severely dehydrated by giving fluid in addition to the feeds. Pinch a fold of skin and observe the return time. If the skin is slow to return to its position the animal is dehydrated.

Colostrum: Young mammals obtain protective antibodies from the milk of their mothers. These young mammals can only absorb the antibodies in the colostrum for the first 24 hours after birth.

If it is known that the animal didn't receive colostrum this should be fed if available, otherwise the animal must be given serum taken from the mother or an animal of the same species. Animals that do not receive colostrum are susceptible to infection.

Use of milk formula: The composition of the milk of various species differs considerably. Carnivores need more fat and protein than ruminants for example, so cow's milk can be used but the addition of cream or eggs is required. Specific formulas are available for various species in Mc Kenzie (1993) or from wildlife care centres and veterinary staff of zoological gardens. Some formulae are available commercially.

The optimal temperature of milk or formula is 35–37 °C and varying the temperature can cause diarrhoea in newborns. Milk temperature is of particular importance in young ruminants because warm milk stimulates the closure of the oesophageal groove which ensures that the milk reaches the stomach instead of the rumen. The general rule of thumb for feeding milk formula is to give 10–15% of its live body weight daily (w/v), divided up into 3–4 feeds. So, if the animal weighs 50 kg it must be fed 5 litre per day divided into 4 x 1.25 litre feeds throughout the day. The percentage needed may be higher in animals with a rapid metabolic rate. It is very important to control the amount of formula since underfeeding can cause slow growth and overfeeding can cause severe diarrhoea which can be fatal. (Mc Kenzie, 1993)

Food equipment: The suitable size and shape of the teats used will differ with species. Dog, calf and sheep teats are available from co-ops or vet shops. If the opening of the teat is too small the animal won't be able to feed properly, whereas if too big the milk may leak out into the lungs resulting in pneumonia. Bottles and teats must be kept scrupulously clean using chemical bottle sterilisers such as Milton. These must be thoroughly rinsed to remove chemical residues.

Hygiene: It is essential, particularly the cleaning of bottles and teats. Do not store the milk mixture after feeding since it will become contaminated with bacteria in the process. Formulas are therefore very handy in this respect.

Orphans of all sizes may require hand-raising.

Anogenital stimulation: Young carnivores in particular need stimulation of the anus after feeding, with a warm damp cloth or wad of cotton wool, otherwise constipation will develop.

Feeding position: Adopt the most natural feeding position for the animal to ensure the maximal intake.

Mineral and vitamin supplement: Supplementation may be needed to prevent deficiencies in specific species.

Weaning: The animal should be weaned at the correct age for the species. This is done by gradually offering the animal natural graze, browse, or prey food, while gradually phasing out the milk feeds.

Problems: Diarrhoea is the most common problem when raising young animals. The most common causes are related to feeding, most often overfeeding or varying the temperature of the milk. Since diarrhoea causes dehydration it must be treated by withdrawing milk and using lime water mixed with saline, and then gradually reintroducing milk formula again. Pneumonia often results from incorrect feeding and this must be treated immediately with antibiotics since it can be fatal. Some specific species requirements for feeding are detailed below to illustrate species differences. Detailed recipes are available from textbooks, veterinarians or nutritionists:

Antelope

Full cream cow's milk or goat's milk (preferable) can be used as a base, enriched with cream or egg yolk as antelope require more energy and protein than cattle.

Alternately, human baby formula can be used since it has a higher fat and protein content than cow's milk. Nespray with the addition of 15 ml of egg yolk and 60 ml cream has been used successfully by "Free-Me".

The smaller the antelope the higher the metabolic rate and the amount of energy required, and therefore the more frequent the feeds must be. It is preferable to feed small amounts more often. Biorem/Biorad can be used when animals develop diarrhoea.

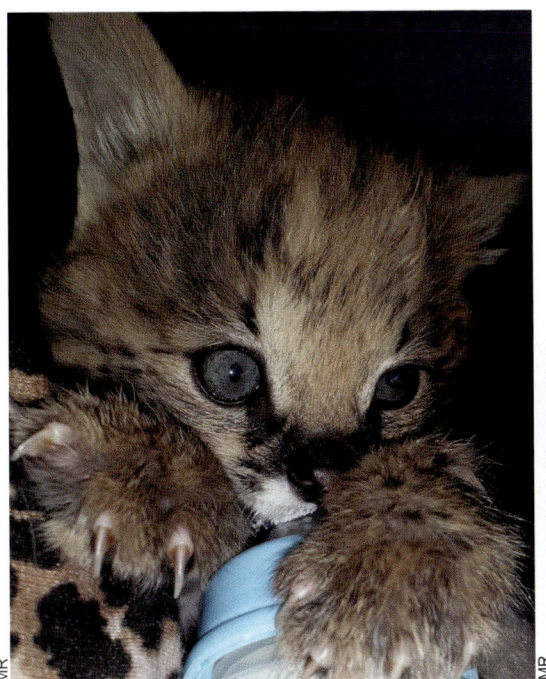

Buffalo

There have been a number of buffalo calf-raising initiatives in recent years in the attempt to raise disease-free buffalo. Cow's milk is suitable for raising buffalo calves. Hand-raised buffalo become aggressive and difficult to manage thus some outfits use Jersey cows as foster mothers. Calves remain with their mothers for the first 48 hours to ensure they take in colostrum before placed with the foster mother (2–3 calves per mother). Calves in these intensive systems may develop diarrhoea due to *E. coli* and coccidiosis.

Primates

Young primates feed on demand in the wild so they need a lot of feeds, 6–8 initially and then gradually reducing to less regular feeds. Primate babies need physical contact since mothers carry them around continually. Human replacement formula and nappies can be used.

Elephants

Elephant calves that have received colostrum can be successfully raised with various plant-based products such as soya milk formulae (Isomil). The calves need to have a body weight increase of 0.5 kg per day.

Hippo

Calves have been successfully raised on evaporated milk and water, or calf formula mixed with eggs.

Rhino

Calf milk replacer can be used because rhino milk has little fat and is high in lactose. The formula must be supplemented with glucose (0.4%). Once they are habituated to being fed, rhino calves will happily drink from large flat containers like baby baths. They need a mud wallow for skin care, and companions in the form of other rhinos, goats or sheep.

Carnivores

Cat and dog formulae are available from vet suppliers for specific carnivore species. Vaccination should be considered with veterinary consultation since wild carnivores are susceptible to the "childhood" diseases of pets.

GENERAL DISEASE CONDITIONS

Abortion and deaths of newborn animals

It is known from studies in domestic animals that a small percentage of abortions or resorptions (3–5%) will occur in populations as a result of defective genes and can therefore be regarded as "normal". This frequency will rise when there is inbreeding within animal populations. Other causes of abortions in wildlife are poor nutrition, injury, stress or disturbance of animals during the hunting season. Abortions may also result from diseases that cause fever reactions (heartwater or babesia) and those that affect the foetus directly, for example brucellosis in buffalo and Rift Valley fever in some herbivores (see more detailed discussion under these sections).

Abortions in wild herbivores and the deaths of young animals have been attributed to the protozoal organism *Neospora caninum* of which the domestic dog is the main host. Deaths in newborn animals are most often due to predation and starvation as a result of being orphaned. Another cause of abortion storms in herbivores is poisoning by mycotoxins (fungus) in stored feed with a high moisture content (see under Nutrition, Chapter 3 for details).

In carnivores such as wild dogs, competition with siblings for food may cause a high percentage of deaths. Carnivores in captive breeding systems may also succumb to "childhood diseases" such as distemper. Hand-raised orphans frequently die as a result of inappropriate nutrition or feeding techniques, which predispose them to diarrhoea and pneumonia.

Lameness

Game animals may develop lameness due to a variety of different causes. Laminitis or the inflammation of the fleshy leaves of the hooves occurs in ungulates as a result of overfeeding of carbohydrates such as maize. It is often seen when grazing species are fed diets composed of high quality lucerne hay with cubes or pellets, which gives the animals a total oversupply of protein and energy with a skewed calcium:phosphorous ratio. An excess of high quality lucerne in the place of veld or grass hay has the same effect. Laminitis is an extremely severe, painful condition which can cause the loss of the hoof. The condition must be avoided at all costs because it is difficult to treat effectively and can have irreversible consequences which necessitate the destruction of the animal.

Nerve injury is sometimes seen when large animals like rhino are left to lie on their sides for extended periods after immobilisation instead of being placed in sternal recumbency (see Capture myopathy). The radial nerve becomes damaged due to the weight of the animal pressing on it resulting in partial paralysis of the front leg, which manifests as drooping of the shoulder.

Stiffness seen in animals that have recently been translocated may be caused by capture myopathy (see later). Newly delivered animals should be observed for at least a week after delivery for signs of this condition.

In foot-and-mouth disease (FMD) infected areas some wild antelope like impala may develop foot lesions as a result of the disease. The condition may cause lameness in the early stage of the disease and later permanent hoof damage which may cause abnormal growth of the hoof. Game ranch owners outside the FMD area should be vigilant for such symptoms since they are often the only visible signs of FMD outbreaks.

Young animals, especially those that are orphaned or kept in unhygienic conditions, may develop polyarthritis which is an infection of

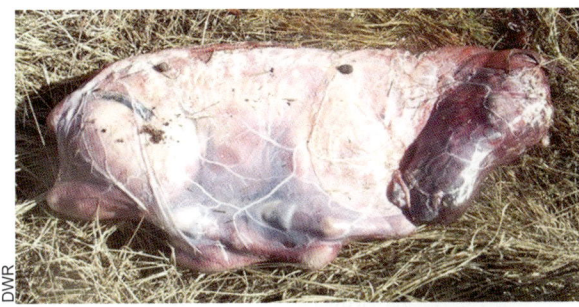

Top left: A zebra foetus aborted close to term possibly due to maternal trauma. Bottom left: Lameness due to damage of the foot caused by a poachers snare. Top right: A laceration on the leg of a giraffe probably caused by a predator.

more than one joint on the limbs. The portal of entry for the infection is the umbilical stump which becomes infected shortly after birth. The infection spreads from the umbilicus to the joints where it causes severe stiffness, with the animals sometimes being unable to feed as a result. These cases are difficult to treat with antibiotics and can become chronic with the result that the animals remain stunted. Polyarthritis in young animals is prevented by providing hygienic pens for calving and raising of young animals. Disinfecting the umbilical stump of newborn animals where possible will reduce the incidence of the condition.

Other causes of apparent lameness may be poisonings with chemicals such as organophosphates which affect the nervous system (see Poisoning).

The tick *Ixodes rubicundus* which occurs in certain areas of the country causes paralysis in antelope due to a toxin which it secretes (see Parasite).

Botulism is a condition caused by the toxin of *Clostridum botulinum*. It is occasionally seen in antelope, as a cause of stiffness and lameness in the initial stages of the disease and this may need to be excluded as a cause (see under Herbivores).

Footrot is a problem encountered in ungulates held in bomas, where conditions may be damp or muddy. Under these conditions the causative bacterium *Fusobacterium necrophorum* which occurs in the faeces of the animals, invades the damp skin between the toes (interdigital space) where it causes swelling and redness. Infection then spreads around the skin adjacent to the hooves and the skin may ooze pus. Affected animals become lame, may stop eating and suffer a severe loss of condition. The condition can be treated with antibiotics, but the hooves may become misformed requiring trimming. Foot rot must be prevented by ensuring that the floors of camps and bomas are kept dry, and faeces must be regularly removed. Regular foot care may be needed for animals kept in bomas where the combined effects of sandy floor and the lack of exercise result in abnormal hoof growth.

Other conditions which can cause lameness are injuries to the feet or limbs from a variety of causes such as wires, fighting, traps, wounding by sharp objects, etc.

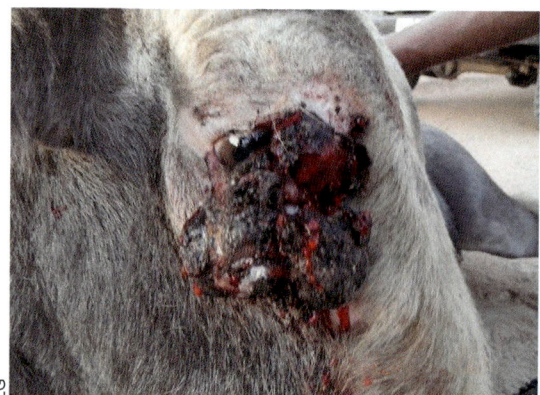
King's Wildebeest with skin cancer due to lack of pigmentation around the eye.

Depigmentation of the skin in a buffalo (vitiligo) caused by stress due to an injury.

Skin conditions

Skin conditions are seen frequently in captive but also in free-living wildlife. One of the most common causes of skin conditions is parasitic infections: Lice can become a problem when animals are confined together or during winter when their resistance is low and there is more direct contact between animals. Sarcoptic mange which is seen in many different wildlife species causes severe irritation resulting in debilitation and sometimes death. Demodectic mange which is usually less severe may also cause hair loss and irritation.

Other parasites that cause skin irritation are louse flies, ticks and biting flies. The larvae of certain flies may be found causing lumps under the skin (*Stephanofilaria*) or their maggots (*Chrysomyia bezziana*) may be found infesting large open wounds. It is usually impossible for the layperson to diagnose these conditions on the basis of observed symptoms, so a veterinarian must be consulted.

The various parasite infestations and their treatments are discussed in more detail under the parasite section.

Bacterial infections of the skin as a result of damp cages or enclosures show reddening, oozing and hair loss. These infections can be treated with antibiotic sprays or ointments. To prevent the condition the cages/pens must be kept dry and clean. Infected darting wounds can lead to abscessation so they must be disinfected after removal of the dart to prevent complications. A highly infectious fungal disease known as ringworm is a common cause of patchy hair loss in both herbivores and carnivores. This condition can also be transmitted to humans. The diagnosis must be confirmed by a veterinarian and treatment instigated with antifungal solutions, such as iodine spray.

Skin cancers such as squamous cell carcinomas are seen in albinos or animals with patchy pigmentation of the skin. As in livestock with lack of pigmentation the action of the sun promotes the development of skin cancers. These can become large, painful and unsightly growths which have to be removed but may also spread to other areas of the body. Colour variants which lack proper pigments should not be bred as this will perpetuate the problem.

Acquired (as opposed to genetic) loss of pigment or vitiligo has been described in a buffalo after an injury. The exact cause is not known but it may be a response to stress.

Capture myopathy

Capture myopathy or "overexertion disease" accounts for the highest numbers of mortalities of translocated ungulates. Under natural conditions animals flee from danger at high

A rhino with capture myopathy showing hind limb stiffness.

speed usually over short distances. When the chase is sustained over long distances or with undue stress as happens with inexpert capture outfits, the pursued animals develop severe muscle damage with systemic complications which is ultimately fatal. The condition is aggravated by stress factors such as strange smells, loud noise, being placed in confined spaces where they continue to struggle and the presence of dogs.

The species most severely affected by capture myopathy are sable, roan, nyala, tssesebe, red hartebeest, springbok, kudu and giraffe, although rhino and some other species can also be affected. Capture myopathy can cause death within 12 hours after capture but chronic cases can die up to 14 days after the ordeal. The symptoms of hyperacute capture myopathy are signs of agitation and distress, and then depression just before death. More chronic cases show lameness, stiffness, depression, unwillingness to eat or drink. Animals typically show torticollis or retraction of the head against the neck. When animals are translocated to new farms deaths due to capture myopathy are often attributed to infectious diseases or poisonings since they occur a few days after delivery. The damaged muscles release a protein called myoglobin which damages the kidneys and other organs. The condition can be confirmed on post mortem examination by demonstrating dark brown myoglobin in the urine, haemorrhages of the muscles and the heart, as well as lung oedema and kidney damage. Histology of the muscles and other organs will reveal damage.

There is no effective treatment for the condition. Because capture myopathy can cause massive losses it is essential to make use of professional, experienced capture teams that use techniques to minimise the stress of capture. The use of tranquilisers after the animal has been captured reduces the struggling and distress of the animal and therefore the stress associated with the experience. Supplementing animals with vitamins and mineral combinations may improve tolerance of capture and transport stress.

Digestive problems

Bloat is a frequent complication of ruminants after capture. When ruminants are immobilised and allowed to lie on their sides for extended periods, they are unable to expel the gas which accumulates in their rumen. The gas accumulation causes distention of the rumen, resulting in severe discomfort and difficulties with breathing. This free gas bloat can be relieved by a veterinarian passing a tube down the oesophagus into the rumen to release the trapped gas. If this is unsuccessful, a sharp instrument called a trocar with a surrounding cannula, is inserted into the paralumbar fossa in the left flank, through the skin and into the rumen. The gas can then be released from the rumen. It is not ideal to do this on an animal to be released into the wild, so must be viewed as an emergency measure. Bloat should be prevented by placing immobilised or tranquilised ruminants on their sternums, lying down but in an upright position.

Frothy bloat occurs in ruminants that have fed on green legumes such as lucerne or clover. These plants contain substances which promote the formation of small gas bubbles

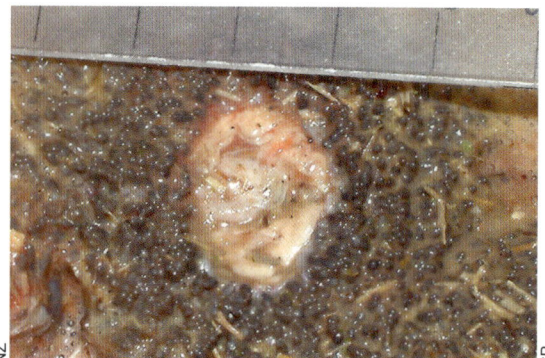
Rumenitis in a springbok as a sequel to acidosis.

The fatal condition red gut is seen in particular when grazers are fed fresh lucerne or green lucerne pellets.

which do not coalesce, and therefore the gas cannot be released by burping (eructation). The symptoms are the same as for free gas bloat but frothy bloat must be treated by administering surfactants which break up the bubbles. Because of the dangers of free bloat and the difficulty of treatment green lucerne and clover should not be fed to wild ruminants.

Acidosis is a digestive problem of ruminants which results when carbohydrates like maize are fed either intentionally or accidentally without a period of adaptation to this dietary change. The ruminal bacteria which digest carbohydrates produce a large amount of acid which produces local and sometimes systemic effects. Depending on how much concentrate is ingested, the symptoms can be mild "indigestion" (see below) to severe fatal systemic disease. Even if the condition isn't fatal, damage to the lining of the rumen can cause chronic problems which affect the animal's performance.

Liver abscessation is often a sequel to rumen acidosis. Wild ruminants should be allowed an adaptation period with gradual feeding of pelleted feed containing carbohydrates like grain. They must be prevented from accidentally accessing any type of grain.

Ruminant "indigestion" is the disturbance of the rumen flora of ruminants which occurs most often as the result of protracted periods of not eating, or due to a change in diet. The symptoms of mild indigestion are subtle, mainly a temporary loss of appetite and reduced faecal output. On veterinary examination the rumen will be found to have reduced motility. Animals being translocated to areas where the grazing is very different from their area of origin may experience indigestion problems, and will do poorly or may even starve to death as a result. It must always be borne in mind that any changes in a ruminant's diet must always be done gradually to prevent indigestion problems (see Nutrition, Chapter 3).

A "red gut"-syndrome has been observed in herbivores, especially when grazers are fed green lucerne without having access to roughage. It is thought to result from an overgrowth of *Clostridium perfringens* type A bacteria, which either cause an enterotoxaemia or a torsion of the gut. Animals with red gut die acutely and the intestines are filled with blood giving rise to the name of the condition. Grazing herbivores must not be fed green lucerne even in pelleted form, and must be allowed sufficient time to adapt to new diets. A new diet must be fed gradually to animals over a period of 21 days to prevent this and other dietary problems.

Colic (abdominal pain) can occur in elephants, rhino and zebra, as a result of constipation, sand ingestion or feeding on mouldy feed. The signs of colic are abdominal discomfort, peering at the flanks, rolling or kicking at the abdomen. This condition must be

A rhino injured by a poacher's snare.

Wire is a constant problem on game farms because it can cause severe injuries and mortalities.

attended to by a veterinarian as it can become serious. Some worm infections may also cause diarrhoea.

"Choke" or oesophageal obstruction has been seen in elephants that are fed fruit such as oranges. Fruit should always be halved or quartered to prevent obstruction of the digestive tract.

Diarrhoea (scours) is a common problem in young animals that are hand-raised, most often due to nutritional problems but sometimes as a result of infectious agents. In adult animals loose faeces can be caused by stress or change in diet. Severe or persistent diarrhoea is likely to be due to coccidial infection (see later) or bacterial infections like salmonellosis which can progress to septicaemia if untreated.

Wounds and fractures

Free-living animals may develop wounds as a result of predator attacks, fighting among competing males and parasite infestations. Ticks with long mouthparts such as the bont tick and the bont-legged tick cause wounding, screwworm infestation and abscess formation at the sites of the bites. Young animals under six months are susceptible to secondary infection of tick bites by the bacterium *Arcanobacterium/Actinomyces pyogenes* (old name *Corynebacterium*) especially when they are in poor condition. These infections may become generalised and cause mortalities.

In areas where oxpeckers are present they help to keep ticks under control, and also clean maggot-infested wounds. Tick control may be necessary if no oxpeckers are present (see Parasite section). The *Corynebacterium* vaccine is unfortunately not useful for the prevention of abscesses. Do not buy in animals with abscesses and avoid contaminating the environment when opening the wounds. Cleaning of wounds should be done with veterinary help, and contaminated material must be discarded appropriately.

Wild animals may sustain injuries in the process of capture and transport, particularly in holding pens with sharp projections or if they are housed with aggressive male animals. The social grouping of animals is important to prevent severe injuries. Inexpert darting can cause massive internal bleeding which is usually fatal.

Poachers' traps or nooses often lead to severe, sometimes fatal, injuries. Treatment of wounds in free-living animals is seldom undertaken unless they are extensive and the animal is particularly valuable. Mild flesh wounds can be treated with a wound ointment which contains an antibacterial and an insecticidal effect, in areas where screwworm is prevalent (see Parasite section). More severe wounds may require the use of long-acting antibiotics. Very serious snaring injuries may affect the underlying bone in which case the prognosis

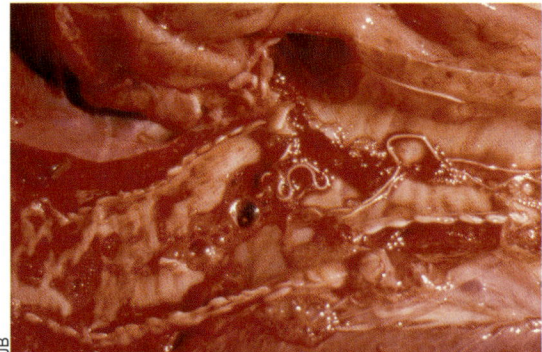
Lungworm infestation may sometimes be the cause of death in antelope and other herbivores during or after translocation.

Blindness in a springbok possibly as a result of eye infection.

for treatment is very poor. Properties should be kept clean of discarded wire in which animals can become entangled and injured.

Darting wounds should routinely be treated by application of wound oil or ointment after the procedure to prevent the development of infections such as abscesses. Bone fractures occur in game animals during capture and translocation, as a result of fleeing from predators or during fighting. Limb fractures in most free-living species cannot be treated, since the use of supportive splints or casts will impede the animal in its natural environment. Antelope with broken horns can be immobilised, the horn sawn off, and the stump treated with wound ointment.

Carnivores are subject to bite wounds due to fighting and these often lead to serious infection. In captive animals extensive fresh wounds should be sutured, otherwise they have to be treated as open wounds which have to be cleaned, and treated with wound ointment or antibiotic administration.

Wild animals may become trapped in veld fires and suffer extensive burn wounds. Heroic treatment is sometimes attempted for valuable or endangered animals but since the condition is very painful, and requires extensive and prolonged treatment, this can prolong the suffering. Euthanasia is often a more humane option. Based on observations on sheep farms after bush fires, Australian veterinarians have observed that animals with burn wounds on the limbs and hooves have a poor prognosis and should be put down, while those with burn wounds to the body will be more likely to survive if these are not too extensive.

Pneumonia

Pneumonia is seen in free-living animals such as kudu when they are subjected to nutrition stress and chilling. Buffalo calves are also said to suffer from pneumonia as a result of infection with *Corynebacterium* bacteria but also under conditions of poor nutrition during droughts or winter. These cases can seldom be treated since they are found dead and the diagnosis made postmortem. Pneumonia is a frequent problem seen in wild animals being transported or kept in confinement or captivity especially if they are subjected to high levels of stress, poor nutrition or drenched with rain.

Aspiration pneumonia occurs when immobilised ruminants are allowed to become bloated and regurgitate rumen contents into the lungs, or when animals are ineptly dosed, delivering the remedies directly into the lungs.

Young animals being hand-fed may also develop pneumonia as a result of aspiration of milk when force-fed by blocking the nostrils, feeding too rapidly or tilting the animal's head too far back thus preventing it from swallowing.

The symptoms of pneumonia are very high fever (42 °C), depression and difficult

A buffalo electrocuted by rubbing on a power cable.

breathing, with neck extension, a typical symptom in antelope. The condition must be treated with antibiotics, keeping the animal warm and ensuring that dehydration doesn't result. However, many pneumonia cases die despite intensive treatment, so all practices that predispose to the development of pneumonia must be minimised. Stress must be minimised during capture and transport, and wetting and bloating must be avoided. Dosing or force-feeding of wild animals must be done only by veterinarians or other suitably trained staff.

Although many antelope species harbour various species of lungworms, most of these animals are unaffected by the parasites. However some lungworm species can cause antelope to develop bronchitis or pneumonia when placed under stress, such as transport. Antelope which harbour lungworms without any adverse signs may nevertheless infect other species when moved to other areas and cause disease (see Internal Parasite section).

Eye conditions

Injuries to the eyes are sometimes seen during capture and translocation, usually lacerations of the conjunctiva or cornea. Predator species and less commonly antelope, may suffer eye injuries due to altercations with porcupines or other prey. Trauma to the eyes can sometimes be treated by suturing the eyelids closed and giving intensive treatment with antibiotics. Bacterial infections of the eyes which cause opacity and eventually blindness may occur in wild antelope. The cause is unknown but may be due to transmission by face flies (*Musca* spp.) of various organisms such as *Moraxella* and *Chlamydiophila* which are known to cause infections in livestock. Injectable antibiotic therapy is the most practical for these conditions as administering eye ointments is impractical and very painful for the animal.

The larvae of nasal flies may cause eye problems in certain antelope species causing a condition called "popeye" or "uitpeuloog" (see Parasite section).

Electrocution and lightning strike

Electric fences are used on game farms to contain large species, predators and crocodiles. Animals receive a non-lethal shock which teaches them to avoid the fence. The electrified strands are placed at various heights depending on the species of animals to be contained (Bothma *et al*, 2002). However, electric fences may unfortunately cause a large number of deaths especially in small animals. Electrified base strands to prevent warthog and other animals burrowing often kill tortoises, pangolins and others. Snakes can also be electrocuted trying to crawl under or over fences.

Power lines may cause electrocution when animals come into contact with poorly insulated or constructed poles. Giraffe may occasionally come into contact with overhead powerlines by standing on termite mounds. An electrocuted animal is usually found dead close to the power line or cable, and the presence of burns on the skin will confirm the cause of death.

Lightning strikes also occasionally cause deaths in an individual or groups of wild animals. Electrocution can usually be diagnosed by the presence of burns on the hair or skin.

INFECTIOUS DISEASES OF MULTIPLE SPECIES

ANTHRAX

Cause

Anthrax is an infectious disease caused by the bacterium *Bacillus anthracis*. When the bacterium is exposed to oxygen it forms resistant spores which can remain dormant in the soil for many years. Anthrax spores isolated from 250 year old bones excavated from an archaeological dig in the Kruger National Park indicate that the disease has been present in southern Africa for a considerable period but early accounts of outbreaks suggest that the distribution of the disease may have expanded as a result of livestock farming.

Prior to the development of the vaccine, anthrax had a devastating effect on livestock farming. It is estimated that in 1923, at the height of anthrax epidemics, 60 000 farm animals were lost due to the disease. With the advent of an effective vaccine developed by the South African scientist Max Sterne, livestock losses declined dramatically and sustained government subsidised campaigns reduced the prevalence on livestock farms to a few outbreaks a year.

For many years major anthrax outbreaks were confined to large wildlife reserves in southern Africa. However, since government vaccination campaigns have ceased, the incidence of outbreaks on private properties has increased again, because the anthrax spores are still present in the soil.

Epidemiology

The conditions which predispose anthrax outbreaks have been studied in wildlife reserves such as the Kruger National Park and Namibian Parks. The ability of anthrax spores to survive in the soil for long periods allows them to lie dormant between outbreaks. Under certain conditions the spores become exposed

> Although the postmortem findings for anthrax are typical, carcasses should never be opened since this will cause the bacteria to sporulate and spread the infection.

either during droughts when there is loss of vegetation due to trampling or overcrowding, or due to water erosion by heavy rains or floods. The specific epidemiology varies in the different wildlife reserves. In the Kruger National Park these outbreaks tend to be at the end of winter when water is scarce and animals crowd around watering points, while in Etosha the outbreaks occur after summer rains.

Herbivores are infected during grazing either by ingesting spores or by inhaling them, and will then die rapidly from the disease. When scavengers open anthrax-infected carcasses they effectively spread the infection in a number of ways. The exposure of anthrax bacteria to oxygen causes them to form resistant spores which are then spread in the environment. Scavengers will spread spores by tearing up carcasses and excreting them in their faeces.

The spores are also spread to water holes where vultures wash after feeding and the birds may even regurgitate infected meat. Blowflies visiting carcasses have been shown to be a major source of infection for browsers since after feeding they roost in tress in the area. Here they regurgitate and excrete blood ingested from carcasses containing anthrax spores, thus exposing animals such as kudu to contaminated browse.

The species involved in anthrax outbreaks depend on local circumstances, and possibly the virulence of the bacterial strain. In the KNP the most susceptible species are kudu, but nyala, bushbuck, zebra and some carnivores such as lion may also be affected. Roan antelope are reported to be highly susceptible and due

Anthrax in a carnivore showing the swelling around the head and neck.

Herbivores usually die acutely from anthrax without showing any symptoms but some carcasses show exudation of blood from the nose.

to their small numbers their populations are severely affected during outbreaks. Outbreaks in Luangwa Valley in Zambia affected mainly hippo while outbreaks in Etosha have affected species such as elephant. Recent outbreaks on game farms in the North West Cape were reported to have affected 632 springbok, 21 mountain rhebok, 4 impala, 33 hartebeest, 8 gemsbok, 28 eland, 42 zebra, 33 kudu, 120 blue wildebeest and 14 black wildebeest.

Symptoms

A number of forms of anthrax are recognised namely peracute, acute, subacute and chronic. The various forms are seen in different animal species.
- The peracute form is seen mainly in kudu, roan and impala. This form has a very rapid course with symptoms seldom being seen and death occurring within hours. Affected animals have a fever, are restless, show muscle tremors, difficult breathing, and collapse with terminal convulsions during which they typically extend the forelegs and retract the head. After death blood may ooze from the body openings.
- The acute form is seen in species such as zebra. Affected animals show depression, lag behind the herd, and they finally lie down due to the difficulty of breathing. Some develop haemorrhagic diarrhoea or may abort. In rare cases thought to be transmitted by the bites of stable flies, swelling may develop along the ventral line (belly). Acute cases die within two to four days.
- Subacute and chronic cases are seen in porcines and carnivores in which the infection becomes localised in the lymph nodes of the throat. The animals are ill for 3–4 days before they either recover or die. Swelling of the head and the neck region can be extensive and may interfere with breathing and eating.

Diagnosis

- Anthrax is most often suspected when one or more dead animals of the same or different species are found with signs such as the oozing of blood from the carcass, and bloating due to rapid decomposition.
- Carnivore carcasses show a severely swollen head and throat area.

Although the postmortem findings for anthrax are typical, carcasses should never be opened since this will cause the bacteria to sporulate and spread the infection. If an anthrax outbreak is suspected a veterinarian must be called out to make a bloodsmear. Finding the brick-shaped anthrax bacilli in the blood smear will confirm the diagnosis. If no bacteria are found the veterinarian may take blood or small tissue samples for laboratory culture.

Treatment

Although the anthrax bacterium is susceptible to penicillin, wild animals usually cannot be

Blowflies feeding on anthrax carcasses rest on leaves where they regurgitate anthrax spores and provide a source of infection for browsers.

treated, since they are generally found when terminally ill or dead. However, long acting penicillin injections can be given to protect valuable captive or boma-held animals during an outbreak. Vaccination can then be done 10 days later to protect these animals.

Control

Anthrax is a controlled disease which must be reported to the veterinary authorities who will then quarantine the affected property.

Movement of the animals is prevented until the outbreak has abated. Various methods have been used in wildlife reserves to stop anthrax outbreaks, including the disposal of carcasses by burying or burning. Burning of carcasses is usually impractical due to unavailability of fuel, and there is also good evidence to suggest that it is not a very effective procedure.

The recommended method to prevent the spread of infection is ensuring that carcasses are not opened by burying them at a depth of 2 m, and adding one part of lime chloride or quicklime [$Ca(OCl_2)$] to three parts of soil. This helps the carcass to decompose more rapidly. These burial areas should then be fenced off to prevent disturbance. Fencing off waterholes and providing artificial drinking holes can also be attempted.

Prevention

The cycle of anthrax outbreaks that occurs in wildlife reserves in southern Africa is regarded by some ecologists as a natural phenomenon. However, under current conditions of fragmented and isolated populations the disease can cause considerable losses of vulnerable species. Since anthrax spores cannot be eliminated from the environment, vaccination is the most practical approach to controlling the disease in livestock. The Sterne spore vaccine is highly effective and sustained annual vaccination has reduced the prevalence of outbreaks considerably.

Vaccination is not usually a practical option for most free-living animals, however, selected populations regarded as vulnerable are sometimes vaccinated. Roan antelope were vaccinated in the KNP using specially formulated "biobullets" containing the Sterne spore vaccine. Captive animals can be vaccinated with the Sterne spore vaccine used in livestock. It should be noted that adverse reactions have been seen in some exotic ruminant species such as llamas with anthrax spore vaccines so this should be done with caution and in consultation with wildlife veterinarians.

Human anthrax infections

Humans are not very susceptible to anthrax under normal circumstances but cases do occur occasionally. Cutting up infected carcasses is the most common source of human infections resulting in the skin form of anthrax which can develop into a fatal septicaemia. Other less common forms of the disease are the respiratory form contacted by inhaling spores contaminating wool or hides, and an intestinal form from eating infected meat. If humans are unwittingly exposed to anthrax infected material, they can be effectively treated with the penicillin group of antibiotics.

RABIES

Cause

Rabies is caused by a lyssa virus which can infect almost all warm-blooded mammals including humans. The virus seems to have been present in southern Africa for centuries and has become established in domestic dogs and certain wildlife species (sylvatic cycle). The "rabies-like" viruses (Mokola, Duvenage, and Lagos bat viruses) are closely related to the true rabies virus but are associated with bats, shrews and rodents, and are much more rarely encountered in Southern Africa with only occasional cases occurring in domestic cats and humans.

Epidemiology

Two main strains of rabies have been identified in South Africa namely the **canine** and the **herpestid** (formerly referred to as vivverid strains).

- **Canine** strain is found in dogs, bat-eared foxes and black-backed jackals. This virus spreads readily within and in-between these species. Domestic animals, other non-vector species and humans are accidental, dead-end hosts. An exception is the outbreaks seen in kudu in Namibia where there is horizontal spread of the virus among these accidental hosts.
- **Herpestid** rabies strain is found in a number of species of mongoose and a rodent *Xerus inauris* (ground squirrel), can spread within these species and between them, but spread to other species is accidental and a dead-end host for the disease, since no further transmission takes place. It is not fully understood how the canid and herpestid biotypes of rabies virus are maintained within their respective sylvatic cycles, and why they remain compartmentalised.

There is at present no evidence for an asymptomatic carrier status for the rabies virus, although studies in the Serengeti have indicated that domestic dogs may be implicated, since rabies antibody has been found in healthy unvaccinated dogs.

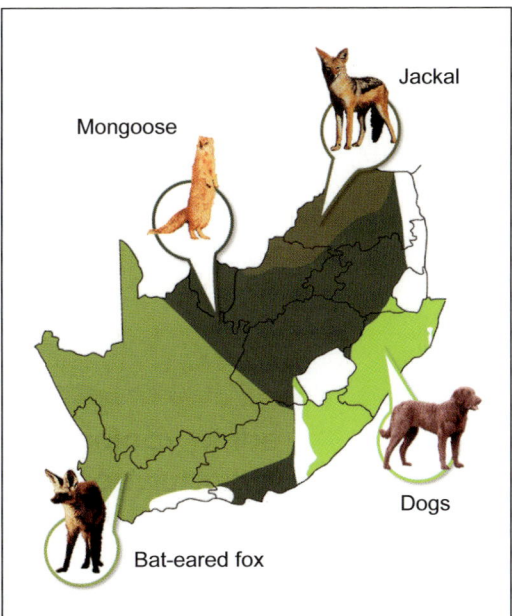

Distribution of the various rabies vectors in South Africa.

Jackals, bat-eared foxes, dogs, and various species of mongoose are the main vectors of rabies in Southern Africa. These vectors are dominant in different geographic areas (see map). The species most commonly infected accidentally are wild felines and canines but occasional cases are seen in herbivores such as duiker, various other antelope and plains zebra.

An extensive outbreak in kudu in Namibia occurred in the 1970s due to a number of predisposing factors. A population explosion of kudu is said to have caused large numbers of these antelope becoming infected through browsing acacia trees. Rabid kudu secrete large amounts of virus in their saliva and the wounding to the mucous membranes of the mouth caused by acacia thorns possibly contributed to effective spread of the disease to others. The outbreak most probably began with a single kudu being infected by a bite from a rabid carnivore.

Rabid kudu entering a house.

Rabies is seldom reported in large game reserves such as KNP except for occasional incursions by rabid domestic dogs from Mozambique. It is not clear whether this is due to the population dynamics of the various species involved, or whether the disease remains undetected due to effective scavenging. The disease has, however, been diagnosed in wild dogs in the Madikwe Game Reserve where the source is thought to be domestic dogs.

Transmission of rabies occurs through biting in almost all cases, but contact with saliva alone may be sufficient to infect an animal. This was typically seen with the kudu outbreaks in Namibia.

Symptoms

After initial infection the rabies virus travels from the bite or infected wound to the nearest nerve ending. It then migrates up the nerve towards the brain and only then are the first symptoms seen. The time taken for this incubation period varies depending on the distance which the virus has to travel.

When animals are bitten on the limbs the incubation period will be longer than those bitten on the face or mouth. The virus progressively affects the brain functions:
- Initially the behavior of the animal is altered but accompanying effects such as weight loss are seen because they stop feeding and the oesophagus becomes paralysed. Later the muscles of the limbs show paralysis and eventually the animal dies due to paralysis of the respiratory muscles.
- The most constant symptom of rabies in animals is a change in behaviour. Typically in wild animals this means loss of fear of humans, but this varies according to the species. Yellow mongoose most often show tame behaviour while some individuals show aggression.
- Rabid jackal may show either aggressive or non-aggressive behaviour. They have been known to attack the wheels of vehicles, enter houses and attack residents, or make attacks on cattle.
- Non-aggressive animals lose their fear of humans and approach farms and people during daylight hours. Rabid badgers become very fierce and are reported to have killed sheep in frenzied attacks.

Kudu with rabies lose their fear and may wander into houses or livestock pens. They show profuse salvation and eventually become paralysed as the disease progresses. Duiker are reported to become aggressive. Wild dogs show extreme aggression and rabid females have been observed biting pups begging for food to death. Like domestic cats, wild cats are typically aggressive, frequently biting humans or other animals.

Diagnosis

A presumptive diagnosis of rabies can be made based on the abnormal behaviour of a wild animal but this must be confirmed by taking a brain specimen from the animal. The suspected case must therefore be quarantined and observed for 10 days if possible, or if this is not practical the animal must be destroyed by a responsible person, taking care not to damage the brain material. A veterinarian or similarly trained person must take the brain samples for laboratory analysis, taking the necessary precautions to prevent becoming infected. The diagnosis is confirmed in the laboratory using a fluorescent antibody test which detects the presence of rabies virus in the brain. It is important to confirm the diagnosis since there are other diseases which can be confused with rabies in all species. There are no typical postmortem signs.

Treatment

Rabies is a fatal disease which cannot be treated in animals. Humans bitten or exposed to rabid animals are treated as early as possible after exposure either by antiserum administration and or vaccination, at the discretion of a medical practitioner.

Control

Extensive hunting and poisoning of jackals and poisoning of mongoose have failed to reduce the prevalence of the disease where cases are seen in cattle. Poisoning has been responsible for massive mortalities in non-target species. These strategies are not a viable control option.

Populations of vulnerable carnivores such as breeding populations of wild dog are effectively vaccinated with the inactivated vaccines available on the market, but there are practical constraints since animals have to be given booster inoculations every 3 years to sustain the immunity. A canary-pox vectored rabies vaccine (Recombitek-Merial) has been used in wild carnivores in zoos, and it has been shown to be safe and gives a life long immunity. It may be useful for the vaccination of captive carnivores and those intended for release. Although rabies vaccination of cats and dogs is compulsory in South Africa it should be borne in mind that there are large populations of unvaccinated animals which serve as a reservoir of infection for adjoining wildlife reserves.

Vaccination of wildlife with various oral bait vaccines has been successful in reducing the incidence of rabies in Europe and the USA. Trials have been done with similar rabies bait vaccines in Southern Africa with good results. Protection was obtained in jackal challenged with wild rabies virus and in addition the vaccine was shown to be safe in non-target animals, namely baboon, civet, mongoose, honey badger, genets, mice, gerbils and crows, with no adverse effects.

The National Department of Agriculture is currently using the SAG 2 double mutant oral rabies vaccine to reduce the prevalence of rabies in township dogs in KwaZulu-Natal, but as yet there has been no extensive oral rabies vaccine campaign in wildlife in South Africa.

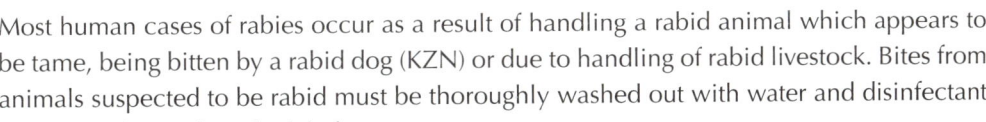

Rabies in humans

Most human cases of rabies occur as a result of handling a rabid animal which appears to be tame, being bitten by a rabid dog (KZN) or due to handling of rabid livestock. Bites from animals suspected to be rabid must be thoroughly washed out with water and disinfectant diluted as directed on the label.

A medical practitioner must be consulted immediately. Based on the history of the species of the animal, prevalence of the disease in the area and the outcome of diagnostic tests the practitioner may decide to institute prophylactic treatment using rabies vaccine or a rabies antiserum. Rabies is a highly unpleasant disease which is with some notable exceptions almost always fatal if not treated timeously.

BOVINE TUBERCULOSIS (BTB)

Cause

The main cause of tuberculosis in African wildlife is *Mycobacterium bovis* which is a cattle-associated disease commonly referred to as bovine tuberculosis or BTB. Cases of *M. tuberculosis* the cause of human TB, are most often seen in zoo collections where the animals have been exposed to infected people. Only a few cases of the human disease have been described in wild animals.

Epidemiology

Bovine tuberculosis affects the lungs of the main or maintenance hosts (see below). The BTB bacteria are spread by the aerosol dispersal of infected droplets from the lungs when the animal coughs or sneezes. These may either be inhaled by another animal or land on the pasture where they can be inhaled as infected dust particles. Sharing infected pastures is therefore sufficient for the spread from one animal to another. The BTB bacteria can survive for up to 6 weeks in the environment.

BTB is considered a primary parasite of domestic cattle which has spread into wildlife populations all over the world, including South Africa. Kudu in the Eastern Cape were diagnosed with the disease as early as 1929 and subsequent diagnoses of infection have been made in buffalo and various other species in the Kruger National Park and the Hluluwe-iMfolozi Park. Two types of hosts have been described for BTB based on their ability to transmit the disease.

Maintenance hosts which are those species that effectively maintain and spread the infection to members of the same, or other species.

Spillover hosts or dead-end species which do not transmit the disease over long periods of time but can nevertheless be severely affected.

Buffalo and kudu are regarded as the major maintenance hosts, while bushbuck and warthog may also play an epidemiological role in the spread of the disease.

Symptoms and effects on populations

- BTB in buffalo is predominantly a chronic progressive pneumonia, but affected animals show no symptoms until the disease is at an advanced stage. In most advanced cases, especially stressed individuals, animals are emaciated, have poor skin condition, and become weak and recumbent shortly before they die. The infection reduces the life expectancy of infected animals and has reduced the growth rate of populations. The disease in buffalo has caused an annual mortality rate of 11% in Hluluwe-iMfolozi.
- As in buffalo, BTB in kudu mainly involves the lung but in addition there is spread via the bloodstream to the lymph nodes around the head and neck. These become massively enlarged and they may rupture to the outside and discharge huge numbers of bacteria into the environment. Infected animals also show weight loss and lethargy.
- Lions in the KNP where there is a high concentration of buffalo-BTB infections, are exposed to the infection when feeding on the carcasses of diseased animals. Infected lion gradually become emaciated, show a rough hair coat with accompanying

---

Epidemiological studies have shown an ongoing, alarming spread in both national parks. Buffalo herds in the southern part of the KNP are said to have a 92% infection rate, and the infection has spread northwards so that currently only a small pool of buffalo in the northern part of the park remain uninfected. Antelope and other smaller species have been diagnosed with *M. bovis* infections in various other regions of the country.

Kudu infected with BTB showing enlarged lymph nodes.

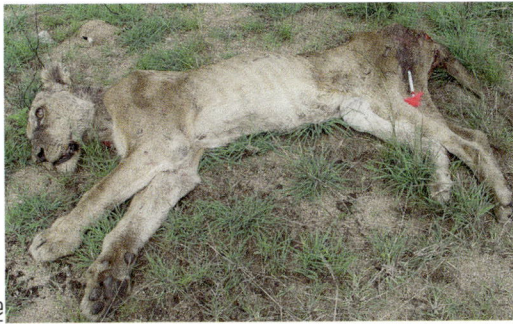
A lion with BTB showing emaciation and skin infection.

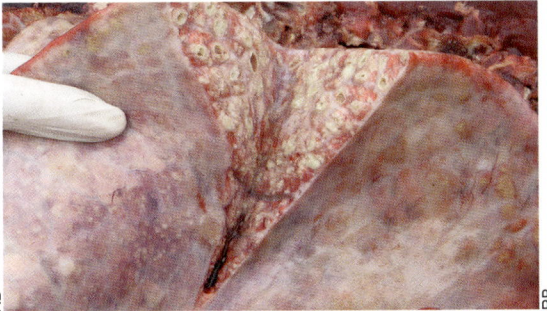
Bovine TB lesions in the lungs of a buffalo.

A buffalo with advanced BTB showing emaciation and skin lesions.

hairlessness, swelling of the joints and sometimes blindness. They show terminal weakness and severe dehydration. The effects on their population dynamics have been observed to be a shorter life span of infected animals which is then compensated for by an increase in birth rates.
- Warthog with BTB show weight loss, coughing and lethargy.
- Leopard, hyaena, cheetah, baboon and honey badgers with BTB show poor condition and abnormal behaviour.

Diagnosis

The diagnosis of tuberculosis in the live animal can be difficult since symptoms usually only appear in advanced cases and these are most often non-specific such as emaciation.

Most commonly the diagnosis is made postmortem when tuberculous lesions are found in the lungs and various other organs. This must be left to veterinarians because a thorough examination must be done and the disease is transmissible to humans. The veterinarian will take organ samples for histopathology and bacterial culture to confirm the diagnosis. Since the bacteria can take up to 3 months to grow in the laboratory, histopathology is useful in making a presumptive diagnosis of tuberculosis. Bacterial culture will allow identification of the mycobacterium to distinguish it from other forms of TB. Suspected and confirmed cases of tuberculosis must be reported to the nearest state veterinarian.

Herd testing for tuberculosis is performed using an intradermal test or a blood test. The intradermal TB testing developed for cattle is performed in buffalo and has been found to be reliable. This test involves the injection of tuberculin, an extract of TB bacteria, into a shaved area on the skin. The skin thickness is measured before injection and is then measured 72 hours after the tuberculin injection. Significant thickening of the skin indicates a positive reaction. However, the test must be done strictly according to set protocols under the supervision of a state veterinarian to avoid false positive results, and requires that the animal be handled twice. The gamma interferon assay specifically developed for buffalo can also be performed to identify BTB in the live animal but blood must be submitted to the lab within 6 hours. The test requires a single blood sampling which is an advantage over the intradermal test. A serological test called the ELISA is sometimes used but does not detect very early cases.

Treatment

While tuberculosis cases are usually treatable in humans it is generally uneconomical to treat wild animals.

Control

Tuberculosis eradication programs in cattle herds involve a test-and-slaughter approach. Positive animals are identified using the available diagnostic tests and then slaughtered. Farmers then focus their efforts on establishing a clean and closed herd in which animals are tested before introduction and no contact with untested animals is permitted. This test-and-slaughter method is costly and probably impractical in large herds.

Prevention

Game farm ranchers are required by the Buffalo Diseases Protocol to purchase only TB-free buffalo in order to stock registered buffalo farms, since the use of infected breeding stock was phased out by law by 2012. A BTB-free herd of buffalo is one in which all individuals have undergone three consecutive negative tests if sourced from a herd with unknown status, or five consecutive tests if sourced from a known infected herd. Game farm owners should bear in mind that livestock kept adjacent to their farms can infect their valuable animals and vice versa.

Since the discontinuation of the TB scheme in 1994 BTB in cattle is becoming more prevalent, and because it is not easily detected even by livestock owners, it is often present without their knowledge. It is therefore essential to prevent contact between infected animals, either buffalo or cattle. Feeding captive populations of lion with infected cattle carcasses is a known cause of introducing BTB onto game and wildlife reserves. As yet there is no effective vaccine for use in livestock or wildlife.

COCCIDIOSIS

Coccidia are single-celled protozoal organisms found in the intestines of many species of animals. The main causes of intestinal coccidiosis are *Eimeria* and *Isospora* spp. although there are many others. These organisms are the most commonly encountered causes of intestinal coccidiosis, causing problems when animals are confined under intensive conditions. Animals become infected with the microscopic oocysts by mouth after which the sporozoites which they contain are released and penetrate the cells of the intestine. Here they undergo a series of multiplication cycles leading to the eventual production of the infective oocysts which are shed into the faeces. The oocysts may survive for some time in the environment and in this way they can infect other animals.

- Under free-living conditions infection is an incidental and uneventful occurrence.
- Under intensive conditions such as when animals are held in bomas, the build-up of faeces, the close contact of animals with each other and moist conditions provided by water troughs promotes the survival and transmission of coccidia.
- Animals under stress are also more prone to develop infections.

Coccidiosis has been reported in buffalo and antelope kept in bomas, while sporadic outbreaks have been recorded on farms and in single animals in captivity. Intestinal coccidiosis typically causes diarrhoea which may be watery or sometimes haemorrhagic. Often the diarrhoea is very severe and results in life-threatening dehydration. High mortalities have been recorded if the animals remain untreated.

- The diagnosis of intestinal coccidiosis is based on the clinical symptoms of diarrhoea, but a definitive diagnosis should be attempted to exclude the involvement of other enteric infections such as salmonellosis.
- Faecal samples from the affected animals must be examined microscopically by a veterinarian or a veterinary laboratory to confirm the diagnosis.

There are two drugs which have been used effectively by veterinarians for the treatment for clinical cases. In addition an anti-coccidial remedy can be used to medicate feed to prevent outbreaks but this must be done with care since toxicity can result if this is not mixed correctly with feed. Both clinical and prophylactic medical treatment should be done under veterinary supervision. Since management factors contribute to outbreaks of coccidiosis these should be optimal to reduce the possibility of infections. Avoid overcrowding in bomas and remove faeces as frequently as possible. Repair leaking water troughs to prevent muddy conditions which will predispose the survival of the coccidial oocysts. If coccidiosis is a problem in breeding or farming projects, feed can be medicated under veterinary supervision to prevent infections.

Sarcocysticosis

Sarcocystis is a protozoan found in the intestine of carnivores. The intermediate host is usually a herbivore in which the *Sarcocystis* parasite occurs as a dormant cyst in the tissues, until eaten by the carnivore. These parasites have been identified in a wide range of African ungulates including antelope, hippos and buffalo, and in carnivores such as wild dog, cheetah and hyena. Although the organism does not cause disease in either the carnivore or herbivore host, the presence of the cysts in carcasses are deemed to make them unfit for human consumption. However, it has yet to be proven whether these parasites are a threat to human health.

Toxoplasmosis

Toxoplasma gondii is an intestinal parasite of domestic cats. They excrete oocysts in the faeces which can be picked up by a wide variety of wild animal species and man. The cysts have been found in the tissues of a wide range of herbivores and carnivores. Although the parasite rarely causes disease in the host animals, toxoplasmosis is a public health concern for certain groups of people, namely pregnant women and individuals with immune suppression either due to AIDS infection, or treatment with immunosuppressive drugs. These groups of people should avoid eating uncooked or undercooked meat from any species. They should also avoid exposure to the faeces of domestic and wild cats.

Neosporosis

Neospora caninum is an intestinal parasite of the domestic dog. The organism has been found in various free-living carnivore and herbivore species. It has been found to be the occasional cause of abortions in wildlife and deaths of newborn animals. The epidemiology and significance for wildlife is, however, still unclear.

Besnoitiosis

Besnoitia is an intestinal parasite of felines which occurs as a cyst in tissues in intermediate wild herbivore hosts. It causes a severe skin condition in cattle in some areas of South Africa. The role of wildlife in the maintenance and transmission of the disease is as yet unknown. A vaccine is available for the prevention of the disease which appears to have a limited distribution.

HERBIVORE DISEASES

RINDERPEST

Cause

Rinderpest is caused by a morbillivirus which causes disease in livestock and various wild animal species. The virus is highly infectious, very contagious and spreads as a true epidemic through populations of animals, causing severe economic losses and devastation of wildlife populations.

History of rinderpest

The rinderpest virus appears to have originated in Asia and swept into Europe along with invading armies, causing epidemic livestock deaths. It is thought to have been introduced into Africa in the 1880s via Ethiopia from where it spread into east and southern Africa causing the so called Great Epidemic which killed 5.2 million cattle. It also caused massive losses of wild animal species. The epidemic was halted by strenuous quarantine and prophylactic inoculations, as well as slaughter of infected animals. By 1905 rinderpest was eradicated from Southern Africa. South Africa has remained free of this disease since then, as a result of strict import regulations for livestock and game animals.

Elsewhere in Africa the disease continued to fulminate during the 1900s, but the development of a highly effective vaccine and a concerted control campaign (Joint Project 15) resulted in the containment of the infection in small focal areas in West and East Africa in Ethiopia by 1976. However, after the Joint Project 15 was halted, vaccination of cattle was relaxed in the countries where it was endemic and a resurgence of the disease occurred, so that the infected zone stretched in a belt from West to East Africa. From 1986 to 1999 the Pan-African Rinderpest Campaign funded by the European Union embarked on a new campaign of vaccination and the implementation of other control measures which was highly successful. However, foci of rinderpest still persist in Southern Sudan and parts of Somalia which were politically unstable and therefore inaccessible for the implementation of control measures. These remaining foci represent a threat to the livestock and wildlife of the rest of Africa should the political situation deteriorates.

Severe diarrhoea caused by rinderpest in a buffalo calf.

Rinderpest causes severe erosive mouth lesions in bovid animals.

Symptoms in wildlife

The symptoms of rinderpest in wildlife vary according to the species.
- Bovid animals like buffalo, eland, giraffe and waterbuck suffer erosive mouth lesions, and severe gastroenteritis which terminates in death from dehydration.
- Antelope species like impala show mild, non-specific symptoms.
- Corneal opacity as a sequel to infection is seen in giraffe and buffalo, and blindness is a typical sequel in buffalo.

Diagnosis

- Animals that have died from rinderpest show soiling of the hindquarters, eye lesions, discharge caked around the eyes, and sunken eyes due to the severe dehydration.
- On postmortem the erosive mouth lesions and severe necrotic lesions of the abomasum can be demonstrated. The diagnosis is confirmed by the isolation of the rinderpest virus from tissue samples.

Treatment

There is no treatment for the disease.

Control

In countries where rinderpest is endemic, vaccination of livestock with the Plowright strain is used to reduce the prevalence of infection. It has been shown that once the infection rate drops in livestock, infection in wildlife populations disappears. In countries free of the disease, outbreaks are contained by quarantine and culling of infected animals. It is vital that introduction of the disease into South Africa be prevented by stringent control of imported animals and control of animal movement.

FOOT-AND-MOUTH DISEASE (FMD)

Cause

Foot-and-mouth disease is a highly contagious viral disease of various domestic and wild animal species. In South Africa the endemic virus types are the Southern African Territories types of foot-and-mouth virus, Sat 1, 2 and 3. The introduction of other FMD virus types such as Asia 1 and Type O have occurred due to the import of infected animal products, but these outbreaks have been contained by quarantine, vaccination and slaughtering-out of infected animals.

Epidemiology

Foot-and-mouth disease can infect a wide variety of domestic animals, including cattle, sheep, pigs and goats. Animals contract FMD by direct contact with infected animals but the virus can also be transmitted indirectly by infected equipment, vehicles, clothing, or the feeding of infected meat in offal to healthy animals.

Dairies are particularly hard hit because the virus causes ulceration of the teats of lactating cows which makes them impossible to milk and causes extensive outbreaks of mastitis. The lesions of the feet and the mouth impair feeding which leads to a dramatic loss of weight.

When an outbreak of FMD occurs in a country all agricultural exports to developed countries are halted. This affects all animal products such as meat, milk products, hides, and wool, as well as all plant materials including maize, fruit and vegetables. This has a major impact on the economy of the FMD-infected country. Government controlled veterinary services and international communities therefore make strenuous efforts to control the disease.

While a number of wild antelope such as impala are susceptible and develop FMD lesions on exposure, the African buffalo (*Syncerus caffer*) acts as an asymptomatic carrier of the SAT 1, 2, and 3 strains. These are specific strains which have developed an effective host-parasite relationship in buffalo. Buffalo calves in FMD-infected herds become

---

Foot-and-mouth disease is caused by a highly infectious virus which spreads through herds in a very short time. While the disease does not cause high mortalities it is greatly feared because it has a devastating effect on the production of commercial farming.

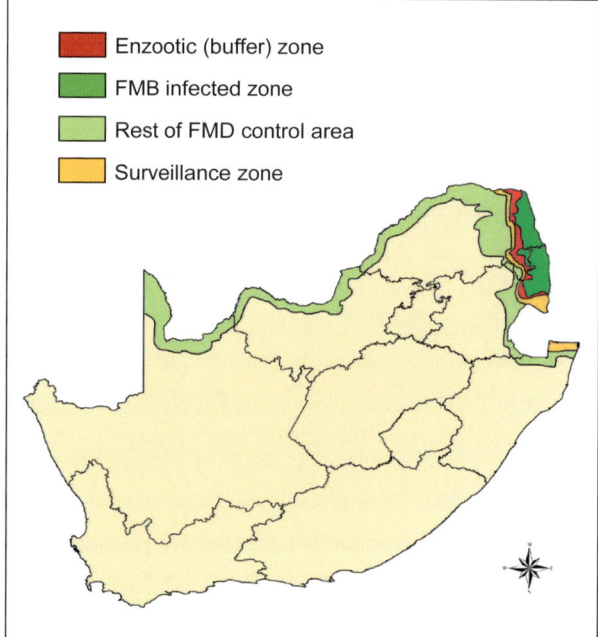

The FMD control area in South Africa.

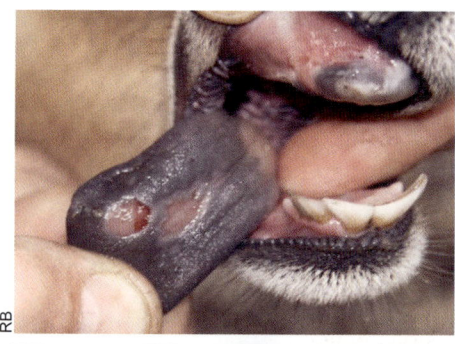

Impala infected with FMD develop lesions of the tongue and mouth, and the feet. Hoof damage may result and permanent lameness can be caused.

infected with the virus when their maternally derived antibodies begin to wane. After an initial systemic infection the virus becomes lodged in the pharynx of the buffalo causing the animal to become subclinically infected (carrier) for many years.

Occasionally under conditions which are still unknown the virus is shed from the pharynx of the carrier animal. In the Kruger National Park this gives rise to sporadic outbreaks in the impala population.

Buffalo therefore serve as a reservoir of infection for other game species as well as livestock. FMD is endemic in the buffalo population in the Kruger National Park and therefore an elaborate control system has been put in place to contain the infection. This is done by fencing, surveillance and vaccination of livestock in part of the buffer zone (see map).

Currently the Kruger National Park is regarded as an infected zone, and is surrounded by a designated buffer zone. The rest of South Africa outside the control zone is regarded as free of the disease once again after a recent outbreak and vaccination may not be practiced in this area. All agricultural products for export originate from the disease free zone.

Symptoms

The FMD virus affects the epithelial cells of the body, typically those in the mouth and between the claws of cloven-hoofed animals.

- Initially a small white vesicle appears on the epithelium of the mouth, tongue or between the claws, which then becomes a blister.
- The blisters rupture and as a result of friction become open raw sores. In the mouth these are seen on the dental pad, on the epithelium inside the mouth and on the tongue.
- The lesions on the feet develop as blisters between the claws of the feet, which then become extensive with the skin finally tearing off the lesions.
- Severe lesions are seen in exotic cattle breeds while small stock such as pigs, sheep and goats show less obvious lesions.

- Indigenous cattle do not develop severe lesions and outbreaks in these herds often go unidentified.

Impala and kudu

Clinical signs of FMD have been observed in impala in KNP, and kudu have been infected experimentally. These species develop mouth lesions on the tongue and dental pad, and foot lesions which can be severe enough to cause a break in the hoof material, which can lead to chronic lameness in recovered animals. Antelope do not become permanent carriers of the disease although kudu have been shown to carry the virus for 140 days, and were alleged to play a role in the dissemination of the disease to livestock in Zimbabwe.

Buffalo

Although buffalo are for the most part inapparent carriers of FMD, clinical lesions have been observed occasionally in boma-held animals, causing signs of depression, lack of appetite and mild fever and "mouth-soaking" in drinking troughs.

On examination buffalo with clinical signs show lesions of the hard palate and tongue. Sloughing of the epithelium leaves large raw ulcers. Salivation is seen in some animals with mouth lesions. Lameness and signs of a painful gait have been seen in animals that show foot lesions, although these are not seen in all cases.

Diagnosis

- To confirm the presence of an FMD outbreak, tissue samples of the lesions of infected animals are submitted for virus isolation.
- The virus samples must be taken by a veterinarian and submitted to the high security laboratory isolation at Onderstepoort which is equipped to handle the FMD virus.
- Carrier animals such as buffalo have to be sampled using a probing – a long probe with a steel cup at its tip, which allows sampling of the tissue at the back of the throat. These samples can be used to grow the virus in the laboratory.
- Serology (blood tests) can be used as a diagnostic tool to monitor exposure of animals in contact with FMD infected cases.

Treatment

There is no treatment for foot-and-mouth disease in wildlife or in livestock.

The importance of FMD in wildlife

African buffalo (*Syncerus caffer*) serve as inapparent carriers for SAT strains of the FMD virus, for protracted periods of time and so serve as a source of infection for other wildlife species and livestock. It is therefore of cardinal importance that the infected buffalo in the Kruger National Park are contained within the FMD Control area and not introduced or escape to the disease-free regions of the country. Wildlife species other than buffalo can be exported from the controlled area after lengthy quarantine and repeated serological tests. All movements of cloven-hoofed animals inside the FMD control zone fall under the control of the veterinary authorities.

Control of FMD

The situation with persistently infected buffalo in Southern Africa has been controlled making use of double fences to separate buffalo from livestock.
- The control area consists of an infected area, which is the Kruger Park and its adjacent properties, delineated by the so-called "red line".
- Bordering on the infected area is a buffer zone in which livestock are vaccinated against FMD to contain possible FMD outbreaks.
- Adjacent to the buffer zone is an inspection zone in which livestock are unvaccinated but are regularly inspected for signs of any infection.

- Outside the buffer zone the rest of South Africa is regarded as a FMD-free zone, with exports of agricultural products to developed countries permitted.

The borders of the control regions are modified from time to time, in consultation with an international body, the Office International des Epizooties (OIE) which designates the FMD-status of all countries. The FMD-status of countries changes should they have outbreaks of the disease, which then causes a huge disruption to the country's economy and presents a serious threat to the wildlife ranching industry.

Although the use of fencing to control animal movements has been severely criticised by conservationists because it prevents the natural migration of certain wildlife species, it has been an effective control measure for preventing livestock from becoming infected. However, fences are vulnerable to natural disasters such as floods and need constant inspection and upkeep. Any breaches can result in contact with infected buffalo and livestock with subsequent outbreaks.

Prevention

Experimental vaccination of buffalo calves with high potency FMD vaccines to protect them from becoming infected with the FMD virus under free-living conditions has been unsuccessful (Anderson and Hunter, unpublished). These results were not unexpected because vaccination of livestock merely protects against clinical disease but does not prevent infection.

The development of novel vaccines which prevent infection could facilitate the prevention of FMD in wildlife species in the future. However, it should be stressed that vaccination of wildlife against FMD is currently prohibited unless done under veterinary supervision.

BOVINE MALIGNANT CATARRH (BMC) (SNOTSIEKTE)

Cause

Bovine malignant catarrh (BMC) is a disease mainly of cattle caused by a gamma herpes virus. There are two different viruses – the alcelaphine virus (AlHV-1) which is wildebeest-associated, and the sheep-associated virus (OvHV-2), although the latter is not of importance in Southern Africa. Neither of these two viruses cause disease in their respective wildebeest or sheep hosts.

Epidemiology

The disease BMC is seen where cattle are kept in proximity to wildebeest, because almost all adult wildebeest in South Africa are infected with the AlHV-1 virus, and both *Connochaetes taurinus* (blue wildebeest) and *C. gnou* (black wildebeest) are carriers.

Wildebeest cows calve from December to February and their calves become almost immediately infected with the virus, within the first few months of life, in spite of the presence of a maternally-derived antibody. The young wildebeest circulate and shed the AlHV-1 virus through nasal secretions for a time, although they show no discernible symptoms. It is at this stage that the wildebeest calves become infective for cattle.

There are two peaks of infection seen in cattle, one in January–May which coincides with the wildebeest calving season, and one later in mid-September when the wildebeest calves are 9–11 months old. The reasons for

> Almost all adult wildebeest in South Africa are infected with the AlHV-1 virus, and both blue wildebeest and black wildebeest are carriers.

BMC or snotsiekte causes severe, usually fatal, respiratory disease in cattle.

the latter peak of infection are thought to be associated with some kind of stress such as weaning which causes calves to shed the virus.

Stress such as continuous hounding by hunters is known to cause shedding in adult wildebeest and this may give rise to sporadic outbreaks.

Bovine calves are highly susceptible to the AlHV-1 virus and develop clinical disease between 8–18 months of age; they can also be infected while in the uterus in which case they die a few weeks after birth.

Both indigenous and exotic breeds of cattle are susceptible to BMC. Cattle do not transmit the virus to each other.

The transmission of the virus is said to be by aerosol since it can spread over distances of roughly 800 m and the virus can survive in the environment for roughly 48 hours. There is no evidence to support claims that insects or other arthropods such as ticks transmit the virus. Experimental attempts at mechanical transmission by infecting face flies (*Musca xanthomelas*) failed to transmit the virus to cattle on which they fed, as the virus survived only for 5 hours in the fly after infection.

Under experimental conditions, cattle housed with infected wildebeest developed the disease within 30 days but occasionally there may be a prolonged incubation period of up to 80 days. This lengthy incubation period seen in some animals may explain so-called anomalies of transmission outside the calving season. The incidence of BMC within cattle herds is sporadic.

Only a small number of animals are usually infected (0.5–5%) and the disease does not spread within the herd.

Symptoms

- The incubation period of BMC in cattle is usually 2–4 weeks but can be as long as 7 months after infection.
- Infected cattle show symptoms of fever, loss of appetite and the inflammation of the mouth, nose and eyes.
- A discharge is seen from the eyes and nose which can be watery in the beginning and then becomes purulent.
- The muzzle becomes dry and crusted, developing raw open sores and a severe nasal discharge which can block the nostrils.
- Ulcers may occur in the mouth.
- A conjunctivitis develops in both eyes and usually causes opacity of the cornea, which results in some degree of blindness.
- Other symptoms such as diarrhoea, skin lesions and nervous symptoms may occur. The disease can be confused with pneumonia, mucosal disease (BVD), and FMD.

Treatment

There is no specific treatment and supportive treatment with antibiotics is usually futile since the disease is almost always fatal.

Diagnosis

A PCR test on a blood sample can be used to confirm the presence of the virus in infected cattle. BMC infection can also be confirmed on postmortem examination, and performing histology on the tissues.

Control

Currently the only feasible control measures to prevent the transmission of AlHV-1 virus to cattle is aimed at keeping a 1 km fenced buffer distance between livestock and wildebeest, especially at the peak seasons of infection.

Occurrence of BMC in cattle often brings game and livestock owners into conflict. Although the Animal Diseases Act states that landowners must prevent the spread of disease to adjoining properties, a recent court appeal was dismissed on the premise that wildebeest posed a very low level threat to neighbouring livestock. The establishment of disease-free wildebeest herds is currently not feasible since practically speaking all wildebeest are infected. Wildebeest calves become infected as foetuses or very soon after birth in spite of the presence of antibodies to the virus.

Vaccination of cattle has up to now been unsuccessful, the recent testing of a live attenuated vaccine by researchers at the Moredun Institute in Scotland has shown protective results in cattle. With the assistance of WRSA, the Faculty of Veterinary Science and the veterinary company Afrivet, this attenuated vaccine will be tested, with the aim of registration for use in South Africa. If successful this will be a major development in the control of BMC in livestock.

BOTULISM

Cause

Botulism is caused by the intake of the toxin produced by the bacterium *Clostridium botulinum*. This bacterium is an anaerobic organism which is typically found in the intestinal tract of animals. When animals die *C. botulinum* toxin is produced in the decaying carcass and can persist here for very long periods. The most important types of botulism in herbivores in South Africa are Types C and D. Type D botulism occurs under free-range conditions when animals chew contaminated carcasses, either bones, skin or old tortoise shells. Poisoning with *C. botulinum* Type C usually occurs as a result of feeding chicken manure, or contamination of feed such as hay or water with rat or cat carcasses.

Epidemiology

Although there are no scientific publications reporting confirmed cases of botulism in game species there is plenty of evidence that these occur.

Pica or bone-chewing behaviour which is seen in livestock and game as a result of phosphate deficiency in savanna regions is a known source of the Type D botulism in cattle and sometimes sheep.

Carcass-eating and bone-chewing behaviour are often observed in giraffe and various antelope species in bushveld areas. It has been shown that botulism toxin can persist in the carcasses of small mammals such as mongoose, hare and birds for 4–6 weeks under field conditions and tortoise shells for 350 days. Rain may leach the toxin from carcasses but tortoise shells protect the toxin more effectively.

Symptoms

Botulism toxin blocks nerve transmission to muscle fibres resulting in the progressive paralysis of various muscles of the body. This is usually an irreversible process once the toxin has bound to the nerves in the body. The typical symptoms of botulism in livestock are initial stiffness with the gradual development of paralysis usually leading to recumbency and death. However the degree and extent of the symptoms depends on the amount of toxin ingested.

> Pica or bone-chewing behaviour as a result of phosphate deficiency is a sourse of the botulism toxin.

A wildebeest showing the paralysis of the skeletal muscles typical of botulism.

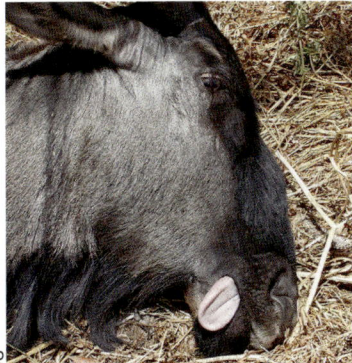
Paralysis of the tongue in a case of botulism.

In suspected cases of botulism in game animals such as sable, roan, buffalo, rhino, buffalo and gemsbok various symptoms are seen:
- Stiffness, lagging behind the herd and hindquarter paralysis which later progresses to complete paralysis forcing the animal to lie down have been reported.
- Wildebeest have been observed showing the typical tongue paralysis, lameness and the typical retraction of the head against the flanks once the animal becomes recumbent.

Cases of botulism are usually progressive and fatal, unless very small amounts of toxin have been ingested.

Diagnosis

At present the diagnosis of botulism depends on the isolation of toxin from the intestinal tract, which is often a difficult and unsuccessful undertaking from carcasses in a state of advanced putrefaction. Botulism in wildlife is suspected when there is a history of grazing winter pastures, bone chewing, or of animals being fed stored feed, or drinking from contaminated water sources. Symptoms of stiffness, lameness or paralysis will add weight to the diagnosis.

There are no typical postmortem findings for botulism but finding tortoise shells, bones or pieces of carcass in the digestive tract will strengthen suspicions of botulism.

Treatment

The administration of botulism antitoxin in early cases can be beneficial at reversing the condition. It is, however, seldom effective in animals in advanced stages of botulism. The antitoxin is administered intravenously at the dose recommended for cattle and horses on the package insert (5ml each of Type C and D antitoxins). Supportive veterinary treatment may be needed in some cases.

Control

A vaccine registered for use in livestock containing Types C and D has been used by veterinarians in valuable wildlife species apparently to good effect. However, this is not always practical in free-living animals since two vaccinations are required initially a month apart and thereafter annual boosting to maintain effective levels of protection. A more practical control measure for free-living animals is to provide phosphate containing licks during winter months, or as advised by nutrition experts. The removal of carcasses and tortoise shells can be attempted but those of small animals may be difficult to find. Game animals should never be fed chicken manure as a supplement because of the dangers of botulism intoxication. Rodent control should be practiced in hay stores to prevent Type C botulism. Water troughs and water holes should be checked frequently for contamination with carcass material.

CLOSTRIDIAL MYOSITIS (SPONSSIEKTE)

Cause

Clostridial myositis (muscle infection) is a common disease syndrome in ruminant domestic livestock in South Africa. It is caused by a group of anaerobic bacteria with an affinity for the muscle tissue of animals.

The most commonly implicated species are *Clostridium chauvoei*, *C. septicum*, and *C. novyi*.

Epidemiology

Clostridia are anaerobic (oxygen sensitive) bacteria commonly found in soil in the form of spores where they can survive for many years.

The organisms involved in myositis cases are part of the intestinal flora of animals, and are thought to penetrate the gut and lodge in the liver or muscles of healthy animals.

Under circumstances such as muscle bruising or deep penetrating wounds, which favour the growth of these anaerobic organisms, the bacteria multiply and secrete a number of toxins. These severely damage the muscle tissue and ultimately cause the death of the animal. Although there are no published scientific reports of gas gangrene in game animals, there is strong evidence that *Clostridium novyi* has caused the disease in a number of free-living species such as elephant, sable, buffalo and giraffe.

> Bruising inflicted by fighting among male animals or high levels of stress may be causes of clostridial myositis.

It is not known what the predisposing factors are for the development of the disease but bruising caused by fighting among male animals has been suggested since there is usually no external sign of wounding.

Other possible precipitating causes that have been suggested are high levels of nutrition and stress. Contact with livestock may contribute to the prevalence of the disease in wildlife because it has been noted that *C. novyi* is becoming a more prevalent cause of clostridial myositis in cattle.

Symptoms

- Clostridial myositis is usually an acute condition with few symptoms likely to be seen.
- Usually the first signs of the presence of the disease are acute deaths in animals.
- In outbreaks among domestic animals affected live animals may show a temperature reaction and muscle stiffness when driven.

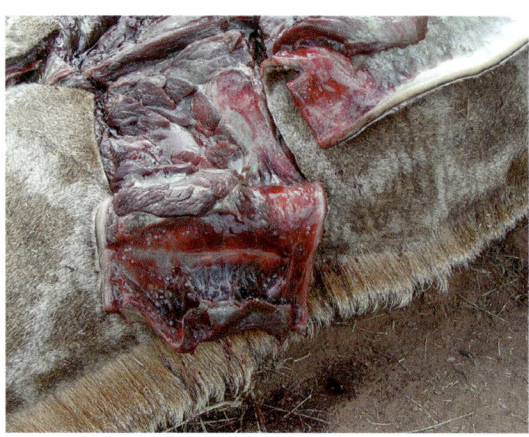

A case of clostridial myositis in giraffe.

Oozing of blood from an elephant that died of clostridial myositis.

Diagnosis

- Most cases of clostridial myositis are diagnosed postmortem because of the acute nature of the disease.
- The carcass is usually bloated due to the rapid decomposition which accompanies clostridial myositis.
- The affected muscles show severe swelling, discolouration, and have a rancid smell.
- *C. novyi* cases typically show a gelatinous swelling of the tissue which is referred to as "malignant oedema" when it occurs in cattle.
- Impression smears made from the muscle lesions can be submitted to veterinary diagnostic laboratories where these specific clostridia can be identified.

Treatment

If the presence of the disease is suspected in captive or boma-held animals an injection of long-acting penicillin may save the animal's life if given early enough, but most cases are found dead because of the acute nature of the disease.

Control

In livestock the various clostridial myositis syndromes are prevented by vaccination with multiclostridials which contain all the implicated strains. Veterinarians may recommend this for game animals if they suspect or confirm that the disease is occurring on the property.

Anecdotal evidence indicates that this prevents or halts outbreaks. It should be noted that at least two vaccinations given 3–4 weeks apart are required for clostridial vaccines to be protective.

Burying of carcasses is recommended by some veterinarians but since the organism is a normal soil inhabitant it may not be sufficient to control the outbreaks.

ENCEPHALOMYOCARDITIS (EMC)

Cause

The disease is caused by a cardiovirus virus of the family Picornidae. It is a robust virus which survives well in the environment and can infect a wide range of species. EMC virus has been the cause of infections in zoo collections usually associated with an increase in rodent numbers.

Epidemiology

In South Africa the virus was first isolated in an outbreak among domestic pigs in which it caused reproductive problems. In 1993 an outbreak of EMC caused mortalities among free-living elephants (*Loxodonta africana*) in the Kruger National Park. It occurred in 4 different clusters in which a total of 64 elephants died, 83% of them large bulls. It was reported that simultaneous to the deaths of elephants due to EMC virus infection, there was an explosive increase in rodent numbers. Serological surveys indicated a high incidence of serological reactions to EMC virus in the multimammate mouse (*Mastomys natalensis)*. This appeared to confirm suspicions that the rodents were the source of infection, probably by the oral route. Mortalities were also seen in tree squirrels and a lion cub.

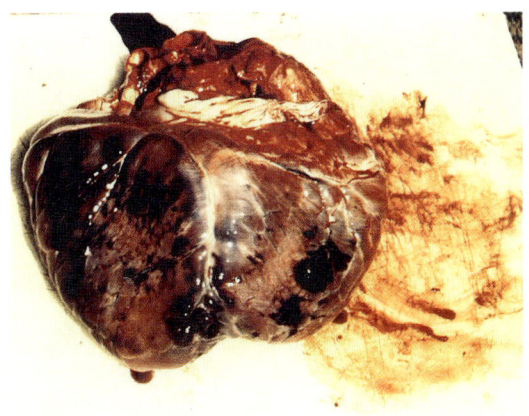

Haemorrhages on the heart of a young elephant caused by the EMC virus.

Symptoms

- During the 1993 outbreak only a single clinical case of EMC was seen in the field. The infected elephant exhibited a disinclination to move, difficult breathing and irritability.
- During a vaccine trial experimentally infected animals showed depression, diarrhoea, trunk-tip sucking and trunk swinging. Two animals died acutely showing terminal paddling of the legs with froth exuding from the external nostrils in the trunk.

Diagnosis

In free-living animals virus isolation for confirmation of the disease was often difficult due to the decomposition of carcasses. However there was a consistent post-mortem finding of heart lesions, specifically haemorrhage of the epicardium and pale streaking of the myocardium. On histology the myocardium showed signs of necrosis and infiltration of inflammatory cells. Immuno-staining showed the presence of EMC virus antigen in a few cases.

Treatment

There is no known treatment for encephalomyocarditis virus infection.

Control

An oil-based experimental vaccine was shown to protect rodents, pigs and elephants in challenge experiments. Although vaccination of free-living elephants is usually impractical, the vaccine was developed with the aim of protecting the large tuskers which were the predominant group affected.

> Rodents have been found to be the normal hosts of the EMC virus since healthy animals excrete it in their faeces.

Prevention

Since outbreaks of EMC in wild animals in zoos are accompanied by an increase in rodent populations, rodent control is very important. The vaccine tested during the elephant trial could be useful in protecting zoo collections under threat from the disease.

BRUCELLOSIS

Cause

Brucellosis of domestic animals is caused by a variety of *Brucella* bacterial species which are usually host specific so *B. abortus* occurs in cattle, *B. ovis* in sheep, *B. melitensis* in goats, and *B. suis* in pigs. The species *B. abortus* and *B. melitensis* can cause clinical disease in humans.

All species are involved in infections of the reproductive tract. *B. abortus*, *melitensis*, and *suis* cause abortions while *B. ovis* causes infection of the epididymis of the testis with resultant infertility.

Epidemiology

Although brucellosis is a disease of livestock, it can spill over to certain wildlife species some of which become maintenance hosts for the disease. A number of wildlife species in South Africa show antibodies to *Brucella* organisms namely buffalo, hippopotamus, zebra, eland, and impala, but this merely indicates contact with the organism and not established infection. So far buffalo are the only species in which *B. abortus* is considered to be maintained, although clinical signs such as hygroma have been seen in eland and sable. Buffalo in Kruger Park show 23% of infection on serology, although abortions are not often noticed. Contact with infected cattle is most likely to have been the original source of infection. Brucellosis is a serious cause of reproductive failure in buffalo.

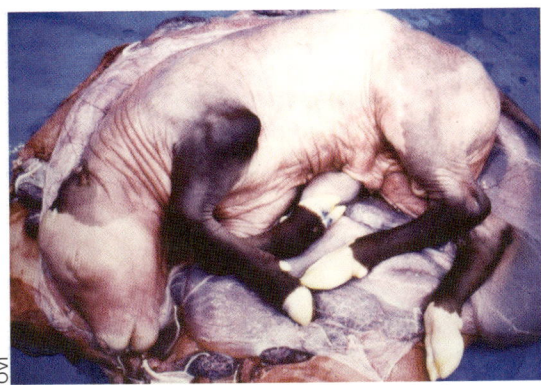
Bovine foetus aborted as a result of brucellosis.

Bursitis in an eland caused by *Brucella abortus*.

Brucella bacteria are transmitted by direct or indirect contact with infected animals or their secretions. Contact with aborted foetuses, foetal membranes or even contaminated pastures will infect susceptible animals. The bacteria can survive well in the environment especially on lush moist pastures. An outbreak of *B. melitensis* has been recorded in sable in the Aberdeen area most likely due to contact with infected goats or cattle.

Symptoms

In cattle *B. abortus* initially causes abortion in susceptible cows. The infection then becomes established and these cows, although they do not abort again are a continuing source of infection for other susceptible cattle, because they shed bacteria on the foetal membranes at each normal calving.

- Cows shed *Brucella* organisms in the milk.
- Abortions occur at 5–7 months of pregnancy in 50% of cows.
- Once infection becomes chronic in the herd, cases of orchitis (testicular inflammation) are seen in bulls.
- Chronically infected animals occasionally develop swellings around the knee joints referred to as hygroma or enlargement of other joint structures (bursitis).

This has been observed in buffalo, eland and sable. Abortions have been observed in infected African buffalo herds, and *B. abortus* organisms have also been isolated from the foetus of a slaughtered pregnant buffalo, as well as from the testes of a male buffalo one of which showed orchitis.

Diagnosis

The diagnosis of brucellosis is based on the symptoms but in buffalo it is unlikely that abortions will be observed in free-living animals.

However, if this is seen, submission of the foetus for further laboratory investigation is useful. Using gloves the foetus should be placed in a strong plastic bag (preferably double to prevent leakages) and submitted on icepacks as soon as possible to the nearest veterinary laboratory.

Bacterial isolation can be attempted from animals that are intended for slaughter.

> Confirmed cases of brucellosis in buffalo must be reported to the local State Veterinarian, and the farm should be placed under quarantine.

The sampling of tissues should be done by a veterinarian. Herds showing signs of joint infection should be investigated for possible brucella infection.

The most convenient method of diagnosis is serology, in which the blood is tested for the presence of *Brucella abortus* antibody. The Serum Agglutination Test (SAT) is used for screening, and positive reactions are confirmed using a Complement Fixation Test (CFT). All suspected and confirmed cases must be reported to the local state veterinarian.

Treatment

Treatment is impractical in livestock and free-living wildlife.

Control

Game ranchers are required to farm with disease-free buffalo which have been tested and certified to be free of brucellosis. However, a clean herd can become infected by contact with infected livestock. It is therefore essential to keep the integrity of fences since the only control measure which can be implemented is to avoid direct contact between livestock and wildlife.

If cattle are run together with buffalo the game rancher must ensure that these cattle are brucella free. Recently large disease-free buffalo herds have become infected from neighbouring cattle farms without direct contact between animals and it is suspected that infection was introduced by scavengers bringing in infected calves or foetal membranes. (See the section on Buffalo in Chapter 4 for examples of perimeter exclusion fences to prevent contact with livestock or infected herds.)

ZOONOSIS

A zoonosis is a disease or parasite that can be transferred from animals to humans. Some examples of zoonoses are:
- brucellosis
- anthrax
- rabies
- echinococcosis
- Rift Valley fever

At present confirmed cases of brucellosis in buffalo must be reported to the local State Veterinarian, and the farm is placed under quarantine. Testing is conducted and currently Veterinary Services require infected buffalo to be slaughtered, unlike infected cattle which may be salvaged by adult vaccination.

Prevention

Vaccination has been used experimentally to protect free-living bison in North America against *B. abortus* using the two vaccines used in cattle, S19 and RB51. The S19-strain failed to give sufficient protection in bison, and RB51 was shed into the environment and caused abortions in some animals. These vaccines have not been tested in African buffalo because their use is currently not permitted as a control measure in South Africa. However, due to the current problems experienced with cattle infecting buffalo herds it may be argued that investigative vaccination trials with RB51 should be permitted particularly in infected herds.

Important!

Brucellosis can potentially infect humans causing fever, wasting and headaches. Take the greatest care with handling foetal tissues and even newborn calves.

INSECT- (ARTHROPOD) TRANSMITTED DISEASES

RIFT VALLEY FEVER

Cause

Rift Valley fever (RVF) is a mosquito-borne viral disease indigenous to Africa, which primarily affects livestock and some wild ruminants under natural conditions. Humans become infected by direct contact with infected animal tissues during handling of infected animals or laboratory work.

Epidemiology

The RVF virus is transmitted by mosquitoes which preferentially feed on livestock and wild vertebrates, as opposed to humans. The virus is maintained within the mosquito population during inter-epidemic periods by transovarial transmission (via eggs).

Outbreaks in southern Africa occur when abnormally heavy spring rains cause an accumulation of surface water which provides ideal conditions for the hatching of the mosquito eggs. This results in a large number of RVF-infected mosquitoes been hatched which then feed on livestock or wildlife species.

Huge epidemics were seen in South Africa during the 1970s when millions of livestock were lost in the outbreak before the availability of vaccines. Since then the disease was sporadically causing a few cases of abortion in buffalo. In 2010 a large outbreak occurred which spread rapidly from the central areas of the country, in a northerly and southerly direction. Most livestock were susceptible as a result of the failure of farmers to vaccinate livestock on a consistent basis, because of the perception that the disease had "disappeared".

Symptoms

The RVF virus is injected into the animal host when an infected mosquito feeds. This causes a viraemia or circulation of the virus through the system. The virus multiplies in some of the tissues, particularly in the liver.

- In adult animals it usually only causes a mild infection with a transient fever.
- In young animals and foetuses, the virus causes severe liver damage and death.
- High mortalities are seen in newborn animals.
- The abortion rate can be as high as 90% in livestock.

Serological studies confirm that a wide range of wildlife species become exposed to the Rift Valley fever virus; in Kenya and Zimbabwe buffalo, rhino of both species and waterbuck showed antibodies to the virus. Clinical symptoms of RVF have also been reported in wildlife although most of the effects seem to be restricted to abortions.

Abortions in springbok and blesbok were seen during the epidemics in the 1950s and

RIFT VALLEY FEVER IN HUMANS

Humans generally do not contract RVF from mosquitoes since the species involved prefer livestock and wild animals, and avoid entering houses. People contract the infection by direct contact with infected animals and their tissues. This usually occurs during the handling of aborted foetuses, cutting up carcasses or performing postmortems, or when handling blood, serum and tissues from infected animals. The disease is therefore seen in veterinarians, farmers, farm labourers, laboratory technicians and wildlife scientists. It causes an influenza-like syndrome characterised by headaches and muscle pains, but a small percentage of individuals may suffer severe, sometimes fatal, liver damage or blindness.

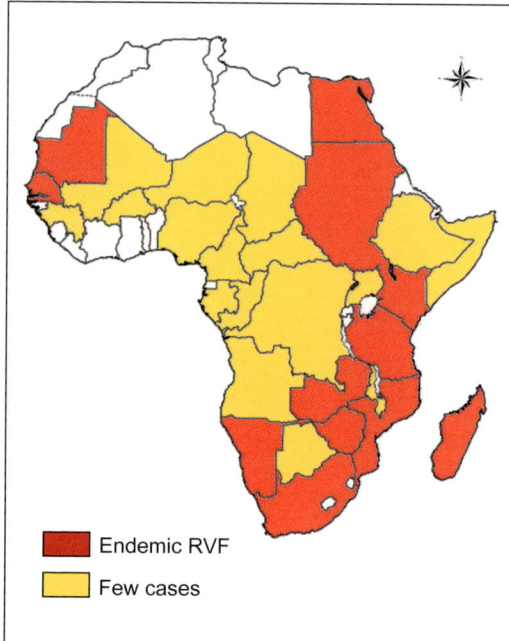

Rift Valley Fever distribution area in Africa.

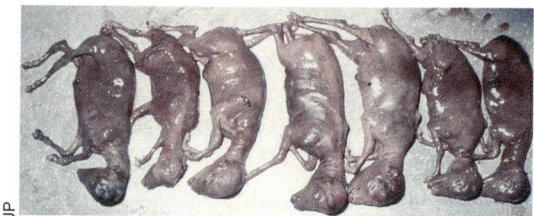

RVF causes abortion "storms" in pregnant livestock.

Control

During RVF outbreaks animals in bomas or quarantine stations can be treated with a pyrethroid spray or pour-on, to prevent been bitten by infected mosquitoes. This will offer more immediate protection than vaccination which can take up to 21 days for immunity to develop.

Prevention

The live RVF vaccines, Smithburn and Clone 13, are effective in protecting livestock against abortions caused by RVF. Smithburn is known to cause a small percentage of abortions and teratogenicity in pregnant sheep, so its use is generally avoided during pregnancy, even though no cases have ever been described in cattle. Vaccination with the live vaccine has been performed in some wildlife species with no adverse reactions described as yet. Inactivated vaccines give poor immunity unless they are given at least three times so are therefore useless in an outbreak situation.

although RVF virus wasn't confirmed as the cause, it seems likely that these were due to the disease. An experimentally infected buffalo of 7 months' old showed transient fever and depression, while one out of two pregnant buffalo showed abortion.

Treatment

There is no treatment for this viral disease.

Diagnosis

Abortions in pregnant animals are probably the only signs of RVF the game ranch owner is likely to see. These can be investigated by submission of the foetus for viral isolation (see Brucellosis). Using gloves the foetus should be placed in a robust plastic bag to exclude possibility of leakages. The foetus must be kept cool by placing it on ice packs (not frozen) and submitted to an investigative laboratory with clear labelling SUSPECTED RVF. Blood samples are of limited value because while a positive serological result indicates exposure, does not confirm the virus as the cause of abortion.

TRYPANOSOMOSIS (NAGANA)

Cause

Trypanosomosis is caused by a number of species of the protozoal blood parasites of the genus *Trypanosoma*. Trypanosomes are leaf-shaped, single-celled parasites which are injected into the bloodstream by the tsetse fly. Examples of diseases caused by these organisms are sleeping sickness and Chagas' disease of humans. In livestock they cause a disease called nagana in southern Africa. Roughly 10

Tsetse flies are the transmitters of trypanosomosis.

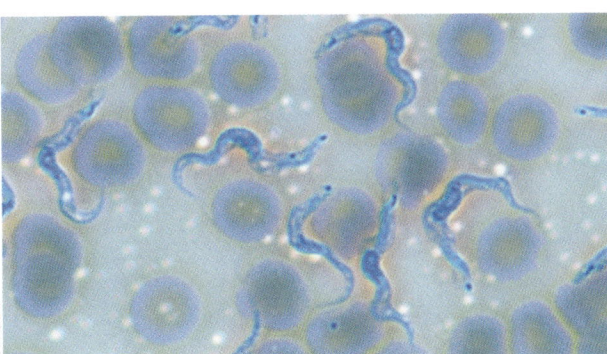
Trypanosomes in the bloodstream.

million km² in 37 African countries are infested by tsetse fly and are thus ravaged by nagana and sleeping sickness. Prior to the 1850s, tsetse fly and nagana infested the Limpopo, KwaZulu-Natal and Mpumalanga Provinces of South Africa. The rinderpest pandemic killed millions of head of game and cattle and led to the disappearance of the tsetse in these regions. Small pockets of tsetse flies survived mainly in the game reserves of KwaZulu-Natal and despite aerial spraying with insecticide in the early 1950s, nagana again threatened livestock in and around those areas for the first time again in 1990.

Epidemiology

Tsetse flies belong to the genus *Glossina* of which there are a number of species limited to Africa. They are big flies with long, piercing mouthparts. Both male and female flies feed on blood only. When hungry, they are attracted to moving objects as well as to odours produced in the hosts breath and urine. While feeding they will inject trypanosomes into the blood stream.

Game animals unlike introduced cattle and other livestock have evolved with the flies and the disease for thousands of years, so game animals harbour the parasite without showing any ill effects or signs of disease. Kudu, warthog, bushbuck, bushpig, African buffalo, African elephant and both species of rhinoceros (white and black) are known reservoirs of the disease. Buffalo appear to be innately resistant while most other species seem to acquire resistance on exposure. Game animals only show clinical disease when under stress or after reintroduction of non-immune game animals into trypanosome endemic areas. "Trypanotolerance" can break down under conditions of stress, particularly reduced nutrition during drought periods. When livestock are introduced into areas where infected tsetse flies and game occur, cattle can experience outbreaks.

Symptoms

Trypanosomosis in cattle in endemic areas is primarily caused by *T. congolense* and *T. vivax*. The clinical signs are not specific to nagana and may vary from acute (fatal within a couple of weeks) to chronic (lasting months).
- The first sign of disease is a fever and malaise which rise and fall with the parasitaemia.
- **Acute cases:** sudden loss of milk production and sometimes abortions. Animals become progressively anaemic, and although they continue to eat they lose weight and body condition becoming recumbent and dying a few days later.
- **Chronic cases:** more common. Animals become emaciated, losing substantial amount of weight. Their condition is poor, and their coat rough and dull. They develop a severe anaemia, with pale membranes and a bounding rapid pulse sometimes

visible in the jugular vein, and rapid breathing. Death is usually sudden as a result of cardiac failure. In endemic areas, herd calving rates are drastically reduced.

- Signs in other species such as horses, dogs, pigs and rarely sheep and goats are generally similar but with some differences, such as ventral oedema (accumulation of fluid) in horses and ocular lesions in dogs and sheep.

Diagnosis

In tsetse infected areas nagana in livestock is diagnosed based on the symptoms. Game animals may develop clinical disease when under stress or if they have been recently introduced into a tsetse infected area. The disease is confirmed by demonstrating the organism microscopically in a blood smear. The presence of parasites does not necessarily indicate disease in game since they can be non-symptomatic carriers. Serological tests will identify the species of *Trypanosoma* involved. At postmortem typical signs are carcass in poor condition, anaemia, enlarged lymph nodes and an excessive accumulation of fluid in the body cavities.

Treatment

Nagana can be relatively easily treated using short-acting trypanocides. Diminazine (Berenil) is given at a dose of 3.5 to 7 mg/kg intramuscularly. Because it is relatively toxic it must not be repeated within a period of three months. Homidium bromide (Ethidium) is given at 1 mg/kg intramuscularly. Other supportive therapy, rest, and good food must be provided. Severely affected animals may recover poorly due to damage to the blood producing cells.

Prevention and control

Tseste fly control: in the form of pyrethoid dips, sprays or pour-ons is used on cattle in tsetse infected areas. However, fly control in game reserves and on game species is not recommended since this will render certain species susceptible to trypanosomosis.

Chemoprophylaxis

Prevention of nagana transmission has been achieved in cattle using trypanocides which have a long action preventing the transmission of nagana. These are homidium bromide (Ethidium) given at a dose of 1 mg/kg intramuscularly, or isometamidium (Samorin) given at a dose of 0,25 to 1,0 mg/kg intramuscularly. The usefulness of chemoprophylaxis in wildlife species is unknown.

TICK-BORNE DISEASES

BABESIOSIS (REDWATER) IN UNGULATES

Babesiosis, caused by the blood parasites *Babesia bigemina* and *B. bovis,* is a very important tick-borne disease of domestic cattle, while *B. equi* and to a lesser extent *B. caballi* are important causes of disease in horses. As a result, much research has focused on the cause, epidemiology, treatment and prevention of these diseases in livestock. Similar blood parasites known as piroplasms have frequently been reported from wild herbivores (and carnivores – see below), the first of these in 1908. Prior to the recent development of molecular characterisation of these parasites, the early reports and species identifications were based only on the species in which they were found and on their microscopic morphology. As a result, the naming and classification of these blood parasites is now very confused and in need of a whole re-identification and reclassification with the help of molecular techniques. However, our knowledge of babesiosis in domestic stock fills in many of the gaps in our knowledge of this disease in game species.

Cause

Babesiosis is caused by piroplasms or teardrop-shaped parasites, of the genus *Babesia*, found in red blood cells. The parasites seem to be fairly species specific, meaning that each mammal host has one or more *Babesia* spp. which parasitises it alone. There are reports of *Babesia* spp. from domestic animals found in wildlife, many of these from before proper identification using molecular techniques could confirm exactly what species were involved. Generally there are two types of *Babesia*:

- **Large babesias:** These are true babesias and while they do cause disease in domestic stock they are usually less virulent and easier to treat than the small babesias.
- **Small babesias:** These are generally more virulent and more difficult to treat. There is some controversy about the nomenclature of the small babesias which some scientists have placed in the genus *Theileria*.

Epidemiology

Babesia-parasites are transmitted by ticks, in the case of domestic cattle and sheep, by the one-host blue ticks, *Boophilus (Rhipicephalus) decoloratus* and *Boophilus (Rhipicephalus) microplus*. In domestic horses the parasite is transmitted by the red-legged tick, *Rhipicephalus evertsi evertsi* (*B.equi* and *B. caballi*), and *Hyalomma truncatum*, (*B. caballi*), both two-host ticks in Southern Africa. The vectors of *Babesia* spp. of wild hosts have not been determined and are open to speculation.

Young animals born in endemic areas are generally protected during the first six to nine months of life from *Babesia*-infections by passively acquired maternal (colostral) antibodies and other non-specific factors. Infection acquired from a tick bite during this early period results in an active immunity developing. If there is a regular, sufficient challenge (infected tick bites), an endemically stable situation develops with most of the animals in the herd being immune to infection. This most likely occurs in free-ranging wild ungulates. Clinical cases may, however, develop when the immune system is compromised by stress. This would explain why babesiosis is so seldom seen as a clinical disease in wild animals and why the clinical cases and deaths are usually only seen in captured, translocated or similarly stressed animals (e.g. during droughts).

When the exposure to infected tick bites is infrequent as in zoo animals or where the animals are treated frequently for ticks when they are translocated to areas where infected vectors are present, the animal will contract the disease. Bearing this in mind, the cases of babesiosis reported in wildlife can more easily be understood:

Babesia bigemina, a large *Babesia* and the cause of African redwater in cattle, has been reported in African buffalo, which were experimentally infected but showed no clinical manifestations, as well as Soemering's gazelle and possibly sable antelope. In 1930 a "new" species called *B. irvinesmithi* was described in sable. This may have been *B. bigemina* but sable re-imported from a European zoo during 1990 died with typical "redwater" symptoms and extracted DNA was found to be of a new *Babesia* sp.

Babesia caballi (large *Babesia*) and *B. equi* (small *Babesia*), the causes of biliary fever in horses, mules and donkeys have both been seen in both plains and mountain zebra.

Babesia trautmanni, the piroplasm of domestic pigs has been reported in both bushpig and warthog which showed no apparent symptoms.

A number of black rhinoceros have been diagnosed as having died of babesiosis and a new species, *Babesia bicornis,* was confirmed by molecular characterisation. While the parasite has been identified in many healthy rhinoceros, all these clinical cases were seen in animals which were stressed either by capture, translocation or severe drought conditions.

There is molecular evidence that this species also occurs in white rhinoceros, although no clinical cases have been reported.

Similarly, a number of stress related deaths in giraffe from babesiosis have been reported.

Symptoms

Although the symptoms of babesiosis may vary in severity depending on the immune status of the affected host and the virulence of the strain, they remain similar regardless of the species of host or parasite involved.

- The babesia parasite causes destruction of red blood cells, with subsequent anaemia, haemoglobinuria (haemoglobin in the urine, hence the name redwater), and jaundice.
- The clinical signs seen after an incubation period of 1–2 weeks, are a fever of > 40 °C, lack of appetite, depression and sometimes diarrhoea.
- Pregnant animals may abort.
- Terminal cases develop muscle wasting, tremors, become recumbent and lapse into a coma.
- If the brain is affected (cerebral form) nervous symptoms will be seen. Non-fatal cases may take many weeks to recover completely.

Diagnosis

Diagnosis can be made on a history of stress or recent introduction to the area, clinical signs and postmortem findings. The diagnosis can be confirmed by demonstrating the pear-shaped parasites in the red blood cells. To determine the exact *Babesia* sp. involved samples need to be sent to a diagnostic laboratory.

Postmortem signs are usually characteristic. Acute cases will show congestion of most organs and small haemorrhages in many internal organs. More protracted cases show pale mucous membranes indicative of anaemia, jaundice, haemoglobinuria (red urine), an enlarged spleen, swollen and yellowish liver.

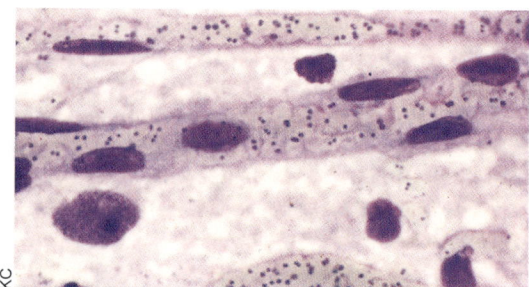

Babesia parasites in red blood cells.

In cases where the brain is involved it will show congestion with the blood vessels being very prominent.

Treatment

Treatment is only feasible in valuable, captured and restrained animals. The remedies that may be used are:

- Diminazine (Berenil/Veriben) at 3.5 mg/kg i/m.
- Imidocarb (Imizol/Forray 65) at 1.2 mg/kg s/c or i/m. Imidocarb may also be used in very specific cases at a higher dose (3 mg/kg) prophylactically to protect valuable susceptible animals of a herd where some animals have already been diagnosed as having babesiosis.
- Other normal supportive therapy such as fluid replacement may be warranted in expensive individual animals.

Prevention and control

Control of babesiosis is only necessary under specific circumstances such as in zoos, intensive breeding programmes or where susceptible animals are introduced into endemic areas. Control and prevention will rely on good tick control (discussed in other chapters) and limited chemotherapy and chemoprophylaxis (see above).

Prevention depends on good management specifically reducing stress by giving supplementary feeding during severe drought when it becomes obvious that the animals are losing condition, keeping only animals adapted to the conditions on the property, not translocating and introducing susceptible animals, e.g from zoos, into endemic areas and preventing a build up of massive tick numbers.

BABESIOSIS IN CARNIVORES

Biliary or babesiosis is an important world wide tick-borne disease of canines and felines caused by a parasite *Babesia* of the red blood cells of infected animals.

As a result the epidemiology, pathogenesis, diagnosis, treatment and control of the disease in domestic pets is well documented. Much of this information can be extrapolated to the disease in wild carnivores.

Cause

While many *Babesia* spp. have been isolated from or seen in a wide variety of carnivores, a true understanding of the species involved in wild carnivores is only now becoming possible due to the newly developed techniques of molecular characterisation.

It has thus only recently been recognised that the virulent South African disease of domestic dogs is caused by the subspecies *Babesia canis rossi* first described in 1910 from a side-striped jackal and not *Babesia canis canis*. The "true" European *Babesia canis canis* has not been recorded in South Africa while a third species, *Babesia canis vogeli,* does occur here. African wild dogs and black-backed jackals artificially infected with *B. canis rossi* showed no ill effects. On the other hand, the Johannesburg Zoo has confirmed the death of an African wild dog pup of biliary.

Although *Babesia felis*, a small babesia parasite, has been reported in Europe (France and Germany), in Thailand and Zimbabwe, it is only in South Africa that it appears to cause disease. This parasite was first described in a blood smear from an African wild cat in 1929. A domestic cat which was given blood from this wild cat showed the presence of parasites in the blood but didn't develop any symptoms. It is thus not clear whether this is a disease of the African wild cat or of domestic cats.

Babesia felis has also been reported in cheetah, lion and serval.

New techniques have shown that free-ranging lion in southern and eastern Africa carry two babesia species, viz. *Babesia felis* and *B. leo*. A splenectomised domestic cat was infected with the latter "new" species and while the parasite did establish itself in the cat for a short period the domestic cat developed no symptoms.

Babesia spp. have been found in a long list of carnivores including leopard, various mongoose species, the spotted hyena, the Cape pole cat, the civet and various genet species. In most cases these were incidental findings and the animals showed no signs of disease.

As with the wild ungulates, babesiosis in carnivores appears to manifest only under conditions of stress. Elsa, the lioness of "Born Free" fame is said to have died of babesiosis. Being a hand-reared animal, the stress of being re-introduced to the wild could have precipitated the clinical manifestation of biliary fever.

Epidemiology

Babesia parasites are transmitted to carnivores only by ticks.

The vectors of the blood parasites of domestic dogs in South Africa are the kennel tick (*Rhipicephalus sanguineus*), and the yellow dog tick (*Haemophysalis leachi*).

Transmission and incidence of disease is highest during the summer months. The precise vector of feline biliary is not known, nor are the vectors of the disease in wild carnivores.

Symptoms and diagnosis

- After an incubation period of 10–21 days following the bite of an infected tick, the signs shown by diseased canines are similar to those described in ungulates.

- In felines it is a more insidious disease, causing a chronic disease with a protracted course during which the animal shows gradual loss of weight and weakness.

Treatment

There are a number of specific treatments available in canines. A single drug is available for the treatment of felines. For both species the anaemia must be reversed by a blood transfusion or at least fluid replacement.

Control and prevention

Babesiosis can be prevented in captive carnivores by controlling the tick vectors. In addition, stress factors must be reduced by providing the most appropriate and natural accommodation and food. Excessive contact with humans should be reduced or the animals should be trained to enter small enclosures where they can be darted and handled. Avoid the introduction of strange animals into a socialised pack. A canine babesiosis vaccine is available for use in domestic dogs, but its usefulness in wild animals has not been determined.

HEARTWATER

Heartwater is a very important tick-borne disease of cattle, sheep, goats and some wild ruminants in Africa. Because of its importance in domestic stock, there is a vast amount of knowledge about the disease in domesticated livestock and its vectors, which may be extrapolated to game animals.

Cause

The causative organism is a rickettsial organism called *Ehrlichia ruminantium* (formerly *Cowdria ruminantium*) which is transmitted to ruminants by various ticks of the genus *Amblyomma* or the "bont" ticks. Different field isolates of *E. ruminantium* vary in their ability to cause disease.

Epidemiology

The disease is seen north of the Magaliesberg range of mountains and down the east and southeast coast of South Africa, southeastern Botswana and most of Zimbabwe wherever the vector *Amblyomma hebraeum* ("bont tick") is found. Newly hatched larval ticks become infected by feeding on the blood of a heartwater-infected animal. These may be susceptible to sick animals or non-susceptible reservoir hosts. Immature bont ticks feed on smaller animals and tortoises, guinea fowl and scrub hares which makes the tick difficult to control. Scrub hares and guinea fowl have been shown to be carriers of the heartwater parasite, and there may be many more as yet unidentified reservoir hosts. The prevalence of the disease in an area therefore depends on tick numbers, the infection rate in the ticks and the presence of reservoir hosts. Adult tick numbers are seasonal, being most numerous during the summer and early autumn. Consequently, this is when most cases of heartwater are seen. *Amblyomma* ticks are found where there is sufficient bush cover and suitable levels of temperature and humidity.

Based on observations made on a wide range of wild ruminants in South Africa a general pattern of heartwater susceptibility can be distinguished:
- **Resistant:** These species have an innate or genetic resistance to heartwater. They include most species which evolved in bushveld such as buffalo, kudu, and nyala.
- **Susceptible but can acquire immunity to the disease or avoid heavy challenge from the ticks:** These species are susceptible but can acquire heartwater immunity when exposed naturally to low dose infections and if vaccinated. They include impala, gemsbok and eland.
- **Highly susceptible:** These are mainly the species which evolved in grassland where they had no historic exposure

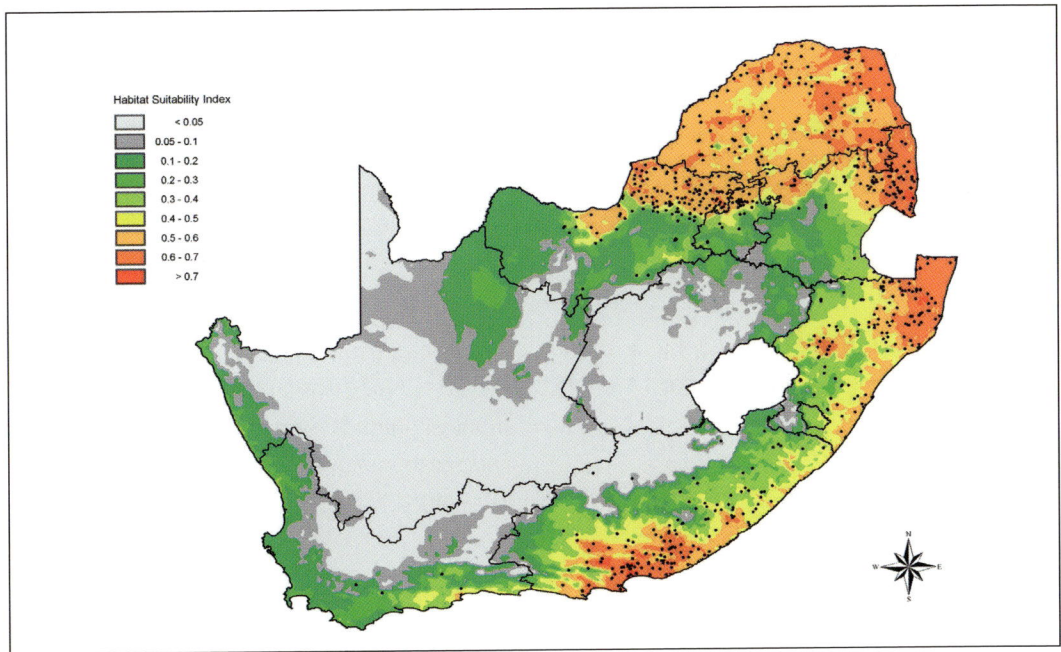

Distribution of heartwater tick (*Amblyomma hebrauem*).

to heartwater. They include springbok, bontebok and black wildebeest. This group can be immunised by natural exposure but this is dose dependent – if they receive a high challenge most animals will die, while a small challenge dose will allow immunisation. Vaccination can give 100% immunity but must be blocked with antibiotic treatment.

- **Exotic ruminants:** Exotic ruminants are totally susceptible to heartwater.

In susceptible species which acquire immunity the offspring will be protected by maternal immunity and will then be able to develop active immunity when exposed to infection by ticks. The immunity acquired by susceptible species is thought to be genetic and may involve immunity to ticks as well as the *Erlichia*-organism.

Symptoms

The heartwater organism replicates in the endothelial cells of the blood capillaries and causes an increased permeability of the blood vessels. As a result blood fluids leak out of the vessels causing an accumulation of straw-coloured liquid into body cavities and soft tissues including in the lungs, pericardial sac and brain.

- Symptoms seen in domestic cattle and sheep are a fever of >40 °C, nervous symptoms such as an exaggerated blinking reflex, staggering with terminal convulsions, lateral recumbency and paddling motions with the legs.
- Other signs such as respiratory distress and haemorrhagic diarrhoea are seen in less acute cases. While the symptoms of heartwater in wild ungulates are not well studied they are likely to be similar to those in livestock.

Diagnosis

Diagnosis should be based on the history of susceptibility of the species, recent translocation into a heartwater area, a history of stress and the tick burden of the animal concerned. Clinical symptoms are fairly typical but can be confused with cerebral babesiosis, cerebral theileriosis, various plant poisonings

Table 1: Showing the susceptibility of various antelope species to heartwater according to the description of the three groups above:

GROUP 1 SPECIES (FULLY SUSCEPTIBLE)	GROUP 2 SPECIES (INTERMEDIATE)	GROUP 3 SPECIES (RESISTANT)
Species evolved in grassland regions where the vector tick and disease never occurred.	Species which more recently moved from regions where heartwater occurred and adapted to non-endemic grasslands.	Species that evolved for millennia in regions where the habitat was bushy enough to sustain the vector tick and hence the disease.
Black wildebeest	Eland	Giraffe
Sitatunga	Bushbuck	African buffalo
Lechwe	Blesbok	Scimitar-horned oryx
Springbok	Impala	Greater kudu
	Oryx	Blue wildebeest
		Tsessebe
		Red hartebeest
		Nyala
		Sable antelope
		Roan
		Common duiker

such as *Albizia tangeniensis*, *Sarcostemma viminale* and *Solanum kwebenzi*.

The postmortem is quite typical with straw-coloured fluid found in the body cavities and the heart sac, lung and brain oedema and signs of a diffuse enteritis.

Microscopic examination of brain smears stained with Giemsa will show colonies of *E. ruminantium* which will confirm the diagnosis.

Treatment

Treatment is only practical in zoo- or boma-kept animals or in exceptional cases where valuable antelope are seen to be showing early signs of heartwater.

At least one intramuscular injection of long-acting oxytetracycline at 20 mg/kg (usually 1 ml per 10 kg) must be given. In very severe cases short acting oxytetracycline must be given intravenously and followed up by an intramuscular injection a day later. A repeat dose, a week later, is advisable if practical. Supportive therapy can be given to increase the chance of survival.

Introduction of animals into heartwater areas

Group 1

This group includes fully susceptible species, such as springbok. When naive animals of this group are introduced into an area within the natural range of the vector and hence the disease, most will contract severe heartwater and die.

The few survivors probably received very few bites from infected ticks and hence have had a low disease challenge and/or are animals which are genetically better adapted to avoid being bitten by ticks and/or overcome heartwater infection. The offspring from the very few survivors, will also be immune and breeding with them will help build a heartwater-resistant herd. In order to limit these huge initial losses, animals from this group can be vaccinated, which is a cumbersome exercise and merely a form of controlled exposure and treatment (see under Vaccination) prior to introduction. Some losses can be expected. These animals

Lechwe showing heartwater symptoms.

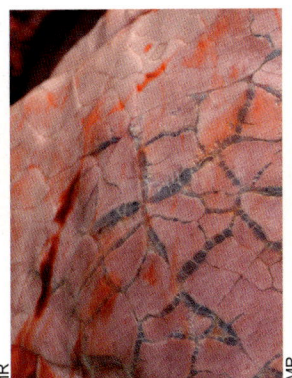
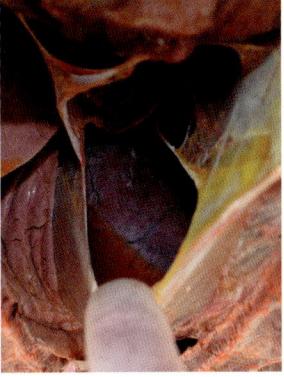
Severe fluid accumulation in the pericard/lungs of an animal that died of heartwater.

will become permanently immune provided they are challenged by natural infection by infected ticks from time to time. Their offspring will not be immune and heavy losses from the second generation can be expected. At this point one will need to "rebuild" the herd from the surviving vaccinated animals and the few surviving second generation animals (as above). It should be noted that animals sold as "heartwater-resistant" springbok may well originate from endemic areas but may never have been exposed because of the absence of ticks in a particular micro-habitat, particular farm or camp system.

All extra-African ruminants tested, such as white-tailed deer, fallow deer, bison, water buffalo, Nilgai and blackbuck have proven to be highly susceptible.

Group 2
This is an intermediate group which if vaccinated, or exposed to the disease, react less severely with less losses experienced. Their offspring seem to be immune and few losses are experienced in the subsequent generations. They adapt far more quickly and better to being in heartwater endemic areas than Group 1.

Group 3
These are animals which are highly unlikely to become ill and or die from heartwater. In most cases heartwater has never been described in these animals. Resistant species can be introduced into heartwater areas from non-endemic areas without losses.

Vaccination
Heartwater vaccination must be done six weeks before introducing animals into an endemic area. Using the currently available blood vaccine it is a rather cumbersome process which involves intravenous administration of infected blood which is stored frozen in liquid nitrogen and transported on dry ice.

The vaccine contains live virulent heartwater organisms so animals may develop a reaction, indicated by the development of a fever which must then be blocked by treatment with tetracyclines. This is a very risky and stressful operation when dealing with wild antelope. However, it has been done with some success by various game ranchers as detailed below (Malan, personal communication; Barnard, personal communication):

- Newly introduced animals, held in a boma, are hand-caught and vaccinated intravenously as directed on the pamphlet.
- From day eight after vaccination the animals are caught by hand and their temperatures are taken, until a significant rise in temperature of 1 °C within one day is seen, or it rises above 40 °C. This usually occurs by day 12 after vaccination.

- When the fever reaction develops the animals are treated with oxytetracyclines as discussed under treatment.
- It should be noted that because field strains of heartwater vary in pathogenicity, the vaccine does not protect equally well against all of them.
- Other preventative measures, such as reducing stress on capture and adequate tick control measures, should be used.

Immunity "certification"

Although laboratory tests are available for heartwater antibody determination (IFAT/ELISA), the presence of antibody against the organism merely indicates that animals have been exposed and does not guarantee immunity (Latif, personal communication).

Game ranchers have reported that animals which have tested positive on IFAT by Onderstepoort Veterinary Institute have developed clinical cases of heartwater on introduction into endemic areas (Jacques Malan, personal communication). Further research is needed to develop a reliable diagnostic test.

A potential buyer should therefore request written proof that animals purchased originated from an endemic heartwater area, but must be aware that not all these animals are necessarily immune.

Future prospects

A new attenuated vaccine which does not require blocking treatment with antibiotics, has been recently developed at Onderstepoort, and shown to be protective in livestock. It has yet to be registered for use and has not yet been tested in highly susceptible game species such as springbok.

THEILERIOSIS

Theileria are small piroplasms or blood parasites transmitted by ticks and found in the red and white blood cells of both wild and domestic ungulates.

Some species in particular like *Theileria parva*, the cause of East Coast Fever are highly pathogenic to domestic cattle and of great economic importance. The nomenclature of the different species occurring in wild game and their host specificity is not well researched, and it is only now with the recent availability of molecular characterisation that the complexities are slowly being unravelled.

Theileria organisms do not generally cause clinical disease in their wild hosts. However, they may cause clinical disease in stressed game animals and game animals introduced into areas where they do not normally occur.

CORRIDOR DISEASE

Cause

The causative organism, *Theileria parva*, is thought to have evolved in buffalo populations in east Africa and is currently universally distributed in African buffalo in eastern, central and southern Africa.

The only "wild" buffalo populations which do not carry the organism in their blood are in the Addo Elephant Park from where the vector tick, *Rhipicephalus appendiculatus*, the brown ear tick, is absent and on private farms where "disease-free" buffalo have been introduced.

Epidemiology

The close relationship between *Theileria parva* and the African buffalo having developed over such a long period has resulted in the parasite and host becoming adapted to each other. Consequently, an endemically stable situation has developed in which, under normal circumstances, African buffalo are not affected by the disease.

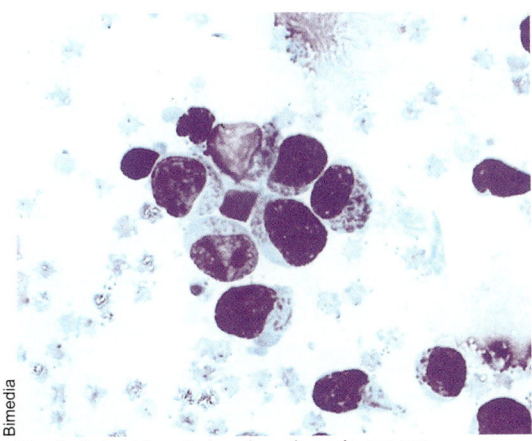
Theilerial schizonts in a lymph node smear.

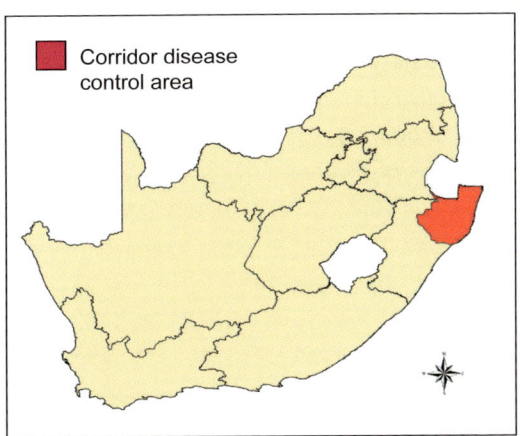
Corridor disease control area in South Africa.

In endemic areas buffalo calves become infected, show no signs of disease and become carriers of *T. parva* organisms. *Rhipicephalus appendiculatus* or the brown ear tick feeding on the carrier buffalo becomes heavily infected with the *Theileria*-organisms.

Cattle sharing pastures with carrier buffalo are soon fed on by infected ticks, and are exposed to the *Theileria parva*-organism, causing Corridor disease. The name of the disease derives from the fact that the first cases of Corridor disease in cattle were described from the "corridor" between the Hluhluwe and uMfolozi Game Reserves.

Symptoms

While African buffalo are generally asymptomatic, cattle become severely affected. Symptoms are similar to those of East Coast fever except that the course is usually shorter, death occurring within a few days of the onset of the first signs.
- The first signs are fever followed by an enlargement of the superficial lymph nodes, severe lung oedema and loss of condition. Mortality in infected cattle is usually about 80%.

Because the organism is not well adapted to cattle, its development and the formation of the infective stages (piroplasms) is slowed, most cattle dying before these have a chance to form in the blood. Ticks can therefore not transmit infection from Corridor infected cattle. The disease is thus self-limiting in a herd of cattle, because African buffalo are the sole reservoir of infection for the ticks.

Diagnosis

Diagnosis in cattle is based on the history of the presence of African buffalo, exposure to infected ticks, and the fact that the outbreak ceases when the buffalo are removed. The typical clinical signs are more acute than those of East Coast fever and the postmortem lesions are more outspoken.

The disease can be confirmed by examining a stained blood or lymph node smear under the microscope and finding the organism. Some laboratories can test blood using PCR techniques to confirm the exact identity of parasites, differentiating them from, for example, *T. taurotragi*.

Treatment

Chemotherapy is not permitted in South Africa because this can create carrier animals.

In neighbouring countries buparvoquone is used at 2.5mg/kg with >90% recovery rates.

When field cases are detected late, a second injection 48 hours after the first is recommended. This is usually necessary with Corridor disease as its course is generally short.

Control

Corridor disease is one of the four diseases including FMD, brucellosis and BTB, for which buffalo to be moved must be tested to ensure they are "disease-free". It is a notifiable disease under the control of the veterinary services who must be advised immediately when the disease is suspected.

The state veterinarian will quarantine the property and isolate the infected herd (two fences, 5 m apart), slaughter infected animals and institute very strict monitoring and tick control on the remainder of the herd. The area will then be destocked for two years to prevent re-infection since the adult ticks will no longer carry the organism.

Prevention

Within the Corridor control area in South Africa, where the disease is a threat to livestock farming, prevention is based on limiting close contact between African buffalo and cattle.

Rigorous tick control is practised with short inter-treatment periods which is necessary due to the rapid engorgement of the brown ear tick. Corridor-free buffalo were produced in a project run by SANParks by removing calves from their mothers and raising them under tick-free conditions. Note that the East Coast fever "vaccine" used in Kenya does not protect against buffalo-adapted theileriosis (Corridor disease).

EAST COAST FEVER (CATTLE-DERIVED THEILERIOSIS)

East Coast fever is a buffalo-derived theilerial disease. It was introduced into South Africa by cattle imported from Kenya and Tanzania for restocking after the rinderpest epidemic of 1896 and the South African war of 1899 to 1902.

By 1955 the disease was eradicated from South Africa by intensive tick control and strict eradication regulations, including stock movement control, destocking of infected pastures and slaughter. It is still present in some neighbouring countries south of the Zambezi. When East Coast fever is introduced into a region it can cause mortalities in susceptible cattle of over 90% if intensive control measures are not instituted.

In areas where it is endemic as with the other tick-borne diseases enzootic stability amongst locally adapted zebu-type cattle develops, resulting in negligible mortalities seen.

Cause

Theileria parva, originally a parasite of buffalo, became adapted to cattle in which it, however, still causes severe disease (ECF).

Epidemiology

The three-host brown ear tick (*Rhipicephalus appendiculatus*) is the only significant vector of the causative organism of East Coast fever. The disease is picked up from the blood of infected cattle by the nymphal ticks and transmitted to new hosts when the adult ticks feed.

Transmission of the disease therefore takes place mainly during the warm, wet season when adult brown ear ticks are numerous. Only cattle and waterbuck are known to be naturally infected and so these are the only animals which can serve as a reservoir of the blood parasite and a source of infection for the ticks.

The potential distribution of East Coast fever is thus restricted to where the brown ear tick occurs, namely the warmer more humid areas of eastern, central and southern Africa.

Symptoms

In the rare cases of clinical disease in waterbuck, the signs are similar to those seen in cattle. After an incubation period of two weeks following attachment of an infected tick the following signs are seen:

- Fever, enlargement of the superficial lymph nodes, severe lung oedema and loss of condition.
- Most cases are fatal with death following about two weeks from signs of fever.

Diagnosis

Diagnosis is based on the history of exposure to infected ticks, the typical clinical signs and the postmortem lesions. The disease is confirmed on demonstrating the organism in blood or lymph node smears. Specialist laboratories can test blood using PCR techniques to differentiate *T. parva* from *T. taurotragi*.

Control

ECF has been eradicated from South Africa, but there is a danger of re-introduction by the importation of infected brown ear ticks, infected livestock or game species. Strict import controls are therefore in place for livestock and game animals from ECF infected countries.

THEILERIOSIS (*T. HIPPOTRAGI*) IN ROAN AND SABLE ANTELOPE

Cause

Theileria spp. have been reported to occur in roan and sable antelope. *Theileria hippotragi* has been recorded as the cause of deaths in roan antelope in which almost 100% of the year's calf crop died. Similarly, it has been identified as the cause of mortalities in young sable calves up to the age of two months. Some clinical cases have been seen in wildebeest calves.

Epidemiology

The red-legged tick (*Rhipicephalus evertsi evertsi*), which has the most widespread distribution of all ticks in South Africa, has been

Newborn roan and sable calves might need treatment with pyrethroid pour-on to control red-legged ticks.

shown to be the main vector of *T. hippotragi*. The immature stages of this two-host tick feed in the ears of antelope and equids such as zebra. The ticks become infected by antelope species and have shown to be benign carriers of *T. hippotragi*, namely reedbuck, blue wildebeest, blesbuck, nyala and bushbuck. Roan and sable calves do not have any immunity to this parasite and will develop clinical, usually fatal, disease if they receive a high enough dose of parasites (Steyl, 2015). Adults seem to be less susceptible, possibly because the dose per body size is less. There is some indication that theilerial susceptibility in roan and sable has a genetic cause.

Symptoms

The clinical signs of *T. hippotragi* are fever and lymph node enlargement. Pulmonary oedema resulting in difficult breathing as well as anaemia and icterus are seen in most acute cases.

Diagnosis

Diagnosis is based on history, stress, the presence of large numbers of red-legged ticks, and postmortem changes typical of theileriosis.

The disease is confirmed by demonstrating the presence of the parasite on stained blood or lymph node smears. DNA probe analysis of frozen spleen, liver, lung and kidney samples by a specialist laboratory will confirm the species of *Theileria* involved.

Treatment

Where the antelope are intensively raised treatment is feasible using buparvoquone at 2.5mg/kg but the use of this drug is not permitted by veterinary authorities. Because of this, prevention of the disease must be focused on controlling the tick vector.

Prevention and control

There are two strategies which can be used or combined to prevent the exposure of roan and sable to ticks:

- **Calving in clean camps:** Pregnant cows can be moved to "tick clean" camps (December) in other words which have not been stocked with antelope for 18 months, in which the chances of exposure of calves to infected ticks are less under these conditions (Steyl, 2015). The cows then calve in February and remain in the clean camps until April, when the young are past the age of susceptibility.
- **Treatment with tick pour-ons:** Roan and sable antelope calves in small breeding camps are usually caught and tagged soon after birth. They can therefore be treated by applying a registered pour-on on the underline, which makes it less likely that the cow will reject her treated calf. Repeat treatments may be needed until the calves are older than two months (E. Davey, 2015).

THEILERIA TAUROTRAGI-INFECTION (*CYTAUZOONOSIS*)

Cause

There are a number of species of *Theileria* that have been identified in various host species but which cause a benign or mild form of theileriosis in cattle. One of these is *Theileria taurotragi*, a benign parasite of eland.

Epidemiology

Various brown ticks (*Rhipicephalus* spp.), including *Rh. appendiculatus* (brown ear tick), *Rh. evertsi evertsi* (red-legged tick), *Rh. pulchellus* and *Rh. zambesiensis* have been shown to transmit *T. taurotragi*.

Symptoms

- A mild, transient febrile reaction and some swelling of the lymph nodes especially the parotid lymph nodes is seen.
- Fatal cases can occur in eland possibly when immunosuppressed by toxicosis induced by very heavy infections of brown ear ticks.
- There is some speculation that the poor performance of gemsbok in the Waterberg is due to this organism.

Diagnosis

Typical, often mild, ECF-like symptoms associated with exposure to *Rhipicephalus*-infestation and the demonstration of parasites in lymphnode smears will confirm the diagnosis of theileriosis. The exact organism involved needs to be confirmed using serological or molecular characterisation techniques.

Treatment and prevention

Tick control may be necessary in heavily infested eland to prevent fatal cases.

VIRAL DISEASES OF CARNIVORES

Wild carnivores are susceptible to most of the viral diseases of domestic carnivores and they may contract these by direct or indirect contact. Captive populations are therefore at risk but free-range populations also come under threat sometimes when domestic animals make incursions into wildlife areas. The most important diseases are discussed here with the exception of rabies which is discussed under the diseases affecting a number of species.

CANINE DISTEMPER VIRUS (CDV)

Canine distemper is an extremely widespread and infectious viral disease of domestic dogs, but a range of wild canids are known to be susceptible, including wild dogs, bat-eared foxes and jackal.

In addition certain felidae and hyaenidae are also susceptible to the disease (see Table 2).

In domestic dogs distemper is a "childhood disease", affecting puppies as soon as the colostral antibodies obtained from their mother begins to fall.

Although there is no carrier state of the disease, infection is maintained in the domestic dog population due to the high density of animals and the fact that there are always susceptible hosts in the form of puppies. Susceptible dogs pick up the virus via direct contact with sick animals or through their excreta or vomit.

- After exposure to the virus dogs develop a fever that may last for 3–6 days.
- A purulent (yellow) discharge is seen from the eyes and the nose.
- The infected dog has a poor appetite and may have severe diarrhoea which leads to dehydration.
- Later in the disease the animal may develop nervous signs such as twitching, paralysis, fits and convulsions of the jaw ("chewing gum fits"). If the animal survives, the neurological signs may nevertheless persist and may interfere with the dog's normal functioning.

Table 2: Viral infections of wild carnivores

Viral disease	Species affected	Affect
Canine distemper	Wild dogs, lions, jackal, aardwolf, brown and spotted hyaena, civet, clawless otter, honey badger	Clinical infection
Canine parvo	Aardwolf, wild dog	Clinical infection
Feline parvo	Cheetah, lion, leopard, caracal, serval	Clinical infection
Feline immunosuppression virus (FIV)	Lion	Positive serology; no clinical cases
Feline rhinotracheitis (herpes)	Cheetah	Clinical infection
Feline infectious peritonitis (Fe Co)	Cheetah	Severe cases in captive animals
Feline leukemia	Cheetah	Severe cases in captive animals

- A hardening of the pads of the feet is usually an accompanying sign to the nervous symptoms. The nervous symptoms are not reversible, and permanent twitches which can impair the dog's normal functioning may persist.
- Wild canines come into contact with CDV when kept in captivity, but free-living animals can also be exposed when coming into contact with infected domestic dogs as recorded in the Serengeti. Wild dog species are highly susceptible to CDV infections and suffer heavy mortalities as seen in some captive populations of wild dogs.
- Hyenas with distemper have been shown to develop respiratory distress, nasal and ocular discharge, listlessness, bloody faeces and in-coordination. Lions with distemper suffer heavy mortalities and survivors show neurological symptoms.

Treatment

Animals suffering from distemper can be treated with antibiotics and fluid therapy, but this can reverse neurological damage caused by the virus.

Prevention

Since vaccination is the only means of prevention domestic dogs are routinely vaccinated from the age of 6–8 weeks to prevent infection. There is still however a high prevalence of the disease in dog populations which poses a threat to captive wild carnivore populations.

Modified live virus (MLV) vaccines developed for domestic dogs, which have been grown on canine or avian cell cultures, are unsuitable for some wild carnivores because they may cause the disease. Because MLVs can be dangerous, killed distemper vaccines have therefore been used because of these safety concerns but have been shown to give poor protection.

A recently developed canary-pox vectored distemper vaccine (Recombitek C4/CV – Merial) is said to be safe in wild carnivores and gives life-long immunity.

CANINE PARVO VIRUS (CPV2)

This virus of domestic dogs which emerged in 1978, is believed to have evolved from the feline parvo virus. It is a highly infectious often fatal disease in domestic dogs causing severe gastroenteritis. Canine parvo virus is highly contagious in dogs and causes a high percentage of mortalities (20–50%). The virus is shed by infected animals for a long time and is very resistant, surviving effectively in the environment. It can therefore be contracted by contact with other dogs but also with objects or infected premises. Most dogs of less than a year old are exposed to the virus.

The first symptoms of parvo virus infection are seen within 3–8 days of exposure to infection. In very young pups the virus may cause infection of the muscle of the heart (myocarditis) which will cause sudden death, although this syndrome is not very common where there is extensive vaccination coverage. The most common form of canine parvo is the gastro-intestinal form. It occurs at the age of 6–20 weeks when the maternal antibody obtained through the milk of the bitch begins to drop. Typically the pup will develop sudden listlessness, lack of appetite, fever, vomiting and diarrhoea. The faeces may contain blood.

At present there is serological evidence that the disease can spread from domestic dogs to wild dog populations (Masai-Mara), although some populations such as those in Kruger National Park and Namibia show no evidence of being exposed to the virus. Vaccination of vulnerable or valuable populations of wild dog should be done on veterinary advice.

FELINE PARVO VIRUS (FELINE PANLEUKOPENIA)

In domestic cats this virus is responsible for the very common disease called feline panleukopenia, sometimes called "cat flu". The virus is highly contagious, stable and very persistent in the environment for up to one year. As a result the disease is widespread. Kittens become infected by contact with infected cats or with an infected environment.
- With acute infections sudden death may be the only sign.
- With less acute but severe cases kittens show a high fever, depression, lack of appetite, vomiting and eventually refuse to eat. Infected cats become severely dehydrated due to the loss of fluid. There is a high mortality rate of infected kittens.
- Queens that become infected during pregnancy give birth to kittens with damage to the cerebellum, which results in permanent tremors.
- FPV causes infection of the respiratory and digestive tracts and is responsible for fairly high mortality especially in young cats.

In urban areas cats are vaccinated as a routine against the disease which has contributed to lowering its prevalence in certain areas. A wide range of wild felids are susceptible to the disease including leopard, cheetah, lynx, serval and lion.

Some zoo and wildlife experts recommend that captive juvenile felidae should be vaccinated against panleukopenia using Felovax (Fort Dodge) which has been shown to be safe. Zoo expert Fowler recommends vaccination every two weeks from 8–16 weeks with a booster given 6–12 months later, and tri-annual boosters.

FELINE IMMUNODEFICIENCY VIRUS (FIV)

This retrovirus of felines causes an immunosuppressive, chronic disease in cats similar to HIV in humans. The highest incidence of FIV occurs in free-roaming male cats since transmission occurs by biting, and not by casual contact such as sharing water bowls.
- A few weeks after infection, the cat will have a mild illness with fever and lymph node enlargement. This disappears without treatment after a week or two.
- The virus then remains dormant and the cat may remain healthy for months or years. However, when the virus becomes reactivated the cat will suffer chronic infections of the mouth, nose, and skin.
- Diarrhoea, neurological symptoms and tumours can also be seen. In domestic cats the disease is eventually fatal.

FIV infection has been detected in free-living populations of lions in South Africa, Namibia, Botswana, Zimbabwe, Kenya and Uganda. The infection appears to be benign in wild carnivores that do not develop the disease syndromes seen in domestic cats. Researchers are of the opinion that the virus evolved in Africa in lions so that existing populations are resistant. However, there is a possibility that infected felines in captivity or under stress may develop disease syndromes seen in domestic cats, but this remains to be confirmed. It is recommended that cat's sero-positive for FIV should not be introduced into sero-negative populations.

FELINE RHINOTRACHEITIS (SNUFFLES)

This is an upper respiratory infection which can be caused by a number of infectious organisms, including a herpes virus (feline infectious rhinotracheitis), calici virus, *Chlamydophila* and *Bordatella bronchiseptica*. The condition is most common where cats are kept in groups such as kennels, breeding units and hospitals.

- Early symptoms of snuffles are fever, sneezing and weepy eyes. At first the secretions from the eyes is watery, but later this becomes purulent and there may be a nasal discharge as well.
- Cats very often lose their appetite once they have blocked noses and are unable to smell. There may also be ulcerations in the mouth. They may develop sinusitis as a complication.
- Animals infected with the herpes virus are permanent carriers and will infect other cats. They may show no symptoms or sometimes a constant weeping of the eyes.

The diagnosis of snuffles is based on the vaccination history and symptoms. Only the secondary infection can be treated with antibiotics. Cleaning the eyes and nose with damp cotton wool helps to make the cat more comfortable. The eye lesions may need veterinary treatment. It can be difficult to get snuffles cases to start eating again.

As a sequel to snuffles cheetah may develop proliferative cutaneous lesions around the eyes, nose and other areas which they groom vigorously. Cryosurgery may be needed to remove these. Kittens at risk from the disease should be vaccinated with Felovax as described under feline panleukopenia.

FELINE LEUKEMIA (FELV)

This condition which is prevalent in domestic cats is caused by the feline leukemia virus. The main effects of the virus are anaemia, immune suppression and the development of tumours of the white blood cells. Infection with FeLv is most prevalent among strays or in multi-cat households since cats become infected by contact with infected cats which shed virus in the saliva, faeces, tears and urine.

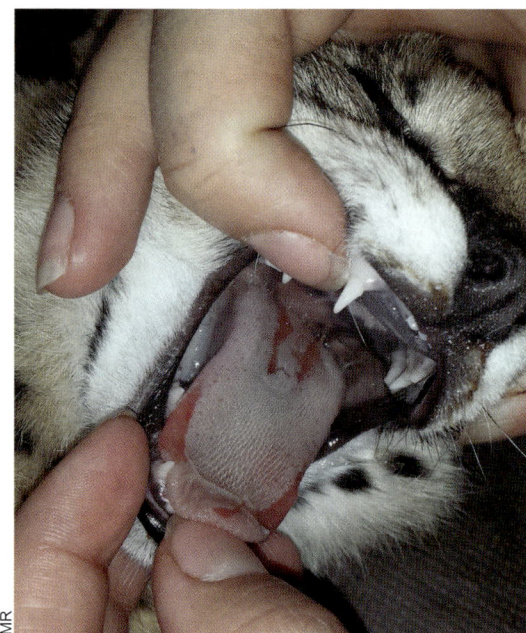

A young hand-raised serval showing calici virus ulceration of the tongue.

Cats grooming each other, sharing bowls and litter boxes will therefore allow transmission of FeLv. Kittens of infected mothers will become infected through the milk or in the uterus.

Kittens under 16 weeks are the most vulnerable since exposure to the virus after this time will cause only a transient infection which is later cleared from the system. Of the cats that become infected before 16 weeks, not all will become permanently infected. Less than one third of infected cats become persistently viraemic, shedding virus and developing clinical signs. The symptoms of FeLv are variable in frequency and severity.

- Because of the immune suppression caused by the virus infected cats develop secondary infections of the skin, eye, mouth and gums, intestines and parasite transmitted diseases.
- They develop tumours such as lymphoma, renal failure, or arthritis.
- Abortions and infertility can occur in queens infected with feline leukemia virus.

The variability of the symptoms of FeLv infection makes the disease difficult to diagnose. Serological surveys of wild felidae

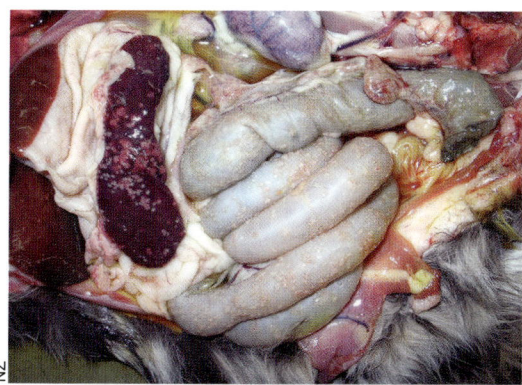
A case of feline infectious peritonitis.

in Southern Africa have shown no evidence for infection with FeLv. However, clinical cases have been seen in cheetah and the virus has been transmitted between cheetah housed together in conservation projects. It is therefore important that the serological status of cheetah be determined before new animals are introduced. Although there are vaccines available, vaccination of wild felidae is not practiced as a general rule.

FELINE CORONA VIRUSES (FECOV)/FELINE INFECTIOUS PERITONITIS (FIP)

Within this group are two closely related viruses, feline enteric corona virus which causes a mild gastroenteritis, and the corona virus which causes the clinical condition called Feline Infectious Peritonitis. Of the two, feline infectious peretonitis is the most important condition since it causes a progressive and fatal disease in domestic cats. A large number of cats become infected but only a small percentage develop the disease syndrome. It is spread by cat-to-cat contact as well as indirect contact, for example, sharing water bowls or bedding. Symptoms develop mainly in young cats less than two years of age and cats older than ten years, as well as those subjected to stress. Initially, when the cat becomes infected, there are often no signs although some cats show a mild upper respiratory infection. This passes and after this initial infection, the subsequent symptoms may take weeks or months to develop.

There are two main clinical syndromes (wet and dry), but combinations of both may also be seen.

- The wet form typically shows a distention of the abdomen owing to fluid accumulation, as well as a fluctuating fever, lack of appetite, weight loss and depression. Fluid can accumulate in the chest cavity causing breathing difficulties.
- The dry form develops more slowly, and no abdominal distension is seen. Vague signs of illness such as loss of appetite, fluctuating fever, weight loss and depression are seen. There may also be failure of the kidney and the liver. Cats with pancreatitis will manifest with vomiting and diarrhoea.
- Other manifestations are neurological and eye disease.

All these symptoms can be seen either singly or in combination, and the variability of these signs makes it difficult to diagnose the primary cause. Diagnosis is made on clinical signs and positive serology to feline corona virus.

The virus has been detected in free-living as well as captive cheetah. The disease FIP has been identified at five separate cheetah facilities as the cause of outbreaks of disease. The prevalence of disease in these cheetah colonies has been higher than is normally seen in domestic cats, with cubs under three months being most severely affected. Analysis of virus from these colonies has shown that there may be a separate cheetah CoV which has evolved.

The high susceptibility of cheetah to this virus is attributed to the narrow genetic base of the cheetah in Southern Africa. The symptoms seen in outbreaks among cheetah include peritonitis and pleuritis. A newly developed feline infectious peretonitis vaccine for cats has not yet been used in cheetah because of safety concerns.

DISEASES OF EQUINES

EQUINE INFLUENZA

Equine influenza is a highly infectious viral disease specifically adapted to equids, which causes disease in horses, donkeys, mules and zebras. The A equine 2 virus (H3N8) was introduced into South Africa in 1986 when infected horses were imported into the country. The disease spread throughout the country within a matter of weeks after infected horses were released from quarantine. The virus spreads rapidly though populations by direct contact with infected horses but also through indirect contact with instruments, clothing, human handlers and feed. It is important mainly in stud and athletic horses.

- The incubation period of equine influenza varies from 1–3 days. This short incubation period is typical of all influenza viruses and contributes to the rapid spread of infection.
- In most horses the infection is acute with a rapid onset characterised by a high temperature, coughing and clear nasal discharge. Occasionally weakness and stiffness may be seen. The infection usually clears up within 2–3 weeks if the horse is allowed to rest and given good nursing.
- However, the virus causes severe infections in young foals, old horses and horses that have some underlying respiratory illness. These horses develop a secondary pneumonia and if they survive, may need six months to recover.

Horses recovering from influenza must be rested for a few weeks to prevent permanent damage to the heart muscle. Equine influenza can be confused with the condition called equine rhinopneumonitis that is caused by a herpes virus. This condition also causes upper respiratory infection but may also cause neurological symptoms.

When equine influenza was introduced into South Africa in 1986 it was feared that

A zebra infected with equine influenza virus showing the characteristic nasal discharge.

indigenous equids, particularly the threatened mountain zebra populations, would be severely affected. However, when young zebra (*Equus quagga*) were infected experimentally they suffered a mild form of the disease from which they recovered without complications within a week or two.

EI vaccines are available for protection against the disease but it is considered unnecessary to vaccinate free-living zebra against the disease since the infection is usually uneventful. However, since foals may develop severe and sometimes fatal infections, EI vaccination could be considered for captive breeding populations of threatened populations, particularly if there is a possibility of contact with domestic horses.

AFRICAN HORSE SICKNESS (AHS)

Horse sickness, or African horse sickness, is a virus disease transmitted by *Culicoides* midges during late summer and autumn. The effects on horses are very severe, while donkeys and mules get mild infections. The disease is endemic (occurs regularly) in the Lowveld, Natal and Gauteng but may extend into other areas (non-endemic) when local conditions become favourable for the multiplication of the midge vector. The disease is reported to be absent from the interior and most of the Western Cape although outbreaks have been recorded sporadically.

The disease is prevalent in the late summer/autumn (Feb–April) when *Culicoides* midges are numerous especially during wet seasons. Low-lying areas such as valleys, vleis and rivers are midge breeding sites and will be sites of heavy attack from the insects. In the areas where the African horse sickness virus occurs it is an extremely important disease which has a mortality rate of 95% in susceptible horses.

- The incubation period is 5–7 days and there are various forms of the disease of differing severity, but in most cases there is fever, accumulation of fluid, either in the lungs ("dunkop") or under the skin ("dikkop").

Zebra species are known to circulate African horse sickness virus while showing no symptoms. Export of healthy zebra to Spain in 1986 caused a severe outbreak in the Spanish horses which took considerable efforts such as slaughter and quarantine to bring under control. Although zebra can be considered to be reservoirs for the disease, and some researchers argue that zebra should therefore not be reintroduced into southwestern areas of the Western Cape Province, donkeys and mules are also able to maintain the infection. Banning zebra will therefore not necessarily prevent the spread of the disease during favourable African horse sickness seasons.

Horses must be protected from the disease by a combination of annual vaccination and midge control during the summer months. Midge control is achieved by stabling horses from dusk to dawn or by using fly repellents registered for use in horses. The latter is especially important in young horses that have received only a few vaccinations.

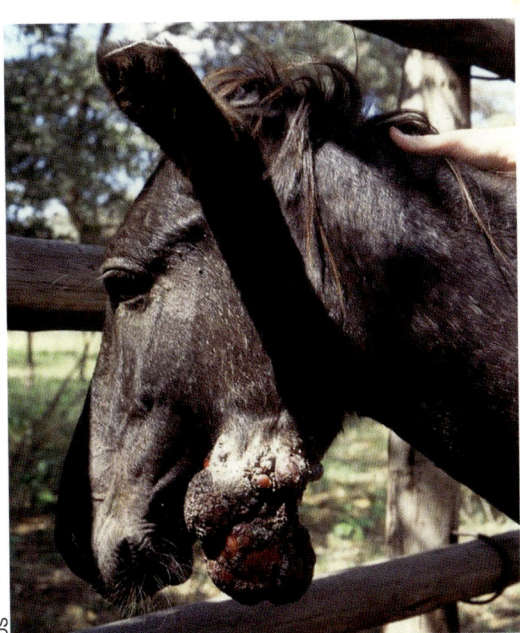
Sarcoids are viral tumours which occur in all equids and can grow to a very large size.

EQUINE SARCOIDS

Sarcoids are skin tumours found in horses, donkeys, mules and zebra. The cause is thought to be a virus, possibly a bovine papilloma virus (BP1 and 2), or a retrovirus. Transmission of the infectious agent is thought to be through skin wounds, possibly those caused by flies or sharp objects such as needles or thorns. Animals younger than four years develop the condition.

- Sarcoids can vary in form, being either flat, wart-like or rounded.
- Although they do not spread into the body they grow very rapidly, are locally invasive and can grow very large, causing great discomfort.
- They may also bleed extensively if injured. The condition occurs in certain families so it is suspected that there is a genetic predisposition to the condition.

Sarcoids have been diagnosed in plains zebra in the Kruger National Park where it is seen at a low incidence (1%) and in mountain zebra populations (*Equus zebra*) in which it occurs at a very high incidence (53%) in various national parks (Gariep and Bontebok).

The high susceptibility of the mountain zebra is probably due to their narrow genetic base, since they were bred up from the brink of extinction from a group of 30 animals. In Cape mountain zebra the lesions are seen chiefly on the ventral abdomen and limbs, and in stallions in the inguinal area in particular. Researchers at the Gariep Nature Reserve initially culled infected animals but this failed to eradicate the problem. Although some sarcoids show regression most need to be surgically excised. A toxic cream has also been used to good effect. Current research on vaccines against the condition may offer some means of protecting the vulnerable populations of Cape mountain zebra.

DISEASES OF SUIDAE (PORCINES)

AFRICAN SWINE FEVER

African swine fever is a severe disease of domestic pigs (*Sus scrofa*). The causative virus is unrelated to any other known viruses and is indigenous to Africa. The African swine fever virus (ASFV) is transmitted by argasid ticks (tampans) and wild suids, especially warthog and bushpigs to a lesser degree. The disease is currently restricted to Limpopo Province where there are state veterinary restrictions on the movements of pigs and pig meat.

The tampan *Ornithodoros porcinus porcinus* live in the walls of warthog burrows, and feed at intervals on the blood of the warthogs. The virus is maintained in a cycle between the warthog and the tampans. When warthog piglets are bitten by the tampans they become viraemic, circulating the virus in their blood for roughly three weeks although they do not develop disease. When warthog come into contact with domestic pigs, the latter develop the disease.

The pigs probably become infected through the tampans carried by the warthog, rather than by direct contact.

- After exposure to the virus (5–15 days later) domestic pigs develop a fever, listlessness, anorexia, lack of coordination and convulsions.
- There may be reddening and then a blue discolouration of the skin, and haemorrhages may also be seen.
- Bloody diarrhoea may occur followed by coma and death.

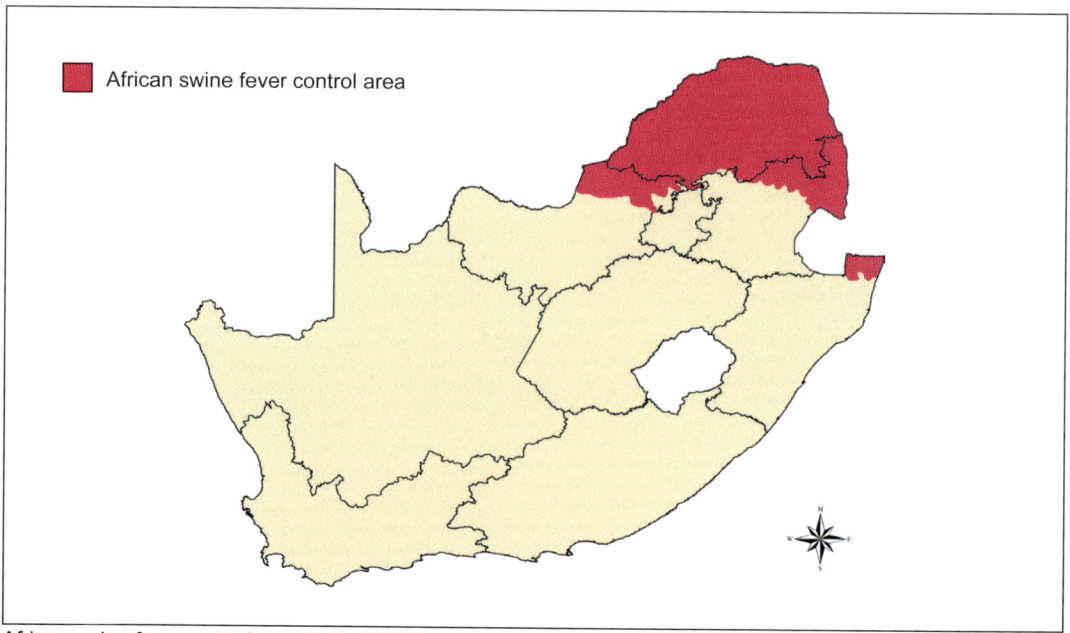

African swine fever control area in South Africa.

Tampans live in warthog holes and are the source of African swine fever virus attacking domestic piglets.

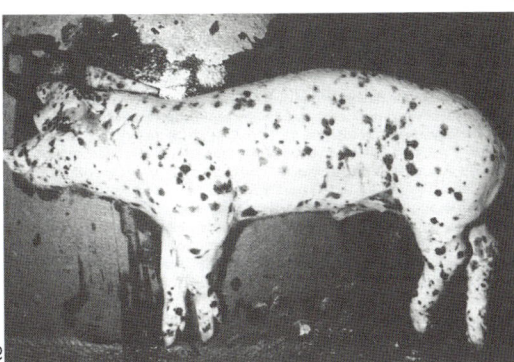
Hog cholera in domestic pigs causes severe disease.

The disease spreads extremely rapidly in domestic piggeries, and causes almost 100% mortalities. The only control measure is to quarantine the premises and slaughter out infected pigs. The African swine fever virus survives in uncooked meat for a period of time and can therefore serve as a source of infection to domestic pigs when fed in swill. It is therefore compulsory to cook swill fed to pigs for 60 minutes. There is no treatment for African swine fever.

In other parts of Africa where feral domestic pigs are kept as a food source, the virus has become endemic (adapted) and these pigs develop subclinical disease with few observable symptoms. This is hampering attempts by these poorer countries to raise domestic pigs more intensively for food production to meet increasing food demands.

In order to prevent the virus becoming endemic in South Africa in feral and domestic pigs, the state veterinary authorities impose restrictions on the movement of wild pigs and their meat in and out of the controlled area.
- Trophies of wild pigs must be dipped for 60 seconds in acaricide to kill off any tampans which could transmit the disease.
- A permit must be obtained for moving wild pigs, wild pig meat and wild pig trophies out of an area.

HOG CHOLERA/CLASSICAL SWINE FEVER

Hog cholera or classical swine fever is a viral disease of pigs which is unrelated to African swine fever. It is a highly contagious disease which can manifest in a range of forms, from acute to clinically inapparent, and the mortality varies from 0–100% depending on various factors. The symptoms are therefore variable depending on the form. Transmission occurs by direct contact between sick and healthy pigs, indirect contact through clothing, equipment or vehicles, or via the feeding of infected swill.

The disease was introduced to South Africa from Europe in 1903, and was eradicated by destroying all infected pigs. It was reintroduced here 87 years later in 2005 and became established in feral pigs in the Eastern Cape.

Epidemiology

Wild boar in Europe are persistently infected with hog cholera, and contact between boars and pigs cause outbreaks of disease. Experimental infection of wild suids in South Africa have revealed that both species can circulate the virus and bushpig can contract very severe clinical disease. Both species can potentially be infected and may act as reservoirs of the disease. So far no natural infection of these species have been reported in the Eastern Cape.

Symptoms

The symptoms of hog cholera are variable due to the variety of forms which can occur.
- In acute cases there is fever, dullness and reluctance to move.
- Reddening of the skin occurs which later progresses to purple discoloration.
- Later haemorrhages are seen on the skin causing a spotted appearance.
- Runny eyes and nose, shivering, diarrhoea and convulsions can also be seen.
- The pig usually dies within 10–20 days. In chronic, subacute and inapparent forms of the disease the animals survive for between 30–100 days. The virus survives in meat and outbreaks can therefore be caused by feeding infected swill.

Treatment

There is no treatment for classical swine fever.

Control

Testing and slaughtering out of infected pigs was the method used to control the spread of the outbreak in the Eastern Cape in 2005. Authorities have now announced that the outbreak is under control, allowing the controlled area to be minimised.

IMPORTANT PARASITES OF GAME ANIMALS

Introduction: How wild animals cope with parasites

Parasites are extremely common in nature to the extent that every animal on earth has a number of species that have adapted to live in or on them. Zoologists believe that sexual reproduction evolved as a strategy to resist parasites since it provides more genetic variation than asexual cloning, and therefore the possibility of more defence mechanisms.

Wild animals use various strategies to counter parasites. Some species use mechanical means such as the friction of rolling, mud-bathing and grooming. Impala use their teeth to effectively remove external parasites from their coat. Some animals allow other individuals to groom them. In savanna areas oxpeckers (*Buphagus* spp.) have exploited the ecological niche of tick infestation on large herbivores. Each bird eats roughly 400 adult ticks per day and therefore have a significant impact on the breeding potential of these parasites. Some animals counter external parasites by an immune reaction: Wildebeest are known to have innate (inborn) resistance to certain species of ticks, which only breaks down when the animals are diseased or stressed. Buffalo, like indigenous cattle, can acquire resistance to certain tick species on exposure, so individuals raised under tick-free conditions will initially be susceptible to ticks.

Internal parasites can be prevented from infecting an animal by an innate immune response, or an acquired immune response after exposure. The immune responses will, for example, block worm larvae by trapping them in the skin, or by preventing attachment to the gut mucosa. These immune abilities are genetic and specific to certain worm species. Resistant animals are therefore selected under natural conditions. Although some internal parasites are able to evade the immune response, from an evolutionary perspective the parasites which are the best adapted to the host will be the most successful since a healthy host is a better food source. Some hosts are able to tolerate parasites, sometimes in enormous numbers, if the parasite does minimal harm or the host is able to compensate for the drain on its resources. A dramatic example of this is seen in zebra, which are able to have massive burdens (42 million) of the roundworm *Probstmayria* and still remain healthy by being in a constant state of red blood cell production,

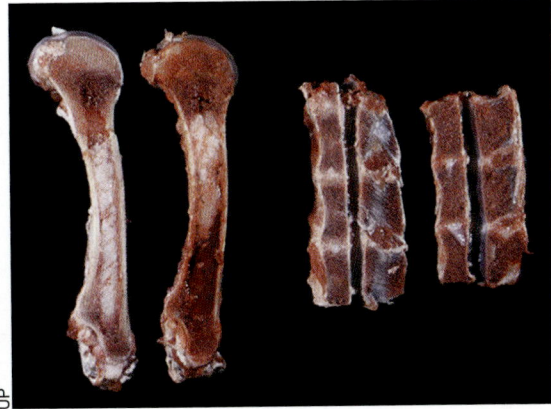

Healthy zebra can survive huge burdens of bloodsucking worms (left) by being in a constant state of red blood cell production, which results in the fat in the bone marrow cavity being replaced by haemopoetic tissue (right).

which prevents anaemia developing. Parasitism is therefore a natural phenomenon in wild animals and applies selection pressure on animal populations to remain resistant. With this in mind it is theoretically undesirable to treat free-living wild animals, unless the animal needs to be transported or bred in captive situations where they cannot move away from a heavily infected environment.

Internal parasites (worms) of wildlife

The biology of internal parasites in free-living animals is complex and is still being unravelled. Preliminary studies have shown that many worm species are host-limited as well as geographically restricted while others may infect more than one host and are widespread.

Other factors which affect the dispersion of worm parasites are climate, feeding habits (grazing vs browsing in antelope), and seasonal effects. In general most internal parasites are host-adapted as a result of being immune to, or other factors. Free-living animals therefore tend not to develop clinical symptoms as a result of worm infections. However, the status of the animal may cause fluctuations in the level of infection: For example, the stress of pregnancy, or presence of disease and injury can predispose animals to heavy worm burdens.

Any factor such as cold, drought, and poor nutrition which may affect the animal's immune system can cause an increase in parasite numbers. Human intervention creates conditions which are favourable for high levels of worm infestation by confining of game in camps, allowing contact with livestock and transporting animals.

For a more detailed discussion see the chapter on helminths of wildlife in *Veterinary Helminthology for South Africa*.

Control of worms in wild animals

Chemical control of internal parasites (use of anthelmintics) in wild animals should always be done under veterinary supervision for the following reasons:
- The active ingredient used must be suitable for the specific parasite.
- The wormer must be safe for use in the target species.
- The regime used must be in compliance with recognised sustainable use principles or "best principles" in order to prevent the development of resistance (see under haemonchosis in antelope).

There are three main groups of internal parasites or worms which affect wild animals: roundworms, trematodes, tapeworms.

ROUNDWORMS (NEMATODES)

Roundworms are cylindrically shaped worms which can either have a direct or indirect life cycle. These worms are mainly found in the gastro-intestinal tract although some may lodge in other organs such as the lungs. Many roundworms attach to mucosa of the gastro-intestinal tract where they suck blood, but some absorb nutrients from the gut cavity or the organ in which they have lodged.

The symptoms caused by roundworms will depend on the specific worm since each has its own particular route of migration and final site where they choose to live.

Roundworms occur in all free-living animals, sometimes in enormous numbers. They are generally more numerous in areas with higher rainfall. For example, kudu sampled in Kruger National Park showed roundworm burdens of 2 251 worms each, while those sampled in Etosha and the Eastern Cape showed burdens of only 289–399 worms per animal.

Roundworms can be species specific or they can be group specific: For example, *Haemonchus vegliai* is a roundworm which is found in many browsing antelope, while *Lasiostrongylus* is found in grazing animals. In general the average worm burden found in browsers is lower (8 000) than in grazers (20 000) because the feeding habits of grazers expose them more effectively to infective larvae. Despite these massive sounding worm burdens, as far as is known these seldom cause mortalities under free-living conditions although the resistance is lowered under stress conditions – for example, impala have been shown to have increased burdens from a normal load of 20 000 to 60 000 during drought conditions. This resistance is most likely as a result of natural selection which will favour animals that are resistant to roundworms. In contrast domestic animals that live in confined spaces are exposed to high numbers of worms and are selected for their production characteristics rather than parasite resistance. Roundworm infestations are therefore most often a cause for concern in animals in intensive farming systems or those raised in captivity. It must be borne in mind that frequent, unnecessary medication of free-living animals can lead to loss of host resistance, wastage of remedies and possibly the selection of anthelminthic resistant parasites if animals are intensively medicated. Resistant worm strains can also be introduced when buying new animals or can be transferred from domestic stock to valuable game animals.

Roundworm resistance to worm remedies is currently a huge problem in certain valuable species such as sable and roan (see discussion under *Haemonchus* for further details).

TREMATODES (FLUKES)

Flukes are worms which are found near water sources such as dams and vleis or even leaky water troughs, because their intermediate host is an aquatic snail. A larval stage of the fluke develops in the snail which then release an infective larval stage into water and the pasture then becomes contaminated.

Liver flukes (*Fasciola hepatica* and *F. gigantica*): found in wet areas such as vleis and dams where they infect livestock and certain wildlife species. After ingestion of the infective stage by the host, young flukes migrate through the liver to the bile ducts where they suck blood causing anaemia and damage to the liver. Clinical signs seen in affected animals: anaemia, weakness, loss of weight. In heavy infestations – death due to massive haemorrhage in the liver tissue.

Conical fluke (*Callicophoron*): found in the rumen where it can cause severe diarrhoea.

Bilharzia parasites (*Schistosoma*): are flukes which are commonly found in wildlife species in the lowveld. They lodge in the blood vessels of the host where cardiovascular problems such as thrombosis can occur.

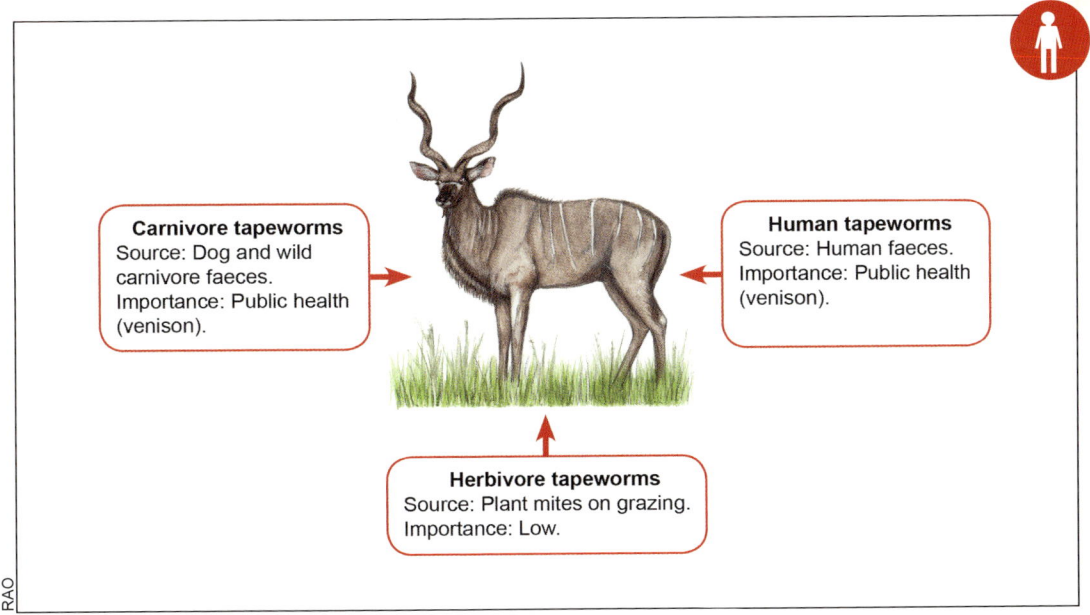

The importance of tapeworms for wild herbivores and humans.

TAPEWORMS (CESTODES)

In the adult form these worms are ribbon-like, segmented worms that can vary in size depending on the species from a few millimeters to a few meters long. They have an indirect life cycle, in which the immature or larval form (cyst) is carried by an intermediate host which is eaten by the main or definitive host. This host is the one in which the adult tapeworm develops in the intestine. There are three main groups of tapeworms which may be encountered in game animals, namely herbivore, carnivore and human tapeworms.

Herbivore tapeworms: Grazers, when they feed, also ingest tiny grass mites which are the intermediate hosts of a number of tapeworms. Once in the stomach of the herbivore the larvae of the tapeworm hatch and grow into adult tapeworms. Although species such as *Moniezia benedini*, *M. expansa*, and *Avittelina* are common in antelope in South Africa, no clinical disease has ever been seen, even in young animals in which they are prevalent.

Carnivore tapeworms: These are tapeworms which occur in the intestine of wild and domestic carnivores without causing their hosts any adverse reactions. They shed the tapeworm eggs in their faeces which are picked up by herbivores, either domestic livestock or wild herbivores. Once ingested by the herbivore the larval form of the tapeworm develops, usually in the form of a bladder-like structure or cyst. The herbivore intermediate host is usually not affected, unless for example as in the case of *Taenia multiceps* which lodges in the brain and can cause nervous symptoms ("gid") in small stock and antelope like sable (see under Nervous system). *Echinococcus* spp. which develop in the liver can infect humans causing hydatid disease, a condition in which the cysts cause problems in the lungs and liver.

Human tapeworms (*Taenia saginata* and *Taenia solium*): Two tapeworm species occur in the intestine of humans, *T. saginata* and *T. solium*. Because they grow very large they absorb large amounts of nutrients from the gut and can cause malnutrition especially in children. Cattle and pigs become infected when their grazing is contaminated with human faeces, and there are reports of blue wildebeest, gemsbok and eland being infested with the measles or cysts of *Taenia saginata* on slaughter. This is a serious problem for game ranchers supplying venison to the market.

A more serious consequence is that these worms can auto-infest humans, in other words the eggs which they shed in the faeces can be ingested, and the developing larval forms lodge in important organs such as the brain (human neurocysticercosis) and liver. Neurocysticercosis (NCC) is one of the most important causes of epilepsy in young children in South Africa, especially in the rural areas of the Eastern Cape.

Humans usually become infected with these tapeworms when eating the immature cysts of the tapeworms in meat, sometimes called "measles" or "pearly pork" (*T. saginata* in beef and *T. solium* in pork). "Measly" pork or beef is condemned at abattoirs because of the public health threat posed by these cysts.

SPECIFIC WORMS OF IMPORTANCE

Some specific worms of importance or interest to game farmers are discussed below. For a complete review of helminths of wildlife see Boomker in *Veterinary Helminthology for South Africa*.

Haemonchus roundworms of antelope

Haemonchus spp., also known as wireworms, are bloodsuckers which can cause severe anaemia and death in herbivores. While wild herbivores are known to be host to various *Haemonchus* species, a serious problem is experienced in intensively farmed valuable species such as sable and roan antelope with *H. contortus*, the wireworm of small stock. Although the worm can usually be effectively treated with anthelmintic remedies, a number of stud breeders have been affected by anthelmintic resistant *H. contortus* strains. This

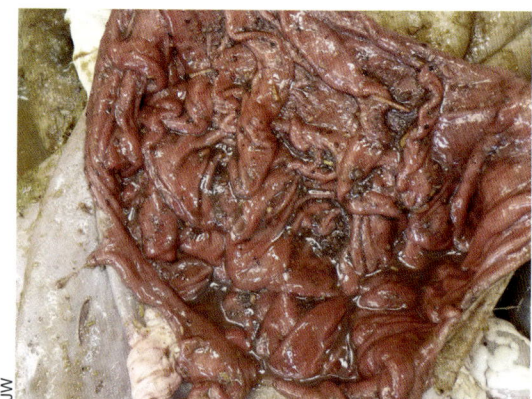

The abomasum of a sable with haemonchosis showing severe congestion.

is a major cause for concern because there are some multi-resistant strains that may spill over from livestock into game and which are untreatable with all the available registered remedies. It is not known whether the infecting *H. contortus* strains of antelope became resistant initially due to poor management by game ranchers themselves, or whether the resistant strains were acquired by contact with small stock. Whatever the source, this problem presents a threat to other farmers of these valuable species because the resistant *H. contortus* can be acquired by buying infected stock. The game farmer must therefore prevent introduction by doing the following, in conjunction with the veterinarian:

- Ensure that antelope are treated and are free of infection before they are introduced onto the farm.
- Avoid contact with livestock, especially those regularly dosed with anthelmintics.
- Dose only when worm egg counts are very high and may possibly affect the health of the animals.
- Do not move treated animals to clean camps until a few weeks after dosing.
- Rotate camps to reduce build-up of infective worm stages which are a hazard in particular for pregnant females and young.
- Ensure camp hygiene, rotate feeding sites if possible and fix all leaking water points.

- Failure to use these "best principles" may cause long term problems of worm resistance in *Haemonchus* spp.

Future developments

A vaccine which has been developed for the control of *Haemonchus contortus* in livestock may be of use in controlling infections in valuable antelope. It is expected that Wirevax will be registered in South Africa soon.

Lungworms in antelope

There are a variety of nematodes that occur in the bronchi and lungs of antelope and wildebeest. Some of these occur commonly in a species but have never been seen to cause clinical problems.

The nematodes *Dictyocaulus africana, D. filaria, D. viviparus* and *Bronchonema magna* occur in the bronchi and trachea of a variety of antelopes. The worms may cause bronchitis, the symptoms of which are coughing, difficult breathing, typically with an extended neck.

Bronchonema magna is considered non-pathogenic for springbok, its natural host. However, when springbok were introduced into the Bontebok National Park near Swellendam, bontebok became infected and mortalities occurred.

Pneumostrongylus calcaratus in impala is common without causing clinical disease while mortalities in bontebok have been recorded as a result of *P. cornigerus* infection. *Protostrongylus capensis* of bontebok and *P. etoshai* of blue wildebeest and gemsbok, respectively, have been found but in the absence of disease.

Worms in the liver of herbivores

Hippopotamus are commonly infected with liver fluke due to them grazing around rivers and vleis where the parasites occur.
- Fluke infestation has also been described in elephant, and certain antelope but

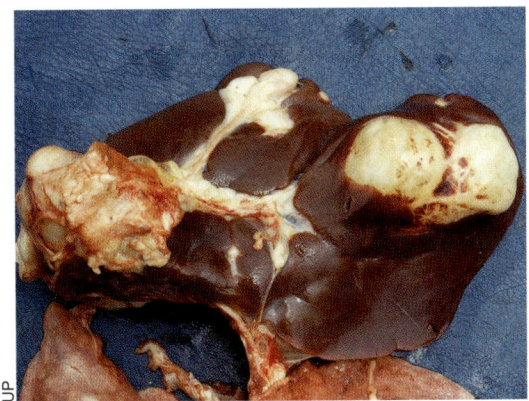
Hydatid cysts of *Echinococcus granulosus* in the liver.

free-living wild species apparently rarely develop clinical signs.
- Animals with clinical liver fluke infestation develop anaemia and a severe diarrhoea.

Treatment can be considered if the condition is diagnosed in valuable animals, but veterinary consultation is essential since some of the flukicides are toxic for herbivores.

The cysts of canine tapeworms are sometimes found in the livers of herbivores. These cysts do not affect the health of the herbivore hosts but those of *Echinococcus granulosus* can be a danger to human health.

Prevent reinfection of carnivores on the farm by feeding infected livers to dogs, by thorough cooking or disposal in sealed drums until the material has decomposed. All domestic dogs and cats on game farms should be regularly dosed. The dewormer used must contain the active ingredient praziquantel.

Worms that infect the cardio-vascular system (blood and heart)

Eleaphora saggita: *Eleaphora saggita* is a filarial worm that infects the arteries in some herbivores such as kudu, bushbuck and buffalo. The presence of the worms in the blood vessels causes aneurysms. Under stress conditions such as the transport of antelope, these aneurysms may cause fatalities.

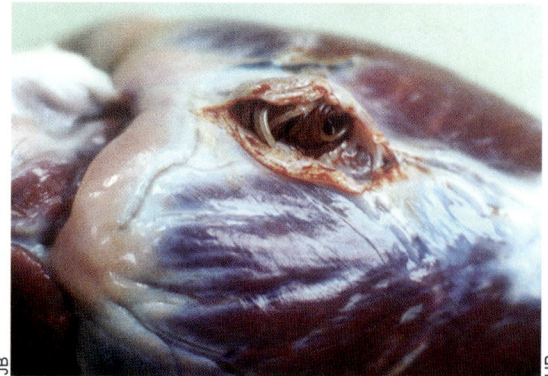
The filarial worm *Eleaphora* in the coronary artery of a kudu.

Human tapeworm cysts (*Taenia saginata*) in herbivore muscle.

Bilharzia (*Schistosoma* sp.): The adult bilharzia worm occurs in the blood vessels of the host where it sucks blood. Many wild ungulates in the Lowveld are apparently infected with biharzia parasites without them causing significant clinical signs. They have also been seen in other species, such as baboons. Humans, however, develop clinical bilharzia, the symptoms dependent on the parasite species.

Worms in the muscles of herbivores

The muscles of herbivores such as antelope and pigs can contain the cysts of carnivore tapeworms, most commonly the *Taenia* spp. which are commonly associated with free-living wildlife (*T. hyaena*, *T. regis*, *T. gonyamai*, and *T. hydatidgena*).

More recently the tapeworm cysts of *T. saginata* have been found in wild antelope species, which since they can cause infection in humans, is of concern. It is essential to prevent contamination of grazing with human faeces by making use of toilets for staff and all visitors The control of human tapeworms on game ranches is very important because it can affect the market value of venison and biltong, and is also a threat to the health of farm inhabitants.

Prevent infections on the farm by providing toilets for staff and casual workers on the property. Human faeces deposited in the veld should be buried so that they cannot contaminate grazing. Encourage staff to be dewormed for tapeworms at local clinics by explaining the importance of the infection and the health benefits.

Worms affecting the central nervous system

The cyst or larval form of *Taenia multiceps* has been recorded as causing the clinical condition known as "gid" in a sable. In this condition the cyst lodges in the brain and if it grows sufficiently large it causes nervous symptoms, which are typically loss of balance, high stepping, blindness, holding the head to one side and paralysis. Some veterinarians have achieved success with treatment of these cases by giving large doses of praziquantel.

SKIN CONDITIONS IN GAME SPECIES

Filarial worms which lodge under the skin and cause tissue damage have been reported in some wildlife species. *Parafilaria* have been reported to infest buffalo and *Stephanofilaria* is seen in rhino in the eastern parts of South Africa, causing similar conditions referred to as

Left: A sable with a *Taenia multiceps* cyst in the brain showing abnormal behaviour (loss of fear of humans).
Top: *Parafilaria bassoni*-lesion in a buffalo.

"summer sores". The lesion is a wound which oozes blood and can be further enlarged by oxpeckers.

In buffalo and rhino blood spots will be noticed in the live animal when it is captured, or at slaughter when the animal is skinned the worm may be seen under the skin, or the "bruising" of the surrounding tissue may be seen. The condition is not life-threatening but may cause wounds which are unsightly and can become secondarily infected. The infestation can be treated using injectable ivermectin, but this must be done under veterinary advice as ivermectin may be toxic in some species such as rhino.

The filarial worm *Onchocerca* is a common cause of lumps under the skin in buffalo but these are of no clinical importance.

Various cysts of the carnivore tapeworms such as *T. multiceps* may be found under the skin of a variety of antelope.

INTESTINAL WORMS IN CARNIVORES

There are two important roundworm species of carnivores which can be problematic in captive animals. Hookworms (*Ancylostoma* spp.) are smallish worms with a direct lifecycle. Newborn puppies and kittens pick these up either through the milk of their mothers or from the faeces of other animals in their surroundings.

These hookworms, which develop in the small intestine, are bloodsuckers which can cause severe, sometimes fatal anaemia in young animals. Ascarid worms are large roundworms with a direct lifecycle, found in canines and felines.

In canines transmission takes place through the placenta and so the worms are found in the small intestine of puppies as young as one week old. They are also transmitted from the mother to the newborns through the milk. Infection with ascarids will cause poor growth, loss of condition, dull coats and a pot belly. These worms are passed in the faeces or vomited up. To prevent problems with these worms in captive carnivores, females should be dewormed before they whelp and puppies need regular deworming. Note that both the larvae of hookworm and ascarid worm can potentially cause infestations in humans because they can migrate through the skin and internal organs.

There are safe and effective combination dewormers for roundworms and tapeworms which can be used for regular deworming of carnivores, but a veterinarian should be consulted since some remedies are toxic in certain species (nitroscanate in felines and piperazine in cheetah).

For the control of carnivore tapeworms the remedy must contain praziquantel for effective control (see later). A veterinarian will also rec-

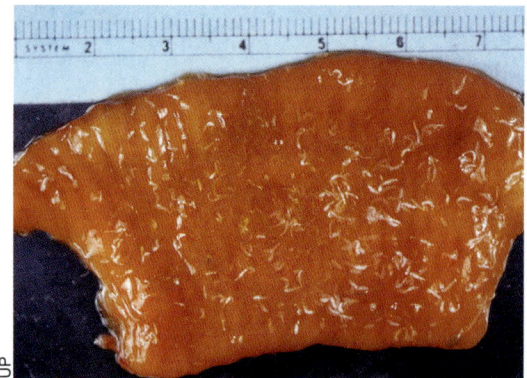

Carnivore tapeworms in the intestine of the host (*T. multiceps*).

ommend an appropriate schedule for the effective control of roundworms. Generally breeding females are dewormed a few weeks before giving birth to prevent transmission to their offspring. The newborns are then dewormed at the age of three weeks, and thereafter every second week until they are two months old. The deworming intervals can then be gradually increased as the animals get older to once every six months.

There is a wide range of carnivore tapeworms which mostly do not cause any clinical disease in the main host. Humans may become infected with *E. granulosus*, the cause of hydatid disease, when handling live carnivores, their intestines, or faeces.

Hydatid disease results from the cysts developing in the liver or lungs, where they cause problems. If humans become infected with *T. multiceps* the larval cysts which develop in the brain can cause nervous symptoms if they are large enough. *T. multiceps* can also cause brain cysts in antelope resulting in "gid" or draaisiekte (see also under central nervous system of antelope)

TRICHINELLA and HUMAN HEALTH

Trichinosis (*Trichinella* spp.)

This roundworm species occurs in many areas of the world, where it infests mainly wild carnivores and wild pigs. The adult worm occurs in the intestine of the animal and its larval stages are found in the muscle tissue of the same animal. In the Kruger National Park the cysts of the worms have been found

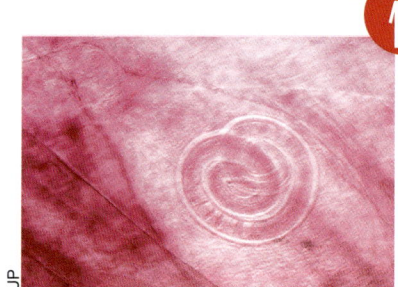

Trichinella worms in the gut of a dog.

in the muscles of species such as hyaena, lion, jackal, mice, civet and warthog, without causing any symptoms. The main significance of trichinellosis is for public health. When humans ingest raw or improperly cooked infected meat, the worms hatch and cause intestinal infections, swelling of the muscles especially of the face, headache, muscular pains, respiratory symptoms and sometimes death. Although the condition has not been identified outside the Kruger National Park, the concern is that the worm can enter domestic pigs where it can become established as a human health hazard. To prevent this, raw offal originating from any species should never be fed to pigs. Currently the main risk to humans is from eating raw warthog meat. Although freezing and drying (biltong) infested meat has been shown to reduce the infectivity of meat these processes are not always successful. It should be noted that infested meat cannot be identified at meat inspection because the cysts are microscopic in size. Diagnosis of suspected infestation of meat must therefore be done using serology or histopathology.

EXTERNAL PARASITES OF WILDLIFE

TICKS

Ticks are eight-legged arthropods closely related to mites, which have various stages in the lifecycle. The tiny newly hatched six-legged larvae or "pepper ticks" feed, moult and develop into eight-legged nymphae, which after feeding, moult and become sexually mature adults which search for mates.

All stages are bloodsucking although the adult female takes a massive meal becoming engorged in order to lay her eggs, which in some species can reach enormous numbers (20 000). Ticks are seasonal breeders that breed during hot wet seasons. The paralysis tick is an exception being most active in autumn and winter. Tick species may spend their lives on one host, or may drop off and feed on other hosts between immature stages. Based on this feeding behaviour they are referred to as one-host, two-host or three-host ticks.

Many of the two- and three-host immature stages feed on small mammals or birds, while the adults prefer larger animals such as antelope or larger mammals. There are 200 known species of tick in sub-Saharan Africa, 37 of which occur in South Africa. Only a small number are vectors of disease or secrete toxins. The vast majority of ticks feed on wild animals, including large and small mammals, birds and reptiles. It is therefore not surprising that wildlife species have developed strategies for defence against heavy tick burdens. In general, ticks that occur in the animal's natural range are generally well tolerated, sometimes in large numbers as long as the property is large enough.

Large herbivores, like buffalo and giraffe, are considered to be multipliers of certain tick species, since they are favoured by the adults. Ticks will become problematic on small

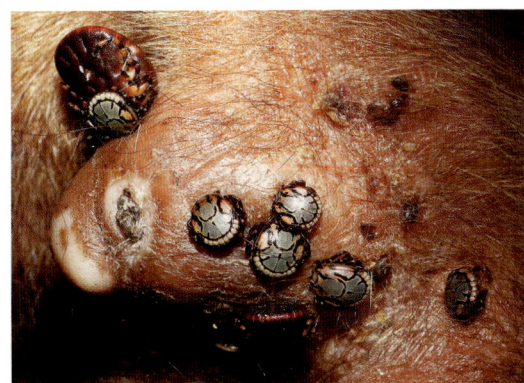

Engorged *Amblyomma hebraeum* or bont ticks.

or overstocked properties giving rise to large tick populations. Most healthy large antelope and equids can harbour large burdens without problems. These large herbivores are the preferred hosts of the adult ticks while small antelope, small mammals and birds are favoured by the immature stages.

A few important tick species are discussed below.

The bont tick (*Amblyomma hebraeum*)

The bont tick adult is large with strong, biting mouthparts that cause deep wounds in the skin, which may result in abscessation or tissue damage.

Bont ticks are also vectors of the disease heartwater (*Rickettsia ruminantium*) which causes fatalities in livestock and some game animals. Species like eland, black wildebeest and springbok that do not occur naturally in the bushveld may become heavily parasitised and are susceptible to heartwater.

Bont ticks are three-host ticks which need a specific microclimate, so are found in the north and eastern parts of South Africa and are absent from the open grasslands of the highveld.

The immatures feed on small animals such as guinea fowl, scrub hares and tortoises which may be reservoirs for the heartwater organism. Adults and nymphs feed on large

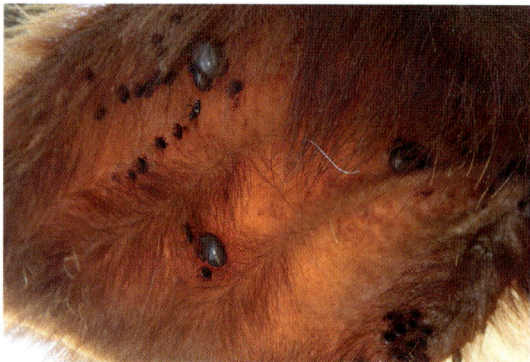 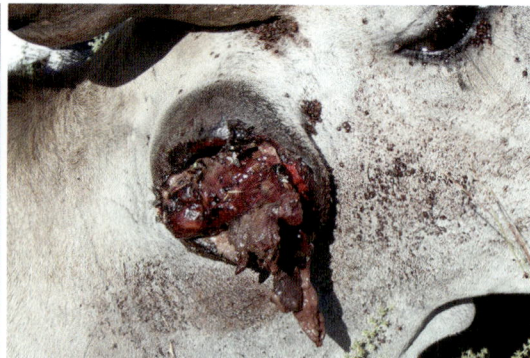

Left: Heavy infestation of brown ear tick (*Rhipicephalus* sp.). Right: Tissue damage cause such as ear loss in susceptible species such as eland (right).

mammals, which act as multipliers of this specific species. When male adult bont ticks attach to their antelope or livestock hosts they give off a pheromone which attracts others and causes clustering of ticks at one site on an infested animal. This behaviour and their long mouthparts result in abscesses developing at the site of their attachment. Bont ticks become troublesome on small properties where certain species, like eland, become heavily parasitised.

Paralysis tick (*Ixodes rubicundus*)

This tick occurs in the Karoo and arid areas of the Eastern, Western and Northern Cape, Free State and small foci in Gauteng and Mpumalanga provinces. It is typically found in hilly, rocky areas where wild olive trees (*Olea africana*), besembos (*Rhus erosa*) and clumps of mountain wire grass (*Merxmuellera disticha*) create the ideal habitat for the small mammal hosts of these ticks, namely elephant shrews and red rock rabbits.

Ixodes ticks are susceptible to dessication and are usually found on the cooler southern slopes of hills or ridges. Paralysis ticks moult from the nymphal stage emerging as adults in the autumn, in response to the first spells of cold weather in May, and may be active until July. The adult ticks attach to their final hosts which are either antelope or livestock species such as sheep, goats or calves, usually on the lower parts of the body – the legs, belly and inguinal areas. The female ticks produce a toxin which is released into the bloodstream of the host when they feed, which results in paralysis. Affected animals initially show lameness or weakness, and then move with difficulty, finally being forced to lie down. The animals usually die unless the paralysis ticks are removed. In livestock the condition can be controlled by applying tick remedies preventatively.

Correct veld management, specifically the prevention of overgrazing, will reduce the numbers of paralysis tick in a game ranching situation.

Brown ear ticks (*Rhipicephalus* spp.)

These ticks occur in the northern and eastern bushveld areas (*Rhip. appendiculatus*) and the fynbos regions of the Western and Eastern Cape (*Rhip. nitens*) respectively. They are three-host ticks, whose larvae and nymphae feed on small ruminants, carnivores and hares.

Adults feed on medium to large ruminants including buffalo, eland, nyala bulls, kudu, and sable which can have heavy burdens. These ticks feed more quickly than other tick species, completing their meal within four rather than seven days. They can therefore attain huge numbers in summer seasons. Their attachment site of choice is the inside of the ear, which can be covered with feeding brown ear ticks. Heavy brown ear tick infestations in the ear can cause severe damage, resulting in bleeding, and secondary screwworm infestation which may finally result in the loss of the ear in some animals. Eland and springbok kept in the bushveld develop heavy infestations particularly when large antelope are kept on small properties, or when there is overstocking with large antelope species or when the species are unsuitable for the area. Brown ear ticks are also the transmitters of the theilerial diseases.

Red-legged ticks (*Rhipecephalus evertsi*).

Red-legged tick (*Rhipicephalus evertsi evertsi*)

These two-host ticks have a wide distribution in South Africa, being present in almost all areas except for the arid west. As the name indicates they can be identified by the bright orange red legs and the male tick has a red outline along the scutum. All stages of this tick prefer wild and domestic equids, but also feed on ruminant livestock and a wide range of antelope. Larvae attach in the ear canal and may therefore not be obvious to the observer, while adults feed under the tail around the anus, the axillae and sternum. They can be active throughout the year in warm areas.

Rhip. evertsi evertsi ticks become infected with *Theileria hippotragi*, the parasites which cause clinical theileriosis in young roan and sable calves. Control of the disease in small-camp breeding systems is aimed at reducing tick exposure of the calves by camp rotation and/or pour-on application on calves shortly after birth (see *Theileria hippotragi*).

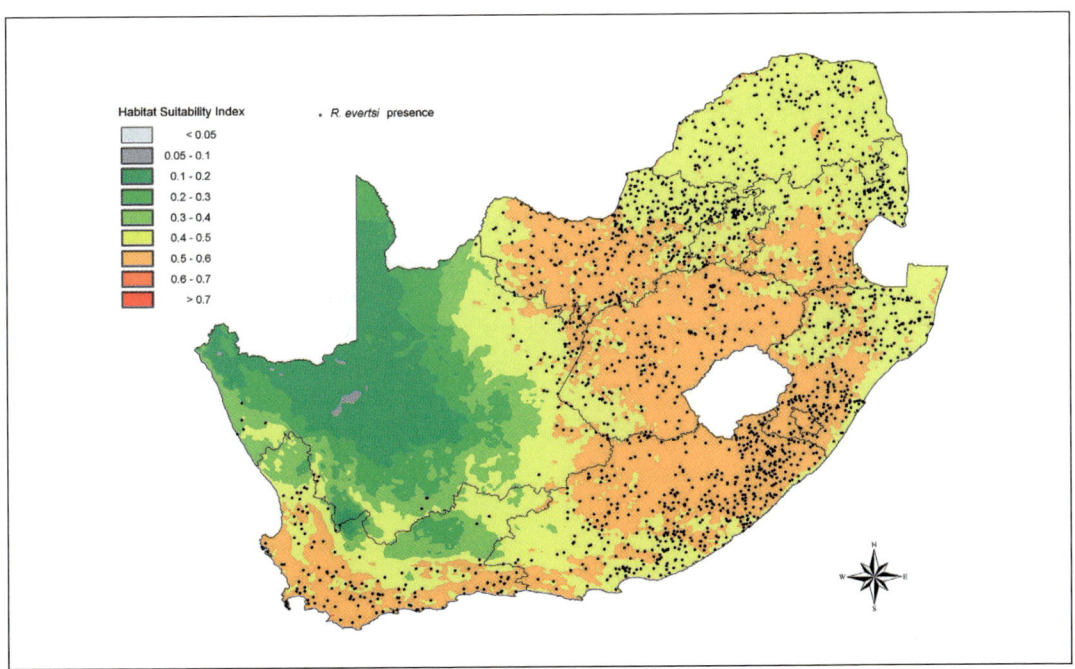

Distribution of red-legged ticks (*Rhipecephalus evertsi*)

Blue ticks (*Boophilus decolaratus* spp.)

These are one-host ticks with a mainly easterly distribution across South Africa, because they are active in warm summer months and dependant on moisture for their multiplication. The immature stages and males are small, insignificant ticks but the engorged females are relatively large, bluish-coloured ticks, hence the common name. The larvae, nymphae and adults all feed on only one animal unlike the two and three-host ticks.

Blue ticks have a preference for cattle but commonly occur in large numbers on wild ungulates including zebra, impala, bushbuck, kudu, eland and sable.

Because they are one-host ticks blue ticks are easier to control on cattle by dipping but also have a higher frequency of developing resistance against tick remedies. They are the vectors of babesiosis in ungulates, but control on wild life is not warranted since animals should be exposed to the ticks on a regular basis to allow them to maintain their immunity to this disease (see Babesiosis section under Diseases).

TICK CONTROL METHODS ON WILDLIFE

As explained before, the more natural the conditions on a game farm with respect to size, suitability to the area, correct stocking rate, good veld management and the presence of large predators, the less tick control will be needed, and the less controls used the better to ensure that animals retain their tick resistance capabilities. However, some property owners have to use some form of tick control when burdens are very high. For example, in the Waterberg game owners implement tick control to prevent eland acquiring heavy burdens which can cause severe local damage to tissues and developing of tick-borne diseases.

Direct application of tick remedies on various game species should be done in consultation with the veterinarian, since only a few are registered for use in game species and some remedies are toxic in certain species. A few of the available methods for tick control on game ranches are discussed below. Bear in mind that dips used in applicators in areas where oxpeckers occur must be non-toxic for birds (see below). Some of the applicators available for tick control in wildlife are discussed below.

Duncan Applicator and AppliGator

These two applicators are designed to deliver a pyrethroid pour-on which can disperse effectively on the surface of the skin. The pour-on is circulated down a central rod set in a drum in which lick is placed to attract the animal. Animals are therefore forced to rub against the dip covered central rod when taking the lick and therefore pick up the dip on the skin in the process. The limitations of the applicator are that the dose size and frequency of application cannot be controlled.

"Tick off" applicator

The Tick Off applicator is a buried electronic scale with a dispenser which measures out the requisite amount of pour-on according to the animal's weight. The applicator is placed in a gap such as in a hedge through which the animal walks, attracted by water or lick. Each time they move across the scale the dose of pour-on is delivered onto the animal's skin. Although the correct dose per weight is applied, the disadvantage is that the frequency of pour-on application cannot be controlled. Various other applicators are available on the market, based on similar principles with the same limitations of dose/and or frequency of application.

Tickball application

The tickball method is intended for the treatment of individual animals. It is based on

CHAPTER 5: DISEASES AND PARASITES

Left: Duncan applicator. Right: Ticks balls are ideal for treating individual animals.

the paintball principle: The ball is filled with a pyrethroid pour-on formulation to which a dye has been added. The tickball is delivered using a paintball gun which has been adjusted to deliver the correct pressure. The dose can be adjusted by delivering more than one paintball to large animals. Tickballs are currently only available under veterinary prescription from Afrivet Business Management.

Plant extract remedies for parasite control

There are various anecdotal reports of game animals self-medicating themselves against tick infestation by eating various plants. This has led to feed/lick manufacturers to add various aloe extracts to antelope feeds and claiming antiparasitic effects. However, the efficacy of aloe extracts for internal and external parasite control has been tested under controlled experiments by different researchers. Fourie *et al.* (2005) found *Aloe ferox* extracts to have no effect on tick burdens on cattle or dogs. Spickett *et al.* (2007) using *A. marlothii* extracts showed no effect on tick burdens in cattle. Despite anecdotal accounts that antelope medicate themselves with tobacco leaves these should never be used for treatment since nicotine is a highly toxic substance with a narrow safety margin.

Diatomaceous earth

Diatomaceous earth (DE) is composed of dried marine diatoms. In South Africa it is marketed by some companies with claims that it is an acaricide and anthelmintic. The manufacturers claim that DE kills ticks by interfering with their respiration. There are no scientific publications to support the use of DE as a safe or effective method for external parasite control. On the contrary, the very sharp particulate nature of DE makes it unacceptable for external use since this can cause lung damage if inhaled during dust application. Note that scientific trials in livestock have shown that there is no efficacy on internal parasites when delivered orally, for example through the feed and may in fact be deleterious to weight gain if the quantity is not restricted (see review by Whitely and Miller, 2015).

Use of cattle for tick control

Cattle grazed along with game can be used as "vacuum cleaners" for ticks but this should always be done using cattle that are free from BTB and brucellosis. Boomker and Horak in Bothma (2002) recommend using European cattle breeds since these are more susceptible to ticks than indigenous cattle. The cattle should be allowed to graze with game species when ticks are active (January–March) because this method will attract the highest number of ticks over the shortest period of time. Treat these cattle for ticks every five days to ensure the ticks don't engorge and drop off before one can control them.

The chosen tick remedy should not have any residual effect because this will prevent maximum attachment, and should be non-toxic for oxpeckers. Cattle can be encouraged to trample and/or graze old unpalatable grass by spraying pastures with diluted molasses or a similar product.

The yellow dog tick (*Haemaphysalis leachi*).

The bont-legged tick (*Hyalomma* sp.).

TICK CONTROL IN CARNIVORES

Ticks are found on free-living carnivores but heavy burdens are usually only found on old or debilitated animals. A large number of tick species have been collected from carnivores in southern Africa but only seven of these are considered to be true parasites of wild carnivores. Some important ticks are discussed below.

Yellow dog tick (*Haemaphysalis leachi*)

They are smallish, yellow-brown, inconspicuous ticks but when the females are engorged they are more easily noticed. They occur in the wetter areas of the country – Gauteng, KwaZulu-Natal, Eastern Cape and focal areas of the Western Cape. They are active most of the year except during the coldest months.

This tick is the chief transmitter of canine biliary and also transmits *Rickettsia conori*, the organism that causes tick bite fever of humans. The favourite site of attachment of the adults is the neck and shoulders but with heavy infestations they can be found all over the body.

Kennel tick (*Rhipicephalus sanguineus*)

The kennel tick is absent from the dry western areas of the Northern Cape. It has adapted to living inside houses and kennels, crawling up walls and hiding away in the nooks and crannies. The female lays up to 3 000 eggs which can hatch within a month. The life cycle can be completed within a short time and during the summer months the numbers of these ticks can become massive. The adult kennel ticks attach on the neck, ears and between the toes while the larvae and nymphae attach anywhere on the body. These ticks transmit canine biliary and the blood parasite *Erlichia canis* which causes erlichiosis which is occasionally seen in wild carnivores.

Bont-legged ticks (*Hyalomma* sp.)

Bont-legged ticks are large brown ticks with legs banded with red and white stripes. They are mainly found on livestock but occasionally attach to dogs. Some of these ticks have a toxin in their saliva which causes their bites to be extremely painful and cause tick bite necrosis which is a local dying off of skin tissue. When toxic bont-legged ticks attach on an animal it will become hypersensitive, and will seem to cry for no reason, often when resting. A careful examination is needed to find the tick especially in a long hair coat but they are most often found on the back or the abdomen. These ticks must be immediately removed, but the toxin it has injected may still cause the skin around the bite to be inflamed and the tissue around it may actually die off, leaving a large gaping hole. The hair should be clipped away from the

The kennel tick (*Rhipicephalus sanguineu*).

wound to keep it clean and wound ointment should be applied to promote healing.

A wide variety of tick remedies are registered for use on domestic cats and dogs, but not all of these are practical for use in captive wild carnivores. Less irritant pyrethoid actives such as flumethrin (Bayticol – Bayer) have been used in wild canines and felines as dips or sprays. However, a number of effective long-acting pour-ons and collars have recently become available which may be safer and more effective. The Seresto collar (Bayer) for canines only prevents tick infestation for up to eight months, and has been used safely and effectively in wild dogs.

The usage of most products in wild carnivores will be off-label and should be done on the advice of a veterinarian. Bear in mind that canines and felines will differ in their susceptibility to anti-parasite remedies.

MITES, LICE, FLEAS AND KEDS (SKIN PARASITES)

These parasites are commonly found on the skin of wild animals. Mites and lice are microscopically small parasites, probably always present but they only reach large numbers when animals become stressed or sick. The condition caused by mites is referred to as mange, a clinical symptom characterised by focal loss of hair, and severe itching, for example, in the case of sarcoptic mange which is commonly seen in species such as lion and various antelope. These infestations can cause severe debilitation and euthanasia is often recommended. Since sarcoptic mange can also spread to humans causing severe itching and debilitation, gloves should always be worn when handling these cases.

Mange in buffalo has been described as a result of two specific mite species, *Demodex cafferi* and *Choriopsoroptes keneyenis*. Except for sarcoptic mange which affects almost all species of mammals, mange mites are usually host species specific, being adapted to living on only one species of animal. They are also permanent parasites, being unable to live off the host in the environment for more than a day or two. Mange is seen in buffalo and wildebeest in winter, especially when the animals are stressed by cold and poor nutrition and often resolves spontaneously.

Louse infestations are most commonly seen in animals that are crowded together, or under stress. Biting lice or red lice can cause severe irritation and hair loss, while sucking or blue lice cause anaemia especially in young animals. Severe sucking lice infestations have been seen in impala. Lice are even more species specific than mites, because their claws are specifically adapted to the thickness of the hosts hairs. They may even confine themselves to a certain body part, for example the feet of certain species. Biting lice are generally quite mobile so are easily controlled by pour-on remedies, while bloodsucking lice are more effectively controlled by injectable products which reach the bloodstream of the host.

It is essential to obtain a veterinary diagnosis and identification of the specific causative parasite since mite and louse infestations cause superficially similar symptoms but are treated with different remedies.

The cat flea (*Ctenocephalides* sp.) is a common problem in captive carnivores and their populations can build up to enormous

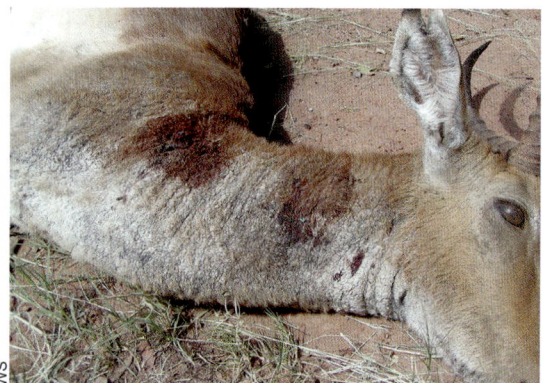
Sarcoptic mange in an impala.

Life cycle of a typical fly.

numbers. Large numbers of fleas sucking blood from young animals can cause weakness and anaemia, and the constant irritation from their bites causes loss of condition. Adult fleas feed on the animal but their immature stages are found in the environment. Excellent veterinary remedies have been developed for flea control in recent years, both for controlling the adult fleas (adulticides) and those in the animal's environment. This treatment should be done under veterinary advice.

Sticktight fleas (*Echidnophaga* sp.) are found embedded under the skin, unlike the jumping fleas discussed above. They can be a problem in warthogs. These fleas can be eliminated by treating the animal with adulticide flea remedies.

Keds or louse flies (hippoboscids) are bloodsucking parasites which are commonly found on a variety of wild animals. A wide range of *Lipoptena* sp. have been found on antelope such as nyala, kudu, duiker and springbok. Louse flies are also found on carnivores such as cheetah. These flies are usually poor fliers, some being totally flightless and spend their lives crawling around in the hair of the animal, keeping close to the body. They reproduce on the animal and the young are able to spread to other animals by direct contact. Heavy ked infestations can cause anaemia and irritation, which causes a loss of general condition. Pyrethroid sprays or carbamates can be used to control louse flies but treatment should be done under veterinary supervision.

FLIES

The fly family includes a wide variety of species, from the familiar house fly and its relatives to very small flies like mosquitoes and midges. The life cycle of flies is roughly the same for most of the species except that the larvae of bot flies and blow flies may spend part of their life cycle feeding inside animals, rather than on them. Fly larvae found in the skin:
- Screwworm fly (*Chrysomya bezziana*).
- Warble fly (*Strobilooestrus* sp.).
- Tumbu fly (*Cordylobia anthrophagia*).

The larval stages of certain fly species can be found on wounds or under the skin. The most important is that of the fly *Chrysomya* which is found in the northern areas of South Africa. They lay their eggs on wounds and when these hatch the larvae or maggots feed on the tissue in the wound, a condition that veterinarians refer to as myaisis. Heavy burdens of the larvae may kill the animal because of a toxin which they produce. These infestations must be treated with wound ointment that contains insecticide.

The larvae of the warble fly (*Strobilooestrus*) are found under the skin of various antelope such as klipspringer, springbok, grey rhebok, steenbok and common duiker, usually at

A wound caused by ear ticks infested with the maggots of the fly *Chrysomya bezziana*.

slaughter. There is no indication that they are problematic and usually need no treatment. Tumbu flies are found in the northern regions of Gauteng, around Brits and Pretoria North as well as in Limpopo Province, but they may spread into other regions as the climate becomes warmer. The female flies lay their eggs on surfaces contaminated by sweat, urine or faeces. Most often this is in sandy or moist soil or bedding stained with urine or faeces. The eggs hatch into larvae when they come into contact with the skin of children or dogs, and then they penetrate the skin and lie just below the surface. Here they breathe through a small opening in the skin and feed on the host's tissues. As they grow and enlarge they become visible as small painful swellings. If the larvae are left alone they will eventually emerge from the skin leaving large wounds. Tumbu fly larvae should be removed by a veterinarian as just squeezing them out can cause severe allergic reactions. To prevent infestations animals can be treated with shampoos, dips or powders containing organophosphates. It is preferable to do this under veterinary supervision as these products are quite toxic.

Nasal bot flies (Oestrus ovis, Kirkioestrus and Gedoelstia)

The term "bot" refers to the worm-like larva which is the immature form of the fly. Nasal bot flies follow alcelaphine antelope which includes blesbok, bontebok, wildebeest and hartebeest. *Oestrus ovis* and *Kirkioestrus* flies deposit tiny live larvae around the nostrils of the antelope and these crawl into the nostrils and then into the sinuses of the animal. Here they live on the secretions of the mucous membranes of the sinuses. When the larvae are mature they are sneezed out, drop onto the ground and pupate in the soil. The bots cause little damage in the alcelaphine antelope which have also developed a head nodding behaviour to try and repel the flies. It is not necessary to treat these antelope for the parasite, however, when the nasal bot flies parasitise livestock they can cause runny noses and loss of production. Non-alcelaphine antelope can be infested with nasal bot fly larvae and may cause nasal discharge or signs of distress. Nasal bots are susceptible to treatment with injectable ivermectin formulations.

Gedoelstia infestations of livestock and non-alcelaphine antelope are much more problematic because the larvae are deposited on, and migrate through, the eyes. In these "abnormal hosts" this migration results in severe inflammation and swelling of the eye sometimes causing protrusion of the eyeball, the so-called "popeye" or "uitpeuloog" and resultant blindness. The problem cannot be treated at this stage. The only feasible control method is to isolate non-alcelaphines from alcelaphine antelope.

Bot flies

- Horse bot fly (*Gasterophilus* sp.).
- Rhino bot fly (*Gyrostigma pavesi*).

These flies lay their eggs on the skin of animals which are then ingested during grooming. They hatch in the gastro-intestinal tract where the larvae then attach to the mucous membranes. The larvae grow quite large and are eventually passed out in the faeces. On postmortem the finding of these in the stomach of zebra and rhino are quite alarming because they can be present in quite large numbers, and the rhino

A horse fly (tabanid).

Note that the stable fly (left) is smaller than the house fly (right) and has biting mouthparts.

bot is very large. However, there is usually little deleterious effect and therefore no need to treat this condition in free-living animals.

Horse flies or tabanids (*Tabanus* and other spp.)

These large robust flies with iridescent eyes, are represented by 227 different species in the southern African region, and are widespread in all habitats including arid regions. The females are aggressive bloodsuckers causing painful bites during the blood-sucking process. They attack a wide variety of large animals including zebra, carnivores, various ungulates and humans. An interesting example is the very large hippo fly *Tabanus biguttatus* which attacks hippo forcing them to spend their days underwater.

The female horse flies lay their eggs in moist organic matter such as mud where the larvae feed on vegetable matter or prey on insect larvae or tadpoles. They are numerous during wet summers, causing annoyance ("fly worry") to wildlife such as kudu but also to guests during game drives.

Using pyrethroid pour-on formulations in Duncan applicators placed near waterholes may reduce horsefly irritation of ungulates. The use of DEET containing insect repellent sprays (e.g. Peaceful Sleep or Tabard) will reduce horse fly worry on game drives.

Stable fly (*Stomoxys calcitrans*)

Stable flies are biting flies that closely resemble the ordinary house fly except they are slightly smaller and have mouth parts adapted for rasping and lapping blood. When they feed on animals their painful bites cause severe "fly worry" which in domestic animals such as dairy cows can reduce their production considerably. Stable flies get their name from the fact that they feed in compost heaps, especially of grass clippings and horse manure. On game farms they attack buffalo and may also be an annoyance in captive or boma held animals. There is no easy way of controlling the life cycle but captive animals can be treated with pyrethroid pour-ons, dips or spray which will have a repellent effect.

House fly (*Musca domestica*)

These flies breed in dung and compost and can reach enormous numbers around households and farm premises. Their multiplication is dependent on heat and moisture. As a result they cause annoyance to animals and people, are unaesthetic and a public health risk because they settle on food. House flies can be controlled by turning compost heaps frequently to kill the maggots, using baited fly traps and using environmental sprays on outhouses where flies tend to settle. These measures must be done early in the spring to prevent them breeding to enormous numbers

Horn flies clustered on a steenbok ram.

in the late summer. Biological control using parasitic wasps is said to be effective.

Face flies (*Musca* spp.)

These are flies which unlike house flies follow animals around in the veld and breed in their dung. They resemble small house flies but have prostomal teeth on the mouthparts which they use to feed on the lacrimal secretions, wounds or the surface of the eye. They may transmit bacterial eye infections and are known to transmit the *Parafilaria* worm (see under Internal parasites). It is seldom necessary to control these flies on game but if necessary they can be controlled by treatment with pyrethroid-containing products.

Tsetse flies (*Glossina* spp.)

These large biting flies were widespread over Africa until the rinderpest epidemic in 1890, followed by the South African war, wiped out large numbers of wild animals on which the flies habitually fed. They also feed on livestock, in the process transmitting the trypanosome parasites which cause nagana (see section on Trypanosomiasis).

The tsetse fly females lay only one live fully developed larva at a time at about 10 day intervals which is a very slow reproductive rate for flies. The larva which is usually deposited in a shady place with soft soil or organic material and never feeds, pupates within an hour of being produced. The time it takes for the pupa to emerge as an adult is temperature dependent. Different tsetse species have specific habitat preferences and climate tolerances. The most abundant species in South Africa are *G. morsitans* and *G. pallidipes*. They have a preference for bush-frequenting hosts like warthog, bushpig, kudu and bushbuck, but also zebra and impala and less frequently, primates. Other species *G. brevipalpis* and *G. austeni* prefer the bushy gorges and thickets of KwaZulu-Natal. Their preferred hosts are unknown. Wildlife are usually refractory to nagana but on livestock farms adjoining tsetse infested areas control measures are taken to prevent tsetse fly bites, using pyrethoid containing products.

Horn flies (*Haematobia*, *Haematobosca*)

These flies resemble the house fly group but are smaller and have slightly elongated wings. They are blood-sucking flies that sit on the host most of the time, only leaving to lay eggs in the dung of the animal. Large numbers are found on buffalo. If animals in bomas are heavily infested the horn flies will be effectively controlled by the use of pyrethroids, applied as sprays or pour-ons. However, it should be mentioned that because these flies have such a short generation time they have reportedly developed rapid resistance to pyrethroids in other parts of the world.

Summary of fly control in wildlife species

For controlling adult flies the application of pyrethroids such as deltamethrin in the form of a dip, spray or pour-ons are effective since they have a repellent effect. However, some game species are sensitive to pyrethroid irritation so the less effective but also less irritant flumethrin is used, for example, on felines and horses. Pyrethoids can be applied using pour-ons in tick applicators like the Duncan applicator, using paintballs or by applying them as sprays where possible. A veterinarian should be consulted about the dosage when using sprays since most of the available products are registered for use in domestic animals. To treat maggot infestations organophosphate containing wound ointments are used, for example, for tumbu fly or blow flies. Organophosphates are relatively toxic, particularly on felines so must be used in consultation with veterinarians.

Nasal and stomach bot flies are treated if necessary with injectable solutions or oral pastes containing macrocyclic lactones such as ivermectin, which are absorbed into the blood stream. However, these may not be suitable for all wildlife species so a veterinarian must be consulted. Pyrethroids, when used in insecticidal wound ointments, are effective for the treatment of fly larvae since they are fairly concentrated.

Environmental control can be practiced for controlling nuisance flies (house flies) by practicing compost hygiene, using baited fly traps, applying environmental pyrethroid sprays around households, applying pyrethroid pour-ons, dips or sprays registered for use in animals. Biological control with parasitic wasps can be used if the use of insecticidal sprays is undesirable.

POISONINGS

PLANT POISONINGS

Although there is little documented experimental work on plant poisonings of game there is some evidence that wild ungulates can safely eat plants that cause poisonings in livestock.

Researchers have suggested that this is due to natural selection which has resulted in these animals being able to detoxify the poisonous components of indigenous plants in the liver. It is known for example that springbok eat karoo

Lantana camara is a common toxic invasive weed on game farms.

bushes that are poisonous to sheep, that rhino and klipspringer eat irritant latex-secreting *Euphorbia* sp., and buffalo and giraffe have been seen to graze tamboti leaves, and giraffe are reported to be refractory to prussic acid poisoning of plant origin. Eland are said to be able to eat highly toxic "gifblaar" (*Dichapetalum cymosum*) which contains flouroacetate and is responsible for extensive poisoning of livestock in the bushveld areas. Nyala in this region have been seen eating milkweed (*Asclepias* sp.) when the veld condition was good, without observable ill effects.

It has been proposed that wild herbivores learn avoidance of poisonous plants such as those containing cardiac glycosides, as do cattle farmed in areas where these plants occurs. As a result poisonings of livestock from cardiac glycoside containing plants occur in newly introduced or starving cattle. However, there are anecdotal reports of plant poisoning in wild ungulates in South Africa, specifically laminitis caused in duiker due to *Crotalaria* and buffalo are reported to have been poisoned by a *Brachiaria* sp.

Generally under good veld conditions wild herbivores are able to avoid a high intake of potentially poisonous plants. But under certain conditions game can be poisoned, for example if animals are unfamiliar with the plants when introduced into a new area or the veld is in poor condition.

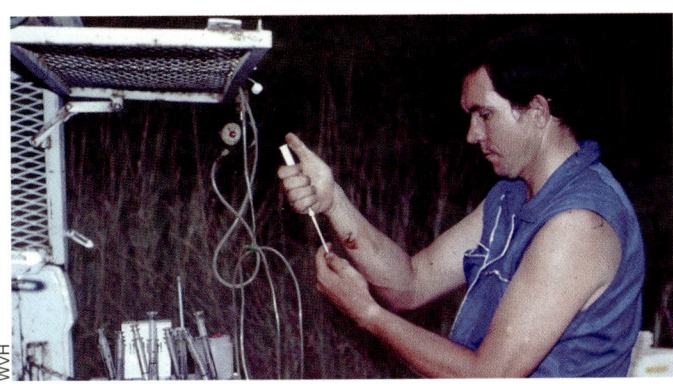

Scientist Wouter van Hoven showed by measuring rumen fermentation rates that tannins in the leaves of various trees were responsible for the deaths of kudu under certain circumstances.

Lantana camara is an exotic weed which is widespread in many biomes. There is evidence that these plants are browsed in the late winter in areas such as the Waterberg despite the fact that they are thorny and have a profusion of small thorns. In cattle one of the symptoms is photosensitivity, an inflammation of unpigmented areas of the skin but this is unlikely to be seen in game, but deaths as a result of wasting due to liver damage should be treated with suspicion. Liver samples can be submitted to make a diagnosis of *Lantana* poisoning. Eradication should be tackled with cost effectiveness in mind since this can be a very expensive undertaking (Bromilow, 2010).

Poisoning has been described in African herbivores in zoological gardens caused by exotic plants such as oleander (*Nerium oleander*), wild tobacco (*Nicotiana glauca*), English oak (*Quercus robur*) most probably because they are unfamiliar with these plants. Herbivores fed in bomas or camps are vulnerable to plant poisoning if the hay becomes contaminated with poisonous plants. Examples that have been seen in domestic animals are contamination with thorn apple (*Datura stramonium*) and bracken fern (*Pteridium aquinlinum*) in horses. Care should therefore be taken that when hay is made poisonous plants are not harvested along with the grasses. Contamination of feed with mycotoxins (fungal poisons) is known to cause poisoning in livestock, so mouldy pellets or hay should never be fed to wildlife.

Game ranch owners should avoid planting potentially poisonous plants in gardens or around camps on game ranches. A comprehensive list of indigenous and exotic plants that are potentially poisonous for herbivores is given in the excellent publication *Poisonous Plants of South Africa*.

Tannic acid "poisoning"

Tannic acid is a plant derived substance which is used in the tanning industry to cure hides. It does this by binding to the proteins in the hides, making them indigestible to microbial activity. "Poisoning" with tannic acid has been described in the bushveld of Limpopo Province under a specific set of circumstances. It specifically affects kudu in late winter on small fenced properties. Although the affected properties appear to have sufficient browse available for the numbers of kudu present, it has been shown that certain trees and shrubs favoured by kudu such as the common hook thorn (*Senegalia* [*Acacia*] *caffra*) and the weeping wattle (*Peltophorum africanum*) produce tannic acid in their leaves in response to heavy browsing. These plants are also able to communicate their stress condition to plants downwind which then produce tannic acid in response. Under normal circumstances animals will move off to browse on other trees

Microcystis bacteria forming a scum on the surface of a dam.

but in winter or during cold spells in spring, kudu on small properties are forced to browse on those that already have high levels of tannic acid. In the rumen of the antelope the tannic acid binds to proteins rendering them indigestible. The kudu therefore literally die of a protein deficiency. On postmortem animals with tannic acid "poisoning" show emaciation but no other abnormalities.

To prevent this syndrome in bushveld areas it is suggested that during winter and drought periods that the maximum stocking rate for kudu should be reduced to 3–4 per 100 hectares. Registered products containing polyethylene glycol can be added to drinking water to counter the effects of tannic acid in browse during the danger periods (Afrivet Game Min Browse and Browse Plus).

Microcystis poisoning

Poisoning as a result of this organism is a well-documented cause of death in livestock and more recently cases have occurred in game in the Kruger National Park. *Microcystis aeruginosa* is a cyanobacterium, a cholorophyll-containing bacterium which grows on the surface of still water bodies. It is therefore sometimes erroneously referred to as an algal bloom. These bacteria grow to large numbers on the surface of still waters under certain conditions such as eutrophication, which is the increase in nitrate content as a result of evaporation or heavy faecal contamination. The bacterial growth is seen as a green scum on the water surface, usually accumulating on the downwind shores of the water body. Millions of these cyanobacteria release a toxin into the water which when drunk by animals or humans causes severe liver damage.

The outbreak seen in Kruger National Park occurred during the late autumn when the level of two specific dams was dropping and there was a high level of hippo activity which caused eutrophication. The growth of *Microcystis* bacteria could be clearly seen on their surfaces. Fifty four animals died clustered around these dams. Herbivores were affected including ruminants, zebra, and rhino, as well as large carnivores such as lion and cheetah. A postmortem carried out on a fresh carcass showed severe liver swelling with an orange-brown discolouration, as well as jaundice throughout the carcass.

Control measures for *Microcystis* will depend on the circumstances on the reserve/ranch but fencing such dams or pans off, or burning grazing around the water body to make it unattractive seem to be the only practical measures that can be taken.

CHEMICAL POISONINGS

Wild animals are still being poisoned maliciously or may become poisoned by accident when exposed to chemical substances in their environment.

Some farmers use poisons to control predators and in the process poisoning not only predators but numerous useful scavengers including endangered species such as vultures. Poisoning jackal with coyote getters, strychnine, or any other poison in bait form is unlawful but farmers continue to do this. See the section on problem animal investigation and management in the general introduction section of the book for more details on how to manage these problems.

Game species are sometimes maliciously poisoned using grain or carcasses treated with highly toxic substances such as carbamates or organophosphates. A typical poison used is aldicarb (Temik) commonly called "Two Step" which is a highly poisonous carbamate used for crop protection. Typically poachers will target rhino by poisoning waterholes with aldicarb, killing large numbers of antelope and others in the process. There is currently no antidote for this poison.

Diazinon an organophosphate still used as a sheep dip, is often used by rural people for "protein gathering" by soaking maize kernels in the dip solution and then scattering this near waterholes. Gamebirds, ducks, geese and guinea fowl are killed and eaten or sold. Hundreds of blue cranes are poisoned in this way annually in the Southern and Western Cape.

A wide array of agricultural products may cause poisoning of wildlife including herbicides, pesticides and stock remedies. Therefore it is essential that agricultural products are used responsibly by applying as directed and storing them under lock and key to prevent malicious poisonings. Dip tanks on game farms should be fenced off to prevent animals like elephants drinking the dip solution. Agricultural chemicals and their containers must never be dumped into water bodies or in landfills. Various organizations such as AVCASA provide an information service with regard to the application of chemicals, training of workers, and disposal of chemicals.

Rodenticides based on warfarin (coumarines) kill rodents by preventing the blood from clotting. Most of these (brodifacoum, etc.) kill rodents rapidly after one feed and animals which eat these poisoned rodents can be poisoned (secondary poisoning). Most often these are owls, small predators and pet cats and dogs. The chemical warfarin derivative coumatetralyl is a multifeed rodenticide which requires a number of feeds to kill the rodent with the result that the amount of poison in the animal's carcass is lower than with the other coumarines, so that secondary poisoning does not occur. Coumatetralyl ("Racumin"-Bayer) is available in bait, paste or liquid form. It must be placed where only the target rodents can access them, for example in bait boxes to prevent other animals and people ingesting the poison.

Other potentially poisonous substances found on farms are fertilisers which contain substances such as nitrates. Even creosote used for preserving poles can cause poisoning in susceptible animals such as rhinos. Avoid storing or dumping these chemicals where they can be accessed by herbivores since they may attempt to lick at these because of the salty taste. Licks or feed supplements registered for farm animals are not always suitable for wildlife as they may contain additives which are poisonous for certain species, for example urea or growth stimulants such as monensin.

Veterinary products such as antibiotics, dewormers and dips must be used with caution on wildlife species, unless they have specifically been registered for use in a particular animal. Certain species have a low tolerance for drugs that are used in other species. For example, rhino are sensitive to amitraz, ivermectin, and tetracycline which are commonly used in antelope species. The uninformed use of immobilising and tranquilising agents can result in the death of animals and these drugs must by law only be handled by veterinarians. They are also a danger to human health.

The use of certain drugs in livestock can result in poisoning of predators and scavengers. An example of this is the poisoning of vultures with the carcasses of livestock injected with phenylbutazone, at vulture restaurants.

Environmental contamination is becoming an increasing problem in game farming areas due to mining, farming, hunting, fishing and industrial activities causing air, water and dust pollution with heavy metals and other chemical substances. Cases of copper poisoning have been identified in wildlife in Limpopo due to air pollution from a nearby foundry. Note also that the use of copper sulphate to supplement deficiencies must be done with utmost care to prevent poisoning. Using commercial mineral supplement injections is a safer method of treatment.

Lead shot used by hunters has been found to be a major source of environmental contamination in wildlife areas. When predators or scavengers take in meat contaminated with lead shot they may suffer acute lead poisoning, or develop chronic lead poisoning which will affect young animals and inhibit reproduction in various species. Studies in various countries have shown that birds are most seriously affected. A specific example is the endangered southern ground hornbill which have been found poisoned by a few lead pellets in the digestive system. Game ranchers are encouraged to switch to non-lead shot to prevent environmental contamination. Humans can also develop lead poisoning if lead shot is not carefully removed from carcasses.

The investigation of suspected poisoning cases should be undertaken by veterinarians, since they will be able to perform post-mortems and take the correct samples for laboratory analysis. This is a highly specialised task as different poisons require the taking of specific organs and samples which must be stored in a specific way. Water samples can be submitted to laboratories for analysis. Suspected environmental contamination should be reported to local government offices and conservation organizations.

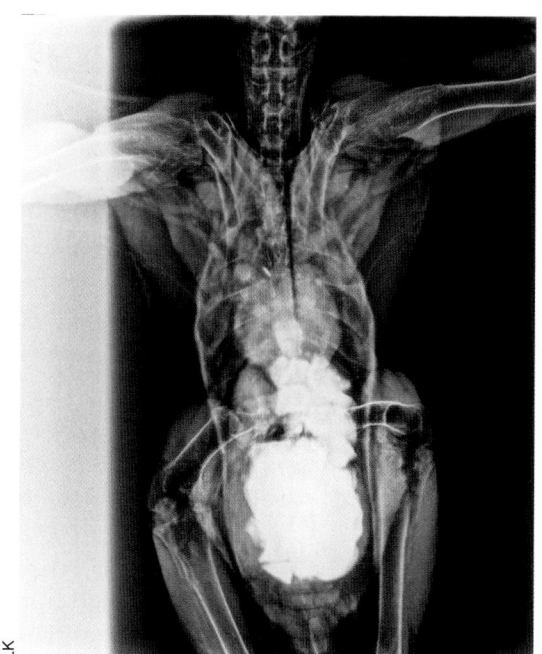

An x-ray of a ground hornbill which developed poisoning due to ingested lead shot.

Very few poisonings in wild animals can be treated timeously or effectively so the emphasis must be on the prevention of poisonings by being informed. There are few specific antidotes for poisons so treatment usually involves heroic attempts to prevent further absorption through the skin or digestive tract and controlling specific symptoms such as violent muscle spasms. Animals suspected of poisonings should be treated by a veterinarian as soon as possible.

REFERENCES AND FURTHER READING

INTRODUCTION AND HISTORY

Beinart, W. 2003. *The rise of Conservation in South Africa. Settlers, livestock, and the environment 1770–1950.* Oxford University Press. First edition.

Dry G. Pers. Comms. 2014.

Fermet-Quinet E et al. OIE PVS Evaluation Report: Republic of South Africa. October 2012.

Laubscher L. & Hoffman L. 2012. *An Overview of Disease-Free Buffalo Breeding Projects with Reference to the Different Systems Used in South Africa.* Sustainability 2012, 4, 3124-3140; doi:10.3390/su4113124.

Phelps, R.J. and Lovemore, D.F. 1994. *Infectious diseases of livestock with special reference to southern Africa.* Edited by: J.A.W. Coetzer, G.R. Thomson & R.C. Tustin. Oxford University Press. First edition 1994. Chapter 2 Page 40.

Rossiter, P.B. 1994. *Infectious diseases of livestock with special reference to southern Africa.* Edited by: J.A.W. Coetzer, G.R. Thomson & R.C. Tustin. Oxford University Press. First edition 1994. Chapter 74 Page 737.

Saayman R. Pers. Comms. 2014.

Simpson I.F. 2012. *Mpunzi, Dawn of a New Era.* First edition.

Skead, C.J. 1987. *Historical Mammal Incidence in the Cape. Vol 1 & 2.* Government Printer, Cape Town.

Skead, C.J 2011. *Historical Incidence of the Larger Land Mammals in the Broader Northern and Western Cape.* Editors: Andre Boschoff, Graham Kerley and Peter Lloyd. Port Elizabeth: Nelson Mandela Metropolitan University.

Van der Merwe, P. 1945. *Trek: Studies oor die Mobiliteit van Pioniersbevolking aan die Kaap.* Nasionale Pers Beperk, Kaapstad.

BREEDING/GAME RANCHING

Du P. Bothma J. (ed). 2002. *Game ranch management.* Van Schaik Publishers, Pretoria.

Du P. Bothma, J. & Van Rooyen, N. (eds). 2005. *Intensive wildlife production in southern Africa.* Van Schaik, Pretoria.

WILDLIFE TOURISM

Allen, G. & Brennan, F. 2004. Tourism in the new South Africa: social responsibility and the tourists experience. New York: I.B. Tauris.

Baldus, R. & Cauldwell. 2004. *Tourist hunting and its role in development of wildlife management areas in Tanzania.* Tanzanian German Development Cooperation, Dar es Salaam, Tanzania. Available from http://www.wildlife-programme.gtz.de/ (accessed October 2006).

Cloete, P.C., Van der Merwe, P. & Saayman, M. 2015. *Game ranch profitability in South Africa.* Second edition. Pretoria: Caxton.

Croal, J. 1995. *Preserve or destroy: tourism and the environment.* Calouste Gulbenkian Foundation, London.

Eagles, P.F.J., Mccool, S.F. & Haynes, C.D. 2002. *Sustainable tourism in protected areas: guidelines for planning and management.* Switzerland & Cambridge, UK: IUCN Gland.

Fredline, I. & Faulkner, B. 2001. Wildlife tourism research report series: no 22. *International market analysis of wildlife tourism.* Edited by Higginbottom, K. Australia: National library of Australia.

Freese, C. 1996. The commercial, consumptive use of wild species: Managing it for the benefit of biodiversity. Discussion Paper, WWF US and WWF International.

Freese, C. 1998. *Wild species as commodities: Managing markets and ecosystems for sustainability.* Washington, D.C.: Island Press.

Higginbottom, K. 2004. *Wildlife tourism: impacts, management and planning.* Edited by Higginbottom, K. Australia: National library of Australia. http://SustainableTourism.Publisher-Site. com. Date of access: 10 February 2014.

Ivins, T. 2007. *A hunter's handbook.* Durban: PenPrint.

Kaltenborn B.P., Nyahongo J.W.& Tingstad, K.M.2005. The nature of hunting around the western corridor of Serengeti National Park, Tanzania. European Journal of Wildlife Research, 7(6): 51:213–222.

Knight R.L. & Cole, D.N. 1995. *Wildlife responses to recreationists.* (In Knight, R.L & Gutzwiller, K.J. *Wildlife and recreation: Coexistence through management and research.* (pp. 71}80). Washington, DC: Island Press.

Mason, P. 2008. *Tourism impacts, planning and management.* 2nd edition. Oxford: Elsevier.

Milner-Gulland, E.J. & Mace, R. 1998. *Conservation of biological resources.* Oxford: Blackwell Science.

Moscardo, G., Woods, B. & Greenwood, T. 2001. *Understanding Visitor Perspectives on Wildlife Tourism.* Wildlife Series Research Report No. 2. Gold Coast: CRC for Sustainable Tourism.

Novelli, M. (Ed) 2005. *Niche tourism: contemporary issues, trends and cases.* Oxford: Elsevier Butterworth – Heinemann.

OECD Publishing. 2009. *Wildlife and Nature-Based Tourism for Pro-Poor Growth*, in Natural Resources; and *Pro-Poor Growth: The Economics and Politics*, OECD Publishing. Available: http://www.oecd-ilibrary.org/development/natural-resources-and-pro-poor-growth/wildlife-and-nature-based-tourism-for-pro-poor-growth_9789264060258-10-en

Page, S.J. & Dowling, R.K. 2002. *Ecotourism*. Harlow: Prentice Hall.

Reynolds, P.C. & Braithwaite, D. 2001. *Towards a conceptual framework for wildlife tourism*. Tourism management. School of Tourism and Hospitality Management, Southern Cross University, Coffs Harbour, New South Wales, Australia.

Shea, A.R., Abbott, I., Armstrong, J.A. & McNamara, K.J. 1997. *Sustainable conservation: a new integrated approach to nature conservation in Australia*. Pp. 39-48 in Hale, P. and Lamb, D. (Eds). 1997. *Conservation outside Nature Reserves*. Centre for Conservation Biology, University of Queensland, Brisbane, Queensland. In Higginbottom, K. 2004. *Wildlife tourism: impacts, management and planning*.)

The International Hotel school, 2004. Web; http://www.hotelschool.co.za/2013/03/hospitality-a-world-of-oppertunities-for-south-african-graduates.com. Date of access: 10 March 2014.

Valentine, P & Birtles, A. 2004. *Wildlife Watching*. (In Higginbottom, K. (ed.). *Wildlife Tourism: Planning, Impacts and Management*. Common Ground Publishing, Melbourne. Pp 15-34).

Van der Merwe, P. 2014. *Introduction to game farm tourism*. (In Van der Merwe, P. & Du Plessis, L. 2014. *Game farm and hunting tourism*. 1st ed. Sun Media. Stellenbosch)

Wearing, S. & Neil, J. 1999. *Ecotourism: impacts, potentials and possibilities*. Oxford; Butterworth-Heinemann.

WWF-SA (WORLDWIDE FUND FOR NATURE-SOUTH AFRICA). 2003. WWF-SA position statement on sustainable use. African indaba, 1(1):14, Jan.

GAME MEAT

Hoffman, L. 2003. *Game meat and South African consumers*. African Indaba, 1(5). September: 8-12.

HUNTING

Harris, W.C. 1844. *The Wild Sports of Southern Africa*. London: Pelham Richardson, Cornhill.

Robertson, K. ("Doctari"). *Nyati: a guide to Hunting Zimbabwe's Most Dangerous Big Game: The Southern Buffalo*. Mag-Set Publications. 1996. Page 8.

Robertson, K. 1999. *The perfect shot*. Safari Press Inc., California.

Selous, F. C., Millais, J.G. & Chapman, A. 1914. *The Gun at Home and Abroad: The Big Game of Africa and Europe*. London: The London and Counties Press Association Ltd.

Ward, R. 2006. *Rowland Ward's Records of Big Game*. 27th edn. Rowland Ward Publications, Johannesburg.

ECO SYSTEMS AND HABITAT

Esler, K.J., Milton, S.J. & Dean, W.R.J. (Eds). 2006. *Karoo Veld*. Briza Publications, Pretoria.

Esler, K.J., Pierce, S.M. & De Villiers, C. (Eds). 2014. *Fynbos – Ecology and Management*. Briza Publications, Pretoria.

Roodt, V. 2015. *Grasses and grazers of Botswana and the surrounding savannah*. Struik Nature, Cape Town.

Tainton, N. 1999. *Veld management in South Africa*. University of Natal Press.

Van Oudstshoorn, F. 1999. *Guide to grasses of southern Africa*. Briza Publications, Pretoria.

Van Wyk, B., Van Heerden, F. & Van Oudtshoorn, F. 2002. *Poisonous plants of south Africa*. Briza Publications, Pretoria.

NUTRITION

Koster, H.H. 1996. Journal of Animal Science 1996. 74: 2473-2481. *The effect of increasing degradable intake protein on intake and digestion of low-quality, tallgrass-prairie forage by beef cows*.

Meissner, H.H. 1981. South African journal of wildlife research 12: 41-47. *Theory and application of a method to calculate forage intake of wild southern African ungulates for purposes of estimating carrying capacity*.

Van Hoven, W. 2010. *Herbivore Nutrition in Game Ranch Management*. 5th edition, Editors J. du Bothma, J.G. du Toit. Pages 367-383. Van Schaik.

Van der Merwe, F.J. & Smith. W.A. 1991. *Dierevoeding*. Animal Science (PTY) Ltd.

GENETICS

Carrol, S.B. 2005. *Endless forms most beautiful: the new science of evolutionary development*. W. W. Norton and Company, New York.

Lubout, P. 2015. *Breeding plan for colour variants that minimizes inbreeding*. Wildlife Stud Services Journal 2015:32-33.

Lubout, P. 2015. *Breeding for horn length*. Wildlife Stud Services Journal 2015:38-39.

Marx, M. 2015. *Basics of DNA genotyping and genomic profiling in game farming*. Wildlife Stud Services Journal 2015:41-48.

Van der Hooft, P. 2015. Buffalo presentation

CAPTURE

Harthoorn, T. 1976. *The chemical capture of animals*.

Harthoorn, T. 1970. *The flying syringe*.

Kock, M.D. & Burroughs, R. 2012. *Chemical and physical restraint of wild animals*. 2nd edition.

Kock, M.D., Melzer, D. & Burroughs, R. (eds). 2006. *Chemical and physical restraint of wild animals*. IWVS (Africa), Greyton.

Mc Kenzie, A.A. (ed). 1993. *Capture and Care Manual*. Wildlife decision support services and SA Veterinary Foundation, Pretoria.

Young, E. 1973. *The capture and care of wild animals*.

PREDATOR MANAGEMENT

Hodkinson, C., Komen, H., Snow, T. & Davies-Mostert, H. 2007. *Predators and Farmers*. Endangered Wildlife Trust, Johannesburg.

SPECIES
General zoology

Du Plessis, S.F. 1969. *The past and present geographical distribution of the Perrisodactyla and Artiodactyla in Southern Africa.* M.Sc. Thesis, University of Pretoria.

Estes, R.D. 1991. *The Behaviour Guide to African Mammals.* University of California Press. Berkley and Los Angeles, California.

IEA (Institute of Applied Ecology), 1998. *African Mammals Databank - A Databank for the Conservation and Management of the African Mammals.* Vol 1 & 2. European Commission Directorate, Bruxelles.

IUCN, 2015. IUCN Red List of Threatened Species. Version 2015.2. Gland, Switzerland. www.iucnredlist.org

Kingdon, J,. 1982. *East African Mammals – Bovids: An atlas of evolution in Africa.* Vol. IIID. Academic Press, London.

Mills, G. & Hes, L. 1997. *The Complete Book of Southern African Mammals.* p. 274. Struik Publishers.

Skinner, J.D. & Chimba, C.T. 2005. *The Mammals of the Southern African Subregion.* 3rd edition. Cambridge University Press.

Smithers, R.H.N. 1983. *The Mammals of the Southern African Subregion.* 1st edition. University of Pretoria, CTP Book Printers, Cape Town.

Wilson, D. E. & Reeder, D. M. (Eds) 1993. *Mammal Species of the World.* 2nd edition. Washington.

Kingdon, J. 1989. *East African Mammals: An atlas of evolution in Africa – Bovids.* Vol 111D. Univ. of Chicago Press, Chicago.

RHINO
ZEBRA

Barnier, F., Grange, S., Ganswindt, A., Ncube, H. & Duncan, P. 2012. Inter-birth interval in zebras is longer following the birth of male foals than after female foals. *Acta Oecologica* 42: 11-15.

Bennet, D.K. 1980. Stripes do not a zebra make, Part I: A cladistics analysis of *Equus. Systematic Zoology* 29: 272-287.

Cabrera, A. 1936. Subspecific and individual variation in the Burchell zebras. *Journal of Mammalogy* 17: 89-112.

Churcher, C.S. 1993. *Equus grevyi. Mammalian Species* 453: 1-9.

Groves, C.P. & Bell, C.H. 2004. New investigations on the taxonomy of the zebras genus *Equus, subgenus Hippotigris.* Mammalian Biology 69: 182-196.

Faith, J.T. 2011. Palaeozoological insights into management options for a threatened mammal: southern Africa's Cape mountain zebra *(Equus zebra). Diversity and Distributions* 18: 438-447.

Georgiadis, N., Hack, M. & Turpin, K. 2003. The influence of rainfall on zebra population dynamics: implications for management. *Journal of Applied Ecology* 40:125–136

Hack, M. A., East, R. & Rubenstein, D. I. 2002. Status and Action plan for the Plains zebra *(Equus burchellii).* Status and Action Plan for the Mountain Zebra *(Equus zebra).* In Equids: Zebras, Asses and Horses: Status, Survey and Conservation Action Plan. (ed. Moehlman, P.), pp. 43-60. IUCN, Gland, Switzerland

Harley, E., Knight, M., Lardner, C., Wooding, B. & Gregor, M. 2009 The Quagga project: progress over 20 years of selective breeding. *South African Journal of Wildlife Research* 39: 155-163..

Hrabar, H. & Kerley, G.I.H. 2013. Conservation goals for the Cape mountain zebra *(Equus zebra zebra)* – security in numbers. *Oryx* 47(3):403-409.

Hrabar, H. & Kerley, G.I.H. 2013. *Selective breeding in the Quagga Breeding Program – the effect of translocations and inbreeding on Plains zebra reproduction.* Nelson Mandela Metropolitan University. Report No. C127.

Jónsson et al. 2014. Speciation with gene flow in equids, despite extensive chromosomal plasticity. *Proceedings of the National Academy of Sciences* 111 (52): 18655-18660.

Joubert, E. 1974. Notes on the reproduction in Hartmann zebra *(Equus zebra hartmannae)* in South West Africa. *Madoqua* 1: 31-35.

Klingel, H. 1965. Notes on the biology of the plains zebra *(Equus quagga boehmi Matschie). East African Wildlife Journal* 3: 86-88.

Klingel, H. 1969. Reproduction in the plains zebra (Equus burchelli boehmi): Behaviour and ecological factors. *Journal of Reproduction and Fertility.* Supplement 6:339-345.

Klingel, H. 1974. Social Organization and behaviour of the Grevy's zebra. *Zeitschrift für Tierpsychologie* 36(36): 36-70.

Leonard, J., Rohland, N., Glaberman, S., Fleischer, R., Caccone, A. & Hofreiter, M. 2005. A rapid loss of stripes: the evolutionary history of the extinct quagga. Biological Letters 1: 291-295.

Smuts, G.L. 1976. Reproduction in the zebra mare Equus burchelli antiquorium from the Kruger National Park. *Koedoe* 19: 89-132.

Trivers, R.L. & Willard, D.E. 1973. Natural selection of parental ability to vary the sex ratio of offspring. *Science* 179: 90-92.

Lloyd, P.H. 1984. The Cape mountain zebra 1984. *African Wildlife* 38: 144-149.

Lloyd, P.D. & Rasa, O.A. E. 1989. Status, reproductive success and fitness in Cape mountain zebra *(Equus zebra zebra). Behavioural Ecology and Sociobiology* 25:411-420.

Millar, J.C.G. 1970a. Census of Cape mountain zebra: part I. *African Wildlife,* 24, 17-25.

Millar, J.C.G. 1970b. Census of Cape mountain zebra: part II. *African Wildlife* 24: 105-114.

Nuñez, C., Asa, C.S. & Rubenstein, D.I. 2011. Zebra Reproduction: Plains Zebra *(Equus burchelli),* Mountain Zebra *(Equus zebra),* and Grevy's Zebra *(Equus grevyi).* Pp. 2851-2865. In: *Equine*

Reproduction, 2nd edition. A.O. McKinnon, E.L Squires, W.E. Vaala & D.D. Varner, eds. Wiley-Blackwell, Ames, Iowa.

Penzhorn, B L. 1985. Reproductive characteristics of a free-ranging population of Cape Mountain Zebra (*Equus zebra zebra*). *Journal of Reproduction and Fertility* 73: 51-57.

Rubenstein, D.I. 2010. Ecology, social behaviour, and conservation in zebras. *Advances in the study of behaviour* 42: 232-258.

Smith, R.K., Marais, A., Chadwick, P., Lloyd, P.H. & Hill, R.A. 2007. Monitoring and management of the endangered Cape mountain zebra (*Equus zebra zebra*) in the Western Cape, South Africa. *African Journal of Ecology* 46: 207-213.

Taplin, M., Zimmermann, D., Hofmeyr, M., Williams, R., Knight, M., Novellie, P., Ferreira, S., Bond, G., Engelbrecht, D. & Gaylard, A. 2015. Hybridization between plains and Cape mountain zebra in the Mountain Zebra National Park: Conservation Implications and Management Recommendations. *SANParks Report*.

Watson, L.H., Odendaal, H.E., Barry, T.J. & Pietersen, J. 2005. Population viability of Cape mountain zebra in Gamka Mountain Nature Reserve, South Africa: the influence of habitat and fire. *Biological Conservation* 122, 173-180.

Westlin-van Aarde, L.M., Van Aarde, R.J. & Skinner, J.D. 1988. Reproduction in female Hartmann's zebra (*Equus zebra hartmannae*). *Journal of Reproductive Fertility* 84: 505-511.

Williams, S.D. 2002. Status and Action Plan for Grevy's Zebra (*Equus grevyi*). In: P. D. Moehlman (ed.), *Equids: Zebras, Asses, and Horses. Status Survey and Conservation Action Plan*, pp. 11-27. IUCN, Gland, Switzerland.

BUFFALO

Basson, P.A., McCully, R.M., Kruger, S.P., Van Niekerk, J.W., Young, E. & de Vos, V. 1970. Parasitic and other diseases of African buffalo in the Kruger National Park. *Onderstepoort Journal of Veterinary Research*, Vol. 37.

Grimsdell, J.J.R. 1973. Age determination of the African buffalo, *Syncerus caffer*. *East African Wildlife Journal*: Vol.11.

Penzhorn, B. L. 1996. Proceedings of a Symposium on The African Buffalo as a Game Ranch Animal. SAVA Wildlife Group, Onderstepoort, South Africa.

Pienaar, U de V. 1969. Observations on developmental biology, growth and some aspects of population ecology of the African Buffalo in the KNP. *Koedoe*, Vol 12.

SABLE

Du Plessis, S.F. 1969. The past and present geographical distribution of the Perrisodactyla and Artiodactyla in Southern Africa. *M.Sc. Thesis*, University of Pretoria.

Estes, R. 2007. Western Zambian sable – the debate. *Game & Hunt* 13(12):29.

Grobler, J.H. 1980b. Breeding biology and aspects of social behaviour of sable *Hippotragus niger niger* in the Rhodes Matopos National Park, Zimbabwe. *S.Afr. J. Wildl. Res.* 10(3/4):150-152.

Grobler, J.H. 1981. Feeding behaviour of sable *Hippotragus niger niger* in the Rhodes Matopos National Park, Zimbabwe. *S.Afr. J. Zool.* 16:50-58.

Kriek, J.C. 2005. The Sable. In: *Intensive Wildlife Production in Southern Africa*, Eds. Bothma, J. Du P. & N. Van Rooyen. Van Schaik Publishers, Pretoria.

Mathee, C.A. & Robinson, T.J. 1999. Cytochrome b phylogeny of the Family Bovidae: resolution within the Alcelaphini, Antilopini, Neotragini and Tragelaphini. *Mol. Phylog. Evol.* 12:31-46.

Mathee, C.A. & Robinson, T.J. 1999. Mitochondrial DNA population structure of roan and sable antelope: implications for the translocation and conservation of the species. *Mol. Ecol.* 8:227-238.

Pitra, C., Hansen, A.J., Lieckfeldt, D. and Arctander, P. 2002. An exceptional case of historical outbreeding in African sable antelope populations. *Molecular Ecology* 11:1197-1208.

Robinson, T.J. & Harley, E.H. 1995. Absence of geographic chromosomal variation in the roan and sable antelope and the cytogenetics of a naturally occulting hybrid. *Cytogenet. Cell. Genet.* 71:363-369.

Wilson, D & Hirst, S. 1977. Ecology and factors limiting roan and sable antelope populations in South Africa. *Wildlife Monogr* 54:1-111.

GEMSBOK

Coe, M.J. & Skinner, J.D. 1993. Connections, disjunctions and endemism in the eastern and southern African mammal faunas. *Trans. R. Soc. S. Afr.* 48:233-256.

Dieckman, R.C. 1980. The ecology and breeding biology of the gemsbok in the Hester Malan Nature Reserve. *M.Sc. thesis*, University of Pretoria.

Dreyer, H van A. 1987. Die gebruik van water en soutlekke deur die groter hoefdiere in die Kalahari-Gemsbok Nasionale Park. *M.Sc. thesis*, University of Stellenbosch.

Du Plessis, S.F. 1969. The past and present geographical distribution of the Perrisodactyla and Artiodactyla in Southern Africa. *M.Sc. thesis*, University of Pretoria.

Eloff, F.C. 1959. Observations on the migration habits of the antelopes of the Kalahari Gemsbok Park. I & II. *Koedoe* 2:1-51.

Feuerrigel, K. 1996. Aspects of oryx behaviour and its relevance to management. *D.Sc. dissertation*, University of Hamburg.

Knight, M.H. 1991. *Ecology of the gemsbok and blue wildebeest in the southern Kalahari*. Ph.D. thesis, University of Pretoria.

Taylor, C.R. 1969. The eland and the oryx. *Sci. Am.* 220:89-95.

Williamson, D.T. & Williamson, J. 1988. *Habitat use and ranging behaviour of Kalahari gemsbok.* In: *Conservation and Biology of Desert Antelope*, pp 114-118. Eds. A. Dixon & D. Jones, Christopher Helm Ltd., London.

KUDU

Boomker, E.A. 1987. Fermentation and digestion in the kudu. *D.Sc. thesis*, University of Pretoria.

Du Plessis, S.F. 1969. The past and present geographical distribution of the Perrisodactyla and Artiodactyla in Southern Africa. *M.Sc. thesis*, Univ. of Pretoria.

Furstenburg, D. 1991. Die invloed van tannien op die voedingsekologie van die kameelperd Giraffa camelopardalis in die Nasionale Krugerwildtuin. *M.Sc. thesis*, University of Pretoria.

Novellie, P.A. 1983. Feeding ecology of the kudu in the Kruger Nationasl Park. *D.Sc. thesis*, University of Pretoria.

Owen-Smith, R.N. 1994. Foraging responses of kudu to seasonal changes in food resources: elasticity in constraints. *Ecology* 75:1050-1062.

Simpson, C.D. 1972. Some characteristics of Tragelaphine horn growth and their relationship to age in greater kudu and bushbuck. *J. South African Wildlife Management Association* 2:1-8.

Van Hoven, W. 1991. Mortalities in kudu populations related to chemical defence in trees. *J. Afr. Zool.* 105:141-145.

NYALA

Anderson, J.L. 1979. Reproductive seasonality of the nyala; the interaction of light, vegetation phenology, feeding style and reproductive physiology. *Mammal. Rev.* 9:33-46.

Anderson, J.L. The social organization and aspects of behaviour of the nyala. *Z. Saugetierk.* 45:90-123.

Anderson, J.L. 1984. Reproduction in the nyala. *J. Zool. Lond.* 204:129-142.

Anderson, J.L. 1985. Age determination of the nyala. *S. Afr. J. Wildl. Res.* 16:82-90.

Pfitzer, S. & Kohrs, H. 2005. *The Nyala.* In: *Intensive Wildlife Production in Southern Africa.* Eds. Bothma, J. Du P. & N. van Rooyen. Van Schaik Publishers, Pretoria.

Rowe-Rowe, D.T. & Mentis, M.T. 1972. Some ageing criteria for nyala. *J. Sn. Afr. Wildl. Mgmt Assoc.* 2(1):17-21.

Seymour, G. 2002. Ecological separation of greater kudu, nyala and bushbuck at Londolozi. *CC Africa Ecological J.* 4:137-145.

Tello, J.L.P.L. & Van Gelder, R.G. 1975. The natural history of nyala in Mozambique. *Bull. Am. Mus. Nat. Hist.* 155:323-385.

Van Rooyen, A.F. 1992. Diets of impala and nyala in two game reserves in Natal, South Africa. *S. Afr. J. Wildl. Res.* 22:98-101.

ELAND

Buys, D. 1987. The ecology of eland Taurotragus oryx in the western Transvaal Highveld. *M.Sc. thesis*, University of Pretoria.

Dalton, D.L., Van Wyk, A. & Kotze, A. 2015. Meshing molecules and management: an overview of hybrid detection in South African wildlife. *Wildlife Stud Services Journal* 2015:49-50.

Hillman, J.C. 1979. The biology of the eland Taurotragus oryx in the wild. *Ph.D. thesis*, University of Nairobi, Kenya.

WILDEBEEST

Frost, W. 2014. *The antelope of Africa.* Jacana Media. South Africa.

TSESSEBE

Brothersa, P.S., Collins, N.E., Oosthuizen, M.C., Bhoora, R., Troskie & Penzhorn, M. BL. 2011 Occurrence of blood-borne tick-transmitted parasites in common tsessebe (Damaliscus lunatus) antelope in Northern Cape Province, *SA Veterinary Parasitology* 183 (2011) 160-165.

Child, G., Robbel, H. & Hepburn, CP. 1972. Observations on the biology of tsessebe in northern Botswana. *Mammalia* 36:342-388.

Dunham, K.M., Robbertson, E.F. & Grant, C.C. 2004. Rainfall and the decline of a rare antelope the tsessebe in Kruger National Park. *Biol. Consev.* 117:83-94.

Dunham, K.M., Robertson, E.F. & Swanepoel, C.M. 2003. Population decline of tsessebe antelope on a mixed cattle and wildlife ranch in Zimbabwe. *Biol. Consev.* 113:111-124.

Grobler, J.H. 1973. Biological data on tsessebe in Rhodesia. *Arnoldia Rhod.* 6(12):1-16.

Joubert, S.C.J. 1972. Territorial behaviour of the tsessebe in the Kruger National Park. *Zool. Afr.* 7:141-156.

BLESBOK

Bigalke, R.C., Hartl, G.B., Hubertus, Van Hensbergen, H.J., Vrahimis, S. & Berry, M.P.S. 1995. Further studies on the population genetics of the blesbok *Damaliscus dorcas phillipsi. Acta Theriologica*, Suppl. 3: 157-164

Du Plessis, S.S., 1968. Ecology of blesbok on the Van Riebeeck Nature Reserve, Pretoria, with special reference to productivity. *D.Sc. Thesis*, University of Pretoria.

Lubout, P. 2015. Breeding plan for colour variants that minimizes inbreeding. *Wildlife Stud Services Journal* 2015:32-33.

Lynch, C.D. 1971. A behavioural study of blesbok *Damaliscus dorcas philipsi* with special reference to territoriality. *M.Sc. Thesis*, University of Pretoria.

Novellie, P.A. 1975. Comparative social behaviour of springbok and blesbok on the Jack Scott Nature Reserve.

Vrba, E.S. 1979. Phylogenetic analysis and classification of fossil and recent Alcelaphini Mammalia, Bovidae. *Biol J Linnaen Soc*. 11:207–228.

Watson, J.P., Skinner, J.D., Erasmus, B.H. & Dott, H.M. 1991. Age determination from skull growth in blesbok. *S. Afr. J. Wildl. Res*. 21(1):6-14.

IMPALA

Anderson, J.L. 1971. Seasonal changes in the social organization and distribution of the impala in Hluhluwe game reserve, Zululand. *J. sth Afr. Wildl. Mgmt. Ass*. 2:16-20.

Brooks, P.M. 1978. Relationship between body condition and age, growth, reproduction and social status in impala, and its application for management. *Sth. Afr. J. Wildl. Res*. 8(4):151-157.

Child, G. 1964. Growth and ageing criteria of impala Aepyceros melampus. *Arnoldia* 27:128-135.

Dalton, D.L., Van Wyk, A. & Kotze, A. 2015. Meshing molecules and management: an overview of hybrid detection in south African wildlife. *Wildlife Stud Services Journal* 2015:49-50.

Fairall, N. & Braack, H.H. 1976. Growth and development of the impala Aypyceros melampus. *Koedoe* 19:83-88.

Green, W.C. & Rothstein, A. 1998. Translocation, hybridization and the endangered black-faced impala. *Conserv. Biol*. 12:475-480.

Hill, R.H. 1982. Effect of dietary extreme of impala rumen epimural flora. *Appl. Enviro. Microbiol*. 44:198-202.

Joubert, E. 1971. Observations on the habitat preferences and populatiuon dynamics of the black-faced impala Aepyceros petersi in S.W. Africa. *Madoqua* 1:55-65.

Lorenzen, E.D. & Siegismund, H.R. 2004. No suggestion of hybridization between the vulnerable black-faced impala (*Aepyceros melampus petersi*) and the common impala (*A. m. melampus*) in Etosha National Park, Namibia. *Molecular Ecology* 13:3007-3019.

Matson, T.K., Goldizen, A.W. & Jarman, P.J. 2005. Microhabitat use by black-faced impala in the Etosha National Park, Namibia. *Journal of Wildlife Management* 69:1708-1715.

Meissner, H.H., Pieterse, E. & Potgieter, J.H.J. 1996. Seasonal food selection and intake by male impala in two habitats. *Sth. Afr. J. Wildl. Res*. 26:56-63.

Van Rooyen, A.F. 1996. Simulated protein requirements and seasonal breeding in impala Aepyceros melampus. *Sth. Afr. J. Wildl. Res*. 26:77-80.

Young, E. 1972. Observations on the movement patterns and daily range size of impala in the Kruger National Park. *Zool. Africana* 7:187-195.

SPRINGBOK

Bednekoff, P.A. & Ritter, R.C. 1994. Vigilance in Nxai pan springbok. *Behaviour* 129:1-11.

Bigalke, R.C. 1972. Observations on the behaviour and feeding habits of the springbok. *Zool. Afr*. 7:333-359.

Child, G. & Le Riche, J.D. 1969. Recent springbok treks (mass movements) in south-western Botswana. *Mammalia* 33:499-504.

Conroy, A.M. 2005. The Springbok. In: *Intensive Wildlife Production in Southern Africa*, pp. 214-226. Eds. Bothma, J. Du P. & Van Rooyen, N. Van Schaik Publishers, Pretoria.

Davies, R.A.G. 1985. *A comparison of springbok and merino sheep on Karoo veld. M.Sc. thesis*, University of Pretoria.

Findlay, G.H. 1989. Development of the springbok skincolour pattern, hair slope and horn rudiments in Antidorcas marsupialis. *S. Afr. J. Zool*. 24:68-73.

Greenwald, L.I. 1967. Water economy of the desert dwelling springbok Antidorcas marsupialis. *M.Sc. thesis*, University of Syracuse.

Hofmeyr, M.D. 1981. Thermal physiology of selected African ungulates with emphasis on the physical properties of the pelage. *Ph.D. thesis*, University of Cape Town.

Hofmeyr, M.D. & Low, G.N. 1987. Thermoregulation, pelage conductance and renal function in desert-adapted springbok, Antidorcas marsupialis. *J. Arid. Environ*. 13:137-151.

Jackson, T.P. 1995. The role of territoriality in the mating system of the springbok Antidorcas marsupialis. *Ph.D. thesis*, University of Pretoria.

Kruger, J.C., Skinner, J.D. & Robbinson, T.J. 1979. On the taxonomic status of the black and white springbok, Antidorcas marsupialis. *S. Afr. J. Sci*. 75:411-412.

Le Roux, J.C. 2015. The springbok migrations of yesteryear: the most spectacular and grandiose historical mammal events in the world. *Wildlife Ranching South Africa Conference*, Sun City 2015.

Mitchell, D., Maloney, S.K., Laburn, H.P., Knight, M.H., Kuhnen, G. Jessen, C. 1997. Activity, blood temperature and brain temperature of free-ranging springbok. *J. Comp. Hpysiol. B* 167:335-343.

Nagy, K.A. & Knight, M.H. 1994. Energy, water, and food use by springbok antelope in the Kalahari desert. *J. Mammal*. 75:860-872.

Novellie, P.A. 1975. Comparative social behaviour of springbok, Antidorcas m. marsupialis and blesbok on the Jack Scott Nature Reserve, Transvaal. *M.Sc. thesis, University of Pretoria*.

Penzhorn, B.L. 1974. Sex and age composition and dimentions of the springbok population in the Mountain Zebra National Park. *J. Sth. Afr. Wildl. Mgmt. Ass*. 4:63-65.

Penzhorn, B.L. 1978. Body growth of the springbok population in the Mountain Zebra National Park. *S. Afr. J. Wildl.Res*. 8:171-172.

Skinner, J.D. 1993. Springbok treks. *Trans. R. Soc. S. Afr*. 48:291-305.

Stapelberg, H., Van Rooyen M.W., Bothma J. du P., Van der Linde, M.J. & Groeneveld, H.T. 2008. Springbok behaviour as affected by environmental conditions in the Kalahari. *Koedoe* 50(1):145-153.

Stapelberg, F.H. 2007. Feeding ecology of the Kalahari springbok Antidorcas marsupialis in the Kgalagadi Transfrontier Park, South Africa. *MSc. dissertation*. University of Pretoria.

Von La Chevallerie, M. & Van Zyl, J.H.M. 1971. Growth and carcass development of the springbok. *Agroanimalia* 3:115-121.

OSTRICH

Western Cape Department of Agriculture Ostrich Manual.

CROCODILES

Blake D. 2006. The Nile crocodile. In: Intensive wildlife production in southern Africa. Ed: J. du P. Bothma & van Rooyen, N. Van Schaik Publishers, Pretoria.

Huchzermeyer F.W. 2003. *Crocodile biology, husbandry and diseases*. CABI publishing, Oxon, UK.

Jensch, B., Baur, M., Brandstaetter, F., Fritz, T., Koelpin, T., Schmidt, F., Sommerland, R. & Voigt, H. 2009. Mindestanforderungen an die artgerechte Haltung von Krokodilen in privaten Terrarien und zoologischen Einrichtungen. *Der Zoologische Garten* 78:193-131.

South African Bureau of Standards (SABS). 2009. Standard on crocodiles in captivity, SANS 631 of 2009.

Trutnau, L. & Sommerland, R. 2006. *Crocodilians. Their Natural History & Captive Husbandry*. Chimaira Buchhandelsgesellschaft mbH, Frankfurt am Main, Germany.

DISEASES

Boomker, J.D. 2015. Helminths of wild animals. Veterinary Helminthology for South Africa. Eds Oberem, P. L., Lange, N. & Kriek. *Agriconnect*, Pretoria.

Bromilow, C. 2010. *Problem plants and alien weeds of South Africa*. Briza Publications Pretoria.

Cleaveland, S. & Dye, C. 1995. Maintenance of a microparasite infecting several host species: rabies in the Serengeti. *Parasitology*, 111 S33-S47.

Coetzer, J.A.W. & Tustin, R.C. 2004. *Livestock diseases in Southern Africa*. Oxford University Press, Cape Town.

Haig, D.M., Grant, D., Deane, D., Campbell, I., Thomson, J., Buxton, D. & Russell, G.C. 2008. An immunisation strategy for the protection of cattle against alcelaphine herpes virus 1 induced by BMC. *Vaccine* 35:4461-4468.

Fourie, J.J., Fourie, L.J. & Horak, I.G. 2005. Efficacy of orally administered powdered aloe juice (*Aloe ferox*) against ticks on cattle, and ticks and fleas on dogs. *Journal of the South African Veterinary Association* 76 (4), 193-196.

Fowler, M.E. & Miller, R.E. 2007. *Zoo and wild animal medicine*. Saunders-Elsevier, Amsterdam.

Horak, I.G., Golezardy, H. & Uys, A.C. 2007. Ticks associated with the three largest wild ruminant species in southern Africa. *Onderstepoort Journal of Veterinary Research*, 74 (3) 231-242.

Kellerman, T.S., Coetzer, J.A.W. & Naude, T.W. 1988. *Plant poisonings and mycotoxicoses of livestock in southern Africa*. Oxford University Press, Cape Town.

Koeppel, K.N. & Kemp, L.V. 2015. Lead toxicosis in Southern Ground hornbills Bucorvus leadbeateri. *Journal of Avian Medicine and surgery*.

Marais, H,J., Nel, P., Bertschinger, H.J., Schoeman, J.P. & Zimmerman, D. 2007. Prevalence and body distribution of sarcoids in South African Cape Mountain Zebra. *Journal of the South African Veterinary Association* 78(3):145-148.

Naude, T., Coetzer, J.A.W. & Kellerman, T.S. 1992. *Variation in animal species' response to plant poisonings and mycotoxicoses in southern Africa*. In: Poisonous Plants. James, L.F. (Ed) 3rd International Symposium Logan, Utah, USA. Iowa State University Press, Ames, Iowa.

Penzhorn, B.L. (ed). 2006. Proceedings of Update on diseases of southern African wildlife. *Wildlife Group of SAVA*, Onderstepoort.

Picker, M., Griffiths, C. & Weaving, A. 2004. *Field guide to insects of South Africa*. Struik, Cape Town.

Reinecke, R.K. 1983. *Veterinary Helminthology*. Butterworths, Durban.

Sandvik, T. *et al*. 2005. Classical swine fever in South Africa after 87 years' absence. *Veterinary Record* (Letters, Aug 27).

Spickett, A.M., Van der Merwe, D. & Mathee, O. 2007. The effect of orally administered *Aloe marlothii* leaves on *Boophilus decoloratus*. *Experimental Applied Acarology* 41(1-2) 139-146.

Steinel, A., Parrish, C.R., Bloom, M.E. & Truyen, U. 2001. Parvovirus infections in wild carnivores. *Journal of wildlife diseases*, 37(3) 594-607.

Van den Heever, L.W. & Du Preez, J.H. 1993. *Zoonoses: animal diseases and man*. Butterworths, Durban.

Vosloo, W., De Klerk, L-M., Boshoff, C.I., Botha, B., Dwarka, R.M., Keet, D. & Haydon, D.T. 2007. Characterisation of a SAT-1 outbreak of foot-and-mouth disease in captive African buffalo: clinical symptoms, genetic characterisation and phylogenetic comparison of outbreak isolates. *Veterinary Microbiology* 120:226-240.

Vosloo, W., Lubisi, B.A., Pardini, A., Botha, B., Gers, S., Everett, H., Gurrala, R., Keet, D.F. & Drew T. *Classical Swine fever virus infection in African wild suids*. (In press)

Whitely, N. & Miller, J.M. 2015. Does diatomaceous earth have a role in worm control? *Proceedings of joint conference of SAVA and the American consortium for small ruminants*.

Woodford, M.H., Keet, D.F. & Bengis, R.G. 2000. *Post-mortem procedures for wildlife veterinarians and field biologists*. Office International des Epizooties, Paris.

GENERAL INDEX

A
Aardwolf 102, 321
Abomassum 78, 293, 334
Acid acetic 78
    amino 78
    butyric 78
    lactic 78
    propionic 78
African buffalo 92, 130, 131, 137, 293, 295, 303, 304, 307, 308, 313, 316–318
African wild cat 29, 97, 311
    wild dog 241, 245, 244, 246, 311
Alcelaphine antelope 196, 217, 347, 347
Alien plants 47, 59, 60, 67, 68
Alternative tourism 38, 39
Anatolian shepherd dog 104
Animal Diseases Act (Act 35 of 1984) 141, 298
Anogenital stimulation 241, 272
APAC (Agricultural Produce Agents Council) 69
AppliGator 342
Arabian oryx 153, 154, 155
Aves 247

B
Baboon 29, 287, 336
Bankrotbos 67
Beisa oryx 153, 155
Besembos 340
Biome 44, 45, 66, 211, 212, 351
Biome forest 45
    fynbos 47
    grassland 46
    Nama Karoo 46
    savanna 46
    succulent Karoo 47
    thicket 46
Bison 304, 315
Black rhinoceros 4–7, 29, 48, 51, 77–97, 121–125, 128, 309
    Eastern 121
    North western 121
    South central 121
    South western
Black seed grass 202
Black wattle 59
Black wildebeest 3–6, 9, 10, 23, 24, 26, 29, 50, 61, 97, 112, 150, 211, 212, 283, 296, 313, 314, 339
Black-backed jackal 100, 101, 285, 311
Blackbuck 315
Black-coated impala 98
Black-faced impala 217–219, 220, 221
Black-footed cat 29
Blackwood 60
Blesbok 4–6, 10, 23, 26, 32, 33, 50, 61, 97, 112, 150, 196–205, 211, 217, 305, 314, 319, 347
    white 197, 199
Blue buffalo 85
Blue crane 10, 105, 353

Blue wildebeest 22, 32, 50, 61, 69, 79, 97–99, 118, 187, 206, 211–214, 221, 230, 241, 283, 296, 314, 319
Blue- (golden) wildebeest 21–23, 178, 213, 224
Boma 70, 71, 78, 80, 84, 85, 87, 89, 106, 107, 109–118, 125, 126, 135, 136, 139, 140, 144, 145, 172, 179, 191, 194, 195, 210, 216, 224, 275, 284, 290, 291, 295, 301, 306, 314, 315, 348, 349, 351
Bongo 97
Bont wildebeest 213
Bontebok 4–7, 9, 10, 18, 24, 26, 29, 50, 97, 152, 196, 197–199, 204, 205, 211, 313, 335, 347
Bontebok National Park 327, 335
Bracken fern 351
Brindled wildebeest 211, 212
Bronze wildebeest 213
Brown ear tick 141, 142, 144, 188, 316–320, 340, 341
Brown hyena 101
Browser 46–48, 53, 60, 63, 66, 69, 77–79, 84, 85, 87, 235, 236, 282, 284, 332
Browsing capacity 69,
Buffalo 4, 5, 7, 14, 15, 17, 23, 48, 51, 53, 61, 70, 71, 73, 77, 83, 84, 89, 93, 95, 110, 111, 116, 121, 130, 131, 133–142, 144–146, 173, 181, 194, 216, 224, 269, 273, 281, 288, 290, 350
    Advisory Committee 145
    breeding 7, 133, 135,
    Corridor-free 318
    disease-free 7, 10, 15, 17, 18, 144, 146, 273, 288, 304, 316
    diseases 140–145, 274, 276, 280, 288–290, 292–296, 299, 300, 302, 303, 305–307, 309, 312–318, 330, 335–337, 339, 340, 345, 348, 349
    Diseases Protocol 290
    grass 122, 150
    hand-raised 273
    management system 135, 137
    nutrition 137
    prices 146
    specific pathogen free (SPF) 7
    TB-free 290
    transportation 139
Burchell's golden gemsbok 153
    zebra 153
Bushbuck 23, 46, 48, 50, 97, 112, 189, 192, 193, 282, 288, 307, 314, 319, 335, 342, 349
Bushpig 307, 309, 328, 329, 349

C
Cape blue buck 165
    buffalo 3, 92, 94, 95, 130
    bushbuck 26
    grysbok 26, 236
    hunting dog 245
    mountain zebra 4–6, 9, 18, 26, 29, 51, 97, 147, 150, 151, 152, 327, 328
    pole cat 311

GENERAL INDEX **363**

Capture drugs 107, 115, 117–119, 139, 263
  administering 117
Capture method 106–108, 117, 118
  cage traps 103, 109, 117
  drop nets 112, 113
  hand capture 106–108, 117
  leg-hold traps 105, 108, 109, 117
  linear nets 112, 113
  mass capture 106, 109, 116–118, 139
  net boma 112–114
  net capture 106–108, 112, 117
  net gun capture 107, 108, 117
  plastic boma capture 106, 109, 110, 117, 118
  pop-up boma 114
  passive 106, 107, 113, 234
    boma 107, 114, 194, 195, 216
    boma traps 113
    drop-down bomas 113
    capture structure 107, 113
    net boma 113
    permanent passive capture structure 113, 114
Caracal 29, 101–103, 162, 164, 214, 238, 321
Carbohydrates 77, 78, 80, 274, 278
Carrying capacity 18–21, 66, 68, 69, 79, 207, 209, 215, 222
Chacma baboon 221
Cheetah 8, 96, 98, 101, 104, 109, 201, 241, 244, 245, 289, 291, 311, 321, 323–325, 337, 346, 352
  king 98, 244, 245
Chemical capture 106, 107, 115, 139
CITES Appendix I 28
  Appendix II 28
Civet 287, 311, 321, 338
Clawless otter 321
Colour variants 3, 12, 17, 23, 91, 98, 99, 154, 173, 189, 197, 211–213, 218, 223, 224, 227, 237, 276
Common hook thorn 351
Common reedbuck 23, 29
Cookson's wildebeest 212
Couch grass 202
Crocodile 18, 29, 109, 253–267, 281
Crow 287

D
Darting 106–108, 111, 112, 116–119, 136–139, 143, 162, 171, 210, 215, 276, 279, 280
Diarrhoea 83, 87, 89, 240, 245, 271, 272–274, 279, 283, 291, 292, 297, 302, 310, 313, 321–323, 325, 328, 330, 332, 335
Diatomaceous earth (DE) 343
DNA 91, 92–96, 98, 129, 173, 180, 191, 197, 204, 309, 320
Domestic dogs 101, 103, 143, 242, 285, 286, 311, 312, 321, 322, 335
Domesticated cat 97
Donkey 43, 97, 99, 104, 244, 309, 326, 327
Drainage lines 53, 56, 57, 63, 66, 157, 158, 170, 181, 208, 220, 233
Dropseed grass 150
Duiker 29, 235, 237–239
  blue 23, 29, 48, 112, 235, 238, 240, 285, 286, 346, 350
  bush 235
  common 51, 235, 314, 346
  grey 235, 238
  Natal red 235
  red 50, 235, 236, 239,
Duncan Applicator 342, 343, 348, 350
Dung beetles 9, 10, 49

E
East African buffalo 146
  greater kudu 180
  sable 165
  topi 205
East Zambian sable 205
Eastern Cape greater kudu 26
  Cape kudu 180, 181, 184, 186
  sable antelope 165
Ecotone 50, 57, 169, 191, 208, 220, 222
Ecotourism 2, 3, 17, 18, 25, 31, 38, 39, 42, 74, 122, 144, 146, 167, 245
Eland 23, 32–34, 48, 50, 61, 70, 97, 112, 116, 161, 173–179, 187, 194, 232, 241, 283, 292, 302, 303, 312, 314, 320, 333, 339, 340–342, 350
  Cape 173, 174, 176–178
  East African 173, 174
  Livingstone's 173, 174
  Lord Derby 173, 174, 178
  Patterson 173
  southern 173
Elephant 3, 4, 8, 28, 29, 48, 51, 61, 78, 116, 273, 278, 279, 283, 300–302, 307, 316, 335, 353
English oak 351
Environmental contamination 353, 354
Eutrophication 89, 352
Evisceration 35

F
Factory farming 33
Fallow deer 315
Fencing 22, 70, 71, 73, 102, 135, 151, 162, 180, 215, 237, 238, 240, 242, 245, 246, 284, 294, 296, 352
Fencing predator- 102, 162
Fire Protection Agency (FPA) 75
Fluorosis 89
Foregut fermenters 77
Forest buffalo 92
Fringe-eared oryx 153

G
Game meat 2, 3, 5, 10–12, 16, 17, 31–36, 226
Gemsbok 13, 18, 23, 32, 46, 47, 50, 69, 71, 96, 153, 155, 156
  Angolan 153
  Burchell's golden 153–160, 232, 283, 299, 312, 320, 333, 335
  royal (red) 153
  southern 155, 156
Genet 287, 311
Genetic diversity 16, 20, 23, 70, 91, 92, 94, 96, 98–151, 166, 175, 181, 230
Gerbil 287
Ghost wildebeest 213

Giant eland 173, 174
   sable 165–167
Gifblaar 216, 350
Giraffe 48, 73, 77, 110, 115, 142, 221, 223, 275, 277, 281, 292, 298, 300, 310, 314, 339, 350
Golden King Wildebeest 213
Golden wildebeest 21–23, 178, 213, 224
Grazers 47, 48, 53–55, 60, 62, 63, 66, 69, 73, 78, 79, 84, 122, 126, 131, 144, 148, 150, 161, 202, 203, 209, 212, 214, 216, 278, 332, 333
Grazing capacity 69
Grevy's zebra 147, 149
Grey rhebuck 48, 51,
Ground squirrel 285

H

Hartebeest 18, 23, 32, 48, 71, 205, 211, 217, 283, 347
   red 54, 97, 171, 196, 207, 232, 241, 277, 314
Hartmann's mountain zebra 29, 147, 150, 151, 152
Heat exhaustion 106, 127
Hind gut fermenters 47, 77
Hippo (hippopotamus) 28, 29, 61, 73, 77, 113, 114–116, 273, 283, 291, 302, 335, 352
Homeostasis 77,
Honey badger 102, 238, 287, 289, 312
Horselike antelope 153
Hunting tourism 6, 18, 26
Hybridisation 97, 99, 150, 165, 173, 174, 197

I

Impala 5, 14, 18, 22, 23, 32, 33, 50, 53, 61, 63, 70, 98, 107, 110, 112, 113, 115, 116, 160, 161, 178, 181, 187, 192–194, 197, 217–227, 230, 274, 283, 292–295, 302, 312, 314, 330, 332, 335, 342, 345, 346, 349,
   black-coloured 21, 218, 221
   black-faced 217–221
   common red-coloured 21, 218
   East African 217–219, 221
   saddle back 21, 218
   southern 217, 220, 221
Inbreeding depression 96
Indian water buffalo 97
International Trade in Endangered Species (CITES) 8, 15, 24, 28, 29, 129, 235, 256

K

King's Wildebeest 213, 276
Klipspringer 23, 51, 236–238, 346, 350
   white saddle 237
Kob 97
Korrigum 196, 205
Kudu 14, 17, 22, 32, 46, 48, 50, 69, 70, 79, 96, 97, 110, 112, 173, 180–183, 185–190, 192, 220, 223, 224, 241, 277, 280, 282, 283, 285, 286, 288, 289, 295, 307, 312, 332, 335, 336, 340, 342, 346, 348, 349, 351, 352
   Abyssinian greater 180
   greater 97, 173, 174, 180, 182–184, 188, 314
   lesser 97, 180, 183,
   northern greater 183
   southern greater 180, 183
   western greater 180
Kweek 216

L

Lantana 60, 351
Lechwe 18, 97, 314, 315
   red 29
Leopard 29, 101, 103, 104, 108, 117, 201, 270, 289, 311, 321, 323
Lion 4, 8, 15, 17, 28, 29, 96, 101, 117, 241–246, 282, 288–290, 301, 311, 321–323, 338, 345, 352
Lipids 78
Llamas 284
Love grass 202
Lynx 323

M

Maluti dog 104
Mass tourism 38, 40
Matetsi/Southern sable 165
Milkweed 350
Mongoose 285, 287, 298, 311
   yellow 285
Mountain nyala 97, 189, 190
   reedbuck 23, 48, 51,
   wire grass 340
   zebra 5, 23, 147, 149–152, 309, 326, 327
Multimammate mouse 301
Mutation 92, 93, 98

N

Nagana 4, 306, 307, 308, 349
Narrow-leaved turpentine grass 150
Nature, Environmental and Adventure Tourism (NEAT) 10
Nile crocodile 29, 253, 254, 256, 258, 260, 264
Nilgai 315
Nutrition 12, 19, 21, 33, 53, 61, 62, 77–80, 82, 83, 86, 134, 137, 148, 152, 162, 164, 171, 172, 174, 178, 183, 185, 187, 188, 193, 195, 202, 208, 214, 216, 231, 239, 242, 244, 248, 252, 254, 255, 263, 264, 269, 270, 272, 274, 278–280, 299, 300, 307, 331, 345
Nyala 18, 23, 46, 50, 53, 69, 70, 77, 96, 97, 107, 112, 172, 173, 178, 181, 187, 189, 190–195, 277, 282, 312, 314, 319, 340, 346, 350
   red 189, 190
Nyala/kudu cross 191
Nyamera 196
Nyasaland gnu 212

O

Oat hay 85, 137
Oleander 351
Oribi 5, 23, 29, 51, 236,
Ostrich 18, 104, 110, 247–250, 252
Oulandsgras 85, 137
Oxpecker 5, 9, 10, 279, 330, 337, 342, 343

P

Painted dog 245
Pangolin 281
Pathogen free (SPF) 7
Pica 81, 127
Plains zebra 3, 4, 23, 51, 97, 147–152, 285, 327
Porcines 283, 328
Porcupine 162, 281
Port Jackson willow 60
Predator management 100, 105
Prince wildebeest 213
Puku 97

Q

Quagga 4, 147, 148, 326

R

Red grass 62, 150, 202
Red wildebeest 97, 214
Rhodes grass 216
Roan antelope 5–7, 9, 24, 29, 57, 161, 164, 165, 172, 282, 284, 319, 334
Rooikrantz 60
Rowland Ward records and trophy status 153, 156, 167, 175, 180–182, 190, 199, 205, 217, 220, 221, 228, 229
Royal sable 165
Ruminant 2, 47, 51, 77, 78, 82, 84, 86, 130, 131, 135, 142, 148, 270, 271, 277, 278, 280, 284, 300, 305, 312, 313, 315, 340, 341, 352

S

Sable antelope 5–7, 10, 22, 79, 96, 164, 165–167, 169,172, 173, 230, 309, 314, 319, 320
Savanna buffalo 3
Scimitar-horned oryx 153–155, 314
Sedatives 115, 116, 119, 139,
Seeplines 55, 56,
Semi-intensive systems 18, 66, 215, 216
Serval 29, 102, 311, 321, 323, 324
Sharpe's grysbok 29, 51
Sicklebush 172
Silver clusterleaf 56
Single nucleotide polymorphisms (SNP) 95, 96
Sink effect 105
Sitatunga 97, 173, 314
Smutsfinger grass 216
Soil health 45
Southern oryx 153
    sable antelope 165
    springbok 226
Special Hunting Permits 29
Spiral-horned antelope 173
Spotted hyena 29, 101, 311
Springbok 3, 18, 22, 23, 32, 33, 35, 46–48, 50, 61, 63, 71, 89, 97, 112, 116, 150, 158, 159, 197, 217, 226–234, 277, 278, 280, 283, 305, 313–316, 335, 339, 341, 346, 350
    Algolan 226
    Damara 226
    Kalahari 226
    northern 226
    southern 226
Steekgras 122
Steenbok 23, 48, 51, 236–239, 346, 349
Suni 23, 29, 51, 112,
Suni Livingstone's 236

T

Tef 137
Thorn apple 351
Tiang 196, 205
Tick off applicator 342
Tickball 342, 343
Topi 196, 205
Topi East coast 205
TOPS (Threatened or Protected Species Regulation) 28–30, 70, 118, 119, 204, 212, 256,
Tortoise 102, 281, 312, 339
Tranquilisers 112, 115–119, 277
Triffid weed 60
Trypanosome 4, 306, 307, 349
Tsessebe 19, 23, 29, 48, 61, 97, 100, 171, 181, 196, 197, 205–211, 225, 234, 314
    Bangwela 205, 206
Turpentine grass 150

V

Vaal rhebok 26
Viscera 35, 36
Voss wildebeest 213

W

Warthog 5, 30, 48, 53, 61, 71, 110, 113, 161, 238, 240, 241, 245, 281, 288, 289, 307, 309, 328, 329, 338, 346, 349,
Water buffalo 315
Waterbuck 23, 48, 50, 70, 192, 206, 221, 293, 305, 318
Weeping wattle 351
White oryx 153
White rhino (rhinoceros) 4–7, 23, 24, 28, 29, 48, 51, 61, 77, 78, 82, 97, 121
    north western 121
White wildebeest 213
White-bearded blue wildebeest 230
    gnu 212
White-tailed deer 315
Wild dogs 241, 245, 246, 274, 286, 311, 321, 322, 345
Wild olive tree 340
Wild tobacco 351
Wildlife Ranching South Africa (WRSA) 13, 14, 16, 32, 34, 36, 204, 240, 267, 298
Wildlife-based tourism 39–43
Wildlife-ecotourism 42

Z

Zambian sable 165
Zebra 5, 18, 32, 46, 48, 53, 54, 61, 77, 78, 82, 97, 99, 121, 143, 147–149, 161, 206, 221, 270, 275, 278, 282, 283, 302, 319, 326, 327, 330, 331, 342, 347, 348, 349, 352,

SCIENTIFIC NAME INDEX

A
Acacia cyclops 60
   karoo 181
   mearnsii 59
   melanoxylon 60
   saligna 60
   spp. 178, 185, 193, 232
Acinonyx jubatus 241
Adansonia digitata 193
Aepyceros melampus 181, 217, 226, 230
   holubi 217
   johnstoni 217
   katangae 217
   melampus 217
   petersi 217
   rendilis 217
   suara 217
Aepycertotidae 217
Albizia tangeniensis 314
Aloe ferox 343
   marlothii 343
Amblyomma hebraeum 142, 312, 339
Antelopini 217
Antidorcas marsupialis 217, 226
   angolensis 226
   hofmeyri 226
   marsupialis 226
Aristida spp. 122
Asclepias sp. 350

B
Bauhinia sp. 178
Boscia albitrunca 178, 232
Brachiaria spp. 233, 350
Burkea africana 178

C
Cacti 232
Capparis sepiaria 193
Cenchrus ciliaris 85, 208
Cephalophini 235
Cephalophus natalensis 235
Ceratotherium simum 121
   simum 7
Chloromelas sp. 202
Chromolaena odorata 60
Chrysoeoma tenuifolia 232
Chrysomya bezziana 346, 347
Colophospermum mopane 193
Combretum apiculatum 185
   spp. 178
Connochaetes gnou 212, 296
   taurinus 212, 221, 296
   albojubatus 212
   cooksoni 212
   johnstoni 212
   taurinus 212
Cordylobia anthrophagia 346
Crocodylus niloticus 253
Crotalaria 350
Cymbopogon pospischilii 150
Cynodon dactylon 202, 216, 232

D
Damalis dorcas 205
Damaliscus jimela 205
   korrigum 205
   lunatus 205
   superstes 205
   tiang 205
   topi 205
Damaliscus pygargus 205
   phillipsi 205
   pygargus 205
Datura stramonium 351
Diceros bicornis 7, 121
   bicornis 121
      micheali 121
      minor 121
Dichapetalum cymosum 350
Dichrostachys cinerea 172, 178, 185, 193
Digitaria eriantha 208
   spp. 232
Diplorhynchus condylocarpon 178

E
Ehretia rigida 178
Enneapogon scoparius 232
Equus grevyi 147
   quagga 4, 147, 326
   spp. 221
   zebra 147, 327
Eragrostis curvula 137, 202
Eragrostis spp. 208, 232
   tef 85, 137
Euclea spp. 178
Euphorbia sp. 350

G
Gedoelstia 347
Giraffa camelopardalis 221
Grewia occidentalis 185
Grewia spp. 178, 193, 232
Gyrostigma 126, 127

H
Haemophysalis leachi 311
Heteropogon contortis 208

SCIENTIFIC NAME INDEX

Hippotragus equinus 161, 172
   equinus 161
Hippotragus leucopaeos 4, 165
Hippotragus niger 165
   nkirkii 165
   niger 165
   roosevelti 165
   variani 165

I
Ischaemum brachyatherum 298
Ixodes rubicundus 234, 275, 340

K
Kirkioestrus 347
Kobus ellipsiprymnus 221

L
Lantana camara 60, 350, 351
Lonchocarpus capassa 178
Loxodonta africana 301
Lycaon pictus 241

M
Mastomys natalensis 301
Merxmuellera disticha 340
Mesembryanthomaceae 340
Microcystis aeruginosa 89, 352
Monechma sp. 232

N
Neospora caninum 274, 291
Neotragini 235, 236
Neotragus moschatus livingstonianus 236
Nerium oleander 351
Nicotiana glauca 351

O
Oestrus ovis 347
Olea africana 340
Oreotragus oreotragus 236
Oribi oribi ourebi 236
Oryx beisa beisa 153
   beisa callotis 153
   blainei 153
   dammah 153
   gazella 153
   leucoryx 153

P
Panicum coloratum 208
   maximum 208
   spp. 232
   stapfianum 150
Panthera leo 241
Papio ursinus 221
Parafilaria bassoni 142, 337
Peltophorum africanum 351

Pennisetum spp. 232
Pentzia incana 232
Philantomba monticola 235
Portulacaria afra 178
Psoralea sp. 232
Psoroptes pienaarii 142
Pteridium aquinlinum 351

Q
Quercus robur 351

R
Raphicerus campestris 236
   melanotis 236
Rhigosum sp. 232
Rhipicephalus appendiculatus 142, 188, 316, 317, 318
   evertsi 164, 309, 319, 341
   sanguineus 311, 344
Rhus ciliata 232
   erosa 340

S
Sarcoptes scabeii 142
Sarcostemma viminale 314
Schmidtia bulbosa 208
Sclerocarya birrea 179
Securingia virosa 178
Senegalia [Acacia] caffra 351
   erubescens 185
   galpinii 185
   mellifera 185
   nigrescens 185
   nigrirostris 202
Setaria woodii 208
Solanum kwebenzi 314
   spp. 232
Sorghum versicolor 208
   verticilaster 208
Spirostachys africana 193
Sporobolus fimbriatus 150
   spp. 232
Stipagrostis uniplumis 232
Stoebe vulgaris 67
Strobilooestrus sp. 346
Struthio camelius 247
Suidae 328
Strychnos sp. 178
Sylvicapra grimmia 235
Syncerus caffer 3, 94, 130, 293, 295
   caffer caffer 3

T
Taurotragus 173
Terminalia sericea 56
   spp. 178
Themeda triandra 150, 202, 208, 232
Tragelaphines 173, 189
Tragelaphus 97

angasii 189
buxtoni 189
derbianus 173
derbianus gigas 173
derbianus derbianus 173
imberbis 180
oryx 173
oryx livingstonii 173
oryx oryx 173
oryx pattersonianus 173
speckii 173
strepsiceros 173
strepsiceros bea 180
strepsiceros chora 180
strepsiceros cottoni 180
strepsiceros strepsiceros 180

U
Urochloa mosambicensis 208

V
Vachellia karroo 185
   sieberana 185
   tortillis 185

X
Xerus inauris 285
Ximenia caffra 178

Z
Ziziphus mucronata 193, 232
Zygophyllum sp. 232

INDEX OF DISEASES AND PARASITES

A
A equine 2 virus (H3N8) 326
Abdominal pain 278
Abortion 141, 142, 203, 274, 291, 302–07, 324
Acidosis 80, 82, 85, 87, 216, 239, 278
Acute hepatitis 266
Adenoviral hepatitis 267
Adenovirus infection 266
Aflatoxicosis 126
African horse sickness (AHS) 326, 327
    redwater 309
    swine fever (ASFV) 328, 329
Alcelaphine herpes virus (Al 1) 216
Aldicarb 353
Amblyomma 312
    hebraeum 142, 312, 313, 339
Anaerobic metabolism 265
Ancylostoma spp. 337
Anthrax 139, 143, 164, 172, 188, 216, 224, 269, 282–284, 304
    acute 283
    bacilli 283
    bacteria 282, 283
    chronic 283
    peracute 283
    spores 164, 282, 284
    subacute 283
Arcanobacterium/Actinomyces pyogenes 279
Arthritis 266, 324
Ascarid worms 337
Aspiration pneumonia 280
Avian influenza 247, 252
Avittelina 333

B
Babesia 274, 309–311
    bicornis 309
    bigemina 308, 309
    bovis 308
    caballi 309
    canis canis 311
    canis rossi 311
    canis vogeli 311
    equi 309
    felis 311
    irvinesmithi 309
    leo 311
    spp. 309, 310, 311
    trautmanni 309
Babesiosis 69, 308–313, 342
Bacillus anthracis 282
Bacterial contamination 36
    culture 289
    disease 5, 141, 252
    eye infection 349
    growth 33, 352
    infection 141, 276, 279, 281

    isolation 303
    load 36
    skin disease 266
    strain 282
Besnoitia 291
Besnoitiosis 291
Bilharzia 332, 336
    parasites 332
Biting flies 276, 348, 349
Bloat 35, 138, 267, 277, 278, 280–283, 301
Blow flies 346, 350
Boophilus (Rhipicephalus) decoloratus 309
    (Rhipicephalus) microplus 309
    decolaratus spp. 342
    bronchiseptica 324
Bot flies 346
    nasal 347
    horse 437
    rhino 347
    stomach 350
Bots 126, 347
Botulism 81, 127, 143, 210, 216, 275, 298, 299
    Type C 299
    Type D 298
Bovine brucellosis 141, 143
    Malignant Catarrh (BMC) 5, 8, 73, 216, 296
    papilloma virus 143, 327
    rhinotracheitis virus 203
    tuberculosis (BTB) 5, 36, 73, 139, 141, 144, 180, 188, 241, 288
Bronchitis 281, 335
Bronchonema magna 335
Brucella 302, 303, 304
    abortus 179, 303, 304
    bacterial species 302
    melitensis 302
    ovis 302
    suis 302
Brucellosis 7, 17, 22, 36, 73, 141, 144, 172, 179, 269, 274, 302–304, 318, 343
Buffalo Diseases Protocol 290
Buphagus spp. 330
Bursitis 303

C
Calici virus 324
Callicophoron 332
Campylobacter jejuni 203
Canine biliary 344
    distemper virus (CDV) 321
    parvo 321, 322
    parvo virus (CPV2) 322
Capture myopathy 108, 118, 186, 195, 210, 234, 240, 274, 276, 277,
    stress 210
Cat flea 345
    flu 323

Cerebral theileriosis 313
Cestodes 333
Chagas' disease 306
Chilling 172, 271, 280
Chlamydiophila 281
Chlamydiosis 266
Chlamydophilia 324
Choke 279
Choriopsoroptes keneyenis 345
Chronic conjunctivitis 266
Chrysomyia bezziana 276
Classical swine fever 329, 330
Clostridia 300, 301
Clostridial enteritis 195
    myositis 127, 172, 216, 300, 301
    l-diseases 143, 164
Clostridium botulinum 298
    chauvoei 300
    novyi 300
    perfringens Type A bacteria 278
    septicum 300
Coccidia 85, 90, 170, 240, 290
Coccidial oocysts 291
    infection 279
Coccidian 279
    parasites 267
Coccidiosis 22, 172, 224, 263, 266, 267, 273, 290, 291,
Colic 83, 87, 126, 127, 172, 278
Colostrum 237, 271, 273
Conical fluke 332
Conjunctivitis 266, 267, 297
Constipation 83, 272, 278
Copper deficiency 81, 172, 203
Corneal opacity 292
Corridor disease (CD)
Corynebacterium 87, 279, 280
    abscessation 87
    bacteria 280
    vaccine 279
Cowdria ruminantium 312
Crocodile pox 266
Ctenocephalides sp. 345
Cyanobacterial poisoning 127,
Cyanobacterium 89, 352
Cyst 36, 291, 333–338
Cyst hydatid 143, 335, 338
Cytauzoonosis 320

D
Dehydration 195, 271, 272, 281, 289, 291–293, 321
Demodectic mange 142, 276
Demodex cafferi 345
Depigmentation 16, 276
Diarrhoea 83, 87, 89, 240, 245, 271–274, 279, 283, 291, 292, 297, 302, 310, 313, 321–323, 325, 328, 330, 332, 335
Dictyocaulus africana 335
    filaria 335

    viviparous 335
Dikkop 327
Distemper 246, 274, 322
Draaisiekte 338
Dunkop 327
Dystocia 83

E
E. coli 243, 267, 273
East Coast Fever 5, 316, 317, 318
Echidnophaga sp. 346
Echinoccocosis 269
    granulosus 335
    spp. 333
Ectoparasites 143
Ehrlichia ruminantium 312
Eimeria spp. 290
Eleaphora saggita 335
Encephalomyocarditis (EMC) 302
Endoparasites 143, 170, 234
Enterotoxaemia 278
Equine influenza 326
    rhinopneumonitis 326
    sarcoids 152, 327
Equus zebra 147, 327
Erlichia canis 344
Erlichiosis 344
Eutrophication 89, 352

F
Face flies 281, 297, 349
Fasciola gigantica 332
Fasciola hepatica 332
Feeding stress 160, 210
Feline corona viruses (FeCoV) 325
    enteric corona virus 325
    immunosuppression virus (FIV) 321
    infectious peritonitis (FeCo) 321
    infectious peritonitis (FIP) 325
    leukemia (FeLv) 321, 324
    panleukopenia 323, 324
    parvo 321–323
    rhinotracheitis (herpes) 321
Filarial worm 335–337
Flukes 142, 332
Foot and mouth disease (FMD) 5, 7, 11–14, 16, 31, 32, 34, 141, 144, 145, 224, 274, 293–295, 296, 297, 318
Footrot 275
Fungal poisons 351
    skin disease 266
Fungus/Fungi 85, 87, 274
Fusobacterium necrophorum 275

G
Gamma herpes virus 296
Gas gangrene 143, 300
Gasterophilus sp. 347
Gastroenteritis 292, 322, 325

Gid 333, 336, 338
Glossina 307
   austeni 349
   brevipalpis 349
   morsitans 349
   pallidipes 349
   spp. 349
Goedoelstia-flies 203
Gyrostigma pavesi 347

H
Haemaphysalis leachi 344
Haematobia 349
Haematobosca 349
Haemoglobinuria 310
Haemonchus contortus 335
   spp. 334, 335
Haemonchus vegliai 332
Haemorrhagic diarrhoea 283, 313
Heart worm 36
Heartwater 69, 144, 160, 179, 195, 229, 234, 274, 312–316, 339
Hepatic lipidosis 244, 245
Hepatitis 266
Hippo fly 348
Hippoboscids 346
Hog cholera 329, 330
Hookworm 337
Horn flies 349
Horse bot fly 347
   flies 348
House fly 346, 348, 349
Houttynia struthionis 252
Human neurocysticercosis (NCC) 334
Hyalomma sp. 344
   truncatum 309
Hydatid disease 333, 338
Hydatids 36
Hygroma 141, 143, 302, 303
Hyperacute capture myopathy 277
Hyperthermia 118

I
Internal parasites 90, 142, 163, 233, 330, 331, 343, 349
Intestinal coccidiosis 172, 290, 291
Isospora spp. 290
Ixodes rubicundus 234, 275, 340

J
Jaundice 310, 352

K
Keds 345, 346
Kennel tick 311, 344, 345

L
Laminitis 164, 274, 350
Lasiostrongylus 332

Libostrongylus douglassi 252
Lice 143, 276, 345
Lipoptena sp. 346
Liver abscessation 278
   flukes 332
Louse 345, 346
   flies 276
Lumpy skin disease 142
Lung oedema 277, 317, 319
Lungworm 224, 280, 281, 335
Lyssa virus 285

M
Maggots 276, 346, 347, 348
Malignant catarrhal fever 144
   oedema 143, 301
Mange 142, 276, 345
   sarcoptic 276, 345, 346
Microcystis 89, 127, 352
   aeruginosa 352
   -poisoning 270, 352
Mineral deficiencies 80, 223
Mite 142, 143, 333, 339, 345
Moniezia benedini 333
   expansa 333
Moraxella 281
Morbilli virus 292
Mucosal disease (BVD) 297
Musca domestica 348
   spp. 281, 349
   xanthomelas 297
Muscle infection 300
Myaisis 346
Mycobacterium bovis 288
Mycoplasma 266
   alligatoria 266
   crocodyli 266
Mycoplasmosis 266, 267
Mycotoxicosis 86
Mycotoxins 83, 86, 87, 274, 351
Myoglobin 277

N
Nasal bot flies 347
   flies 281
Nematodes 332, 335
Neospora caninum 274, 291
Neosporosis 291
Nodular demodectic mange lesions 142

O
Oesophageal obstruction 279
Oestrid fly 9
Onchocerca 337
Oocysts 143, 290, 291
Opacity 267, 281, 292, 297
Orchitis 303
Ornithodoros porcinus porcinus 328
Overexertion disease 276

P

Pancreatitis 325
Parafilaria 142, 336, 349
   bassoni 142, 337
Paralysis tick 339, 340
Parasitic infections 276
Pathogens 7, 85, 240, 266
Pepper ticks 339
Peritonitis 321, 325
Picornidae 301
Piroplasms 308, 309, 316, 317
Pleuritis 325
Pneumonia 87, 164, 172, 188, 210, 224, 240, 266, 271, 272, 274, 280, 281, 288, 297, 326
Pneumostrongylus calcaratus 335
   cornigerus 335
Poisoning aflatoxin 127
   chemical 352
   Microcystis 270, 352
   tannic acid 81
Polyarthritis 274, 275
Popeye 281, 347,
Probstmayria 330
Protostrongylus capensis 335
   etoshai 335
Protozoal organism 274, 290
Protozoan sarcocysts 143
Proventriculitis 252

Q

Quarter evil 143

R

Rabies 188, 246, 269, 285–287, 304, 321
   canine strain 285
   herpestid strain 285
Red gut 82, 85, 163, 164, 278
Redwater 164, 179, 308, 309, 310
Rhino bot fly 347
Rhipicephalus appendiculatus 142, 188, 316–318, 355
   evertsi evertsi 309, 319, 341
   nitens 340
   pulchellus 320
   sanguineus 311, 344
   spp. 320, 340
   zambesiensis 320
Rickettsia conori 344
   ruminantium 339
Rift Valley fever (RVF) 142, 143, 274, 304–306
Rinderpest 4, 94, 180, 228, 292, 293, 307, 318, 349R
Ringworm 276
Roundworm 142, 203, 224, 330–332, 334, 337, 338
Rumen acidosis 278
Rumenitis 278
Runting 252, 259, 267

S

Salmonella 36, 243
   spp. 35
Salmonellosis 267, 279, 291
Sarcocysticosis 291
Sarcocystis 291
   parasite 291
Schistosoma 332
   sp. 336
Screwworm 279, 341, 346
Septicaemia 263, 279, 284
Skin cancer 227, 276
Screwworm fly 346
Sleeping sickness 306, 307
Snotsiekte 5, 8, 73, 144, 216, 297
Snuffles 323, 324
Sponssiekte 127, 172, 300
Squamous cell carcinoma 276
Stable fly 348
Staphylococcus 36
Steatitis 263
Stephanofilaria 276, 336
Sticktight fleas 346
Stomach ulcers 124, 126
Stomoxys calcitrans 348
Streptococcus 36
Summer sores 337
Sus scrofa 328

T

Tabanid 348
Tabanus biguttatus 348
   gonyamai 336
   hyaena 336
   hydatidgena 336
   multiceps 333
   regis 336
   saginata 333
   saginata 333
   solium 333
   spp. 336
Tampan 328, 329
Tapeworm 36, 142, 143, 252, 331, 333–338
   carnivore 36, 333, 336–338,
   herbivore 333
   human 333, 336
Testicular inflammation 303
Theileria 309, 316, 317, 320
   hippotragi 160, 164, 172, 319, 341
   parva 316, 317, 318
   schizonts 317
   spp. 22, 23, 319
   taurotragi 178, 320
Theileriosis 171, 172, 216, 313, 316, 318–320, 341
Tick 5, 22, 143, 144, 188, 210, 224, 234, 276, 279, 309, 311–320, 328, 330, 339–344
   bite necrosis 344
   blue 309, 342
   bont 142, 279, 312, 339, 340
   bont-legged 344
   -borne diseases 69, 179, 210, 240, 269, 308, 318, 342

brown ear 141, 142, 144, 188, 316–320, 340, 341,
  paralysis 234
  red-legged tick 164, 309, 319, 320, 341
  vector 314, 316
Tongue worm 143
Torticollis 277
Toxoplasma gondii 291
Toxoplasmosis 291
Trematode 331, 332
Trichinella 36, 263, 338
  spp. 338
Trypanosoma 306, 308
  congolense 307
  vivax 307
Trypanosome 4, 306, 307, 349
Trypanosomosis 306, 307, 308
Tsetse fly 4, 5, 306, 307, 349
Tumbu fly 346, 347, 350
Tuberculosis 7, 22, 36, 269, 288–290
  mycobacterium 288
Two Step 353

U
Uitpeuloog 203, 281, 347

V
Vaccination 14, 16, 73, 135, 143, 242, 252, 270, 273, 282, 284, 287, 292–294, 296, 298, 299, 301, 302, 304, 306, 313–315, 322–327
Vibrionic abortion 203
Vitamin deficiensies 80
  B deficiency 216
Vitiligo 276

W
Warble fly 346
Wireworm 4, 22, 172, 252, 334
Worm eggs 143, 240, 333
  larvae 330
Worms 22, 49, 85, 216, 331–338

Y
Yellow dog tick 311, 344
  fat disease 263

Z
Zoonoses 269, 304
Zoonosis 304

NOTES